W9-APU-428

Fundamentals of Mortgage Lending

Fundamentals of Mortgage Lending

Marshall W. Dennis

Institute of Financial Education

Reston Publishing Company, Inc.
A Prentice-Hall Company
Reston, Virginia

Library of Congress Cataloging in Publication Data

Dennis, Marshall W.
    Fundamentals of mortgage lending.

    Includes bibliographies and index.
    1. Mortgage loans—United States. I. Title.
HG2040.5.U5D43   332.7'2   78-5451
ISBN 0-8359-2153-0

©1978 by
Reston Publishing Company, Inc.
A Prentice-Hall Company
Reston, Virginia

All rights reserved. No part of this book may be reproduced in any way or by any means
without permission in writing from the publisher.

10 9 8 7 6 5 4 3 2 1

Printed in the United States of America

This book is dedicated with love to my wife Marilyn. The inspiration for this book has come from my past students.

Contents

Preface

Few people realize the tremendous effect mortgage lending has on the entire economy of the United States. The fundamentals of mortgage lending are understood by even fewer.

The purpose of this book is to communicate and explain these fundamentals in as simple and concise a manner as possible. It is designed either for a new employee of a mortgage lender, or a college student studying real estate finance and wanting to supplement that study with practical mortgage lending fundamentals.

A new employee of any mortgage lender will probably need at least the first six months to understand the specific job requirements and the larger complexities of mortgage lending. This book is for that individual, whether the employing mortgage lender be a commercial bank, a savings and loan association, a mutual savings bank, or a mortgage company.

The academic backgrounds of those entering the mortgage lending field today will range from solid real estate finance training to no formal academic training. Whatever the background, all of these students can and will succeed if they have the ability to learn and apply what they have learned. No prior knowledge of any part of mortgage lending is assumed. The reader is assumed to possess only the ability and willingness to learn.

This text will discuss each topic beginning with the fundamentals and will develop them to the point where the reader will have a basic understanding of that topic. Not all topics will be applicable to every mortgage lender, nor even be of interest to all readers, but to understand the basics of modern mortgage lending each subject included needs to be comprehensively understood. Changes occur so rapidly in this segment of the economy, that an area in which a particular mortgage lender is not involved today may be where the growth and profit scene is tomorrow. All mortgage lenders should prepare for growth and change by employing suitably educated personnel.

The major mortgage lenders may hold different financial philosophies, but when they make a mortgage loan they all deal with the same product. The financing of real estate requires productive origination, careful underwriting, and effective servicing to allow for profitable marketing. While explaining the fundamentals, this book also examines the similarities and differences which exist among mortgage lenders.

This text is designed to fulfill the need mortgage lenders have for a basic text to prepare new employees for the important job of helping finance the growing real estate needs of this country.

Acknowledgments

I am deeply indebted to a number of people for valuable assistance in preparing this book. These recognized experts in their field have read portions of the book and suggested appropriate improvements.

James R. Carlin, Jr., Loan Officer, Perpetual Federal Savings and Loan, Washington, D.C.

Martin R. Eggers, Regional Manager, Northwestern Mutual Life Insurance Co., Washington, D.C.

John Fitzmaurice, Vice President, Mortgage Guaranty Insurance Corp., Milwaukee, Wisconsin.

Edward R. Godwin, Senior Vice President, Mortgage and Trust, Inc., Houston, Texas.

Dr. William Heuson, Chairman, Department of Finance, University of Miami, Coral Gables, Florida.

Raymond R. Holland, Senior Vice President, The Philadelphia Saving Fund Society, Philadelphia, Pennsylvania.

Thomas J. Kelly, Department of Education and Training, Mortgage Bankers Association of America, Washington, D.C.

James Kozuch, Vice President, Government National Mortgage Association, Washington, D.C.

Thomas L. Lowe, Jr., Vice President and Partner, Mason-McDuffie, Berkeley, California.

Robert F. MacSwain, Secretary, Hartford Life Insurance Co., Hartford, Connecticut.

Vincent G. Maher, Vice President, 20th Century-Fox Realty and Development Co., Los Angeles, California.

Thomas C. Martin, President, Kennedy Mortgage Co., Camden, New Jersey.

Donna J. Pillard, Assistant Vice President, Carruth Mortgage Co., New Orleans, Louisiana.

Dr. James Porterfield, Professor of Finance, Graduate School of Business, Stanford University, Stanford, California.

Thomas A. Ronzetti, Vice President, Federal National Mortgage Association, Washington, D.C.

Donald D. Wipf, Assistant Vice President, Perpetual Federal Savings and Loan, Washington, D.C.

Finally, I must extend my deepest appreciation to Douglas E. Metz of Mid-Lantic Mortgage Corporation, Cherry Hill, New Jersey, who reviewed and edited the final manuscript and offered many important suggestions.

For those possible errors, omissions, or faulty analyses, the author assumes full and sole responsibility.

Marshall W. Dennis
Chicago, Illinois

Introduction

Any attempt to analyze or answer all of the many questions inherent to mortgage lending would result in a series of treatises too complex to be of value or benefit to the student or the new practitioner. Instead, this book is designed to provide the theoretical and practical framework necessary to begin understanding the increasingly complex field of mortgage lending.

Throughout this book additional readings are listed which the more advanced student may want to review. Reference will be made to other publications for review and study regarding subjects not related directly to the design of this book or which are too complex to be included.

Real Estate Decisions

Many important real estate decisions must be made by a potential mortgage borrower before seeking a mortgage loan. These decisions are basic, yet complex. For example, a potential borrower (whether the loan is for a residential or income property) must analyze at least six issues:

1. The general benefits of renting as compared with owning real estate

2. Tax aspects

3. The leverage factor

4. The cost of money

5. Location, timing and feasibility

6. The risk factor

Although a mortgage loan officer may want to review these issues with a borrower, an analysis and the necessary decisions usually are made by the borrower before the loan is sought. Of course a mortgage loan officer must analyze all relevant material to determine whether the loan should be made. However, since these decisions should occur before seeking a mortgage loan, they will not be discussed in this book. The subject of this book concerns those questions or issues that occur after the decision to borrow has been made and a mortgage loan sought.

Major differences exist among mortgage lenders regarding the actual mortgage lending process. For example, the origination of mortgage loans, whether for residential or income property, is possibly the most important phase of morgage lending. But the manner in which a commercial bank originates mortgages is often radically different from that of a mortgage company or savings and loan. In fact, even within an industry group, the origination function is most often performed according to company policy or philosophy rather than industry custom.

The marketing of mortgage loans is another difficult area to discuss adequately in a book of this nature. Many mortgage lenders, such as small savings and loan associations, still originate mortgages only for their own portfolio and consequently engage in no secondary marketing. Others, such as mortgage companies, originate all mortgage loans for sale to others. Among mortgage lenders active in marketing loans, each establishes its own individual methods and policies. Although marketing of mortgage loans will not be discussed specifically, the important secondary mortgage market and its institutions will be examined.

Mortgage Lenders

Some of the basic philosophies of mortgage lenders are at opposite extremes of the real estate financing spectrum. In general, all mortgage lenders have worked diligently to provide for the real estate financing needs of this nation and their success has made this the best housed nation in the world. Yet, more could be done and greater cooperation among mortgage lenders could prepare the way for greater accomplishments.

All mortgage lenders are dealing with the same product and rendering the same service—financing real estate. Although they may obtain funds for lending in different ways and have varying degrees of regulation, the result is the same. Some commentators on the mortgage industry claim that the inability of mortgage lenders to work more closely together is the result of competition and, therefore, it cannot be expected that one lender would assist another when the result could be lost business. If the industry is going to solve the major real estate finance problems of today (such as the inability of the average family to afford the average priced home), all lenders will have to combine their financial expertise and political influence.

Mortgage lenders include:

1. Savings and loan associations

2. Commercial banks

3. Mortgage companies

4. Mutual savings banks

5. Real estate investment trusts

The total number of such lenders and their branches is about 50,000. And at some point in 1978, one of these lenders will originate a loan which will push the nation's outstanding mortgage debt beyond the mind-boggling $1 trillion mark. Regardless of which mortgage lender originates a mortgage, all perform basically the same function for a mortgage borrower.

Mortgage Lending Functions

All mortgage lenders perform some or all of the following functions:

1. Mortgage loan origination
    a. residential
    b. income property

2. Mortgage loan processing
   a. government insured or guaranteed
   b. conventional

3. Real estate appraisal

4. Mortgage loan underwriting
   a. residential
   b. income property

5. Mortgage loan administration
   a. loan approval
   b. loan closing
   c. loan servicing
   d. collections
   e. tax and insurance account processing

6. Marketing
   a. packaging
   b. fulfilling commitments
   c. secondary mortgage market operations

Special Areas of Emphasis

The first chapter in this book concerns the history and evolution of mortgage lending. It provides essential material for a serious student of mortgage lending. Unless past problems and failures of mortgage lending are understood and resolved, they will occur again. Further, it would be difficult to comprehend the present position of mortgage lending without examining its evolution.

A chapter on real estate law is included to provide the reader with both a basic review of law as it relates to real estate and mortgage lending, and as a reference for material covered in other chapters.

The last three chapters are supplements for training purposes. The first is an extensive glossary of the language of the industry. An important first step toward becoming a competent practitioner is understanding the vocabulary used.

The second supplemental chapter contains three residential case studies and the third an income-property case study. Many people in mortgage lending do not have the opportunity to see the complete product of the mortgage lending process. The packaging of these loans should be studied not for adoption purposes but to determine what should be included for the protection of both the borrower and lender.

SUGGESTED READINGS

Bagby, Joseph R. *Real Estate Financing Desk Book*, Englewood Cliffs, New Jersey: Institute for Business Planning, Inc., 1975.

Beaton, William R. *Real Estate Finance.* Englewood Cliffs, New Jersey: Prentice-Hall, Inc., 1975.

_____. *Real Estate Investment.* Englewood Cliffs, New Jersey: Prentice-Hall, Inc., 1971.

Clark, William Dennison. "Leverage: Magnificent Mover of Real Estate," *Real Estate Review* (Winter 1972), pp. 8-13.

Cooper, James R. *Real Estate Investment Analysis.* Lexington, Massachusetts: Lexington Books, D. C. Heath & Co., 1974.

Graaskamp, J. A. *A Guide to Feasibility Analysis.* Chicago: Society of Real Estate Appraisers, 1970.

Maisel, Sherman J., and Roulac, Stephen E. *Real Estate Investment and Finance.* New York: McGraw-Hill Book Co., Inc., 1976.

Martin, Wendall H. "Tax Shelter and the Real Estate Analyst," *The Appraisal Journal* (January 1975), pp. 17-28.

Robinson, Gerald J. *Federal Income Taxation of Real Estate.* Boston: Warren, Gorham & Lamont, Inc., 1974.

Roulac, Stephen E. "Life Cycle of a Real Estate Investment," *Real Estate Review* (Fall 1974), pp. 113-17.

Wendt, Paul F., and Cerf, Alan R. *Real Estate Investment Analysis and Taxation.* New York: McGraw-Hill Book Co., Inc., 1969.

Chapter 1

The History of Mortgage Lending

Mortgage lending, as presently utilized in the United States, is a relatively recent development, although many of the basic concepts date back to the beginning of recorded history.

The underlying product in all real estate activities is land. Some sociologists claim that the use of, the desire to acquire, and the need to regulate the transfer of land were the fundamental reasons for the development of governments and laws. As government units developed, laws were formulated to govern the ownership and use of land. Because of the importance of land, it was soon being used as security for the performance of an obligation, such as repaying debts or the fulfillment of military service.

ANCIENT CONCEPTS OF MORTGAGE LENDING

Evidence of transactions involving land as security has been uncovered in such ancient civilizations as Babylonia and Egypt. Many of the basic principles of mortgage lending, including the essential elements of naming the borrower and the lender and describing the property, were developed in these early civilizations. For example, there is evidence that the Egyptians were the first to use surveys to describe mortgaged land. This was undoubtedly necessitated by the annual flooding of the Nile River, which often obliterated property markers.

During the period when Greek civilization was at its peak, the temple leaders loaned money with real estate as security. In fact, throughout history organized religion has taken a strong interest in real estate.

The Roman Empire developed mortgage lending to a high level of sophistication, beginning with the *fiducia*. This transaction was an actual transfer of possession and title to land. It was subject to an additional agreement stating that if the borrower fulfilled the obligation, a reconveyance would occur. As Roman government became stronger and the law more clearly defined, a new concept of security, called the *pignus*, was developed. No title transfer occurred. Instead the land was "pawned." According to this concept, title and possession remained with the borrower, but the lender could take possession of the property at any time if it was deemed a possibility of default existed.

However, the most important Roman development regarding mortgages was the *hypotheca*, which was a pledge. The hypotheca was similar to the lien theory (described later) that exists in most states in this country today. The title remained with the borrower, who was also allowed to retain possession of the property. Only if an actual default occurred, i.e., a failure on the part of the borrower to perform, was the lender entitled to take possession of and title to the land.

As the Roman Empire receded throughout Europe during the Dark Ages, a Germanic law introduced a new concept. A borrower was given a choice whether to fulfill an obligation or lose the security. If the mortgagor defaulted, the mortgagee had to look exclusively to the property itself. This security system was called a *gage* in Germanic law; something was deposited for the performance of an agreement. As the Dark Ages continued and the governmental authority of Rome weakened to the point where lenders were not sure they would have support from the central authorities in securing their debts, the *hypotheca* system decayed and died, and the more primitive concept of the *fiducia* returned.

ENGLISH DEVELOPMENTS

Later, in Europe, a new system of government and social structure, the feudal system, became widespread. The feudal system was an all-encompassing form of government that affected the economy, the military and the administration of government. The essential element of the feudal system was the totality of the king's control. He was the owner of all lands. He would grant the *use* of this land to certain lords in return for military fealty. Lords given the use of the land were permitted to continue on the land as long as they fulfilled a military obligation to the king. If this obligation was not fulfilled, or if the lord died, the use of the land was revoked and given to others. In this situation, land served as a security for the performance of an obligation—military service.

Along with the feudal system of land tenure, the Germanic system of the *gage* was introduced into early English law by William of Normandy in 1066 following the successful invasion of England. The word *mortgage* was not found in English literature until after the Norman invasion. It derives from the French words *mort*, which means "dead" or "frozen" (the land is "dead," since the mortgagor could not use or derive income from it), and *gage*, which means "pledge".

During the early years after the Norman invasion, it was the Catholic Church that primarily established the civil law in England. The Church stated that the charging of any interest for money loaned was *usury*; therefore, mortgage lending (along with other business transactions) was not an important feature in the economic system of that time.

Throughout the development of the common law in England, there occurred a gradual shift from a concept of favoritism or protection of the mortgagee, to favoritism or protection of the mortgagor. Finally, the common law reached a more balanced position. The initial concept (mortgagee favoritism) was dictated by the realities of the economic and legal systems that existed at this early stage of mortgage development. Mortgage lending was not a common occurrence during this period for two reasons: 1) there was very little need for it, and 2) no incentive to lend existed without the ability to collect interest. The mortgage lending that did occur was not for the purpose of providing funds to purchase real estate, but usually to finance large purchases, for example, of a new mill, or livestock, or perhaps to prepare a dowry for a daughter. Since lenders could not collect interest on these loans, they would take both title *and* possession of a designated portion of the borrower's land and thus be entitled to all rents and profits. When the obligation was fulfilled, title was reconveyed to the mortgagor. If the mortgagor defaulted, the mortgagee would permanently retain title and possession of the mortgaged land. The mortgagee was also still entitled to expect performance of the underlying obligation.

During the 15th century, courts of equity allowed the mortgagor to perform the obligation, even after the required date, and redeem the property. This concept was expanded and by 1625 nearly all existing mortgage lending practices had ended because a mortgagee never knew when a mortgagor might perform and thus redeem the property. To alleviate this problem, mortgagees would petition the court for a decree requiring the mortgagor to redeem the property within six months or lose the right to do so.

A more balanced position resulted which required the mortgagor to still relinquish title to the land, but to retain possession. If a default occurred, the mortgagor had a specified period of time in which to redeem the property.

This concept, called *title theory*, was brought to America and formed the basis of American mortgage law. After the Revolutionary War, however, the concept was changed by some states to the more modern *lien theory*. Under this theory, title remains with the mortgagor, and the mortgagee has only a lien against the property which can be exercised if the underlying obligation is not fulfilled.

AMERICAN DEVELOPMENTS

The American Revolutionary War was followed by a westward expansion which was financed by land development banks borrowing primarily in Europe to finance their land purchases in the developing West. Much of this land acquisition was speculative and eventually culminated in the bankruptcy of nearly all these early land development banks. Little, if any, real estate financing was done on an organized basis from the early 1800s until after the Civil War.

During the first 75 years of this country's history, the population was located primarily on small farms passed down through families.

Little need existed for mortgage lending except for an occasional purchase of new land or for seed money. The small amount of mortgage lending that did occur during this period was provided primarily by family and friends. It is important to realize that until the 1920s, the largest category of mortgage lenders in the United States was individuals, not financial institutions.

Thrift Institutions

The birth of various thrift institutions provided a change in mortgage lending. The first mutual savings bank, the Philadelphia Savings Fund Society, was started Dec. 2, 1816. Of greater long-term importance to mortgage lending was the organization of the first building society in the U.S. Modeled after societies that had existed in England and Scotland for 50 years, the Oxford Provident Building Association was organized Jan. 3, 1831 in Frankford, Penn. This association, like the ones that soon followed, was intended to exist only long enough for all the organizers to obtain funds to purchase homes. Ironically, the first loan made by this association became delinquent and another member of the association assumed the debt and took possession of the house.

Later, other associations were formed, providing a popular means for the expansion of building associations across the United States.

Even with these new financial institutions, mortgage lending was still not an important part of the economy in the first half of the 19th century. Most families still lived on farms, which met basically all their requirements. No urgent need for savings existed. Away from the farm there were few employment opportunities where excess cash could be accumulated for savings. The concept of saving was still new, and the number of active savers was very small. Then, as now, the impetus for mortgage lending was the inflow of savings to the institutions that would lend funds.

Mortgage Companies

After the Civil War, expansion continued and change resumed. Starting with a new westward expansion which opened virgin lands for farming, a regular farm mortgage business developed in the predominantly rural Midwest. The Midwest is an area where many mortgage companies began, and it still has one of the heaviest concentrations of mortgage companies.

Most of these companies did not originate mortgage loans for their own portfolios, as did the thrift institutions. Rather, such loans were for direct sale to wealthy individuals or to institutional investors such as life insurance companies. Most of these individual and institutional investors were located on the East coast and needed local mortgage companies to originate loans for them. This need resulted in the mortgage loan correspondent system.

The bulk of the mortgage business consisted of financing farms, usually with a prevailing loan-to-value ratio of 40 percent. An occasional 50 percent loan might be made on a farm in a well-developed area. The term of the loan was short (less than five years), with interest payable semi-annually and the principal paid at the end of the term. By 1900, outstanding farm mortgages originated by these mortgage companies totalled more than $4 billion.

During this period of time, the move to urban areas began to increase, swelled by ever-mounting numbers of immigrants. In 1892, the United States League of Savings Associations was founded in response to the expanding savings and loan industry. These institutions provided urban residents a place to save money and a source of funds to use in purchasing homes. These mortgages made by savings and loans associations usually were repaid on an installment basis, not at the expiration of the term as were mortgages from other types of lenders.

Commercial Banks

Commercial banks made few real estate loans until after the Civil War when a sudden demand for loans to finance new farmsteads encouraged state-chartered commercial banks to make low-ratio farm mortgages. Except for a brief period of time, federally-chartered commercial banks could not make real estate loans. This competition from state-chartered banks eventually forced a change in federal banking law. In 1913 the *Federal Reserve Act* authorized federally-chartered banks to lend money on real estate. This initial authorization limited mortgage loans to improved farms for a five-year term with the loan-to-value ratio of 50 percent. This authorization was extended in 1916 to include one-year loans on urban real estate.

Many changes have occurred in both state and federal laws relating to the types and terms of mortgage loans made by commercial banks. These changes tended to lag behind advances made by other mortgage lenders, but the contribution made by commercial banks has been meaningful, especially in those areas of the country where they function as the principal mortgage lender.

Turn of the Century

During the period from 1870 to the early 1900s, a few mortgage companies in or near urban areas began to make loans on single-family houses. This initially constituted a very small percentage of their business but gradually grew to account for more and more total origination volume. The Farm Mortgage Bankers Association, which was formed in 1914, was changed to the Mortgage Bankers Association in 1923 to reflect the increasing accent on residential lending.

In the first two decades of this century the typical loan made by a mortgage company on a single-family dwelling called for no more than a 50 percent loan-to-value ratio, with a three-to-five-year mortgage term. There were no provisions for *amortization* of the loan and interest was generally payable semi-annually. The majority of these mortgages were renewed upon maturity, since few families had the money to retire the debt. The mortgage companies originating these mortgages charged from one to three percent of the amount of the loan as a fee. Upon renewal, an additional one percent fee would be charged.

As the 20th century progressed, thrift institutions, especially savings and loan associations, continued to expand. The mutual savings banks, which had their greatest growth after the Civil War, remained principally in the New England states, but the savings and loans continued to grow and spread across the country. During this time, thrift institutions originated short-term mortgage loans for their own portfolios, with some installment-type mortgages.

All mortgage lenders participated in the real estate boom years of the 1920s. This was a period of unrestrained optimism. Most Americans believed growth and prosperity would continue forever. Real estate prices appreciated 25 to 50 percent per year during the first half of the decade. Many lenders forgot their underwriting standards, believing that inflating prices would bail out any bad loan. As with any speculative period, the end came and, along with it, many personal fortunes were dissipated.

Depression Era

The real estate boom of the 1920s began to show signs of weakening long before the stock market crash. By 1927, real estate values that had appreciated in the early 1920s declined dramatically. Following the disastrous dive of the stock market in 1929 the entire economy of the United States was in danger of collapse. Real estate values plunged to less than half the level of the year before. The ability of both the individual borrower and the income property mortgagor to meet quarterly or semi-annual interest payments was reduced by the large-scale unemployment that followed the collapse of the stock market and by the loss of economic vitality throughout the nation.

Because periodic amortization of mortgages was not common, a six-month lag often occurred before an institutional investor realized a mortgage was in trouble. In addition, the various financial institutions were faced with a severe liquidity problem which sometimes required them to sell vast real estate and mortgage holdings under very unfavorable conditions. This need to sell real estate holdings to obtain cash, coupled with a rise in foreclosures and tax sales, severely depressed an already-crumbling real estate market. Many individual homeowners were threatened with property loss even if they retained their jobs, because when their five-year mortgages expired, many were unable to refinance their mortgages because lenders were caught in a liquidity crisis and did not have the funds to lend.

Thrift institutions also experienced problems during this period even though some of their mortgagors had installment type mortgages. As many workers lost their jobs and unemployment reached 25 percent, the savings inflow diminished drastically. All types of financial institutions began to fail, savers withdrew funds and the liquidity crisis worsened for all lenders. In the early 1930s, many savings and loan associations failed due to financial problems associated with heavy withdrawals by savers and a high foreclosure rate. This foreclosure rate reached such a high level that by 1935, 20 percent of all savings and loan mortgage assets were in the "real estate owned" category.

The vast majority of all foreclosures during the 1930s were made by second and third mortgagees, who needed to foreclose immediately on a defaulted property to protect what little security they may have had. The highest number of foreclosures occurred from 1931-1935, averaging 250,000 each year. The increasing number of foreclosures, especially on family farms in the Midwest, forced the beginning of compulsory moratoria. In the Midwest, where economic deterioration was aggravated by the dust bowl storms, the cry for moratoria reached the stage of near rebellion, and some violence occurred. Reacting to the hysteria sweeping the farm belt and some of the larger cities, many mortgagees voluntarily instituted forbearance, some for as long as two years. The first law requiring a mortgage moratorium became effective in Iowa on Feb. 8, 1933. In the next 18 months, 27 states enacted legislation suspending nearly all foreclosures. Most of the moratorium laws enacted during this period were to last for two years or less, although many were re-enacted and allowed to continue as law until the early 1940s.

It is important to note that during the period when these laws were in effect, there still were some foreclosures. The determining factor on whether to grant relief was the soundness of a debtor's fundamental economic position. If it were determined that a debtor would eventually lose the land anyway, it was considered a waste of time and an injustice to the creditor to postpone the foreclosure or grant a moratorium. The moratoria of the early 1930s did not provide an actual solution to the underlying economic problems, but they did provide time in which public unrest could be soothed and the federal government could introduce some economic remedies.

GOVERNMENTAL INTERVENTION

The federal government realized that the drop in real estate values would continue to add to the depression of the entire economy, preventing its revitalization. Therefore, the government instituted a series of programs designed to help stabilize real estate values and, hopefully, the entire economy. This marked the beginning of a drastic reversal in previous governmental-political philosophy, which had more or less been laissez-faire. The first step was taken in the last year of the Hoover Administration and involved the creation of the Reconstruction Finance Corporation (RFC) in January 1932. The RFC was meant to stabilize the economy by providing funds to financial institutions, mostly commercial banks, to help with the liquidity crisis.

Shortly after the creation of the RFC, new legislation creating the Federal Home Loan Bank System (FHLB) was enacted, but only after heated debate within the mortgage lending community. The FHLB established 11 regional banks to provide funds for member savings and loan associations and similar institutions engaged in home financing. The FHLB generated these funds by selling bonds and notes on the open market and making the funds available to member banks at a nominal markup.

Next the Home Owners' Loan Corporation (HOLC) was established during the summer of 1933. Before the creation of the HOLC, more than 40 percent of the nation's home mortgage debt of $20 billion was in default. To alleviate this problem, the HOLC provided 1) the exchange of HOLC government-backed bonds to mortgagees for home mortgages in default, and 2) some cash loans to mortgagors for payment of real estate taxes.

The importance of this governmental agency cannot be overstated. It provided the opportunity for mortgagees to receive something of value (HOLC bonds) for a debt instrument that was diminishing in value almost daily. By providing a system of refinancing, the defaulted mortgages did not have to be foreclosed during a time of decreasing real estate values, preventing a further decline in property values.

One often-overlooked HOLC program gave aid to homeowners to help pay local real estate taxes. Without the tax revenue paid by these homeowners, many municipalities would have been bankrupt.

The mortgages HOLC obtained usually were refinanced for a 15-year term on an installment plan. During its three-year lending period, HOLC refinanced more than one million non-farm homes. This action by the government not only helped to restabilize the economy, but also prevented the foreclosure of thousands of homes.

Federal Housing Administration

In 1934 the federal government created the Federal Housing Administration (FHA) and gave it three primary objectives:

1. To encourage the improvement of the nation's housing standards and conditions.

2. To provide an adequate home financing system.

3. To exert a stabilizing influence on the mortgage and residential real estate markets.

This program furthered the concept of installment or amortized loans begun by the thrift institutions (and encouraged by HOLC). This type of loan is practically the only one in existence today.

FHA was not popular with the financial communities when it first appeared. The concept of government-guaranteed mortgages was suspect because many companies and individuals had suffered financially as a result of the mortgage guaranty companies of the 1930s. (See Chapter 7, Mortgage Insurance—Government and Private.) Others felt that this intrusion by the government into the housing market eventually would be detrimental to private capitalism.

The FHA-insured mortgage provided the elements of dependability, transferability and minimal risk vital to the development of a national mortgage market. Prior to FHA, only local mortgage markets existed in which most loans were made either by individuals who wanted to keep their loans local, or by thrift institutions which were limited to specific lending areas and originated loans only for their own portfolios.

The correspondent system between mortgage companies and insurance company, which was already in existence to a limited extent, helped establish a national mortgage market by using FHA standards for homes and borrowers to move funds from capital-rich areas to capital-poor areas of the nation. Today, the mortgage banking industry undoubtedly owes its success and growth to the basic decision by life insurance companies to engage in national lending, with FHA providing the insurance. About 80 percent of all mortgage companies now in existence were formed after the creation of FHA. This fact alone is dramatic evidence of the effect FHA has had on the mortgage industry.

Thrift institutions did not use the FHA-insured mortgage to any great extent because they were primarily local organizations which promoted local home ownership. The legal limitations on lending activity also had an effect, as did the belief by some thrift institution leaders that the government should not become involved in insuring home mortgages.

The other important residential lender—commercial banks—did participate in FHA-insured mortgages, but not as extensively as mortgage companies, which have originated more than 75 percent of such mortgages. Other residential lenders (excluding mortgage companies) have originated practically all conventional mortgages, usually on a local basis.

Until the creation of FHA, mortgage lenders serviced few if any loans. However, with the practice of monthly loan amortization being reinforced by FHA and the requirement of escrowing taxes and insurance, the need became evident for lenders to service loans. Servicing now is considered an integral part of mortgage lending and one of the means by which mortgage lenders persevere despite fluctuating financial conditions. (See Chapter 11, Closing and Administering the Mortgage Loan.)

In 1938, Congress created the Federal National Mortgage Association (FNMA) to provide a secondary mortgage market for FHA-insured loans. FNMA became active after World War II and provided the necessary facilities for a truly national market. FNMA has been reorganized as a private corporation and is now the largest holder of single-family mortgages, including FHA-insured, VA-guaranteed and conventional mortgages. (See Chapter 6, Secondary Mortgage Markets and Institutions.)

THE GROWTH ERA

A minimal amount of single-family construction occurred from 1926 to 1946 as a result of the Depression and World War II. At the end of the war, however, five million servicemen returned home, and a tremendous demand for housing was created. The government, as part of its responsibility to returning veterans, passed the Servicemen's Readjustment Act of 1944. One of the major products of this act was a program which provided a desirable means of financing homes for veterans, the most distinguishing feature of which is the lack of a downpayment requirement for eligible veterans. Rates have been set at or slightly below the FHA rate. No mortgage insurance premiums are collected from the participants, since the program is not meant to be self-supporting, as is the FHA.

The highly liquid position of financial institutions was the second great impetus to the rapid expansion of single-family dwelling construction following World War II. In 1945, more than half of their assets were tied up in the no-risk but low-yielding securities they were obligated to purchase during World War II. At the end of the war, these bonds could be sold and the cash converted into higher returns through mortgage loans.

The greatest boom in housing construction in the history of this country and possibly the world became a reality with these two government programs (FHA and VA), the built-in demand for housing and the liquid position of lenders. Since that time, the mortgage market has been the largest user of long-term credit in the entire American economy.

During the period of 1946 to 1955, almost all new dollars invested in real estate mortgages were used to finance single-family housing. However, as the demand for housing peaked and began to diminish, some lenders realized that the new suburban communities would need shopping centers, office buildings and even apartment houses. A new investment philosophy began to emerge with the income-property mortgage market.

This change in investment philosophy among lenders, especially life insurance companies, resulted from the need for these new properties and a realization that higher yields could be obtained with less expense. For example, it was less expensive for an institutional lender to make a $1 million apartment loan than to make 50 $20,000 single-family loans. The change in some lenders' investment philosophy is further illustrated by the fact that in 1955, three out of every four dollars being invested by life insurance companies in long-term mortgages were in single-family loans. By 1960, the ratio had changed to two out of every four dollars, and during the first half of the 1970s almost all new dollars invested were for income-property mortgages.

MORTGAGE LENDING TODAY

The most productive boom in real estate construction and financing in the United States has occurred during the past 25 years. More housing units have been constructed during this period than in all the years since this country was founded. Much of the credit must be given to the availability of capital at a reasonable rate and the corresponding creation of the secondary mortgage market. For example, FNMA was given expanded purchasing authority in 1970, and was joined by the Federal Home Loan Mortgage Corporation (FHLMC) in that year to provide secondary market facilities for conventional mortgages originated by savings and loan associations. While the housing boom changed the landscape of the American countryside, new office buildings, apartment complexes and the shopping centers provided the amenities and services needed by the new families in these homes.

In the early 1970s direct governmental stimulation of the real estate field, unparalleled since the 1930s, brought the Housing and Urban Development Act of 1968 which committed the government to a goal of 26 million new housing starts in the next decade. At the time, many argued that this goal was not practical on either fiscal or political grounds. However, the act introduced a new concept in government programs for residential real estate by adopting the principle of subsidizing interest rates. The two major subsidy programs of the 1968 act were a) Section 235, which encouraged home ownership for low and moderate income families by providing special mortgage insurance and by subsidizing the mortgage interest rate in excess of one percent, and b) Section 236, which was basically the same as 235 but was geared to multi-family rental units.

These government subsidy programs combined with a general national growth to stimulate housing production in 1972 to more than three million units (housing starts of 2.4 million plus mobile home shipments of .6 million). Problems began almost immediately. In 1971, when news reports of possible scandals in subsidized housing began to appear, the concept was in grave danger. The scandals were followed by congressional investigations which spotlighted the unforeseen high program costs. In January of 1973, President Nixon ordered a freeze on all subsidy programs which was partially lifted later, but only after a thorough review of government programs by a special task force created by the Department of Housing and Urban Development (HUD). This task force reviewed the history of government involvement in real estate and analyzed the impact of the various subsidy programs on housing. One result of the task force effort was a change in the basic government philosophy regarding shelter for the poor. The task force concluded that the goal of providing home ownership for everyone was neither practical nor desirable when weighed against the cost. The report stated:

> "Although home ownership has been encouraged by a variety of Federal laws, no major programs offering home ownership to the poor in the 20th century were enacted until the 1960s. Since that time, the problems that have arisen from the operation of these programs—principally the Section 235 and Section 221(d)(2) programs—are so serious that they raise questions about the validity of the concept itself."[1]

The government's concept changed from subsidizing ownership to subsidizing rent. The Housing and Community Development Act of 1974 formalized this change with the "Section 8" program. This program allows low and moderate income families to choose the rental unit in the community in which they want to live with the government subsidizing the amount of "fair market rent" that is in excess of 25 percent of the family's monthly income. This program provided assistance to families who could not afford the minimal housing expenses stipulated in prior programs and to families whose incomes were just over the maximum income limit qualifying them for assistance in home purchasing.

The federal government was not the only government in the 1970s involved in either providing or stimulating housing for low and moderate income families. Before 1960, the state of New York had the only state housing agency, but by 1975 nearly all states had some type of housing agency. Although some have used tax-exempt bonds to raise revenue to lend to home buyers at below-market interest rates, many have fulfilled their social responsibility by providing financing for multi-family units.

During the 1970s, the rapid growth and equally rapid decline of a new mortgage lender—the real estate investment trust, or REIT— occurred. Authorized by a 1960 amendment to the tax laws, REITs were originally designed to provide a type of "mutual fund" interest or equity ownership in real estate for the investing public. By purchasing a share of stock, a shareholder had an interest in a trust that owned and managed real estate. The concept grew slowly through the 1960s and then exploded in the early 1970s with the introduction of a new type of REIT on Wall Street. This new REIT was a mortgage-type (as contrasted with the older, equity type) and was designed to make construction loans, land development loans, and some long-term mortgage loans. The primary means of growth for these mortgage-type trusts was by maximizing leverage (lending borrowed funds) in order to increase the book value of stock. This allowed the sale of more equity. During the REIT growth period (1971-1973) the demand for commercial loans at commercial banks was low and excess funds were used to finance these trusts. The number of REITs increased at a phenomenal rate until more than 200 existed in 1973; but then the real estate bubble burst and many REITs suffered serious financial problems that sent a few into bankruptcy.

A combination of inexperienced management, poor underwriting of loans, the oil embargo, a recession, and the unforeseeable dramatic increase in the prime interest rate brought disaster to the REITs. Most short-term trusts charged an interest rate that floated from three to five percent above the prime rate. The increase in the prime rate to 12 percent in 1973 forced many builder/developers into default, since few projects could carry an interest rate of 17 percent. The result was massive foreclosure and loss to the REITs. Although only a few trusts became bankrupt, most had substantial portions of their assets in an "interest non-accrual" category for a period of time. Most REITs will probably survive past reversals, but the public's confidence in them may have been shattered by the spectacular drop in REIT share prices.

The 1970s will be remembered as the time when recession and inflation (normally at opposite phases within the business cycle) combined to produce the worst recession since the 1930s. The 1974-75 recession had a crippling effect on the demand for many consumer goods, but the credit crunch of 1973 was devastating on real estate finance. Throughout the 1970s, the inflation rate and periodic capital shortages (and therefore higher interest rates) were the major problems for real estate finance. These problems led to some basic changes in mortgage lending that will be discussed later in the text.

SUGGESTED READINGS

Bryant, Willis R. *Mortgage Lending Fundamentals and Practices.* New York: McGraw-Hill Book Co., Inc., 1962.

Colean, Miles L. *Mortgage Companies: Their Place in the Financial Structure.* Englewood Cliffs, New Jersey: Prentice-Hall, Inc., 1962.

Dennis, Marshall W. "Mortgage Banking: Steeped in History and Bright with Promise," *The Mortgage Banker* (October 1973), pp. 88-105.

Downs, Anthony. *Federal Housing Subsidies: How Are They Working?* Lexington, Massachusetts: Lexington Books, D. C. Heath & Co., 1973.

Halperin, Jerome Y., and Brenner, Michael J. "Opportunities Under the New Section 8 Housing Program," *Real Estate Review* (Spring 1976), pp. 67-75.

Harriss, C. Lowell. *History and Policies of the Home Owners' Loan Corporation.* New York: National Bureau of Economic Research, Inc., 1951.

Hoffman, G. J., Jr. *The Mortgage Banker of Yesterday and Today.* Jacksonville, Florida: Stockton, Whatley, Davin & Company, 1956.

Klaman, Saul B. *The Postwar Rise of Mortgage Companies.* New York: National Bureau of Economic Research, Inc., 1959.

Lodge, Edgar A. *A Mortgage Analysis 1906-1934.* Home Title Guaranty Company, 1935.

Pease, Robert H. and Kerwood, Lewis O., eds., *Mortgage Banking.* New York: McGraw-Hill Book Co., Inc., 1965.

Ring, Alfred A. *Real Estate Principles and Practices.* Englewood Cliffs, New Jersey: Prentice-Hall, Inc., 1972.

Skilton, Robert H. *Government and the Mortgage Debtor* (1929 to 1939). Philadelphia: University of Pennsylvania, 1944.

Unger, Maurice A. *Real Estate.* Cincinnati, Ohio: South-Western Publishing Co., 1974.

Weimer, Arthur M., Hoyt, Homer, and Bloom, George F. *Real Estate.* New York: The Ronald Press Co., 1972.

NOTES

1.   Housing in the Seventies, *National Housing Policy Review*, Department of Housing and Urban Development, Washington, D.C. 1974, p. 136.

Chapter 2

The Role of Mortgage Lending in the Economy

Mortgage lending, in addition to fulfilling certain sociological demands, is a principal and essential ingredient of our nation's economy. Viewed in another perspective, mortgage lending allows for the fruition of one of the "American Dreams," that is, owning a home. It also provides a process through which an attractive return on savings can be realized and needed funds can be borrowed.

Mortgage lending could not fulfill these functions without many and varied types of mortgage lenders. The common requisite for all mortgage lenders is the accumulation of sufficient savings to produce the capital needed for mortgage loans. Unless financial institutions have sufficient savings on deposit, capital shortages result and credit restraints occur, affecting all mortgage lenders, often with disastrous results. This was the situation during 1973-74. Secondary mortgage markets can assist during these periods of credit restraint but cannot solve the basic problem of a lack of savings inflow to the mortgage lenders. (See Chapter 6, Secondary Mortgage Markets and Institutions.

CAPITAL FORMATION

The funds required by the financial market are derived primarily from the savings of individuals and businesses. Savings of individuals, in the form of either deposits at financial institutions or reserves that accumulate in whole life insurance policies, account for approximately 90 percent of total savings. Savings inflows are not constant and the savings function must compete with food, shelter, clothing, transportation, recreation and other real or perceived demands for the after-tax income of an individual. Those individuals who do save are motivated by such needs and desires as accumulating funds for retirement, future security, major purchases, college, and others.

Changes in the economy directly affect savings in some manner. For example, if the business cycle is down and unemployment increases, individuals may increase savings because of uncertainty over their employment. The result could be a savings inflow which theoretically should cause interest rates to decline as more dollars chase less demand. On the other hand, with the downturn in the business cycle and increase in unemployment, those unemployed may have to withdraw savings for living expenses.

If the economy is expanding, savings may also accumulate since the demand for funds could reach a point where high interest rates attract more savings. On the other hand, if the economy is expanding, the demand for funds and interest rates may reach the legal limit on interest financial intermediaries can pay on savings. This could influence savers to reinvest elsewhere at a higher rate. This is known as *disintermediation*. The effect is a massive savings outflow devastating to mortgage lending. (See Figure 2-1.) Although future economic cycles may change the result, the past seems to indicate that when the economy overheats, disintermediation will occur as savers seek the highest return on their funds.

During periods of high demand for credit (the apex of a business cycle) the capital markets are usually unable to satisfy the combined demands for credit of individuals, government and business. Mortgage lending usually suffers during such periods since the price of money, as indicated by the interest rate, is too high for most mortgage loans to be economically feasible. Because real estate in general and mortgage lending in particular are the losers in a credit crunch, they have often been classified as countercyclical. This means that real estate activity, and consequently mortgage lending, usually expands when the general business cycle is down and credit demands are low. Conversely, as the economy begins to improve and demand

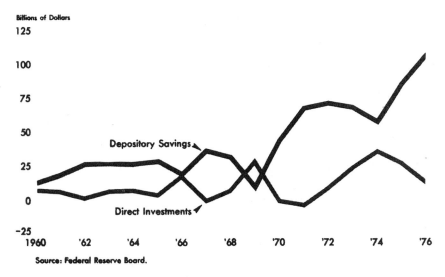

Billions of Dollars

125

100

75

50

Depository Savings

25

0

Direct Investments

−25

1960   '62   '64   '66   '68   '70   '72   '74   '76

Source: Federal Reserve Board.

Figure 2-1. Annual change in depository savings and direct investments of households

for credit from other users increases, real estate activity begins to slow down as interest rates increase. This somewhat simplified explanation demonstrates the direct relationship between the availability of credit and real estate activity.

MORTGAGE MARKETS

Two general markets, capital and money, comprise the total financial market.[1] The mortgage market is only a part of the complete capital market. Within the capital market, a specific demand for funds, e.g. mortgages, must compete with other instruments, such as corporate bonds. Yet, mortgage lending has used more credit in the past 25 years than any other segment of the American economy, exceeding even the staggering credit demands of the federal government. (See Table 2-1.)

If the composite demand for available funds is high, the price for these funds (the interest rate) will probably also be high as well. Therefore, the price of money is subject to supply and demand like any other commodity. For example, if those who are demanding funds for mortgages are willing to pay the price for the funds, credit will be made available. But if corporate demand is also high and corporations are willing to pay a price equal to that offered by mortgages, funds will generally flow to bonds to the detriment of

TABLE 2-1
Growth of Selected Types of Credit

(Billions of Dollars)

Type of Credit	1950	1976*	Increase
Total Credit Outstanding	$427.0	$2,903.1	$2,476.1
Residential Mortgage Loans:			
One- to Four-Family Homes	45.2	554.0	508.8
Multifamily Units	9.3	101.7	92.4
Total	54.5	655.7	601.2
Corporate and Foreign Bonds	39.2	355.5	316.3
State and Local Government Obligations	24.4	248.7	224.3
Consumer Credit	21.5	217.8	196.3
Mortgages on Commercial Properties	12.5	172.0	159.5
Federal Debt	218.4	645.2	426.8

*Preliminary.
Sources: Federal Reserve Board; United States League of Savings Associations.

mortgage lending. The explanation for this relative attractiveness of corporate capital instruments lies in the unique characteristics of mortgage debt which requires a higher yield because of the lack of uniformity in mortgages, lower liquidity and the problems and delays of foreclosure. Although inflation and demand and supply of funds are the most important factors in the rise and fall of interest rates, the degree of risk inherent in any mortgage loan or bond offering also is influential.

PUBLIC DEBT VS. PRIVATE DEBT

When any federal, state, or local government spends more money than it collects, it must borrow in the same markets in which the issuers of bonds and mortgages borrow. In this manner they provide greater competition for the available capital. The federal government in particular has been in a deficit position recently, a condition which many economists believe was the basic cause of the persistent inflation in the 1970s. The inflation and resulting high interest rates have played havoc both in the money markets and capital markets, and all users of credit have suffered.

Many times the fiscal policy of the federal government forces the Federal Reserve to act in an attempt to moderate the inflationary impact of federal borrowing.

FEDERAL RESERVE

In addition to its banking functions, the Federal Reserve has credit control responsibility over the nation's economy through commercial banks. The Federal Reserve has several methods of implementing this control.

Reserve requirements. By increasing the amount of money a member bank must have in its reserve account, less money is available to be loaned. Conversely, if the Federal Reserve policy is to increase the amount of money in order to make credit easier to obtain, it can lower the reserve requirement.

Open Market Operations. This commonly-used method allows the Federal Reserve to decrease the supply of money by selling treasury securities on the open market. The securities are paid by checks drawn on commercial banks. This decreases their reserves, therefore reducing the amount of funds which can be loaned.

Discount Rate. The Federal Reserve operates a service of discounting (paying less than par) commercial paper from member banks. By discounting, the Federal Reserve provides funds which can be loaned. If the discount rate is increased, (considered as the interest rate that a member bank pays the Federal Reserve), it becomes more difficult for a commercial bank to borrow to obtain necessary reserves. Consequently, the interest rate a member bank must then charge a borrower increases. If the discount rate is lowered, borrowing is easier for a commercial bank and the interest rate charged to a borrower could be lowered.

FINANCIAL INTERMEDIARIES

Although the savings of individuals are the most important part of capital formation and mortgage lending, these individual savers are not investing or lending their money directly. Most individuals have neither the time nor the expertise to make sound investment decisions regardless of whether their investment vehicle is mortgages or stocks and bonds. Instead of direct investments, most savers use financial experts who can accumulate the funds of many savers and then invest them at a higher net yield to the saver. These experts are called *financial intermediaries* and include:

1. Commercial banks

2. Credit unions

3. Life insurance companies

4. Mutual savings banks

5. Savings and loan associations

These financial intermediaries have various alternatives for investing the accumulated funds of individuals and others, depending upon laws, regulations and custom. One of the attractive alternatives in addition to stocks and bonds is mortgages, and these intermediaries and others, such as mortgage companies, are the principal mortgage lenders.

MORTGAGE LENDERS

The primary economic function of a mortgage lender is to facilitate the flow of money into and through the mortgage market. A mortgage lender obtains funds accumulated by institutions such as savings and loan associations, commercial banks and life insurance companies and makes these funds available to borrowers in the form of mortgage loans. By bringing together borrowers and lenders from different economic sectors and geographic locations, a mortgage lender contributes to a more efficient allocation of the economy's resources.

The classification *mortgage lender* is used to describe those institutions or organizations at least partially engaged in the primary mortgage market; that is, the extending of funds directly to a borrower. Mortgage lenders may also purchase mortgages originated by other mortgage lenders either directly through fulfilled commitments or the secondary markets. This classification includes:

1. Savings and loan associations

2. Commercial banks

3. Mortgage companies

4. Mutual savings banks

5. Life insurance companies

6. Real estate investment trusts

These mortgage lenders originate nearly all mortgage loans, including all types of residential and income-producing property loans, and hold about 75 percent of the total outstanding mortgage debt.

TABLE 2-2

1977 Approximate Percentage Holdings of
Major Mortgage Lenders of the
Total Outstanding Mortgage Debt

	Percentage
Savings and Loan Associations	36
Commercial Banks	17
Mutual Savings Banks	10
Life Insurance Companies	10
Real Estate Investment Trusts	2
	75
Others	25
	100

Source: Federal Reserve Bulletin, June 1977

A complete discussion on the development of these mortgage lenders, how they are organized and their mortgage lending activity is included in Chapter 3, The Mortgage Lenders.

MORTGAGE INVESTORS

The classification *mortgage investor* is used to describe those institutions that usually do not originate mortgage loans but are important holders of mortgage debt. This classification includes:

1. Federal National Mortgage Association (FNMA)

2. Government National Mortgage Association (GNMA)

3. Retirement and pension funds

4. Credit unions[2]

5. Federal agencies

6. State housing agencies

These mortgage investors acquire the mortgages they hold either directly from the mortgage lenders or through the operations of the secondary market. Historically, the most important of these mortgage investors, FHLMC, FNMA and GNMA, will be discussed in detail in Chapter 6, Secondary Mortgage Markets and Institutions. The others will be discussed briefly at the end of Chapter 3, The Mortgage Lenders.

TRENDS IN MORTGAGE LENDING

More changes currently are influencing mortgage lending than at any other time since the 1930s. These changes affect how needed funds for mortgage financing are raised and loaned. After the turmoil in real estate finance of the 1970s, many borrowers and lenders questioned both the traditional manner of obtaining funds for mortgage lending and the mortgage instruments. The recent history of high inflation and unsettled monetary conditions has increased the need for modernization of the basic mortgage lending industry.

Mortgage lenders have difficulty with the traditional fixed interest rate mortgage when interest rates fluctuate rapidly because of excessive demands for credit, the advent of abnormal inflation, or a combination of both. If interest rates throughout the economy increase, thrift institutions must increase the rate of interest paid on deposits to hold those deposits. If the rate of interest on deposits does not keep pace with general interest rate increases, disintermediation occurs and depositors withdraw their funds and reinvest elsewhere. Disintermediation for mortgage lenders and particularly thrift institutions results in no available funds for mortgage loans. And a credit crunch occurs as it did in 1973-74. (See Figure 2-2.)

Billions of Dollars

Source: United States League of Savings Associations.

Figure 2-2. Net savings gains at insured associations (seasonally adjusted)

On the other hand, if a thrift institution attempts to keep deposits by increasing the rate of interest paid to depositors, its cost of capital and lending increases. The problem is that while a thrift institution must pay the increased rate to all depositors, it is limited on its return to previously-negotiated interest rates on mortgages in its portfolio. Since the return on the mortgage portfolio remains constant or only slightly increases as the rate paid for deposits increases, the net return becomes tenuous.

When the market rates drop, a mortgage lender still may suffer, since a borrower many times simply refinances at a lower rate after paying any prepayment penalty. If lenders are to remain in the mortgage market during periods of extended inflation or rapid interest rate fluctuation, alternate forms of finance must be used.

ALTERNATIVE MORTGAGE INSTRUMENTS

One of the attempted solutions to this problem has been the *due-on-sale clause* whereby a lender can accelerate the loan by calling all payments due if an attempt is made to assign the mortgage when the property is sold. Many courts allow for the enforcement of this clause, recognizing the possibility of a different risk in the borrower who assumes the loan as opposed to the original mortgagor.

A more equitable solution to the lender's problem is the *variable rate mortgage*. Variable rate mortgages are the direct result of inflation and are designed to provide a sufficient return to mortgage lenders to induce them to stay in the mortgage market. This type of mortgage has existed in other countries for many years and has proven satisfactory to both borrower and lender. This alternative recently gained wide acceptance among state-chartered savings and loan associations and commercial banks in California. Although federally-chartered savings and loans currently may not use this type mortgage instrument, other states probably will follow California's example.

The rate on the underlying mortgage will change according to the prevailing market interest rate as fixed by an acceptable standard. An example of this is the cost of money index at a Federal Home Loan Bank. Changes in the underlying rate can occur periodically, usually quarterly or semi-annually, by at least a 0.10 percent rate but not more than a 0.25 percent rate. If a borrower is not satisfied with the rate change, prepayment is allowed with no penalty.

Another alternative is a return to the three-to-five year *short-term mortgage* which was popular prior to the 1930s. The liquidity problem of financial institutions then forced many homeowners to lose their homes because refinancing was not available. Since this situation does not exist today, the mortgage would become due at the end of the three-to-five year term and the mortgagor could pay the balance due or accept a new mortgage—which the mortgagee is obligated to make—at the current interest rate.

A third alternative to the fixed rate mortgage is the *graduated payment mortgage* on which FHA has been authorized to conduct an experimental lending program. Although this program is not designed to encourage mortgage lenders to remain in the long-term mortgage market, it does provide a means for young couples to purchase homes at an initially lower-than-normal monthly debt service. This program recognizes that incomes do increase, and that a larger payment could be made later to offset the initial lower debt service and fully amortize the mortgage loan within the normal 25- to 30-year term.

MORTGAGE-BACKED BONDS

As real estate in general, and single-family units in particular, rebounded from the lows of 1975-76, the need for new sources of mortgage money produced new vehicles for generating the needed capital. The most important innovation was the private mortgage-backed bond with no governmental guarantee. This allows both thrift institutions and commercial banks to raise new funds by pooling existing mortgages and selling a bond backed by these mortgages. The mortgages in these pools are either FHA-insured, VA-guaranteed, or have private mortgage insurance. Standard and Poor's has given many of these bonds the top AAA rating because of the existence of private or governmental insurance and because the bonds are over-collateralized from 150 to 200 percent of face value. (One issuer pledged $340 million of mortgages to collateralize the $200 million worth of bonds.) Other issues insured by private mortgage insurance were not over-collateralized.

SUGGESTED READINGS

Aaron, Henry J. *Shelter and Subsidies: Who Benefits from Federal Housing Policies?* Washington, D.C.: The Brookings Institution, 1972.

Brueggeman, William B., and Baesel, Jerome B. "The Mechanics of Variable Rate Mortgages and Implications for Home Ownership as an Inflation Hedge," *The Appraisal Journal* (April 1976), pp. 236-46.

Candilis, Wray O. *Variable Rate Mortgage Plans.* Washington, D.C.: The American Bankers Association, 1971.

Grebler, Leo, "The New System of Residential Mortgage Finance," *The Appraisal Journal* (April 1976), pp. 434-48.

Hoagland, Henry E., Stone, Leo D., and Brueggeman, William B. *Real Estate Finance*, 6th Ed. Homewood, Illinois: Richard D. Irwin, Inc., 1977.

Jacobs, D. P., Farwell, and Neave, E. H. *Financial Institutions.* Homewood, Illinois: Richard D. Irwin, Inc., 1972.

Meltzer, Allan H. "Credit Availability and Economic Decisions: Some Evidence from the Mortgage and Housing Markets," *Journal of Finance* (June 1974), pp. 763-77.

Seldin, Maury, and Swesnik, Richard H. *Real Estate Investment Strategy.* New York: Wiley-Interscience, 1970.

Stansell, Stanley R., and Miller, James A. "How Variable Rate Mortgages Would Affect Lenders," *Real Estate Review* (Winter 1976), pp. 116-18.

Tucker, Donald P. "The Variable-Rate Graduated-Payment Mortgage," *Real Estate Review* (Spring 1975), pp. 71-80.

Vitt, Lois A., and Berstein, Joel H. "Convertible Mortgages: New Financing Tool?" *Real Estate Review* (Spring 1976), pp. 33-37.

Wiedemer, John P. *Real Estate Finance*, 2nd Ed. Reston, Virginia: Reston Publishing Company, 1977.

NOTES

1. The basic difference between the two markets is the maturity of the financial instruments. Money market instruments (U.S. Treasury Bills, corporate commercial paper, etc.) mature in less than one year. Capital market instruments (bonds and mortgages) mature in more than one year.

2. Although state-chartered credit unions have had the authority to make long-term mortgage loans for a number of years, they have not been a significant factor in mortgage lending. Federally-chartered credit unions were given the authority in 1977 to make long-term mortgage loans but only to their own members.

Chapter 3

The Mortgage Lenders

About 75 percent of the nation's outstanding mortgage debt is held by four major mortgage lenders. (See Table 2-2.) It is important to note that holding mortgage debt does not mean that the institution necessarily originated the mortgage. For example, mortgage companies have originated more than 75 percent of all FHA-VA mortgages made, yet mortgage companies are not listed as holders of any mortgage debt. On the other hand, life insurance companies are listed as holding a substantial amount of mortgage debt although most of this debt was originated by mortgage companies and then sold to life insurance companies.

As contrasted with mortgage holdings, 95 percent of the mortgage loan originations are by four types of mortgage lenders. These will be discussed in the order of their historical origination volume.

SAVINGS AND LOAN ASSOCIATIONS (S&Ls)

The unique role of savings and loan associations in the nation's economy concerns the pooling of savings of individuals for investment in residential mortgages. S&Ls number about 5,000 and are the largest of all mortgage lenders in total mortgage debt held and in annual origination volume. Although the percentage held may vary from year to year depending on savings inflow, S&Ls originate about

50 percent of all residential mortgages and 20 percent of all income-property mortgages each year.

Development

From the founding of the first association in 1831 (Oxford Provident Building Association in Frankfort, Penn.), S&Ls have continued to grow and provide funds for the growth of the nation as well. Although the greatest number of associations was reached in 1927 when more than 12,000 were in existence, the contribution they have made toward providing housing finance has continued to increase. S&Ls provided much of the financing for urban homes for middle-income Americans before the Depression.

The 1930s were years of dramatic change for S&Ls. More than half of those in existence failed during this time and more than 25 percent of S&L mortgage assets were in default. In addition to the general economic depression, the major problem for S&Ls during the early '30s was a lack of liquidity. As non-amortized, short-term mortgages came due, many creditworthy mortgagors were unable to refinance their mortgages because the associations had no funds. Many homes were lost as a result. To help alleviate this liquidity problem, the Federal Home Loan Bank System (FHLB) was created by Congress on July 22, 1932. The FHLB has provided liquidity during periods of credit restraint for member associations and has served the industry in the way that the Federal Reserve System has served the needs of commercial banks. The law provided for the creation of 12 regional banks to serve each geographical area.[1]

Another important step toward the development of the modern S&L occurred with the creation of the Federal Savings and Loan Insurance Corporation (FSLIC) as authorized by Title IV of the *National Housing Act of 1934*. This step was vital for the restoration of faith in the safety of deposits in S&Ls and paved the way for new deposits which were needed before any new mortgage loans could be made. This also increased the assets of S&Ls.

In member S&Ls, the maximum insurance protection for each depositor is currently $40,000.

Organization and Regulation

Savings and loan associations may be chartered by either a state or the federal government and can be either mutual or stock associations. State charters account for about 60 percent of existing associations, with 40 percent operating under Federal charter. In a mutual association all depositors automatically become shareholders of the association, whereas a stock association is owned by private stockholders. Since 1975 federally-chartered associations have been allowed to be stock associations.

Federal associations are required to belong to both the FHLB and the FSLIC. Although state-chartered associations are not so required, most belong to one or both. If a state-chartered association does not belong to the FSLIC, state insurance is usually available. Those state-chartered associations that join the FHLB are subject to the regulations of the FHLB, but they also have access to funds for lending during periods of tight credit. During those periods when savings inflows are not sufficient to meet the demand for mortgage credit, member S&Ls can turn to the FHLB. One of the ways that the FHLB assists S&Ls in tight credit periods is by changing the liquidity requirement. The liquidity, or cash on hand requirement, set by law to range from four to ten percent of total assets, assures that sufficient assets are available if a depositor wants to make a withdrawal. These liquidity reserves are usually held in United States government securities. By lowering the liquidity requirement, more money becomes available for lending. The ability to borrow directly from a regional bank has allowed member associations to continue to make mortgage loans even during periods of severe savings outflow. For example, in 1973 member associations borrowed in excess of $7 billion to offset deposit withdrawals. The FHLB acquires the funds through the sale of bonds and notes in the open market.

Those associations chartered by states but which do not belong to the FHLB are regulated by the respective state on lending area, types of loans, loan-to-value ratio and maximum loan amount. These regulations normally are similar to federal regulations although state regulations usually are more liberal.

The lending area for federally chartered S&Ls is currently limited to 100 miles from any branch within the same state, although these S&Ls may have up to 20 percent of their assets in out-of-state mortgages or mortgage participations.

S&Ls' ability to compete for deposits is increased by their authority (Regulation Q) to offer a .25 percent higher interest rate than commercial banks. Another competitive edge is derived from special treatment under current tax law which grants an incentive for providing residential financing. As long as no more than 18 percent of assets are in commercial mortgages, an S&L may transfer earnings to a nontaxable surplus account. This allows more funds to accumulate for loans.

Mortgage Lending Characteristics

Unlike other private financial institutions, savings and loan associations basically exist to accumulate savings from individuals which are then used to finance home ownership. Originally, S&Ls were concerned only with local housing needs, and this is still their primary interest. Some of the larger S&Ls have become active in the secondary mortgage market, both as buyers and sellers, although this activity is normally attributable to periodic changes in savings inflow, thus making it quite cyclical.

Because of acquired local expertise and legal limitations on their lending area, most S&Ls seldom become involved in either FHA-insured or VA-guaranteed mortgages. Instead, S&L funds are invested in local conventional mortgages originated primarily for association portfolios. This type of mortgage comprises 90 percent of the total number of mortgages held by S&Ls.

General economic conditions locally or nationally can affect the volume of origination of mortgages by S&Ls more than other lenders. If unemployment is high in an S&L primary market, deposits may be low and lending limited. If interest rates are high, disintermediation may occur with similar results.

With respect to mortgage lending, S&Ls have historically given primary emphasis to residential lending and secondary emphasis to income-property lending. All thrift institutions are encouraged by federal tax benefits to invest at least 80 percent of assets in residential mortgages. Current regulations for federally chartered S&Ls (state regulations may be different) allow mortgage loans for the following:

Residential. Maximum term, 30 years; maximum loan amount, a) 80-90 percent loan-to-value, conforming loans (must be 80 percent of portfolio) up to $75,000 with no limit on non-conforming loans, but subject to $75,000 limit in the secondary market, and b) 90-95 percent loan-to-value, $60,000 limit on conforming loans. Loans over 90 percent must have private mortgage insurance. (Alaska, Hawaii, and Guam are slightly higher.)

Income property. Maximum term 25 years; maximum loan-to-value is 75 percent; no limit on mortgage amount.

Leasehold.   Loan limited to those leasehold interests that extend 10 years past loan maturity.

Real estate.   May invest two percent of assets in real estate in urban renewal area.

Home improvement.   Loan limit is $15,000.

COMMERCIAL BANKS (CBs)

Commercial banks have the largest collective membership at about 15,000, and total assets with just under 50 percent of the total assets of all financial institutions. CBs are second only to S&Ls in their holdings of the total outstanding mortgage debt. They are first in origination of income-property loans and construction mortgages, and are second to S&Ls in origination of residential mortgages.

A commercial bank is a private financial institution organized to accumulate funds primarily through time and demand deposits and to make these funds available to finance the nation's commerce and industry. In recent years, commercial banks have expanded their real estate finance operations from mostly short-term mortgage loans to include long-term loans.

Development

Except for a one-year period following the enactment of the National Bank Act of 1863, federally-chartered commercial banks were not allowed to make real estate loans until relatively recently. During the period from 1863 to 1913 state-chartered banks thrived since they were able to make real estate loans. Then in 1913, the Federal Reserve Act provided the authorization for federally-chartered commercial banks to make mortgage loans. The typical CB mortgage loan during this early period was a 50 percent loan-to-value ratio for a five-year term with the principal payable at the end of the term and with interest payable semiannually.

Commercial banks in the 1930s were in a position similar to that of other financial institutions—distressed by being illiquid—and consequently many failed. (In fact, the number of commercial banks decreased from more than 30,000 to about 16,000.) During the early months of President F. D. Roosevelt's first term, many new federal laws affecting the economy were enacted. The Federal Deposit Insurance Corporation (FDIC), authorized by the Banking Act of 1933, helped restore confidence in commercial banks and encouraged badly needed funds to flow back into bank vaults to provide liquidity for new loans. Currently, the FDIC insures deposits in all commercial banks up to $40,000.

Organization and Regulation

Commercial banks are chartered by either the federal government through the comptroller of the currency, or a state banking agency. State-chartered banks outnumber federally-chartered banks by about two to one, although more assets are in the federally-chartered CBs. State-chartered CBs may be members of the Federal Reserve System but only 1,000 or 10 percent are members. All federally-chartered must be members, however. This central banking system, comprising 12 Federal Reserve Districts,[2] provides many services to its members such as issuing currency, holding bank reserves, discounting loans, and serving as a check clearinghouse. (For a discussion of how the Federal Reserve operates to control economic developments, see page 29.)

Mortgage Lending Activity

Commercial banks are quite different from S&Ls. They are neither organized for nor economically inclined toward mortgage lending. CB funds are short term and derived mainly from passbook savings and deposits in checking accounts. Long-term lending is generally not attractive. CBs are interested in commercial loans which are normally short-term and provide a better match between the maturity of assets (loans) and liabilities (deposits). When commercial loan demand is high, practically all CB funds flow to meet that demand and mortgage loans are neglected. During those periods in the business cycle when commercial loan demand is light, CBs have recently placed excess funds in real estate. This excess credit of CBs can be damaging to real estate in general as some unsound mortgage loans result. The CB problem loans in the 1970s, primarily to real estate investment trusts, can be traced directly to 1972-73 when CBs held funds with little commercial loan demand. Much of the current real estate assets of CBs resulted from these poor loan judgments made during that time.

Some CBs holding companies have recently become more active in mortgage lending either by purchasing a mortgage company or establishing their own, while others have formed REITs.

The mortgage lending activity of commercial banks is more diverse than other lenders. Banks not only engage in both government and conventional residential mortgage lending, but also are the largest income-property lender. They are the largest mortgage lender for construction loans and help finance other lenders, especially mortgage companies, by issuing lines of credit which allow for the "warehousing" of loans until needed for delivery to an investor.

Currently, construction loans on residential and income-properties comprise a large percentage of mortgage financing activity by banks. These loans are normally classified as ordinary commercial loans, not real estate loans on the bank's books. The interest rate on these loans is generally two to five points above the prime rate depending on the borrower. These loans are attractive to CBs because of the yield and because the loan is short term (6 to 36 months) making it similar to the bank's source of funds.

The board of governors of the Federal Reserve System issues regulations affecting real estate lending activity by member banks. State-chartered banks are governed by the regulations of the responsible state agency. These regulations usually are similar to those of the Federal Reserve. The current regulations of the Federal Reserve allow loans up to 90 percent of value to be amortized up to 30 years with no limit on the loan amount, although they are subject to a $75,000 limit in the secondary market. A bank can lend up to 70 percent of its deposits or 100 percent of capital and surplus, whichever is greater. CBs may have up to 10 percent of real estate loan units in a "basket," or nonconforming classification. Leasehold loans are allowed if the lease extends at least 10 years past the date of full amortization.

MORTGAGE COMPANIES

A mortgage company usually is identified as a mortgage banker, but that term is somewhat misleading since it implies that the lender is a depository for funds like other banks. Mortgage companies are not depositories but can be classified as intermediaries since they serve as financial bridges between borrowers and lenders.

Less than 1,000 mortgage companies exist throughout the United States although the majority are located in traditional capital-deficit areas such as the South and West. They render a valuable service to both the borrower and the ultimate investor by moving funds by means of mortgage originations and sales from capital-surplus areas to areas where insufficient capital exists for needed growth.

Unlike previously discussed mortgage lenders, a mortgage company does not intentially hold mortgages for its own benefit. All mortgages originated are sold to mortgage investors either directly or through the secondary market. Mortgage companies originate about as many residential mortgages as commercial banks although both originate far less than savings and loan associations. Mortgage companies originate about 75 percent of all FHA-VA mortgages, most of which are currently being pooled in mortgage-backed securities guaranteed by GNMA. Only commercial banks originate more income-property loans than mortgage companies.

Development

Mortgage companies developed to fulfill a need for farm financing in the second half of the 19th century. Following the Civil War, new farm lands were opened in the Ohio Valley and further west which required an infusion of credit from the capital-surplus areas in New England. Originally, a few real estate agents, attorneys and some commercial bankers made the needed mortgage loans and then sold the mortgages either to wealthy individuals or institutions in the east. This practice grew until farm mortgage lending specialists developed and formed the first mortgage companies. At the turn of the century approximately 200 mortgage companies were originating 50 percent loan-to-value ratio farm mortgages with five-year maturities and principal paid at maturity.

Following World War I, the migration from the farms to the developing urban areas accelerated, and a few of the more aggressive mortgage companies began to make single-family mortgage loans. Regarding loan ratio and term, this type of loan was similar to the farm mortgage loans made by mortgage companies for the previous 50 years. The non-amortized mortgage, which normally required refinancing at the expiration of the term, was one of the principle reasons for the large number of families who lost their homes in the depression of the 1930s. The liquidity crisis which prevented other financial institutions from refinancing mortgage loans as they became due had a multiplied effect for mortgage companies.

In the early 1930s, officials of the federal government realized that to prevent more basic political changes from occurring some basic economic changes were needed. The first step taken toward stabilizing the economy was to put a floor under depreciating real estate values. Not only was demand at a low point, but values were being forced down by an ever-increasing foreclosure rate. The Federal Home Loan Bank System was begun in 1932 to help the savings and loan associations, but the Home Owners Loan Corporation (HOLC) in 1933 allowed all lenders to exchange defaulted mortgages for government bonds. This program helped save many family homes as HOLC restructured the mortgage and put it on an amortized basis. It also helped stabilize real estate values since foreclosed mortgages were not forced on the market.

The Federal Housing Administration (FHA), created by the National Housing Act of 1934, provided the main stimulus to the formation of modern mortgage companies. Approximately 80 percent of current mortgage companies were formed after 1934. FHA established minimum standards for both the borrower and the real estate before it would insure a mortgage loan. FHA insurance protected mortgage lenders. FHA minimum standards prompted life insurance companies to seek permission from state insurance commissioners to make out-of-state loans with higher loan-to-value ratios and longer terms. State regulatory authorities eventually agreed to the request and mortgage companies soon began originating FHA-insured mortgages for sale to life insurance companies.

FHA adopted the HOLC practice of amortizing mortgage loans, thus creating a need to service loans sold to investors. Servicing meant that a mortgage company would collect the monthly principal and interest and then forward it to an investor, in addition to ascertaining that taxes and insurance were paid and the property generally maintained. If a default occurred, the mortgage company had the responsibility of curing it, if possible. If not, the mortgage company would handle the foreclosure. The servicing function is what clearly separates the mortgage company from the mortgage broker, who simply handles the sale of a mortgage loan and is then finished with the transaction.

Mortgage companies grew slowly during the slow-growth period of the Depression and World War II. But at the end of the war three factors led to one of the greatest real estate booms this country has ever seen:

1. Pent-up demand for housing because of minimal housing construction for nearly 20 years.

2. The Veterans Administration's mortgage guarantee for eligible veterans.

3. The bountiful financial capacity created by the sale of previously-obligatory government bonds.

This single-family housing boom lasted well into the 1950s, and mortgage companies originated the vast majority of the FHA-VA mortgages made. By the 1960s, the interest of permanent investors (particularly life insurance companies) turned toward income-property loans. So the mortgage companies developed the expertise that also enabled them to originate these multi-million dollar loans.

The evolution of mortgage companies has produced a modern financial institution that is capable of adapting to changes in financial conditions and government activity. Today, most mortgage companies have dual capabilities—single-family housing and income-property production—while some companies specialize in one or the other.

Some of all of the following functions are performed by the modern mortgage company:

1. Originates mortgages on single-family and/or income-property for sale to investors

2. Arranges construction financing, gap financing and interim financing

3. Warehouses single-family loans

4. Services loans sold to investors

Organization and Regulation

The mortgage banking function is performed primarily by mortgage companies, but some commercial banks and savings and loans serve basically the same function. Some of these latter institutions have purchased mortgage companies in order to compete with other mortgage companies.

Unlike the other mortgage lenders, mortgage companies are not chartered by either state or federal government but simply follow either the partnership or incorporation laws and requirements of the state in which the respective company is located. The mortgage company is also unique by not being subject to direct regulation and supervision. If a mortgage company is an approved FHA lender or an FNMA-approved seller/servicer, it is subject to periodic audits. HUD has recently attempted to exercise more control by issuing regulations governing several areas of concern, among them how a mortgagee handles delinquency problems with a mortgagor. During the early 1970s when activity in mergers and acquisitions between commercial banks and mortgage companies were common, the Federal Reserve attempted to exercise some control by requiring approval prior to ownership changes.

Mortgage Lending Activity

The manner in which a mortgage company conducts its residential lending business differs considerably from other lenders. The principal reason for this difference is that mortgage companies usually do not have their own funds to close residential loans. Life insurance companies and other depository institutions can attract their funds needed for mortgage lending directly, but mortgage companies must borrow before they can lend.

Financing the Mortgage Company

Mortgage companies finance lending activity either by the sale of *commercial paper* or by drawing on a line of credit with a commercial bank. Historically, the latter was the primary way of obtaining funds, but commercial paper has recently become equally important. Commercial paper is a short-term debt instrument for which the maximum term is usually 180 or 270 days and that carries a fixed rate for a fixed term. Mortgage companies use this alternative during those periods in the economic cycle when the rate for commercial paper is lower than the prime rate. In addition to the lower cost of borrowing, the need for *compensating balances*—funds left on deposit with a commercial bank to provide increased incentive to lend funds—is either diminished or non-existent. If a commercial bank lends its support to the commercial paper by backing it with an irrevocable letter of credit, the bank will require a fee and some compensating balances. On the other hand, if commercial paper is sold under the name of a holding company of the mortgage company, no compensating balances are required, but the parent company must have a recognizable credit rating before it can render this valuable service to a subsidiary mortgage company. The problem with selling commercial paper is that the market is quite volatile, and during periods of tight money only high-cost funds can be obtained and then only by those companies with the highest credit ratings.

The second alternative for obtaining funds needed by a mortgage company is by drawing on a line of credit with a commercial bank. The loan from the commercial bank will be fully collateralized by closed mortgage loans and repaid from the proceeds of a periodic sale of a group of mortgages to either a permanent investor or in the secondary mortgage market. This process is called *warehousing*. It aptly describes the constant flow of closed mortgages which secure the bank loan into the commercial bank. There the closed mortgages remain until a group, or pool of mortgages, typically $1 million worth, is sold to an investor.

Commercial banks are attracted to this type of loan because it is short-term, involves little risk and because the mortgages that serve as collateral are usually obligated by a commitment to an investor. Commercial banks require this line of credit to be supported by compensating balances usually of 20 percent of the maximum line of credit. These required compensating balances sometimes are tax and insurance escrows collected by a mortgage company and deposited with the lending bank until needed.

A mortgage company pays the prime rate or higher for the borrowed funds, depending on its credit rating and the money market. This often allows for a small marketing profit between the cost of borrowing and the interest rate on the underlying mortgage.

Because of its unique financial characteristics, a mortgage company usually obtains a *commitment* from either a permanent investor, such as a mutual savings bank, or government agency, such as GNMA. That investor agrees to purchase the originated mortgages. A commitment is a contractual agreement between an investor, who agrees to purchase a certain amount of mortgages at a stated interest rate with certain maturities and type of property, and a mortgage company, which agrees to supply them. The commitment agreement may also stipulate whether servicing is to be granted, how it is to be handled, and the fee involved. A commitment, depending on the terms, can require delivery, which is a *take-out commitment*, either immediately or in the future, usually within four months. It may not require delivery at all. This is called a *stand-by commitment*. The commitment may be supported by a fee payable by the mortgage company to the investor and which may be refunded if the commitment is fulfilled. If it is a stand-by commitment the fee is not refunded.

Mortgage companies earn revenue from four sources:

1. An origination fee charged to each borrower

2. A servicing fee charged to the investor

3. Any marketing difference between the interest rate of the underlying mortgage and the rate required by the commitment

4. Any warehousing difference between interest rate of funds borrowed and loaned

Both residential (FHA-VA and conventional) and income-property loans are originated by mortgage companies for sale to the following investors:

1. Life insurance companies—primarily income-property

2. Mutual savings banks—primarily residential

3. Savings and loan associations—all types of loans

4. Federal National Mortgage Association—primarily residential

5. Government National Mortgage Association—primarily residential

6. Commercial banks—primarily income-property

7. Pension funds—all types of loans

Since mortgage companies are not directly regulated on mortgage limits, ratios, lending areas or types of loans, their only limitations are those imposed by purchasers of mortgages or insuring or guaranteeing agencies or companies.

MUTUAL SAVINGS BANKS (MSBs)

Mutual savings banks often have been categorized as commercial banks and at other times as S&Ls. Although an MSB has some of the characteristics of both, it actually is a thrift institution. MSBs are unique, private financial institutions where many individuals keep their savings. Approximately 475 exist in 17 states and Puerto Rico, although more than 60 percent of the total are located in New York and Massachusetts. MSBs, which had total assets of $135 billion at the end of 1976, hold just under 10 percent of the total outstanding mortgage debt and originate about six to eight percent of all residential and commercial mortgages each year. Since MSBs are thrift institutions, this percentage is quite cyclical, depending on savings inflows.

Development

The first mutual savings bank was founded in the same state as the first savings and loan association—Pennsylvania. The Philadelphia Saving Fund Society, the nation's largest mutual savings bank, began in 1816 and was followed in 1817 by the Provident Institute for Savings in Boston. The Boston facility was the first savings bank in New England.

Unlike the early building societies, these institutions were organized to provide facilities to encourage saving by the small wage earner who was being thoroughly ignored by the other financial institutions. They were well received and began to spread throughout the New England states. By 1875 the number of MSBs had reached a peak of 674. The MSB concept never spread far from its origins, probably due to the change in building societies that encouraged savings, and to the development of savings deposits at commercial banks.

Organization and Regulation

Since these institutions are mutual organizations, no stockholders exist. Instead, all depositors share ownership. An MSB is managed by a board of trustees, usually comprised of prominent local and business leaders.

MSBs are chartered only by states and therefore the regulations that govern their operations vary from state to state. These state regulations establish guidelines for deposits, reserves, the extent of mortgage lending allowed, as well as maximum loan amounts, loan terms and loan-to-value ratios. These limits are usually similar to those of S&Ls.

An MSB may be a member of the FHLB but only a few hold membership. All provide federal insurance (FDIC) to depositors.

Mortgage Lending Activity

MSBs differ from other thrift institutions in that they are not obligated to invest a set amount of assets in mortgages. Some may make personal loans and consumer loans, and all MSBs buy government and private securities and make mortgages on residential and income properties. MSBs have always considered mortgage lending to be important and currently about 65 percent of their assets is in mortgages. This percentage has varied throughout the years as the risk in mortgage lending changed and alternate investments became available. The percentage of assets invested in mortgages dropped after the Depression but began to climb again with the rapid growth of the low-risk FHA-VA mortgage loan program after World War II.

In the current mortgage market, MSBs originate both conventional and FHA-VA mortgages for their own portfolios. Since the majority of MSBs are located in capital-surplus areas and therefore have more funds than are demanded locally, they normally purchase low-risk FHA-VA and conventional mortgages from other mortgage lenders, particularly mortgage companies, in capital-short areas of the country.

LIFE INSURANCE COMPANIES (LICs)

There are about 1,750 life insurance companies in the United States. LICs have a long history of mortgage lending and currently hold about 10 percent of the outstanding mortgage debt. Their total assets exceed $320 billion of which about 30 percent is in the form of mortgages.[3] The mix of mortgages between residential (1–4 family) and income-property has changed drastically in the past 30 years. During the residential boom years of the late 1940s and early 1950s, more than 60 percent of the mortgages held were residential, but this mixture is now reversed and more than 80 percent of mortgages held are income-property. LICs differ significantly from other mortgage lenders in the way mortgage loans are acquired. Practically all residential mortgages and many income-property mortgages are originated by other mortgage lenders, primarily mortgage companies, who then sell to a LIC. However, LICs are considered to be mortgage lenders rather than investors because some income-property mortgages loans are made directly to borrowers such as builders and developers without the aid of an intermediary. In addition, some LICs will make mortgage loans only if they are originated by their own regional offices.

Development

The first 25 years of the 20th century witnessed the development and public acceptance of life insurance as major repositories for savings. As more and more American families sought the protection of life insurance, the assets of LICs increased dramatically—ten-fold since 1940. Most life insurance contracts written today, as in the past, are ordinary life insurance policies in which cash value accrues in addition to the death protection. The death protection is the sole feature of term insurance.

Life insurance premium payments provide a steady and substantial cash inflow which life insurance companies can project into the future to balance long-term liabilities, such as death benefits, with safe long-term assets such as mortgages. Mortgages, of course, must compete with other investment alternatives—stocks, bonds and, in some situations, real estate ownership. In any given year, for example, bonds may provide a greater yield to LICs with less risk and greater liquidity than other investment alternatives. Therefore, funds will flow to bonds. Mortgage holdings of LICs as a percentage of total assets have been relatively constant over the past 20 years, although currently only about 30 percent of total assets are in mortgages, down about five percent since 1970.

An LIC's cash inflow comes from premiums on policies, earnings on investments, and repayments of investment principal. This inflow is usually well-regulated and anticipated, but it occasionally puts pressures on a company to put these funds to work immediately.

Until the Depression of the 1930s, the farm mortgage was the primary interest of LICs. Some of these loans were originated directly, but most were originated by mortgage companies which then sold the mortgages to LICs located primarily in the Northeast. This was the beginning of one of the most successful, mutually beneficial business relationships in the U.S. economy. This relationship still continues and is referred to as the *correspondent system.*

The correspondent system became an important way of transacting the mortgage lending business for LICs after the creation of the FHA in 1934. Following the changes in state regulation of LICs, due in a major part to the FHA, they relied heavily on correspondents in various parts of the country to originate loans. The rationale for this system was that the lender could rely on the local expert to originate financially sound loans and in this way the lender would not have the expense of attempting to duplicate that local expertise. In return for this assistance, an LIC would commit to buy a certain dollar amount of mortgages on a periodic schedule, providing a ready market for all loans originated. The LIC would also agree to buy only from one mortgage company and in return expect its commitments to be satisfied. A mortgage company, depending on its size, may have a correspondent relationship with only one investor or with several at the same time.

"The understanding between the loan correspondent who originates and sells loans and the investor who buys such loans is usually covered by a servicing contract. This contract may be one covering all loans which are sold by a correspondent, or each loan may be covered by an individual short form of servicing contract. Such a contract is usually made with the expectation that it will be a continuing arrangement over a long period of time and that it will result in a steady submission of new loans. Its purpose is to avoid misunderstandings about the rights and duties of those who are bound by it."[4]

Regulations

Life insurance companies are regulated by state laws which control either the activities of those LICs located within the state, those doing business within the state, or both. As a general rule, LICs located elsewhere but doing business in a state are limited to the same extent as those within the state.

LICs are considered national lenders because they are not limited to a certain geographical area, as are S&Ls. As a general rule, LICs may make a loan-to-value ratio loan up to 75 percent as established by an appraisal. Most states do not limit the term of the loans, although a term in excess of 30 years is highly unlikely.

The loan amount as established by state regulation is usually a factor based on total assets. For example, in New York, an insurance company is limited on any one loan to two percent of total assets.

Mortgage Lending Activity

LICs have an advantage over other mortgage lenders—the predictable inflow of funds. This advantage may be partially off-set by policy loans during periods of disintermediation, but allows for more orderly planning of mortgage investments by LICs.

Most insurance companies, especially the larger ones, are not currently purchasing residential mortgages. Instead, all new dollars invested in mortgages are for income-property mortgages. (For additional information on this subject, see Chapter 8, Fundamentals of Income-Property Mortgage Lending.)

Some LICs only invest in mortgage loans originated by their regional offices while other LICs rely completely on the correspondent system. Many LICs will consider a *direct placement* in which a builder or developer sends the loan application directly to a life insurance company. But many others expect most loans to come from intermediaries such as mortgage companies.

REAL ESTATE INVESTMENT TRUSTS (REITs)

The real estate investment trust is of recent origin and the smallest in the percentage of total outstanding mortgage debt held (about two percent) of the major mortgage lenders. At the beginning of 1977, 218 REITs held more than $16 billion in total assets.[5]

Development

The forerunner of the modern REIT existed in Massachusetts for many years before changes in federal tax law in 1960 allowed for the development of shareholder-owned trusts that could be treated as conduits for tax purposes in which trusts would not be taxed on those earnings passed to shareholders. The key provisions to the Internal Revenue Code were:

1. A trust, in order to qualify for conduit status, must distribute 90 percent of annual net income to shareholders

2. 75 percent of assets must consist of either mortgages or real estate equities and

3. 75 percent of the trust's earnings must come from those assets.

REITs grew slowly until 1968 when total assets reached $1 billion. This amount doubled in 1969 and by the end of 1970 assets were nearly $5 billion. Growth in the number of REITs and their total assets exploded after 1970, peaking in 1974 when more than 200 REITs had total assets in excess of $21 billion. The success story changed after 1974 because of a combination of overbuilding, poor and improper underwriting, construction material shortages and record-high interest rates. The outlook in general for REITs has been blurred ever since.

During the early 1960s, the REIT industry was dominated by equity trusts which purchased and operated existing income proper-ties. These early trusts provided professionally selected and managed real estate investment opportunities for the small investor, similar to the way mutual funds operated in stocks and bonds. During this same period of time, a few mortgage trusts existed which invested in long-term mortgages. Following the credit crunch of 1966, these trusts became more active in the short-term construction and development (C&D) market, which, until that time, had been dominated by commercial banks. The earnings of these short-term trusts allowed for an increase in their book value which facilitated the sale of additional shares of stock at a premium, the proceeds of which could be used for future leverage.

These short-term trusts produced such phenomenal results that many mortgage companies, commercial banks and life insurance companies followed the trend and formed their own REITs to share in the attractive earnings. From 1970 to 1973 the total assets of all REITs increased from $4.7 billion to more than $20 billion and the number of REITs increased from less than 100 to more than 200.

Much of the real estate construction boom of the early 1970s was funded by these REITs and consequently, when the boom ended in 1974, the result was devastating for most REITs. Without a doubt, a lot of real estate construction occurred in the early 1970s because some REITs were forced to put all available funds to work immediately to produce the earnings necessary to pay high dividends to expectant shareholders. To accomplish this task, many REITs turned to short-term, variable-cost bank loans on which interest rates floated at or above the prime, and to the sale of commercial paper to finance lending operations and increase leverage. The burden of satisfying the debt service requirements of these bank loans forced many trusts into more aggressive lending. This resulted both in a lowering of underwriting standards and massive overbuilding of certain types of properties in some areas, such as condominiums in Florida.

In 1974, several events combined to produce a general economic recession which was actually a depression for the real estate industry:

1. The oil embargo which made recreational properties located far from population centers unattractive

2. A shortage of construction materials which resulted in costly construction delays

3. Record-high interest rates which made construction mortgages floating three to five percent over prime uneconomical.

Massive losses to REITs resulted with corresponding losses to their shareholders. Many of the larger short-term trusts had more than 70 percent of assets in a nonaccruing interest status, which resulted in no dividends being paid to shareholders. As a result, stock prices plummeted and many investors became disillusioned with REITs. Some economic commentators expected many REITs to become bankrupt during these difficult years but only a few did. The reason many survived was that creditor banks did not want to transfer real estate losses from REITs' balance sheets to their own by demanding payment on past due loans. Some REITs recently relinquished their tax-free status to become publicly-owned companies. This allows them to carry forward losses to balance future earnings.

The future for REITs is blurred, but it appears many will probably survive past problems, possibly in a merged form, and again make an important contribution to the real estate finance needs of this nation. In 1977 some of the stronger trusts began making new loans and paying dividends to their shareholders. Many of the pure equity trusts experienced little difficulty during the dark days of 1974 and 1975 and have continued to pay dividends on a regular basis.

Organization and Regulation

The trustees of a REIT, elected by the shareholders, have a function similar to the board of directors of a corporation. Trustees have a responsibility to formulate the trust's general investment philosophy, although the implementation usually is entrusted to an independent advisor. This advisor, which may also lend its name to the trust, is normally a mortgage company, a commercial bank or a life insurance company. In return for its professional services involving originating, underwriting and servicing of loans, the advisor receives a fee, usually ranging from 0.5 to 1.25 percent of the dollar value of the assets managed.

REITs are not directly regulated by either the federal government or state governments. However, they must satisfy the securities law. Since REITs have no restrictions on types of loans, loan amounts, loan-to-value ratios or locations, they can fill a void in real estate finance that other mortgage lenders cannot.

Mortgage Lending Activity

A unique source of funds for mortgage lending exists with REITs. Unlike most other mortgage lenders, which, except for mortgage companies, are depository-type institutions, REITs raise funds through the sale of shares and debt securities or bank borrowing. As a result, the cost of funds to REITs is considerably higher than the cost to other mortgage lenders. Consequently, REITs have tended to focus their lending in those areas of real estate finance that offer higher returns even though higher risks may be involved. An example would be construction and development loans. A few REITs make C&D loans for tract homes, but because of their yield requirements, REITs usually do not make long-term single-family mortgages. In addition to C&D loans, REITs make sale-leaseback loans, long-term income-property loans and short-term gap or interim loans.

OTHER MORTGAGE INVESTORS

Although the previously-discussed mortgage lenders originate practically all mortgage loans and hold a large percentage of the nation's outstanding mortgage debt, they are not the only mortgage investors. Others will be discussed in their order of importance.

Federal National Mortgage Association (FNMA)

This one-time governmental agency, which is now a privately-owned corporation, is the largest single holder of residential mortgage debt, owning in excess of $33 billion in 1977. FNMA does not originate any mortgages directly and is normally associated with the secondary mortgage market. A complete discussion of FNMA appears in Chapter 6, Secondary Mortgage Markets and Institutions.

Governmental National Mortgage Association (GNMA)

GNMA is a governmental agency created in 1968 when FNMA became privately-owned. It is another important mortgage investor that does not originate mortgages. In addition to engaging in the secondary mortgage market, GNMA is the principal means by which the federal government subsidizes home ownership or stimulates the housing industry. The GNMA mortgage-backed security has brought traditionally non-mortgage investors into the mortgage market. A complete discussion of GNMA appears in Chapter 6, Secondary Mortgage Markets and Institutions.

Federal Home Loan Mortgage Corporation (FHLMC)

This is a relatively new (1970) secondary mortgage market participant and does not hold as much mortgage debt in its own name as others in the secondary mortgage market, such as FNMA. A complete examination of FHLMC and its role in supporting the conventional mortgage market appears in Chapter 6, Secondary Mortgage Markets and Institutions.

Retirement and Pension Funds

The funds accumulated in these retirement programs are for the future security of the participants; therefore, the primary investment objective is security for the funds invested. The number of funds and assets of retirement and pension funds are growing and in the near future should equal the life insurance industry.

Until recently, mortgages have not been a significant investment alternative to stocks and bonds for these funds. The reasons are:

1. These funds have not had the technical expertise necessary to invest in mortgages

2. The need to reinvest the monthly payment of principal and interest did not appeal to them

3. The lack of market quotations on mortgages was contrary to their daily needs.

The Employee Retirement Income Security Act of 1974 (ERISA) placed an increased duty on trustees of these funds to exercise greater care in selecting investments to achieve greater diversification and reduce the chances of substantial losses. The lack of performance in the stock and bond markets in recent years has forced fund trustees to consider mortgages as investment alternatives. The GNMA mortgage-backed security provided a bond-type investment that eliminated most of the previous objections to mortgage investments while still providing a yield comparable to high-rated stocks and bonds. Many retirement and pension funds are currently acquiring the expertise to consider long-term mortgages originated by various mortgage lenders as investments.

Credit Unions

A credit union is a specialized thrift institution and one of the fastest growing financial organizations in the American economy. A recent change in federal regulations may stimulate this growth. Since April, 1977 federal credit unions have been authorized to make residential mortgage loans to their members. State-regulated credit unions have had this authority for many years. This activity is expected to begin slowly, but at some future point credit unions could become a significant factor in residential mortgage finance. The problems credit unions will have to overcome are basically the same ones retirement and pension funds are facing.

Federal Agencies

In addition to GNMA and FHLMC, other federal agencies hold about three percent of the total outstanding mortgage debt.[6] The Federal Land Bank held more than $20 billion farm mortgages and the Farmers Home Administration held in excess of $1 billion in 1977. The Federal Housing Administration and the Veterans Administration held more than $5 billion of mortgages they either insured or guaranteed.

State Housing Agencies

Most states now have a state housing agency of one type or another that has the responsibility of providing shelter for low and moderate income families. The funds used in the various programs are often raised from the sale of tax-exempt bonds. The resulting cost of funds for these agencies is relatively low. Many of the state programs subsidize only the mortgage interest rates without the state purchasing the mortgage. Other programs authorize the state to purchase the mortgage and then resell it in the secondary market. These state housing agencies could become more important in the future depending on the position taken by the federal government on providing shelter for low and moderate income families.

SUGGESTED READINGS

Bryant, Willis R. *Mortgage Lending Fundamentals and Practices.* New York: McGraw-Hill Book Co., Inc., 1962.

Campbell, Kenneth D. *Mortgage Trusts: Lenders with a Plus.* New York: Audit Publications, Inc., 1969.

Friend, I., et al. *Study of the Savings and Loan Industry*, Vols. 1–4. Washington, D.C.: Federal Home Loan Bank Board, 1969.

Haverkampf, Peter T. "The Pension Trusts Move into Real Estate Slowly," *Real Estate Review* (Spring 1974), pp. 126-29.

Hines, Mary Alice. "The REIT Shakeout in 1974," *Real Estate Review* (Winter 1975), pp. 56-59.

Hoagland, Henry E., Stone, Leo D., and Brueggeman, William B. *Real Estate Finance*, 6th Ed. Homewood, Illinois: Richard D. Irwin, Inc., 1977.

Jacobs, D. P., and Neave, E. H. *Financial Institutions.* Homewood, Illinois: Richard D. Irwin, Inc., 1972.

Klaman, Saul B. *The Postwar Rise of Mortgage Companies.* New York: National Bureau of Economic Research, Inc., 1959.

McMichael, Stanley L., and O'Keefe, Paul T. *How to Finance Real Estate.* Englewood Cliffs, New Jersey: Prentice-Hall, Inc., 1967.

NOTES

1. These regional banks are located in Boston, New York, Pittsburgh, Indianapolis, Chicago, Cincinnati, Greensboro (N.C.), Little Rock, Topeka, Des Moines, San Francisco, and Seattle.

2. Federal District Banks are located in Boston, New York, Philadelphia, Richmond, Atlanta, Cleveland, St. Louis, Chicago, Minneapolis, Kansas City, Dallas, and San Francisco.

3. Life Insurance Fact Book, 1977.

4. Pease and Kerwood, Editors, *Mortgage Banking*, McGraw-Hill, New York, 2nd Ed., 1963, page 315.

5. REIT Fact Book, 1977, National Association of Real Estate Investment Trusts, Washington, D.C.

6. Federal Reserve Bulletin, September 1977, page A41.

Chapter 4

Security Instruments

PART ONE

MORTGAGES AND DEEDS OF TRUST

A mortgage and a deed of trust (sometimes called a trust deed or trust indenture) are alternate forms of real estate finance instruments used in many states. The purpose of each is to provide an instrument for the lender of money to obtain a security interest in that real estate which is securing the debt.

An excellent definition of a mortgage, which could be expanded to include a deed of trust, is found in Black's Law Dictionary, 4th Edition:

"... a pledge or security of particular property for the payment of a debt or the performance of some other obligation, whatever form the transaction may take, but is not now regarded as a conveyance in effect, though it may be cast in the form of a conveyance."

As it exists today in the United States, the mortgage is unique in many features, but its fundamentals are based on the common law as it developed in England over the past 900 years.

HISTORICAL DEVELOPMENT

The classic common law mortgage, which developed in England after the Norman invasion in 1066, was well developed and established by 1400. Basically it was an actual conveyance, and title transfer, of the real estate serving as security for the debt. For a conveyance to be effective under the common law, possession of that real estate actually had to pass, putting the mortgagee in possession of the real estate.

The instrument conveying the real estate title to the mortgagee contained a *defeasance clause* whereby the mortgagee's title was defeated if payment was made on the due date, called the *law day*. Originally, when title and possession were in the hands of the mortgagee, all rents and profits generated by the land could be retained by the mortgagee. This practice was established because a mortgagee could not charge interest on a loan; any interest was usury, which was illegal. After this law changed and interest could be charged, the mortgagee was forced to credit all rents and profits to the credit of the mortgagor.

Early common law mortgages did not require any action on behalf of mortgagees to protect their rights if a mortgagor failed to perform. Since a conveyance had already been made, the mortgagee had title and possession, and thus the only effect of the mortgagor's nonperformance was the termination of the possibility of *reversion* through the defeasance clause.

The harsh result of a mortgagor not performing after the due date, even when not personally at fault, led mortgagors to petition the king for redress from an inequitable practice. Eventually, the courts of equity gave relief to mortgagors by allowing them to redeem their real estate through payment with interest of the past due debts. This was called the *equity of redemption*. By 1625, this practice had become so widespread that mortgagees were reluctant to lend money with real estate as security since they never knew when a mortgagor might elect to redeem the real estate. Mortgagees attempted to to change this by inserting a clause in mortgages whereby the mortgagor agreed not to seek this redress. But courts of equity refused to allow the practice and would not enforce the clause. In order to restore an equitable balance, the courts began to decree that a mortgagor had a certain amount of time after default, usually six months, in which to redeem the real estate. If this were not done, the mortgagor's equity of redemption would be cancelled or foreclosed.

This action soon became known as a foreclosure suit and is still used in some states today. (See Part 2 of this chapter, Foreclosure and Redemption.)

AMERICAN MORTGAGE LAW

The most important change in the common law that has occurred in American law relates to the concept of who actually owns the real estate that is serving as security for the performance of an obligation. The common law held that the mortgagee was the legal owner of the real estate while it served as security. This was called the *title theory*; the mortgagee had the title. Shortly after the Revolutionary War, a New Jersey court held that a mortgagor did not lose title to real estate serving as security. The court's reasoning was since the law already recognized the right of a mortgagor to redeem the real estate after default, the law had to accept a continuing ownership interest in the mortgagor. The court held that a mortgage created only a security interest in the mortgagee and that title should therefore remain with the mortgagor. This is the law in 28 of the United States today and is called the *lien theory*. Although 23 states still classify themselves as either intermediate or title theory states, actually all states recognize the mortgagor as the legal owner of the real estate. The principal difference between these two theories is in the manner of foreclosure. Currently, mortgagors are able to do as they please with mortgaged real estate as long as the activity does not interfere with the security interest of a mortgagee.

According to current law, any interest in real estate that can be sold can be mortgaged, including a fee simple, a life estate or a lease. The determining factor is whether a mortgagee can be found willing to lend money with that particular interest as security.

THE SECURITY INTEREST

The Mortgage Debt

The debt secured by a mortgage is evidenced by either a promissory note or a bond (Figure 4-1). Normally, the mortgage and the note

NOTE

US $. . . . ., Montana

City

. . . ., 19. . . .

FOR VALUE RECEIVED, the undersigned ("Borrower") promise(s) to pay. . . . .
. . . ., or order, the principal sum of
. . . . .Dollars, with
interest on the unpaid principal balance from the date of this Note, until paid, at the rate of. . . . .
. . . . .percent per annum. Principal and interest shall be payable at. . . . .
. . . ., or such other place as the Note holder may
designate, in consecutive monthly installments of. . . . .
. . . . .Dollars (US $. . . . .), on the. . . . .
. . . . .day of each month beginning. . . . ., 19. . . . . Such monthly installments
shall continue until the entire indebtedness evidenced by this Note is fully paid, except that any remaining indebtedness, if not sooner paid, shall be due and payable on. . . . .

If any monthly installment under this Note is not paid when due and remains unpaid after a date specified by a notice to Borrower, the entire principal amount outstanding and accrued interest thereon shall at once become due and payable at the option of the Note holder. The date specified shall not be less than thirty days from the date such notice is mailed. The Note holder may exercise this option to accelerate during any default by Borrower regardless of any prior forbearance. If suit is brought to collect this Note, the Note holder shall be entitled to collect all reasonable costs and expenses of suit, including, but not limited to, reasonable attorney's fees.

Borrower shall pay to the Note holder a late charge of. . . . . .percent of any monthly installment not received by the Note holder within. .days after the installment is due.

Borrower may prepay the principal amount outstanding in whole or in part. The Note holder may require that any partial prepayments (i) be made on the date monthly installments are due and (ii) be in the amount of that part of one or more monthly installments which would be applicable to principal. Any partial prepayment shall be applied against the principal amount outstanding and shall not postpone the due date of any subsequent monthly installments or change the amount of such installments, unless the Note holder shall otherwise agree in writing. If, within five years from the date of this Note, Borrower make(s) any prepayments in any twelve month period beginning with the date of this Note or anniversary dates thereof ("loan year") with money lent to Borrower by a lender other than the Note holder, Borrower shall pay the Note holder (a) during each of the first three loan years . . . . .percent of the amount by which the sum of prepayments made in any such loan year exceeds twenty percent of the original principal amount of this Note and (b) during the fourth and fifth loan years . . . . .percent of the amount by which the sum of prepayments made in any such loan year exceeds twenty percent of the original principal amount of this Note.

Presentment, notice of dishonor, and protest are hereby waived by all makers, sureties, guarantors and endorsers hereof. This Note shall be the joint and several obligation of all makers, sureties, guarantors and endorsers, and shall be binding upon them and their successors and assigns.

Any notice to Borrower provided for in this Note shall be given by mailing such notice by certified mail addressed to Borrower at the Property Address stated below, or to such other address as Borrower may designate by notice to the Note holder. Any notice to the Note holder shall be given by mailing such notice by certified mail, return receipt requested, to the Note holder at the address stated in the first paragraph of this Note, or at such other address as may have been designated by notice to Borrower.

The indebtedness evidenced by this Note is secured by a Deed of Trust, dated. . . . .
. . . ., and reference is made to the Deed of Trust for rights as to acceleration of the indebtedness evidenced by this Note.

. . . .

. . . .

. . . .

Property Address   *(Execute Original Only)*

MONTANA—1 to 4 Family—6/75—**FNMA/FHLMC UNIFORM INSTRUMENT**

FIGURE 4-1. Note

are separate documents, but in some jurisdictions they are combined. The note should be negotiable so that the originating mortgagee can assign it. This is normal practice for some mortgage lenders such as a mortgage company. The mortgage must, in one way or another, acknowledge and identify the debt it secures. When the entire debt has been paid, the mortgage that secured it loses its effectiveness and no longer creates a lien. A *notice of satisfaction*, or notice of full payment of a mortgage, should be recorded when a debt is paid to clear the *cloud on the title* created by the mortgage.

The Mortgage Instrument

The mortgage instrument, like a deed, does not have to appear in any particular form. There are no set requirements except that it must be in writing. Any wording that clearly indicates the purpose of the instrument, which is to create a security interest in described real estate for the benefit of a mortgagee, is sufficient.

If a conveyance is made to a mortgagee that appears to be a *deed absolute* but is actually intended to be a *conveyance* as security for a debt, all state courts have uniformly held that transaction to be a mortgage even if a defeasance clause is missing. If the parties agree in writing that money will be advanced with the debt for those funds secured by a later mortgage and a mortgage is not executed, the law holds that a creditor has a security interest in the real estate. This interest is called an *equitable mortgage*.

A valid mortgage instrument should include (Figure 4–2):

1. Names of the mortgagor and mortgagee

2. Words of conveyance or a mortgaging clause

3. Amount of the mortgage, interest rate, terms of payment and, in some jurisdictions, a repeat of the provisions of the promissory note or bond

4. Description of the real estate securing the debt

5. Clauses to protect the rights of the parties

MORTGAGE

THIS MORTGAGE is made this.........................day of.........................,
19...., between the Mortgagor,...
.....................................(herein "Borrower"), and the Mortgagee,..................
...., a corporation organized and
existing under the laws of......................................, whose address is..................
....(herein "Lender").

WHEREAS, Borrower is indebted to Lender in the principal sum of...............................
....Dollars, which indebtedness is evidenced by Borrower's
note dated.......................(herein "Note"), providing for monthly installments of principal and
interest, with the balance of the indebtedness, if not sooner paid, due and payable on.......................
....................;

To SECURE to Lender (a) the repayment of the indebtedness evidenced by the Note, with interest thereon, the payment of all other sums, with interest thereon, advanced in accordance herewith to protect the security of this Mortgage, and the performance of the covenants and agreements of Borrower herein contained, and (b) the repayment of any future advances, with interest thereon, made to Borrower by Lender pursuant to paragraph 21 hereof (herein "Future Advances"), Borrower does hereby mortgage, grant and convey to Lender the following described property located in the County of......................................, State of Indiana:

which has the address of..,.........................,
                       [Street]   **[City]**
.........................(herein "Property Address");
      [State and Zip Code]

TOGETHER with all the improvements now or hereafter erected on the property, and all easements, rights, appurtenances, rents, royalties, mineral, oil and gas rights and profits, water, water rights, and water stock, and all fixtures now or hereafter attached to the property, all of which, including replacements and additions thereto, shall be deemed to be and remain a part of the property covered by this Mortgage; and all of the foregoing, together with said property (or the leasehold estate if this Mortgage is on a leasehold) are herein referred to as the "Property".

Borrower covenants that Borrower is lawfully seised of the estate hereby conveyed and has the right to mortgage, grant and convey the Property, that the Property is unencumbered, and that Borrower will warrant and defend generally the title to the Property against all claims and demands, subject to any declarations, easements or restrictions listed in a schedule of exceptions to coverage in any title insurance policy insuring Lender's interest in the Property.

INDIANA—1 to 4 Family—6/75—FNMA/FHLMC UNIFORM INSTRUMENT

IN WITNESS WHEREOF, Borrower has executed this Mortgage.

....(Seal)
                                           —Borrower

....(Seal)
                                           —Borrower

STATE OF INDIANA,......................................County ss:

On this...............day of.........................., 19...., before me, the undersigned, a
Notary Public in and for said County, personally appeared...
...., and acknowledged the execution of the foregoing instrument.

WITNESS my hand and official seal.

My Commission expires:

....
                                  Notary Public

This instrument was prepared by:...

FIGURE 4-2. Mortgage

6. Date

7. Signature of the mortgagor

8. Any additional requirements particular to the jurisdiction, such as acknowledgment.

Clauses to Protect the Rights of the Parties

The above-mentioned elements are the framework upon which a complete mortgage instrument is built. A mortgage instrument should contain clauses to solve all foreseeable problems, and they should be sufficient to protect both parties (Figure 4–3). Of course there are many types of clauses; but the most typical and important ones are the acceleration clause, the prepayment clause and the payment clause. Other clauses, such as those relating to *eminent domain* or *assignment of rent*, for example, are recommended if either party considers it necessary.

Acceleration clause. The acceleration clause is the most important clause in the entire mortgage for the protection of the mortgagee. This clause is generally found in both the mortgage and the instrument that evidences the debt. It states that the entire amount of the debt can be accelerated at the mortgagee's election if the mortgagor defaults or breaches any stated covenant (paragraph 18, Figure 4–3).

(In some states, automatic acceleration clauses are allowed, but these should be avoided if possible, because other options for curing defaults or breaches are available to the mortgagee and may be more beneficial.)

The most common defaults or breaches of covenants by a mortgagor that could trigger acceleration are:

1. Failure to pay principal and interest when due

2. Failure to pay taxes or insurance when due

3. Failure to maintain the property

4. Committing waste (destructive use of property)

UNIFORM COVENANTS. Borrower and Lender covenant and agree as follows:

1. Payment of Principal and Interest. Borrower shall promptly pay when due the principal of and interest on the indebtedness evidenced by the Note, prepayment and late charges as provided in the Note, and the principal of and interest on any Future Advances secured by this Mortgage.

2. Funds for Taxes and Insurance. Subject to applicable law or to a written waiver by Lender, Borrower shall pay to Lender on the day monthly installments of principal and interest are payable under the Note, until the Note is paid in full, a sum (herein "Funds") equal to one-twelfth of the yearly taxes and assessments which may attain priority over this Mortgage, and ground rents on the Property, if any, plus one-twelfth of yearly premium installments for hazard insurance, plus one-twelfth of yearly premium installments for mortgage insurance, if any, all as reasonably estimated initially and from time to time by Lender on the basis of assessments and bills and reasonable estimates thereof.

The Funds shall be held in an institution the deposits or accounts of which are insured or guaranteed by a Federal or state agency (including Lender if Lender is such an institution). Lender shall apply the Funds to pay said taxes, assessments, insurance premiums and ground rents. Lender may not charge for so holding and applying the Funds, analyzing said account, or verifying and compiling said assessments and bills, unless Lender pays Borrower interest on the Funds and applicable law permits Lender to make such a charge. Borrower and Lender may agree in writing at the time of execution of this Mortgage that interest on the Funds shall be paid to Borrower, and unless such agreement is made or applicable law requires such interest to be paid, Lender shall not be required to pay Borrower any interest or earnings on the Funds. Lender shall give to Borrower, without charge, an annual accounting of the Funds showing credits and debits to the Funds and the purpose for which each debit to the Funds was made. The Funds are pledged as additional security for the sums secured by this Mortgage.

If the amount of the Funds held by Lender, together with the future monthly installments of Funds payable prior to the due dates of taxes, assessments, insurance premiums and ground rents, shall exceed the amount required to pay said taxes, assessments, insurance premiums and ground rents as they fall due, such excess shall be, at Borrower's option, either promptly repaid to Borrower or credited to Borrower on monthly installments of Funds. If the amount of the Funds held by Lender shall not be sufficient to pay taxes, assessments, insurance premiums and ground rents as they fall due, Borrower shall pay to Lender any amount necessary to make up the deficiency within 30 days from the date notice is mailed by Lender to Borrower requesting payment thereof.

Upon payment in full of all sums secured by this Mortgage, Lender shall promptly refund to Borrower any Funds held by Lender. If under paragraph 18 hereof the Property is sold or the Property is otherwise acquired by Lender, Lender shall apply, no later than immediately prior to the sale of the Property or its acquisition by Lender, any Funds held by Lender at the time of application as a credit against the sums secured by this Mortgage.

3. Application of Payments. Unless applicable law provides otherwise, all payments received by Lender under the Note and paragraphs 1 and 2 hereof shall be applied by Lender first in payment of amounts payable to Lender by Borrower under paragraph 2 hereof, then to interest payable on the Note, then to the principal of the Note, and then to interest and principal on any Future Advances.

4. Charges; Liens. Borrower shall pay all taxes, assessments and other charges, fines and impositions attributable to the Property which may attain a priority over this Mortgage, and leasehold payments or ground rents, if any, in the manner provided under paragraph 2 hereof or, if not paid in such manner, by Borrower making payment, when due, directly to the payee thereof. Borrower shall promptly furnish to Lender all notices of amounts due under this paragraph, and in the event Borrower shall make payment directly, Borrower shall promptly furnish to Lender receipts evidencing such payments. Borrower shall promptly discharge any lien which has priority over this Mortgage; provided, that Borrower shall not be required to discharge any such lien so long as Borrower shall agree in writing to the payment of the obligation secured by such lien in a manner acceptable to Lender, or shall in good faith contest such lien by, or defend enforcement of such lien in, legal proceedings which operate to prevent the enforcement of the lien or forfeiture of the Property or any part thereof.

5. Hazard Insurance. Borrower shall keep the improvements now existing or hereafter erected on the Property insured against loss by fire, hazards included within the term "extended coverage", and such other hazards as Lender may require and in such amounts and for such periods as Lender may require; provided, that Lender shall not require that the amount of such coverage exceed that amount of coverage required to pay the sums secured by this Mortgage.

The insurance carrier providing the insurance shall be chosen by Borrower subject to approval by Lender; provided, that such approval shall not be unreasonably withheld. All premiums on insurance policies shall be paid in the manner provided under paragraph 2 hereof or, if not paid in such manner, by Borrower making payment, when due, directly to the insurance carrier.

All insurance policies and renewals thereof shall be in form acceptable to Lender and shall include a standard mortgage clause in favor of and in form acceptable to Lender. Lender shall have the right to hold the policies and renewals thereof, and Borrower shall promptly furnish to Lender all renewal notices and all receipts of paid premiums. In the event of loss, Borrower shall give prompt notice to the insurance carrier and Lender. Lender may make proof of loss if not made promptly by Borrower.

Unless Lender and Borrower otherwise agree in writing, insurance proceeds shall be applied to restoration or repair of the Property damaged, provided such restoration or repair is economically feasible and the security of this Mortgage is not thereby impaired. If such restoration or repair is not economically feasible or if the security of this Mortgage would be impaired, the insurance proceeds shall be applied to the sums secured by this Mortgage, with the excess, if any, paid to Borrower. If the Property is abandoned by Borrower, or if Borrower fails to respond to Lender within 30 days from the date notice is mailed by Lender to Borrower that the insurance carrier offers to settle a claim for insurance benefits, Lender is authorized to collect and apply the insurance proceeds at Lender's option either to restoration or repair of the Property or to the sums secured by this Mortgage.

Unless Lender and Borrower otherwise agree in writing, any such application of proceeds to principal shall not extend or postpone the due date of the monthly installments referred to in paragraphs 1 and 2 hereof or change the amount of such installments. If under paragraph 18 hereof the Property is acquired by Lender, all right, title and interest of Borrower in and to any insurance policies and in and to the proceeds thereof resulting from damage to the Property prior to the sale or acquisition shall pass to Lender to the extent of the sums secured by this Mortgage immediately prior to such sale or acquisition.

6. Preservation and Maintenance of Property; Leaseholds; Condominiums; Planned Unit Developments. Borrower shall keep the Property in good repair and shall not commit waste or permit impairment or deterioration of the Property and shall comply with the provisions of any lease if this Mortgage is on a leasehold. If this Mortgage is on a unit in a condominium or a planned unit development, Borrower shall perform all of Borrower's obligations under the declaration or covenants creating or governing the condominium or planned unit development, the by-laws and regulations of the condominium or planned unit development, and constituent documents. If a condominium or planned unit development rider is executed by Borrower and recorded together with this Mortgage, the covenants and agreements of such rider shall be incorporated into and shall amend and supplement the covenants and agreements of this Mortgage as if the rider were a part hereof.

FIGURE 4-3. FNMA/FHLMC uniform covenants

7. Protection of Lender's Security. If Borrower fails to perform the covenants and agreements contained in this Mortgage, or if any action or proceeding is commenced which materially affects Lender's interest in the Property, including, but not limited to, eminent domain, insolvency, code enforcement, or arrangements or proceedings involving a bankrupt or decedent, then Lender at Lender's option, upon notice to Borrower, may make such appearances, disburse such sums and take such action as is necessary to protect Lender's interest, including, but not limited to, disbursement of reasonable attorney's fees and entry upon the Property to make repairs. If Lender required mortgage insurance as a condition of making the loan secured by this Mortgage, Borrower shall pay the premiums required to maintain such insurance in effect until such time as the requirement for such insurance terminates in accordance with Borrower's and Lender's written agreement or applicable law. Borrower shall pay the amount of all mortgage insurance premiums in the manner provided under paragraph 2 hereof.

Any amounts disbursed by Lender pursuant to this paragraph 7, with interest thereon, shall become additional indebtedness of Borrower secured by this Mortgage. Unless Borrower and Lender agree to other terms of payment, such amounts shall be payable upon notice from Lender to Borrower requesting payment thereof, and shall bear interest from the date of disbursement at the rate payable from time to time on outstanding principal under the Note unless payment of interest at such rate would be contrary to applicable law, in which event such amounts shall bear interest at the highest rate permissible under applicable law. Nothing contained in this paragraph 7 shall require Lender to incur any expense or take any action hereunder.

8. Inspection. Lender may make or cause to be made reasonable entries upon and inspections of the Property, provided that Lender shall give Borrower notice prior to any such inspection specifying reasonable cause therefor related to Lender's interest in the Property.

9. Condemnation. The proceeds of any award or claim for damages, direct or consequential, in connection with any condemnation or other taking of the Property, or part thereof, or for conveyance in lieu of condemnation, are hereby assigned and shall be paid to Lender.

In the event of a total taking of the Property, the proceeds shall be applied to the sums secured by this Mortgage, with the excess, if any, paid to Borrower. In the event of a partial taking of the Property, unless Borrower and Lender otherwise agree in writing, there shall be applied to the sums secured by this Mortgage such proportion of the proceeds as is equal to that proportion which the amount of the sums secured by this Mortgage immediately prior to the date of taking bears to the fair market value of the Property immediately prior to the date of taking, with the balance of the proceeds paid to Borrower.

If the Property is abandoned by Borrower, or if, after notice by Lender to Borrower that the condemnor offers to make an award or settle a claim for damages, Borrower fails to respond to Lender within 30 days after the date such notice is mailed, Lender is authorized to collect and apply the proceeds, at Lender's option, either to restoration or repair of the Property or to the sums secured by this Mortgage.

Unless Lender and Borrower otherwise agree in writing, any such application of proceeds to principal shall not extend or postpone the due date of the monthly installments referred to in paragraphs 1 and 2 hereof or change the amount of such installments.

10. Borrower Not Released. Extension of the time for payment or modification of amortization of the sums secured by this Mortgage granted by Lender to any successor in interest of Borrower shall not operate to release, in any manner, the liability of the original Borrower and Borrower's successors in interest. Lender shall not be required to commence proceedings against such successor or refuse to extend time for payment or otherwise modify amortization of the sums secured by this Mortgage by reason of any demand made by the original Borrower and Borrower's successors in interest.

11. Forbearance by Lender Not a Waiver. Any forbearance by Lender in exercising any right or remedy hereunder, or otherwise afforded by applicable law, shall not be a waiver of or preclude the exercise of any such right or remedy. The procurement of insurance or the payment of taxes or other liens or charges by Lender shall not be a waiver of Lender's right to accelerate the maturity of the indebtedness secured by this Mortgage.

12. Remedies Cumulative. All remedies provided in this Mortgage are distinct and cumulative to any other right or remedy under this Mortgage or afforded by law or equity, and may be exercised concurrently, independently or successively.

13. Successors and Assigns Bound; Joint and Several Liability; Captions. The covenants and agreements herein contained shall bind, and the rights hereunder shall inure to, the respective successors and assigns of Lender and Borrower, subject to the provisions of paragraph 17 hereof. All covenants and agreements of Borrower shall be joint and several. The captions and headings of the paragraphs of this Mortgage are for convenience only and are not to be used to interpret or define the provisions hereof.

14. Notice. Except for any notice required under applicable law to be given in another manner, (a) any notice to Borrower provided for in this Mortgage shall be given by mailing such notice by certified mail addressed to Borrower at the Property Address or at such other address as Borrower may designate by notice to Lender as provided herein, and (b) any notice to Lender shall be given by certified mail, return receipt requested, to Lender's address stated herein or to such other address as Lender may designate by notice to Borrower as provided herein. Any notice provided for in this Mortgage shall be deemed to have been given to Borrower or Lender when given in the manner designated herein.

15. Uniform Mortgage; Governing Law; Severability. This form of mortgage combines uniform covenants for national use and non-uniform covenants with limited variations by jurisdiction to constitute a uniform security instrument covering real property. This Mortgage shall be governed by the law of the jurisdiction in which the Property is located. In the event that any provision or clause of this Mortgage or the Note conflicts with applicable law, such conflict shall not affect other provisions of this Mortgage or the Note which can be given effect without the conflicting provision, and to this end the provisions of the Mortgage and the Note are declared to be severable.

16. Borrower's Copy. Borrower shall be furnished a conformed copy of the Note and of this Mortgage at the time of execution or after recordation hereof.

17. Transfer of the Property; Assumption. If all or any part of the Property or an interest therein is sold or transferred by Borrower without Lender's prior written consent, excluding (a) the creation of a lien or encumbrance subordinate to this Mortgage, (b) the creation of a purchase money security interest for household appliances, (c) a transfer by devise, descent or by operation of law upon the death of a joint tenant or (d) the grant of any leasehold interest of three years or less not containing an option to purchase, Lender may, at Lender's option, declare all the sums secured by this Mortgage to be immediately due and payable. Lender shall have waived such option to accelerate if, prior to the sale or transfer, Lender and the person to whom the Property is to be sold or transferred reach agreement in writing that the credit of such person is satisfactory to Lender and that the interest payable on the sums secured by this Mortgage shall be at such rate as Lender shall request. If Lender has waived the option to accelerate provided in this paragraph 17, and if Borrower's successor in interest has executed a written assumption agreement accepted in writing by Lender, Lender shall release Borrower from all obligations under this Mortgage and the Note.

If Lender exercises such option to accelerate, Lender shall mail Borrower notice of acceleration in accordance with paragraph 14 hereof. Such notice shall provide a period of not less than 30 days from the date the notice is mailed within which Borrower may pay the sums declared due. If Borrower fails to pay such sums prior to the expiration of such period, Lender may, without further notice or demand on Borrower, invoke any remedies permitted by paragraph 18 hereof.

FIGURE 4-3. FNMA/FHLMC uniform convenants continued

NON-UNIFORM COVENANTS. Borrower and Lender further covenant and agree as follows:

18. Acceleration; Remedies. Except as provided in paragraph 17 hereof, upon Borrower's breach of any covenant or agreement of Borrower in this Mortgage, including the covenants to pay when due any sums secured by this Mortgage, Lender prior to acceleration shall mail notice to Borrower as provided in paragraph 14 hereof specifying: (1) the breach; (2) the action required to cure such breach; (3) a date, not less than 30 days from the date the notice is mailed to Borrower, by which such breach must be cured; and (4) that failure to cure such breach on or before the date specified in the notice may result in acceleration of the sums secured by this Mortgage, foreclosure by judicial proceeding and sale of the Property. The notice shall further inform Borrower of the right to reinstate after acceleration and the right to assert in the foreclosure proceeding the non-existence of a default or any other defense of Borrower to acceleration and foreclosure. If the breach is not cured on or before the date specified in the notice, Lender at Lender's option may declare all of the sums secured by this Mortgage to be immediately due and payable without further demand and may foreclose this Mortgage by judicial proceeding. Lender shall be entitled to collect in such proceeding all expenses of foreclosure, including, but not limited to, reasonable attorney's fees, and costs of documentary evidence, abstracts and title reports.

19. Borrower's Right to Reinstate. Notwithstanding Lender's acceleration of the sums secured by this Mortgage, Borrower shall have the right to have any proceedings begun by Lender to enforce this Mortgage discontinued at any time prior to entry of a judgment enforcing this Mortgage if: (a) Borrower pays Lender all sums which would be then due under this Mortgage, the Note and notes securing Future Advances, if any, had no acceleration occurred; (b) Borrower cures all breaches of any other covenants or agreements of Borrower contained in this Mortgage; (c) Borrower pays all reasonable expenses incurred by Lender in enforcing the covenants and agreements of Borrower contained in this Mortgage and in enforcing Lender's remedies as provided in paragraph 18 hereof, including, but not limited to, reasonable attorney's fees; and (d) Borrower takes such action as Lender may reasonably require to assure that the lien of this Mortgage, Lender's interest in the Property and Borrower's obligation to pay the sums secured by this Mortgage shall continue unimpaired. Upon such payment and cure by Borrower, this Mortgage and the obligations secured hereby shall remain in full force and effect as if no acceleration had occurred.

20. Assignment of Rents; Appointment of Receiver. As additional security hereunder, Borrower hereby assigns to Lender the rents of the Property, provided that Borrower shall, prior to acceleration under paragraph 18 hereof or abandonment of the Property, have the right to collect and retain such rents as they become due and payable.

Upon acceleration under paragraph 18 hereof or abandonment of the Property, Lender shall be entitled, to the extent provided by applicable law, to have a receiver appointed by a court to enter upon, take possession of and manage the Property and to collect the rents of the Property including those past due. All rents collected by the receiver shall be applied first to payment of the costs of management of the Property and collection of rents, including, but not limited to, receiver's fees, premiums on receiver's bonds and reasonable attorney's fees, and then to the sums secured by this Mortgage. The receiver shall be liable to account only for those rents actually received.

21. Future Advances. Upon request of Borrower, Lender, at Lender's option prior to release of this Mortgage, may make Future Advances to Borrower. Such Future Advances, with interest thereon, shall be secured by this Mortgage when evidenced by promissory notes stating that said notes are secured hereby. At no time shall the principal amount of the indebtedness secured by this Mortgage, not including sums advanced in accordance herewith to protect the security of this Mortgage, exceed the original amount of the Note plus US$.............................

22. Release. Upon payment of all sums secured by this Mortgage, Lender shall release this Mortgage without charge to Borrower.

23. Waiver of Valuation and Appraisement. Borrower hereby waives all right of valuation and appraisement.

FIGURE 4-3. FNMA/FHLMC uniform convenants continued

For the past 15 years, some mortgagees have inserted clauses providing for acceleration if a mortgagor either further mortgages the secured real estate or sells the real estate with the mortgage still attached (paragraph 17, Figure 4–3). This clause ostensibly protects the mortgagee from a change in risk.

Prepayment clause. A mortgagee, especially an institutional investor, lends money with the expectation that it will be repaid over a period of time at a certain, usually fixed rate as stipulated in the mortgage. The mortgagee relies on this schedule of repayment to determine future financial strategy, and could be at an economic disadvantage if forced to accept early payments. This disadvantage would be the result of either having to give up a high interest rate or having to reinvest the funds immediately.

The law is clear; a mortgagee does not have to accept early payment unless so obligated in the mortgage itself. If a mortgagor desires the option of early payment, the provision should be negotiated before the mortgage is executed and be included in the mortgage. Many mortgagees will stipulate in the mortgage that prepayment can be made if a penalty is paid—usually a certain percentage of the outstanding debt. Mortgagees may waive this penalty if they want to remove low-yielding mortgages from their portfolios, but a mortgagor would normally have no desire in prepaying a mortgage with a low interest rate.

Payment clause. The most obvious clause in a mortgage is the one by which a mortgagor agrees to pay the obligation in an agreed-upon manner. Reference usually is made to the note or bond whereby a mortgagor was obligated to pay a certain amount of money. A separate clause may stipulate a covenant to pay taxes and hazard insurance (with a mortgagee payable clause) as they became due on the encumbered real estate. However, this often is a part of the payment clause. A mortgagee may require taxes and insurance to be placed in escrow and collected monthly as part of the mortgage payment.

Deeds of Trust

Before deeds of trust can be used in any state, special enabling legislation must be enacted, since the deed of trust was not known in the common law. One of the basic legal differences between a mortgage and a deed of trust is that a mortgage is a two-party instrument between a mortgagor and a mortgagee, while a deed of trust is a three-party instrument between a borrower, a lender and a third party, called a *trustee* (Figure 4-4). If a deed of trust is used, a borrower conveys title for the real estate securing a debt to a trustee who holds it until the obligation is satisfied, at which time title is conveyed back to the borrower. This is for the benefit of the lender.

Another theoretical difference is the necessity of a mortgagee foreclosing on a mortgage if there has been a default. On the other hand, in most states there is no requirement for a foreclosure with its time-consuming court proceedings if a deed of trust is used. Instead, the trustee has the power of sale to satisfy the debt. Some states, however, require a foreclosure even if the financing vehicle is a deed of trust. Regardless of the situation, there is always a requirement for a public sale. (See Part 2 of this chapter, Foreclosure and Redemption.)

In using a deed of trust there is generally no statutory right of redemption as there is with a mortgage. This is one of the most important reasons for a mortgagee to use a deed of trust rather than

DEED OF TRUST

THIS DEED OF TRUST is made this.........................day of........................,
19...., among the Trustor,..
....................................(herein "Borrower"),...........................
....(herein "Trustee"), and the Beneficiary,
...., a corporation organized and
existing under the laws of....................................., whose address is.................
....(herein "Lender").

BORROWER, in consideration of the indebtedness herein recited and the trust herein created, irrevocably grants and conveys to Trustee, in trust, with power of sale, the following described property located in the County of
................................., State of California:

which has the address of.., ...,
                                            [Street]   **[City]**
..........................(herein "Property Address");
[State and Zip Code]

TOGETHER with all the improvements now or hereafter erected on the property, and all easements, rights, appurtenances, rents (subject however to the rights and authorities given herein to Lender to collect and apply such rents), royalties, mineral, oil and gas rights and profits, water, water rights, and water stock, and all fixtures now or hereafter attached to the property, all of which, including replacements and additions thereto, shall be deemed to be and remain a part of the property covered by this Deed of Trust; and all of the foregoing, together with said property (or the leasehold estate if this Deed of Trust is on a leasehold) are herein referred to as the "Property";

To SECURE to Lender (a) the repayment of the indebtedness evidenced by Borrower's note dated.........
.........................(herein "Note"), in the principal sum of................................
....Dollars, with interest thereon, providing for monthly installments of principal and interest, with the balance of the indebtedness, if not sooner paid, due and payable on
...................................; the payment of all other sums, with interest thereon, advanced in accordance herewith to protect the security of this Deed of Trust; and the performance of the covenants and agreements of Borrower herein contained; and (b) the repayment of any future advances, with interest thereon, made to Borrower by Lender pursuant to paragraph 21 hereof (herein "Future Advances").

Borrower covenants that Borrower is lawfully seised of the estate hereby conveyed and has the right to grant and convey the Property, that the Property is unencumbered, and that Borrower will warrant and defend generally the title to the Property against all claims and demands, subject to any declarations, easements or restrictions listed in a schedule of exceptions to coverage in any title insurance policy insuring Lender's interest in the Property.

CALIFORNIA—1 to 4 Family—6/75—**FNMA/FHLMC UNIFORM INSTRUMENT**

FIGURE 4-4. Deed of trust

IN WITNESS WHEREOF, Borrower has executed this Deed of Trust.

. . . .
—Borrower

. . . .
—Borrower

STATE OF CALIFORNIA, ...County ss:

On this. . . . . .day of. . . . . , 19. . . ., before me, the undersigned, a Notary Public in and for said State, personally appeared. . . . ., known to me to be the person(s) whose name(s). . . . . subscribed to the foregoing instrument and acknowledged that. . . . . .executed the same.

WITNESS my hand and official seal.   Signature:. . . . .

(Reserved for official seal)   . . . .
Name (typed or printed)

My Commission expires:

REQUEST FOR RECONVEYANCE

TO TRUSTEE:

   The undersigned is the holder of the note or notes secured by this Deed of Trust. Said note or notes, together with all other indebtedness secured by this Deed of Trust, have been paid in full. You are hereby directed to cancel said note or notes and this Deed of Trust, which are delivered hereby, and to reconvey, without warranty, all the estate now held by you under this Deed of Trust to the person or persons legally entitled thereto.

Dated:. . . . .

FIGURE 4-4. Deed of trust continued

a mortgage. In many jurisdictions, a mortgagor has a period of time to redeem the property after default and foreclosure. If the right to redeem exists, this period varies from six months to two years, depending on the state. To a mortgagor, the advantage of a deed of trust is that a mortgagee does not have the right to a deficiency judgment. A deficiency judgment is the result of a lawsuit to make up the difference between the amount obtained at a foreclosure sale and the mortgage obligation.

TRANSFERS OF MORTGAGED REAL ESTATE

In all jurisdictions, whether the title or lien theory is followed, the mortgagor has the ability to transfer real estate that is serving as security for a debt and has options on the method of transfer.

   Free and clear. The grantor (the one transferring) could transfer the land free and clear. This would occur if a mortgagor satisfied the obligation secured by the real estate and presumes the mortgage could be prepaid. In such an event, a prepayment penalty might be required. Most mortgaged real estate sold today is transferred in this manner, with a new owner obtaining new financing, since inflation has produced greater equity in real estate than a purchaser would want to buy for cash. Therefore, a new purchaser would rather finance the purchase price than assume the mortgage and pay cash for the equity.

Subject to the mortgage. The grantor could transfer the real estate subject to the mortgage, with the grantee (the one to whom the property is transferred) paying the grantor for any equity. If this occurs, the original mortgage remains effective and the personal liability of the original mortgagor to pay the mortgage continues, although the mortgage payment will probably be made by the grantee from that point on. The grantee becomes the legal owner of the real estate after the sale, although it continues to serve as security for the original mortgage. The grantee assumes no personal liability for the original mortgage payment and could decide to abandon the real estate with no danger of contingent liability. If the grantee stops the mortgage payment and the mortgagee forecloses, the grantee loses only equity in the real estate while the original mortgagor is liable for any amount of the obligation not satisfied by the sale of the mortgaged real estate.

Assumption of the mortgage. The real estate could be transferred to the grantee who would buy the grantor's equity and assume the mortgage. This is the most common manner in which real estate is transferred in those cases where the existing mortgage remains intact. In this situation, the grantee assumes personal liability for satisfying the mortgage debt, while the original mortgagor retains only secondary liability.

Recently some mortgagees have inserted clauses into conventional mortgages to either prohibit the transfer of the mortgage or make the transfer conditional on the approval of the mortgagee. Other mortgagees, especially savings and loan associations, have inserted *due-on-sale clauses* in conventional mortgages, accelerating the entire debt if the real estate is sold with the mortgage still intact. The stated rationale for such a clause is to protect the mortgagee's security interest by forcing the new mortgagor to meet the mortgagee's underwriting requirements. Often, however, the real reason is to force the grantee to assume an increase in the interest rate from the rate on the assumed mortgage to the higher current rate. The validity of these clauses has evolved to the point that courts currently enforce the mortgagee's right to accelerate. This trend could change if alternative mortgage instruments become common, providing mortgagees some protection on their yields.

Many mortgagors, after selling the real estate to the grantee who assumes the mortgage, have requested that the mortgagee sign a *novation contract* which would end any secondary liability on the part of the original mortgagor. Many mortgagees have agreed to sign, but normally the assuming grantee must agree to an increase in the interest rate to the prevailing rate.

Assignments of Mortgages

Many originators of mortgage loans, such as mortgage companies, originate loans for sale to other investors. Any mortgage lender has the right to assign a mortgage even if the mortgagor is unaware of the assignment.

The instrument by which mortgages are assigned should be in writing and the assignment should be recorded immediately to protect the assignee from another possible assignment.

At the time of assignment, the mortgagor may be required to sign an *estoppel certificate*. This is a statement by the mortgagor that there is a binding obligation not yet satisfied, and that the mortgagor has no defenses against the mortgagee. An assigned mortgage has full effect and the mortgage payments may be made directly to the assignee or through the original mortgagee.

PART TWO

FORECLOSURE AND REDEMPTION

DEFAULT

A mortgagor who breaches any of the covenants in a mortgage is considered to be in default. A default is normally caused by a non-payment of principal and interest, but could also result from a failure to pay taxes, provide hazard insurance or maintain the premises. A mortgage instrument is usually worded in such a manner that the mortgagee has certain options in the event of a default. Even if automatic acceleration is required in a mortgage it may not be the best choice for a mortgagee and is certainly not the best alternative for a mortgagor.

There are many reasons why a mortgagor defaults on mortgage obligations. The more common reasons for residential mortgage defaults read like a list of personal tragedies, and usually are:

1. Loss of employment

2. Strike

3. Death of a wage-earner

4. Credit over-extension or bankruptcy

5. Illness of a wage-earner or mounting family medical expenses

6. Marital problems

Income-property mortgage defaults could occur from the reasons listed above, plus:

1. Economic slowdown

2. Inflation

3. Loss of top management

4. Loss of a key industry

In practically all situations, a mortgagee does not want to foreclose if it can be prevented. Although the average American may not believe it, mortgagees not only dislike foreclosure, but generally lose money if they must foreclose.[1] After all, most mortgagees are in the business of lending money, not owning or managing real property.

Typically, a loan is delinquent 30 days before a mortgagee or its agent (e.g., a mortgage company) takes any action. This is primarily because of the awareness that people may occasionally miss a payment because of vacation, forgetfulness or some other logical reason. Although most mortgages provide for acceleration 30 days after the due date for a payment, few are immediately accelerated.

After 30 days, a mortgagee or the agent will attempt to contact the mortgagor to determine why a required payment has not been received. This initial inquiry may enable a mortgagee to resolve the problem and, after charging a late fee to partially offset additional expenses, allow the mortgage to continue. If the mortgage is FHA-insured, however, the mortgagee may not be able to accelerate if the mortgagor has submitted at least 50 percent of past due amounts. (See HUD Handbook 4191.1, Revised 1977.)

If a mortgagee does not require a late fee or accelerates and reinstates the mortgage, it still retains all options, including the right to accelerate for future defaults. Together, a mortgagee and mortgagor are normally able to handle any personal problems that may have led to the delinquency. For example, in a case where a borrower is sick and cannot work for six months, a mortgagee may choose:

1. To collect just a portion of the past due amount immediately

2. To make a second mortgage to bring the loan current

3. To extend the term

4. To look to other solutions tailored to the needs of both parties that will rectify the problem.

The percentage of single-family loans that are delinquent 30 days or more changes with swings in the economy and unemployment. But the percentage in foreclosure is near an historic low. (Table 4–1.) This is due in part to the fact that the inflationary period of the early

TABLE 4-1

National Delinquency Survey Ratios
Not Seasonally Adjusted
U.S. Totals
All 1–4 Family Mortgage Loans

		DELINQUENCY				In Foreclosure
Year	Qtr.	30	60	90 or More	Total	During Quarter
1971	1	2.26	.56	.39	3.21	.20
	2	3.27	.53	.38	3.27	.18
	3	2.59	.62	.43	2.59	.20
	4	2.82	.65	.46	3.93	.21
1972	1	2.21	.58	.37	3.16	.22
	2	2.38	.53	.36	3.27	.22
	3	2.74	.65	.43	3.82	.22
	4	2.42	.78	.45	4.65	.21
1973	1	2.52	.68	.43	3.63	.26
	2	2.81	.64	.39	3.84	.25
	3	3.10	.78	.48	4.36	.23
	4	3.42	.79	.49	4.70	.25
1974	1	2.80	.76	.45	4.01	.25
	2	2.95	.67	.39	4.01	.23
	3	3.03	.77	.43	4.23	.22
	4	3.36	.85	.48	4.69	.25
1975	1	2.90	.81	.51	4.22	.25
	2	2.91	.70	.42	4.03	.23
	3	3.08	.81	.48	4.37	.20
	4	3.49	.83	.53	4.85	.19
1976	1	2.83	.71	.51	4.05	.19
	2	3.20	.72	.51	4.43	.15
	3	3.39	.81	.56	4.76	.16
	4	3.70	.86	.59	5.15	.19
1977	1	2.91	.74	.56	4.21	.21
	2	3.15	.71	.49	4.35	.17

Source: Economics and Research Department, Mortgage Bankers Association of America, Washington, D.C.

1970s has given most homeowners enough equity in their homes to sell (thus keeping their equity) if they have problems making the mortgage payment rather than let it be sold at foreclosure.

FORECLOSURE

After all attempts to cure a default fail, a mortgagee must move to foreclose and protect its investment. It is important for all to realize that when a mortgagee or its agent forecloses a defaulted mortgage, it is only fulfilling its fiduciary responsibility to protect the funds loaned which are actually the savings public's money, whether in the form of passbook savings or life insurance.

There are various forms of foreclosure, depending on state law. Any time before a foreclosure sale or other disposition, a mortgagor or anyone claiming through the mortgagor, such as a spouse or junior lienholders, may exercise the equitable right of redemption. This right is exercised by paying the mortgagee the outstanding balance plus interest and costs and applies to all foreclosures.

As mentioned previously, the first judicial method of cutting off a mortgagor's equity of redemption was known as *strict foreclosure.* If not redeemed within a set time, a court decree transferred the mortgagor's interest to the mortgagee irrespective of any equity of the mortgagor in the property. This result was grossly unfair to the mortgagor. Therefore, a more balanced approach followed which provided for selling the property to secure the debt. The proceeds of the sale went first to satisfy the mortgagee, then other lienholders, and then to the mortgagor.

The four modern methods of foreclosure, depending on the law of a state, are: (See Figure 4-5.)

1. Judicial proceeding

2. Power of sale

3. Strict foreclosure

4. Entry and possession

Judicial Proceeding

Most states provide for mortgage foreclosure through a court pro-ceeding. This method best protects the interests of the various

STATE BY STATE COMPARISON OF SELECTED ASPECTS OF FORECLOSURE

State	Nature of Mortgage	Customary Security Instrument	Predominant Method of Foreclosure	Redemption Period (Months) (If customary security instrument used)	Possession During Redemption	Deficiency Judgment Allowed?
Alabama	Title	Mortgage	Power of Sale	12	Purchaser	Yes
Alaska	Lien	Trust Deed	Power of Sale	None	–	No
Arizona	Lien	Trust Deed	Judicial	None	–	Yes
Arkansas	Intermediate	Mortgage	Power of Sale	12	Purchaser	Yes
California	Lien	Trust Deed	Power of Sale	None	–	No
Colorado	Lien	Trust Deed	Power of Sale	2½	Mortgagor	Yes
Connecticut	Intermediate	Mortgage	Strict Foreclosure	None	–	No
Delaware	Intermediate	Mortgage	Judicial	None	–	No
Dist. of Columbia	Intermediate	Trust Deed	Power of Sale	None	–	Yes
Florida	Lien	Mortgage	Judicial	None	–	Yes
Georgia	Title	Security Deed	Power of Sale	None	–	Yes
Hawaii	Title	Trust Deed	Power of Sale	None	–	Yes
Idaho	Lien	Trust Deed	Power of Sale	None	–	Yes
Illinois	Intermediate	Mortgage	Judicial	12	Mortgagor	No
Indiana	Lien	Mortgage	Judicial	3	Mortgagor	Yes
Iowa	Lien	Mortgage	Judicial	6	Mortgagor	No
Kansas	Lien	Mortgage	Judicial	12	Mortgagor	Yes
Kentucky	Lien	Mortgage	Judicial	None	–	Yes
Louisiana	Lien	Mortgage	Judicial	None	–	Yes
Maine	Title	Mortgage	Entry and Possession	12	Mortgagor	Yes
Maryland	Title	Trust Deed	Power of Sale	None	–	Yes
Massachusetts	Intermediate	Mortgage	Power of Sale	None	–	Yes
Michigan	Lien	Mortgage	Power of Sale	6	Mortgagor	Yes
Minnesota	Lien	Mortgage	Power of Sale	12	Mortgagor	Yes
Mississippi	Intermediate	Trust Deed	Power of Sale	None	–	Yes
Missouri	Intermediate	Trust Deed	Power of Sale	12	Mortgagor	Yes
Montana	Lien	Mortgage	Judicial	12	Mortgagor	Yes
Nebraska	Lien	Mortgage	Judicial	None	–	No
Nevada	Lien	Mortgage	Power of Sale	None	–	Yes
New Hampshire	Title	Mortgage	Power of Sale	None	–	Yes
New Jersey	Intermediate	Mortgage	Judicial	None	–	No
New Mexico	Lien	Mortgage	Judicial	1	Purchaser	Yes
New York	Lien	Mortgage	Judicial	None	–	Yes
North Carolina	Intermediate	Trust Deed	Power of Sale	None	–	No
North Dakota	Lien	Mortgage	Judicial	12	Mortgagor	Yes
Ohio	Intermediate	Mortgage	Judicial	None	–	Yes
Oklahoma	Lien	Mortgage	Judicial	None	–	Yes
Oregon	Lien	Trust Deed	Power of Sale	None	–	Yes
Pennsylvania	Title	Mortgage	Judicial	None	–	Yes
Rhode Island	Title	Mortgage	Power of Sale	None	–	No
South Carolina	Lien	Mortgage	Judicial	None	–	Yes
South Dakota	Lien	Mortgage	Power of Sale	12	Mortgagor	Yes
Tennessee	Title	Trust Deed	Power of Sale	None	–	No
Texas	Lien	Trust Deed	Power of Sale	None	–	Yes
Utah	Lien	Mortgage	Judicial	6	Mortgagor	Yes
Vermont	Intermediate	Mortgage	Strict Foreclosure	6	Mortgagor	Yes
Virginia	Intermediate	Trust Deed	Power of Sale	None	–	Yes
Washington	Lien	Mortgage	Judicial	12	Purchaser	Yes
West Virginia	Intermediate	Trust Deed	Power of Sale	None	–	Yes
Wisconsin	Lien	Mortgage	Power of Sale	None	–	Yes
Wyoming	Lien	Mortgage	Power of Sale	6	Mortgagor	Yes

CAVEAT This chart only lists the customary form of security instrument used in each state and not all the forms that could be used. Therefore, the method of foreclosure and period of redemption (if allowed) will be listed only for the customary form and not for all possible security instruments. The reader is further cautioned that many states have extensive qualifications and limitations on the period of redemption and for obtaining a delinquency judgment.

Consult a local attorney for details.

FIGURE 4-5. State by state comparison of selected aspects of foreclosures

parties. The action is much like any other civil suit in that the case must be brought in the court with jurisdiction, either a circuit or district court of the state where the real estate is located. The procedure involved requires a complaint naming the borrower, who now is the defendant, alleging that a mortgage was executed by the defendant using specifically described real estate as security for a loan and that a default has occurred whereby the mortgagee has had to accelerate. The complaint will request foreclosure.

The defendant always has an opportunity to answer the allegations with any defenses available. For example, the defendant may attempt to prove that:

1. no mortgage existed

2. the mortgage was satisfied

3. no default occurred

4. the interest rate was usurious

If the decision of a court is in favor of a mortgagee, the decree of foreclosure terminates the equitable right of redemption at the time of sale, and a mortgagor loses all rights to the real property except the right to any excess proceeds from sale after secured parties are paid. The exception is if a state has a statutory right of redemption. The court decree will order a sale and the manner for its execution. Many courts will include an *upset price* in the decree which is the acceptable minimum bid at the sale. The court usually specifies the officer, such as a sheriff or referee, who will conduct the sale after giving the statutory notice of the sale. To encourage purchasers, a successful bidder acquires title to the property unencumbered by any interest, except that of the mortgagor's statutory right of redemption, if allowed.

With one possible exception, anyone who can contract can purchase property at a foreclosure sale. Some states prevent a defaulting mortgagor from purchasing since the unencumbered title would cut off the rights of junior lienholders. Probably the best laws are those that allow a mortgagor to repurchase at a foreclosure sale where all liens on the real estate prior to foreclosure reattach.

The key element in this form of foreclosure is that the sale must be accepted or confirmed by the court retaining jurisdiction. This requirement is for the protection of both the mortgagor and junior lienholders since a court will not approve a price which is unconscionably low.

Power of Sale

This method is sometimes called *foreclosure by advertisement* since the clause creating a power of sale calls for an advertisement to give notice of the sale. This method is used primarily with deeds of trust, but it can be used with mortgages.

The power to use this method rather than the more cumbersome judicial proceeding comes from a clause that is part of the securing instrument. The clause specifically explains how the sale will be carried out. This method does not preclude a mortgagor's statutory right of redemption if it exists, although many states do not allow such a right if the instrument is a deed of trust.

Foreclosure by advertisement requires procedures which vary among the states. Therefore, extreme care should be taken to insure that proper notice is given and that other requirements are fulfilled. The proceeds from the sale are distributed in the same way as those in a judicial proceeding.

Strict Foreclosure

As mentioned earlier, this was the original method of foreclosure. It is still used in some states which classify themselves as title theory states. The action involves a court of equity and requests a decree giving a mortgagor a period of time to exercise the equitable right of redemption or lose all rights to the property with title vesting irrevocably in the mortgagee. When requesting this type of relief, a mortgagee must be able to prove all allegations just as it must in judicial proceedings.

Entry and Possession

Entry and possession is used only in Maine, Massachusetts, New Hampshire and Rhode Island. After default, a mortgagee gives the mortgagor notice that possession will be taken. If the mortgagor does not agree peacefully to relinquish possession, the mortgagee will have to use a judicial method. This "peaceful possession" needs to be witnessed and recorded. If the mortgagor does not redeem in the statutory period, title vests with the mortgagee.

An alternative to foreclosure which may be of benefit to both the mortgagor and mortgagee would be the execution of a deed transferring the secured real estate to the mortgagee in lieu of foreclosure. The benefits to a mortgagor would include not being subject to the embarrassment of a foreclosure suit or possibly being liable for a deficiency judgment. A mortgagee would benefit by immediately acquiring title to the real estate for a quick sale.

For a deed in lieu to be effective in transferring title, the existing mortgage liability of the mortgagor must be extinguished. If not, the transaction and deed will be considered as nothing more than a new security agreement.

The mortgagee must carefully consider the consequences of this alternative before it is used. If a mortgagee decides to take a deed in lieu of foreclosure, the rights of junior lienholders will not be extinguished. On the other hand, if a mortgagee forecloses, junior lienholders' rights are extinguished if not satisfied by the proceeds of the sale, but the mortgagor has the right of redemption which can be of serious consequence to a mortgagee.

Redemption

In addition to the equity of redemption already discussed, 26 states provide another form of redemption right which begins to accrue to a mortgagor or those claiming through the mortgagor after foreclosure and sale depending on the type of security instrument. This is called the statutory right of redemption because it only exists if created by statute. This redemption period ranges from six months to two years depending on the state.

There are two reasons for a statutory right of redemption: 1) to provide a mortgagor with a chance to keep the real estate, and 2) to encourage bidders at foreclosure sales to bid the market value. The first is more important in agricultural states where a bad growing season can be followed by bumper crops. This right would provide a method for a mortgagor to keep the farm. This same reasoning applies in some income-property situations, but rarely in a residential case. The second reason is equally important for all types of real estate since a bidder at a forced sale would more likely bid the true market value rather than chance later divesture by the mortgagor.

The right of redemption currently has a limited impact on single-family transactions since most of these transactions use a trust deed rather than a mortgage. This makes a difference because many states do not allow the statutory right of redemption with a trust deed based on the concept that a grantor had conveyed all interest to the trustee at the creation of the transaction and consequently had nothing on which to base the redemption.[2] Other states allow it, regardless of what the transaction is called, because if real estate secures a debt, then the transaction is a mortgage and all rights attach. Even if the redemption right exists for a mortgagor, it is seldom exercised by single-family mortgagors who are more likely to sell their property before foreclosure if there is equity to protect.

The right, as previously mentioned, is important to agricultural or income-property mortgagors. If a mortgagor wants to redeem, it must be done within the statutory period by paying the purchaser the price paid at the foreclosure sale, not the outstanding balance on the mortgage, plus interest and costs.

One of the problems inherent with this right usually emerges in a jurisdiction that allows a mortgagor to retain possession during the redemption period. This is necessary if a farmer is to have the advantage of a good year, but it can be catastrophic with income-property if a mortgagor with financial difficulties cannot or will not properly maintain the property. Mortgagees so deeply dread this possibility that many will "trade" their right to a deficiency judgment for immediate possession, possibly by taking a *deed in lieu* of foreclosure.

Other Considerations

In some states, a mortgagee could elect to sue rather than foreclose, based on the promissory note the mortgagor signed. If allowed, the decision might be based on the fact a mortgagee does not believe a forced sale would yield sufficient compensation, but a judgment based on the note could attach to all the debtor's property, and yield full compensation.

Some states allow a mortgagee to sue on the mortgage and force a sale and if not fully compensated, also sue on the note and get a deficiency judgment.

SUGGESTED READINGS

Hebard, Edna L., and Meisel, Gerald S. *Principles of Real Estate Law.* Cambridge, Massachusetts: Schenkman Publishing Co., 1967.

Kratovil, Robert. *Modern Mortgage Law and Practice.* Englewood Cliffs, New Jersey: Prentice-Hall, Inc., 1972.

_____. *Real Estate Law.* Englewood Cliffs, New Jersey: Prentice-Hall Inc., 1974.

Lusk, Harold F. *The Law of the Real Estate Business.* Homewood, Illinois: Richard D. Irwin, Inc., 1975.

NOTES

1. "It is perhaps the normal situation to find any project in foreclosure to be in need of substantial repair. Many mortgagors, during a period of diminishing income, utilize the net income to keep the mortgage current as long as possible, keeping maintenance expenses to a bare minimum. When the evil day arrives that the income will no longer cover the mortgage payments, he falls into default and the subject of the foreclosure action is a property which requires substantial expenditures to place it in properly inhabitable condition, and to make it attractive to the rental market." Court quoting FHA comments in *U.S. vs. Stadium Apartments, Inc., 425F. 2d 358, 365 (1970).*

2. Comment, Comparison of California Mortgages, Trust Deeds, and Land Sales Contracts, 7 *U.C.L.A. Law Review* 83 (1959).

Chapter 5

Underwriting the Residential Loan

The term *underwriting* is used in many segments of the American economy to describe the process of analyzing information relating to risk and making a decision whether or not to accept that risk. In real estate, underwriting is an integral part of the mortgage lending process, regardless of the type of loan or the type of property securing the mortgage. Although similarities exist in the underwriting of all types of real estate loans, the differences are fundamental and of great importance. This chapter examines the steps in underwriting a residential loan. The underwriting of an income-producing property loan will be covered in Chapter 8, Fundamentals of Income-Property Mortgage Lending.

INTRODUCTION

All mortgage loans involve the risk of a possible loss to a mortgage lender or investor. The underwriting involved to determine this risk on a residential mortgage loan requires the gathering and analysis of much information about both the applicant and the real estate which will secure the loan.

This underwriting could involve more than that accomplished by a mortgage lender. On any one residential loan, three separate underwriting reviews could occur at various stages on the mortgage lending cycle:

1. A *mortgage lender* may analyze the risk and determine whether to lend funds to a borrower for a period of time secured by a certain piece of real estate.

2. A *mortgage insuror or guarantor* may determine if mortgage insurance will be written, or a guarantee made based on the loan as submitted.

3. A *permanent investor* may determine if the mortgage or mortgages as submitted will be purchased.

Each of these underwriters will analyze the submission and estimate the risk to the institution being represented and determine if the benefits are sufficient to balance the risk. Mortgage lending is a risk business and a lender must be willing to take a business risk to earn a fee or make a profit and satisfy the real estate financing needs of the nation. All mortgage lenders have a responsibility to attempt to satisfy a request for a mortgage loan as long as the risk is fully analyzed and acceptable. The duty to make a loan if at all possible must be balanced by a mortgage lender's duty to protect funds loaned, which are the savings of depositors or life insurance policy holders.

Of the three mentioned underwriting stages, mortgage lenders have the most difficult underwriting task because they face the delinquency problems that can result from improperly-underwritten mortgages.

A mortgage company also has a unique problem. Unlike other mortgage lenders, a mortgage company must underwrite a loan knowing the loan must be sold to a permanent investor either directly or through the secondary market. If a loan is not attractive as made, a substantial discount may be needed to make it marketable. This can involve considerable loss to a mortgage company. Since most other mortgage lenders have the option of placing mortgages they originate in their own portfolios, their marketing loss potential for a poorly underwritten mortgage is less than that of a mortgage company. All lenders, of course, share the danger that a poorly underwritten mortgage can become delinquent.

If a default occurs, the cost of either curing the default or foreclosing could eliminate present or future profit made from either marketing or servicing. For example, loss could result from a poorly underwritten mortgage if the defaulted loan is in a pool of mortgages securing a GNMA mortgage-backed security. In this situation, the originating mortgage lender must pay the monthly accrued principal and interest to the security holder from its own funds. As is evident, the underwriting phase in the mortgage lending cycle can have a lasting effect, obligating the originating mortgage lender to exercise professional expertise in underwriting.

Unfortunately, no uniform underwriting guidelines exist for all residential mortgage loans. Mortgage lenders have had to adopt and follow different underwriting rules, regulations and formulas depending on whether a residential mortgage loan was conventional, FHA-insured or VA-guaranteed.[1] Many of these differences are not of major significance in underwriting but instead affect loan processing. If a specific difference exists on an important point, it will be explained; otherwise a composite of these underwriting guidelines will be used. It is important to realize only guidelines exist, not specific, precise formulas that can be applied to every applicant. Underwriting is an art, not a science, and the successful underwriter is one who can analyze all relevant material and make a mortgage loan if justified while protecting the assets of others.

INITIAL INTERVIEW

The underwriting process for a residential loan begins with the initial interview between the lender and a potential borrower. The importance of this face-to-face interview cannot be emphasized enough since it allows for counseling if the borrower is attempting to borrow more than he or she can handle. It also allows a mortgage lender to save future time and paperwork if the borrower is obviously not qualified.

During the interview, a lender should apply the various general guidelines to establish whether the underwriting process should continue. For a lender, these guidelines are not absolute formulas but are used only to assist in establishing whether a borrower is qualified. Typical guidelines include:

1. Monthly principal, interest, taxes, insurance and others (such as condominium or homeowners' association fees) should *not* exceed 25 percent of gross monthly income: if FHA-insured, 35 percent of net effective income

2. Monthly mortgage debt service, taxes, insurance and other fixed monthly obligations extending eight to 10 months or more into the future should not exceed 33 percent of gross monthly income: if FHA-insured, 50 percent of net effective income

3. Stable employment history

4. Adequate liquid assets for closing and moving expenses

5. Strong mortgagor motivation

6. Acceptable real estate

If a mortgage lender determines that a borrower is apparently qualified and seriously interested and not just shopping for the lowest interest rate, a mortgage loan application should be taken.

At this point, the underwriting begins in earnest and a mortgage lender will request supporting documentation and necessary verifications. (See Chapter 14, Residential Mortgage Loan Case-Studies.)

An underwriter will be particularly interested in:

1. Financial capability of a borrower

2. Credit characteristics of a borrower

3. Real estate securing the mortgage

FINANCIAL CAPABILITY OF THE BORROWER

A borrower's income provides the means for the repayment of the mortgage debt and other household and long-term debts. Not only is current income important, but the prospect for continuation of that income must be determined. The *Request for Verification of Employment* form (Figure 5-1) requests from an employer the amount of current income, type of income, tenure of employment and probability of continued employment.

The amount of income usually is not an item of controversy, but the type of income can be. If all income is derived from commissions or bonuses, an obvious problem exists regarding the possibility of lower sales income in a subsequent year which would not support the continuation of the commission income at the present level. As a rule, if the past two or three years establish the current level as "normal," the income should be given full weight. If income derived from overtime or part-time work is necessary to qualify the loan, a lender should establish whether the additional income is expected to continue and whether the amount of that income is reasonable for the additional employment.

Self-employed applicants should be required to furnish a copy of federal income tax returns for the last two or three years to support the claim of income received. Tax returns also may be requested in other situations to verify income claims, such as if income from securities is the main support for mortgage payments.

FHA-insured Mortgage

HUD-FHA uses *net effective income*, or monthly income minus estimated federal income tax, in analyzing a mortgagor's financial capacity for an FHA-insured loan. HUD-FHA applies a guideline of 35 percent of net effective income as the maximum amount that should be applied to housing expense.

Housing expenses, according to HUD-FHA regulations, include:

1. Principal and interest

2. Mortgage insurance

3. Hazard insurance

4. Taxes and special assessments

5. Maintenance

6. Utilities

7. Homeowner association fees

Conventional Mortgage

A conventional mortgage utilizes *gross monthly income*, which is income before any deductions, in analyzing a mortgagor's financial capacity to carry the mortgage debt. The suggested guideline is that principal, interest, taxes and insurance, and homeowner's association fees if applicable, should not exceed 25 percent of gross monthly income.

Long-term Debts

It is recognized that different mortgagors with the same income and the same housing expenses may have other financial obligations which will affect their future financial capacity. The permissible ratio of these other liabilities against income varies according to the type of mortgage sought. For an FHA-insured mortgage, the guideline suggests prospective housing expenses and other recurring expenses should not exceed 50 percent of net effective income. FHA defines recurring expenses as those extending a year or more into the future. For a conventional mortgage, the relationship of total monthly obligations (obligations extending eight to 10 months or more into the future) should not exceed 33 percent of gross monthly income.

CREDIT CHARACTERISTICS OF THE BORROWER

Of great concern to any mortgage lender is the answer to the question of the applicant's credit record. If an applicant has demonstrated an inability to handle financial obligations, the amount of current income and its relationship to outstanding obligations is more crucial. In some situations, a mortgage lender may not be able to justify a loan to an applicant regardless of current income because of past credit problems. In all situations, an applicant should be given the opportunity to explain and possibly justify credit problems.

Federal National Mortgage Association

REQUEST FOR VERIFICATION OF EMPLOYMENT

INSTRUCTIONS LENDER Complete items 1 thru 7. Have applicant complete item 8. Forward directly to employer named in item 1

EMPLOYER Please complete either Part II or Part III as applicable. Sign and return directly to lender named in item 2.

PART I · REQUEST

1 TO *(Name and address of employer)*	2 FROM*(Name and address of lender)*		
3 SIGNATURE OF LENDER	4 TITLE	5 DATE	6 LENDER'S NUMBER *(optional)*

I have applied for a mortgage loan and stated that I am now or was formerly employed by you. My signature below authorizes verification of this information.

7 NAME AND ADDRESS OF APPLICANT *(Include employee or badge number)*	8 SIGNATURE OF APPLICANT

PART II · VERIFICATION OF PRESENT EMPLOYMENT

EMPLOYMENT DATA		PAY DATA			
9 APPLICANT'S DATE OF EMPLOYMENT	12A BASE PAY ☐ ANNUAL ☐ HOURLY ☐ MONTHLY ☐ OTHER *(specify)* ☐ WEEKLY			12C FOR MILITARY PERSONNEL ONLY PAY GRADE	
10 PRESENT POSITION				TYPE	MONTHLY AMOUNT
	12B EARNINGS			BASE PAY	$
11 PROBABILITY OF CONTINUED EMPLOYMENT	TYPE	YEAR TO DATE	PAST YEAR	RATIONS	$
13 IF OVERTIME OR BONUS IS APPLICABLE, IS ITS CONTINUANCE LIKELY?	BASE PAY	$	$	FLIGHT OR HAZARD	$
	OVERTIME	$	$	CLOTHING	$
	COMMISSIONS	$	$	QUARTERS	$
OVERTIME ☐ YES ☐ NO				PRO PAY	$
BONUS ☐ YES ☐ NO	BONUS	$	$	OVER SEAS OR COMBAT	$

14. REMARKS *(if paid hourly, please indicate average hours worked each week during current and past year)*

PART III · VERIFICATION OF PREVIOUS EMPLOYMENT

15 DATES OF EMPLOYMENT	16 SALARY/WAGE AT TERMINATION PER (Year) (Month)(Week) BASE _____ OVERTIME _____ COMMISSIONS _____ BONUS _____
17 REASON FOR LEAVING	18 POSITION HELD

The above information is provided in strict confidence in response to your request

19 SIGNATURE OF EMPLOYER	20 TITLE	21 DATE

The information on this form is Confidential. It is to be transmitted directly to the lender, without passing through the hands of the applicant or any other party.

PREVIOUS EDITIONS MAY BE USED UNTIL OCT 1, 1977

FNMA Form 1005
Feb 77

FIGURE 5-1. Request for verification of employment

A mortgage lender must be aware of two important limitations on credit information gathering. The first is the *Fair Credit Reporting Act*[2] which is designed to insure fair and accurate reporting of information regarding consumer credit. A mortgage lender seeking credit information from a consumer reporting agency must certify the purpose for which the information is sought and use it for no other purpose. The act prohibits investigative reports which are based on interviews with neighbors and others relating to character, general reputation, mode of living and other subjective areas. Certain previous credit information (such as a bankruptcy more than seven years before) is also prohibited unless the principal is $50,000 or more. If credit is denied, the consumer *must* be notified if the denial is based on information contained in a credit report.

A more recent federal law of far reaching effect is the *Equal Credit Opportunity Act (ECOA)*[3] which became law on Oct. 28, 1975 and was substantially changed by amendments effective March 23, 1977. ECOA prohibits a creditor from discriminating in the extending of credit based on:

1. Race

2. Color

3. National origin

4. Sex

5. Marital status

6. Age (provided borrower can legally contract)

7. The fact that all or part of income is derived from a public assistance program

A loan application form may ask if the applicant is unmarried, married or separated, but not whether the applicant is divorced. Questions concerning an applicant's spouse are prohibited unless:

1. Spouse will be contractually liable

2. Spouse's income will be used to qualify

3. Applicants live in a community property state

4. Applicant will use child support, alimony or separate maintenance payments from a spouse or former spouse to qualify.

Questions concerning fertility, birth control practices or the possibility of children in the future may not be asked, although the age and current number of children may be asked.

The act further states that no classification of income such as part-time or retirement may be rejected automatically, but must be analyzed in view of its probable continuation. In addition, if a woman's income is being relied upon, it cannot be assumed she will become pregnant or, that it will prevent further employment if she does.

Finally, a mortgage lender must notify an applicant within 30 days of receipt of a completed application whether the loan has been approved substantially as submitted or rejected. If the loan is rejected, the applicant must be informed of the specific reasons.

Within the legal framework of the credit information limitations, a mortgage lender should gather as much information as possible on an applicant's credit record. The analysis of the information supplied in a credit report by a reputable reporting agency (Figure 5-2) should be directed at four key areas:

1. History of past credit: how much credit has the applicant had and what have been the repayment terms?

2. Type of credit: has the applicant had a past real estate loan, an auto loan or other installment type loans?

3. Attitude toward credit: are the active accounts current, and is there any recent bankruptcy or judgment?

4. Lapses in employment or debt repayment history: how many unexplained lapses, and for how long?

AVAILABLE ASSETS

The size of the equity or down payment is of great importance to an underwriter. The experience of many investors has shown that less risk is present in loans with a higher equity or down payment. The applicant must have sufficient assets not only to make the required down payment, but to close the transaction as well. Sufficient assets for both can be ascertained by a *Request for Verification of Deposit* (Figure 5-3). In some situations, a down payment may be made

EQUIFAX / RETAILERS COMMERCIAL AGENCY   CONFIDENTIAL
MORTGAGE LOAN REPORT   SPECIMEN - ALL ENTITIES FICTITIOUS

| Acct. No. | 00000 | | Report Made By Equifax ☐ Retailers ☒ | Atlanta OFFICE |

Date 00-0-00   REPORT FROM (If not city in Heading) (State whether former addr., etc.)
NAME (& Spouse) JONES, RICHARD C. (JULIA)
Address Atlanta, Ga., 234 Lark Street Case or File Number M-276589
Emp-Occ XYZ Corporation - Manager
Bus Add Atlanta, Ga., 456 Peachtree St. Property Address 18 Meadow Lane, Atlanta, Ga.

1. Time known by each source?	1. 3yrs., 5yrs., Intv. Wife
2. Are name & addresses correct as given?	2. Yes
3. About what is age? (If around 21, verify if possible.)	3. 34
4. Is applicant married? How long married? No. dependents (including spouse)?	4. Yes How long? 7yrs. No. of deps.? 3
5. Name of Employer.	5. XYZ Corporation
6. What is nature of business? (State kind of trade or Industry.)	6. Building Material Mfg.
7. Position held—how long with present employer?	7. Manager How long? 5yrs.
8. Is present employment reasonably secure?	8. Yes
9. Work full time steadily? (If not, how many days per week?)	9. Yes
10. Employment status changed within the past two years?	10. No
11. Annual earned income from employment or business?	11. $ 17,000 Exact ☒ Estimated ☐
12. Approximate annual income, if any, from other sources. (Investments, rentals, pensions.)	12. 250 Source: Invest.
13. What would you estimate net worth?	13. $ 35,000
14. Does applicant own home or rent?	14. Own Home
15. If rents home, what is amount of monthly rental?	15. $ -
16. If spouse employed, give name of employer.	16. Housewife
17. Position held—approximate ANNUAL INCOME.	17. - Income $ -
18. Approximate number of years employed.	18. -
19. Do you learn of any failures, bankruptcies, mortgage foreclosures, suits, judgments or garnishments? (If so, state which. Give details.)	19. None

REMARKS. 20. CREDIT RECORD: Set out CREDIT RECORD in tabular form below.
(Please write a separate paragraph on each)

21. BUSINESS—FINANCES: Cover business history for minimum of two years. If any change in employment within 2 years, list names and locations of former connection. Cover financial position, giving breakdown on worth. Cover income from investments, rentals, pensions, etc., showing source and regularity.

22. RESIDENCE: Show how long subject has lived at this address and former addresses if developed. Comment when information developed during report as to responsibility or financial difficulties may affect earnings or paying ability. (DO NOT REPORT INVESTIGATIVE CONSUMER INFORMATION.)

Trade Line	How Long Selling	Date Last Sale	Highest Credit	Terms of Sale	Amount Owing	Amount Past Due	Paying Record
Bank-Mtge.	6-73	-	$26,102	$96.45/Mo.	$21,472	None	Satis.-J
Dept. Store	4-75	5-78	550	Revolving	None	None	30 Day Slow-I
Bank-Auto	3-77	-	4,000	100/Mo.	2,200	$100	30 Day Slow-J
Oil Card	7-75	4-78	76	Revolving	None	None	Prompt-I

BUSINESS-FINANCES: Richard.C. Jones is employed as a manager for the XYZ Corporation at the above captioned address and has been so employed for the past 5 years, earning $17,000 per year as verified by employer. Subject has $250 annual additional income from stock dividends. The subject's net worth consists of equity in home, savings, automobile and household effects.

RESIDENCE: The subject is married to Julia for the past 7 years and has two children, ages 5 years and 3 years. They have resided at 234 Lark Street, Atlanta, Ga. for the past 5 years where they are buying.

WFG/st
2cc

Equifax Inc.
Form 1667—2-76 U.S.A.

FIGURE 5-2. Sample credit report for mortgage loan purposes. Use of this form by courtesy of Retailers Commercial Agency, Inc., Atlanta.

Federal National Mortgage Association

REQUEST FOR VERIFICATION OF DEPOSIT

INSTRUCTIONS   LENDER - Complete Items 1 thru 8   Have applicant(s) complete Item 9   Forward directly to
depository named in Item 1

DEPOSITORY - Please complete Items 10 thru 15 and return DIRECTLY to lender named in Item 2

PART I - REQUEST

1 TO (Name and address of depository)	2 FROM (Name and address of lender)		
3 SIGNATURE OF LENDER	**4 TITLE**	**5 DATE**	**6 LENDER'S NUMBER** (Optional)

7 INFORMATION TO BE VERIFIED

TYPE OF ACCOUNT	ACCOUNT IN NAME OF	ACCOUNT NUMBER	BALANCE
			$
			$
			$
			$

TO DEPOSITORY   I have applied for a mortgage loan and stated in my financial statement that the balance on deposit with you is as shown above   You are
authorized to verify this information and to supply the lender identified above with the information requested in Items 10 thru 12   Your response is solely
a matter of courtesy for which no responsibility is attached to your institution or any of your officers

8	NAME AND ADDRESS OF APPLICANT(s)	9	SIGNATURE OF APPLICANT(s)

TO BE COMPLETED BY DEPOSITORY

PART II - VERIFICATION OF DEPOSITORY

10 DEPOSIT ACCOUNTS OF APPLICANT(s)

TYPE OF ACCOUNT	ACCOUNT NUMBER	CURRENT BALANCE	AVERAGE BALANCE FOR PREVIOUS TWO MONTHS	DATE OPENED
		$	$	
		$	$	
		$	$	
		$	$	

11 LOANS OUTSTANDING TO APPLICANT(s)

LOAN NUMBER	DATE OF LOAN	ORIGINAL AMOUNT	CURRENT BALANCE	INSTALLMENTS (Monthly/Quarterly)	SECURED BY	NUMBER OF LATE PAYMENTS
		$	$	$ per		
		$	$	$ per		
		$	$	$ per		

12 ADDITIONAL INFORMATION WHICH MAY BE OF ASSISTANCE IN DETERMINATION OF CREDIT WORTHINESS
(Please include information on loans paid-in-full as in Item 11 above)

Subject to the requirements of the Fair Credit Reporting Act, the information provided in Items 10 thru 12 is furnished to you in strict confidence in response
to your request   The accuracy of such information is not guaranteed

13 SIGNATURE OF DEPOSITORY	14 TITLE	15 DATE

This form is to be transmitted directly to the lender and is not to be transmitted through the applicant or any other party.

FNMA Form 1006
Rev Dec 75

★ ★ ★ ★ THIS FORM MUST BE REPRODUCED BY LENDER ★ ★ ★ ★

FIGURE 5-3.   Request for verification of deposit

from funds supplied by parents or relatives of the applicants. This is acceptable as long as funds are legally a gift not to be repaid and the donors sign an affidavit to that effect. (Figure 5-4.)

REAL ESTATE SECURING THE MORTGAGE

The third stage in underwriting a residential mortgage loan involves an analysis of the real estate which will secure the mortgage debt. Although it is expected that the income of a borrower will be available to fulfill the mortgage obligation, a mortgage lender must protect both its own position and that of any ultimate investor by having adequate security for the debt. The adequacy of the security will be established by an appraisal.

An appraisal is an opinion or estimate of value made by an appraiser who is either an independent fee appraiser or employed by a mortgage lender. The appraisal not only helps establish the adequacy of the security but also establishes the value of the security upon which the loan-to-value ratio will be applied.[4] (See Chapter 10, Appraising Real Estate for Mortgage Loan Purposes.)

An underwriter will use the appraisal and other information—such as city growth plan—to evaluate the following:

1. *Physical security.* The age, equipment, architectural design, quality of construction, floor plan and site features are considered in establishing the adequacy and future value of the physical security.

2. *Location.* The type of neighborhood in which the subject property is located, its condition and its proximity to amenities is of paramount importance. The availability of public transportation and public utilities will add to the attractiveness of the location.

3. *Local government.* The amount of property tax can have a great effect on future marketability. Building codes, deed restrictions and zoning ordinances help to maintain housing standards and promote a high degree of homogeneity.

THE UNDERWRITING DECISION

When all information relating to a borrower's financial capabilities, credit characteristics and the physical security are present, a decision

GIFT LETTER

TO WHOM IT MAY CONCERN:

I, _____, do hereby certify that I have
                donor

made a gift of $_____ to my _____
                                          relationship

to be applied toward the purchase of the property located at

_____

I further certify that there is no repayment expected or implied

on this gift either in the form of cash or future services from

_____ and/or _____
        recipient   co-recipient

                        _____
                                      donor

                    Date _____

ACKNOWLEDGMENT

I, _____, and I, _____

hereby certify to the receipt of the gift made by_____

in the amount of $_____to be applied toward the purchase of

the referenced property.

                        _____
                        Purchaser

                        _____
                        Purchaser

                    Date_____

FIGURE 5-4. Typical gift letter

must be made to accept, reject or modify the mortgage loan application.

All of the items must be reviewed individually and in conjunction with other items being considered. For example, a number of credit characteristics may have deficiencies that are not serious when considered alone, but when combined with other characteristics could affect a mortgagor's ability or willingness to pay, possibly leading to a future default. Although all underwriters should attempt to approve a loan application if at all prudently possible, the approval of a loan that will become delinquent is a disservice to the borrower, the mortgage lender and those it represents.

HUD-FHA has an *Evaluation of Mortgagor Risk Report* which an examiner can use to rate a mortgagor's credit characteristics (Figure 5-5). An underwriter must exercise care in using a checklist of this type in order not to miss the reason for a rejection. For example, if an applicant is rejected because of a bad attitude toward credit, the loan should not become acceptable by reducing the amount of the loan.

EVALUATION OF MORTGAGOR RISK REPORT

	Mortgagor Features	Rating
1.	Credit Characteristics of Mortgagor	_____
2.	Motivating Interest in Ownership of the Property	_____
3.	Importance of Monetary Interest to Mortgagor	_____
4.	Adequacy of Available Assets for Transaction	_____
5.	Stability of Effective Income	_____
6.	Adequacy of Effective Income for Total Obligations	_____
	Mortgagor Rating	_____

RATING FEATURES. Each feature will be classified as "Accepted" or "Rejected" based on the thorough analysis of the elements that comprise that feature. The over-all risk is reflected in the Mortgagor Rating which is completed only after each feature has been classified. Although the risk in each feature may be border-line, at least one feature must be rated "Rejected" to justify a rejected classification for the Mortgagor Rating.

FIGURE 5-5. Evaluation of mortgagor risk report. Source: Mortgage Credit Analysis Handbook (4155.1), U.S. Department of Housing and Urban Development, Washington, D.C., July 1972.

UNDERWRITING WORKSHEET

	Verified	Acceptable
I. Financial Capability		
A. Of the applicant		_____
1. Primary employment	_____	_____
2. Self-employed	_____	_____
3. Secondary employment	_____	_____
4. Other income	_____	_____
B. Of the co-applicant (if any)		_____
1. Primary employment	_____	_____
2. Self-employed	_____	_____
3. Secondary employment	_____	_____
4. Other income	_____	_____
II. Credit Characteristics		_____
A. Past real estate loans	_____	_____
B. Installment loans	_____	_____
C. Bankruptcy, judgments	_____	_____
D. Lapses	_____	_____
III. Real Estate (Security)		_____
A. Structure		_____
1. Age ____ years		_____
2. Amenities		_____
3. Condition		_____
B. Neighborhood		_____
C. Local Government		_____

Underwriting worksheet

SUGGESTED READINGS

Pease, Robert H., and Kerwood, Lewis O., eds. *Mortgage Banking.* New York: McGraw-Hill Book Co., Inc., 1965.

Shenkel, William M. *Modern Real Estate Principles.* Dallas, Texas: Business Publications, Inc., 1977.

_____. *Real Estate Finance.* Washington, D.C.: American Bankers Association, 1976.

Unger, Maurice A. *Real Estate.* Cincinnati, Ohio: South-Western Publishing Co., 1974.

Weimer, Arthur M., Hoyt, Homer, and Bloom, George F. *Real Estate.* New York: The Roland Press Co., 1972.

LOAN ANALYSIS

	LOAN NUMBER

SECTION A – LOAN DATA

1. NAME OF BORROWER	2. AMOUNT OF LOAN $	3. CASH DOWN PAYMENT ON PURCHASE PRICE $

SECTION B – BORROWER'S PERSONAL AND FINANCIAL STATUS

4. APPLICANT'S AGE	5. OCCUPATION OF APPLICANT		6. NUMBER OF YEARS AT PRESENT EMPLOYMENT	7. LIQUID ASSETS (Cash savings, bonds, etc.) $	8. CURRENT MONTHLY RENTAL OR OTHER HOUSING EXPENSE $
9. IS SPOUSE EMPLOYED? ☐ YES ☐ NO	10. SPOUSE'S AGE	11. OCCUPATION OF SPOUSE	12. NUMBER OF YEARS AT PRESENT EMPLOYMENT		13. AGE OF OTHER DEPENDENTS

SECTION C – ESTIMATED MONTHLY SHELTER EXPENSES (This Property)

SECTION D – DEBTS AND OBLIGATIONS (Itemize and indicate by (✓) which debts considered in Section E, Line 42)

	ITEMS	AMOUNT		ITEMS	(✓)	MO. PAYMENT	UNPAID BAL.
14.	TERM OF LOAN: YEARS		23.			$	$
15.	MORTGAGE PAYMENT (P&I)(@____%)	$	24.				
16.	REALTY TAXES		25.				
17.	HAZARD INSURANCE		26.				
18.	SPECIAL ASSESSMENTS		27.				
19.	MAINTENANCE		28.				
20.	UTILITIES (Including heat)		29.				
21.	OTHER		30.	JOB RELATED EXPENSE (Child care, etc.)			
22.	TOTAL	$	31.	TOTAL	$		$

SECTION E – MONTHLY INCOME AND DEDUCTIONS

	ITEMS		SPOUSE	BORROWER	TOTAL
32.	GROSS SALARY OR EARNINGS FROM EMPLOYMENT		$	$	$
33.	DEDUCTIONS	FEDERAL INCOME TAX			
34.		STATE INCOME TAX			
35.		RETIREMENT OR SOCIAL SECURITY			
36.		OTHER (Specify)			
37.		TOTAL DEDUCTIONS	$	$	$
38.	NET TAKE-HOME PAY				$
39.	PENSION COMPENSATION OR OTHER NET INCOME (Specify)				
40.	TOTAL (Sum of lines 38 and 39)		$	$	$
41.	LESS THOSE OBLIGATIONS LISTED IN SECTION D WHICH SHOULD BE DEDUCTED FROM INCOME				
42.	TOTAL NET EFFECTIVE INCOME				$
43.	LESS ESTIMATED MONTHLY SHELTER EXPENSE (Line 22)				$
44.	BALANCE AVAILABLE FOR FAMILY SUPPORT				$

45. PAST CREDIT RECORD ☐ SATISFACTORY ☐ UNSATISFACTORY	46. DOES LOAN MEET VA CREDIT STANDARDS? (Give reasons for decision under "Remarks," if necessary, e.g., borderline cases) ☐ YES ☐ NO

47. REMARKS (Use reverse, if necessary)

SECTION F – DISPOSITION OF APPLICATION

☐ Recommend that the application be approved since it meets all requirements of Chapter 37, Title 38, U.S. Code and applicable VA Regulations and directives.

☐ Recommend that the application be disapproved for the reasons stated under "Remarks" above.

48. DATE	49. SIGNATURE OF EXAMINER

50. FINAL ACTION ☐ APPROVE APPLICATION ☐ REJECT APPLICATION	51. DATE	52. SIGNATURE AND TITLE OF APPROVING OFFICIAL

VA FORM
SEP 1974 **26-6393**   EXISTING STOCK OF VA FORM 26-6393, JUL 1973, WILL BE USED.

Veterans Administration loan analysis form

NOTES

1. For FHA-insured single-family mortgage, see HUD Handbook, *Mortgage Credit Analysis Handbook* (4155.1), July 1972 as amended pages 1–29. For VA-guaranteed mortgage, see VA *Lenders Handbook*, December 1969.

2. Effective April 25, 1971, Title VI of the *Consumer Credit Protection Act*, as amended, 15 USC 1601 et. seq.

3. Also known as *Regulation B*, effective March 23, 1977, Title VII of the *Consumer Credit Protection Act*, as amended, 15 USC 1601 et. seq. Please note: This brief review is *not* intended in any way to be a complete discussion of ECOA. Competent counsel should be consulted concerning all laws governing the granting of credit in your jurisdiction.

4. All financial institutions are limited by federal or state laws to certain loan-to-value ratios for loans in their portfolios.

Chapter 6

Secondary Mortgage Markets and Institutions

One of the most important reasons for the sharp increase in real estate lending activity since the end of World War II has been the general availability of mortgage money at reasonable rates. This availability, although sporadic at times, has been largely the result of the development of a secondary market for mortgages. During periods of tight money or credit restraints such as existed in 1966, 1969-70 and 1974, the activity of the secondary market, especially that of the Federal National Mortgage Association, accounted for a large portion of the residential lending that did occur.

Primary vs. Secondary

The distinction between what is known as the *primary* and *secondary* mortgage markets is not always clear, and one is often used to describe activity in the other. The term *secondary market* is not used often in regard to income-property loan mortgage transactions, although the possibility exists for a true income-property loan secondary market in the future.

Most authorities agree that a primary market exists when a lender extends funds directly to a borrower. This would occur whether the lender is originating the mortgages for its own portfolio (e.g., most thrift institutions) or for sale to another investor (e.g., a mortgage company). (See Chapter 3, The Mortgage Lenders.)

The secondary market exists when primary lenders and permanent investors buy and sell existing mortgages from each other. This activity could occur as part of the normal course of business for the mortgage lender, or be utilized only during periods of credit restraints.

> "The secondary market for residential mortgages is that part of the mortgage market in which existing mortgages are bought and sold. The primary market, on the other hand, is that part of the market in which mortgages are originated. Thus, the primary market involves an extension of credit and the secondary market a sale of the credit instrument." [1]

The authors of this statement further limit this definition by excluding mortgages originated with a prior commitment from an investor.

> "This definition excludes transactions from the secondary market that were preceded by the buyer's promise to purchase the loans prior to their acquisition by the seller. In such "sales" the transaction is no more than a transfer from agent to principal and is, therefore, assigned to the primary market. Thus, the definition of the secondary market is limited to sales of mortgages without prior commitment from the buyer." [2]

When these quotes were published the type of commitment used was a firm commitment which established contractually the obligation the originator had to deliver and the investor had to buy. The current practice of many institutions active in the secondary market is to use a *standby commitment* which provides an originator with the opportunity to deliver if no better price is available elsewhere. A fee is charged for the service.

ECONOMIC FUNCTIONS OF THE SECONDARY MORTGAGE MARKET

In order to provide the needed economic assistances to mortgage lending, a secondary mortgage market should perform these four important economic functions:

1. *Provide liquidity.* Many investors who have traditionally not invested in mortgages, such as pension funds, trust accounts and

credit unions, are now beginning to invest in mortgages because the required liquidity is present. These investors are interested in the relatively higher yields available with mortgages, and realize that a ready market exists if they are forced to liquidate their holdings.

2. *Moderate the cyclical flow of mortgage capital.* During periods of general capital shortage, the funds available for mortgages are usually very scarce (e.g., 1966, 1969-70, 1974) and real estate activity slows down. The financial institutions operating in the secondary market during these periods can purchase existing mortgages from the primary mortgage lenders, and in this way provide funds for additional mortgages to be originated.

3. *Assist the flow of capital from surplus areas to deficit areas.* The operations of the secondary market allow an investor in a capital-surplus area, such as New England, to invest in mortgages originated in a capital deficit area such as the South and West, thus providing capital for needed growth. (Figure 6-1.)

4. *Lessen the geographical spread in interest rates and allow for portfolio diversification.* The mobility of capital allows for a moderation of the geographical differences in mortgage interest rates to the borrower since capital will flow to areas of high interest, pressuring the rate downward. In addition, regional risk, e.g., a large industry closing, is spread to more investors, lessening its effect.

FINANCIAL INSTITUTIONS ACTIVE IN THE SECONDARY MARKET

Federal National Mortgage Association (FNMA)

Any discussion of secondary markets must start with the Federal National Mortgage Association, also known as "Fannie Mae". FNMA is the most active participant historically and currently is also the largest single owner of residential mortgage debt.

The importance of an effective secondary market has been recognized since 1924, when a bill was introduced in Congress to establish a system of national home loan banks which could purchase first mortgages. The legislation failed to become law. The first federal attempt to establish and assist a national mortgage market was the Reconstruction Finance Corporation (RFC), created in 1935, followed in 1938 by a wholly-owned subsidiary, the National Mortgage

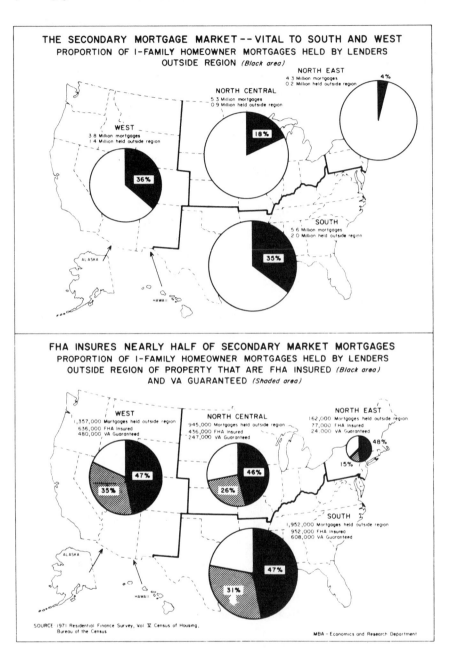

FIGURE 6-1. Sectionalized maps from the Mortgage Bankers Association of America, Economics and Research Department

Association of Washington, soon renamed the Federal National Mortgage Association.

In 1950, FNMA was transferred to the Department of Housing and Urban Development (HUD)[3], and was partitioned into two separate corporations by amendments to the Housing and Urban Development Act of 1968. This was done to permit the new FNMA to support more actively the mortgage market outside the federal budget.

One of these corporations, named the Government National Mortgage Association (GNMA, or "Ginnie Mae") remained in HUD and retained the special assistance and loan liquidation functions of the old FNMA. GNMA will be discussed in greater detail in a later section.

The second corporation was to be basically private, though some regulatory control remained with HUD. It retained the Federal National Mortgage Association's name, as well as the assets and responsibility for secondary market operations.

Today, the corporation is run by a 15-member board of directors, consisting of 10 selected by the stockholders and five appointed by the President of the United States. Approximately 50 million shares are currently outstanding and traded regularly on the New York Stock Exchange.

At the end of 1976, FNMA held approximately $33 billion in mortgages and earned $203 million on that portfolio before taxes and after deducting all borrowing costs.[4] This income was 83 percent of FNMA's gross income that year with the remaining 17 percent derived principally from commitment fees.

FNMA finances its secondary market operations by tapping the private capital markets using both short and long-term obligations. The short-term obligations are discount notes, which, as the term implies, are sold to investors at a price less than the face amount at maturity. At the end of 1976, FNMA had $1.6 billion outstanding in such discount notes. The long-term obligations are called *debentures* and are generally issued with maturities ranging from two to 25 years. At the end of 1976, $29 billion was outstanding. The average cost of all debt was 7.46 percent.

FNMA must produce its earnings from the spread between its borrowing cost and the yield on its mortgage investment, since it is a stockholder-owned corporation. It must keep the cost of borrowing below its portfolio yield, although for a brief period the rates for short-term funds were higher than mortgage rates. This occurred in 1974 (Table 6-1).

TABLE 6-1

	1976	1975	1974	1973	1972
Average yield on portfolio (%)	7.94	7.79	7.58	7.35	7.25
Average cost of debt (%)	7.46	7.41	7.27	6.72	6.67
Average port-folio spread (%)	.48	.38	.31	.63	.58

Source: 1976 Annual Report, Federal National Mortgage Association

Secondary Market Operations

Mortgages are purchased by FNMA only from approved seller/servicers that number approximately 3,000 and who have outstanding commitments to deliver mortgages.

An approved seller/servicer can obtain a commitment from FNMA by participating in the Free Market System (FMS) auction usually held every two weeks. Participants are charged one basis point or .01 percent of the offer as an offering fee to bid competitively by phone against other seller/servicers. Each bid is to deliver up to $3 million mortgages at a stated yield to FNMA. After analyzing the bids, the trends in the capital markets, and the cost of borrowing, FNMA accepts bids representing a range of yields and issues contracts obligating itself for a four-month period to buy mortgages at the yield specified in the accepted bid.

The commitment the successful bidder obtained from FNMA does not obligate the seller/servicer to deliver to FNMA. Instead, it gives the seller/servicer the right to deliver if no better price can be obtained elsewhere, and this is known as an optional delivery commitment or a "put" option. A fee of .5 percent of the commitment amount is charged to the seller/servicer.

In addition to the competitive bid, a seller/servicer may submit a noncompetitive bid limited to $250,000 by which the yield to FNMA will be the weighted average of all accepted competitive bids at that particular auction.

Another program allows a seller/servicer to obtain a forward 12-month *convertible standby commitment* at a yield established by FNMA. Usually used to protect builders of new construction against sharp interest rate changes, this commitment can be converted after the first four-month period to match the weighted average yield of the most recent FMS auction. In addition to the .01 percent processing fee, FNMA also charges a .5 percent (1/2 point) fee at commitment and an additional .5 percent fee at conversion or delivery. The latter fee is calculated on the dollar amount delivered to FNMA, not the original commitment amount.

In April 1977, FNMA added a participation loan purchase and sale program. This program currently is limited to single-family mortgages submitted by an approved seller/servicer that executes a participation loan agreement.

This program has two basic plans:

1. FNMA purchases a majority interest of 60 to 90 percent from an originating lender that retains servicing. The remaining interest may be retained by the originating lender or sold to another investor.

2. FNMA receives the entire package of mortgages from the originator and purchases a minority interest of 10 to 40 percent while simultaneously selling a majority interest to another investor according to a commitment secured by the originator. The originator services the package and FNMA passes the pro rata share of principal and interest to the majority investor.

Types of Mortgages FNMA Purchases. Prior to 1970, the only mortgages FNMA was authorized to purchase were FHA-insured and VA-guaranteed loans. This requirement was based on FNMA being a federally-chartered corporation charged with the responsibility of supporting the nation's goal of providing adequate housing for low and moderate income families through a degree of supplemental liquidity to the residential mortgage market. This responsibility was fulfilled by dealing only with FHA-insured and VA-guaranteed mortgages which provided the financing for most families in low to moderate income levels because of the limit set by Congress on the size of the mortgages.

The law was changed by the Emergency Home Finance Act of 1970, and FNMA was authorized to purchase conventional mortgages—those not guaranteed or insured by the federal government. Its prime responsibility was still to support the government programs. The first purchases under the new convention program began in early 1972 after a lengthy study to determine the correct underwriting procedure for these non-government insured loans.

The dollar amount of conventional mortgages in the FNMA portfolio has increased dramatically since the program began in 1972. In 1976, more conventional mortgages were purchased than FHA/VA, and the commitments issued were about equal (Table 6-2).

Table 6-2

For The Year Dollars in millions	1976	1975	1974	1973	1972
Commitments Issued:					
FNMA Direct:					
Home—Government insured or					
guaranteed	**$3,827**	$ 4,695	$ 4,333	$ 3,793	$3,047
—Conventional	**2,168**	982	1,051	2,332	319
Total home mortgage commitments . . .	**5,995**	5,677	5,384	6,125	3,366
Project	**1**	10	5	41	79
Total FNMA direct commitments					
issued	**5,996**	5,687	5,389	6,166	3,445
Tandem Plans (a)	**241**	419	5,376	2,748	5,478
Total commitments issued	**$6,237**	$ 6,106	$10,765	$ 8,914	$8,923
Mortgages and Loans Purchased:					
Home—Government insured or					
guaranteed	**$ 824**	$ 3,099	$ 3,617	$ 3,231	$2,541
—Conventional	**2,513**	547	1,129	939	55
Total home mortgages purchased	**3,337**	3,646	4,746	4,170	2,596
Project	**269**	616	2,208	1,957	1,104
Participations in project construction					
loans	**26**	58	65	125	164
Total mortgages and loans purchased .	**$3,632**	$ 4,320	$ 7,019	$ 6,252	$3,864
Debt Issued:					
Discount notes	**$3,650**	$ 5,254	$ 6,396	$ 4,124	$2,782
Debentures	**5,600**	6,450	6,600	6,061	4,314
Subordinated capital debentures	**300**	300	—	—	250
Mortgage backed bonds	**—**	—	—	278	—
Total debt issued	**$9,550**	$12,004	$12,996	$10,463	$7,346

Source: 1976 Annual Report of the Federal National Mortgage Association

FNMA added another program in 1974 to purchase mortgages on condominiums and planned unit developments (PUDs). It is expected that FNMA will expand its residential lending programs by purchasing conventionally financed apartment mortgages.

Government National Mortgage Association (GNMA)

The Government National Mortgage Association, known as Ginnie Mae, was organized within HUD under the authority of the Housing and Urban Development Act of 1968 which split the old FNMA into two separate entities—FNMA and GNMA.

GNMA was given authority to operate in the following three areas, the first two of which were inherited from the old FNMA:

1. *The special assistance function (SAF).* Under this function, GNMA was authorized to make available below-market interest rate loans to low-income families who normally could not obtain loans through private means. An example would be one of the tandem plans through which GNMA purchases below-market interest rate mortgages for sale to FNMA at market yield with GNMA absorbing any loss.

2. *The management and liquidation of previously originated (old FNMA) mortgages.*

3. *The mortgage-backed security program.* Under this new program, GNMA will guarantee the timely payment of principal and interest on mortgage-backed securities composed of FHA-insured, VA-guaranteed or Farmers Home Administration mortgages and issued by an FHA-approved mortgagee and sold to an investor.

It is in this last area that GNMA has had its greatest effect on the secondary markets.

The primary purpose behind the rebirth of a mortgage-backed security was to attract more funds into the housing markets by providing a liquid instrument with a governmental guarantee to traditional nonmortgage investors.

A mortgage lender usually is a mortgage company since most FHA/VA mortgages are originated by this type of lender. This lender seeks a commitment from GNMA to guarantee a pool of acceptable mortgages.[5] When the commitment is received, a mortgage lender can rely on GNMA's guarantee of the certificate when the underlying mortgages are originated, purchased and packaged. These certificates are sold to investors with the full faith and credit of the United States behind the monthly payment of principal and interest.

In addition to the better-known, single-family mortgage-backed security, GNMA is authorized to guarantee pools of FHA/VA mobile home mortgages, FHA-insured hospital mortgages and securities backed by a single FHA-insured multi-family mortgage.

The mortgage-backed security has been well received by both traditional and non-traditional mortgage investors (Table 6–3). Many credit unions, pension funds, trusts and individuals who never had invested in mortgages before now have a vehicle to do so. These security instruments, usually purchased from a securities dealer that also will make a market in the security, provide the holder with:

1. High yielding government security

2. Liquidity

3. Safety

4. Monthly cash flow

TABLE 6-3

Estimated Volume of GNMAs Held by Type of Investor (By Percent)

Date: Outstanding Volume:	Dec. 1974 $13.3 billion	Dec. 1976 $34.5 billion	Feb. 1977 $37.4 billion
Savings Banks	18.03%	13.02%	12.75%
Savings and Loans	30.40	19.62	18.08
Credit Unions	4.01	2.59	2.42
Commercial Banks	5.92	5.34	5.21
Pension Funds	7.72	9.98	9.54
Mortgage Bankers/Dealers	10.58	20.30	21.60
Nominees and others	21.70	28.05	29.35
Individuals	1.64	1.10	1.05

Source: Government National Mortgage Association.

The coupon rate on the security will be 50 basis points (1/2 percent) less than the internal rate of the underlying mortgages. Of this, 44 basis points are to compensate the issuer for servicing the loan and six to GNMA as a guarantee fee.

Although others exist, the most popular form of mortgage-backed security is the *modified pass-through security*. Under this program, the issuer must pay the scheduled monthly payment of principal and interest to the holder whether or not the mortgagors pay the issuer. This risk to the issuer is partially compensated by the increase in servicing income from 37 1/2 basis points (3/8 of one percent) to 44 basis points. If the issuer defaults on the obligation to the holder, GNMA will take over the pool and make the payment.

During periods of extreme credit restraint GNMA has been authorized to purchase mortgages as a means of stimulating the housing industry. The Emergency Home Purchase Assistance Act of 1974 is an example of this authorization. It authorized GNMA to purchase conventional mortgages at a below market interest rate. Initially $3 billion worth was purchased. This was the first time GNMA was authorized to purchase mortgages not insured or guaranteed by the government.

Federal Home Loan Mortgage Corporation (FHLMC)

The Emergency Home Finance Act of 1970, in addition to giving FNMA the power to purchase conventional mortgages, authorized the establishment of the Federal Home Loan Mortgage Corporation, also known as "Freddie Mac" or The Mortgage Corporation. It provided secondary market facilities for members of the Federal Home Loan Bank System.

Although FHLMC can purchase FHA/VA loans, its particular function is to provide secondary market support for conventional mortgages originated by lenders whose deposits or accounts are insured by an agency of the United States. This limitation effectively excludes mortgage companies. FHLMC has two mortgage purchase programs:

1. *Whole Loan Program*

Single-family. FHLMC will purchase the entire interest in a group of mortgages of which total value can range from $100,000 to $5 million depending on contract and consisting of either conventional or FHA/VA mortgages.

Until May 1977, the yield to FHLMC was administratively set by FHLMC, but now a bid price system similar to FNMA's auctions is used to set a net yield[6] to FHLMC. Noncompetitive offers up to $500,000 will be accepted at a weighted average based on previous weeks' bidding.

Multi-family. FHLMC will purchase the entire interest in conventional multi-family in a program similar to the single-family. The servicing fee is less than the single-family servicing.

2. *Participation Program*

Class A. FHLMC will purchase up to 85 percent interest in a conventional multi-family loan with a maximum loan amount of $5 million.

Class B. FHLMC will purchase from 50 to 85 percent interest in a group of conventional mortgages that can contain both single-family and multi-family loans, up to 50 percent of the total.

Unlike FNMA, all of those programs call for mandatory delivery. Failure to deliver could bring a two-year suspension of the right to sell to FHLMC.

Like FNMA, FHLMC does have a forward commitment program for optional delivery of six to 24 months. All types (conventional, FHA/VA) are eligible to be purchased under this program.

FHLMC finances its secondary market operations somewhat differently than FNMA. Rather than finance its purchases with debt securities in the capital market, as does FNMA, FHLMC finances its mortgage purchases with capital generated from the sale of either whole mortgages or participations in groups of mortgages. Thus, FHLMC is not as large a corporation as FNMA, since it effectively buys and sells mortgages.

The total FHLMC mortgage purchase activity of $1.1 billion in 1976 was funded by the sale of Mortgage Participation Certificates (PCs) of $1.5 billion.[7] These PC securities are sold to thrift institutions and give them an undivided interest in the pooled mortgages. The monthly payment of principal and interest is guaranteed by FHLMC.

In addition to the PC program, FHLMC periodically issues guaranteed mortgage certificates (GMC) for sale to traditional non-mortgage investors such as bank trusts and pension funds. Interest is payable semi-annually with the GMCs and principal annually. In the PC program, interest and principal are payable monthly.

To fulfill its balanced purchase and sale strategy FHLMC sold more mortgages out of its portfolio than it acquired (Figure 6–2). This is radically different from FNMA's corporate philosophy of retaining practically all mortgages purchased.

Automated Mortgage Market Information Network (AMMINET)

AMMINET is a nonprofit corporation created by the joint efforts of many mortgage lenders and investors as a centralized, nationwide secondary mortgage market. Traders can communicate offers to buy or sell whole loans, participations or commitments through the net-

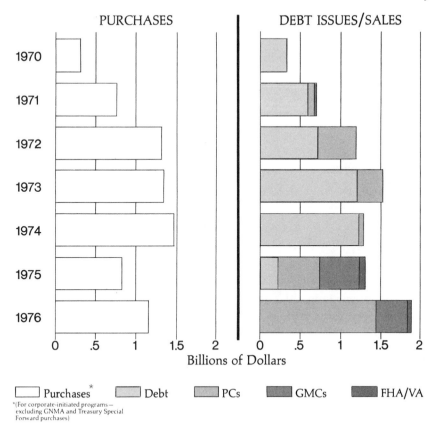

PURCHASES   DEBT ISSUES/SALES

Billions of Dollars

☐ Purchases* ☐ Debt ☐ PCs ■ GMCs ■ FHA/VA

*(For corporate-initiated programs—
excluding GNMA and Treasury Special
Forward purchases)

FIGURE 6-2. Purchases and Financing, 1970-76 from the 1976 FHLMC Annual Report

work. Currently about 100 subscribers are using the service but the concept has not produced many consummated transactions as many use it only to test the market.

Uniform Documentation

In order for mortgages to be readily saleable in a secondary market a degree of uniformity must exist. Before FHLMC joined FNMA in the secondary market the required uniformity existed because all mortgages sold in the secondary market were either FHA-insured or VA-guaranteed. After 1970, conventional mortgages could also be bought and sold in the secondary market and a need developed for uniform documentation.

Both FNMA and FHLMC have worked diligently to produce the state-by-state uniform documents that all mortgage lenders needed. GNMA has also adopted these forms which include:

1. Mortgage note

2. Deeds of trust

3. Mortgage

4. Loan application

5. Appraisal form

These forms can also be used for VA-guaranteed mortgages if a VA guaranteed loan rider is added to the mortgage or deed of trust to make the mortgage instrument conform to special VA requirements. These forms regrettably cannot be used for FHA-insured loans; FHA-approved forms must be used. This may change in the future.

These uniform forms may contain some minor variations to comply with different state laws.

SUGGESTED READINGS

Harrington, Philip N. "Freddie Mac: Big Man in Mortgages," *Real Estate Review* (Winter 1974), pp. 102-04.

Jacobs, Steven, and Kozuch, James R. "Is There a Future for a Mortgage Futures Market?" *Real Estate Review* (Spring 1975), pp. 109-13.

Wiggin, Charles E. "Doing Business in the Secondary Market," *Real Estate Review* (Summer 1975), pp. 84-95.

NOTES

1. Jones, Oliver H., and Grebler, Leo. *The Secondary Mortgage Market: Its Purpose, Its Performance and Its Potential.* Los Angeles: Real Estate Research Program, UCLA, 1961, p. 4.

2.   Ibid.

3.   It was originally called the Housing and Home Finance Agency until 1965 when the present cabinet-level department was created.

4.   1976 Annual Report of the Federal National Mortgage Association.

5.   An acceptable pool of mortgages (in an aggregate amount of at least $1 million) would contain only the same type of mortgage (such as all single-family with the same interest rate and maturity). The government-insured or guaranteed mortgage cannot be older than one year at the time of the GNMA commitment.

6.   A net yield means the originating lender must add on any servicing fee. However, FNMA purchases on a gross yield basis and pays for servicing at 3/8 percent of the principal balance. FHLMC, on the other hand, purchases on a net servicing basis and, consequently, is not concerned with specific servicing fees.

7.   1976 Annual Report of the Federal Home Loan Mortgage Corporation.

Chapter 7

Mortgage Insurance– Government and Private

The function of mortgage insurance, whether government or private, is to make mortgage investments more attractive by lessening risk and providing liquidity. With mortgage insurance, a permanent mortgage investor has an alternative to foreclosed real estate, releasing the investor from an asset that might decline in value.

Mortgage insurance offers lenders the opportunity to make higher percentage loans with lower downpayments to more people because of less risk. The variations on this basic concept can be traced to whether the insurance is government or private, and whether it is for a single-family loan or an income-property loan.

Before examining government and private insurance programs, a brief review of the historical development of this concept will be helpful to an understanding of present mortgage insurance practices.

HISTORICAL DEVELOPMENT

Although some of the early title insurance companies insured the mortgage in addition to the title, the first law providing statutory authority for this type of insurance was not enacted until 1904 in New York.

The social and demographic changes that emerged after 1900 (particularly following World War I) led mortgage lending into a more important position in the American economy. As mortgage lending became more prevalent and important, mortgage insurance became more accepted and desired and mortgage companies began taking an interest in the concept.

It was customary during this period for a mortgage company either to exchange a new mortgage for a defaulted one or to buy back a troubled loan sold to an investor. As the real estate boom of the 1920s continued, this custom gave way to the actual guaranteeing of principal and interest by a new entity—a mortgage guaranty company. During their peak years (1925-1932), as many as 50 of these companies were in operation, located primarily in the state of New York.

These companies prospered by originating and selling mortgages with a guaranty either as whole loans to institutional investors or as mortgage participation bonds to individual investors. The units sold to individual investors were usually in $500 or $1,000 denominations. Yield and apparent safety made the units very attractive. A trustee would hold the mortgage and be responsible for foreclosure if any default in payment occurred. The prevailing viewpoint during this period of time was that real estate values would continue to appreciate, and if any lax underwriting or appraising occurred, the resulting questionable mortgage would be saved by inflation. This optimism affected the investing public. Large portions of accumulated savings were invested in mortgage bonds issued by apparently successful mortgage guaranty companies.

Due to the general optimism about the economy and the *laissez-faire* attitude of the government, these mortgage guaranty companies were virtually unregulated. This lack of regulation often led to poor underwriting, self-dealing, fraud, and ultimately to a lack of adequate reserves to meet any meaningful emergency.

Before the stock market crash of 1929, the real estate industry was in serious trouble. As real estate values started to drop, the emergency the mortgage guaranty companies could not survive had arrived, and it was inevitable that these companies would not survive the bank holiday declared by President F. D. Roosevelt in March 1933. Many billions of dollars were lost by institutional investors with similarly tragic results to private investors because of the failure of these companies. The collapse left such an ugly mark on the real estate finance industry that private mortgage insurance did not reappear for almost 25 years.

Government (FHA) Insurance

The years immediately following the stock market crash witnessed much debate on the advisability and proper role of the government in the nation's economy. One segment of the economy that many agreed could benefit from government action was real estate. Those in favor of stimulation reasoned that expanding waves from a healthy real estate industry would have a multiplied effect on the remainder of a depressed economy. The National Housing Act of 1934 contained provisions to help stimulate the construction industry and created the Federal Housing Administration (FHA) to encourage lenders to make real estate mortgages, again by providing government-backed mortgage insurance as protection. Title I of this law provided initially free insurance to lenders who loaned money for home improvements and repairs.

Title II provided for the establishment of a Mutual Mortgage Insurance Fund to be funded by premiums paid by mortgagors out of which any claims by the protected lenders could be satisfied. Initially, the mortgagor paid an annual insurance premium of .5 percent based on the original amount. (The premium is now computed on the unpaid balance.)

The basic program under this Act was Section 203(b), designed to provide government insurance to lenders who made loans on 1–4 family houses. (Most have been single-family.) This program is still successfully meeting national housing needs after helping to provide housing for more than 10 million families.

Now a part of the Department of Housing and Urban Development (HUD), the FHA has other insurance programs (Figure 7–1), each designed to meet a specific problem. But the Mutual Mortgage Insurance Fund remains the largest and most important.

It should be understood that the legislation to establish FHA was faced with opposition from some thrift institutions that believed the federal government should not get involved in housing. Even after enactment, FHA did not meet with great acceptance among the financial centers, since many felt mortgage insurance as a concept was discredited, and even if not discredited, the government should not get involved in what was basically a private enterprise.

<u>HUD-FHA MORTGAGE INSURANCE PROGRAMS</u>

203 Mutual Mortgage Insurance and Insured Improvement Loans.

(b) One-to-four Family Housing.

(h) One-Family Housing for Disaster Victims.

(i) Outlying Properties; One-Family Non-farm or Farm Housing.

(m) Vacation Homes.

207 Multifamily Housing Mortgage Insurance.

Rental Housing of eight or more Units.

Mobile Home Parks.

213 Cooperative Housing Mortgage Insurance.

Dwelling Unit Released from a Cooperative Project-Sales Mortgage.

Management-type Cooperative Projects of five or more Units.

Sales-type Cooperative Projects of five or more Units.

Investor-sponsored Cooperative Projects of five or more Units.

220 Urban Renewal Mortgage Insurance and Insured Improvement Loans.

One-to-eleven Family Housing in Urban Renewal Areas.

Construction of two or more Units in Approved Urban Renewal Area.

221 Low Cost and Moderate Income Mortgage Insurance.

(d)(2) One-to-four Family Housing for Low and Moderate Income Families
and Displaced Families.

(h) Individual Units Released from 222(h) Project Mortgage.

(i) Conversion of 221(d)(3) Below Market Interest Rate Rental Project
into Condominium Plan.

(d)(3) Housing Projects (Below Market Interest Rate) for Housing
Moderate Income Families, Individuals 62 or Older, or Handicapped.

(d)(3) Same as above, but with Market Interest Rate Program and
Rent Supplement Program.

(d)(4) Housing Projects for Moderate Income Families. Market Interest
Rate Program for Profit-motivated Sponsors.

(h) Substandard Housing for Subsequent Resale after Rehabilitation.

(j) Conversion of 221(d)(3) Rental Project into a Cooperative Project.

222 Servicemen's Mortgage Insurance

One-Family Housing for Servicemen.

FIGURE 7-1. HUD-FHA mortgage insurance programs

223 Miscellaneous Housing Insurance.

Housing and Mortgage Insurance for Housing in Declining Neighborhoods

Insurance for Government-Acquired Properties.

231 Housing Mortgage Insurance for the Elderly.

Housing Project of eight or more Units for Occupancy by Elderly or

Handicapped.

232 Nursing Homes and/or Intermediate Care Facilities Mortgage Insurance.

Housing for 20 or more Patients.

233 Experimental Housing Mortgage Insurance.

Proposed or Rehabilitated Housing Using Advanced Technology.

Rental Housing Using Advanced Technology.

234 Condominium Housing Mortgage Insurance.

(c) Individual Units in Condominium Projects.

(d) Condominium Projects with four or more Units.

235 Mortgage Insurance and Assistance Payments.

(i) One-Family Unit in Single- or Two-Family Dwelling. Open-end

advances permitted in connection with previously insured mortgage.

(j) Individual Units Released from 235(j) Rehabilitation Sales Project

Mortgage.

(j) Housing for Lower Income Families.

236 Mortgage Insurance and Interest Reduction Payments.

Rental and Cooperative Housing for Lower Income Families, Individuals

62 or over, or Handicapped.

237 Special Mortgage Insurance for Low and Moderate Income.

Special Credit Risks; Single-Family Units.

240 Mortgage Insurance on Loans for Title Purchase.

Purchase of Fee Simple Title.

241 Supplementary Financing for FHA Project Mortgages.

242 Mortgage Insurance for Hospitals.

Construction or Rehabilitation of Non-profit and Proprietary Hospitals.

803/809/810 Armed Services Housing.

809 One-to-Four Family Housing for Civilian Employees at or near

R & D Installations.

FIGURE 7-1. HUD-FHA mortgage insurance programs continued

```
810(h) Individual Units Released from 810(g) Mutlifamily Mortgage.

810(f) Rental Housing with eight or more Units for Military or Civilian

Personnel.

810(g) Same as above, but for Later Resale as Single-Family Housing.

1000 Mortgage Insurance for Land Development.

Purchase of Land for Development of Building Sites for Subdivisions

or New Communities.

1100 Mortgage Insurance for Group Practice Facilities.

Constrction of Rehabilitation of Facilities for Dentistry, Medicine or

or Optometry Practice.

Note: This chart is intended for quick reference to HUD-FHA insurance programs.

Check for specific details in the appropriate FHA issuances.

Source: Department of Housing and Urban Development, Housing in the Seventies,

A report of the National Housing Policy Review, Washington, D.C., 1974.
```

FIGURE 7-1. HUD-FHA mortgage insurance programs continued

History, however, has proven this to be a shortsighted belief, especially in view of the many changes for which FHA has paved the way in real estate finance. As an example, FHA insurance has allowed for the development of a national mortgage market by providing for the transferability, and thus the liquidity, of mortgage instruments. The FHA-insured mortgage was attractive to many investors because it established property and borrower standards with a corresponding reduction in risk.

The FHA mortgage insurance program allowed life insurance companies to justify a successful request to offer loans with higher loan-to-value ratios with lower downpayments to state insurance commissioners. The program also gave them the opportunity to lend across the nation. With this new authorization, life insurance companies could lend in those areas of the country that desperately needed capital. Subsequently they could receive a higher yield than what was previously available in the capital-surplus area of New England, where most of the major life insurance companies were located. Mortgage companies were the principal intermediaries for moving this capital from capital-surplus areas to capital-poor areas by originating mortgages with FHA insurance and selling them to life insurance companies.

One of the primary reasons for the increase in home ownership from about 40 percent of all homes occupied in 1930 to about 65 percent today is the leadership provided by FHA that led to:

1. Established property and borrower standards

2. Mortgage insurance

3. Amortized mortgage payments

4. Higher loan-to-value ratios

5. Longer terms

These factors have contributed to the higher percentage of home ownership and to a financial environment conducive to a rebirth of private mortgage insurance.

The loans to be insured by FHA could be originated by any of the various mortgage intermediaries, although as a practical matter about 75 percent have been originated by mortgage companies. Initially, this high percentage of origination was due to the local lending philosophy of the other mortgage lenders and the correspondent system that developed between mortgage lenders and life insurance companies. Most FHA-insured mortgages are still originated by mortgage companies.

FHA INSURANCE TODAY

Although the various FHA programs have performed admirably and have allowed for changes in real estate finance that have affected all mortgage lenders whether FHA insurance was used or not, the percentage of homes insured by FHA declined in the early 1970s to an alarming point (Table 7–1).

The reasons for this precipitous decline are many, but would have to include:

1. The unjustified length of time it takes to get a commitment from FHA

TABLE 7–1

One-to-Four-Family Originations by Type of Loan

One-to-Four-Family Mortgages

Year	FHA	VA	Conventional
1975	8.2%	11.8%	80.1%
1974	6.7	11.7	81.6
1973	6.6	9.6	83.9
1972	11.2	10.1	78.7
1971	19.0	11.8	69.2
1970	24.6	10.8	64.6
1965	16.7	6.2	76.6
1960	18.4	8.4	73.6
1955	12.7	29.5	58.2
1950	19.5	26.0	55.3

Source: Adapted from HUD's Monthly Gross Mortgage Flow Series, Arnold H. Diamond, *The Supply of Mortgage Credit*, 1970-1974 (Washington, D.C.: U.S. Department of Housing and Urban Development, 1975) and Arnold H. Diamond, *Mortgage Loan Gross Flows* (Washington, D.C.: U.S. Department of Housing and Urban Development, December 1968).

2. The previously low FHA maximum insured loan amount ($45,000) for Section 203(b), which precluded large areas of the country from the program because of the high cost of real estate

3. The maximum interest rate limit for FHA-insured loans set by HUD, which is usually far below the market rate, thus requiring discount points

Since October 1977, under the basic Section 203(b) program for a fee of .5 percent which is paid by the borrower, FHA will insure a lender for 97 percent of the first $25,000 of the appraised value and 95 percent of the remainder, up to a maximum insured amount of $60,000.

As an example, if Mr. and Mrs. Jones want to purchase a home appraised for $47,000, their downpayment would be as follows:

3% (non-insured) of $25,000 = $ 750
5% (non-insured) of $22,000 = $1,100
                                      ────────
               Total Downpayment $1,850

With FHA insurance on $45,150 loan ($47,000 – $1,850), the monthly payment of principal and interest including .5 percent FHA insurance at 9 percent for 30 years would be $382.09.

Chapter 5, Underwriting the Residential Loan, discusses the requirements the property must meet and the income the family must have to obtain this mortgage insurance.

VETERANS ADMINISTRATION

As a gesture to returning World War II veterans, Congress enacted the Servicemen's Readjustment Act of 1944, which authorized the Veterans Administration (VA) to guarantee loans (among other benefits) made to eligible veterans.[1] The original guarantee was for the first 50 percent of the loan amount or $2,000, whichever was less. This has been increased through the years to the current guarantee of $17,500, or 60 percent of the loan. The VA issues a *Certificate of Reasonable Value* (CRV) that establishes the amount on which these figures are based. A veteran borrower does not pay a premium for the mortgagee's protection as with an FHA-insured loan. Instead, any loss is paid by the government without benefit of a premium-supported fund. The maximum interest rate for a VA-guaranteed mortgage, like the FHA rate, is an artificially-set rate which normally requires that discount points be charged to a seller.

Originally, this program was designed to allow a veteran to buy a home with no money down, and it still operates on that concept. Consequently, a veteran now can buy a home costing up to $70,000 with no downpayment, assuming income is sufficient to support the payment. The $17,500 guarantee is the reason no downpayment is required. It means that although the lender is lending $70,000, only $52,500, or 75 percent of value, is made with any risk. If foreclosure is necessary, the real estate typically should bring at least the $52,500 the lender had as a risk, which, combined with the $17,500 guarantee, will make the lender whole.

If a veteran wanted to buy a home appraised at more than $70,000, a lender would probably require a downpayment equal to the amount in excess of $70,000 to keep the loan within the 75 percent loan-to-value ratio.

Veterans who believe they are eligible for a VA-guaranteed loan must apply to the VA for a certificate of eligibility which establishes eligibility and the amount of the guarantee available. The 1974 law which increased the guarantee to $17,500 also provided for re-entitlement of benefits if all prior VA-guaranteed mortgages had been repaid or, if assumed, released.

PRIVATE MORTGAGE INSURANCE

After a quarter of a century, private mortgage insurance companies (MICs) returned as FHA insurance programs proved successful. The first of the reborn MICs was Mortgage Guarantee Insurance Corporation (MGIC), organized in 1957 under a Wisconsin state law passed in 1956. As the first, MGIC remains the largest of the current 11[2] MICs and receives about 60 percent of all the premium dollars.

Protection for insured mortgage lenders and the general public that was missing with the old mortgage insurance companies is present now because all MICs are carefully regulated by the laws of the state in which they are organized as well as the states where they do business. The regulating entity is normally the state insurance commission or department. According to a recent study,[3] the result of this careful regulation has been an industry that is strong and capable of weathering any foreseeable economic calamity.

The specific requirements vary among the states but generally provide that a MIC can insure only a fully amortized first lien on a 1–4 family residence that does not exceed 95 percent of fair market value. This originally was 90 percent but was changed by the Emergency Home Loan Financing Act of 1970, which allowed FNMA and FHLMC to purchase 95 percent conventional mortgages. Before an MIC can begin insuring loans, it must meet minimum limits for paid-in capital and surplus. Then its insurance exposure is limited to 25 times the value of the capital.

Three types of reserves must be maintained by MICs:

Unearned Premium Reserves. Premiums received but unearned for the term of a policy are placed in this reserve.

Loss Reserves. This reserve is established for losses or potential losses on a case-by-case basis as the company learns of defaults and foreclosures. It also includes a reserve for losses incurred, but not reported.

Contingency Reserve. This is a special reserve required by law to protect mortgage lenders against the type of catastrophic loss that can occur in severe economic periods. Half of each premium dollar received goes into this reserve and cannot be used by an MIC for 10 years, unless losses in a calendar year exceed 35 percent of earned premiums and the insurance commissioner of the state where the insurer is domiciled concurs in the withdrawal.

Before a mortgage lender can do business with an MIC, the lender must be approved in regard to its capacity to underwrite, appraise and service (if required) the high-ratio loans to be insured. An approved lender can get a commitment to insure within a day or two of submitting the application. The contents of the application and underwriting standards for MICs is discussed in Chapter 5, Underwriting the Residential Loan.

COMPARISON OF GOVERNMENT AND PRIVATE MORTGAGE INSURANCE

The differences between FHA mortgage insurance, a VA guarantee and private mortgage insurance are many and, in some cases, debatable as to which is preferable. These would include:

Premium. The VA-guaranteed mortgage requires no premium from the borrower. An FHA-insured mortgage requires the borrower to pay .5 percent of the outstanding balance for the life of the loan. MICs will provide insurance for .25 percent of the principal balance after the first year. At the lender's option, the premium can be dropped any time, although probably not until the loan-to-value ratio reaches 70 percent. MICs charge a premium in the first year that ranges from .25 to 1.0 percent, depending on the loan-to-value ratio.

Downpayment required. If the mortgage is VA-guaranteed, veterans do not need to make a downpayment unless the mortgage exceeds $70,000. For an FHA-insured mortgage, the borrower must put up equity of three percent of the first $25,000 of appraised value and five percent of the remainder up to a maximum insured amount of $60,000. If the insurance comes from an MIC, the downpayment could be as little as five percent with no loan limit, except the secondary market limits, as long as the borrower has the capacity to repay.

Coverage. The VA guarantee protects the lender to the extent of 60 percent of the mortgage or $17,500, whichever is less. A mortgage insured by FHA under the basic 203(b) program protects the lender on the whole loan up to the insured amount to a maximum of $60,000. A mortgage insured by an MIC protects the top 20 or 25 percent of the lender's exposure.

Processing time. With VA allowing approved mortgagees to make commitments, the time for processing is now quite reasonable. The FHA processing time is supposed to be five working days, but instead is usually several weeks. An approved MIC lender is normally able to get a commitment within a day or two.

Interest rate. Both the VA and FHA programs have a maximum interest rate which is set administratively. This interest rate is often below the market rate requiring discount points to increase the investor's yield to the market.[4] Since an MIC-insured loan is normally made on a conventional mortgage, the market rate is used and points generally are not required.

Assumption. Neither VA nor FHA mortgages have a due-on-sale clause. Because of this the mortgage can be transferred to a new buyer and the mortgage lender can charge only a reasonable fee for transferring the records. Practically all conventional mortgages, whether insured by an MIC or not, contain due-on-sale clauses which could prevent the transfer of the mortgage upon sale.

Prepayment penalty. Neither FHA nor VA mortgages contain a prepayment penalty. Most conventional mortgages do.

INCOME-PROPERTY MORTGAGE INSURANCE

Following the success of the home mortgage insurance programs by the various MICs, the predictable expansion into income-property mortgage insurance occurred in 1967 when MGIC offered both income-property mortgage insurance and lease guarantees.

This original income-property mortgage insurance to protect mortgage lenders provided for coverage on the top 20 percent of an income-property loan. If a default occurred, a protected lender had to foreclose and then tender title to the insurer. The insurer, at its election, could decide on whether to pay 100 percent of the amount due under the loan and take title or pay 20 percent of the loan and leave title with the lender. The five-year premium for this insurance ranged from 1.75 to 2.90 percent of the loan, depending on the type of property.

As originally offered, the lease guarantee program guaranteed the total mount of fixed rent over a period ranging from a minimum of five years to a maximum of 20 years. Although percentage rents were excluded, additional rent from tax increases were allowed if a proper tax escalation clause existed.

The guarantee extends to the landlord after an eviction and protects until a new tenant is found. If the new tenant pays less rent than the guaranteed amount, the insurer pays the difference. In reality, this program was designed for the benefit of a mortgage lender who decided to make a mortgage loan based on a loan guarantee which would allow for an uninterrupted flow of income to amortize the mortgage.

Depending on the lease term, the premium for this guarantee ranged from 2.80 to 5.40 percent of the amount of rent guaranteed.

Both of these programs were profitable for insurance until the recession of 1974. This national recession was actually a depression for the real estate industry and resulted in tremendous underwriting losses for those MICs engaged in income-property mortgage insurance and lease guarantee. In 1975 the losses were so massive that most existing programs were scrapped, forcing a complete re-examination of the basic concepts and underwriting criteria.

The involved MICs realized that insuring an income property mortgage was far riskier and involved more variables than were present in home mortgage insurances. In addition, many mortgage lenders, especially those only interested in credit transactions, took the position that if a particular mortgage or lease needed to be insured or guaranteed to be attractive, it was better not to become involved at all.

Faced with mounting underwriting losses and the poor acceptance by lenders, most MICs reconsidered their approach to income-property mortgage insurance and instituted new programs which provided for less exposure to the insurer. As an example, CLIC,[5] with about 85 percent of the market, abolished the lease guarantee program and decreased its exposure on income-property mortgage insurance to either the top 10 or 15 percent, depending on which program was selected, and dropped its set premium schedule.

The current program offers a 10-year policy followed by annual renewals. The premium is established by CLIC after reviewing the risk. If a default occurs, the insured lender must foreclose and offer a merchantable title to CLIC which, at its option, can either pay 10 percent (or 15 percent depending on program) of the claim[6] or the original amount of the loan, whichever is less, or pay 100 percent of the claim and take title.

Income-property mortgage insurance's future is clouded by the severe recession of 1974-75 and the losses suffered by both mortgage lenders and insurers. The acceptability of income-property mortgage insurance by most lenders has not occurred yet, but a period of relatively stable economic progress should provide the opportunity.

SUGGESTED READINGS

Rapkin, Chester. *The Private Insurance of Home Mortgages*. New York: Columbia University, 1973.

Starr, John O. "Lease Guarantee Insurance," *The Appraisal Journal* (April 1972), pp. 175-87.

NOTES

1. A VA guarantee is not technically mortgage insurance, although the effect is the same, because a mortgage lender is protected and thus encouraged to make loans.

2. The other eleven are American Mortgage Insurance Co., Continental Insurance Co., Foremost Guaranty Corp., Home Guaranty Insurance Corp., Investor Mortgage Insurance Co., Mortgage Guaranty Insurance Corp., PMI Mortgage Insurance Co., Republic Mortgage Insurance Corp., Secura Insurance Co., Ticor Mortgage Insurance Co., and United Guaranty Corp.

3. Arthur D. Little, Inc., *The Private Insurance Industry*, Final Report to the Federal National Mortgage Association and the Federal Home Loan Mortgage Corporation (2 vols., 337 pp.), Cambridge, Massachusetts, April 1975.

4. Discount points (or "points") are used to increase the effective yield of an FHA or VA mortgage (with administratively set interest rates) to a current level. For example, assume the FHA interest rate is 9 percent while the current market yield required is 9.5 percent. In order to induce an investor to purchase the 9 percent FHA mortgage rather than one at 9.5 percent, the 9 percent FHA mortgage would have to be discounted to increase the investor's yield. If the FHA mortgage is for $10,000 at 9 percent for 30 years, the investor would discount the mortgage by 3.41 (341 basis points) and purchase it at 96.59; that

is $9,659. (The discount amount can be obtained from typically available tables.) The investor will pay $9,659 for the mortgage (while the mortgagor repays the entire $10,000), thereby increasing the yield from the 9 percent coupon rate to 9.5 percent (assuming the average 12 years before prepayment). The $341 difference will be paid by the seller of the home the mortgage is being used to finance because the law prohibits an FHA or VA buyer from paying discount points.

5. Commercial Loan Insurance Corporation, a subsidiary of MGIC Investment Corporation.

6. A claim includes the unpaid principal balance, accumulated interest, real estate taxes and hazard insurance premiums advanced, cash for repairs and foreclosure costs.

Chapter 8

Fundamentals of Income–Property Mortgage Lending

INTRODUCTION

The classification of real estate known as income property (or commercial) can be defined as that real estate conceived, built and operated for the purpose of producing income. This income is realized either as actual cash or on the income-property owner's balance sheet as a tax shelter. This income can be *actual*, (e.g., if an owner has leased the property) or *imputed* (e.g., if an owner occupies the property). This is contrasted with residential real estate which is an *amenity* property.

Another major difference between residential and income property is how the income of a borrower is treated. In financing residential real estate, the income of a borrower, and the stability of that income, are of primary importance in determining whether the loan is made. The income-producing capability of commercial real estate itself establishes the value and thus the amount of financing available.

The income property classification can be divided further into *general use* and *special use* property. A general use property could be a retail space in a shopping center since that space could be used by many different types of retail outlets. Churches, factories, bowling alleys and grain elevators are examples of special use properties because their special architectural requirements are useable only for a specific purpose. As a general rule, permanent mortgage investors would rather lend on a general use property than on a special use property since the alternate use potential provides greater security if an occupying tenant does not renew the lease or if a lender has to foreclose. Since permanent mortgage investors take a greater risk with a special use property, they insist on greater protection through such items as a higher interest rate, personal or corporate guarantees or pre-leasing requirements.

General use properties include:

1. Apartment buildings

2. Office buildings

3. Retail outlets

4. Shopping centers

5. Industrial (multi-purpose)

6. Some warehouses

Special use properties include:

1. Hotels and motels

2. Mobile home parks

3. Churches

4. Banks

5. Nursing homes and hospitals

6. Theaters

7. Restaurants

Another classification of income property is based on whether the lender is looking primarily to the real estate as the security for the mortgage loan, as in a real estate loan, or is looking to the credit of either the mortgagor or the tenant who has signed a long-term *net lease.*[1] This would be a credit loan. A credit loan is of increasing importance to many long-term investors who have learned through experience that real estate values can depreciate as well as appreciate.

The ideal credit loan for a permanent investor would be one that fully amortizes over a period of time during which the property is completely leased by an AAA tenant (national credit) with a net lease obligating the tenant for that period and with the rent equal to or exceeding the debt service. In this situation, the lender's risk exposure is limited to the extreme improbability of the tenant declaring bankruptcy. (Leases and their important clauses are discussed in Chapter 9, The Lease and Leasehold Financing.)

Unlike a credit loan where a lender has the security of a valuable tenant and the real estate, a pure real estate mortgage loan offers only the real property as security. Normally this is sufficient security but the risk to a lender is greater. This increased risk is derived from the possibility that the real estate may not be aesthetically or economically attractive to tenants in the future. If that occurs, existing tenants may not renew their leases and new tenants may be difficult to attract. The result of such a situation is usually that a mortgagor defaults on the mortgage because insufficient funds are generated by the property, thereby forcing the lender to foreclose.

ANALYZING THE INCOME PROPERTY LOAN

The analysis of this type of loan must be extensive to protect and provide information for all parties involved. A borrower must be satisfied that the property to be bought or built will provide a reasonable return on the investment. This of course will vary according to each borrower's unique financial position after consideration of taxes, leverage, cash flow and depreciation. No single income property arrangement will satisfy all needs or all borrowers.

Typically, this type of loan involves a mortgage intermediary such as a mortgage company. This intermediary, between the borrower and the permanent mortgage investor, must be convinced that the concept is sound and possible to place before time and effort is invested in underwriting and packaging the deal. A permanent mortgage investor is not involved at this stage unless the loan is being made directly.

Of particular importance to all parties is whether this arrangement creates more value than it will cost to produce. Disregarding tax considerations for the moment, a project costing $10 million to build but which is worth only $10 million or less at completion is one that should never have been started. Of course, a borrower may intend to get only tax benefits from a particular transaction.

Every income property loan should be analyzed according to:

1. Feasibility

2. Location

3. Timing

4. Borrower

5. Real estate

Feasibility

Although a permanent investor will regard location as the paramount issue because of concern for the safety of its investment, both the borrower and the mortgage intermediary are initially concerned with the concept. Questions must be answered, such as: Will this project work at any cost? Does a need exist that this project can satisfy on a practical basis? If the answer is yes then it must be determined if the transaction can create value and give the borrower the requested loan while protecting the interest of the permanent investor.

Figure 8-1 is an example of an analysis made after the acceptance (positive feasibility) of a concept.

Location

Although a few deals will work almost anywhere, good location usually is required. The garden apartment proposal in Figure 8-1 is a good example of a type of loan that requires a good location.

As the location for the proposed construction is analyzed, particular emphasis should be placed on competing properties, population growth, income level, stability of employment, accessibility by automobile and public transportation, and any other factor which will affect the project at this location. This is often called a *market analysis.*

Timing

Assuming that the concept is financially sound, the figures work and a good location exists, the timing of the project is of crucial importance. If three months before the project is completed a similar one is opened elsewhere, in all probability this so-called good deal will fail, or at best have trouble renting. A rent cut may be necessary to attract tenants. The mortgage intermediary *must* investigate to determine whether or not other, similar projects are being planned.

Borrower

An entrepreneur is the most important link in the whole income-property financing chain. Without an entrepreneur's skill and a desire to create value where none existed or to increase existing value, the entire field of income property financing would be entirely different.

It is imperative that this entrepreneur have a successful track record. This record should be indicative of the entrepreneur's ability as a manager, because many developers want to manage the completed project to save management fees which normally are five percent of gross income.

The permanent mortgage investor is interested only in the bor-

Assume Joe Developer has plans for a 150-unit garden apartment. He provides the following information:

COST

Hard cost (land and construction)	
$17,000 per unit x 150	$2,550,000
Soft cost (architectural and engineering)	
10% of hard cost	255,000
Financing cost (construction interest and points)	127,000
Total Cost	$2,932,000

INCOME

Average rent for 1 & 2 bedroom units	
(tenant pays utilities)	
$300 per month x 12 x 150	$ 540,000
Vacancy factor - 5 percent	- 27,000
Effective Gross Income	$ 513,000

EXPENSES

Real estate taxes (est.)	15%
Insurance	4%
Maintenance	10%
Management	6%
Reserve & Misc.	5%

40% of Effective Gross Income

Income	$ -205,200
NET INCOME	$ 307,800

FINANCING

Capitalization rate[1]   10¼%

$$\frac{307,800}{.1025} = \$3,002,926 \text{ value}[2] \text{ established by } \underline{\text{Income Capitalization Method}[3]}, \text{ say } \$3,000,000.$$

75% <u>Loan-to-value ratio</u>[4]

     $3,000,000 x .75 = $2,250,000 loan

<u>Rate</u>[5] 9½ for 28 years

Monthly principal and interest, $19,163 x 12 = $229,950 <u>debt service</u>[6]

<u>Constant</u>[7] $\frac{229,950}{2,250,000}$ = 10.22

<u>Debt coverage</u>[8] $\frac{307,800}{229,950}$ = 1.34

FIGURE 8-1. Step-by-step income-property analysis

Break-even point[9] $\dfrac{435,150}{540,000} = .80$

Cash flow[10] $513,000 - 205,200 - 229,950 = \$77,850$

[1] Capitalization rate - a rate used to convert into present value a series of future installments of net income. Used to establish value. (See Chapter Ten, Appraising Real Estate for Mortgage Loan Purposes, for an explanation of how this rate is established.

[2] Value - an estimate arrived at by dividing the net income by the capitalization rate. Required in order to apply maximum legally allowed loan-to-value ratio.

[3] Income Capitalization Method - the most important appraisal technique used to establish an estimate of value based on a capitalization of net income.

[4] Loan-to-value ratio - in most cases, permanent investors are limited by law to lending only 75 percent of the value of an interest in real estate.

[5] Rate - the interest rate upon which the loan is to be repaid over a specific term, normally established by money market conditions.

[6] Debt service - the annual amount of principal and interest necessary to amortize the loan over its term.

[7] Constant - the percentage of the original loan paid in equal, annual payments (monthly principal and interest x 12) that provides for repayment of the loan over the term. In other words, the percentage that the annual debt service is to the original loan amount.

[8] Debt coverage - the amount of times (stated as a ratio) the net income covers (is over) the debt service.

[9] Break-even point - a percentage of occupancy required to produce sufficient income to meet operating expenses and debt service.

[10] Cash flow - the amount of cash derived from the real estate after debt service and expenses but before depreciation and income taxes.

FIGURE 8-1. Step-by-step income-property analysis continued

rower's ability to build the project according to plans and specifications and, most importantly, within budget. After the project is completed and funding by the permanent mortgagee has occurred, the borrower takes on secondary importance behind the tenants and the real estate.

Some permanent investors will attempt to get personal endorsements which obligate a borrower to repay the mortgage debt if a default occurs. Although these have questionable value in some jurisdictions, the entire financial condition of the borrower must be open to examination. An audited financial statement of the borrower's personal and professional status should be obtained.

Real Estate

For many years the value of the real estate served as the matrix for establishing the mortgage loan. It was assumed that a lender should be able to appraise the value of the real estate against which it was lending and by lending 75 percent of value have sufficient protection against any possible loss through the 25 percent equity if problems developed. Normally this is a valid assumption, but lenders have learned that most of the value created has a direct correlation to the general economic climate. A change in the economy could affect spending, which in turn could affect the mortgaged premises. Because of these problems, many lenders started to consider not only the real estate as security, but also the credit of both the borrower and long-term tenants.

THE INCOME-PROPERTY LENDING PROCESS

The stages through which an income property loan progresses are not always in the same order. But for the purpose of this text, the stages will be organized in a typical sequence.

The origination of this type of loan by a mortgage lender is generally quite different from the origination of a typical residential mortgage loan. The tract business, which is important to residential mortgage lending, is normally not available. Instead, origination resembles the residential spot business as satisfied builder-developers return for additional or new financing. Income property borrowers tend not to remember who helped finance their last deal. If your competitor is quoting rates an eighth or a quarter point lower, they will probably get the business.

If a mortgage lender such as a mortgage company has a correspondent relationship with an institutional investor (e.g., life insurance company) that investor may refer business directly received to the mortgage company.

The feasibility stage usually follows in which the mortgage lender analyzes the data to determine if a proposed transaction is possible. The format is much like the method previously suggested.

Assume a transaction looks like a deal that can be structured and placed. At this stage a mortgage lender will take an application from the borrower and may also require a good faith deposit of one or two percent of the amount sought. In addition to showing that a borrower has some cash to begin the project, this deposit prevents a borrower from shopping a commitment—that is, trying to get one at a lower interest rate or for a longer term. A mortgage intermediary will earn its fee when a commitment is obtained from a permanent lender according to the application, irrespective of whether the borrower accepts it.

An application gives an originator a period of time in which to place the loan—usually 30 to 90 days. Since an application insures a fee if the loan is placed, time can be spent to underwrite the loan completely. This stage requires a complete analysis of the projected numbers and the estimation of value by an appraiser using the income approach primarily and the cost and market data approaches as a check. (See Chapter 10, Appraising Real Estate for Mortgage Loan Purposes.)

The *capitalization rate* and the *constant* are figures that can be used as pawns in negotiations with a permanent mortgage investor. A permanent lender may require a high capitalization rate and be willing to trade a longer mortgage term for it, or the borrower may want a lower constant and be willing to accept a higher interest rate in return. All factors should be negotiable, as long as both parties feel protected. An investor who insists on getting as much out of a loan as possible may end up being the owner—something it does not want.

All supporting data and documentation should be submitted to the investor in a carefully prepared loan submission. (See Chapter 15, Income-Property Mortgage Loan Case-Study.) In some cases, this is all the investor will see, although all income property real estate should be inspected before a loan is funded.

Assuming a loan as submitted, or modified, is acceptable to the permanent mortgage investor, a *firm commitment* will be offered. At this point the mortgage intermediary's fee is earned. The closing of a loan, or *preclosing* if construction must still occur, normally terminates the production phase.

The last stage is the important one of servicing the mortgage loan. Many times, a permanent investor will require a few loans from a mortgage intermediary before granting servicing—others never grant it. (See Chapter 11, Closing and Administering the Mortgage Loan.)

PERMANENT MORTGAGE INVESTORS

Four main groups of permanent investors hold approximately 84 percent of all long-term mortgages on income-producing real estate

(Table 8-1). These same four groups have been active for many years in all types of long-term mortgage lending, although their emphasis has shifted periodically from one type of loan to another.

All mortgage investors are concerned and motivated by *return on* and *return of* investment. Return on investment is the interest that is charged for the use of the money for the term of the loan. This interest rate is determined by the marketplace and the risk involved. Return of the investment is the repayment of the principal and is of primary concern to a mortgage investor.

As an investor reviews a potential loan, it is concerned with the degree of risk involved, because the risk element will affect the interest rate. If the risk is high, probably no interest rate will balance it, but if the risk is only moderate, a higher than normal interest rate may make the investment attractive. At this point, an investor would have to decide if the higher interest rate might jeopardize the basic deal and force foreclosure in the future.

TABLE 8-1

Major Income-Property Long-Term Mortgage Holders

	Income-Property Mortgages Held (Millions of Dollars)	Percent of Total Income-Property Holdings	Total Mortgage Holdings (Millions of Dollars)	Percent of Income-Property Loans to Total Mortgage Holdings
Life Insurance Companies	63,716	29%	86,656	73%
Savings & Loan Associations	51,204	23%	295,887	17%
Commercial Banks	43,759	20%	122,774	35%
Mutual Savings Banks	27,129	12%	78,879	34%
Subtotal	185,808	84%	584,196	32%
Others	35,683	16%	154,940	23%
Total	221,491	100%	739,136	30%

Source: Hud Newsletter #76-444, Dec. 13, 1976 (as of September, 1976)

SUGGESTED READINGS

Aronsohn, Alan J. B. "The Real Estate Limited Partnership and Other Joint Ventures," *Real Estate Review* (Spring 1971), pp, 43-49.

Britton, James A. and Kerwood, Lewis O., eds. *Financing Income-Producing Real Estate*. New York: McGraw-Hill Book Co., Inc., 1977.

Chesborough, Lowell D. "Do Participation Loans Pay Off?" *Real Estate Review* (Summer 1974), pp. 94-100.

Halper, Emanuel M. "What is a New Net Net Net Lease?" *Real Estate Review* (Winter 1974), pp. 9-14.

Kempner, Paul S. "Investments in Single-Tenant Net Leased Properties," *Real Estate Review* (Summer 1974), pp. 131-34.

Robinson, Gerald J. *Federal Income Taxation of Real Estate*. Boston: Warren, Gorham & Lamont, Inc., 1974.

Sillcocks, H. Jackson. "Financing Sense in Real Estate Sales and Leasebacks," *Real Estate Review* (Spring 1975), pp. 89-95.

Unger, Maurice A. *Real Estate*. Cincinnati, Ohio: South-Western Publishing Co., 1974.

NOTES

1. A net lease is one where the tenant is responsible for all taxes, insurance, maintenance and operating expenses.

Chapter 9

The Lease and Leasehold Financing

INTRODUCTION

The business side of real estate is normally concerned with the building, sale, financing or leasing of real estate. The leasing aspect of real estate is extensive considering all the various and often complicated types of leases and leasing arrangements. Consumers and members of the real estate fraternity alike are exposed to leasing in one form or another. As a result everyone needs to be aware of the legal and financial aspects of leasing. The legal term for the interest or estate created by a lease is *leasehold estate*. (See Chapter 12, Fundamentals of Real Estate Law.)

The Importance of Leases

A lease fulfills various economic functions. To the tenant,[1] a lease establishes the contractual right to use and possess the real property of another. To the landlord, it creates the contractual right to collect rent. To a landlord, rent represents either a return on the investment, income to pay the mortgage on the leased real property, or both. The second alternative takes on greater importance when discussing income-producing real property, because a primary reason for the construction of income-producing real estate is to lease to a tenant whose rent will retire the mortgage and produce a reasonable net profit.

The law historically has considered a lease to be both a *conveyance* of real estate and a *contract*. It is considered a conveyance because the landlord is parting with a possessory right to the real estate for a period of time. Under a lease, a landlord gives up the right to use the real estate and, until the expiration of the lease, has only limited rights of a reversionary nature unless further rights have been reserved. For example, under common law, nonpayment of rent did not give a landlord the right to dispossess a tenant because the lease conveyed possession of the land to a tenant for the period of the lease. This rule, of course, has been modified by statute in all states. Another common law rule was that a tenant could not use lack of repairs to justify nonpayment of rent. But this has also been changed by statute in many states to alleviate the problems of slum landlords who continue to collect rent without making repairs.

A lease is considered a contract because it includes clauses containing certain covenants which are guarantees or promises. Since a lease is a contract as well as a conveyance, suit can be brought for breach of contract without terminating the lease. For example, if a tenant has a lease with a covenant requiring the landlord to make repairs to the leased premises but no repairs are made, the tenant can sue for breach of contract to repair, without destroying the lease. In another example, if a shopping center landlord has a valuable tenant who breaches a covenant, the landlord can retain that valuable tenant and still enforce the lease by suing for breach of contract on the appropriate covenant.

All leases, whether for a simple apartment or a complex industrial park, are basically the same. One lease may contain more clauses than another to resolve particular problems, but all will have the same basic elements. A review of the various clauses follows with an explanation of their function and importance. The clauses discussed will be examined from the viewpoint of understanding the different needs of both the landlord and tenant. It is important to emphasize that real estate laws differ among the states, and a local attorney should be consulted about any specific questions regarding leases.

The key to working with leases is to understand the lease itself. Any landlord or tenant should be able to find an answer to any question that could conceivably arise in the wording. The primary reason for a lease is to establish the *rights and duties* of both the landlord and tenant. The Statute of Frauds (each state has a statute named after the original English statute) requires that all leases for a period of more than one year be in writing. But as a practical matter all leases should be in writing for the protection of the parties involved.

Credit Loans

Due to recent and rapid fluctuations in the cost (interest rate) and value of money (inflation), long-term mortage investors have been extremely hesitant to make loans based only on the real estate securing the debt. They have turned to making credit loans and in some cases, exclusively.

As mentioned previously, a permanent investor may look primarily at the credit of a tenant in determining whether to make the loan and how much to lend when analyzing an income property loan application. Accordingly, the real estate takes on a secondary role as security. This lender is interested in determining whether the tenant is a recognizable credit—with either a national or regional reputation. In this way the lender can reasonably determine whether or not the tenant's net lease[2] will be sufficient to meet the debt service, which includes mortgage interest and principal. For example, if a major auto manufacturer executes a 30-year net lease at X dollars a year, a lender probably will make a mortgage loan to be amortized within 30 years if the debt service is also X dollars or, ideally, less. The ability to analyze a lease in a credit transaction is very important for both a mortgage originator and a permanent investor.

THE LEASE

An effective lease should include the following:

1. The parties to the lease

EQUIFAX / RETAILERS COMMERCIAL AGENCY
CREDIT FIRM REPORT

SPECIMEN - ALL ENTITIES FICTITIOUS
CONFIDENTIAL

Acct. No. 00000   File No. Y-2567548   Report Made By Equifax ☐ Retailers ☒   Atlanta _____ OFFICE

00-0-00
ACME CARD SHOP, INC.
Atlanta, Ga., 1675 Grady Street

Transaction: Lease of Space
Amount: $ 18,000/3 years

BUSINESS RECORD: ☒ Corporation—List names of officers.
Check type business organization: ☐ Partnership—List names of partners.
☐ Individual Proprietorship—List owner's name.

FULL NAME	TITLE	AGE	HOW LONG IN FIRM?	IF LESS THAN 2 YEARS WHAT WAS FORMER JOB?
Marvin Brown	President	43	5yrs.	
Louis Carter	Vice-Pres.	46	5yrs.	
Jane Lewis	Treasurer	41	5yrs.	

1. No. Years Known. 5yrs., 3yrs., 5yrs.
2. Date Business Started. 5-1-73
3. Line of business (Mfg., Wholesale, Retail) Retail Sales
4. Type products or services rendered. Greeting cards, magazines, novelty items
5. Any suits, judgments, foreclosures, repossessions, bankruptcy against firm or members' earned? None

6. Is Character of firm and members as to honesty and fair dealing good? If No, explain. Yes
7. Estimated Net Worth. $ 25,000
8. Estimated Gross Annual Sales. $ 175,000
9. Is firm regarded as operating profitably at present? If not, explain. Yes
10. Any factors which will adversely affect future success? If yes, explain. No

REMARKS: Amplify any irregular features above. Write separately if necessary on the following.
CREDIT RECORD: Sources: banks, Commercial Houses. Set out separately the experience and how regarded as a credit risk. Quote any actual records in the Comment on any suit's judgments or bankruptcies developed through sources.
BUSINESS HISTORY: Describe size and nature of business products manufactured or sold or services rendered and scope of operations (local, state, national). Comment on firm's success and stability and future prospects for success. Cover experience and previous connection of each member of firm if in business less than 2 years. Show number of employees if developed. Comment on location of business—whether inside city, uptown, suburban or out of the way. Cover any unusual competition which might affect this business.
FINANCES: Show kind of property that makes up worth of business. Try to develop assets and liabilities. Do they own or lease the building? Secure and attach or quote up-to-date financial statement if available. (If individually owned business, cover total net worth of owner in addition to net worth of business.)
FARM: If firm operating as firm, also cover information on farm.

CREDIT RECORD:
Bank of Atlanta: Bank officer reports paid unsecured loan in 4 figures, paid as agreed.
Bank of Athens: Bank officer reports open unsecured loan in 4 figures since 6-76, paying as agreed.
ABC Card Co.:   Dealing with this firm for 5 years, high credit $3500, pays 30 days, good account.
Business Landlord: Rental of business space paid promptly, $700 per month, satisfactory tenant.

BUSINESS HISTORY: The Acme Card Shop, Inc. is a moderate size retail greeting card store which was incorporated in the State of Georgia in 1973 and the above named officers have been with this firm since its inception. The firm engages in the sale of greeting cards, magazines and novelty items and employs 10 people. The firm has operated from the above location for the past 5 years and is a closed corporation. The firm has operated on a local level only and has been successful at this location.

FINANCES: The firm's net worth is estimated at $25,000 based upon bank account, inventory and equipment. Gross annual sales are estimated at $175,000 and these figures were obtained from the firm's accountant. This firm appears to be financially sound and prospects for the future appear favorable.

WFG/st
2cc

Equifax Inc.
Form 63-256 U.S.A.

Sample credit report on a business for leasing purposes. Use of this form by courtesy of Retailers Commercial Agency, Atlanta.

2. An agreement to lease

3. A description of the leased premises

4. The term of the lease

5. A rental agreement

6. The rights and duties of all parties

7. Signatures

Lease Check List

I. **Parties**	C. Who is responsible for:		Repairs and main-		
A. Landlord		**Lessor Lessee**	tenance	—— ——	
B. Tenant	Real estate		Other	—— ——	
II. **Premises**	taxes —— ——		VI. **Assignment and subletting**		
A. Location	Hazard		A. Allowed?		
B. If less than all, what part	insur- ance —— ——		B. Novation, or keep ten- ant liable		
III. **Term**	Public lia-		C. Increase rental to whom		
A. Lease signed	bility in- surance —— ——		VII. **Mortgages**		
B. Commences	Janitorial —— ——		A. Leasehold mortgages allowed		
C. Expires	Electricity —— ——		B. Subordination		
IV. **Rent**	Elevators —— ——		C. Limit of fee mortgage to lease income		
A. Base rent	Water —— ——		D. Future mortgages sub- ordinated		
B. Percentage	Fuel —— ——		VIII. **Condemnation**		
i. Of gross income	Trash		A. Tenants' share		
ii. Any offsets	removal —— ——		B. Landlord share		
C. Covenant to pay	Landscap-				
D. Assignments of rent	ing —— ——				
i. To investor	Parking				
ii. After foreclosure	area —— ——				
V. **Expenses**	Air cond. —— ——				
A. Escalation					
B. Base year					

Parties to the lease. It is necessary to identify the parties to the lease. When dealing with a corporation, reference should be made to the articles of incorporation which give the corporation the power to be either a landlord or a tenant. It is important that neither landlord nor tenant be a minor because a minor has the legal right to disaffirm a contract.

Agreement to lease. This is a contract between the parties whereby a landlord agrees to give possession of the premises to the tenant in return for certain promises by the tenant, including payment of rent, for a period of time.

Description of the premises. It is advisable to examine a landlord's title to the premises to prevent a tenant being evicted because of a title defect. The leased premises must be clearly identifiable. A description of the premises is usually sufficient, such as, the building at 727 South 3rd Street, or a legal description which identifies and locates the property being leased. If a part of a building is leased, the tenant has the right to use other parts of the building, including stairs, halls, toilets and other areas, even if not so stated within the lease.

Term of the lease. Although the vast majority of leases, especially residential leases, are for periods of less than 10 years, many commercial leases are for longer periods and may last for generations. Many states require that a lease last no longer than 99 years, making it important to determine at the time the lease is drawn how long it will last.

Although a landlord is not obligated to renew a lease unless contracted to do so, it is typical to include in the lease the option to renew if the tenant is in good standing. If the option to renew exists, it will not benefit a sub-tenant. If the mortgage is based on the credit of a tenant, the option to renew would be critical if the lease term was less than the term of the mortgage. However, this would be an unusual situation since the mortgagee would normally require the protection of the lease.

If the option is exercised, the rental amount due under a renewed lease must be determined or the option to renew at a rent to be fixed in the future will be unenforceable because of uncertainty. Some courts have held *contra* if the rent can be established by a reasonable method such as an appraisal, formula, or equation. Under all circumstances, a lease should stipulate how the tenant is to give notice to renew and how much notice is to be given.

Rental agreement. As far as a landlord is concerned, the reason a lease exists is to produce income. Under the common law, rent was payable at the end of a rental period. Today, most landlords require that rent be paid at the beginning of the rental period. A tenant should realize rent paid in advance is not refundable if the premise is not occupied, unless the contract is contra. A lease should not only state the amount of the rent and when it is due, but also include a covenant to pay the rent. Then, if nonpayment occurs, the landlord can sue on the breach of the covenant to pay, instead of having to terminate the lease. Of course, nonpayment can justify termination of the lease if the landlord determines that it is the best alternative. If a tenant with the right to sublet does so, then the landlord has the right to sue the original tenant for any unpaid rent by the subtenant.

Rights and duties of the parties. As mentioned earlier, if a lease is prepared correctly, it should answer as many potential questions as possible regarding the rights and duties of the landlord and tenant. A discussion of some of the more common clauses designed to solve lease problems follows.

1. *Assignment of rent clause.* When dealing with commercial leases, one of the clauses that often creates conflicts involves rent assignments to the landlord's mortgagee. A permanent mortgage investor may require a direct assignment of rent clause because it is not confident of the financial stability of the landlord and, in effect, has made the mortgage on the credit of the tenant. In this case, the investor may insist on a direct assignment of the rents, although this would be unusual, whereby the tenant pays the investor who then takes out principal and interest. Some money may be placed in escrow for taxes and insurance and the difference rebated to the landlord. A more common type of direct assignment occurs when an investor requires a landlord to include a clause that obligates the tenant to forward all rent to the investor rather than to the landlord if there is a default on the mortgage.

2. *Tax clause.* Real estate taxes are a landlord's responsibility, but the lease can require a tenant to pay these taxes and often does. For example, if the lease is a net lease, the tenant is obligated to pay the real estate taxes, among other expenses. (See the section on the escalation clause for an additional explanation.)

3. *Insurance clause.* The landlord and tenant should clearly state in the lease who is responsible for obtaining and paying insurance. In a commercial lease, this could include public liability insurance, rental insurance, fire insurance, boiler insurance, glass insurance, elevator insurance, and any other type of insurance needed. For the protection of the landlord, the lease should require that insurance policies cannot be cancelled for nonpayment of premiums or materially amended unless the landlord has been given sufficient notice.

   If a tenant has the obligation to pay taxes, insurance, etc., the lease should contain a requiring covenant. These obligations could be included as additional rent allowing a landlord to sue for nonpayment of rent if a tenant pays the contract rent but not the additional rent.

4. *Assignment clause.* In an assignment of a lease, a tenant is transferring all interests in the lease and, in effect, creating a

new lease. This creates a new tenant who pays rent directly to the same landlord. With an assignment, the original tenant retains the obligation to the landlord. Therefore, a tenant cannot disregard an obligation to pay rent simply by assigning the lease to another party. If a tenant sublets, then the tenant in effect becomes a landlord since the entire interest under the lease is not being transferred. In this situation, as with an assignment, the prior tenant retains the obligation to the landlord.

Any tenant has the right to assign a lease unless the landlord has restricted the right. Most sophisticated landlords hold back the right to assign or sublet, except with their approval. Normally, this approval will be given because many landlords realize that without the right to transfer a particular lease, a tenant might not be able to sell a business (such as a restaurant) located on or in the leased premises. If a lease allows a transfer with approval, the approval cannot be capriciously withheld. Any increase in rent should go to the landlord if a landlord does allow a tenant to assign or sublet.

5. *Escalation clauses.* The basic reason for escalation clauses is to protect a landlord from inflation and in this way protect the investment. Although most residential leases do not include escalation clauses, many commercial leases now contain them. A few apartment leases also have such clauses. A tenant should insist that an escalation clause affect all tenants on an equal basis.

The escalation clause based on the escalation of taxes is most common. At the time a lease is drawn, it is impossible to predict the level of future taxes. Taxes will probably rise at least at the rate of inflation, which also is indeterminable. If taxes are to be paid completely by the tenant, no need exists for an escalation clause. The clause is required only if increases are to be paid by the tenant. Any increase should be calculated on a base year, and the lease should clearly define the base year. The first three years after the building is completed and 80 percent occupied could be the base year for determining the amount of taxes to be passed on to the tenant. A tenant may want a landlord to agree that the tenant can contest tax increases in the landlord's name.

Escalation clauses for operating expense exist for the same reason as those for taxes. Escalation clauses should include the increases in wages, supplies, repairs or similar expenses. A base year again is advisable if the increases are to be paid by the tenant. Some experts have suggested an operating expenses escalation clause based on the government cost-of-living index, but this index does not always reflect the items included under operation expenses. It seems better to have actual increases passed through to the tenant, especially in an inflationary economy.

6. *Percentage clause.* Another way to protect a landlord against inflation is through the use of percentage leases. These can also exist for the benefit of a tenant. In a percentage lease, any additional rent generally is computed over a base rent or a base amount. This base rent is usually lower than what both parties expect a business to normally pay for a similar premise (economic rent) that has no percentage lease. After a certain gross income level has been reached, a percentage of the excess amount becomes additional rent to the landlord.

A percentage lease allows a tenant to stay in business during adverse economic times, since the rent being paid for the premises is actually less than the rent paid if it were based purely on current economics or the rent of competing businesses. On the other hand, a percentage lease allows a landlord to participate in good times through the increased income a tenant is generating by the use of the real property owned by the landlord.

It is important for all parties to understand that a percentage lease is not a partnership, even though profits are shared. A partner is liable for losses. Consequently, courts have been clear in stating that a percentage lease does not make a landlord a partner with a tenant. Suppose the base rent is $5,000 per year and, if the business grosses more than $100,000 for the year, the landlord will receive five percent of the amount over $100,000 as additional rent. If the business grosses $500,000, the additional rent to the landlord would be $20,000 (.05 x $400,000 = $20,000), or a total rent of $25,000.

Percentage leases should be based on the gross income of a business. Gross income rather than net income is suggested because a tenant might include improper expense items to arrive at net income. Another reason for using gross income is that there may be additional income generated from the premises but still related to the lease, such as repairs. Therefore, a lease should explicitly define gross income.

The percentage a landlord would receive over the base amount varies from area to area and from business to business. The range may be anywhere from half of one percent for a chain supermarket to 60 percent for a parking lot. The base rent is usually payable monthly, while the percentage rent based on gross income will probably be calculated and made payable at the end of the calendar or fiscal year.

7. *Other clauses.* A covenant to do business is necessary with a percentage lease, and it should clearly state that a tenant has an obligation to continue in business. The reason for this clause is clear. Business might be too good and a tenant will realize that the percentage rent is higher than expected. Business may be bad and the tenant will not want to continue in business. Either way, the landlord is affected. Therefore, a continuous operation clause should be made part of the covenant to do business requiring that the tenant remain in business the entire year to insure that a peak period is not missed. It also should prevent a tenant from operating only when business is good, then closing shop for the remainder of the year and prorating income over the entire year.

In addition to the clauses that make a percentage lease operative, a radius clause should be used. Under a radius clause, a tenant cannot operate a second business within a certain area if that business would compete with the one under lease. The radius might be determined in miles if a small community is involved, or by blocks in a large urban area. This clause prevents a tenant from competing with its own business. Such competition would keep income and the percentage rent down. A problem with radius clauses and competition is the questionable legality of preventing a tenant from advertising its other stores.

Mortgages and Leases

Whenever these two topics are discussed, the paramount issue is one of priorities. The simplest rule is the first to be recorded will have a superior position, meaning that if a lease exists on real estate in question before a mortgage encumbers that real estate, the lease is protected and will continue even if a mortgage forecloses.

If the lease is subsequent to the mortgage, then the lease is in jeopardy. If the need to foreclose occurs, in most states the lease would be terminated by a foreclosure proceeding. The legal reason for this is that a tenant is in possession of the premises based on a landlord's (mortgagor's) right to possession. But upon foreclosure the landlord is no longer entitled to possession. This is not the case if the lease predates the mortgage since the mortgagee is bound by the mortgagor's contract with the tenant.

Termination of a lease as a result of foreclosure is not always the desired result for a mortgagee. As mentioned, some mortgages are made based either on the fact that tenants are available or on the credit rating of a tenant. To lose such a tenant could make the property less valuable. A solution to this problem is to make the mortgage subordinate to the important subsequent lease so if the need to foreclose should arise, the valuable tenant will not be lost.

LEASEHOLD FINANCING

As leasehold interests have become more common and important in commercial real estate, various techniques have developed which enable sophisticated landlords, developers and tenants to realize the maximum value from their real estate interest. These techniques include the use of the sale-leaseback and the use of the leasehold interest as security for a mortgage.

A leasehold interest has sufficient determinable value to be one of these financing techniques if the term of the lease is long enough, the rent reasonable, and the real estate desirable. However, many of the decisions on financing the lease and which technique to use are based on tax considerations. A complete explanation of these tax considerations is beyond the scope of this text, but the more obvious ones will be discussed.

Sale-Leaseback

This technique has been used for many years but in the past 25 years or so has become a common financing technique. It gained acceptance when various state laws were amended to allow insurance companies to purchase real estate for investment rather than be limited solely to legally-prescribed loan-to-value mortgages.

A sale-leaseback simply is a sale of real estate to a buyer who simultaneously leases it back to the seller. For example, assume Ajax Steel owns a smelter and the land on which the smelter is located and wants to sell the land, then immediately lease it back. The reasons for this apparently simple transaction are many, but could include any or all of the following:

1. The seller, who did not want its capital tied up in real estate, would rather use the capital to expand its business or acquire additional inventory.

2. The transaction allows a seller to obtain 100 percent of the value of the land sold. If the seller had decided to mortgage, it could have received only up to a maximum of 75 percent of value.

3. The rent the seller has to pay for the leased premises is deductible for income tax purposes and usually less, ideally, than the debt service on a mortgage.

For the buyer, the several advantages of this transaction would include:

1. Greater security for an investment since title is held by the buyer.

2. Normally higher yield than could be obtained from making a mortgage loan because of no usury limitations. Also the buyer often becomes a participant in gross income.

3. An appreciating asset.

This technique also can be used in many situations that require additional financing. For example, assume a developer owns land upon which an office building has been constructed and a permanent mortgage obtained for 75 percent of value. The developer could sell the land under the building and lease it back using the proceeds from the sale to obtain what amounts to 100 percent financing of the office building.

During the prosperous days of 1971-1973 of the Real Estate Investment Trusts, the purchase of land under income-producing real estate, with a net lease back to the seller/tenant, provided an investment without any management problems associated with the land itself. This desirable investment also produced the yield REITs needed on their investments.

If a sale-leaseback is successfully negotiated, a question may arise later concerning whether the transaction was really a sale or a disguised 100 percent mortgage. All aspects of the transaction must be carefully analyzed including sale price, rent, and the amount of the repurchase price. The required documents also must be carefully drafted to prevent one of the parties or, more probably, the Internal Revenue Service, from alleging the transaction was a mortgage. If a court holds the transaction was a disguised mortgage, then the tenant/mortgagor is the legal owner and the landlord/mortgagee has merely a security interest. In addition to the tax consequences of the transaction being a mortgage, the existence of a usurious interest rate is probable. Courts have held that the test for determining whether a sale-leaseback transaction is a sale or a mortgage is the intent of the parties.[3]

Financing the Leasehold Interest

A lease can be mortgaged just as any other interest in real estate that can be sold. The danger of lending money on a lease is that there may be no tangible security. The mortgagee of a fee can always foreclose and obtain the real property, if necessary, but the mortgagee of a lease may only have the lease as security. If the leasehold mortgagor also owns the building on the leased land, then the leasehold mortgagee will have a much stronger security position.[4]

A leasehold mortgagee faces two dangers: 1) the lease could be cancelled by the landlord for some nonperformance by the tenant; or 2) the lease could be cancelled by foreclosure by a feehold mortgagee if the lease is subsequent to a mortgage on the fee.[5] Usually, the mortgagee of a leasehold interest will require an estoppel certificate from the landlord which states that there is no back rent due, no set-offs, no liens, no prior default, nor any other reason why the lease would be vulnerable. The best protection for a leasehold mortgagee would be an agreement that any nonperformance by the tenant would allow the lease to continue until the mortgagee is given a chance to cure the default.

If a lease is prior to a mortgage on the fee, the tenant, and thus its mortgagee, need not be concerned about a foreclosure of the fee mortgage, but if the fee mortgage is prior to the lease, foreclosure could terminate the lease. Even if the lease is subsequent to the fee mortgage, a leasehold interest could be protected by a nondisturbance agreement which states that the fee mortgagee will not destroy the lease if a foreclosure of the fee mortgage occurs. A nondisturbance agreement is useless in some states, since their laws require that if a foreclosure occurs, all subsequent leases are terminated. In those states, a subordination agreement is needed by which the fee mortgagee subordinates its mortgage to the lease.

Normally, a mortgagee of a fee would be willing to subordinate since the lease makes the security more valuable. In some situations a mortgagee may not want to subordinate, because it may feel a property unencumbered by leases would be easier to sell.

This concept is not always easy to understand especially in those situations where mortgages exist on both the fee interest and the leasehold interest. For example, assume ABC is the owner of a shopping center, upon which the PDQ Insurance Company has a mortgage. ABC leases a quarter acre on the edge of the parking lot to XYZ to build a coffee shop. XYZ's coffee shop is constructed and XYZ obtains a permanent mortgage on its leasehold interest from the LUV Insurance Company. At the request of LUV, PDQ Insurance Company subordinated its mortgage on the fee to XYZ's lease in order that XYZ could get the leasehold mortgage. This subordination was acceptable to PDQ because it then had greater security for its mortgage in the lease payment from XYZ.

An example which combines a sale-leaseback and a mortgage of a leasehold interest and also portrays the conflicting claims and motivations of the parties involved follows:

Mr. A owns a parcel of valuable real estate which has been in the family for a number of years and upon which he plans to build an office building. Mr. A does not have the cash to begin construction although a local commercial bank will provide a construction mortgage if Mr. A can obtain sufficient cash.

In order to obtain this cash, Mr. A decides to sell the land to B Investment Company which will simultaneously lease the land back to him under a long-term net lease at a rental amount which provides B with an attractive yield on its investment and a participation in future rental income. Mr. A receives 100 percent of the value of the land in cash—as contrasted with a typical 50 percent of value loan on an unimproved real estate—and is therefore able to get a construction loan for the construction of the office building. The office building is then constructed on his leasehold estate (interest).

Mr. A now wants to obtain a permanent mortgage from C Insurance Company to pay off the construction mortgage and get his cash out. C is willing to make the leasehold mortgage with the building and leasehold interest as security but only if B will subordinate its fee interest to the mortgage. The reason for this demand is that C, the leasehold mortgagee, is concerned about its security which in reality is the leasehold interest of Mr. A. This interest could disappear if the lease is terminated by a default by the tenant, Mr. A.

This security interest of C could be protected by requiring B to notify C of any default and allowing C a chance to cure the default, but this is not acceptable to C. C's primary fear is the possibility that the office building will be difficult to rent and consequently Mr. A would probably default on his lease payment. B would then notify C to cure the default or lose the lease and, for all practical purposes, the building. C does not want to be in a situation where it would have to foreclose the mortgage and become the owner of a leasehold interest, which is uneconomical. C will therefore insist that B's fee be subordinated in order that a foreclosure of the leasehold interest will wipe out the fee interest of B allowing for the sale of the land and building. The B Investment Company will probably agree to subordinate its interest because it realizes its fee will be more valuable with an improvement and its participation in rent can only occur if an improvement exists.

SUGGESTED READINGS

Bohon, Davis T. *Complete Guide to Profitable Real Estate Leasing.* Englewood Cliffs, New Jersey: Prentice-Hall, Inc., 1969.

Dennis, Marshall W. "Close Scrutiny Helps Avoid Legal Troubles in Commercial Leases," *The Mortgage Banker* (December 1974), pp. 27-34.

Friedman, M. R. *Friedman on Leases.* New York: Practicing Law Institute, 1974.

Levy, Daniel S. "ABC's of Shopping Center Leases," *Real Estate Review* (Spring 1971), pp. 12-16.

McMichael, Stanley L., and O'Keefe, Paul T. *Leases: Percentage, Short and Long Term.* Englewood Cliffs, New Jersey: Prentice-Hall, Inc., 1974.

NOTES

1. The term landlord (lessor) and tenant (lessee) will be used in place of the less understood legal terms.

2. The term net lease will be used to define the situation where the tenant is obligated to pay all taxes, insurance, operating, and maintenance expenses.

3. See, In Re San Francisco Industrial Park, Inc., 307 F. Supp. 271, 274 (N.D. Calif. 1969).

4. Normally, the only time a leasehold mortgage is made with only the lease as security is when the purpose of the loan is to finance inventory, or other short-term capital needs.

5. A mortgagee will only make a leasehold mortgage if the loan is fully amortized before the expiration of the lease. Some require that the loan be fully amortized before 75 percent of the term of the ground lease expires.

Chapter 10

Appraising Real Estate for Mortgage Loan Purposes

The purpose of this chapter is to provide an overview of the fundamentals of real estate appraisal, define the standard terminology used, and explain the common methods of estimating value. An appraisal of real estate is a supportable estimate of value made by a technically trained specialist as of a specific date.[1] The value being sought could be insurable value or assessed value, but is most often market value.

An appraisal may be required to provide an estimate of value in almost any stage of a real estate transaction or activity. For example, at any given moment an appraisal of real estate may be needed to estimate:

1. Assessed value for taxation purposes

2. Insurance value

3. Market value for sale or exchange purposes

4. Market value for mortgage loan purposes

5. Compensation in condemnation proceedings

6. Rental value

The value determined for the same piece of real estate can vary according to the purpose of the appraisal; the estimated value for insurance purposes could be much different from the value estimated for condemnation purposes. In this chapter the value to be estimated will be market value since most mortgage lenders are permitted by law or regulation to lend only a certain percentage of market value.

VALUE

A clear, concise definition of value is difficult if not impossible to obtain because the concept of value means many different things. One of the classical definitions holds that value is the capacity of an economic good to command other goods in exchange. In other words, the value of an object is established by what it can get in exchange, or value represents that point stated as a price where supply and demand coincide or intersect.

Market value of real estate is that price a property would bring on the open market if offered for sale during a reasonable period of time by a seller not forced to sell and if sought by a purchaser not forced to buy. The *market price* is that price for which the real estate actually sells. In theory, market value and price should be the same, but they rarely are. For example, a seller may decide to accept less (market price) than asked (market value) in order to facilitate the sale if the seller believes time is more valuable than the difference in money.

PRINCIPLES OF REAL ESTATE VALUE

Value of a given piece of real estate does not remain the same. The value can be changed by:

1. Shifts in social standards and ideals such as population growth or decline

2. Economic developments such as the opening or closing of a large industrial plant

3. Modifications of governmental regulations affecting zoning or building codes

4. Shifts in traffic patterns or road networks

If these factors remain constant, the market value of a given piece of real estate may still change as a result of the following more basic value determinants:

1. *Supply and demand.* Real estate is similar to all other marketable commodities in that its value is increased or decreased by supply and demand.

2. *Highest and best use.* Market value of real estate is influenced most by whether the real estate is being put to its highest and best use. This use is defined as that providing the greatest net return over a period of time. This return could be in terms of money or amenities (living in a house as opposed to renting it).

3. *Diminishing returns.* This principle recognizes that continuing additions to the whole will not continue to increase the value of the whole by the value of the addition after a certain point.

4. *Substitution.* This basic principle perceives that the upper limit of the value of the real estate tends to be established by the cost of acquiring an equally-desirable substitute property.

THE APPRAISAL PROCESS

Since an appraisal is intended to solve a problem; that is, to estimate value, the problem must be clearly stated as to what type of value is sought. The process required to provide this estimate of value necessitates identification of the following:

1. The real estate to be appraised

2. Property rights involved

3. Type of value to be estimated

4. Function or use of the appraisal

To accomplish the assigned task, an appraiser must review and analyze all data relating to the economic background of the region, city and neighborhood of the subject property, the demographic profile, amenities and, finally, of the subject property itself (Figure 10-1). The next step in the process is the application of one or more of the three approaches to value.

THE APPRAISAL PROCESS

DEFINITION OF THE PROBLEM

| Identify Real Estate | Identify Rights | Date of Value | Objective of Appraisal | Definition of Value |

PRELIMINARY SURVEY AND APPRAISAL PLAN

| Data Needed | Data Sources | Personnel Needed | Time Schedule | Completion Flow Chart |

DATA COLLECTION AND ANALYSIS

General Data   **Specific Data**

SUBJECT
LOCATIONAL ECONOMIC PROPERTY COMPARATIVE

Region	Market	Title	Costs
City	Analysis	Site	Sales
Neighborhood	Financial	Physical	Rentals
etc.	Economic Base	Highest and Best Use	Expenses
	Trends		

APPLICATION OF THE THREE APPROACHES

Cost   Market Data   Income

RECONCILIATION OF VALUE INDICATIONS

FINAL ESTIMATE OF DEFINED VALUE

FIGURE 10-1. The appraisal process. Reprinted by permission of the American Institute of Real Estate Appraisers of the National Association of Realtors.

Market Data Approach

This approach to value, often referred to as the *direct sales comparison approach*, uses market data on sales prices of similar properties to estimate value. This is the most common approach used for single-family residential properties. The principle of substitution is evident since the value of a property similar to the subject property should closely approximate the value of the subject property. The market value for the comparables is best substantiated by the actual recent sales prices.

An appraiser will use as many recent sales of similar or comparable properties as possible and the more used, the better will be the estimate. The market price will be adjusted for whatever physical differences exist between the comparables and the subject property. Any features of a comparable that are not found in the subject property are subtracted from the value of the comparable to suggest the value of the subject property. On the other hand, features in the subject property not present in the comparable are added to the value of the comparable to adjust the value. The basic formula is as follows:

Value of comparable property ± adjustments = Value of subject property

For example, if house A with a finished basement worth $6,000 currently sells for $61,000 and is otherwise comparable to house B, then the estimate of value for house B would be $55,000: The house A value of $61,000–$6,000 for finished basement = House B value of $55,000.

Cost Approach

This approach to estimating value often is referred to as the *summation approach.* It combines the cost of replacing or reproducing the improvements with the value of the land and is often considered most important when dealing with nonresidential, nonincome-producing, special purpose real estate, such as a public library, or when used as a check against other approaches. The concept behind this approach is that an investor would not pay more for an improvement on the open market than it would cost to build a new one.

The cost that is estimated to arrive at a value of a subject property by the cost approach is either reproduction cost or replacement cost.

1. *Reproduction cost.* The current amount of money needed to construct a new duplicate structure.

2. *Replacement cost.* Some structures cannot be duplicated at any reasonable cost. Therefore, the cost sought is the cost to construct a structure with the same utility.

When figuring cost for either reproduction or replacement, both direct costs such as supplies, labor and profits, and indirect costs including fees, taxes and financing costs, are listed.

The appraiser considers the fact that the subject property will not be the same as a reproduced structure because of depreciation or loss in value to the subject property. Therefore, adjustments must be made to either the reproduction or replacement cost reflecting existing depreciation. Depreciation includes:

1. *Physical deterioration.* A loss in value from the cost of a new structure is made equal to the loss of economic life in the subject property caused by wear and tear. This physical deterioration may or may not be curable.

2. *Functional obsolescence.* A loss in value resulting from structural components, such as bathrooms, kitchens or in the overall layout, that are outmoded or inefficient as judged by current desires or standards.

3. *Economic obsolescence.* A loss in value resulting from changes external to the property such as changes in zoning classifications, sharp increases in property taxes or other negative influences.

The cost approach can be explained simply:

Cost of reproduction or replacement – depreciation + land value =
Value of subject property

For example, assume the problem is to estimate the value of an old public library which has depreciated 50 percent. The cost to build a new public library (reproduction cost) is $1.5 million and the land is valued at $100,000. The estimate of value is made in this way:

Cost $1,500,000 – depreciation of $750,000 + land, $100,000 =
$850,000 value of subject property

This approach to estimating value uses the net operating income of the property. Although the other two approaches can be used for residences and other types of property, this approach can be used only to arrive at the value for income-producing real estate such as office buildings, apartments and other commercial establishments. The concept is that an ascertainable relationship exists between the income a property earns and the price, or value, someone would be willing to pay for that property.

Obviously, this approach can be used only for those properties that have or will have income, but a special technique called the *gross rent multiplier* (GRM) can be used either to estimate value for a single-family residence or to serve as a check against the other approaches. The theory behind GRM is that the same market will influence both the sales price and the rental price and, therefore, both tend to move up or down in tandem. This relationship can be expressed as a ratio:

$$\frac{\text{Sale price}}{\text{Gross income}} = \text{GRM}$$

Thus, if a house recently sold for $72,000 and rented for $500 a month, the GRM would be:

$$\frac{\$72,000}{\$500} = 144$$

Thus, if the appraisal assignment is to estimate the value of a house comparable to another property being rented at $450 a month, the result would be:

$450 \times 144 = \$64,800$—value of subject house by the income approach.

However, before considering the final estimate of value, the other approaches must be considered.

With respect to income-producing properties, the first step in the income approach is to ascertain the *net operating income* of the property being appraised. This requires establishing *gross income* from which an allowance for vacancy is deducted to arrive at *effective gross income*. Net operating income is derived by deducting *operating expenses* from effective gross income. Operating expenses include all expenses necessary to produce the income, such as utilities, repairs, insurance, real estate taxes and wages, but does not include indirect expenses such as financing costs, income taxes and depreciation.

When net operating income is known, an appraiser can use various techniques to convert this income into a present value. This process is called *capitalization*, and the desired result is to discount the future income to a present value. In other words, the discounting of the future income determines the *present value* of that stream of income (Figure 8–1).

Analyzing the concept from a basic position, this process is used to establish how much money a person would pay for, or value, the right to receive a certain amount of income for a period of time. For example, if a person could receive $100 per year on an investment for 10 years and wanted a 10 percent return on the investment, the worth, or present value, of that future stream of income would be calculated:

$$\text{Value} = \frac{\text{income}}{\text{rate of return}} \quad \text{or} \quad V = \frac{I}{R} \quad \text{or} \quad \$1,000 = \frac{\$100}{.10}$$

The 10 percent return the investor sought in this example is called the *capitalization rate* and the process of converting the income stream to present value is called *capitalization*.

The capitalization rate, or cap rate, to be applied to the income stream is at times a difficult figure to establish, since it is a reflection of market conditions. A small change in the expected rate of return can have an appreciable effect on value as the following example demonstrates:

$$\frac{\$1,000 \text{ annual income}}{.10 \text{ return}} = \$10,000 \text{ value}$$

$$\frac{\$1,000 \text{ annual income}}{.09 \text{ return}} = \$11,111 \text{ value}$$

$$\frac{\$1,000 \text{ annual income}}{.11 \text{ return}} = \$9,090 \text{ value}$$

Many students of real estate have been confused by academic

explanations of how a capitalization rate is established and given false hope by practitioners who explain it simply as "whatever the market will bear." An analysis of capital investment motivation reveals that an investor wants two returns:

1. Return on investment—the interest an investor wants to earn on an investment

2. Return of investment—the return of capital or the recapture of invested capital

Since in theory land does not depreciate in value, it should return the capital invested at some time in the future when it is sold. Therefore, no present need exists to provide for recapture of the capital in land. In land only situations, the capitalization rate would consist solely of the interest, or discount rate, an investor wanted as a return on the investment. Requirements by investors for rates of return vary according to their needs and many outside influences, but the most important influence is the competition for investment dollars from other sources, in addition to real estate. One method by which an individual interest rate can be constructed is the *summation method* which reflects the various risks inherent in an investment that are summed up or added together. For example, the return on land only that is necessary to attract capital is computed by assigning to each element of risk an interest rate that is indicative of its relative weight. For example:

safe rate of interest (as established by a "safe" investment, e.g., U.S. Treasury bills)	.06
risk rate (a need for a greater return as risk increases)	.02
non-liquidity rate (an interest penalty because of lack of liquidity)	.01
management burden (an interest penalty because of a need to manage the investment)	.01
	.10

This 10 percent interest rate would be the capitalization rate for the stream of income from land only.

If the land is improved with a structure, the capitalization rate will include the interest rate as the return on capital and a *recapture rate* as the return of capital. The capital must be partially recaptured each year to provide for a complete return of the capital investment over the life of the improvement. There are three methods of computing recapture—straight-line, sinking-fund, and annuity. If a property had an economic life of 25 years, the recapture, figured on the straight-line method, would require a four percent (100 percent ÷ 25 years = 4 percent) recapture per year. The sinking-fund and annuity methods add back to the amount recaptured the value of the interest the recaptured capital can earn.

Therefore, if the net operating income is produced by both the improvements and the land, the capitalization rate to capitalize that income will include the interest rate or discount rate and the recapture rate. For example:

Interest rate (return on)	.10
Recapture rate (return of)	.04
Capitalization rate	.14

There are other techniques for applying a capitalization rate to various segments of income, but those techniques are beyond the sope of this text.

CORRELATION OF VALUE

An appraiser should always strive to use the three approaches—market data, cost and income—in estimating value to provide as valid an estimate as possible. In most situations, the estimates of value after using all three approaches should be fairly similar. (See Figure 10-2, Valuation Section, for an example of a residential appraisal that embraces all three approaches.) If the estimates are widely divergent, the data-gathering method and analysis for each approach must be carefully reviewed. If the estimates remain far apart, the appraiser must consider the purpose of the appraisal. If the appraisal is to estimate value for a condemnation suit, the market data is most important. For insurance purposes, the replacement cost is most important. If the appraisal is for mortgage loan purposes on an income-producing property, then the income approach should be emphasized. It is in the correlation of value that an appraiser's skill is recognized and the problem of estimating value answered.

RESIDENTIAL APPRAISAL REPORT   File No. _____

Borrower/Client **Martin, John R. & Pamela S.**	Census Tract _____ Map Reference _____

Property Address **2800 Linden Lane**

City **Springfield**   County **Fairfax**   State **Virginia**   Zip Code **22132**

Legal Description **Lot 42, Section 2, Olde Forge Subdivision**

Sale Price $ **35,000**   Date of Sale **current** Property Rights Appraised [X] Fee ☐ Leasehold ☐ DeMinimis PUD(FNMA only ☐ Condo ☐ PUD)

Actual Real Estate Taxes $ **700**   (yr) Loan charges to be paid by seller $ _____   Other sales concessions _____

Lender **Blake Mortgage Company**   Lender's Address **Lendertown, Virginia**

Occupant **R. J. Miller**   Appraiser **Jones & Co.**   Instructions to Appraiser _____

To be completed by Lender

NEIGHBORHOOD

						Good	Avg.	Fair	Poor
Location	[X] Urban	☐ Suburban	☐ Rural		Employment Stability	[X]	☐	☐	☐
Built Up	[X] Over 75%	☐ 25% to 75%	☐ Under 25%		Convenience to Employment	☐	[X]	☐	☐
Growth Rate ☐ Fully Dev.	☐ Rapid	[X] Steady	☐ Slow		Convenience to Shopping	☐	[X]	☐	☐
Property Values	☐ Increasing	[X] Stable	☐ Declining		Convenience to Schools	[X]	☐	☐	☐
Demand/Supply	☐ Shortage	[X] In Balance	☐ Over Supply		Quality of Schools	[X]	☐	☐	☐
Marketing Time	[X] Under 3 Mos.	☐ 4–6 Mos.	☐ Over 6 Mos.		Recreational Facilities	☐	☐	[X]	☐

Present Land Use **75**% 1 Family ___% 2–4 Family ___% Apts. **25**% Condo ___% Commercial   Adequacy of Utilities [X] ☐ ☐ ☐

___% Industrial ___% Vacant ___%   Property Compatibility ☐ [X] ☐ ☐

Change in Present Land Use [X] Not Likely   ☐ Likely (*)   ☐ Taking Place (*)   Protection from Detrimental Conditions [X] ☐ ☐ ☐

(*) From _____ To _____   Police and Fire Protection [X] ☐ ☐ ☐

Predominant Occupancy [X] Owner   ☐ Tenant ___% Vacant   General Appearance of Properties ☐ [X] ☐ ☐

Single Family Price Range $ **31,000** to $ **40,000** Predominant Value $ **36,000**   Appeal to Market ☐ [X] ☐ ☐

Single Family Age **17** yrs to **20** yrs   Predominant Age **18** yrs

Note: FHLMC/FNMA do not consider the racial composition of the neighborhood to be a relevant factor and it must not be considered in the appraisal.

Comments (including those factors adversely affecting marketability) **None**

SITE

Dimensions **70' X 150'** = **10,500** Sq. Ft. or Acres   ☐ Corner Lot

Zoning classification **A-1**   Present improvements [X] do   ☐ do not conform to zoning regulations

Highest and best use: [X] Present use   ☐ Other (specify) _____

	Public	Other (Describe)	OFF SITE IMPROVEMENTS	Topo	**level**
Elec.	[X]		Street Access: [X] Public ☐ Private	Size	**average**
Gas	[X]		Surface **asphalt**	Shape	**rectangular**
Water	[X]		Maintenance: [X] Public ☐ Private	View	**satisfactory**
San.Sewer	[X]		[X] Storm Sewer [X] Curb/Gutter	Drainage	**good**

☐ Underground Elect. & Tel. [X] Sidewalk [X] Street Lights   Is the property located in a HUD identified Flood Hazard Area? [X] No ☐ Yes

Comments (favorable or unfavorable including any apparent adverse easements, encroachments or other adverse conditions) **None**

IMPROVEMENTS

[X] Existing (approx. yr. blt.) 19 **59** No. Units **1**   Type (det, duplex, semi/det, etc.) **detached**   Design (rambler, split level, etc.) **rambler**   Exterior Walls **brick**

☐ Proposed ☐ Under Construction No. Stories **1**

Roof Material **comp. shingle**   Gutters & Downspouts **aluminum** ☐ None   Window (Type): **wood sash**   Insulation ☐ None ☐ Floor

   ☐ Storm Sash ☐ Screens [X] Combination   [X] Ceiling ☐ Roof [X] Walls

Foundation Walls **cinder block**   **50** % Basement [X] Floor Drain   Finished Ceiling **full**

☐ Crawl Space   [X] Outside Entrance ☐ Sump Pump   Finished Walls **full**

☐ Slab on Grade   ☐ Concrete Floor ___% Finished   Finished Floor **full**

   Evidence of: ☐ Dampness ☐ Termites ☐ Settlement

BSMT

Comments _____

ROOM LIST

Room List	Foyer	Living	Dining	Kitchen	Den	Family Rm.	Rec. Rm.	Bedrooms	No. Baths	Laundry	Other
Basement							X			X	
1st Level	X	X	X	X				3	2		
2nd Level											

Total **6** Rooms **3** Bedrooms **2** Baths in finished area above grade.

INTERIOR FINISH & EQUIPMENT

Kitchen Equipment: [X] Refrigerator [X] Range/Oven [X] Disposal [X] Dishwasher [X] Fan/Hood ☐ Compactor ☐ Washer ☐ Dryer ☐

HEAT: Type **for air** Fuel **gas** Cond. **good** AIR COND: [X] Central ☐ Other _____ [X] Adequate ☐ Inadequate

			Good	Avg.	Fair	Poor
Floors	[X] Hardwood [X] Carpet Over **75%**	Quality of Construction (Materials & Finish)	[X]	☐	☐	☐
Walls	[X] Drywall ☐ Plaster	Condition of Improvements	[X]	☐	☐	☐
Trim/Finish	☐ Good [X] Average ☐ Fair ☐ Poor	Rooms size and layout	☐	[X]	☐	☐
Bath Floor	[X] Ceramic ☐	Closets and Storage	☐	[X]	☐	☐
Bath Wainscot	[X] Ceramic ☐	Plumbing–adequacy and condition	☐	[X]	☐	☐
Special Features (including fireplaces): **fireplace**		Electrical–adequacy and condition	☐	[X]	☐	☐
		Kitchen Cabinets–adequacy and condition	☐	[X]	☐	☐
ATTIC: [X] Yes ☐ No ☐ Stairway ☐ Drop-stair [X] Scuttle ☐ Floored		Compatibility to Neighborhood	☐	[X]	☐	☐
Finished (Describe) _____ ☐ Heated		Overall Livability	☐	[X]	☐	☐
CAR STORAGE: ☐ Garage ☐ Built-in ☐ Attached ☐ Detached [X] Car Port		Appeal and Marketability	☐	[X]	☐	☐
No. Cars **1** [X] Adequate ☐ Inadequate Condition **good**		Effective Age **10** Yrs. Est. Remaining Economic Life **40** Yrs.				

PROPERTY RATING

PORCHES, PATIOS, POOL, FENCES, etc. (describe) **None**

COMMENTS (including functional or physical inadequacies, repairs needed, modernization, etc.) **None**

FHLMC Form 70 Rev. 9/75   ATTACH DESCRIPTIVE PHOTOGRAPHS OF SUBJECT PROPERTY AND STREET SCENE   FNMA Form 1004 Rev. 9/75

FIGURE 10-2. FNMA/FHLMC Residential Appraisal Report

VALUATION SECTION

Purpose of Appraisal is to estimate Market Value as defined in Certification & Statement of Limiting Conditions (FHLMC Form 439/FNMA Form 1004B). If submitted for FNMA, the appraiser must attach (1) sketch or map showing location of subject, street names, distance from nearest intersection, and any detrimental conditions and (2) exterior building sketch of improvements showing dimensions.

COST APPROACH

Measurements		No. Stories		Sq. Ft.
55' x 25'	x	1	=	1,375
19' x 12	x	1	=	228
x	x		=	
x	x		=	
x	x		=	
x	x		=	

Total Gross Living Area (List in Market Data Analysis below) _____

Comment on functional and economic obsolescence: _____

ESTIMATED REPRODUCTION COST – NEW – OF IMPROVEMENTS:

Dwelling	1,600 Sq. Ft. @ $ 19.00	=	$ 30,400
	Sq. Ft. @ $		
Extras	bsmt. rec. room	=	600
		=	
		=	
Porches, Patios, etc.		=	
Garage/Car Port	140 Sq. Ft. @ $ 5.00	=	700
Site Improvements (driveway, landscaping, etc.)		=	800
Total Estimated Cost New		=	$ 32,500

	Physical	Functional	Economic	
Less Depreciation $ 4,000	$	$	= $ (4,000)

Depreciated value of improvements . . . . = $ 28,500

ESTIMATED LAND VALUE . . . . = $ 7,000
(If leasehold, show only leasehold value)

INDICATED VALUE BY COST APPROACH . . . . $ 35,500

The undersigned has recited three recent sales of properties most similar and proximate to subject and has considered these in the market analysis. The description includes a dollar adjustment, reflecting market reaction to those items of significant variation between the subject and comparable properties. If a significant item in the comparable property is superior to, or more favorable than, the subject property, a minus (-) adjustment is made, thus reducing the indicated value of subject; if a significant item in the comparable is inferior to, or less favorable than, the subject property, a plus (+) adjustment is made, thus increasing the indicated value of the subject.

MARKET DATA ANALYSIS

ITEM	Subject Property	COMPARABLE NO. 1		COMPARABLE NO. 2		COMPARABLE NO. 3	
Address	2800 Linden	2463 Brinkley		2765 Lemen		3215 Essex	
Proximity to Subj.		2 blocks		1 block		2 blocks	
Sales Price	$ 35,000	$33,900		$36,000		$ 34,990	
Price/Living area	$	$		$		$	
Data Source	MLS	MLS		MLS		MLS	
Date of Sale and Time Adjustment	DESCRIPTION	DESCRIPTION	+(-)$ Adjustment 500	DESCRIPTION	+(-)$ Adjustment 500	DESCRIPTION	+(-)$ Adjustment
Location	good	good		good		exc	-200
Site/View	good	good		good		good	
Design and Appeal	good	good		exc	-250	good	
Quality of Const.	good	good		good		good	
Age	19 yrs	19 yrs		17 yrs		18 yrs	
Condition	good	good		good		good	
Living Area Room Count and Total	Total 6 · B-rms 3 · Baths 2	Total 6 · B-rms 3 · Baths 2		Total 6 · B-rms 3 · Baths 2		Total 6 · B-rms 3 · Baths 2	
Gross Living Area	1600 Sq.Ft.	1600 Sq.Ft.		1700 Sq.Ft.	-1000	1650 Sq.Ft.	-500
Basement & Bsmt. Finished Rooms	½-1	½ open	600	½-2	-350	½ open	600
Functional Utility	good	good		good		good	
Air Conditioning	central	central		central		central	
Garage/Car Port	c/p	c/p		none	600	c/p	
Porches, Patio, Pools, etc.	none	none		patio	-400	none	
Other (e.g. fireplaces, kitchen equip., heating, remodeling)	fireplace	fireplace		fireplace		fireplace	
Sales or Financing Concessions	13% down	10% down		15% down		10% down	
Net Adj. (Total)		☒ Plus; ☐ Minus $ 1100		☐ Plus; ☒ Minus $ 900		☐ Plus; ☒ Minus $ 100	
Indicated Value of Subject		$35,000		$35,100		$34,890	

Comments on Market Data These sales are the three most recent rambler transactions. The adjusted price range is very narrow ($34,890 to $35,100). The sales price of the subject is just at mid-point; which is reasonable in the present market.

INDICATED VALUE BY MARKET DATA APPROACH . . . . $ 35,000

INDICATED VALUE BY INCOME APPROACH (If applicable) Economic Market Rent $ 235 /Mo. x Gross Rent Multiplier 150 = $ 35,250

This appraisal is made ☐ "as is" ☐ subject to the repairs, alterations, or conditions listed below ☐ completion per plans and specifications.

Comments and Conditions of Appraisal: This appraisal includes the usual amount of loan charges, which have no affect on value because similar charges are reflected in comparable sales.

Final Reconciliation: Market approach is most indicative of subject's current market value and was given most weight. Cost approach estimate supports that conclusion.

This appraisal is based upon the above requirements, the certification, contingent and limiting conditions, and Market Value definition that are stated in

☐ FHLMC Form 439 (Rev. 9/75)/FNMA Form 1004B filed with client _____ 19 _____ ☐ attached.

If submitted for FNMA, the report has been prepared in compliance with FNMA form instructions.

I ESTIMATE THE MARKET VALUE, AS DEFINED, OF SUBJECT PROPERTY AS OF _____ 19 ____ to be $ 35,000

Appraiser(s) *L. D. Smith* Jones & Co. Review Appraiser (If applicable) _____
☐ Did ☐ Did Not Physically Inspect Property

FHLMC Form 70 Rev. 9/75　　　　REVERSE　　　　FNMA Form 1004 Rev. 9/75

FIGURE 10-2. FNMA/FHLMC Residential Appraisal Report continued

SUGGESTED READINGS

Graaskamp, J. A. *A Guide to Feasibility Analysis.* Chicago: Society of Real Estate Appraisers, 1970.

Kahn, Sanders A., and Case, Frederick E. *Real Estate Appraisal and Investment.* New York: The Ronald Press Co., 1976.

Kinnard, William N., Jr. *Income Property Valuation.* Lexington, Massachusetts: Lexington Books, D. C. Heath & Co., 1971.

Ratcliff, Richard U. *Real Estate Analysis.* New York: McGraw-Hill Book Co., Inc., 1961.

Ring, Alfred A. *The Valuation of Real Estate.* Englewood Cliffs, New Jersey: Prentice-Hall, Inc., 1970.

Thorne, Oakleigh J. "Real Estate Financial Analysis—The State of the Art," *The Appraisal Journal* (January 1974), pp. 7-37.

Troxel, Jay C. "Rates: Capitalization and Interest," *The Appraisal Journal* (January 1975), pp. 71-80.

Wendt, Paul F. *Real Estate Appraisal: Review and Outlook.* Athens, Georgia: University of Georgia Press, 1974.

————, and Cerf, Alan R. *Real Estate Investment Analysis and Taxation.* New York: McGraw-Hill Book Co., Inc., 1969.

NOTES

1. A trained specialist is one certified by either The Society of Real Estate Appraisers or The American Institute of Real Estate Appraisers.

Chapter 11

Closing and Administering the Mortgage Loan

PART ONE

CLOSING THE MORTGAGE LOAN

INTRODUCTION

The term *loan closing* as used in mortgage lending refers to the process of formulating, executing and delivering all documents required by a permanent investor, the disbursement of the mortgage funds, and the protection of the investor's security. A clear distinction should be drawn between this type of closing and a real estate sales closing in which a different set of documents would be required, such as a purchase agreement, sales contract, and a closing statement, among others. Of course, if the sale also includes financing, both sets of documents or a combination of the two would be required. The process of loan closing begins with the taking of the mortgage application, the issuance of a commitment letter, and concludes in the exchanging of documents and funds and the recording of all pertinent instruments. It is important to realize that a loan closing is not the end of the mortgage lending cycle, which continues through servicing until the loan is finally repaid or refinanced.

Essential documents that should be contained in a complete mortgage file vary by state and also by property type; that is, residential or commercial. A lender's peculiar requirements can also add or delete from this. As in any discussion involving legal documents, state law requires caution. When establishing a loan closing process, competent counsel should be consulted on state law concerning any of the documents discussed.

Loan closing, depending on the custom in the jurisdiction, can be handled by either an outside attorney, an escrow agent, a title insurance company, or the closing staff of the mortgage lender. At one time, most closings were handled by an outside attorney, but now more and more mortgage lenders have staff members who are qualified loan closers to prepare and analyze all necessary closing documents. This is probably true only for residential property. An income property investor may want to close the loan in-house. Care should be exercised to determine whether state law requires a licensed attorney to close a loan. There are many types of loan closings, including the closing of construction loans, loans to be warehoused and loans with the permanent investor. This chapter is concerned primarily with the closing of permanent loans.

CLOSING A RESIDENTIAL LOAN

The following documents are discussed relative to the closing of a residential mortgage loan. The documents needed for a commercial mortgage loan will be discussed in a separate section to follow. The documents need not appear in any particular order in a loan file. Therefore, they are listed here in alphabetical order with a discussion of the reason for the required document. A few examples of these documents can be found as exhibits in this chapter; others can be found in the case studies of Chapters 14 and 15.

Appraisal. The appraisal is necessary for all real estate loans. It is usually made by a designated appraiser who may be either a fee appraiser or an in-house appraiser. The amount of the loan is established by the appraised value of the property and the loan-to-value ratio requirement of the investor. The appraisal is also needed to prove that the permanent investor has satisfied the legal loan-to-value ratio established in the particular state.

If the loan is guaranteed by the Veterans Administration, a Certificate of Reasonable Value (CRV) establishes the maximum loan amount. If the loan is insured by the Federal Housing Administration, FHA Form 2800, Mortgagee's Application for Property Appraisal, is required. Page 5 informs the mortgagee of the final FHA approval. If the mortgage loan is not guaranteed by VA or insured by FHA, the appraisal will probably be on FNMA Form 1004.

Assignment of Mortgage. If the mortgage is being purchased from a mortgage lender who originated it for later sale, an instrument assigning the mortgage to a permanent investor and an estoppel certificate should be included in the loan file.

Building restrictions. Any local building restrictions that affect the mortgaged premise should be contained in the loan file with a statement as to whether this property meets local building restrictions. This may be contained in a lawyer's opinion.

Cancelled mortgage. If the loan being closed is for the purpose of refinancing a previous loan, the original mortgage and note should appear in the file and be cancelled, with the satisfaction of that mortgage recorded.

Certificate of occupancy. In all new construction and refurbishing that requires it, a certificate issued by the local authorities should appear declaring that the building is habitable.

Closing statement. The closing statement for a mortgage closing (like a closing statement for the sale) will determine how the proceeds are to be apportioned to the parties. A receipt signed by the mortgagor is required, indicating that loan proceeds have been disbursed according to instructions.

Commitment letter. A commitment letter should be examined closely since it establishes the contractual rights and obligations between the lender and the borrower. Comparison should be made between this commitment letter and the application for the loan to determine if the applicant is receiving everything required. If the mortgage is to be insured, guaranteed, or sold to FHA, VA, FNMA, GNMA, FHLMC or one of the MICs, their commitment letter should also appear.

Contract of sale. If a loan is requested for the purchase of an existing property, the contract of sale should be in the loan file to verify an actual sale and to assist later in verifying the appraisal of the property.

Credit report. A credit report on the borrower is normally required in all loans. This report is usually accomplished by a local company if the loan is for a residential borrower (Figure 5-2).

Chattel lien. If personal property is serving as security in addition to the real estate, a financing statement or other document creating the lien is required.

Deed. If a loan is to purchase property, a copy of the deed should be included in the loan file, along with instructions to record.

Disbursement papers. Instructions are required on how funds are to be delivered to the mortgagor or to other involved parties.

Escrow. If the transaction involved has been closed in escrow, a copy of the escrow agreement should be in the loan file; and when the term *escrow*, or impoundment, is used to describe the way mortgage payments are to be made, this agreement should also be in the loan file.

FHA/VA. All documents required by an FHA-insured or VA-guaranteed loan—e.g., credit report, verification of employment, building certificate, certificate of occupancy, flood insurance, etc.—should be in the loan file for both residential and multifamily properties.

Insurance policies. In a residential file, the required insurance policies covering losses for fire, theft, liability, and any other hazard should exist with a mortgagee loss payable clause.

Loan application. At the time of closing, both the mortgagor and the mortgagee should review the loan application to determine that the loan is delivered as requested. The application is important to a mortgage lender because it establishes various fees and who is to pay them.

Mortgage or deed of trust. A mortgage or a deed of trust creating the security interest must appear in the loan file. Any chattel liens on personal property, or any financing statements should also appear. Recording instructions are required to protect all parties.

Note. It is essential to include a properly-executed promissory note. The note creates the obligation to repay the debt which is secured by the mortgage and it should state the amount of the loan, the term, the interest rate, and any other pertinent conditions. This note may also be recorded.

Mortgagor's affidavit. A mortgagor should be required to sign certain affidavits attesting to any current position regarding divorce proceedings, judgments or liens, or any recent improvement on the real estate or other pertinent facts that would affect the mortgage loan.

Photographs.   Photographs of good, clear quality are required to adequately show the mortgaged real estate.

Survey.   Since the real estate is the loan security, it is in the mortgagee's interest that a survey be made to identify correctly the property and determine if any encroachments exist.

Private mortgage insurance documents.   All documents required by a mortgage insurance company to issue their insurance as well as a copy of their commitment should appear in the loan file.

Title insurance or examination.   In all loans, it is essential that title be examined, or that an approved ALTA title insurance policy or binder be included. This requirement establishes who has right to the real estate and therefore, who must execute the mortgage to encumber it. The title examination should also disclose any prior encumbrances, tax liens or other interests.

Verification reports.   The mortgage lender should verify all relevant statements made on the loan application by obtaining verifying documentation. The most commonly used verification forms are those for employment and deposits.

Uniform Settlement Statement (HUD-1).   This statement is required at loan closings by the Real Estate Settlement Procedures Act of 1974 (RESPA). The statement offers the borrower and seller a full disclosure of known or estimated settlement costs (Figure 11-1).

CLOSING AN INCOME PROPERTY LOAN

Many of the documents required to close a residential loan are the same as those required to close an income property loan. A few, such as the various RESPA documents, are not needed, but other documents are required. These will be discussed in the following section, along with the different functions that some documents perform in a commercial loan closing.

The commitment is one of the documents that has a much more sophisticated function to perform in an income property loan closing than in a residential loan. In today's market, where interest rates experience wide fluctuations and institutional investors need to protect their future income stream, new concepts have been developed to prevent a builder or other mortgagor from "walking" a commitment.

HUD-1 Rev. 5/76

Form Approved
OMB NO. 63-R-1501

A.		B. TYPE OF LOAN
U. S. DEPARTMENT OF HOUSING AND URBAN DEVELOPMENT		1. ☐ FHA 2. ☐ FmHA 3. ☐ CONV. UNINS.
		4. ☐ VA 5. ☐ CONV. INS.
SETTLEMENT STATEMENT		6. File Number: 7. Loan Number:
		8. Mortgage Insurance Case Number:

C. **NOTE:** *This form is furnished to give you a statement of actual settlement costs. Amounts paid to and by the settlement agent are shown. Items marked "(p.o c.)" were paid outside the closing; they are shown here for informational purposes and are not included in the totals.*

D. NAME OF BORROWER:	E. NAME OF SELLER:	F. NAME OF LENDER:
G. PROPERTY LOCATION:	H. SETTLEMENT AGENT:	I. SETTLEMENT DATE:
	PLACE OF SETTLEMENT:	

J. SUMMARY OF BORROWER'S TRANSACTION		K. SUMMARY OF SELLER'S TRANSACTION	
100. GROSS AMOUNT DUE FROM BORROWER:		**400. GROSS AMOUNT DUE TO SELLER:**	
101. Contract sales price		401. Contract sales price	
102. Personal property		402. Personal property	
103. Settlement charges to borrower *(line 1400)*		403.	
104.		404.	
105.		405.	
Adjustments for items paid by seller in advance		*Adjustments for items paid by seller in advance*	
106. City/town taxes to		406. City/town taxes to	
107. County taxes to		407. County taxes to	
108. Assessments to		408. Assessments to	
109.		409.	
110.		410.	
111.		411.	
112.		412.	
120. GROSS AMOUNT DUE FROM BORROWER		420. GROSS AMOUNT DUE TO SELLER	
200. AMOUNTS PAID BY OR IN BEHALF OF BORROWER:		**500. REDUCTIONS IN AMOUNT DUE TO SELLER:**	
201. Deposit or earnest money		501. Excess deposit *(see instructions)*	
202. Principal amount of new loan(s)		502. Settlement charges to seller *(line 1400)*	
203. Existing loan(s) taken subject to		503. Existing loan(s) taken subject to	
204.		504. Payoff of first mortgage loan	
205.		505. Payoff of second mortgage loan	
206.		506.	
207.		507.	
208.		508.	
209.		509.	
Adjustments for items unpaid by seller		*Adjustments for items unpaid by seller*	
210. City/town taxes to		510. City/town taxes to	
211. County taxes to		511. County taxes to	
212. Assessments to		512. Assessments to	
213.		513.	
214.		514.	
215.		515.	
216.		516.	
217.		517.	
218.		518.	
219.		519.	
220. TOTAL PAID BY/FOR BORROWER		520. TOTAL REDUCTION AMOUNT DUE SELLER	
300. CASH AT SETTLEMENT FROM/TO BORROWER		**600. CASH AT SETTLEMENT TO/FROM SELLER**	
301. Gross amount due from borrower *(line 120)*		601. Gross amount due to seller *(line 420)*	
302. Less amounts paid by/for borrower *(line 220)*	( )	602. Less reductions in amount due seller *(line 520)*	( )
303. CASH (☐ FROM) (☐ TO) BORROWER		603. CASH (☐ TO) (☐ FROM) SELLER	

FIGURE 11-1. HUD settlement statement

L. SETTLEMENT CHARGES		
700. TOTAL SALES/BROKER'S COMMISSION based on price $ a % =	**PAID FROM BORROWER'S FUNDS AT SETTLEMENT**	**PAID FROM SELLER'S FUNDS AT SETTLEMENT**
Division of Commission (line 700) as follows:		
701. $ to		
702. $ to		
703. Commission paid at Settlement		
704.		
800. ITEMS PAYABLE IN CONNECTION WITH LOAN		
801. Loan Origination Fee %		
802. Loan Discount %		
803. Appraisal Fee to		
804. Credit Report to		
805. Lender's Inspection Fee		
806. Mortgage Insurance Application Fee to		
807. Assumption Fee		
808.		
809.		
810.		
811.		
900. ITEMS REQUIRED BY LENDER TO BE PAID IN ADVANCE		
901. Interest from to @ $ /day		
902. Mortgage Insurance Premium for months to		
903. Hazard Insurance Premium for years to		
904. years to		
905.		
1000. RESERVES DEPOSITED WITH LENDER		
1001. Hazard insurance months @ $ per month		
1002. Mortgage insurance months @ $ per month		
1003. City property taxes months @ $ per month		
1004. County property taxes months @ $ per month		
1005. Annual assessments months @ $ per month		
1006. months @ $ per month		
1007. months @ $ per month		
1008. months @ $ per month		
1100. TITLE CHARGES		
1101. Settlement or closing fee to		
1102. Abstract or title search to		
1103. Title examination to		
1104. Title insurance binder to		
1105. Document preparation to		
1106. Notary fees to		
1107. Attorney's fees to		
(includes above items numbers:		
1108. Title insurance to		
(includes above items numbers:		
1109. Lender's coverage $		
1110. Owner's coverage $		
1111.		
1112.		
1113.		
1200. GOVERNMENT RECORDING AND TRANSFER CHARGES		
1201. Recording fees: Deed $; Mortgage $; Releases $		
1202. City/county tax/stamps: Deed $; Mortgage $		
1203. State tax/stamps: Deed $; Mortgage $		
1204.		
1205.		
1300. ADDITIONAL SETTLEMENT CHARGES		
1301. Survey to		
1302. Pest inspection to		
1303.		
1304.		
1305.		
1400. TOTAL SETTLEMENT CHARGES (enter on lines 103, Section J and 502, Section K)		

HUD-1 Rev 5/76

FIGURE 11-1. HUD settlement statement continued

When an investor, including a life insurance company or other investor such as a REIT, issues a commitment to fund a loan, it normally asks for either a *standby deposit* or a *commitment fee.* A standby deposit is for a commitment issued by an investor to a builder who needs a hedge against being able to locate either a permanent investor, or one at an attractive interest rate. The investor will probably not have to fund this commitment since the interest rate is substantially higher than the market.

The builder may expect interest rates to decline before the permanent financing is needed, but in order to secure a construction loan, the builder will need some type of takeout. The standby commitment can be used for this purpose, in addition to being an escape if the interest rates move up dramatically. An investor will charge one or two nonrefundable points for such a commitment.

On a regular commitment, with a fee of one or two points, an investor fully expects to fund the commitment. This commitment fee may or may not be refundable. In the past, with a commitment fee of one or two percent of the loan amount, an investor was normally assured that the loan would be delivered; but in the past few years, with the interest rate changing abruptly, a one- or two-point fee has not meant necessarily that the investor who made the commitment would get the loan. In such a market, the forfeiture of two points can be recovered easily by a borrower who has walked away from a loan commitment to take advantage of a rapid drop in interest rates. For example, this could occur if the builder subsequently obtained another commitment from another investor that was one percent lower. The builder would be able to make up the forfeited two-point commitment fee within a couple of years because of the lower interest rate. Everything after that would be profit. Today, due to the extreme difficulty in assuring the deliverability of a loan for which a commitment has been issued, lenders have developed other methods to protect their interest. These would be in addition to the agreement in the commitment itself not to place the loan with another investor.

One such method investors have developed to protect their interests and assure delivery of the loan is the tripartite agreement, or buy/sell. There are three essential parties to this agreement:

1. The construction lender who agrees and contracts to sell the loan to the permanent investor upon completion

2. The permanent investor who agrees to buy the loan from the construction lender upon completion

3. The borrower or developer who promises to do nothing to interfere with the transaction.

Many investors now require a loan to be preclosed to assure that a builder takes down the permanent loan. This, in effect, closes the loan even though the building has not been constructed. As a result, the builder is precluded from going to another investor for financing since the new investor could not get a first lien—and the builder would also be in default to the first investor.

Other documents needed in an income property loan file, in addition to those already mentioned in the residential file, include:

Articles of incorporation. If the mortgagor is a corporation, the articles of incorporation should be included in the loan file to establish corporate powers, in addition to a copy of the by-laws or minutes empowering the officer to sign a mortgage.

Financial statement. Audited or certified financial statements of the borrower's financial position for the past fiscal year should be in the file, and in some instances, W-2 Forms.

Insurance policies. In an income property loan, the required insurance policies covering losses for fire, theft, personal injury, rent and any other hazard should exist with a mortgagee loss payable clause.

Lawyer's opinion letter. A local attorney's opinion letter concerning usury, zoning, and any other issues determined by local law is required by most investors in income-property loans.

Leases. A list of key tenants, lease arrangements and tenants' ability to sublet or assign, plus any subordination agreement, is essential in a commercial loan file. Any assignment of a rent clause applicable to the particular lease should also be documented. If the mortgage loan is based on the credit of the tenants, the leases may require prior approval of the investor and this approval should be in the loan file.

Partnership agreement. If the mortgagor is a partnership, a copy of the partnership agreement creating the partnership and its authority to act should be in the loan file.

Personal endorsement. If a permanent lender requires a mortgagor to become personally liable on the note, the personal endorsement must be in the loan file.

Plans and specifications. The permanent loan is based on the improvements being constructed according to agreed plans and specifications. Therefore, the agreement to any changes should be in the loan file.

Subordination agreement. In an income property loan, agreements should appear in the loan file if there is a requirement for a subordination of a previous mortgage to the current mortgage or the subordination of a current lease to a subsequent mortgage.

Tax bills. A permanent lender will want to make certain that all taxes are current on the security. This can be established by the stamped tax bills.

Tripartite or buy/sell agreement. If there is an interceding construction loan, this agreement involving a borrower, a construction lender, and a permanent investor should be present to establish the rights and duties of the parties.

PART TWO

MORTGAGE LOAN ADMINISTRATION

INTRODUCTION

"The modern concept of mortgage loan administration includes all activities which complement mortgage loan production and enhance its profitability."[1]

The purpose of this section is to discuss briefly the basic principles of mortgage loan administration. Mortgage loan administration involves all of the essential mortgage loan activities necessary to:

1. Render the required service to the mortgagor

2. Protect the security of the mortgagee

3. Produce a profit for the servicer

Therefore, mortgage loan administration can be defined as the total effort required to perform both the day-to-day management or administrative function, and the servicing of mortgage loans.

Mortgage loan administration is required of all mortgage lenders (except possibly mortgage brokers), whether they originate residential or income-property loans and whether some or all of the loans are sold to other investors. Mortgage companies have been closely associated with the servicing part of mortgage loan administration because of the volume of mortgage loans they have originated and sold to other mortgage investors while continuing to service the same loans. Mortgage companies were servicing in excess of $160 billion of mortgage loans sold to other mortgage investors at the end of 1977. Other mortgage lenders were also servicing for other mortgage investors, but not as extensively as mortgage companies since most other mortgage lenders retain most of the mortgages they originate for their own servicing portfolio.

SERVICING RESPONSIBILITY

If mortgages to be serviced have been sold to another mortgage investor such as FNMA, the servicing relationship is established by either a *commitment letter* or a *servicing contract.* This contractual relationship should continue for the life of the mortgage loans, but it can be terminated. Termination can be either for cause—some failure to perform on the part of the servicer—or, in some cases, without cause. If servicing is withdrawn without cause, then it is common for an investor to pay a fee, typically one percent of amount serviced, as compensation.

The responsibilities of a servicer are usually described in detail in a servicing contract or in a servicing manual supplied by an investor. These responsibilities typically include:

1. Monthly collection of principal and interest from the mortgagor and disbursement to the investor

2. Collection and periodic payment of real estate taxes

3. Collection and periodic payment of required insurance

4. Any other activity necessary to protect the investor's security interest

To successfully fulfill these responsibilities, a servicer of a mortgage loan will need either trained people or separate departments to perform five functions:

1. *Cashier.* The cashier is responsible for a) receiving payments, b) depositing these payments and, c) transmitting this information to loan accounting.

2. *Loan Accounting.* This function is responsible for notifying investors that a deposit has been made to their account, or drawing a check (payable to an investor) to distribute principal and interest less any servicing fee.

3. *Collection.* The purpose of this function is to collect those payments past due. In many ways, this is the most difficult function, but it is also the most essential for a successful servicing operation.

4. *Insurance.* The mortgage lender is responsible for protecting an investor's security interest by determining that adequate insurance exists and is current with a mortgagee payable clause. Some mortgage lenders sell this insurance as a service to their borrowers.

5. *Taxes.* To protect an investor's first lien, a mortgage lender must collect and pay all real estate taxes and assessments due on the security.

SERVICING INCOME

In addition to origination fees and possible marketing profits, the fee a mortgage lender receives from an investor for servicing a mortgage provides practically all income of a mortgage lender. During those periods of the business cycle when mortgage loan demand is low, the servicing income often provides a mortgage lender with the means to stay in business. In the current mortgage market, many mortgage lenders are unable to generate a profit from the origination process, especially if a large percentage of total originations are either FHA or VA. This is because the origination fee for those mortgages by law is only one percent of the loan amount. These mortgage lenders must look to servicing income to offset origination losses, and sometimes marketing losses, to produce a net profit from mortgage lending.

This servicing income is generated by a servicer retaining a previously agreed upon fraction of one percent of the payment collected monthly. The fraction is applied only if the payment is collected. After receiving the monthly payment of principal and interest, a servicer forwards that amount less the *servicing fee* to the investor.

The servicing fee is typically 3/8 of one percent per month for residential mortgages and ranges from 1/10 to 1/8 of one percent for income property loans. Some investors put a maximum on annual servicing income from one mortgage loan at $4,000 to $5,000.

Other fees that a mortgage lender can generate from servicing include late payment fees when a mortgage payment is 15 days past due and transfer fees if the mortgage is being assumed.

SUGGESTED READINGS

Britton, James A., and Kerwood, Lewis O., eds. *Financing Income-Producing Real Estate.* New York: McGraw-Hill Book Co., Inc., 1977.

DeHuszar, William I. *Mortgage Loan Administration.* New York: McGraw-Hill Book Co., Inc., 1972.

Duffy, Robert E., Jr. "The Real Estate Settlement Procedures Act of 1974," *Real Estate Review* (Winter 1976), pp. 86-93.

NOTES

1. William I. DeHuszar. *Mortgage Loan Administration*. New York: McGraw-Hill Book Co., Inc., p. 3.

Chapter 12

Fundamentals of Real Estate Law

This chapter provides reference material for other chapters of the book, as well as a fundamental review of the basic principles of American real estate law.

Possibly no other segment of the U.S. social-economic system is more involved with law than real estate. Whether as a homeowner, a developer or a financier, those involved with real estate must understand the legal framework upon which real estate is defined and the interests therein protected relating both to the business and the commodity. Obviously, mortgage lenders who rely on legally-defined and enforced rights must be aware of their own and possibly other conflicting rights to the real property securing the obligation. This can occur only if the legal principles involved are understood.

Law and real estate have been inseparable since the early days of the development of Anglo-American jurisprudence. This close relationship continues because of custom and the perception that real estate is normally its owner's most precious possession. However, this also has hindered the changes in real estate concepts needed in an evolving society.

A fundamental review of how this relationship between law and real estate developed and a discussion of the interests a person can have in real estate appear in the following sections. Nonlegal terminology is used where the meaning or concept is not altered or affected in any way.

In light of broad differences in state law, this review covers only the general principles of real estate law with no discussion of the unique features of any one state's law. In those situations where there is a basic conflict in the general principles, the majority position is reviewed. Nevertheless, the laws of individual jurisdictions should be carefully determined. This is best accomplished by consulting a competent local attorney.

ENGLISH COMMON LAW

The real estate laws of the 50 jurisdictions, including the District of Columbia but excluding Louisiana, which is based primarily on French civil law, are based almost entirely in the English common law as it existed at the time of the American Revolutionary War. As individual state laws were changed by statute or court decisions, the chief problem of American real estate law was 50 different bodies of law written in an archaic language often difficult to understand, with a conceptual basis different from that which exists in modern America. A short review of this development is vital since our current real estate laws evolved from the English common law.

Before the Norman invasion of England in 1066, there was no well-developed system of land ownership in England. Land was owned by the family unit rather than the individual, and when the head of the household died, the new head of the household would represent the ownership of the family in a particular piece of land. In 1066, when William the Conqueror invaded England, he imposed a European concept of land ownership upon the English called the feudal system of land tenure, an economic, military and political system of government which held that the King exclusively owned all land. The most valuable and important commodity in such a society was land. Land represented wealth, and all wealth came from the land. Money hardly existed and barter was the means of exchange. Since the King owned all land, he had complete control over the country and the economy.

A king, of course, needed arms for protection of the realm. For this he depended on the loyalty, fidelity, and allegiance of the lords. In return for their allegiance and military service, the King allowed the lords to use the land, although no ownership was being conveyed. The lords, in turn, allowed lesser lords to use a portion of this land in return for a share of the profits and for swearing allegiance to them. Finally, these lesser lords allowed serfs, who were nothing more than slaves indentured to the land, to use the land in return for a promise of military service. In this pyramid of military allegiance, the serfs owed military service to the lesser lords, who in turn owed service to the lords, who swore allegiance to the King.

The right to own land didn't exist for many years, but one of the incidents of ownership, the inability to pass the use of land to heirs, produced a confrontation with King John in 1215. The result was the Magna Carta, which provided greater rights for the lords, including the right to pass the use of the land on to their sons. Land was passed on to sons only as a result of the doctrine of primogeniture, which dictated that the oldest male child had the right to inherit the land. This was desirable at the time, since it prevented estates from being broken up into smaller tracts and allowed for the development of a landed gentry, which eventually developed the English society. Out of this society evolved the common law and, eventually, English real estate law. Although modified over the years, the feudal system survived until 1660 when it was abolished by law.

As contrasted with the feudal system, the allodial system recognizes that an owner of real estate has title irrespective of the sovereign and thus owes no duty, such as rent or the rendering of military service, to the sovereign. This system developed throughout the world with the exception of Western Europe and certain other areas where the feudal system remained.

The feudal system was an early part of the American land-ownership system in a few locations such as New York and Maryland. With those exceptions, the allodial system was paramount in America based on either conquest, discovery or purchase.

PRINCIPLES OF REAL ESTATE LAW

The first step in understanding the principles of real estate law is to define terms. *Real property* is land and everything permanently attached to it. Under the common law, and as a general rule today, this included ownership from the center of the earth, the surface, and up to the heavens. All other property is *personal property*. *Real estate* is used to denote both real property and the business of real estate, including financing.

Property can change from one classification to another fairly rapidly. For example, a tree standing in a forest is real property. When it is felled, it becomes personal property and, finally, after being made into lumber and becoming part of a house, it is real property again. The term *fixture* is used to describe a piece of personal property that has been attached in such a manner that it is now considered real property. This distinction is important, since title to real property is normally transferred by a deed, while personal property is transferred by a bill of sale.

Estate

Today, when people talk about their ownership of land, they are legally talking about the type of estate they have in real estate. This is as true in America as it was in England 500 years ago. An estate is defined as *an interest in real property which is measured by its potential duration.* There are two recognized classifications of estate in real property; *freehold*, and *leasehold*, sometimes referred to as non-freehold. The classification *freehold estate* is the highest form of interest possible in real property, as it involves all the rights in real property including use, passing the property to one's heirs, or selecting who is going to take it in a transfer. It is an estate of infinite duration, in that the chain of title could theoretically last forever. An example of a freehold estate would be a *fee simple absolute.*

On the other hand, the classification *leasehold estate* is an inferior interest in real property, because the owner of a leasehold interest only has the right of possession for a period of time. The owner of this interest does not have *seisin*, which is defined as the ability to pass title to one's heirs or assigns. An example of a leasehold estate would be a tenant's interest in leased property.

Fee Simple Absolute

There has never been nor will there ever be complete ownership of land. Examples of the restraints or limitations on ownership of land include, among others, eminent domain, adverse possession and easements.

The greatest interest a person can have in real property is known as a *fee simple absolute.* Any owner of real property, whether it be a large corporation or John Doe, has a fee simple absolute if all possible rights to that piece of real property are possessed.

In order to explain a fee simple absolute, legal pedagogues use the *bundle of rights* concept. For example, assume that all rights, such as the right to sell, mortgage and build on, among others, to a piece of real property are represented by "sticks," contained in this bundle of rights. If all of the "sticks" are present and the owner has all possible rights to the real property, then the bundle of rights is complete and is called a *fee simple absolute.* If a "stick" is missing, such as the right to use the property the way one wants, then the interest is less than a fee simple absolute.

Defeasible or Conditional Fee

A freehold estate, which is similar to a fee simple absolute but minus a "stick" (or a right) from the bundle of rights, is the *defeasible fee simple.* This is a freehold estate that could but will not necessarily last forever. An example of a defeasible fee simple occurs when conditions are placed on how the property may be used.

Grantors of land may put any restrictions they desire on how the land is to be used after it has been conveyed. There are, of course, a few exceptions, such as those that are racially oriented. Grantors can always give less than the full interests they own in conveying land, but never more. They can give possession for any desired period of time, or for any specific use—only as a church, for example. If so conveyed, a defeasible fee simple is created that could last forever, but it could also be terminated.

An example of a defeasible fee simple that would automatically end if a certain event occurs is when A grants land to B church on condition that the premises are used only for church purposes. The church has a defeasible fee simple that could last forever but will automatically end if the property ceases to be used for church purposes. When that happens, the title automatically reverts to A or A's heirs. This interest is classified as a fee simple since it could last forever if the property is always used for church purposes.

A distinction is made legally between two types of defeasible fee simple. They are a fee simple subject to a condition subsequent, and a fee simple determinable. The typical person involved in real estate does not need to know the distinction, but counsel for that person should. An example of a fee simple subject to a condition subsequent would occur when A conveys property to B as long as liquor is never sold on the premises. In this situation, the grantee B (the person to whom the land has been conveyed) has a fee simple, but it is subject to a condition subsequent in that if liquor is ever sold on the premises the land will revert to the grantor (the one making the conveyances). The grantor must make an affirmative action for the property to revert, that is, re-enter the property and sue to terminate the estate.

The fee simple determinable has been described. Most courts lump these together as being basically the same. If forced to distinguish, courts attempt to find a fee on a condition subsequent in order that the grantor must re-enter to terminate rather than have the estate terminate automatically.

Fee Tail

This type of estate came into being from a desire in feudal England to keep land in whole parcels within the family. A fee tail is an estate of potentially infinite duration, but is inheritable only by the grantee's lineal descendants, such as children or grandchildren. For a fee tail to be created under the common law it was necessary to state in the conveyance that the land was being transferred to A and "the heirs of his body." This differed from the wording of any other common law transfer, which required only "and his heirs" to be used.

There were various types of the fee tail. The *fee tail general* meant the property was inheritable by any issue of the grantee. A *fee tail special* meant the land was inheritable only by the issue of the grantee and a specifically named spouse. (*A conveyance to A and the heirs of his body, by his wife Mary*, would be an example.) A fee tail general could specify whether the issue need be male or female, and there also was the possibility of a fee tail special, male or female. Although the fee tail is still allowed in some New England states, the practical effect of it has been abolished in all states today.

A *life estate* is a freehold estate like the fee simple absolute and others already mentioned, but it is not inheritable. Life estates can be either conventional (created by the grantor) or legal (created by operation of law). The creation of a life estate is a tool often used in estate planning and is fairly common interest in real estate. By the creation of a life estate the life tenant (the one granted the right) has the use of real estate for a period of time measured by a human life. The human life used to measure the duration of the life estate may be that of another human life, but is most commonly measured by the life of the life tenant. An example is: A conveys a life estate to B for life, and as long as B is alive, B has the right to use the real estate, with certain exceptions, as if he owned it. The only incident of ownership that B lacks is the power to pass a fee simple absolute. The right to sell or mortgage the interest is not given but a person could acquire only that which B had, which was the use of the land for a period measured by a life.

When A created this life estate, only a part of the complete interest was transferred. In other words someone else was allowed to use the land for a period of time. However, at the expiration of that period of time, the remaining rights to the real estate are with the grantor. A may have retained it to pass the real property to someone else. In the example given, where A conveyed land to B for B's life, the land will revert to A (the grantor) or the heirs upon the death of B (the life tenant) since no other conveyance was made.

When A created the life estate in B, the remainder could have been transferred in this way: A to B for life, and then to C. In this situation, C is the *vested remainderman*, because the grantor has transferred the remaining interest to C. The rights of C are vested irrespective of whether C survives the life tenant or not. If a vested remainderman does die before a life tenant, then the vested remainderman's heirs would inherit the fee interest.

On the other hand, a life estate could be created this way: A to B for B's life, and then to C if C is alive, in which case C must survive B to acquire any rights to the land. If C dies before B, the land reverts to the original owner. If it is impossible to determine at the time of the creation of the life estate who definitely will take the fee simple after the death of the life tenant, the remainderman is referred to as a *contingent remainderman*.

Another common example of this situation would be: A to B for life, and then to B's children. B may not have any children; therefore, their interest is contingent upon being born. To complicate it even further, the conveyance could read: A to B for B's life, and then to B's surviving children. The children, if any, must survive B before they can acquire any interest.

In summary, a conventional life estate is an interest which an individual has in real estate providing most of the incidences of ownership, with the exception of the ability to pass a fee simple absolute. The person who takes possession after the life tenant dies could be either the grantor, if the grantor did not convey the remainder, or it could be a third person who would be classified as either a contingent or a vested remainderman, depending on whether the identify can be determined precisely at the time of the creation of the life estate.

In contrast with the conventional life estate, created intentionally by the grantor, a *legal life estate* is created by operation of the law. An example of a legal life estate is the *right of dower*. Dower was originally conceived to prevent a widow from being penniless during a period of English history when life insurance, welfare and social security were unknown. Dower is a common-law right of a widow still present in many jurisdictions. The equivalent right of the husband is *curtesy*, which has either been abolished or merged with dower in nearly all states.

Basically, the right of dower gives a wife, at her husband's death, a life estate in one-third of the real estate owned by her husband during marriage. Generally, the widow has a choice of which real estate will be subject to her dower right and this right is applicable to all real estate owned by the husband during the marriage, even if he had transferred it before death. In those states where this right exists, a wife's potential dower interest is extinguished if she executes a deed with her husband transferring the land to another.

Currently, in some states, the right of dower has been abolished as unnecessary. This is probably because the need for a right such as dower has been eliminated in most states by the creation of a statutory right of each spouse to a minimum one-third share of the decedent's estate, and because of life insurance, social security and other benefits.

Leasehold Estates (non-freehold estates)

As mentioned earlier, this estate gives the owner the right to possession of real estate for a period of time. The actual duration may or may not be ascertainable at the beginning, but it does not carry with it the ability to pass title to the real estate. The owner of the land (the fee) has given up possession for a period of time, but retains the legal title to the real estate, and the owner (or heirs or assigns) will eventually retake possession. The legal term to describe the missing element in a leasehold estate is seisin.

Although the use of leases can be traced to the beginning of written history, the leasehold estate in England was originally used to circumvent the prohibition against lending money for interest since any interest was usury under early Church law. The person borrowing money would allow the lender to use some or all of the land for a period of time in lieu of interest. Therefore, under the common law, a leasehold was considered personal property, but now is considered an estate in real estate. A lease, which creates the leasehold estate, is a peculiar instrument in that it is both a conveyance giving the tenant possession for a period of time, and a contract establishing rights and duties for the parties. The essential elements for a lease are:

1. Name of landlord and tenant

2. Agreement to lease

3. Description of leased property

4. Duration of lease

5. Rental agreement

6. Rights and duties of the parties

7. Signature

A lease for a year or less may be verbal or in writing, but one for more than a year must be in writing. For the safety of both the landlord and tenant, all leases should be in writing. Most states have a 99-year limitation on a lease, although the vast majority of leases are for less than 10 years. The degree of complexity in leases increases from the relatively simple residential lease to the very complex shopping center lease. The type of tenancy acquired form a lease depends on whether or not the term is renewable and whether notice to terminate must be given by either party. (See Chapter 9, The Lease and Leasehold Financing, for more details.)

Additional Interests in Real Estate

In addition to the freehold and leasehold estates in real estate, there are certain other limited interests or rights to real estate. These include easements, profits and covenants. The effect of these interests is to create a limited right to the real estate of another, although the fact that a piece of real property is subject to an easement, for instance, does not prevent it from being owned in fee simple absolute.

Easements.   An easement is a non-possessory interest in the real estate of another, giving the holder the right to a limited use of real estate. An example is the right to drive across the real estate of another to reach a highway. An easement is either in gross (a personal right) or appurtenant (belonging to whoever owns the benefitted real estate). Although most easements are expressed in writing, they can be simply implied. The right of a gas company to install a gas line on a back property line is an example of an expressed easement appurtenant.

Profit.   A profit resembles an easement because the holder has an interest in the real estate of another. However, a profit creates the right to enter the property of another and take a portion of the property, such as the soil, or the product of the property such as trees or oil.

Covenant.   Like the previous interests discussed, this interest is in the real estate of another. The difference between a covenant or a promise to do or not to do something and other interests is that it restricts or limits how the owner can use the real estate. An example of a covenant is the requirement a farmer may put on the part of a farm being sold that the grantee use the real estate only for residential purposes. This interest is of benefit to the grantor because it allows control of the use of the real estate. Therefore, it is an interest in the real estate of another. This interest can be either in gross or appurtenant, although the term often used with covenants is *running with the land.* This interest should not be confused with a defeasible fee simple since title cannot be lost if a covenant is breached—only damages or an injunction can be sought.

JOINT OR CONCURRENT OWNERSHIP

Joint Tenancy

Ownership in land can be and usually is held by more than one person. The most common type of joint or concurrent ownership is the joint tenancy, which can exist between any two or more persons. Although joint tenants share a single title to the real estate, each owns an equal share of the whole. Joint tenancies are quite common, but a few states have abolished or limited them for reasons that will be discussed later. Most states will allow the creation of a joint tenancy by simply referring to A and B as joint tenants. But other jurisdictions require reference to A and B as joint tenants with the right of survivorship. This interest can be created only by affirmative action of the grantor, not by operation of law. The right of survivorship is the key concept of a joint tenancy. Upon the death of one of the joint tenants, all the deceased's interests in the real property terminate and the ownership in the land is retained by the surviving joint tenant or tenants. In other words, a joint tenancy is not an inheritable estate. Therefore, it does not pass through the estate of the decedent and does not pass to the heirs. Instead, it passes to or is possessed automatically by the surviving joint tenants. For this reason, some states have abolished joint tenancy, and most courts disfavor joint tenancy because it automatically prevents property from flowing through the estate of an individual to the heirs. Therefore, if one wishes to create a joint tenancy, it is mandatory to follow the strict statutory requirements of the respective state. To avoid the possibility that a court could misunderstand a grantor's intention, a joint tenancy should be created by using this phrase: *to A and B, as joint tenants with right of survivorship and not as tenants in common.*

During the time a joint tenancy is in existence, the portion of the whole belonging to any one of the joint tenants usually may be attached to satisfy that individual's legal debts. But the portion belonging to the other joint tenant(s) may not. Some states have laws that modify this approach if the joint tenants are man and wife and the property in question is their home.

Although any joint tenant may sell or mortgage interest (with some exceptions for married joint tenants), the effect is a termination of the joint tenancy by either a voluntary or involuntary transfer. It is also terminated by the death of one of two joint tenants, but not by the death of one of more than two. The survivors in that case still have a joint tenancy among themselves.

Under the common law, if both parties did not acquire ownership to real estate at the same time, a joint tenancy could not exist. Consequently, a husband owning property before marriage could not create a joint tenancy with his wife. One method devised to circumvent this requirement was the usage of a "straw man". For instance, the husband would convey title to his real estate to a friend or relative (the so-called "straw man") who would then transfer the title back to the husband and wife as joint tenants and the unity of time requirement would be satisfied.

Tenancy by the Entirety

A form of concurrent ownership much like the joint tenancy is the *tenancy by the entirety*, which is allowed in about 20 states. The reason for its existence is because of a vestige from the common law of some technical requirement for a joint tenancy, such as the unity of time, or the state had abolished joint tenancy. The primary difference between this form of ownership and the joint tenancy is a tenancy by the entirety can exist only between a legally-married husband and wife, while a joint tenancy can exist between any two or more persons.

Another important feature of a tenancy by the entirety is that the interest of one of the parties cannot be attached for the legal debts of that person. Only if the debts are of both parties can an attachment be made. For this reason, both a husband and wife in some states will be asked to sign the mortgage note if the form of ownership to the real estate is to be as tenants by the entirety, even if only one has income. Many states allowing tenancy by the entirety presume that a conveyance to a husband and wife, silent as to the type of ownership, will be a tenancy by the entirety.

The surviving tenant becomes the sole owner like the surviving joint tenant, but this survivorship right stems from the concept that the husband and wife were one, so ownership was already with the survivor. Divorce or annulment will terminate this tenancy.

Tenants in Common

Tenancy in common is a concurrent estate with no right of survivorship. Therefore, when a person dies, the interest held in the real property passes through the estate. This interest can exist between any two or more individuals and, in effect, jointly gives them the rights and duties of a sole owner. Each of the co-tenants is considered an owner of an undivided interest (not necessarily equal) in the whole property, and each has separate legal title, unlike joint tenants who share a single title. Courts of law look with favor on a tenancy in common, because a co-tenant's share of ownership passes upon death to the heirs and is not forfeited. As contrasted with a joint tenancy or a tenancy by the entirety, a tenancy in common can arise by operation of law, e.g., when a person dies intestate (without a will), heirs automatically inherit as tenants in common.

Any Tenant in common can sell his interest, mortgage it and have it attached for debts without destroying the joint interest. A grantee of a tenancy in common acquires only the percentage of the whole owned by the grantor. A tenancy in common is terminated by agreement between the parties or upon a petition to a court.

Community Property

Another form of concurrent ownership is community property, which is the law primarily in those states located in the western part of the United States.[1] Basically, the concept is that half of all property, personal and real, created during marriage belongs to each spouse. The underlying theory of this concept is that both have contributed to the creation of the family's wealth, even though only one was gainfully employed. There are three exceptions to this rule:

1. Property acquired from separate funds, such as a trust account

2. Property acquired individually before the marriage

3. Property inherited from another's estate.

With these exceptions, if the necessity of terminating the marriage occurs, each should receive a one-half share. Since each has equal interests, both must sign a mortgage note and security agreement.

Tenancy in Partnership

The last form of concurrent ownership is tenancy in partnership. Under the common law, a partnership could not own real estate in its partnership name. Therefore, one of the partners had to own the real estate in his or her own name. This presented the possibility of fraud. The Uniform Partnership Act, as adopted by many states, provides that a partnership can own real property in its firm name. Upon the death of a partner in a partnership, the surviving partners are vested with the share of the decedent or a percentage ownership of all property owned by the partnership. One partner's share of ownership may not necessarily be equal to that of another. It is quite common for partnerships to provide for a means of compensation for a deceased partner's estate, usually by insurance or a buy-sell agreement.

TRANSFER OF LAND

All title to real estate in America can be traced to one of three origins; conquest, discovery, or purchase. Today, title to real property can be transferred either voluntarily or involuntarily.

Voluntary Transfers

Most transfers of land are voluntary in that a grantor usually intends to transfer title to land to a grantee by the use of a deed or possibly a will. A deed is a legal instrument that purports to transfer a grantor's interest. If a grantor had no actual interest in a particular piece of real estate, an executed deed would transfer nothing. In addition, a properly executed deed from a grantor who did have title but lacked legal capacity (the grantor was legally insane, for example) would also transfer nothing. The validity of the title of the grantor can be determined by *abstracting* or checking the chain of title for defects.

All states have a law known as a statute of frauds requiring written transfers of real estate. Today, technical words are not needed in a deed, since any words that clearly show the grantor's intention to transfer are sufficient.

There are eight essential elements of a modern deed:

1. Grantor's name

2. Grantee's name

3. Description of real estate to be conveyed

4. Consideration (does not have to be actual amount paid)

5. Words of conveyance

6. Signature of grantor

7. Delivery and acceptances

8. Proper execution

Three basic types of deed are used, each having a specific purpose and function to perform. The least complicated is a quit claim deed which is used to clear title to real estate. A person signing this deed makes no title guarantee. Instead, a grantor is simply transferring whatever interest owned, if any. This deed can be used to clear a cloud on the title caused by a widow having a potential right of dower. She would be requested to execute the deed, possibly for a fee, whereby she transferred whatever interest she had (in this case dower), thus clearing the title.

A general warranty deed is the most common deed used to transfer interest in real estate. With this deed a grantor guarantees to a grantee that the title transferred is good against the whole world. This guarantee extends past the grantor to those in the chain of title. If a grantor refuses to use this deed, it may be an indication that the title is defective.

The special warranty deed is a relatively rare deed used in situations where a grantor wants to limit the guarantee. This instrument would be used by an executor of an estate to convey real estate to those specified in a will. By this deed the grantor only guarantees that nothing was done to interfere with the title to the real estate while under the grantor's control and makes no guarantee about a decedent's claim to the real estate.

Real estate that passes according to a will is also a voluntary conveyance, since it passes as the testator or the one making the will intended.

Involuntary Transfers

An involuntary conveyance occurs when a legal owner of real estate loses title contrary to the owner's intention. An example of this would be *eminent domain.* Any sovereign in the United States (federal, state, city or county) and some quasi-public entities (such as the telephone company or gas line company) can exercise the right of eminent domain. This right is inherent in a sovereign and is not granted by a constitution, although it is limited by it. The key elements are that it must be exercised for a valid public purpose or use, and that it requires compensation to be paid the legal owner.[2]

Another example of involuntary transfer of title is *adverse possession.* The public policy behind the doctrine of adverse possession is the encouragement of the usage of land, in addition to settling old claims to real property. Normally, a person possessing the real property of another holds that real estate for the legal owner's benefit. But if certain requirements are satisfied, the one occupying the real property could acquire legal title.

To claim title to real property by adverse possession, the one occupying the real property must prove:

1. Actual possession

2. Hostile intent

3. Notorious and open possession

4. Exclusive and continuous possession

5. Possession for a statutory period (which ranges from five to twenty years)

Some states also require that the party claiming title by adverse possession base the claim on some written instrument—even if the instrument is not valid. Other states require the claimant to pay real estate taxes for the statutory period.

Other examples of the possibility of involuntary transfer would include *foreclosure and subsequent sale* if an owner of real estate does not pay the mortgage, real estate tax or other encumbrances.

When a person dies intestate the title to real property along with the personal property passes, not according to the dictates of the owner, but according to the statutes of that particular state. If the individual had no discernable heirs, the property would escheat (pass) to the state.

Recording

Any time an interest in real estate is being created, transferred or encumbered, that transaction should be recorded. As in England centuries ago, the reason for recording is to prevent fraud. For example, situations existed where the owner of land would sell, possibly inadvertently, the same real estate to two or more innocent purchasers. Therefore, it was necessary to develop a system by which fraudulent transactions could be prevented. This was accomplished by devising a system of recording transactions affecting real estate. In order to protect a buyer's interest, recording statutes require purchasers of real estate to record the instrument by which they acquired the interest. If recorded, any subsequent purchaser will have either actual knowledge of the prior interest (because he checked the record), or constructive notice (because if he did check he would have discovered the interest).

If the party (the prior purchaser, for instance) who could have prevented a subsequent fraud by recording does not record, then that party will suffer the loss. An individual who wants to purchase real property has an obligation to check the record, usually in a county court house, to determine if there have been any transactions involving that particular real estate. Recording gives constructive notice to the whole world that a party has acquired an interest in a particular real property. Therefore, any subsequent purchaser could not acquire the same interest. If no transaction appears, an innocent purchaser acquiring an interest will be protected against the whole world, even against a prior purchaser.

In summary, a prior purchaser is protected if a record is made, whether a subsequent purchaser checks the record or not. The same is true if there is actual notice. If A sold land to B, and B failed to record, and C, knowing of that transaction, buys the same land and records, B will be protected since C had actual notice of the transaction between A and B. If C did not have actual notice and recorded before B, C would be protected in any dispute between B and C.

All states have a "race statute" which dictates that the first of two innocent parties to record will be protected.

SUGGESTED READINGS

Hebard, Edna L., and Meisel, Gerald S. *Principles of Real Estate Law.* Cambridge, Massachusetts: Schenkman Publishing Co., 1967.

Kratovil, Robert. *Modern Mortgage Law and Practice.* Englewood Cliffs, New Jersey: Prentice-Hall, Inc., 1972.

————. *Modern Real Estate Documentation.* Englewood Cliffs, New Jersey: Prentice-Hall, Inc., 1975.

————. *Real Estate Law.* Englewood Cliffs, New Jersey: Prentice-Hall Inc., 1974.

Lusk, Harold F. *The Law of the Real Estate Business.* Homewood, Illinois: Richard D. Irwin, Inc., 1975.

NOTES

1. Arizona, California, Idaho, Louisiana, Nevada, New Mexico, Oklahoma, Texas, and Washington.

2. This should not be confused with the exercise of police power, such as zoning, which does not require compensation.

Chapter 13

Residential Mortgage Loan Case Studies

INTRODUCTION

Both the practitioner and student of residential mortgage lending should be aware of and fully understand the essential elements and documents in a mortgage loan submission. This chapter discusses those documents required for each of the three types of residential mortgage loan:

1. Veterans Administration guaranteed loan (VA)

2. Conventional loan

3. Federal Housing Administration insured loan (FHA)

Preceding chapters explained that the type of mortgage loan made depends on the qualifications of the borrower as well as the classification of the mortgage lender. For example, a mortgage company typically originates either VA or FHA mortgage loans, while a savings and loan almost exclusively originates conventional loans, and a commercial bank typically originates all three types.

Since the VA case requires more unique and complete documentation than the others it is covered first. Some of the documents common to all residential cases (e.g. survey, title binder, among others) will not be exhibited in the other two cases to avoid repetition, but will be included in the VA case. The listing of required documents for each case will be complete, however, even if the document is deleted from the text discussion.

All of these cases are actual requests for mortgage loans which were made to the mortgagees whose names appear on the documents. These mortgage lenders provided invaluable assistance in preparing the cases for this chapter. The identities of the borrowers have been disguised and a few facts changed for clarity.

The reader is cautioned that the forms used are those currently required but which could change at any time. Some states may have particular requirements which are not included in these cases.

CASE STUDY: VETERANS ADMINISTRATION GUARANTEED MORTGAGE LOAN

The following case contains all the required information and documents necessary for a mortgage loan to be made to a qualified veteran. The loan will be guaranteed by the Veterans Administration and placed in a pool of mortgages backing a GNMA-guaranteed security.

A mortgage loan application by the borrowers on the mortgagee's own application form begins the case. This form complies with all current regulations and is therefore acceptable, although most mortgage lenders use the FNMA-FHLMC form.

After the application is made, a loan processor, or underwriter, must determine the veteran's eligibility for a VA-guaranteed loan. Many veterans already have a *certificate of eligibility* on hand. However, if they don't, one can be ordered for the veteran by submitting Form 26-1880, Request for Determination of Eligibility and Available Loan Guaranty Entitlement. This form is completed from information taken from the veteran's DD214, Report of Transfer or Discharge. If the veteran is eligible, a certificate of eligibility will be sent to the mortgagee by the Veterans Administration within a short period of time. In order to save time, a loan processor, prior to taking the application, should instruct the veteran to bring the DD214 or the certificate of eligibility, the purchase agreement, and all asset and liability account numbers.

Assuming all is in order to qualify, the processor would follow the *general credit questionnaire* to obtain the necessary data to begin the preliminary stages of underwriting. The *estimated statement of cost of loan and customer's memo* is a form used by the VA to reflect both an approximate annual percentage rate of interest to the borrower and an estimate of proposed monthly payments. This form also serves as a receipt for any funds collected at the time of application, such as fees for credit reports and appraisals. A good faith estimate of closing costs is given to the borrowers and the sellers to comply with RESPA.

The next step is to order an appraisal by submitting the *request for determination of reasonable value*. This form is sent to the VA which in turn has a VA-approved appraiser visit the property. The resulting estimate of value is placed on a *certificate of reasonable value (CRV)* and returned to the mortgagee. It is important to note that the CRV establishes the conditions under which the loan should be closed to assure the VA guaranty. Pictures of the property as well as a credit report, and verifications of employment and deposit are required for a VA guaranty.

Since an interest rate change occurred between the time of application and loan approval, two other forms are required in this particular case. The first informs the purchaser of this change and the second indicates the annual percentage rate based on the new interest rate. Every loan application taken faces the possibility of an interest rate change and all prospective mortgagors are asked to sign a letter protecting all parties against such a possibility.

Upon receipt of all verifications, credit reports and other documents, an *application for home loan guaranty* is prepared by the mortgagee and signed by the veteran. A cover letter is sent to the VA indicating the documentation being set for VA review.

After the VA underwrites and approves the loan submission, it returns a *certificate of commitment* to the mortgagee. The mortgage lender then notifies the mortgagor of the loan approval by letter and sends closing instructions to the closing attorney. All documents needed by the attorney for closing are attached to the *closing data sheet* for completion.

When the loan is ready to close, the closing attorney must furnish the mortgage lender with all items necessary to satisfy the conditions of the loan set forth by the Veterans Administration and mortgage lender. A *termite certificate* and evidence of *flood insurance* are required by VA as indicated on the CRV. A *title binder* and *survey* are required prior to the act of sale to assure clear title. Along with these documents, the closing attorney must submit a *request for authority to close* and a *statement of sellers' and buyers' costs.* These costs and the rate derived from the calculation of annual percentage rate required by the Federal Consumer Protection Act allow the mortgage lender to prepare the *disclosure statement.* The disclosure statement and the *authority to close letter* are sent back to the attorney with the funds for the sale.

At the sale, the borrower is required to sign a note, mortgage, HUD-1 settlement sheet and the *supplement to the disclosure-settlement statement* along with various other documents. In the state of Louisiana, a *credit sale of property* is the accepted mortgage form. It conveys the land and dwelling simultaneously and provides for a more expeditious foreclosure proceeding, if necessary. In other states a mortgage or trust deed would serve the same purpose.

After all documents are returned to the mortgage lender, they are checked for compliance and the loan is assigned to an investor commitment. This particular loan was placed in a GNMA mortgage pool. The original note, mortgage and *assignment of note and mortgage* are forwarded to a custodian to initiate the pool proceedings.

Within this same time frame, the loan file is transferred to the loan administration area to be computerized for proper maintenance of the account. Once the loan is "set up", a *first payment letter* is sent to the mortgagors, congratulating them on their purchase.

The following documents are required for a mortgage loan guaranteed by the Veterans Administration and placed in a mortgage pool guaranteed by GNMA:

1. Residential loan application-general credit questionnaire

2. Purchase agreement

3. Estimated statement of cost of loan and customer's memo

4. Good faith estimates of closing costs

5. Equal Credit Opportunity Act notice and additional disclosure

6. VA Form 26-1880, Request for Determination of Eligibility and Available Loan Guaranty Entitlement

7. Certificate of eligibility

8. VA Form 26-1805, Request for Determination of Reasonable Value

9. VA Form 26-1843, Certificate of Reasonable Value

10. Photographs

11. VA Form 26-8497, Request for Verification of Employment

12. VA Form 26-8497a, Request for Verification of Deposit

13. Credit Reports

14. Mortgagee's cover letter for submission to VA

15. Processing check sheet

16. VA Form 26-1802a, Application for Home Loan Guaranty

17. VA Form 26-1866a, Certificate of Commitment

18. Mortgagee's notification of approval letter

19. No commitment to lend letter

20. Interest rate change letter

21. Mortgagee's closing instructions

22. Title insurance commitment

23. Survey

24. Hazard insurance policy (not included in this case)

25. Flood insurance policy

26. Termite certificate

27. Request for authority to close and statements of costs

28. Calculation of annual percentage rate

29. Disclosure statement

30. Authority to close letter

31. VA Form 26-6316a, note

32. VA Form 26-6316b, mortgage (credit sale of property)

33. HUD-1, settlement statement

34. Supplement to disclosure-settlement statement (HUD)

35. Assignment of note and mortgage

36. First payment letter to mortgagor(s)

CARRUTH MORTGAGE CORPORATION
GENERAL CREDIT QUESTIONNAIRE

( ) FHA Section _____ __ ( ) Proposed (X) Existing
( ) FHA-VA Applicant 123-45-6789
(X) VA Social Security #
( ) Conventional Co-Applicant 762-34-7788

SOURCE ____ Homes Inc. _____ Phone No. 468-9555

AGENT ____ Edith Sims _____ Phone No. 468-2301

A. PROPERTY AND PURCHASER
1. Name of Applicant (x) Married ( ) Unmarried* ( ) Separated
   GEORGE EARL SMITH Age 29
   First Middle Last (Print) (Maiden)

2. Name of Co-Applicant (x) Married ( ) Unmarried* ( ) Separated
   PATRICIA SMITH HOLMES Age 29
   First Middle Last (Print) (Maiden)

3. Property being purchased ____ 1325 Tarrington Dr., Marrero, La.
   Sq. ____ Lot ____ Subdivision _____ Sales Price $ 38,500.00
   Loan(s) Amount $ 38,500.00
   First Mortgage $ _____ Interest Rate 8 % Term 30 years
   Second Mortgage $ _____ Interest Rate ____ % Term ____ years

4. Present address ____ 1325 Genius St., Harahan, La. 70123 ____ 2 ____ years
   Home Phone 737-3743 Business Phone 885-6320
   Former Address
   From _____ to _____ _____
   From _____ to _____ _____
   From _____ to _____ _____
   (Must cover 2 years, including present address)

5. If Applicant owns or partially owns the lot, complete the following:
   Contract Price $ _____ Land Cost $ _____ Balance Due $ _____

B. EMPLOYMENT STATUS Applicant Co-Applicant
   (Must cover 2 year period. If not in present position 2 years, show prior employment.)
   1. Employed By | Clearview Motor Co. | Clearview Motor Co.
   2. Address of Employer | Marrero Texaco | Clearview Gulf
   3. Type of Business | 900 Ave. C, Marrero | 3112 Clearview
   4. Position Occupied | Manager | Bookkeeper
   5. Name of Superior | |
   6. Length of Employment | From ____ to | From ____ to
   7. Length in this Occupation | 2 yr | 2 yr.

C. MONTHLY INCOME Applicant Co-Applicant
   1. Base Pay | $1,000 | $600
   2. Overtime | |
   3. Bonus or Commission | 400 |
   4. VA Disability Pension | |
      Extras | Company Truck | Car insurance & gas free
   5. Other Source of Income ** | NEITHER HAVE FINANCIAL INTEREST

D. COST OF DEPENDENT CARE
   1. Monthly Expense $ ____ NONE

   FUTURE RENTAL $200/ mo.

E. EDUCATION
   1. Applicant _____
   2. Co-Applicant _____

F. UNION Applicant Co-Applicant
   1. Name | |
   2. Address | |
   3. Badge No. | |
   4. Length of membership | From ____ to | From ____ to

*Unmarried includes single, divorced & widowed.
**NOTICE: Alimony, child support, or separate maintenance income need not be revealed if
applicant or co-applicant does not choose to have it considered as a basis for repaying this
loan. Alimony, child support, separate maintenance under court order ____,
written agreement ____, oral understanding ____.

		Applicant	Co-Applicant
G.	**SECONDARY EMPLOYMENT**		

G. **SECONDARY EMPLOYMENT**
1. Employed by
2. Address of Employer
3. Type of Business
4. Position Occupied
5. Name of Superior
6. Length of Employment   From_____ to_____   From_____ to_____
7. Base Pay

H. **PRIOR EMPLOYMENT**
1. Employed by
2. Address
3. Type of Business
4. Position Occupied
5. Name of Superior
6. Length of Employment   From_____ to_____   From_____ to_____

1. Employed by
2. Address
3. Type of Business
4. Position Occupied
5. Name of Superior
6. Length of Employment   From_____ to_____   From_____ to_____

1. Employed by
2. Address
3. Type of Business
4. Position Occupied
5. Name of Superior
6. Length of Employment   From_____ to_____   From_____ to_____

1. Employed by
2. Address
3. Type of Business
4. Position Occupied
5. Name of Superior
6. Length of Employment   From_____ to_____   From_____ to_____

I. ASSETS
1. I have bank accounts with

Name, Branch and Address of Bank	Name of Account and Number	Amount	Type of Account
Commercial Bank	1353630	$400	checking
Delivery Homestead	124222	$1500	savings

2. Cash Value of U. S. Savings Bonds $___NONE___ Life Insurance _____
3. Cash on Hand $_____ I own securities worth $___NONE___ (If over $100 attach schedule)
4. My personal effects (clothing, jewelry, furniture) are valued at $_8,000_
5. I own a car: Make____AMC____ Year_1973_ Present Value $_____
                         Make_____ Year_____ Present Value $_____
6. Earnest Money deposited with Seller/Agent $_____
7. Other Assets _____

The cash required for the payment of loan closing costs and the down payment(difference between sales price and loan applied for, if any) will be provided from the following:
                    BANK

J. LIABILITIES
I have the following debts:

			MO.	AMT.
PAYABLE TO	ACCT.#	PURPOSE	PAYMENT	OWED
First Federal Bank	32219015	Home Improvement	$215.19	$3,000
Holmes	3192333121200		30 day account	

	APPLICANT	CO-APPLICANT
a) Are you obligated to pay alimony, child support or separate maintenance?	NO	NO
b) If so, to whom paid?		
c) Amount		
d) Do you have any loans outstanding from credit unions?		

K. LIST PAID OUT CREDIT REFERENCES (THREE)

L. ITEMS ESSENTIAL FOR ELIGIBILITY
1. It is my intention to occupy this property or a unit thereof as my home (X) Yes ( ) No
2. Have you incurred, or do you intend to incur, any indebtedness, secured or unsecured, other than that of the mortgage loan applied for for any purposes connected with this transaction ( ) Yes ( ) No

M. TAX EXEMPTIONS
1. Are you a Veteran of ( ) WWII   ( ) Korean   ( ) Post Korea
                    (12/7/41-12/31/46) (6/27/50-1/31/55) (8/5/64 -   )
2. If a veteran, have you used any of your 5 year veterans homestead exemption
    ( ) Yes   ( ) No   If yes - how many _____ _____ years.

N. REAL ESTATE OWNED
1. Address 1325 Genius Acct. No. 100-20282   Value $ 30,000
2. Mortgage Balance $ 11,500   Orig. Amt. $ 15,300   Monthly Payment $ 107.63
3. Company Holding Mortgage   PENAMCO
    Address
4. Type of Loan   VA ( )   FHA (X)   Conventional ( )
5. Disposition of Property:
    To be sold _____ Under Agreement of Sale _____ To be rented _____
    If to be rented, anticipated gross rental income per month $ 200

    If home to be sold by refinancing or assumption, we need copy of closing statement, signed by closing attorney, showing net proceeds to seller.

O. PAST CREDIT EXPERIENCE
1. Have any claims for collections, suits, judgments or liens ever been placed against you and/or are you now involved in a bankruptcy proceeding, or have you ever been adjudged a bankrupt in the past? ( ) Yes   (X) No
    If yes, explain by letter in triplicate
    Have you ever had any credit problems including repossessions? ( ) Yes   (x) No
    If yes, explain

2. Have you owned and sold any property within the last 2 years on which you had an ( ) FHA or ( ) VA mortgage. ( ) Yes (x) No. If answer is yes, give the following information.
    (a) Was your loan assumed? ( ) Yes ( ) No
    (b) Address of property _____
    (c) Original Mortgage Amount $ _____
    (d) Unpaid Balance when sold $ _____
    (e) Date Sold _____ _____ _____
                      Month   Day   Year
    (f) Name and address of firm holding mortgage if sold on assumption basis
    _____
    (g) Account Number _____

3. Have you ever been obligated on a VA Guaranteed Home Loan, or an FHA Insured Mortgage on which default of payments resulted in foreclosure or voluntary deed in lieu of foreclosure; or have you ever been obligated on an FHA property improvement loan on which default of payments resulted in the payment of a claim by FHA? ( ) Yes (X) No. If answer is yes, please give the following information.
   (a)   Address of Property _____
   (b)   Name and address of Mortgagee _____
   _____

P. FHA LOANS ONLY
   1. Life Insurance Amount $_____ Annual Premium $_____
      Loans against Policy _____
   2. Do you own 4 or more dwelling units which are subject to mortgages insured under any title of the National Housing Act? ( ) Yes ( ) No
      If anwer is "Yes" or this application involves a property consisting 2, 3 or 4 family dwellings, FHA FORM 2561 WILL BE REQUIRED.
   3. HAVE YOU SOLD PROPERTY ON AN FHA ASSUMPTION WITHIN THE LAST SIX MONTHS?
      ( ) Yes   ( ) No   If answer is yes, the following information is needed:
      Did Purchaser intend to occupy the property as his or her home? ( ) Yes ( ) No
      Name of Assumptor _____
      Address of Assumptor _____
      Place of Employment:
      Name of Employer _____
      Address _____
      and any other pertinent information which can be obtained to assist the credit bureau in making a credit check _____
      _____

      (We must collect credit report fee from applicant to order credit report on assumption.)

Q. HOUSING EXPENSES (MONTHLY)
   (a)   Mortgage Payment or Rent $ 107.63
   (b)   Taxes and Insurance   Included
   (c)   Water, Gas, Electricity   50.00
   (d)   Maintenance
   TOTAL HOUSING EXPENSES (MONTHLY) $ 157.63

R. MY DEPENDENTS NAMES AND AGES ARE: (235 Only)
   Lisa – 5 years
   _____ Brian – 10 years _____
   _____

S. CONVENTIONAL LOANS ONLY:
   Are there any outstanding judgments against you? Yes ( ) No ( ). If Yes, explain
   _____

   Are you co-maker or endorser on any notes? Yes ( ) No ( ). If Yes, explain
   _____

   Are you the defendant/participant in a law suit? Yes ( ) No ( ). If Yes, explain
   _____

   Have you owned a home before? Yes ( ) No ( ). If Yes, date sold_____
   Name and address of company holding mortgage _____
   _____

   Do you have health and accident insurance coverage? Yes ( ) No ( )
   Do you have major medical coverage? Yes ( ) No ( )
   Will the property you are purchasing be your primary residence? Yes ( ) No ( )

I have been advised that flood insurance is, or may be in the future, available in this area in which I am purchasing property, and it has been recommended that I obtain this type of coverage when available from the insurance agent of my choice.

THIS IS TO ACKNOWLEDGE that I am aware of my right to select the insurance company or agent of my choice, provided they meet the requirements of Carruth Mortgage Corporation to write the hazard insurance on the home on which I am applying for financing through Carruth Mortgage Corporation.

I am aware that I have the right to select the carrier of my private mortgage insurance (if applicable) and the carrier of required Mortgage Title Insurance, subject to the approval of Carruth Mortgage Corporation. However, I hereby designate Carruth Mortgage Corporation as my agent to select such companies.

I have applied to you for a loan and you have made a commitment which you have advised me is purely tentative and is subject to approval by the Federal Housing Administration or the Veterans Administration and/or your investor. I understand the present interest rate on this type of loan is _____8_____% per annum. In the event the interest rate is increased prior to passing of the Act of Sale, I realize that my loan would be closed at the increased interest rate. In the event I elect not to close because of the foregoing, the only adverse consequence I would realize as far as Carruth Mortgage Corporation is concerned would be the loss of the amount paid to you for the application and appriasal fee, if any.

If this application is approved by Carruth Mortgage Corporation, I agree to pay to Carruth Mortgage Corporation _____1_____% of the amount of the loan applied for as a lender's fee for services rendered.

THIS STATEMENT (including that on the foregoing pages) is made by the undersigned for the purpose of obtaining the benefits of a mortgage loan which may be insured under the provisions of the National Housing Act and/or the Servicemen's Readjustment Act of 1944 as amended and/or Conventional Financing, and the undersigned hereby represents that to the best of the undersigned's knowledge and belief, the statements and information contained herein are, in all respects, true and correct and complete. The Federal Housing Administration Commissioner and/or the Administrator of Veterans Affairs and Carruth Mortgage Corporation or their representative, may verify the items contained herein by communicating with any of the persons or institutions named in this statement. The statements will otherwise be treated as confidential. The undersigned further understands that the information furnished herewith will be transcribed to the Veterans Administration, or the Federal Housing Administration and/or Carruth Mortgage Corporation investor forms as applicable in order to complete the processing of the application. The undersigned has read the statements contained over the affixed signature on such forms and hereby authorizes Carruth Mortgage Corporation to complete the forms with the information furnished herewith.

SIGNED_*George Earl Smith*_____ SIGNED_*Patricia Holmes Smith*_____

DATE_____*5.24.77*_____ DATE_____*5-24-77*_____

DATE_____*5.24.77*_____ INTERVIEW TAKEN BY:_*Christine Larue*_____

(FHA 235 Only)

I certify that a Home Buyer's Information Kit was delivered to me prior to signing my home purchase agreement.

SIGNED_____ SIGNED_____

DATE_____ DATE_____

Agreement

To Purchase

Or Sell

Agreement

To Purchase

Or Sell

_____ Agent   ~~Sell~~   New Orleans, La._____ 19____

1.   ___I___offer and agree to purchase__1325 Tarrington Street, Marrero, Louisiana__
2.   house, lot and all improvements thereon All electric, plumbing air-cond.
3.   & heating and all built ins to be in working order. Termite inspection at
4.   purchasers expense.·50 X 100_____or as per title, and subject to title restrictions if any,
5.   for the sum of _Thirty eight thousand five hundred_38,500_____) Dollars, on the terms of
6.   _____no_____Cash_and balance by a VA loan. Subject to
7.   satisfactory roof.inspection at purchaser's expense. Seller to furnish
8.   clear termite certificate.
9.   This sale is conditioned upon the ability of the purchaser to borrow upon this property as security the sum of $_38,500_
10. by a mortgage loan or loans at a rate of interest not to exceed_8.5_% per annum, interest and principal payable in equal
11. _____; installments, over a period of_____30_____years.
     (monthly) (quarterly) (semi-annual) (annual)
12. Should the loan stipulated above be unobtainable by the purchaser, seller or agent within _____days from date of accept-
13. ance hereof, this contract shall then become null and void, and the agent is hereby authorized to return the purchaser's deposit
14. in full.
15. Property sold subject to the following lease or leases:
16. Tenant_____ Rental_____ Expiration_____ Options_____
17. _____   _____   _____   _____
18. Occupancy_At act of sale_____
19. Paving charges bearing against the property, if any, to be paid by____Seller_____
20. Real Estate Taxes and rentals (if any) to be prorated to date of Act of Sale.
21. All proper and necessary certificates and revenue stamps to be paid by seller.
22. Cost of survey by_Purchaser_____
23. _____
24. _____
25. _____
26. Act of Sale to be passed before_Purchaser's_____.Notary, on or prior to__July 1st___19 77
27. at expense of purchaser.
28. If this offer is accepted, purchaser must deposit with seller's agent immediately in cash_____% of purchase price
29. amounting to $__300.00_____
30. This deposit is to be non-interest bearing and may be placed in any bank in the City of New Orleans, without
31. responsibility on the part of the agent in case of failure or suspension of such bank.
32. The seller shall deliver to purchaser a merchantable title.
33. In the event the purchaser fails to comply with this agreement within the time specified, the seller shall have the
34. right to declare the deposit, ipso facto, forfeited, without formality beyond tender of title to purchaser; or the seller may de-
35. mand specific performance.
36. In the event the seller does not comply with this agreement within the time specified, the purchaser shall have the
37. right either to demand the return of his deposit in full plus an equal amount to be paid as penalty by the seller; or the
38. purchaser may demand specific performance, at his option.
39. In the event the deposit is forfeited, the commission shall be paid out of this deposit, reserving to the seller the right
40. to proceed against the purchaser for the recovery of the amount of the commission.
41. If this offer is accepted, seller agrees to pay the agent's commission of__6%_____which commission is earned by
42. agent when this agreement is signed by both parties and when the mortgage loan, if any, has been secured.
43. Sellers agree to pay no more than 5% discount.
44. Either party hereto who fails to comply with the terms of this offer, if accepted, is obligated and agrees to pay the
45. agent's commission and all fees and costs incurred in enforcing collection and damages.
46. This offer remains binding and irrevocable through_____
47. Submitted to_Margie Reading_____   (Signed)_George E. Smith_____
         (Listing Agent) (Owner)   _Patricia Smith____
48. By_Edith Sims_____   New Orleans, La.__5/20_____19 77
         Selling Agent

I/We accept the above in all its terms and conditions.

(Signed)_Frederick Jones_____

INCOMPLETE ITEMS

(X) Bank Account Numbers ~~xxxxxxxxxx~~ Dixie

(X) Charge Account Numbers ~~xxxxxxxxxxxxx~~ 1st Metropolitan
                                                        Pennamco

( ) W-2 Forms for last 3 years

( ) Letter(s) of recommendation from employer(s)

( ) Closing Statement on sale of home
         (prior or present)

( ) Certificate of Eligibility

( ) DD 214   ( ) DD 1747   ( ) DD 802

( ) Statement of Services

( ) Copy of Divorce Decree

(X) Applicants forms _____

( ) _____

( ) _____

( ) _____

APPLICATION FEE AND RECEIPT

1. Application Fee $ 10.00

2. Appraisal Fee
    (a) FHA ($_____)
    (b) VA   ($_____) or more   55.00
         Mileage ($_____)   _____
    (c) Conventional ($_____)   _____

3. Underwriter's Fee ($_____)   _____

4. Origination Fee ($_____)   _____

5. TOTAL $ 65.00

Receipt is hereby acknowledged from Patricia Smith
of $ 65.00   Check (X) Cash ( )

Date 5/24/77

BY: _____ C. Pearse _C. Pearse_ _____
          CARRUTH MORTGAGE CORPORATION

ESTIMATED STATEMENT OF COST OF LOAN AND CUSTOMER'S MEMO

LOAN TYPE (X) VA   NAME Patricia & George Smith
          ( ) FHA
          ( ) CONVENTIONAL   PROPERTY 1325 Tarrington Drive

                                     Marrero, La.

MONTHLY PAYMENT ESTIMATE

Principal and Interest $ 282.59   Loan Amount $ 38,500.00

Hazard Insurance   18.00   Interest Rate of 8 % for 30 years

Flood Insurance   6.00   CLOSING COSTS:
  (if appropriate)   Estimated $ 1,540.00
                        (Items of closing costs when appropriate
                        are Mortgagee's Title Insurance and Exam-
Taxes   3.00   ination, Origination Fee, Survey, Notary
                        Fee, Mortgage and Conveyance Certificates,
Mortgage Insurance   Credit Report, Appraisal Fee, Recording
  (FHA or Private)   Fees, 1st year's Hazard Insurance Premium,
                        1st year's Flood Insurance Premium, Escrow
                        for Taxes, Insurance and Mortgage Insur-
                        ance.)
TOTAL PAYMENT $ 309.59   ESTIMATED ANNUAL PERCENTAGE
                                RATE 8.25   %
                          ESTIMATED TOTAL PREPAID FINANCE
                          CHARGES $ 2,263.75

LOAN INFORMATION

1. Lender's security interest in this transaction is to be a first lien on the property.
2. Finance charge on this loan will begin to accrue on the date of closing.
3. Fire and Extended coverage (Hazard Insurance), in a maximum amount which does not need to be greater than the loan amount and which includes a loss payable clause to Carruth Mortgage Corporation, is requested as a condition of this loan.
4. Payments are due on the 1st of each month.
5. In the event of late payment, a late charge equivalent to 4 % of each payment more than fifteen (15) days in arrears must be paid by the borrower(s) to the lender.
6. You will receive a letter from us after your loan is closed giving the details of payments to be made on your loan and an Amortization Schedule on which you may maintain a record of your payments.
7. Interest is paid on the Unpaid Principal Balance.
8. You may make additional payments with your regular monthly payment at any time as long as the amount paid is in accordance with the Amortization Schedule.
9. There *is ( ) is not (X) a penalty for prepaying your loan.
*PREPAYMENT PENALTY:

10. Annual payments for hazard insurance, mortgage insurance, flood insurance (if applicable) and real estate taxes are accumulated by us from your monthly payments and paid by us from the escrow account in which these funds are kept. Any bill or correspondence you receive for these items should be promptly delivered to us.
11. IT IS IMPORTANT THAT YOU APPLY FOR YOUR HOMESTEAD EXEMPTION EACH YEAR. You may check with your Parish Tax Assessor's Office to ascertain the time when you make application. The Homestead Exemption should be promptly delivered to us so that we may adjust the taxes to be collected each month on your property.
12. ( ) This is to formally notify you that the above named property is located in an area that has been identified by the Secretary of Housing and Urban Will Development as an area having special flood hazards. Accordingly, flood advise insurance under the National Flood Insurance Program is a requirement of this loan. The insurance shall be in an amount at least equal to either the outstanding balance of the mortgage or the maximum amount of NFIP insurance available, and which contains a loss payable clause to Carruth Mortgage Corporation.
( ) At the present time, this property is not located in an area that has been identified by the Secretary of Housing and Urban Development as an area having special flood hazards nor is it a requirement, at this time, to carry Flood Insurance. However, Flood Insurance is or may be in the future, available in your area, and it is recommended that you check with your insurance agent regarding this type of coverage and seriously consider the purchase of it, when available. The original policy is to be sent to our office and will be handled the same as your hazard insurance.

RECEIPT IS HEREBY ACKNOWLEDGED OF THE ESTIMATED STATEMENT OF COST OF LOAN TOGETHER
WITH A COPY OF THE CUSTOMER'S MEMO SIGNED BY ME THIS DAY,

Date 5-24-77   Signature *George Earl Smith*, Applicant
Page 1 of 2   Signature *Patricia Holmes Smith*, Applicant

Counseling

CARRUTH Mortgage Corporation

3601 I-10 SERVICE ROAD   METAIRIE, LOUISIANA   PHONE 885-4811

MAILING ADDRESS
P. O. BOX 53334
NEW ORLEANS, LA. 70153

GOOD FAITH ESTIMATES
OF BORROWER'S CLOSING COSTS

TO: Patricia & George Smith   RE: 1325 Tarrington Drive
                                        Marrero, La.
Loan Amount $ 38,500.00

801.	Loan Origination Fee 1%	$ 385.00
802.	Loan Discount %	$
803.	Appraisal Fee	$ 55.00
804.	Credit Report	$ 10.00
805.	Lender's Inspection Fee	$
806.	Mortgage Insurance Application Fee	$
807.	Assumption Fee	$
808.	F.N.M.A. Underwriting Review Fee	$
809.	Private Mortgage Insurance Review Fee	$
810.		$
811.		$
901.	Interest for 15 days @ $ 8.56 Day	$ 128.40
902.	Mortgage Insurance Premium for ___ mo.	$
904.		$
1101.	Settlement or Closing Fee	$
1102.	Abstract or Title Search	$
1103.	Title Examination	$ 385.00
1104.	Title Insurance Binder	$
1105.	Document Preparation	$
1106.	Notary Fees	$ 90.00
1107.	Attorney's Fees	$
1108.	Title Insurance	$
	1109. Lender's Coverage $	
	1110. Owner's Coverage $ 20.00	
1201.	Recording Fees:	$ 35.00
1301.	Survey	$ 75.00
1302.	Pest Inspection	$
1400.	TOTAL ESTIMATED SETTLEMENT CHARGES	$ 1,163.40

THIS FORM DOES NOT COVER ALL ITEMS YOU WILL BE REQUIRED TO PAY IN
CASH AT SETTLEMENT; FOR EXAMPLE, DEPOSIT IN ESCROW FOR REAL ESTATE
TAXES AND INSURANCE. YOU MAY WISH TO INQUIRE AS TO THE AMOUNTS OF
SUCH OTHER ITEMS. YOU MAY BE REQUIRED TO PAY OTHER ADDITIONAL
AMOUNTS AT SETTLEMENT.

NOTE: It is the policy of Carruth Mortgage Corporation not to
       require a particular provider of legal services, title
       examination services or title insurance or to conduct
       settlement. We have a list of the attorneys and notaries
       whom we have approved to handle the above services and
       we reserve the right to reject the use of any provider
       not on our approved list. This list is available for your
       review in nay of our offices. Unless advised otherwise,
       we normally allow the selling agent or builder to choose
       the closing agent.

***** The line numbers in the left hand column above are the
       same as those that will be on the HUD-1 Settlement
       Statement you will receive at loan closing. For further
       explanation of these charges, refer to your Settlement
       Cost Booklet.

227

Date: _____5-24-77_____

Carruth Mortgage Corporation
P.O. Box 53334
New Orleans, La. 70153

RE: EQUAL CREDIT OPPORTUNITY ACT (ECOA) NOTICE AND ADDITIONAL
    DISCLOSURE

The Board of Governors of the Federal Reserve System have issued
Regulation B implementing the Equal Credit Opportunity Act, and
require that the public be alerted to the existence of the general
rule prohibiting discrimination on a prohibited basis. Below is
the (1) Notice and (2) Additional Disclosures required by Regulation
B:

    (1)   EQUAL CREDIT OPPORTUNITY ACT NOTICE
        The Federal Equal Credit Opportunity Act prohibits
        creditors from discrimination against credit appli-
        cants on the basis of race, color, religion, national
        orgin, sex, marital status, age (provided that the
        applicant has the capacity to enter into a binding
        contract); because all or part of the applicant's
        income derives from any public assistance program;
        or because the applicant has in good faith exercised
        any right under the Consumer Credit Protection Act.
        The Federal agency that administers compliance with
        this law concerning this creditor is the Federal
        Trade Commission, Equal Credit Opportunity, Washington,
        D.C. 20580.

    (2)   ADDITIONAL DISCLOSURE
        Alimony, child support, or separate maintenance income
        need not be revealed if applicant does not wish to have
        it considered as a basis for repaying a loan.

Receipt is hereby acknowledged of the above ECOA Notice and Additional Disclosure as made to me this date.

George Earl Smith _____   _Patricia Holmes Smith_____
           Applicant   Co-Applicant

_____5-24-77_____   _____5-24-77_____
        Date   Date

CMC#435
(Rev 3/77)

Form Approved
OMB No. 76-RO371

VETERANS ADMINISTRATION		TO	VETERANS ADMINISTRATION
REQUEST FOR DETERMINATION OF ELIGIBILITY AND AVAILABLE LOAN GUARANTY ENTITLEMENT			ATTN: Loan Guaranty Division

NOTE: Please read instructions on reverse before completing this form. If additional space is required, attach separate sheet.

1. FIRST-MIDDLE-LAST NAME OF VETERAN	2. ADDRESS OF VETERAN (No., street or rural route, city or P.O., State and ZIP code)
George Earl Smith	1325 Genius St.
3. DATE OF BIRTH	Harahan, La. 70123
28, Jan, 1948	

4. MILITARY SERVICE DATA—I request the Veterans Administration to determine my eligibility and the amount of entitlement based on the following period(s) of active military duty: (Start with latest period of service and list all periods of active duty since September 16, 1940.)

PERIOD OF ACTIVE SERVICE		NAME (Show your name exactly as it appears on your separation papers (DD Form 214) or statement of service)	SERVICE NUMBER	BRANCH OF SERVICE
DATE FROM	DATE TO			
4A. 03 Jan 68	03 Oct 69	SMITH, George Earl	872 95 40	Navy
4B.				
4C.				
4D.				

5A. WERE YOU DISCHARGED, RETIRED, OR SEPARATED FROM SERVICE BECAUSE OF DISABILITY, OR DO YOU NOW HAVE ANY SERVICE-CONNECTED DISABILITIES? ☐ YES ☒ NO (If "Yes," complete Item 5B)	5B. VA FILE NUMBER C-	6. IS THERE A CERTIFICATE OF ELIGIBILITY FOR LOAN GUARANTY OR DIRECT LOAN PURPOSES ENCLOSED? ☒ YES ☐ NO (If "No," complete Items 7A and 7B)

7A. HAVE YOU PREVIOUSLY APPLIED FOR A CERTIFICATE OF ELIGIBILITY FOR LOAN GUARANTY OR DIRECT LOAN PURPOSES? ☐ YES ☒ NO	7B. HAVE YOU PREVIOUSLY RECEIVED SUCH A CERTIFICATE OF ELIGIBILITY? ☐ YES ☒ NO (If "Yes," give location of VA office(s) involved)

8A. HAVE YOU PREVIOUSLY SECURED A VA DIRECT HOME LOAN? ☐ YES ☒ NO (If "Yes," give location of VA office(s) involved and complete Items 9 through 18)	8B. HAVE YOU PREVIOUSLY OBTAINED HOME, FARM, CONDOMINIUM OR BUSINESS LOAN(S) WHICH WERE GUARANTEED OR INSURED BY VA? ☐ YES ☒ NO (If "Yes," give location of VA office(s) involved and complete Items 9 through 18)	8C. HAVE YOU PREVIOUSLY OBTAINED A VA MOBILE HOME AND/OR LOT LOAN(S)? ☐ YES ☒ NO (If "Yes," give location of VA office(s) involved)

NOTE: Complete Items 9 through 18 only if you have previously acquired property with the assistance of a GI Loan.	9. ADDRESS OF PROPERTY PREVIOUSLY PURCHASED WITH GUARANTY ENTITLEMENT	10. DATE YOU PURCHASED PROPERTY
		11. DO YOU NOW OWN THE REAL PROPERTY DESCRIBED IN ITEM 9? ☐ YES ☐ NO (If "Yes," do not complete Items 12 through 18)

12. CHECK WHETHER YOU ☐ ENTERED INTO AN INSTALLMENT SALE CONTRACT WITH THE PURCHASER, OR ☐ EXECUTED AND DELIVERED A DEED TO THE PURCHASER CONVEYING ALL YOUR RIGHTS, TITLE, AND INTEREST IN THE PROPERTY	13. NAMES OF PERSONS TO WHOM SOLD THE PROPERTY	14. DATE THE DEED, IF ANY, WAS DELIVERED TO PURCHASER
		15. IS THERE ANY UNDERSTANDING OR AGREEMENT WRITTEN OR ORAL BETWEEN YOU AND THE PURCHASERS THAT THEY WILL RECONVEY THE PROPERTY TO YOU? ☐ YES ☐ NO

NOTE: It will speed processing if you can furnish the information in Items 16, 17, and 18.	16. NAME AND ADDRESS OF LENDER TO WHOM LOAN PAYMENTS WERE MADE	17. LENDER'S LOAN OR ACCOUNT NO.
		18. VA LOAN NO. (LH)

19. Check only if this is a request for a DUPLICATE Certificate of Eligibility ▶	☐ PLEASE ISSUE A DUPLICATE CERTIFICATE OF ELIGIBILITY IN MY NAME. THE CERTIFICATE PREVIOUSLY ISSUED TO ME IS NOT AVAILABLE BECAUSE IT HAS BEEN LOST, DESTROYED OR STOLEN. IF IT IS RECOVERED, IT WILL BE RETURNED TO THE VA FOR CANCELLATION.

I certify that the statements herein are true to the best of my knowledge and belief.	20. SIGNATURE OF VETERAN George Earl Smith	21. DATE 5-24-77

FEDERAL STATUTES PROVIDE SEVERE PENALTIES FOR FRAUD, INTENTIONAL MISREPRESENTATION, CRIMINAL CONNIVANCE, OR CONSPIRACY PURPOSED TO INFLUENCE THE ISSUANCE OF ANY GUARANTY OR INSURANCE BY THE ADMINISTRATOR.

THIS SECTION FOR VA USE ONLY			
DATE CERTIFICATE ISSUED AND DISCHARGE OR SEPARATION PAPERS AND VA PAMPHLETS GIVEN TO VETERAN OR MAILED TO ADDRESS SHOWN BELOW	TYPE OF DISCHARGE OR SEPARATION PAPERS RETURNED	SIGNATURE AND TITLE OF APPROPRIATE OFFICIAL (If applicable)	STATION NUMBER
			CERTIFICATE NUMBER

VA FORM 26-1880, JAN 1977   DO NOT DETACH

IMPORTANT—You must complete Item 22, since the certificate of eligibility together with all discharge and separation papers will be mailed to the address shown in Item 22 immediately below. If they are to be sent to you, your current mailing address should be indicated, or if they are to be sent elsewhere, the name and address of such person or firm should be shown in Item 22.

The amount of loan guaranty entitlement available for use is endorsed on the reverse of the enclosed Certificate of Eligibility. This certificate must be returned to the VA at the time a loan application or loan report is submitted.

22. RETURN TO (Enter name and address below dots)

Carruth Mortgage Corporation
P O. Box 53334
New Orleans, La. 70153

[PLEASE DELIVER THE ENCLOSED PAMPHLETS AND DISCHARGE OR SEPARATION PAPERS TO THE VETERAN PROMPTLY. THANK YOU.]

VA FORM
JAN 1977 **26-1880**

VETERANS ADMINISTRAT...ON

№ 1933917 Certificate of Eligibility
FOR LOAN GUARANTY BENEFITS

Name of Veteran	Service Serial Number	Social Security Number
George Earl Smith	872 95 40	123-45-6789

Date Issued	Entitlement	Branch of Service	Date of Birth
5/30/1977	☐ WW II ☐ PL 550 ☒ PL 358	Navy	Jan. 28, 1948

IS ELIGIBLE FOR THE BENEFITS OF CHAPTER 37, TITLE 38, U.S. CODE, AND HAS THE AMOUNT OF ENTITLEMENT SHOWN AS AVAILABLE ON THE REVERSE SUBJECT TO THE ITEMS CHECKED:

☐ 1. Eligibility restricted per VA Regulation 4349.

☐ 2. Valid unless discharged or released subsequent to the date of this certificate. A certification of continuous active duty as of date of note required.

CANCEL

ADMINISTRATOR OF VETERANS AFFAIRS

(Signature) (Title & Agent)

Veterans Benefits Office
2033 M Street N. W.
(Issuing Office)
Washington, D. C. 20421

Form Approved
OMB No. 76-R0231

VETERANS ADMINISTRATION
REQUEST FOR DETERMINATION OF REASONABLE VALUE (Real Estate)

CASE NUMBER
176354

On receipt of "Certificate of Reasonable Value" or advice from the Veterans Administration that a "Certificate of Reasonable Value" will not be issued, we agree to forward to the appraiser the approved fee which we are holding for this purpose.

1. STATUS OF PROPERTY
- A. PROPOSED
- B. EXISTING, NOT PREVIOUSLY OCCUPIED
- [X] C. EXISTING, PREVIOUSLY OCCUPIED
- D. ALTERATIONS, IMPROVEMENTS, OR REPAIRS
- E. OWNED AND OCCUPIED BY VETERAN APPLICANT AS HIS HOME
- REFINANCING—RESIDENCE

2. CONSTRUCTION COMPLETED BEFORE DATE HEREOF
- A. WITHIN 12 CALENDAR MOS.
- B. MORE THAN 12 CALENDAR MOS.

3. NAME AND ADDRESS OF FIRM OR PERSON MAKING REQUEST (Complete mailing address. Include ZIP Code)

Carruth Mortgage Corporation
P.O. Box 53334
New Orleans, Louisiana 70153

4. PROPERTY ADDRESS (Include ZIP Code)

1325 Tarrington Drive
Marrero, Louisiana

5. TYPE OF PROPERTY [X] HOME ☐ FARM ☐ BUSINESS

6. NO. BLDGS. 1

7. NO. LIVING UNITS 1

8. LOT DIMENSIONS 50 x 100.01 / 100

9. DESCRIPTION									
[X] DETACHED	WOOD SIDING	CINDER BLOCK	SPLIT LEVEL	6 NO. ROOMS	[X] DINING ROOM	CAR GARAGE	[X] GAS	[X] CEN. AIR COND.	
SEMI-DET.	WOOD SHINGLE	STONE	% BASEMENT	3 BEDROOMS	1 KITCHEN	CAR CARPORT	UNDERGRD WIRE	TYPE HEAT. & FUEL GFWA	
ROW	ALUM. SIDING	[X] BRICK & BLOCK	[X] SLAB	2 BATHS	[X] FAMILY RM.	WATER (Public)	[X] SEWER (Public)	ROOFING DESCRIP.	
	ASB. SHINGLE	STUCCO	CRAWL SPACE	1/2 BATHS	[X] UTILITY RM.	WATER (Comm.)	SEWER (Comm.)	Seal Tab	
CONDOMINIUM	[X] BRICK VENEER	1 STORIES	10 YRS. EST. AGE	1 LIVING RM.	FIREPLACE	WATER (Ind.)	SEPTIC TANK		

10. LEGAL DESCRIPTION

Lot 7, Sq. 26
Valley Realty Company S/D, Extended
Parish of Jefferson, La.

11. TITLE LIMITATIONS, INCLUDING EASEMENTS, RESTRICTIONS, ENCROACHMENTS, HOMEOWNERS ASSOCIACATION ASSESS., ETC.

12. TYPE OF STREET PAVING
concrete
[X] CURB
[X] SIDEWALK
[X] STORM SEWER

13. VETERAN PURCHASER'S NAME AND ADDRESS (Complete mailing address. Include ZIP Code)

George Earl Smith
1325 Genius St.
Harahan, Louisiana 70123

14. REMOVABLE EQUIPMENT INCLUDED IN PURCHASE PRICE OR COST
- [X] RANGE OR COUNTER TOP UNIT
- [X] DISHWASHER
- ☐ REFRIGERATOR
- ☐ AUTOMATIC WASHER
- ☐ DRYER
- ☐ WALL-TO-WALL CARPETING
- [X] OTHER(S) (Specify) fenced, storage shed

15A. OCCUPANT'S NAME
Owners both work

15B. TELEPHONE NO.

16A. BROKER'S NAME
Contact Margie Reading of Star Realty – office 366-6446 or home 361-1410

16B. TELEPHONE NO.

17. DATE AND TIME AVAILABLE FOR INSPECTION MADE BY AM PM

18. KEYS AT (Address)

19. NAME OF OWNER
Frederick Jones

20. COMPLIANCE INSPECTIONS WILL BE OR WERE MADE BY
☐ FHA ☐ VA ☐ NONE MADE

21. NUMBER OF MASTER CERTIFICATE OF REASONABLE VALUE (If any)

22. PROPOSED SALES CONTRACT ATTACHED [X] YES ☐ NO

23. CONTRACT NO. PREVIOUSLY APPROVED BY VA THAT WILL BE USED

24A. NAME AND ADDRESS OF BUILDER (Include ZIP Code)

24B. TELEPHONE NO.

25A. NAME AND ADDRESS OF WARRANTOR (Include ZIP Code)

25B. TELEPHONE NO.

26. PLANS (Check one)
☐ FIRST SUBMISSION ☐ REPEAT CASE (If repeat case, complete Item 27)

27. PLANS PREVIOUSLY PROCESSED UNDER VA CASE NO.

28. ANNUAL REAL EST. TAXES (If exist. construction)
$ 40.00

29. COMMENTS ON SPECIAL ASSESSMENTS

30. SHOW BELOW: Shape, location, distance from nearest intersection, and street names. Mark N at north point.

1 3 t h.

Tarrington Drive

S T

EQUAL OPPORTUNITY IN HOUSING – NOTICE

Federal laws and regulations prohibit discrimination because of race, color, religion or national origin in the sale or rental or financing of residential property. Numerous state statutes and local ordinances also prohibit such discrimination.

Non-compliance with applicable antidiscrimination laws and regulations in respect to any property included in this request shall be a proper basis for refusal by the VA to do business with the violator and for refusal to appraise properties with which the violator is identified. Denial of participation in any program administered by the Federal Housing Administration because of such violation shall constitute basis for similar action by the VA.

CERTIFICATION REQUIRED ON CONSTRUCTION UNDER FHA SUPERVISION (Strike out inappropriate phrases in parentheses)

I hereby certify that plans and specifications and related exhibits, including acceptable FHA Change Orders, if any, supplied to VA in this case, are identical to those (submitted to) (to be submitted to) (approved by) FHA, and that FHA inspections (have been) (will be) made pursuant to FHA approval for mortgage insurance on the basis of proposed construction under Sec.

31A. NAME AND ADDRESS OF PROSPECTIVE LENDER (Include ZIP Code)
Carruth Mortgage Corporation
P.O. Box 53334, New Orleans, Louisiana 70153

31B. TELEPHONE NO. OF LENDER
885-4811

32. SALE PRICE OF PROPERTY
$ 38,500.00

33. REFINANCING AMT. OF PROPOSED LOAN
$

34. SIGNATURE OF PERSON AUTHORIZING THIS REQUEST
Donna Pillard *Donna Pillard*

35. TITLE
Ass't. Vice President

36. DATE
5/27/77

Federal statutes provide severe penalties for any fraud, intentional misrepresentation, or criminal connivance or conspiracy purposed to influence the issuance of any guaranty or insurance or the granting of any loan by the Administrator.

DO NOT WRITE IN THIS SPACE – FOR VETERANS ADMINISTRATION USE ONLY

37. DATE OF ASSIGNMENT

38. NAME OF APPRAISER

VA FORM 26-1805
NOV 1972

SUPERSEDES VA FORM 26-1805, OCT 1969, WHICH WILL NOT BE USED.

VA FILE COPY 1

Form Approved
OMB No. 76–R0231

The Reasonable Value as set forth herein is predicated upon conditions recited below as may be applicable.	VETERANS ADMINISTRATION **CERTIFICATE OF REASONABLE VALUE**	CASE NUMBER 176354

1. ESTABLISHED REASONABLE VALUE OF PROPERTY	2. REMAINING ECONOMIC LIFE OR PROPERTY IS ESTIMATED TO BE NOT LESS THAN	3. BUILDING SIZE *(Check and enter no.)*	4. EXPIRATION OF VALIDITY PERIOD
$ 38,500	45 YEARS	☐ CUBIC ☒ SQUARE 1534 FT.	12 9 77

5. STATUS OF PROPERTY
☐ A. PROPOSED ☐ B. PREVIOUSLY OCCUPIED ☒ C. PREVIOUSLY OCCUPIED ☐ D. ALTERATIONS, IMPROVEMTS. OR REPAIRS ☐ E. REFINANCING–RESIDENCE OWNED AND OCCUPIED BY VETERAN APPLICANT AS HIS HOME

6. CONSTRUCTION COMPLETED BEFORE DATE HEREOF
☐ A. WITHIN 12 CALENDAR MOS. ☒ B. MORE THAN 12 CALENDAR MOS.

7. NAME AND ADDRESS OF FIRM OR PERSON MAKING REQUEST *(Complete mailing address, Include ZIP Code)*

CARRUTH MORTGAGE CORPORATION
P. O. Box 53334
New Orleans, Louisiana   70153

8. PROPERTY ADDRESS *(Include ZIP Code)*
1325 Tarrington Drive
Marrero, LA   70072

9. TYPE OF PROPERTY
☒ HOME ☐ FARM ☐ BUSINESS

10. NO. BLDGS. 1

11. NO. LIVING UNITS 1

12. LOT DIMENSIONS
50 X 100.01/100

13. DESCRIPTION										
☒ DETACHED	WOOD SIDING	CINDER BLOCK	SPLIT LEVEL	6 NO. ROOMS	X DINING area	CAR GARAGE	X GAS	X CEN. AIR COND.		
SEMI-DET.	WOOD SHINGLE	STONE	% BASEMENT	3 BEDROOMS	1 KITCHEN	CAR CARPORT	UNDERGD. WIRE	TYPE HEAT. & FUEL GFWA		
ROW	ALUM. SIDING	BRICK & BLOCK X SLAB		2 BATHS	1 FAMILY. RM.	X WATER *(Public)* X	SEWER *(Public)*			
CONDOMINIUM	X ASB. SHINGLE BRICK VENEER 1	STUCCO STORIES 10	CRAWL SPACE YRS. EST. AGE 1	1/2 BATHS X LIVING RM.	UTILITY RM. FIREPLACE	WATER *(Comm.)* WATER *(Ind.)*	SEWER *(Comm.)* SEPTIC TANK	ROOFING DESCRIP. Seal Tab		

14. LEGAL DESCRIPTION
Lot 7, Square 26
Valley Realty Company S/D, Extended
Parish of Jefferson, Louisiana

15. TITLE IS IN FEE SIMPLE, FREE OF ALL ENCROACHMENTS, EASEMENTS AND OTHER LIMITATIONS WITH THE EXCEPTION OF THE FOLLOWING.

16. TYPE OF STREET PAVING
Con.
X CURB
X SIDEWALK
X STORM SEWER

17. VETERAN PURCHASER'S NAME AND ADDRESS *(Complete mailing address, Include ZIP Code)*

George E. Smith
1325 Genius Street
Harahan, Louisiana   70123

18. REMOVABLE EQUIPMENT IN VALUE
☒ RANGE OR COUNTER TOP UNIT ☒ DISHWASHER ☐ REFRIGERATOR
☐ AUTOMATIC WASHER ☐ DRYER ☐ WALL-TO-WALL CARPETING
☒ OTHER(S) *(Specify)* Fence, Storage Shed

GENERAL CONDITIONS

(NOTE: THE VETERANS ADMINISTRATION DOES NOT ASSUME ANY RESPONSIBILITY FOR THE CONDITION OF THE PROPERTY. THE CORRECTION OF ANY DEFECTS NOW EXISTING OR THAT MAY DEVELOP WILL BE THE RESPONSIBILITY OF THE PURCHASER.)

1. This certificate will remain effective as to any written contract of sale entered into by an eligible veteran within the validity period indicated.
2. This dwelling conforms with the Minimum Property Requirements prescribed by the Administrator of Veterans Affairs.
3. The aggregate of any loan secured by this property plus the amount of any assessment consequent on any special improvements as to which a lien or right to a lien shall exist against the property, except as provided in Item 29 below, may not exceed the reasonable value in Item 1 above.
4. Proposed construction shall be completed in accordance with the plans and specifications identified below, relating to both on-site and off-site improvements upon which this valuation is based and shall otherwise conform fully to the VA Minimum Property Requirements. Satisfactory completion must be evidenced by either
   A. VA Final Compliance Inspection Report (VA Form 26-1839), or
   B. VA Acceptance of FHA Compliance Inspection Reports (FHA Forms 2051) or other evidence of completion under FHA supervision applicable to proposed construction.
5. By contracting to sell property, as proposed construction or existing construction not previously occupied, to a veteran purchaser who is to be assisted in the purchase by a loan made, guaranteed, or insured by VA, the builder or other seller agrees to place any down payment received by the seller or agent of the seller in a special trust account as required by section 1806 of Title 38, U.S. Code.

SPECIFIC CONDITIONS *(Applicable when checked or completed)*

19. THE REASONABLE VALUE ESTABLISHED HEREIN FOR THE RELATED PROPERTY IS
☒ BASED UPON OBSERVATION OF THE PROPERTY IN ITS "AS IS" CONDITION
☐ PREDICATED UPON COMPLETION OF REPAIRS LISTED IN ITEM 22
☐ PREDICATED UPON COMPLETION OF CONSTRUCTION (If checked complete item 20)

20. PROPOSED CONSTRUCTION TO BE COMPLETED *(Identify plans, specifications and exhibits)*

21. INSPECTIONS REQUIRED
☐ FHA COMPLIANCE INSPECTIONS FOR PROPOSED CONSTRUCTION
☐ VA COMPLIANCE INSPECTIONS ☐ LENDER TO CERTIFY

22. REPAIRS TO BE COMPLETED

23. NAME OF COMPLIANCE INSPECTOR

24. HEALTH AUTHORITY APPROVAL – Execution of VA Form 26-6395 by the Health Authority indicating approval of the water supply and/or sewage disposal installation is required. (Approval by letter or Health Authority Form may be used.)

25. This document is subject to the provisions of Executive Orders 11246 and 11375, and the Rules and Regulations of the Secretary of Labor in effect this date, and VA Regulation 4390 through 4393, and also the provision of the certification executed by the builder, sponsor or developer named herein which is on file in this office.

26. TERMITE CERTIFICATE – The seller shall furnish the veteran-purchaser at no cost to the veteran prior to settlement a written statement (or certification) from a recognized exterminator that based on careful visual inspection of accessible areas and on sounding of accessible structural members, there is no evidence of termite ☒ or other wood-destroying insect infestation in the subject property, and, if such infestation previously existed, it has been corrected and any damage due to such infestation has also been corrected or alternatively been fully disclosed as follows . . . .

27. WARRANTY
☐ (If checked, complete Item 28)

28. NAME OF WARRANTOR

29. SEE GENERAL CONDITIONS ABOVE

30. OTHER REQUIREMENTS

"Since this property is located in a Special Flood Hazard Area, flood insurance will be required in accordance with VA Regulation 4326."

31. DATE 6 9 77

32. ADMINISTRATOR OF VETERANS AFFAIRS, BY *(Signature of authorized agent)* J. Brown

33. VA OFFICE NOLA

VA FORM NOV 1972 **26-1843**

REQUESTER'S COPY 2

SUBJECT PROPERTY

STREET SCENE

1325 Tarrington Drive
Marrero, Louisiana

Previous Editions Obsolete

FHA FORM NO. 2004-G Rev. 5/75 VA FORM NO. 26-8497 Rev. 5/75	VETERANS ADMINISTRATION and U. S. DEPARTMENT OF HOUSING AND URBAN DEVELOPMENT FEDERAL HOUSING ADMINISTRATION	FORM APPROVED OMB NO. 63-R1288

REQUEST FOR VERIFICATION OF EMPLOYMENT

INSTRUCTIONS: Lender – Complete Items 1 through 6. Have applicant complete Items 7 and 8. Forward the completed form directly to the employer named in Item 1.
Employer – Complete Items 9A through 15 and return form directly to lender named in Item 2.

PART I   REQUEST

1. TO: (Name and Address of Employer):

Clearview Mtr, Co., Inc.
d/b/a Marrero Texaco
900 Ave. C, Marrero, Louisiana 70072

2. FROM: (Name and Address of Lender):

Carruth Mortgage Corporation
P.O. Box 53334
New Orleans, Louisiana   70153

3. Signature of Lender *Marlene Malley*

I certify that this verification has been sent directly to the employer and has not passed through the hands of the applicant or any other interested party.

4. Title of Lender: Loan Processor

5. Date: 5/27/77

6. HUD-FHA or VA Number:

I have applied for a mortgage loan and stated that I am employed by you. My signature below authorizes verification of this information.

7. Name and Address of Applicant:

George Earl Smith
1325 Genius St.
Harahan, La.

8. Employee's Identification Number: 762-34-7788

George Earl Smith
Signature of applicant

PART II   VERIFICATION

9 A. Is applicant now employed by you?
☒ Yes ☐ No

9B. Present Base Pay is $ 1000.00
This amount is paid:
☐ Annually ☐ Hourly
☒ Monthly ☐ Other (Specify)
☐ Weekly

10A. Position or Job Title:
Manager of Texaco - Marrero

10B. Length of Applicant's employment:
2 years

11. TO BE COMPLETED BY MILITARY PERSONNEL ONLY.

Pay Grade:

9C. EARNINGS LAST 12 MONTHS

Amount $ 14,000.00

Basic Earnings $ 1,000.00

Normal Hours worked per Week: 40-50

Overtime Earnings $
☐ Regular
☐ Temporary

Other Income $
☐ Regular
☐ Temporary

10C. Probability of continued employment:
excellent

10D. Date Applicant left:

10E. Reason for leaving:

Base Pay	$
Rations	$
Flight or Hazard	$
Clothing	$
Quarters	$
Pro-Pay	$
Overseas or Combat	$

12. REMARKS:

guaranteed $400 per month for net profits

13. Signature of Employer:

Mimi Rhodes

14. Title of Employer:

Secretary-Treasurer

15. Date:

6/2/77

RETURN DIRECTLY TO LENDER

Previous Editions Obsolete

FHA FORM NO. 2004-G Rev. 5/75 VA FORM NO. 26-8497 Rev. 5/75	VETERANS ADMINISTRATION and U. S. DEPARTMENT OF HOUSING AND URBAN DEVELOPMENT FEDERAL HOUSING ADMINISTRATION	FORM APPROVED OMB NO. 63-R1288

REQUEST FOR VERIFICATION OF EMPLOYMENT

INSTRUCTIONS: Lender – Complete Items 1 through 6. Have applicant complete Items 7 and 8. Forward the completed
form directly to the employer named in Item 1.
Employer – Complete Items 9A through 15 and return form directly to lender named in Item 2.

PART I   REQUEST

1. TO: (Name and Address of Employer):	2. FROM: (Name and Address of Lender):
Clearview Motor Co., Inc. d/b/a Clearview Gulf 3112 Clearview, Metairie, La.	Carruth Mortgage Corporation P.O. Box 53334 New Orleans, Louisiana 70153

3. Signature of Lender: *Philyne Mille*	4. Title of Lender: Loan Processor	5. Date: 5/27/77	6. HUD-FHA or VA Number:

I certify that this verification has been sent directly to the employer and has not passed through the hands of the applicant or any other interested party.

I have applied for a mortgage loan and stated that I am employed by you. My signature below authorizes verification of this information.

7. Name and Address of Applicant:	8. Employee's Identification Number: 123-45-6789
Patricia Smith 1325 Genius Harahan, Louisiana	*Patricia Holmes Smith* Signature of applicant

PART II   VERIFICATION

9 A. Is applicant now employed by you? ☒ Yes ☐ No	10A. Position or Job Title: BOOKKEEPER	11. TO BE COMPLETED BY MILITARY PERSONNEL ONLY.	
9B. Present Base Pay is $ 600.00 This amount is paid: ☐ Annually ☐ Hourly ☒ Monthly ☐ Other (Specify) ☐ Weekly	10B. Length of Applicant's employment: 2 years	Pay Grade:	
		Base Pay	$
9C. EARNINGS LAST 12 MONTHS	10C. Probability of continued employment: excellent	Rations	$
Amount $ 7,200.		Flight or Hazard	$
Basic Earnings $ 600.00		Clothing	$
Normal Hours worked per Week: 35	10D. Date Applicant left:		
Overtime Earnings $ none ☐ Regular ☐ Temporary	10E. Reason for leaving:	Quarters	$
		Pro-Pay	$
Other Income $ none ☐ Regular ☐ Temporary		Overseas or Combat	$

12. REMARKS:

13. Signature of Employer: *Mimi Rhodes*	14. Title of Employer: Secretary-Treasurer	15. Date: 5/31/77

RETURN DIRECTLY TO LENDER

FHA FORM NO. 2004-F (Rev. 12/75) VA FORM NO. 26-8497a (Rev.12/75)	VETERANS ADMINISTRATION AND U. S. DEPARTMENT OF HOUSING AND URBAN DEVELOPMENT FEDERAL HOUSING ADMINISTRATION	OMB NO. 63-R0266 Approval Expires 4/76

REQUEST FOR VERIFICATION OF DEPOSIT

INSTRUCTIONS: LENDER - Complete Items 1 through 7. Have applicant complete Items 8 and 9. Forward directly to bank or other depository named in Item 1.
BANK or DEPOSITORY - Please complete Items 10 through 13. Return directly to Lender named in Item 2.

PART I - REQUEST

1. TO: (Name and Address of Bank or other Depository) Delivery Homestead 230 Carondelet New Orleans, Louisiana 70130	2. FROM: (Name and Address of Lender) Carruth Mortgage Corporation P.O. Box 53334 New Orleans, Louisiana 70153

3. I certify that this verification has been sent directly to the bank or other depository and has not passed through the hands of the applicant or any other interested party.

4. Title:	5. Date: 5/31/77
	6. FHA or VA Number:

Signature of Lender: *Marlyne Malley*   Loan Processor

7. STATEMENT OF APPLICANT:

7A. Name and Address of Applicant: George or Patricia Smith 1325 Genius St. Harahan, La.	7B. TYPE OF ACCOUNT	BALANCE	ACCOUNT NUMBER
	CHECKING	$	
	SAVINGS	$ $1500	124222
	CERTIFICATE OF DEPOSIT	$	

8. I have applied for a mortgage loan and stated that I maintain account(s) with the bank or other depository named in Item 1. My signature below authorizes that bank or other depository to furnish the lender named in Item 2 the information set forth in Part II. Your response is solely a matter of courtesy for which no responsibility is attached to your institution or any of your officers. *George Earl Smith* Signature of Applicant	7C. TYPE OF LOAN	BALANCE	ACCOUNT NUMBER
	SECURED	$	
	UNSECURED	$	
	9. Date:		

PART II - VERIFICATION

10A. Does Applicant have any outstanding loans ? ☐ Yes ☒ No (If Yes, enter total in Item 10B.)	CURRENT STATUS OF ACCOUNTS			
	11A. Is account less than two months old? (If Yes, give date account was opened in Item 12B)	CHECKING ☐ Yes ☐ No	SAVINGS ☒ Yes ☐ No	CERT. of DEPOSIT ☐ Yes ☐ No

10B. TYPE OF LOAN	MONTHLY PAYMENT	PRESENT BALANCE	11B. Date the account was opened.		3-3-77	
SECURED	$	$	11C. Present Balance	$	$1,432.64	$
UNSECURED	$	$	11D. Is account other than individual, e.g., Joint or Trust? (If Yes, explain in Remarks.)	☐ Yes ☐ No	☒ Yes ☐ No	☐ Yes ☐ No
10C. Payment Experience: ☐ Favorable ☐ Unfavorable (If Unfavorable, explain in Remarks.)			11E. Is account satisfactory?	☒ Yes ☐ No		

12. REMARKS:

The above information is provided in response to your request.

13A. Signature of Official of Bank or other Depository: *Sue Miller*	13B. Title: Branch Manager	13C. Date: 6/7/77

THIS INFORMATION IS FOR THE SOLE PURPOSE OF ASSISTING THE APPLICANT IN OBTAINING A MORTGAGE LOAN.

RETURN DIRECTLY TO LENDER

e43—16—83508-1   GPO

FHA FORM NO. 2004-F (Rev. 12/75) VA FORM NO. 26-8497a (Rev.12/75)	VETERANS ADMINISTRATION AND U. S. DEPARTMENT OF HOUSING AND URBAN DEVELOPMENT FEDERAL HOUSING ADMINISTRATION	OMB NO. 63-R0266 Approval Expires 4/76

REQUEST FOR VERIFICATION OF DEPOSIT

INSTRUCTIONS: LENDER - Complete Items 1 through 7. Have applicant complete Items 8 and 9. Forward directly to bank or other depository named in Item 1.
BANK or DEPOSITORY - Please complete Items 10 through 13. Return directly to Lender named in Item 2.

PART I - REQUEST

1. TO: (Name and Address of Bank or other Depository)

Commercial Bank & Trust
8120 Severn
Metairie, Louisiana 70002

2. FROM: (Name and Address of Lender)

Carruth Mortgage Corporation
P.O. Box 53334
New Orleans, Louisiana 70153

3. I certify that this verification has been sent directly to the bank or other depository and has not passed through the hands of the applicant or any other interested party.

Signature of Lender: *Marilyn Malley*

4. Title: Loan Processor

5. Date: 5/27/77

6. FHA or VA Number:

7. STATEMENT OF APPLICANT:

7A. Name and Address of Applicant

George or Patricia Smith
1325 Genius St.
Harahan, Louisiana

7B. TYPE OF ACCOUNT	BALANCE	ACCOUNT NUMBER
CHECKING	$ 400.00	1353630
SAVINGS	$	
CERTIFICATE OF DEPOSIT	$	

8. I have applied for a mortgage loan and stated that I maintain account(s) with the bank or other depository named in Item 1. My signature below authorizes that bank or other depository to furnish the lender named in Item 2 the information set forth in Part II. Your response is solely a matter of courtesy for which no responsibility is attached to your institution or any of your officers.

George Earl Smith
Signature of Applicant

7C. TYPE OF LOAN	BALANCE	ACCOUNT NUMBER
SECURED	$	
UNSECURED	$	NO LOANS LISTED

9. Date:

PART II - VERIFICATION

10A. Does Applicant have any outstanding loans?
☐ Yes ☒ No (If Yes, enter total in Item 10B.)

CURRENT STATUS OF ACCOUNTS			
11A. Is account less than two months old? (If Yes, give date account was opened in Item 12B)	**CHECKING** ☒ Yes ☐ No	**SAVINGS** ☐ Yes ☐ No	**CERT. of DEPOSIT** ☐ Yes ☐ No
11B. Date the account was opened.	7/75 846.33		
11C. Present Balance	$ 846.33	$	$
11D. Is account other than individual, e.g., Joint or Trust? (If Yes, explain in Remarks.)	☐ Yes ☒ No	☐ Yes ☐ No	☐ Yes ☐ No
11E. Is account satisfactory?	☒ Yes ☐ No		

10B. TYPE OF LOAN	MONTHLY PAYMENT	PRESENT BALANCE
SECURED	$	$
UNSECURED	$	$

10C. Payment Experience:
☐ Favorable
☐ Unfavorable (If Unfavorable, explain in Remarks.)

12. REMARKS:

The above information is provided in response to your request.

13A. Signature of Official of Bank or other Depository:

Melody Jones

13B. Title: Vice President

13C. Date: 5-31-77

THIS INFORMATION IS FOR THE SOLE PURPOSE OF ASSISTING THE APPLICANT IN OBTAINING A MORTGAGE LOAN.

RETURN DIRECTLY TO LENDER

e43—16—83508-1   GPO

NAME AND ADDRESS OF CREDIT BUREAU MAKING REPORT	TYPE OF REPORT:
CREDIT BUREAU SERVICES 1539 JACKSON AVENUE NEW ORLEANS, LA. 70130 01	FACT DATA JOINT INQUIRY CROSS REF 01-ID-05036888

CONFIDENTIAL *Factbilt* ® **REPORT**

FOR INQUIRER NO.   01--3027

BUREAU NO.	DATE RECEIVED	DATE MAILED
90--20700	5/31/77	06/08/77

DATE TRADE CLEARED	DATE EMP. VER. (MO.-YR.)	INCOME VERIFIED
6/08/77	6/77	x YES NO

CARRUTH MORTGAGE CORP
P. O. BOX 53334
NEW ORLEANS, LA. 70153

This information is furnished in response to an inquiry for evaluating credit risks. It has been obtained from reliable sources, the accuracy of which is not guaranteed. The inquirer agrees to indemnify the reporting bureau for any damage arising from misuse of this information, and this report is furnished in reliance upon that indemnity. It must be held in strict confidence, and must not be revealed to the subject reported upon. If adverse action is taken based on this report, the subject reported on must be so advised and the reporting agency identified.

FILE SINCE (MO.-YR.)	COMPUTER I.D. NO.	SOCIAL SECURITY NO.
7/76	01-19661857	762-34-7788

REPORT ON (SURNAME):   GIVEN NAME:

SMITH, PATRICIA

SPOUSE'S NAME:

GEORGE

ADDRESS:

1325 GENIUS ST. HARAHAN, LA. 70123   S 5/75 VER

COMPLETE TO HERE FOR TRADE REPORT AND SKIP TO CREDIT HISTORY

PRESENT EMPLOYER:	POSITION HELD:	SINCE: (MO.-YR.)	MONTHLY INCOME:
CLEARVIEW MTR CO INC	BOOKKPR	1/75	$ 600

COMPLETE TO HERE FOR SHORT REPORT AND SUMMARY REPORT AND SKIP TO CREDIT HISTORY

DATE OF BIRTH: (MO.-YR.) --/47	NUMBER OF DEPENDENTS INCLUDING SELF ⟶ -	OWNS OR BUYING HOME	RENTS HOME

FORMER ADDRESS: ---		FROM: (MO.-YR.)	TO: (MO.-YR.)

FORMER EMPLOYER: ---	POSITION HELD:	FROM: (MO.-YR.) TO: (MO.-YR.)	MONTHLY INCOME: $

SPOUSE'S EMPLOYER: ---	POSITION HELD:	SINCE: (MO.-YR.)	MONTHLY INCOME: $

CREDIT HISTORY   *(Complete this section for all reports)*

KIND OF BUSINESS AND IDENTIFICATION	DATE REPORTED	DATE OPENED	DATE OF LAST SALE	HIGHEST CREDIT	BALANCE	AMOUNT PAST DUE	TERMS AND USUAL MANNER OF PAYMENT	REMARKS
REPORTING BUREAU CERTIFIES COMPLIANCE WITH CONTRACTUAL REQUIREMENTS GOVERNING CHECK OF PUBLIC RECORDS AS WELL AS CREDIT INFORMATION INVOLVING SUBJECT								
B	6/77	-/75	-	7746	4343	00	I-1	IND
B	6/77	7/75		LOW 3			CHECKING	JNT
B	6/77	3/77					SAVINGS	JNT

MISCELLANEOUS INFORMATION--IND 5/77,
NO PUBLIC RECORDS FOUND AS OF 5-31-77

NAME AND ADDRESS OF CREDIT BUREAU MAKING REPORT

CREDIT BUREAU SERVICES
1539 JACKSON AVENUE
NEW ORLEANS, LA. 70130
01

TYPE OF REPORT:
FACT DATA   JOINT INQUIRY
CROSS REF 01-ID-19661857

BUREAU NO.	DATE RECEIVED	DATE MAILED
90--20700	5/31/77	06/08/77

CONFIDENTIAL *Factbilt* ® **REPORT**
FOR INQUIRER NO.   01--3027

CARRUTH MORTGAGE CORP
P.O. BOX 53334
NEW ORLEANS, LA. 70153

DATE TRADE CLEARED	DATE EMP. VER. (MO.-YR.)	INCOME VERIFIED
6/08/77	6/77	X YES NO

This information is furnished in response to an inquiry for evaluating credit risks. It has been obtained from reliable sources, the accuracy of which is not guaranteed. The inquirer agrees to indemnify the reporting bureau for any damage arising from misuse of this information, and this report is furnished in reliance upon this indemnity. It must be held in strict confidence, and must not be revealed to the subject reported upon. If adverse action is taken based on this report, the subject reported on must be so advised and the reporting agency identified.

FILE SINCE (MO.-YR.)	COMPUTER I.D. NO.	SOCIAL SECURITY NO.
9/71	01-05036888	123-45-6789

REPORT ON (SURNAME):   GIVEN NAME:

SMITH, GEORGE EARL

SPOUSE'S NAME:
PATRICIA

ADDRESS:
1325 GENIUS ST, HARAHAN, LA. 70123

S 5/75 VER

COMPLETE TO HERE FOR TRADE REPORT AND SKIP TO CREDIT HISTORY			
PRESENT EMPLOYER:	POSITION HELD:	SINCE: (MO.-YR.)	MONTHLY INCOME:
CLEARVIEW MTR CO INC	MANAGER	2/75	$1,000

COMPLETE TO HERE FOR SHORT REPORT AND SUMMARY REPORT AND SKIP TO CREDIT HISTORY			
DATE OF BIRTH: (MO.-YR.) 1/48	NUMBER OF DEPENDENTS INCLUDING SELF ➔ 2	— OWNS OR BUYING HOME	— RENTS HOME
FORMER ADDRESS: 729 RIVER., METAIRIE, LA.		FROM: (MO.-YR.) —	TO: (MO.-YR.) 5/75
FORMER EMPLOYER: MARRERO TEXACO CO	POSITION HELD: MANAGER	FROM: (MO.-YR.) — TO: (MO.-YR.) —	MONTHLY INCOME: $800
SPOUSE'S EMPLOYER:	POSITION HELD:	SINCE: (MO.-YR.)	MONTHLY INCOME: $

CREDIT HISTORY	(Complete this section for all reports)							
KIND OF BUSINESS AND IDENTIFICATION	DATE REPORTED	DATE OPENED	DATE OF LAST SALE	HIGHEST CREDIT	BALANCE	AMOUNT PAST DUE	TERMS AND USUAL MANNER OF PAYMENT	REMARKS

REPORTING BUREAU CERTIFIES COMPLIANCE WITH CONTRACTUAL REQUIREMENTS GOVERNING CHECK OF PUBLIC RECORDS AS WELL AS CREDIT INFORMATION INVOLVING SUBJECT

KIND OF BUSINESS	DATE REPORTED	DATE OPENED	DATE OF LAST SALE	HIGHEST CREDIT	BALANCE	AMOUNT PAST DUE	TERMS	REMARKS
A	6/77	9/67	7/75	291	00	00	R-1	IND
D	6/77	12/75	3/77	92	00	00	R-1	IND
D	6/77	3/73	2/77	387	93	00	R$10-1	IND
D	6/77	8/73	8/75	1014	454	00	I$28-1	IND
D	6/77	7/76	8/75	52	00	00	R-1	IND
E	6/77	-/75	-	7746	3232	00	I-1	IND
M	6/77	12/76	5/77	87	00	00	R-1	IND
F	6/77	12/76	4/77	150	00	00	R$15-1	IND
B	6/77	7/75	-	LOW 3			CHECKING	JNT
B	6/77	3/77	-				SAVINGS	JNT

MISCELLANEOUS INFORMATION--IND 5/77,
NO PUBLIC RECORDS FOUND AS OF 5-31-77

COMMON LANGUAGE FOR CONSUMER CREDIT

TERMS OF SALE

Open Account (30 days or 90 days) .... O
Revolving or Option (Open-end a/c) .... R
Instalment (fixed number of payments) I
    *Where the monthly payment is known, it should be
    shown as in the following examples: R$20 I$78

USUAL MANNER OF PAYMENT	TYPE ACCOUNT		
	O	R	I
Too new to rate; approved but not used	0	0	0
Pays (or paid) within 30 days of billing; pays accounts as agreed	1	1	1
Pays (or paid) in more than 30 days, but not more than 60 days, or not more than one payment past due	2	2	2
Pays (or paid) in more than 60 days, but not more than 90 days or two payments past due	3	3	3
Pays (or paid) in more than 90 days, but not more than 120 days, or three or more payments past due	4	4	4
Account is at least 120 days overdue but is not yet rated "9"	5	5	5
Making regular payments under Wage Earner Plan or similar arrangement	7	7	7
Repossession. (Indicate if it is a voluntary return of merchandise by the consumer.)	8	8	8
Bad debt; placed for collection; skip	9	9	9

KIND OF BUSINESS CLASSIFICATION

Code	Kind of Business
A	Automotive
B	Banks
C	Clothing
D	Department and Variety
F	Finance
G	Groceries
H	Home Furnishings
I	Insurance
J	Jewelry and Cameras
K	Contractors
L	Lumber Building Material, Hardware
M	Medical and Related Health
N	National Credit Card Companies and Air Lines
O	Oil Companies
P	Personal Services Other Than Medical
Q	Mail Order Houses
R	Real Estate and Public Accommodations
S	Sporting Goods
T	Farm and Garden Supplies
U	Utilities and Fuel
V	Government
W	Wholesale
X	Advertising
Y	Collection Services
Z	Miscellaneous

A in remarks section of credit history indicates item reported via **Auto Data** (automatically reported ledger information via tape)

INQUIRIES LISTED As an aid to subscribers, inquiries involving the subject are listed. Many of these are received from national credit grantors who have no local credit offices from which credit history information can be obtained. Examples of this type of inquirer by Kind of Business Classification are C, FM, O, OC, R, V, CBR, CSI. In addition inquiries from other credit bureaus are identified by the abbreviation ACB. LOCAL INQUIRIES ARE UPDATED ON REVISED REPORTS.

**Competent
Mortgage
Counseling**

CARRUTH Mortgage Corporation

3601 I-10 SERVICE ROAD   METAIRIE, LOUISIANA   PHONE 885-4811

MAILING ADDRESS
P. O. BOX 53334
NEW ORLEANS, LA. 70153

June 1 , 1977

Chief, Examining Section
Loan Guaranty Division
Veterans Administration
701 Loyola Avenue
New Orleans, Louisiana

Re: George Earl Smith
Case# 176354
Lot 7, Sq. 26
S/D Valley Realty Co. S/D Extended

Gentlemen:

In order that you may issue your Certificate of Commitment for the
above captioned case, we enclose herewith the following documents:

(X) Certificate of Eligibility (1870)
(X) Application for Home Loan Guaranty (1802)
( ) Copy of Committee Appraisal # CA_____
(X) Credit Report
(X) Employment Verification
(X) Bank Verification of Deposit
(X) Letter re: No Commitment To Lend
( ) Borrower's Statement of Liability
(X) Purchase Agreement
(X) Copy of VA Certificate of Reasonable Value
( ) Veterans Certification of Nondiscrimination
(X) Rating letter
( )
(X) ECOA Notice
( )

Your attention to this matter will be greatly appreciated.

Yours very truly,

Christine M. Pearse

Christine M. Pearse
Supervisor

Enc.
CMC 4

SET UP DATE __5-31-77__

RESET _____

CARRUTH MORTGAGE CORPORATION   RESET _____

PROCESSING CHECK SHEET

APPLICANT: ___George Earl Smith___   CO-APPLICANT ___Patricia___

PROPERTY ADDRESS: __1325 Tarrington Dr.__   TYPE: ____VA____

_____Marrero, Louisiana_____   TERM: __30 years__

DATE OF APPLICATION: __May 24, 1977__   S.P.: __$38,500__

SOURCE: __Homes Inc.__   LOAN: __$38,500.00__

X	REQUIRED ITEMS		DATE REQUESTED	DATE RECEIVED	REMARKS
	APPRAISAL & APPLIC. FEES			5/24/77	
	PURCHASE AGREEMENT			5/24/77	
	PLANS & SPECS. (PROPOSED)				
	TITLES (EXISTING)			5/31/77	
	CREDIT REPORT Shirley		5/31/77	6/8/77	ok
	EMPLOYMENT	APPLICANT	5/27/77	6/2/77	0k
	VERIFICATIONS	CO-APPLICANT	5/27/77	5/31/77	ok
	PREVIOUS	APPLICANT			
	EMPLOYMENT	CO-APPLICANT			
	VERIFICATIONS				
	UNION VERIFICATION				
		1. Commercial	5/27/77	5/31/77	0k
	DEPOSIT	2. Delivery	5/31/77	6/7/77	0k
	VERIFICATIONS	3.			
		4.			
	APPRAISAL - TYPE				
	FHA APPRAISAL ACKNOWLEDGEMENT LETTER SENT TO APPLICANT				
	APPRAISAL SENT TO LISTING AND SELLING AGENT (Where permitted)				
	DIVORCE DECREES/DEATH CERT.				
	W-2 FORMS				
	FIN. & P & L STATEMENTS				
	PROP. INSP. & PHOTOGRAPHS		5/31/77	6/4/77	
	INS. PREFERENCE LETTER				
	CUSTOMER MEMO			5/31/77	
	CERTIFICATE OF ELIGIBILITY		5/24/77	5/31/77	
	DD-802 (FHA IN SERVICE)				
	DD-214				
	DD-1747				
	STATEMENT OF SERVICE				
		1.			
	MORTGAGE	2.			
	RATING	3.			
	LETTERS	4.			
	LOAN APPROVAL		6/9/77	6/15/77	

CMC 89
(Rev. 3/77)

VETERANS ADMINISTRATION **APPLICATION FOR HOME LOAN GUARANTY**	1. VA LOAN NUMBER 176354	2. LENDER'S LOAN NO. 13-760531

3. NAME AND PRESENT ADDRESS OF VETERAN (Include ZIP Code)	5A. VETERAN: If you do not wish to complete Items 5B or 5C, please initial here	INITIALS

George Earl Smith
1325 Genius St
Harahan, Louisiana 70123

5B. RACE/NATIONAL ORIGIN — ☐ AMERICAN INDIAN ALASKAN NATIVE ☐ ASIAN, PACIFIC ISLANDER ☐ BLACK ☐ HISPANIC ☒ WHITE ☐ OTHER (Specify)

5C. SEX — ☐ FEMALE ☒ MALE

4. NAME AND ADDRESS OF LENDER (Include No., street or rural route, city, P.O., State and ZIP Code)

Carruth Mortgage Corporation
P.O. Box 53334
New Orleans, Louisiana 70153

6A. SPOUSE OR OTHER CO-BORROWER If you do not wish to complete Items 6B or 6C, please initial here INITIALS

6B. RACE/NATIONAL ORIGIN — ☐ AMERICAN INDIAN ALASKAN NATIVE ☐ ASIAN, PACIFIC ISLANDER ☐ BLACK ☐ HISPANIC ☒ WHITE ☐ OTHER (Specify)

6C. SEX — ☒ FEMALE ☐ MALE

7. PROPERTY ADDRESS INCLUDING NAME OF SUBDIVISION, LOT AND BLOCK NO., AND ZIP CODE	8A. LOAN AMOUNT	8B. INTEREST RATE	8C. PROPOSED MATURITY

1325 Tarrington Dr.
Lot 7, Sq. 26
Valley Realty Company S/D Extended
Marrero, Jefferson Parish, La.

8A. $ 38,500 8B. 8½ % 8C. 30 YRS. MOS.

DISCOUNT: (Only if veteran to pay under 38 U.S.C. 1803 (c) (3) (C) or (D)) 8D. PERCENT % 8E. AMOUNT $

The undersigned veteran and lender hereby apply to the Administrator of Veterans' Affairs for Guaranty of the loan described here under Section 1810, Chapter 37, Title 38, United States Code to the full extent permitted by the veteran's available entitlement and severally agree that the Regulations promulgated pursuant to Chapter 37, and in effect on the date of the loan shall govern the rights, duties, and liabilities of the parties.

SECTION I—PURPOSE, AMOUNT, TERMS OF AND SECURITY FOR PROPOSED LOAN

9. PURPOSE OF LOAN–TO:
☒ PURCHASE EXISTING HOME PREVIOUSLY OCCUPIED ☐ CONSTRUCT A HOME–PROCEEDS TO BE PAID OUT DURING CONSTRUCTION ☐ PURCHASE EXISTING HOME NOT PREVIOUSLY OCCUPIED ☐ PURCHASE NEW CONDOMINIUM UNIT ☐ PURCHASE EXISTING CONDOMINIUM UNIT

10. TITLE WILL BE VESTED IN: ☐ VETERAN ☒ VETERAN AND SPOUSE ☐ OTHER (Specify)

11. LIEN ☒ 1ST MORTGAGE ☐ OTHER (Specify)

12. ESTATE WILL BE ☒ FEE SIMPLE ☐ LEASEHOLD (Show explanation data)

13. IS THERE A MANDATORY HOMEOWNERS ASSOCIATION? ☐ YES ☒ NO (If "YES", complete Item 14F)

14. ESTIMATED TAXES, INSURANCE AND ASSESSMENTS		15. ESTIMATED MONTHLY PAYMENT	
A. ANNUAL TAXES	$ 36.00	A. PRINCIPAL AND INTEREST	$ 296.07
B. AMOUNT OF HAZARD INSURANCE ON SECURITY	32,750.00	B. TAXES AND INSURANCE DEPOSITS	20.92
C. ANNUAL HAZARD INSURANCE PREMIUMS	215.00	C. OTHER Flood Insurance	6.00
D. ANNUAL SPECIAL ASSESSMENT PAYMENT			
E. UNPAID SPECIAL ASSESSMENT BALANCE			
F. ANNUAL MAINTENANCE ASSESSMENT		D. TOTAL $	322.99

SECTION II—PERSONAL AND FINANCIAL STATUS OF VETERAN

16. PLEASE CHECK THE APPROPRIATE BOX(ES). IF ONE OR MORE ARE CHECKED, ITEMS 18B, 21, 22 AND 23 MUST INCLUDE INFORMATION CONCERNING THE VETERAN'S SPOUSE (OR FORMER SPOUSE IF BOX "D" IS CHECKED). IF NO BOXES ARE CHECKED, NO INFORMATION CONCERNING THE SPOUSE NEED BE FURNISHED.

☒ A. THE SPOUSE WILL BE JOINTLY OBLIGATED WITH THE VETERAN ON THE LOAN

☒ B. THE VETERAN IS RELYING ON THE SPOUSE'S INCOME AS A BASIS FOR REPAYMENT OF THE LOAN

☐ C. THE VETERAN IS MARRIED AND THE PROPERTY TO SECURE THE LOAN IS LOCATED IN A COMMUNITY PROPERTY STATE

☐ D. THE VETERAN IS RELYING ON ALIMONY, CHILD SUPPORT, OR SEPARATE MAINTENANCE PAYMENTS FROM A SPOUSE OR FORMER SPOUSE AS A BASIS FOR REPAYMENT OF THE LOAN

17A. MARITAL STATUS OF VETERAN	17B. MARITAL STATUS OF CO-BORROWER OTHER THAN VETERAN'S SPOUSE	17C. MONTHLY CHILD SUPPORT OBLIGATION	17D. MONTHLY ALIMONY OBLIGATION	18A. AGE OF VETERAN	18B. AGE OF SPOUSE	18C. AGE(S) OF DEPENDENT(S)
☒ MARRIED ☐ UNMARRIED ☐ SEPARATED	☐ MARRIED ☐ UNMARRIED ☐ SEPARATED	NONE	NONE	29	29	7 years

19. NAME AND ADDRESS OF NEAREST LIVING RELATIVE (Include telephone number, if available)	20A. MONTHLY PAYMENT ON RENTED PREMISES VETERAN NOW OCCUPIES	20B. UTILITIES INCLUDED?
Ray Smith 729 Sidewalk Ave., Metairie, La.,	$ 107.63	☐ YES ☒ NO

21. ASSETS		22. LIABILITIES (Itemize all debts)		
		NAME OF CREDITOR	MO. PAYMENT	BALANCE
A. CASH (Including deposit on purchase)	$ 2778.97			
B. SAVINGS BONDS–OTHER SECURITIES		Pennamco – to be rented	$ 107.63	$ 11496.21
C. REAL ESTATE OWNED	30000.00	First Federal Bank	215.19	3232.00
D. AUTO	2000.00	Holmes	28.00	454.00
E. FURNITURE AND HOUSEHOLD GOODS	8000.00	Maison Blanche	30 day	
F. OTHER (Use separate sheet, if necessary)	65.00			
G. TOTAL	$ 42843.97	JOB-RELATED EXPENSE (summer only) 108.33		
		TOTAL	$ 459.15	$ 15275.21

23. INCOME AND OCCUPATIONAL STATUS			24. ESTIMATED TOTAL COST	
ITEM	VETERAN	SPOUSE	ITEM	AMOUNT
			A. PURCHASE EXISTING HOME	$ 38,500.00
A. OCCUPATION	Manager	Bookkeeper	B. ALTERATIONS, IMPROVEMENTS, REPAIRS	
			C. CONSTRUCTION	
B. NAME OF EMPLOYER	Clearview Motor Co. Inc	Clearview Motor Co., Inc.	D. LAND (If acquired separately)	
			E. PURCHASE OF CONDOMINIUM UNIT	
C. NUMBER OF YEARS EMPLOYED	2 years	2 years	F. PREPAID ITEMS	340.84
			G. ESTIMATED CLOSING COST	1100.16
D. GROSS PAY	MONTHLY $1400. HOURLY $	MONTHLY $600. HOURLY $	H. DISCOUNT (Only if veteran permitted to pay)	
			I. TOTAL COST (Add Items 24A through 24H)	40040.00
E. OTHER INCOME (Disclosure of child support, alimony and separate maintenance income is optional)	Future Rental $ 200.00	$	J. LESS CASH FROM VETERAN	1540.00
			K. LESS OTHER CREDITS	
			L. AMOUNT OF LOAN	$ 38,500.00

NOTE - IF LAND ACQUIRED BY SEPARATE TRANSACTION, COMPLETE ITEMS 25A AND 25B.	25A. DATE ACQUIRED	25B. UNPAID BALANCE $

READ CERTIFICATIONS ON REVERSE CAREFULLY

VA FORM JUN 1977 **26-1802a** SUPERSEDES VA FORM 26-1802a, DEC 1975, WHICH WILL NOT BE USED VA 2

TERMS OF COMMITMENT

The documents submitted in connection with the loan described on the face of this certificate have been examined and the loan has been determined to be eligible under Chapter 37, Title 38, U.S.C., and the regulations effective thereunder.

Upon receipt of a duly executed "Certificate of Loan Disbursement"* showing full compliance with the applicable regulations, the Administrator will issue: A Loan Guaranty Certificate as indicated on the face of this Certificate; subject to any adjustment necessary under Section 36:4303(g) of the Regulations upon ascertainment of the exact principal amount of the loan, or upon submission of the loan disbursement report under Section 36:4305 thereof.

In the case of a joint loan as defined in Section 36:4307 of the Regulations the portion of such loan eligible for guaranty shall be as provided therein. This Certificate of Commitment will expire and will be invalid 6 months from the date hereof, unless the loan described herein is closed prior to such expiration date. The expiration date is not applicable if this Certificate relates to a loan which was heretofore closed and so reported to VA.

*If the loan described on the face of this Certificate is made by the lending institution named herein this certificate need not be returned to the VA. Otherwise this certificate or a copy of the agreement assigning this certificate must accompany the Certificate of Loan Disbursement.

VETERANS ADMINISTRATION **CERTIFICATE OF COMMITMENT**	1. VA LOAN NUMBER LH 176354	2. LENDER'S LOAN NO. 13-760531
3. NAME AND PRESENT ADDRESS OF VETERAN *(Include ZIP Code)* George Earl Smith 1325 Genius Drive Harahan, Louisiana 70123		
4. ISSUED TO: *(Name and address of lender)* CARRUTH MORTGAGE CORPORATION P. O. Box 53334 New Orleans, Louisiana 70153	X	X X
	X	

5. PROPERTY ADDRESS INCLUDING NAME OF SUBDIVISION, LOT AND BLOCK NO., AND ZIP CODE	6A. LOAN AMOUNT	6B. INTEREST RATE	6C. PROPOSED MATURITY
1325 Tarrington Drive Lot 7, Square 26 Valley Realty Co. S/D Extended Marrero, Jefferson Parish, Louisiana 70072	$ 38,500 DISCOUNT ▶	8½ % 6D. PERCENT %	30 YRS. 0 MOS. 6E. AMOUNT $

PERCENT OF GUARANTY
45 %

FOR VA USE ONLY ▶

(NOTE: To be completed by VA and returned to Lender.)

☐ CERTIFICATION OF ACTIVE DUTY STATUS AS OF DATE OF NOTE REQUIRED.

THE TERMS OF THIS COMMITMENT ARE ON THE REVERSE

Administrator of Veterans Affairs

By: Mary C. Wilson
(AUTHORIZED AGENT)

Vaso Nola
(ISSUING OFFICE)

6/15/77
(DATE)

VA FORM JUN 1977 **26-1866a**   SUPERSEDES VA FORM 26-1866a, DEC 1975, WHICH WILL NOT BE USED.   LENDER'S COPY   3

Competent
Mortgage
Counseling

CARRUTH Mortgage Corporation

3601 I-10 SERVICE ROAD   METAIRIE, LOUISIANA   PHONE 885-4811

MAILING ADDRESS
P. O. BOX 53334
NEW ORLEANS, LA. 70153

June 15, 1977

George & Patricia Smith
1325 Genius Street
Harahan, La. 70123

> Re: 1325 Tarrington Drive
> Marrero, La.

Dear Customers:

We are pleased to advise that your application for loan on the above referenced property has been approved by the <u>Veterans Administration</u>.

This approval was based upon the information you furnished at the time your application was taken and our subsequent review of your financial standing and credit rating.

As you were previously advised, Flood Insurance under the National Flood Insurance Program is a requirement for the life of your loan. If you have not already made arrangements with your insurance agent to have your flood insurance policy presented to the closing attorney at the time of your Act of Sale, please do so immediately.

This mortgage approval is subject to the condition(s) checked on the attached page. As soon as these conditions have been met and a date has been set for the Act of Sale, you will be notified in writing of the time and place.

Yours very truly,

Barbara Blanchette by cp

Barbara Blanchette
Manager

BB/mm
cc: Edith Sims
    Homes, Inc.
    Margie Reading
    Star Realty, Inc.

CMC 99A (Flood) HO

Date: 5-24-77

Carruth Mortgage Corporation
P.O. Box 53334
New Orleans, La.   70153

RE: NO COMMITMENT TO LEND

I have applied to you for a loan and you have made a commitment
which you have advised me is purely tentative and is subject to
approval by the Federal Housing Administration or Veterans
Administration and/or your investor.

I understand the present interest rate on this type of loan is
_____8_____% per annum.   In the event the interest rate is
increased prior to passing of the Act of Sale, I realize that
my loan will be closed at the increased interest rate.   In the
event that I elect not to close because of the foregoing, the
only adverse consequence I would realize as far as Carruth
Mortgage Corporation is concerned would be the loss of the
amount paid to you for the appraisal, credit report, and any

other out-of-pocket expenses.

Yours very truly,

George Earl Smith

Patricia Holmes Smith

CMC #8
Rev. 8/77

Competent
Mortgage
Counseling

CARRUTH Mortgage Corporation

3601 I-10 SERVICE ROAD   METAIRIE, LOUISIANA   PHONE 885-4811

MAILING ADDRESS
P. O. BOX 53334
NEW ORLEANS, LA. 70153

June 08, 1977

Patricia & George Smith
1325 Genius Street
Harahan, Louisiana   70123

RE: 1325 Tarrington Drive
Marrero, Louisiana

Dear Customers:

This interest rate on FHA/VA loans has been increased from 8% to $8\frac{1}{2}$%, hence your loan will close at the $8\frac{1}{2}$% rate, unless the rate is further increased before your Act of Sale. Due to this, the principal and interest portion of your total monthly payment (based on $8\frac{1}{2}$%) will be $296.07.

At the time you made application, your ESTIMATED ANNUAL PERCENTAGE RATE given to you on our Customer Memo was 8.25. However, based on a $8\frac{1}{2}$% interest rate, the ESTIMATED ANNUAL PERCENTAGE RATE will be 8.75.

Please sign the copy of this letter where indicated and return to us in the enclosed self addressed envelope.

Yours very truly,

CARRUTH MORTGAGE CORPORATION

Harold A. Glazer
Senior Vice President

HAG/dp

This is to acknowledge receipt of your letter dated 6/08/77 concerning increase in interest and ESTIMATED ANNUAL PERCENTAGE RATE, and we accept the terms.

_____   _____
          Applicant   Co-Applicant

CARRUTH MORTGAGE CORPORATION
P. O. BOX 53334
NEW ORLEANS, LOUISIANA 70153
Phone (504) 885-4811

CLOSING DATA SHEET
CMC CASE # 13-760531

June 17, 1977
DATE

TO: John Doe, Attorney   TITLE COMPANY: Green Title Insurance Corp.

MORTGAGOR(S): Patricia Holmes wife of/and George Earl Smith
MARITAL STATUS: Attorney to obtain
REALTOR: Homes, Inc.   CONTRACTOR:

SELLER-OWNER: Frederick Jones   SURVEY FROM: Attorney

MORTGAGEE: CARRUTH MORTGAGE CORPORATION, AN ARKANSAS CORPORATION

LEGAL DESCRIPTION: LOT 7   SQ. 26   SUBDIVISION Valley Realty Co. S/D Extended

STREET ADDRESS 1325 Tarrington Drive   CITY Marrero   STATE Louisiana
CHANGES IN TERMS OF SALE & LOAN RECITED BELOW ARE NOT TO BE MADE (SEE REVERSE
ITEM #2)

SALE PRICE: $ 38,500.00 CONTRACT PRICE: $_____ SALE PRICE OF LOT: $_____

LOAN AMOUNT: $ 38,500.00 RATE 8 1/2 % TERM 30 YRS. MO. PRIN. & INT. $ 296.07
Purchaser to pay closing costs & prepaid items.   ATTORNEY TO VERIFY
HAZARD INSURANCE AGENT/AGENCY: Will Advise   COVERAGE: $ 32,750.00
   FIRST MORTGAGEE CLAUSE
      (X) CARRUTH MORTGAGE CORPORATION, P. O. BOX 53334, NEW ORLEANS, LA. 70153

FLOOD INSURANCE AGENT/AGENCY: Will Advise   COVERAGE: $ 32,750.00
   FIRST MORTGAGEE CLAUSE
      (X) CARRUTH MORTGAGE CORPORATION, P. O. BOX 53334, NEW ORLEANS, LA. 70153

NOTE PREPARED ON:
   (X) VA FORM 26-6316a   ( ) FHA FORM 9123   ( ) FNMA/FHLMC UNIFORM INSTRUMENT

MORTGAGE PREPARED ON:
   (X) VA FORM 26-6316b   ( ) FHA FORM 2123m V-L   ( ) FNMA/FHLMC UNIFORM INST.

PREPAYMENT CLAUSE IN THE CONVENTIONAL NOTE SHOULD BE COMPLETED AS FOLLOWS:
_____ DURING EACH OF THE FIRST THREE LOAN YEARS
_____ DURING EACH OF THE FOURTH AND FIFTH LOAN YEARS
THE ENTIRE PREPAYMENT PARAGRAPH OF THE NOTE SHOULD BE INCORPORATED IN THE CON-
VENTIONAL MORTGAGE FORM.

THE FUNDS FOR ITEMS MARKED BELOW WILL BE COLLECTED AT CLOSING AND FORWARDED TO
CARRUTH MORTGAGE CORORATION.
(X) PHOTOGRAPHS _____ By Seller _____ $ 8.00
(X) AMORTIZATION SCHEDULE _____ By Seller _____ $ 1.50
(X) CREDIT REPORT FEE _____ $ 7.20
(X) APPRAISAL FEE _____ $ 55.00
(X) ORIGINATION FEE _____ 1% _____ $ 385.00
( ) 2 MO. FHA/PMI MTG. INS. _____ @ _____ PER MO. $_____
(X) 2 MO. FLOOD INS. ESCROW _____ @ _____ PER MO. $_____
(X) HAZARD INSURANCE PREMIUM PAYABLE TO ISSUING
      INSURANCE AGENCY _____ $_____
(X) DISCOUNT PAID BY Seller 4 1/4 ____% OF LOAN
      (ATTORNEY TO VERIFY COMPUTATIONS) _____ $ 1732.50
(X) ACCRUED INTEREST IF APPLICABLE — ATTORNEY TO COMPUTE (SEE
      ITEM #3 ON REVERSE SIDE) _____ $_____
(X) ESCROW FUNDS FOR TAXES FOR CURRENT YEAR FROM SELLER & PURCHASER,
      IF NOT BEING PAID BY ATTORNEY.
( ) _____ OF 1%, FIRST YEARS PRIVATE MORTGAGE INSURANCE PREMIUM $_____
( ) PRIVATE MORTGAGE INSURANCE REVIEW FEE _____ $_____
( ) FNMA UNDERWRITING FEE _____ $_____
( ) PROPERTY INSPECTION FEE _____ $_____

ALLOW CREDIT TO: Purchaser _____ FOR FUNDS IN THE AMOUNT OF $ 65.00 _____ PAID
TO CARRUTH MORTGAGE CORPORATION. (C.R.-$10.00, Appr.-$55)

ALL CONDITIONS OF VA CRV AND VA CERTIFICATE OF COMMITMENT AND/OR FHA CONDITIONAL
COMMITMENT WITH ATTACHMENT(S) AND FHA FIRM COMMITMENT MUST BE SATISFIED PRIOR
TO CLOSING THIS LOAN.

ENCLOSURES:
(X) PURCHASE CONTRACT
(X) VA CERTIFICATE OF REASONABLE VALUE
(X) VA CERTIFICATE OF COMMITMENT
(X) VA FORM 1876 FOR SIGNATURE OF VETERAN
( ) DIVORCE DECREES
( ) WARRANTY OF COMPLETION OF CONSTRUCTION
      (MUST BE COMPLETED)
(X) HUD-1 FORM AND ADDENDUM
(X) LOAN CLOSING SETTLEMENT SHEET CMC
      FORM 118 (MUST BE COMPLETED)
( ) FHA FIRM COMMITMENT FOR MORTGAGOR'S
      SIGNATURE (2)
(X) CMC 218

( ) ATTACHMENT "A" FIRM COMMITMENT
      WITH CONDITIONS
( ) FHA CONDITIONAL COMMITMENT
( ) ATTACHMENT "A", "B" OF CONDI-
      TIONAL COMMITMENT
(X) TERMITE STATEMENT CMC FORM 33
      FOR SIGNATURES
( ) CONVENTIONAL NOTE & MORTGAGES
( ) BUILDER & PURCHASER AFFIDAVIT
(X) CMC 157   ( ) FNMA 1009
(X) CMC 176   ( ) CMC 1009A
( ) PREVIOUS TITLE EVIDENCE

FINAL/REPAIR INSPECTION REQUIRED: ( ) YES (X) NO: TERMITE CERTIF. REQUIRED: (X) YES ( ) NO

ADDITIONAL INSTRUCTIONS & REMARKS: Flood Insurance policy must be submitted
with closing papers. Equipment in value must be included in mortgage.

Lawyers Title Insurance Corporation

A STOCK COMPANY
Home Office—Richmond, Virginia

COMMITMENT FOR TITLE INSURANCE

SCHEDULE A

1. Effective date   July 14, 1977

   Case No. 98765

2. Policy or policies to be issued:

   (a) ALTA Owner's Policy—Form B-1970 (Rev. 10-17-70)
   Proposed insured:

   Amount $_____

   Patricia Holmes, wife of/and
   George Earl Smith

   (b) ALTA Loan Policy, 1970 (Rev. 10-17-70)
   Proposed insured:

   Amount $ 38,500

   Carruth Mortgage Corporation

   (c)
   Proposed insured:

   Amount $_____

3. Title to the   fee simple   estate or interest in the land
   described or referred to in this Commitment is at the effective date hereof vested in:

   Frederick Jones

4. The land referred to in this Commitment is described as follows:

   1325 Tarrington St.
   Marrero, Louisiana

   Lot 7, Square 26
   Valley Realty Company S/D Extended
   Marrero, Jefferson Parish, La.

SPECIMEN COPY

Countersigned at New Orleans, La.

Paul Romero
Authorized Officer or Agent

Schedule A—Page 1—No.

Form No. 91-88 (SCH. A)
035-1-088-0099

(over)
ORIGINAL

Lawyers Title Insurance Corporation
A Stock Company
Home Office ~ Richmond , Virginia

COMMITMENT FOR TITLE INSURANCE

LAWYERS TITLE INSURANCE CORPORATION, a Virginia corporation. herein called the Company, for valuable consideration, hereby commits to issue its policy or policies of title insurance, as identified in Schedule A, in favor of the proposed Insured named in Schedule A, as owner or mortgagee of the estate or interest covered hereby in the land described or referred to in Schedule A, upon payment of the premiums and charges therefor; all subject to the provisions of Schedules A and B and to the Conditions and Stipulations hereof.

This Commitment shall be effective only when the identity of the proposed Insured and the amount of the policy or policies committed for have been inserted in Schedule A hereof by the Company, either at the time of the issuance of this Commitment or by subsequent endorsement.

This Commitment is preliminary to the issuance of such policy or policies of title insurance and all liability and obligations hereunder shall cease and terminate six (6) months after the effective date hereof or when the policy or policies committed for shall issue, whichever first occurs, provided that the failure to issue such policy or policies is not the fault of the Company. This Commitment shall not be valid or binding until countersigned by an authorized officer or agent.

IN WITNESS WHEREOF, the Company has caused this Commitment to be signed and sealed, to become valid when countersigned by an authorized officer or agent of the Company, all in accordance with its By-Laws. This Commitment is effective as of the date shown in Schedule A as "Effective Date."

Lawyers Title Insurance Corporation

Robert C. Dawson

President

Attest:

Roy Brushead

Secretary.

SQUARE 26
VALLEY REALITY Co. SUBD. EXT.
JEFFERSON PARISH, LA.

EAST BOUNDARY OF SUBD.

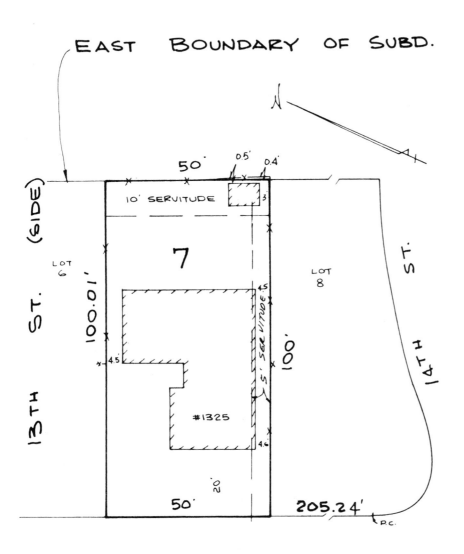

Regular Flood Insurance Program
Application and Declarations Form
(For Use Only With the Flood Insurance Policy)

R REGULAR FLOOD
INSURANCE PROGRAM

Insurance Companies Members of
National Flood Insurers Association
(In Cooperation with the U.S. Government)

Insurance is provided only (1) against the peril of flood as defined in the policy to which this form is attached, (2) with respect to those items specifically described herein and for which a specific amount of insurance is shown below, and (3) for the policy term specified below; and, unless otherwise provided, all conditions and provisions of this form and of the policy to which it is attached shall apply separately to each item covered.

Important Notices: This Policy does not cover loss resulting from a flood or mudslide occurrence already in progress on the date of this application. It is a condition of this insurance that property is not in violation of any Flood Plain Law or Ordinance.

DUMMY POLICY

Space for Agent's Name and Mailing Address (Sticker)

Republic Insurance Agency
P. O. Box 8861
Metairie, La   70011

Policy No. FL

RENEWAL: YES ☐   NO ☒
(IF RENEWAL, USE SAME NUMBER)

Insured's Name and Mailing Address
Number, Street, City or Town, County, State, Zip Code)

Patricia Holmes Smith wife of/and
George Earl Smith
1325 Tarrington Drive
Marrero, La   70072

Policy Term 1 Year, from __8/12/77__ to __8/12/78__

Inception (Mo. Day Yr.) Expiration (Mo. Day Yr.) 12:01 AM. Standard Time at location of the property involved, and thereafter for successive policy terms of 1 year, provided the then current premium payable by the Insured for each successive policy term is paid prior to the expiration of the then current policy term, and if not so paid this policy shall then terminate; provided, however, with respect to any mortgagee (or trustee) named below, this insurance shall continue in force only for the benefit of such mortgagee (or trustee) for 20 days after written notice to the mortgagee (or trustee) of termination of this policy, and shall then terminate.

Community # ____225199B____   FIRM Zone # ____A____

ITEM NO.	AMOUNT OF INSURANCE	RATES AND PREMIUMS				Description and Location of Property Covered
		ACTUARIAL		PAYABLE BY THE INSURED		(Location same as mailing address above unless otherwise indicated)
		RATES	PREMIUMS Check Box ☐ If $15 Expense Constant Included.	RATES	PREMIUMS	
1. Bldg.	a) First Layer $ 33,000	.35	$131.	a) .25	a) $83.	Occupied as Single Family Dwelling
	b) Second Layer $		$	b)	b) $	Located at ☒ 1325 Tarrington Dr
	$ 33,000 Total		$131. Total		$83. Total	Marrero, La 70072
						On Contents consisting principally of_____
						in the Enclosed Building Described Above ☐: or____
2. Conts.	a) $	$ ☐	a)	a) $ ☐		Located at____
	b) $	$	b)	b) $		
	$ Total	$ Total		$ Total		Loss Payee (Contents):____

Notice: The Premium for this Policy has been subsidized by the U.S. Government under the National Flood Insurance Act.	$131.	Grand Total Premium Payable By Insured →	$ 83.

INSERT NAME(S) AND MAILING ADDRESS(ES)

Mortgagee (Building): Insert name(s) and Mailing Address(es)   Carruth Mortgage Corporation, P. O. Box 53334, New
Orleans, La   70153

Second Mortgagee Exists   Yes ☐   No ☐

Mortgagee pays new and renewal ☐ 1 renewal only ☒ 2

Base Flood Elevation from FIRM = ____	Masonry walls-slab foundation ☒ 1
First Floor Elevation — Certify = ____	Masonry walls-other foundation ☐ 2 Check only
Dift. Plus (+) or Minus (−) To Nearest Foot = ____	All other walls-slab foundation ☐ 3 one box
Does Insured Qualify as "Small Business?" Yes ☐ Y No ☒ N	All other walls-other foundation ☐ 4

Is Structure Single   2-4   Other
Family ☒; Family ☐ 2; Residential ☐ 3; All Other ☐ 4

Is This a Motel or Hotel Structure with normal occupancy of less than six (6) Months?
Yes ☐ Y   No ☒ N

Is this "New Construction or Substantial Improvement"?   Yes ☐ Y   No ☒ N

Date New Construction or Substantial Improvement started____

Is structure within ☐ corporate limits or ☒ unincorporated area of county.

One Story — Basement	☐ 1	No Basement ☒ 2
Two or more Stories — Basement	☐ 3	No Basement ☐ 4
Split Level — Basement	☐ 5	No Basement ☐ 6
Mobile Home on Foundation	☐ 7	

Contents Rated as:	Residential	All Other
All in Basement —	☐ 04	☐ 13
All on First Floor —	☐ 05	☐ 14
All on First Two Floors —	☐ 06	☐ 15
All on First Floor & Basement —	☐ 07	☐ 16
All on First Two Floors & Basement —	☐ 08	☐ 17
All above First Floor —	☐ 09	☐ 18
All in Mobile Home on Foundation —	☐ 03	☐ 19

TO BE COMPLETED BY N.F.I.A. SERVICING OFFICE

SERVICING COMPANY NAME AND ADDRESS

COUNTERSIGNATURE DATE   AUTHORIZED REPRESENTATIVE

__7/28/77__
DATE OF APPLICATION

The above statements are correct to the best of my knowledge. I understand that any false statement may be punishable by fine or imprisonment under 18 U.S. Code, Sec. 1001.

Jackie Jeffries, Agent

SIGNATURE OF INSURED OR AGENT

__72-0740533__
Agent's Tax Number____

Agent Certifies that following matters have been discussed with insured:
1) That loss already in progress on date of application is not covered;
2) Advantages of insuring the single family dwelling to at least 80% of the replacement cost of structure, at the time of loss.

NFIA-2 (Ed. 7-74)

PEST CONTROL SYSTEMS
12 Fat City
Metairie, Louisiana

Date ___7/18/77_____

RE: Property Address_____1325 Tarrington Dr.____

_____Marrero, La._____

I certify that I am an authorized agent of the Firm of Business indicated above
and operating under State License No. _ZZ-3____ and Indemnity Bond
expiring ___Dec. 31, 1977_____ and that as a result of an examination
made at Municipal No. _1325 Tarrington Dr._____City of Marrero on
_7/18/77___ We submit the following statement:

This is to cerify that based on careful visual inspection of accessible
areas and on sounding of accessible structural members there is no evidence
of termite or other wood destroying insect infestation in subject property and if
such infestation previously existed the infestation has been corrected and any
damage due to such infestation has been corrected and/or alternatively been
fully disclosed as follows: NONE

SIGNED_____*Manye Nores*_____

George Earl Smith

REQUEST FOR AUTHORITY TO CLOSE AND STATEMENT
OF SELLERS' AND BUYERS' COSTS

The information furnished by you on this form will be used by Carruth Mortgage Corporation in preparation of the "DISCLOSURE OF COST OF LOAN" as required by the federal Consumers Protection Act (Truth in Lending). This form should be prepared as soon as you are able to determine the date of closing and actual costs.

The figures below must be accurate and represent all costs to buyer and seller incident to this transaction.

Receipt of this form in our office will be considered as your formal request for the authority to close this loan. We will furnish to you, within two (2) working days from receipt in our office, written authority to close this loan in accordance with our General Loan Closing Instructions along with a completed "DISCLOSURE OF COST OF LOAN" statement to be signed by the borrower(s) PRIOR TO THE CLOSING.

You are NOT to close this loan under any circumstances without our prior written authority.

Borrower(s) ___SMITH, George Earl___ Sales Price $ __38,500__

Address of Property __1325 Tarrington Drive__ Cash Down _____

_____Marrero, LA 70072_____ Payment - _____

FHA/VA Case No. _____ Loan Amt. $ __38,500__

DATE OF CLOSING 9/27/77 (9:00 am)
Date of First Payment __9/1/77__ Date of Final Payment __8/1/2007__
Hazard Insurance Type _____ Amt. Coverage $ __33,000__

COST OF LOAN TRANSACTION	SELLER	BORROWER
1. Lender's Discount-4½ ---------------------- $	1,732.50	$
2. Photographs ---------------------------	8.00	
3. Amortization Schedule ---------------------	1.50	
4. Termite Inspection ----------------------		
5. Lender's Origination Fee ------------------		385.00
6. VA Funding Fee -------------------------		
7. Appraisal Fee (FHA-VA-Conv.) -------------		55.00
8. Inspection Fees Flood Insurance _____		83.00
9. __2__/12 FHA Mortgage Ins. Premium ------		13.84
10. 1st years Hazard Insurance ----------------		236.00
11. __2__/12 Hazard Insurance Reserve --------		39.34
12. ____/12 Tax Escrow, City 19___ ----------		
13. __9__/12 Tax Escrow, State 19 77 --------	10.20	56.70
14. Tax Pro Ration, City ----------------------		
15. Tax Pro Ration, State and Parish ------------		
16. Interest for __4__ days at $ 8.97 per day-----		35.88
17. Recording and Filing Fees ------------------	4.00	22.50
18. Ordering Certificates ---------------------	82.50	
19. Notary Fee ---------------------------	70.00	90.00
20. Title Examination -----------------------		
21. Title Insurance Premium ------------------		252.25
22. Credit Report --------------------------		7.20
23. Survey -------------------------------		75.00
24. Owners Title Policy ----------------------		
25. Copy of Sale to Assessor ------------------		
26. Real Estate Commission -------------------	2,310.00	
27. Other --------------------------------		

The above statement represents actual costs incurred by buyer and seller pertinent to this transaction. This loan will not be closed by me if these figures do not agree with the acutal charges at the time of the loan closing.

DATE ___July 22, 1977___   ATTORNEY _____
                                              (Signature)
                                              John Doe

CMC Form 178 (6/69)

CALCULATION OF ANNUAL PERCENTAGE RATE
REQUIRED BY FEDERAL CONSUMER CREDIT PROTECTION ACT

NAME _____ George Smith _____

ADDRESS OF PROPERTY ___ 1325 Tarrington Drive, Marrero, La. _____

FHA/VA CASE NO. ___ 202878 _____

A. First Payment Due _____ B. Loan Amount $ __ 38,500.00 __
   Final Payment Due _____   Prepaid Finance
   Total No. of   Charges   − __ 430.38 __
   Payments Due _____   Amount Financed $ __ 38,069.62 __

                          C. Monthly P & I $ __ 296.07 __
                             Total No. of
                             Payments   x __ 360 __
                             Total P & I $ __ 106,585.20 __
                             Loan Amount   − __ 38,500.00 __
                             Interest for
                             Life of Loan $ __ 68,085.20 __

CONVENTIONAL LOANS ONLY   FHA LOANS ONLY
Loan Amount $ _____   Interest for Life of Loan $ _____
PMI factor   FHA Factor   x _____
(2–10yr at .25%)   FHA Mtg Ins. for Life
  times 9 years _____   of Loan $ _____

PMI factor
(11–30 yr at .125%)
  times 20 years _____
Total for life of
  Loan (1–30 yr) $ _____
                             FHA/PMI Mtg. Ins.
                             for life of Loan $ _____
                             Interest for Life
                               of Loan   + _____
                             Continuing Finance
                               Charge $ _____

                          D. Continuing Finance
                             Charge $ __ 68,085.20 __
                             Prepaid Finance
                             Charge + __ 430.38 __
                             Total Finance
                             Charges $ __ 68,515.58 __
                                     x __ 100 __
                             Total $ __ 6851558.00 __
                             Amount Financed $ __ 38,069.62 __
                             Finance Charge per
                             $100 of Amount
                             Financed $ __ 179.98 __
                       ANNUAL PERCENTAGE RATE
                       FROM FEDERAL RESERVE
                             CHART   __ 8.75 __ %

Prepared by __ M. Malley _____ Date ____ 6/28/77 _____

Checked by ___ Christine Pearse _____ Date ____ 6/28/77 _____
COMMENT:

NOTE: If this loan has a co-maker, endorser, guarantor, or surety, the Disclosure Statement
should indicate a place for their signatures under the borrower(s) and additional copies sent
to the attorney to be given to them.

CMC Form 177
(REV. 5/1/77)

CARRUTH MORTGAGE CORPORATION
DISCLOSURE STATEMENT

First Lien to Finance   ☐ FHA ☒ VA ☐ Conventional
Purchase of a Dwelling   Case # __176354__

Name(s) of Borrower(s) __Patricia Holmes wife of/and George Earl Smith__

Mailing Address __1325 Tarrington Drive, Marrero, Louisiana__

1. CARRUTH MORTGAGE CORPORATION, hereinafter called Lender, will lend to Borrower(s) the amount of $ __38,500.00__. Borrower(s) will be obligated to repay the said principal amount at __8.5__% per annum (exclusive of mortgage insurance premiums and payments for escrowing of real estate taxes and hazard insurance premiums), payable in __360__ monthly installments of principal and interest in the amount of $ __296.07__ commencing on __Sept. 1__, 19 __77__ and due on the 1st day of each month thereafter. In addition, monthly installments one through __n/a__ will require additional amounts for mortgage insurance premiums ranging from $ __n/a__ with the first installment to $ __n/a__ for the final installment. FINANCE CHARGE will begin to accrue on __July, 28__, 19 __77__.

THE ANNUAL PERCENTAGE RATE IS __8 3/4__ %.

2. While most of the finance charges will be spread out over the life of the loan and paid as part of the aforementioned monthly installments, certain ones included in the finance charge will be prepaid at closing. Estimated **PREPAID FINANCE CHARGES** for this loan transaction are:

Origination Fee	$ __385.00__	Photographs	$ __8.00__
Loan Discount Fee Paid by Borrower(s)	$ _____	Amortization Schedule	$ __1.50__
Prepaid ___ mortgage insurance prem.	$ _____	Termite Certificate	$ _____
Int. on New Loan (__4__ days)	$ __35.88__	Other: _____	$ _____

           TOTAL PREPAID FINANCE CHARGES $ __430.38__

3. The Total of Payments scheduled to repay this loan is $ __106,585.20__

4. FINANCE CHARGE:

     Interest .... $ __68,085.20__

     Mortgage Insurance Premium .... $ _____

     Other _____ $ _____

           TOTAL FINANCE CHARGES $ __68,085.20__

5. The AMOUNT FINANCED consists of:

     Amount of Loan .... $ __38,500.00__

     Less Prepaid Finance Charges .... $ __430.38__

           AMOUNT FINANCED $ __38,069.62__

6. There will be certain costs to the Borrower(s) which are not part of the finance charge. Among these are:

Appraisal Fees	$ __55.00__	Credit Report	$ __7.20__
Recording Fees (Certificates, Research)	$ __22.50__	Hazard Ins. Prem.	$ __236.00__
Notarial Fee	$ __90.00__	Flood Ins. Prem.	$ __83.00__
Survey	$ __75.00__	Escrows: Taxes & Ins.	$ __54.86__
Mortgage Title Ins.	$ __252.25__	Other:	$ _____

           Total $ __875.81__

7. In the event of late payment, a late charge equivalent to 4% of each payment more than fifteen (15) days in arrears must be paid by borrower(s) to lender.

8. Lender's security interest in this transaction is a first lien on the property located at _____
__1325 Tarrington Drive, Marrero, La.__
more particularly described in the recorded security instrument creating said lien, a copy of which will be furnished to borrower(s) as promptly as practicable. Said security instrument covers all after-acquired property and future advances, the terms for which are described therein.

9. Prepayment Penalty: (FHA and/or VA-borrower(s) may repay the mortgage in whole or in part at anytime without prepayment charge). (Conventional-borrower(s) _____

10. Credit life, accident, health, or loss of income insurance is not required in connection with this transaction, but may be purchased by the borrower(s) through any insurance company of borrower(s) choice.

11. Fire and extended coverage insurance (or Homeowner's Insurance) in the minimum amount of $ __32,750.00__ with mortgage clause in favor of CARRUTH MORTGAGE CORPORATION, or as designated by them, is required as a condition of this loan and must be kept in effect during the existence of the loan. The insurance may be purchased from any insurance agent, of borrower(s) choice, acceptable to lender, but may be purchased through lender at a cost of $ __216.00__ for a __1__ year term, based on current rates and classifications.

12. Flood insurance under the National Flood Insurance Program is/is not a requirement of this loan, and must be purchased in the minimum amount of $ __32,750.00__ with mortgage clause in favor of CARRUTH MORTGAGE CORPORATION, or as designated by them, and must be kept in effect during the existence of the loan. The insurance may be purchased from any insurance agent of the borrower(s) choice, acceptable to lender, but may be purchased through lender at a cost of $ _____ for a _____ year term, based on current rates and classifications.

13. We, the borrower(s) hereby acknowledge under oath that the purpose of said loan is to finance the purchase or construction of a residence for the borrower(s) and acknowledge receipt of a fully executed copy of this statement prior to signing any documents or papers whatsoever, and we approve all disbursements set forth above, and authorize these payments and disbursements.

SWORN TO AND SUBSCRIBED by the borrower(s) before me, Notary, and the undersigned witnesses at this __28__ day of __July__, 19 __77__.

Witnesses:

Donna Willard   _George Earl Smith_
                                     Borrower
_____   _Patricia Holmes Smith_
                                     Borrower

                                       Endorser/Guarantor

               John Doe
                  Notary Public

CMC #176
Rev. 5-21-77

CARRUTH Mortgage Corporation

3601 I-10 SERVICE ROAD   METAIRIE, LOUISIANA   PHONE 885-4811   MAILING ADDRESS
                                                                                    P. O. BOX 53334
                                                                                    NEW ORLEANS, LA. 70153

July 25, 1977

Mr. John Doe, Attorney
3201 Veterans Blvd.
Metairie, La.   70002

RE: Authorization to Close
George Smith

Dear   Sir:

Enclosed is Disclosure of Cost of Loan (CMC Form 176) which we have
prepared for the above captioned transaction in accordance with information furnished by you on CMC Form 178. The enclosed form is to be
completed, properly executed, and distributed in accordance with our
General Loan Closing Instructions, as supplemented and amended, and
in accordance with instructions below.

AFTER the enclosed Disclosure of Cost of Loan Form has been properly
executed, you are authorized to close this loan on _____
_____July 27_____, 19_77___.

Yours very truly,

CARRUTH MORTGAGE CORPORATION

Donna Pillard

Donna Pillard
Assistant Vice President

Enclosure

INSTRUCTIONS

1. Verify that there has been no change in the figures given to us on
CMC Form 178, and the figures indicated on the attached agree with figures
as shown on all statements in connection with this loan transaction.

2. Borrower(s) are to sign Form 176 where indicated, and the form is to
be properly dated, witnessed and notarized.

3. Distribution is to be made in accordance with General Loan Closing
Instructions.

4. Copy of the termite certificate to be signed by the veteran at the act of sale
and included in our closing package.

CMC179

VA Form 26-6316a (Home Loan)
Rev. Apr. 1974. Use Optional. Section 1810, Title 38, U.S.C. Acceptable to Federal National Mortgage
Association.

LOUISIANA

NOTE

$ 38,500.00   Metairie   , Louisiana.

July 28   , **19** 77

FOR VALUE RECEIVED, without grace, the undersigned, in solido, promise(s) to pay to the order of

B E A R E R

the principal sum of THIRTY EIGHT THOUSAND AND FIVE HUNDRED AND NO/100----**Dollars** ($ 38,500.00--), with interest from date at the rate of eight and one half per centum (8.50%) per annum on the unpaid balance until paid. The said principal and interest shall be payable at the office of CARRUTH MORTGAGE CORPORATION in New Orleans , Louisiana , or at such other place as the holder hereof may designate in writing delivered or mailed to the debtor, in monthly installments of -------------------- TWO HUNDRED NINETY SIX & 07/100--Dollars ($ 296.07----), commencing on the first day of September , 19 77, and continuing on the first day of each month thereafter until this note is fully paid, except that, if not sooner paid, the final payment of principal and interest shall be due and payable on the first day of August , 2007.

Privilege is reserved to prepay at any time, without premium or fee, the entire indebtedness or any part thereof not less than the amount of one installment, or $100, whichever is less. Prepayment in full shall be credited on the date received. Partial prepayment, other than on an installment due date, need not be credited until the next following installment due date or thirty days after such prepayment, whichever is earlier.

If any deficiency in the payment of any installment under this note is not made good prior to the due date of the next such installment, the entire principal sum and accrued interest shall at once become due and payable without notice at the option of the holder of this note. Failure to exercise this option shall not constitute a waiver of the right to exercise the same in the event of any subsequent default. In the event of default in payment of this note, and if the same is collected by an attorney at law, I, we, or either of us, in solido, further agree to pay all costs of collection, including a reasonable attorney's fee actually incurred or paid by the holder of this note.

This note is secured by Mortgage or Notarial Act of even date on certain property described therein and represents money actually used for the acquisition of said property or the improvements thereon.

The undersigned hereby waive presentment, protest, and notice.

"NE VARIETUR" in conformity with an act
of mortgage passed this day before me, Notary.

GEORGE EARL SMITH

PATRICIA HOLMES SMITH

Metairie . La., July 28 , 19 77

John Doe
Notary Public.

Jefferson   Parish, La.

THIS IS TO CERTIFY that this is the note described in and secured by mortgage of even date herewith and in the same principal amount as herein stated and secured by real estate situated in Jefferson
Parish, State of Louisiana.

Dated   July 28   , **19** 77 .

John Doe   *Notary Public.*

VA Form 26-6316b (Home Loan)
Revised December 1976. Use Op-
tional. Section 1810, Title 38 U.S.C.
Acceptable to Federal National
Mortgage Association.

CREDIT SALE OF PROPERTY

BY
Frederick Jones

TO
Patricia Holmes wife of/and
George Earl Smith

July 28 , 1977

STATE OF LOUISIANA
PARISH OF

BE IT KNOWN, That on this   28th   day of
July   in the year nineteen hundred and
seventy seven

Before me, the undersigned authority, a notary public
in and for said PARISH and STATE duly commissioned
and qualified, and in the presence of witnesses hereinafter named and undersigned,

PERSONALLY CAME AND APPEARED:

FREDERICK JONES being of full age of majority and resident of the Parish of Jefferson,
State of Louisiana, who declared under oath unto me, Notary, that he is single and
never been married.

[VENDOR], who declared that he does, by these presents, sell, convey, and deliver, with full guaranty of
title, and with complete transfer and subrogation of all rights and actions of warranty against all former pro-
prietors of the property herein conveyed, together with all rights of prescription, whether acquisitive or libera-
tive, to which said vendor may be entitled unto
Patricia Holmes wife of/and George Earl Smith, both persons of the full age of
majority and residents of the Parish of Jefferson, State of Louisiana , who declared
under oath unto me, Notary, that their marital status is as follows: Both have
been married once and then to each other.

MAILING ADDRESS: 1325 Tarrington Dr., Marrero, Louisiana

[PURCHASER], here present, accepting and purchasing for said purchaser, his heirs and assigns, who
acknowledges due delivery and possession thereof, the following described property, to-wit:
A CERTAIN PORTION OF GROUND, together with all the buildings and improvements
thereon, and all of the rights, ways, privileges, servitudes, appurtenances and
advantages thereunto belonging or in anywise appertaining, situated in the Parish
of Jefferson, State of Louisiana, Valley Realty Company Subdivision Extended,
all in accordance with a plan of subdivision by Midler Inc., C.E., dated October 26,
1964, revised November 19, 1964, approved by the Jefferson Parish Council under
Ordinance Number 6877 on November 19, 1964, registered in C.O.B. 603, folio 861
on December 7, 1964, which portion of ground is designated as follows:

LOT 7 in Sq. 26, which is square is bounded by 13th St. Tarrington Drive,
14th St. and the East Boundary of the Subdivision. Lot 7 measures 50 feet front
on Tarrington Drive, same width in the rear, by a depth on the side line of Lot
6 of 100.01 feet and a depth on the side line of Lot of 100 feet. All in accordance
with annexed survey by Midler Inc., C.E., dated July 21, 1977.

VA CLAUSES ANNEXED BY RIDER

To Have and to Hold the above-described property and its appurtenances to the said purchaser, his heirs and assigns, forever.

This sale is made and accepted for and in consideration of the sum of THIRTY EIGHT THOUSAND FIVE HUNDRED DOLLARS AND NO/100-----------Dollars ($ 38,500.00----), paid by

payable as follows   NONE

($ NONE_____)

DOLLARS, cash in hand paid, the receipt of which is hereby acknowledged, and the balance represented in one note of said purchaser in the amount of Thirty Eight Thousand five hundred and no($ 38,500.00) DOLLARS, which is dated with this act, made payable to the order of bearer, with interest from date at the rate of eight and one half centum (8.50 %) per annum on the unpaid balance until paid, the principal and interest thereon being payable at the office of CARRUTH MORTGAGE CORPORATION New Orleans in Louisiana , or at such other place as the holder thereof might designate in writing delivered or mailed to the purchaser, in monthly installments of TWO HUNDRED NINETY SIX AND 07/100 ---($ 296.07)

DOLLARS, commencing on the first day of September , 19 77, and continuing on the first day of each month thereafter until the principal and interest are fully paid, except that, if not sooner paid, the final payment of principal and interest shall be due and payable on the first day of August ,2007. Said promissory note, after having been paraphed "Ne Varietur" by me, notary, to identify it herewith, was delivered unto the said vendor, who, after acknowledging receipt therefor, for value received, the receipt and sufficiency of which value was acknowledged, transferred, assigned, and delivered said note, without recourse as to said vendor, together with all of his rights and actions as vendor herein, including those relating to the vendor's lien and privilege, to CARRUTH MORTGAGE CORPORATION [CREDITOR], through its undersigned agent, who acknowledges receipt thereof.

In order to secure the payment of said promissory note, in capital and interest, according to its tenor and the provisions herein contained, and to secure the faithful performance of all of the obligations contained herein, and the reimbursement and payment of attorneys' fees, taxes, paving assessments, premiums of insurance, costs, fines, late charges, and all advances and expenses as herein authorized, the said purchaser does, by these presents, specially mortgage, affect, and hypothecate the above-described property, unto and in favor of the said creditor, the purchaser hereby confessing judgment in favor of the creditor, and any future holder or holders of said note, for the full amount of the said promissory note or obligation, together with all interest, taxes, paving assessments, premiums of insurance, fines, penalties, attorneys' fees, and all costs, late charges, advances, and expenses, as authorized herein.

Said creditor retains this vendor's lien and privilege as security for all of the purchaser's obligations hereinunder, and the said purchaser hereby binds and obligates himself not to sell, alienate, or encumber the said property to the prejudice of these presents.

(XXXXXXXXXXXXXXXXXXXXXXXXXXXXXXXXXXXXXXXXXXXXXXXXXXXXXXXXXXXXXXXXXXXXXXXXXXXXXXXX XXXXXXXXXXXXXXXXXXXXXXXXXXXXXXXXXXXXXXXXXXXXXXXXXXXXXXXXXXXXXXXXXXXXXXXXXXXXXXXX XXXXXXXXXXXXXXXXXXXXXXXXXXXXXXXXXXXXXXXXXXXXXXXXXXXXXXXXXXXXXXXXXXXXXXXXXXXXXXXX XXXXXXXXXXXXXXXXXXXXXXXXXXXXXXXXXXXXXXXXXXXXXXXXXXXXXXXXXXXXXXXXXXXXXXXXXXXXXXXX XXXXXXXXXXXXXXXXXXXXXXXXXXXXXXXXXXXXXXXXXXXXXXXXXXXXXXXXXXXXXXXXXXXXXXXXXXXXXXXX XXXXXXXXXXXXXXXXXXXXXXXXXXXXXXXXXXXXXXXXXXXXXXXXXXXXXXXXXXXXXXXXXXXXXXXXXXXXXXXX)

The purchaser further covenants and agrees:

1. That he will pay the indebtedness as hereinbefore provided. Privilege is reserved to prepay at any time, without premium or fee, the entire indebtedness or any part thereof not less than the amount of one installment, or one hundred dollars ($100.00), whichever is less. Prepayment in full shall be credited on the date received. Partial prepayment, other than on an installment due date, need not be credited until the next following installment due date or thirty days after such prepayment, whichever is earlier.

2. He will pay to said creditor, as trustee (under the terms of this trust as hereinafter stated) together with and in addition to the monthly payments hereinbefore specified, on the first day of each month until the note is fully paid:

 (*a*) A sum equal to the ground rents, if any, next due, plus the premium that will next become due and payable on policies of fire and other hazard insurance covering the mortgaged property, plus taxes and assessments next due on the mortgaged property (all as estimated by creditor, and of which the purchaser is notified) less all sums already paid therefor divided by the number of months to elapse before one month prior to the date when such ground rents, premiums, taxes, and assessments will become delinquent, such sums to be held by creditor in trust to pay said ground rents, premiums, taxes, and special assessments.

 (*b*) The aggregate of the amounts payable pursuant to subparagraph (*a*) and those payable on the note secured hereby, shall be paid in a single payment each month, to be applied to the following items in the order stated:

  (I) ground rents, taxes, special assessments, fire and other hazard insurance premiums;

  (II) interest on the indebtedness secured hereby; and

  (III) amortization of the principal of said indebtedness.

 Any deficiency in the amount of such aggregate monthly payment shall constitute an event of default under this act.

(XXXXXXXXXXXXXXXXXXXXXXXXXXXXXXXXXXXXXXXXXXXXXXXXXXXXXXXXXXXXXXXXXXXXXXXXXXXXXXXX XXXXXXXXXXXXXXXXXXXXXXXXXXXXXXXXXXXXXXXXXXXXXXXXXXXXXXXXXXXXXXXXXXXXXXXXXXXXXXXX)

3. If the total of the payments made by the purchaser under (*a*) of paragraph 2 preceding shall exceed the amount of payments actually made by creditor as trustee for ground rents, taxes or assessments or insurance premiums, as the case may be, such excess shall be credited on subsequent payments due or to become due by the purchaser for such items or, at the creditor's option, as trustee shall be refunded to the purchaser. If, however, such monthly payments shall not be sufficient to pay such items when the same shall become due and payable, then the purchaser shall pay to creditor as trustee any amount necessary to make up the deficiency. Such payments shall be made within thirty (30) days after written notice stating the amount of the deficiency, which notice may be given by mail. If at any time the purchaser shall tender to the creditor in accordance with the provisions of this act full payment of the purchaser's entire indebtedness the creditor as trustee shall, in computing the amount of such indebtedness, credit to the account of the purchaser the credit balance accumulated under the provisions of (*a*) of paragraph 2 hereof. If there shall be a default under any of the provisions of this act resulting in a public sale of the premises covered hereby, or if creditor acquires the property otherwise after default, creditor as trustee shall apply, at the time of the commencement of such proceedings, or at the time the property is otherwise acquired, the amount then remaining to credit of purchaser under (*a*) of paragraph 2 preceding, as a credit on the interest accrued and unpaid and the balance to the principal then remaining unpaid on said note.

(Note.—If lender is *not* a Building and Loan or Homestead Association delete paragraphs (X) and (Y) above.)

4. He will promptly pay all taxes, assessments, water rates, and other governmental or municipal charges, fines, or impositions, and ground rents, except when payment for all such items has theretofore been made under (a) of paragraph 2 hereof, and he will promptly deliver the official receipts therefor to creditor. If the purchaser fails to make such payment creditor may make them, and any sums so advanced shall bear interest at the same rate as and become a part of the principal debt from the date of payment, and shall be secured by the pledge and mortgage herein granted and by the vendor's lien herein retained.

5. Sums advanced by creditor for the payment of any taxes, special assessments, premiums on insurance, or any other charges, expense or costs herein authorized to be made shall bear interest at the same rate as and become a part of the principal debt from the date of payment, and the reimbursement thereof shall be ratably secured by the pledge and mortgage herein granted and the vendor's lien herein retained.

6. Upon the request of creditor, the purchaser shall execute and deliver a supplemental note or notes for the sum or sums advanced by creditor for any alteration, modernization or improvement made at the purchaser's request; or for maintenance or repair of said premises or taxes, assessments against the same or hazard insurance premiums and for any other purpose elsewhere authorized hereunder. Said note or notes shall be secured hereby on a parity with as fully as if the advance evidenced thereby were included in the note first described above. Said supplemental note or notes shall bear interest at the same rate as the principal debt and shall be payable in approximately equal monthly payments of such period as may be agreed upon by the creditor and debtor. Failing to agree on the maturity, the whole of the sum or sums so advanced shall be due and payable thirty (30) days after demand by the creditor. In no event should the aggregate of the sums so advanced, together with interest, exceed fifty (50%) percent of the original principal amount of the note secured hereby, nor shall the ultimate maturity of the said secured note first described above be extended. The mortgaging and confession of judgment clauses herein shall be deemed to include all such advances in the event the same are not specifically included therein. The holder of the note shall have no obligation to make any such advances.

7. He will continuously maintain hazard insurance, of such type or types and amounts as creditor may from time to time require, on the improvements now or hereafter on said premises, and except when payment for all such premiums has theretofore been made under (a) of paragraph 2 hereof, he will pay promptly when due any premiums therefor. All insurance shall be carried in companies approved by the creditor and the policies and renewals thereof shall have attached thereto standard mortgagee or loss payable clauses in favor of and in form acceptable to creditor. He will transfer and deliver the policy or policies of such insurance or insurances, and their renewals, to creditor; in default of which the creditor is hereby authorized, at its option, to avail itself of the rights hereafter set forth, or to cause such insurance to be made and effected at the cost, charge, and expense of said purchaser.

8. If the property covered hereby, or any part thereof, shall be damaged or destroyed by fire or other hazard against which insurance is held, the amounts due by any insurance company shall, to the extent of the indebtedness then remaining unpaid, be paid to creditor, and, when so paid, may, at its option, be applied to the debt or be used for the repairing or rebuilding of the said property.

9. The lien of this instrument shall remain in full force and effect during any postponement or extension of the time of payment of the indebtedness or any part thereof secured hereby.

10. If any of the monthly payments provided for in paragraph (2) (b) preceding shall not be paid when due, he will, at creditor's option, pay to creditor a "late charge" not exceeding four per centum (4%) of any installment which is paid more than fifteen (15) days after the due date thereof, to cover the extra expense involved in handling delinquent payments, but such "late charge" shall not be payable out of the proceeds of any sale made to satisfy the indebtedness secured hereby, unless such proceeds are sufficient to discharge the entire indebtedness and all proper costs and expenses secured thereby.

11. He will not commit or permit waste; and shall maintain the property in as good condition as at present, reasonable wear and tear excepted. Upon any failure so to maintain, creditor, at its option, may cause reasonable maintenance work to be performed at the cost of the purchaser. Any amounts paid therefor shall bear interest at the same rate as, and become a part of, the principal debt from the date of payment, and the reimbursement thereof shall be secured by the pledge and mortgage herein granted and the vendor's lien herein retained.

12. The balance due by the purchaser, at any time, on his note shall be the face of said note, together with the interest herein stipulated, plus any amount which may have been advanced by or be due to the creditor for taxes, insurance premiums, paving assessments, late charges, or for any other charge or expense elsewhere authorized herein, minus proper credits.

13. In the event of default in any of the terms, conditions, or covenants under this act, creditor shall have the right and is hereby authorized, at its option, to collect and receipt for all rents and revenues from the property, and to apply the same to the purchaser's indebtedness.

14. If purchaser violates any of the conditions of this act, or fails promptly to perform any obligation hereunder, or fails to make any installment or installments on the above described promissory note in accordance with its terms, or upon the cancellation of any insurance covering the property, for whatever reason, if the purchaser fails immediately to replace said insurance in a company, or companies satisfactory to creditor, the creditor may, at its option, without demand, and without putting in default, purchaser having by these presents waived the demand and delay provided for by Article 2639 of the Code of Civil Procedure of Louisiana, declare the entire balance immediately due, exigible and payable together with interest, costs, attorney's fees, advances, and all proper expenses and charges.

15. In the event of any default or the violation of any of the conditions of this act, or the happening of any one or more of the events hereinabove mentioned, the creditor shall have the right, without the necessity of demand or of putting in default, to cause the property herein described, together with all the improvements thereon, to be seized and sold under executory or other process issued by any competent court, or it may proceed to the enforcement of its rights in any other manner provided by law, and the property may be sold with or without appraisement, at the option of the creditor, to the highest bidder for cash, the present purchaser herein waiving hereby the benefit of all laws relative to the appraisement of property seized and sold under executory or other process.

16. If legal proceedings are instituted for the recovery of any amount due hereunder, or if any past due claim hereunder is placed in the hands of an attorney for collection, the purchaser agrees to pay the reasonable fees of the attorney at law employed for that purpose.

17. The failure of creditor to exercise any of its privileges or options at any time shall not constitute a waiver of its right to exercise the same in the event of any subsequent default.

18. Nothing in this act contained shall be so construed as to limit any right or remedy otherwise granted or available to the creditor.

The covenants herein contained shall bind, and the benefits and advantages shall inure to, the respective heirs, executors, administrators, successors, and assigns of the parties hereto. Whenever used, the singular number shall include the plural, the plural the singular, the use of any gender shall be applicable to all genders, and the term "creditor" shall include any payee of the indebtedness hereby secured or any transferee thereof, whether by operation of law or otherwise.

The production of Mortgage, Conveyance, and United States District, and Circuit Court Certificates is hereby waived by the parties hereto, who relieve and release me, Notary, from all responsibility and liability in the premises for such nonproduction.

This conveyance is subject to any paving or other special assessment lien for public improvements, charged against the herein conveyed property. All State and city taxes up to and including taxes due and exigible in 19 76, are paid as per tax research.

All taxes for year 19 77 are assumed by the present purchaser.

THUS DONE AND PASSED in my office in the Parish and State aforesaid on the day, month and year first above written and in the presence of the undersigned competent witnesses of lawful age, who have signed their names with the said appearers, and me, Notary, after reading thereof.

WITNESSES:

FREDERICK JONES   *Vendor*

Vendor

Lucy Sells

Ann Allen

GEORGE EARL SMITH   *Purchaser*

PATRICIA HOLMES SMITH   *Purchaser*

CARRUTH MORTGAGE CORPORATION

By

Agent JOHNNY MILLER   *Creditor*

JOHN DOE   *Notary Public*

STATE OF LOUISIANA

Credit Sale of Property

To

VA Form 26-6316b, mortgage (credit sale of property) contd.

STATE OF LOUISIANA
PARISH OF JEFFERSON

ASSIGNMENT OF NOTE AND MORTGAGE

BE IT KNOWN, That on this _____ day of the month of _____
_____, 19_____, before me, a Notary Public duly commissioned
and qualified, in and for the Parish and State aforesaid, and therein residing, personally
came and appeared _____ J. O. Hecker, Jr._____, who declared unto me,
Notary, that he is _____President_____ of CARRUTH MORTGAGE CORPORATION
and who, acting in said capacity and duly authorized hereunto, declared that, for value
received, the said CARRUTH MORTGAGE CORPORATION does herein and hereby assign,
transfer, sell and deliver to

GOVERNMENT NATIONAL MORTGAGE ASSOCIATION,

without recourse, one certain mortgage note made and subscribed by __George Earl_____
_____Smith and Patricia Holmes Smith_____, dated____July 28, 1977_____,
in the original principal sum of $__38,500_____,payable to the order of_____
_____Bearer_____ Paraphed Ne Varietur by __John Doe_____,
Notary Public and the said CARRUTH MORTGAGE CORPORATION does hereby assign,
transfer and deliver to

GOVERNMENT NATIONAL MORTGAGE ASSOCIATION,

the mortgage, passed before ___John Doe_____, Notary Public, by which the
aforesaid note is secured, recorded in _____Jefferson_____
_____ Parish, Louisiana, on the _____ day of _____
_____, 19_____, in MOB _____, Folio _____, and the said
CARRUTH MORTGAGE CORPORATION does hereby warrant that the principal remaining unpaid on the aforesaid note as of this date is the sum of $_____, that CARRUTH
MORTGAGE CORPORATION has full power and authority to assign, transfer and deliver
same; that it has executed no prior assignment thereof; that it has executed no release,
discharge satisfaction or cancellation of said note or mortgage and that it has not released any portion of the security or released the liability of the maker or makers thereof.

To fully accomplish, effectuate and evidence said assignment and transfer, the
CARRUTH MORTGAGE CORPORATION, through its proper officer, endorsed the hereinabove
described note, without recourse, to the order of

GOVERNMENT NATIONAL MORTGAGE ASSOCIATION,

whereupon I, Notary, did paraph said note for identification herewith.

THUS DONE AND PASSED IN __D U P L I C A T E_____ ORIGINALS IN MY
OFFICE IN THE CITY OF METAIRIE, STATE OF LOUISIANA, on the day and in the month
and year first hereinabove written in the presence of the undersigned competent witnesses
who have affixed their signatures hereto with said appearer and me, Notary, after due
reading of the whole.

WITNESSES:

_Donna J Pillard_____

_Nancy C Cocoun_____

                                                CARRUTH MORTGAGE CORPORATION

                                                By_____
                                                   J. O. Hecker, Jr.,
                                                   President

_____John Doe_____
           NOTARY PUBLIC
     My commission expires at death

HUD-1 REV. 5/76

FORM APPROVED
OMB NO. 63-R-1801

A.		B.		TYPE OF LOAN	
U. S. DEPARTMENT OF HOUSING AND URBAN DEVELOPMENT		1. ☐ FHA	2. ☐ FmHA	3. ☐ CONV. UNINS.	
		4. ☒ VA	5. ☐ CONV. INS.		
SETTLEMENT STATEMENT		6. FILE NUMBER: 4102		7. LOAN NUMBER:	
		8. MORTGAGE INSURANCE CASE NUMBER:			

C. *NOTE:* *This form is furnished to give you a statement of actual settlement costs. Amounts paid to and by the settlement agent are shown. Items marked "(p.o.c.)" were paid outside the closing; they are shown here for informational purposes and are not included in the totals.*

D. NAME OF BORROWER:	E. NAME OF SELLER:	F. NAME OF LENDER:
SMITH, George Earl SMITH, Patricia Holmes	Frederick Jones	Carruth Mortgage Corporation

G. PROPERTY LOCATION:	H. SETTLEMENT AGENT:	I. SETTLEMENT DATE:
1325 Tarrington Drive Marrero, Louisiana	John Doe Green Title Insurance Corp. PLACE OF SETTLEMENT:	7/28/77

J. SUMMARY OF BORROWER'S TRANSACTION		K. SUMMARY OF SELLER'S TRANSACTION	
100. GROSS AMOUNT DUE FROM BORROWER:		400. GROSS AMOUNT DUE TO SELLER:	
101. Contract sales price	38,500.00	401. Contract sales price	38,500.00
102. Personal property		402. Personal property	
103. Settlement charges to borrower *(line 1400)*	1,351.71	403.	
104.		404.	
105.		405.	
Adjustments for items paid by seller in advance		*Adjustments for items paid by seller in advance*	
106. City/town taxes to		406. City/town taxes to	
107. County taxes to		407. County taxes to	
108. Assessments to		408. Assessments to	
109.		409.	
110.		410.	
111.		411.	
112.		412.	
120. GROSS AMOUNT DUE FROM BORROWER	39,851.71	420. GROSS AMOUNT DUE TO SELLER	38,500.00
200. AMOUNTS PAID BY OR IN BEHALF OF BORROWER:		500. REDUCTIONS IN AMOUNT DUE TO SELLER:	
201. Deposit or earnest money	500.00	501. Excess deposit *(see instructions)*	
202. Principal amount of new loan(s)	38,500.00	502. Settlement charges to seller *(line 1400)*	4,218.70
203. Existing loan(s) taken subject to		503. Existing loan(s) taken subject to	
204. funds paid to lender	65.00	504. Payoff of first mortgage loan –Carruth	14,387.29
205.		505. Payoff of second mortgage loan	
206.		506.	
207.		507.	
208.		508.	
209.		509.	
Adjustments for items unpaid by seller		*Adjustments for items unpaid by seller*	
210. City/town taxes to		510. City/town taxes to	
211. County taxes to		511. County taxes to	
212. Assessments to		512. Assessments to	
213.		513.	
214.		514.	
215.		515.	
216.		516.	
217.		517.	
218.		518.	
219.		519.	
220. TOTAL PAID BY/FOR BORROWER	39,065.00	520. TOTAL REDUCTION AMOUNT DUE SELLER	18,605.99
300. CASH AT SETTLEMENT FROM/TO BORROWER		600. CASH AT SETTLEMENT TO/FROM SELLER	
301. Gross amount due from borrower *(line 120)*	39,851.71	601. Gross amount due to seller *(line 420)*	38,500.00
302. Less amounts paid by/for borrower *(line 220)*	39,065.00	602. Less reductions in amount due seller *(line 520)*	18,605.99
303. CASH (☒ FROM) (☐ TO) BORROWER	786.71	603. CASH (☒ TO) (☐ FROM) SELLER	19,894.01

Frederick Jones

George Earl Smith

Patricia Holmes Smith

L.	SETTLEMENT CHARGES		PAID FROM BORROWER'S FUNDS AT SETTLEMENT	PAID FROM SELLER'S FUNDS AT SETTLEMENT
700. TOTAL SALES/BROKER'S COMMISSION based on price $ @ % =				
Division of Commission (line 700) as follows:				
701. $ to				
702. $ to				
703. Commission paid at Settlement				
704.				
800. ITEMS PAYABLE IN CONNECTION WITH LOAN				
801. Loan Origination Fee %			385.00	
802. Loan Discount %				
803. Appraisal Fee to			55.00	
804. Credit Report to			7.20	
805. Lender's Inspection Fee				
806. Mortgage Insurance Application Fee to				
807. Assumption Fee				
808.				
809.				
810.				
811.				
900. ITEMS REQUIRED BY LENDER TO BE PAID IN ADVANCE				
901. Interest from 7/28 to 8/1 4 @ $ 8.97 /day			35.88	
902. Mortgage Insurance Premium for months to				
903. Hazard Insurance Premium for 1 years to			236.00	
904. Flood Ins. Prem. 1 years to			83.00	
905.				
1000. RESERVES DEPOSITED WITH LENDER			tax 10.20	
1001. Hazard insurance 2 months @ $ 19.67 per month			39.34	
1002. Mortgage insurance months @ $ per month				
1003. City property taxes 9 months @ $ 6.30 per month			56.70	
1004. County property taxes months @ $ per month				
1005. Annual assessments months @ $ per month				
1006. Flood Insurance 2 months @ $ 6.92 per month			13.84	
1007. months @ $ per month				
1008. months @ $ per month				
1100. TITLE CHARGES				
1101. Settlement or closing fee to				
1102. Abstract or title search to				
1103. Title examination to				
1104. Title insurance binder to				35.00
1105. Document preparation to				35.00
1106. Notary fees to Vendors Closing Fee			90.00	
1107. Attorney's fees to				
(includes above items numbers;)				
1108. Title insurance to			252.25	
(includes above items numbers;)				
1109. Lender's coverage $				
1110. Owner's coverage $				
1111. Mortgage Conveyance, Tax, Paving, & Tax Sale Cert.				82.50
1112.				
1113.				
1200. GOVERNMENT RECORDING AND TRANSFER CHARGES				
1201. Recording fees: Deed $; Mortgage $ 22.50 ; Releases $ 4.00			22.50	4.00
1202. City/county tax/stamps: Deed $; Mortgage $				
1203. State tax/stamps: Deed $; Mortgage $				
1204.				
1205.				
1300. ADDITIONAL SETTLEMENT CHARGES				
1301. Survey to			75.00	
1302. Pest inspection to				
1303.				
1304.				
1305.				
1400. TOTAL SETTLEMENT CHARGES *(enter on lines 103, Section J and 502, Section K)*			1,351.71	4,218.70

HUD-1 REV. 5/76

Frederick Jones

George Earl Smith
Patricia Holmes Smith

CARRUTH MORTGAGE CORPORATION

Supplement to Disclosure/Settlement Statement (HUD-1)

```
Loan Number.........................
Borrower............................  SMITH, George Earl
Property Address....................  1325 Tarrington Dr.
Amount of Loan....................$   38,500.00
Date of Disbursement...............  7/28/77
Date of First Payment..............  9/1/77

Monthly Payment Amount:
Principal and Interest............$   296.07
Tax Reserve........................  10.62
Insurance Reserve..................  19.67
FHA Mortgage Insurance Res........
TOTAL PAYMENT.....................$   333.28
```

This is to certify that we have examined and received a copy of the Disclosure/Settlement Statement, HUD-1 form, on the above captioned transaction and that no other fees, deposits or commissions other than those stated therein have been paid by the seller and/or borrower either directly or indirectly and that the disbursements listed there-on have been made with our approval.

Frederick Jones
Seller

George Earl Smith
Borrower

_____
Seller

Patricia Holmes Smith
Borrower

_____
Date

_____
Date

The Disclosure/Settlement Statement, HUD-1 form, on the above caption-ed transaction is a complete, true and correct account of the funds received and disbursed by me in the closing of this loan.

John Doe
Attorney/Notary

_7/28/77_
Date

CMC 424

CASE STUDY: CONVENTIONAL RESIDENTIAL LOAN WITH PRIVATE MORTGAGE INSURANCE

This conventional residential mortgage loan submission is typical of one processed normally by a savings and loan association and at times, by other mortgage lenders. It is presented because of several peculiarities. The borrower represents a growing factor in the market—a one-person household. Unlike a VA-guaranteed or an FHA-insured loan, this loan (or more specifically, the top 25 percent of this loan) is insured by a private mortgage insurance company. The cost of the insurance in this case is one percent of the unpaid principal balance the first year (prepaid) and one-quarter of one percent for the remainder of the term.

This particular residence is new, and because of the comparable properties recently sold, the appraisal was relatively straightforward. An unusual expense associated with a property such as a townhouse, condominium or cooperative housing is the *homeowner association dues*. This is levied to pay for the upkeep of the commonly-owned areas and is usually managed for the homeowner by the builder until the completion of the project. Typically, the homeowner association will subsequently choose a professional management firm to perform this task. A typical title insurance policy is included to illustrate the easements, rights-of-way and covenants typically associated with a title and which are recorded in public records. A relatively new innovation, a *home-owners warranty* which is paid by the builder is also included. A *deed of trust* serves as the security instrument, in this case with Suburban Trust Company designated as trustee. In the event of a default on the part of the borrower, this instrument allows the trustee, after due public notice, to sell the property at an auction.

After execution of the note and trust deed this loan was sold to the Federal Home Loan Mortgage Corporation.

The following documents are required for a conventional loan with private mortgage insurance which is sold to FHLMC:

1. Residential loan application

2. Purchase agreement

3. Estimated statement of completion cost of townhouse

4. Good faith estimate of closing costs

5. Request for verification of employment

6. Request for verification of deposit

7. Credit report

8. FHLMC Form 70 Residential Appraisal Report

9. Photographs

10. Private mortgage insurance application

11. Private mortgage insurance certificate

12. Loan commitment

13. Disclosure statement

14. Hazard insurance certificate

15. Title insurance commitment

16. Survey

17. Home owner's warranty

18. Closing instructions

19. Owner's affidavit

20. Disclosure statement

21. Note

22. Deed of trust

23. Settlement statement

24. FHLMC Form 13 SF, Mortgage Submission Voucher

PERPETUAL FEDERAL SAVINGS AND LOAN ASSOCIATION
Eleventh and E Streets, N.W.
Washington, D. C. 20004

RESIDENTIAL LOAN APPLICATION

MORTGAGE APPLIED FOR	☒ Conventional ☐ FHA ☐ VA	Amount $ 35,900	Interest Rate 9.2%	No. of Months 360	Monthly Payment Principal & Interest $ 295.35	Escrow/Impounds (to be collected monthly) ☒ Taxes ☐ Hazard Ins. ☒ Mtg. Ins. ☐ _____
Prepayment Option					Census Tract	

SUBJECT PROPERTY

Property Street Address #3 Ridgeline Drive	City Gaithersburg	County Montgomery	State Maryland	Zip 20760	No. Units 1

Legal Description (Attach description if necessary)
Lot #3, Clubside, Montgomery Village   Year Built

Purpose of Loan: ☐ Purchase ☐ Construction-Permanent ☐ Construction ☐ Refinance ☐ Other (Explain)

Complete this line if Construction-Permanent or Construction Loan ☛	Lot Value Data	Original Cost	Present Value (a)	Cost of Imps. (b)	Total (a + b)	ENTER TOTAL AS PURCHASE PRICE IN DETAILS OF PURCHASE.
	Year Acquired _____ $ _____	$ _____	$ _____	$ _____		

Complete this line if a Refinance Loan

Year Acquired	Original Cost	Amt. Existing Liens	Purpose of Refinance	Describe Improvements [ ] made [ ] to be made
	$	$		Cost: $ _____

Title Will Be Held In What Name(s) Victoria E. Fowler	Manner In Which Title Will Be Held Sole

Source of Down Payment and Settlement Charges
Savings

This application is designed to be completed by the borrower(s) with the lender's assistance. The Co-Borrower Section and all other Co-Borrower questions must be completed and the appropriate box(es) checked if ☐ another person will be jointly obligated with the Borrower on the loan, or ☐ the Borrower is relying on income from alimony, child support or separate maintenance or on the income or assets of another person as a basis for repayment of the loan, or ☐ the Borrower is married and resides, or the property is located, in a community property state.

BORROWER				CO-BORROWER			
Name Victoria E. Fowler		Age 33	School Yrs 12	Name		Age	School Yrs
Present Address	No. Years	☐ Own	☐ Rent	Present Address	No. Years	☐ Own	☐ Rent
Street 1804 Seminary Road				Street			
City/State/Zip Falls Church, Virginia 22041				City/State/Zip			
Former address if less than 2 years at present address				Former address if less than 2 years at present address			
Street 9621 Fillmore Avenue				Street			
City/State/Zip Alexandria, Virginia				City/State/Zip			
Years at former address 2		☐ Own	☒ Rent	Years at former address		☐ Own	☐ Rent
Marital Status ☐ Married ☐ Separated ☐ Unmarried (incl. single, divorced, widowed)				Marital Status ☐ Married ☐ Separated ☐ Unmarried (incl. single, divorced, widowed)			

Name and Address of Employer C & P Telephone Company 8858 Georgia Avenue Potomac, Maryland 20795	Years employed in this line of work or profession? 15 years Years on this job 1 ☐ Self Employed*	Name and Address of Employer	Years employed in this line of work or profession? _____ years Years on this job _____ ☐ Self Employed*
Position/Title Staff Associate	Type of Business Utility	Position/Title	Type of Business
Social Security Number*** 323-19-5644	Home Phone 304-598-8426 Business Phone 304-927-8197	Social Security Number***	Home Phone Business Phone

GROSS MONTHLY INCOME				MONTHLY HOUSING EXPENSE **			DETAILS OF PURCHASE	
Item	Borrower	Co-Borrower	Total		PRESENT $ 266	PROPOSED		
Base Empl. Income	$1,600	$	$	Rent		$ 295.35	a. Purchase Price	$38,538
Overtime				Other Financing (P&I)			b. Total Closing Costs (Est.)	1,900
Bonuses				Hazard Insurance	34	12.00	c. Prepaid Escrows (Est.)	
Commissions				Real Estate Taxes		72.17	d. Total (a + b + c)	$ 40,438
Dividends/Interest				Mortgage Insurance		7.48	e. Amount This Mortgage	(35,900)
Net Rental Income				Homeowner Assn. Dues		18.00	f. Other Financing	( )
Other† (Before completing, see notice under Describe Other Income below.)				Other			g. Present Equity in Lot	( )
				Total Monthly Pmt.	$ 300	$ 405.00	h. Amount of Cash Deposit	(1,500)
				Utilities		80.00	i. Closing Costs Paid by Seller	( )
Total	$	$	$ 1,600	Total	$ 300	$ 485.00	j. Cash Reqd. For Closing (Est.)	$ 3,038

DESCRIBE OTHER INCOME

☞ B—Borrower C—Co-Borrower	NOTICE: † Alimony, child support, or separate maintenance income need not be revealed if the Borrower or Co-Borrower does not choose to have it considered as a basis for repaying this loan.	Monthly Amount
		$

IF EMPLOYED IN CURRENT POSITION FOR LESS THAN TWO YEARS COMPLETE THE FOLLOWING

B/C	Previous Employer/School	City/State	Type of Business	Position/Title	Dates From/To	Monthly Income
						$

THESE QUESTIONS APPLY TO BOTH BORROWER AND CO-BORROWER

If a "yes" answer is given to a question in this column, explain on an attached sheet.

	Borrower Yes or No	Co-Borrower Yes or No		Borrower Yes or No	Co-Borrower Yes or No
Have you any outstanding judgments? In the last 14 years, have you been declared bankrupt?	no				
			Do you have health and accident insurance?	yes	
Have you had property foreclosed upon or given title or deed in lieu thereof?	no		Do you have major medical coverage?	yes	
Are you a co-maker or endorser on a note?	no		Do you intend to occupy this property?	yes	
Are you a party in a law suit?	no		Will this property be your primary residence?	yes	
Are you obligated to pay alimony, child support, or separate maintenance?	no		Have you previously owned a home?	no	
Is any part of the down payment borrowed?	no		Sales Price of previously owned home? $	no	$

*FHLMC requires self employed to furnish signed copies of one or more most recent Federal Tax Returns or audited Profit and Loss Statements. FNMA requires business credit report, signed Federal Income Tax returns for last two years, and, if available, audited P/L plus balance sheet for same period.
**All Present Monthly Housing Expenses of Borrower and Co-Borrower should be listed on a combined basis.
***Neither FHLMC nor FNMA requires this information.

FHLMC 65 Rev. 3/77   FNMA 1003 Rev. 3/77

This Statement and any applicable supporting schedules may be completed jointly by both married and unmarried co-borrowers if their assets and liabilities are sufficiently joined so that the Statement can be meaningfully and fairly presented on a combined basis; otherwise separate Statements and Schedules are required (FHLMC 65A/FNMA 1003A). If the co-borrower section was completed about a spouse, this statement and supporting schedules must be completed about that spouse also. ☐ Completed Jointly ☐ Not Completed Jointly

ASSETS			LIABILITIES AND PLEDGED ASSETS			
Indicate by (*) those liabilities or pledged assets which will be satisfied upon sale of real estate owned or upon refinancing of subject property.						
Description	Cash or Market Value		Creditors' Name, Address and Account Number	Acct. Name if Not Borrower's	Mo. Pmt. and Mos. left to pay	Unpaid Balance
Cash Deposit Toward Purchase Held By	$1,500		Installment Debts (include "revolving" charge accts)		$ Pmt./Mos.	$
Checking and Savings Accounts (Show Names of Institutions/Acct. Nos.)					/	
First Va. Trust Co. Checking/29-36808-4	700				/	
Savings Account—————	2,700				/	
Stocks and Bonds (No./Description)					/	
AT & T	2,500				/	
Life Insurance Net Cash Value	-0-		Automobile Loans		/	
Face Amount ($ 30,000)						
SUBTOTAL LIQUID ASSETS	$7,400					
Real Estate Owned (Enter Market Value from Schedule of Real Estate Owned)			First Virginia Trust Co. Real Estate Loans		140 /18	$2,520
Vested Interest in Retirement Fund						
Net Worth of Business Owned (ATTACH FINANCIAL STATEMENT)	12,499					
Automobiles (Make and Year)			Other Debts Including Stock Pledges			
1976 Volkswagon	3,300				/	
Furniture and Personal Property	3,000		Alimony, Child Support and Separate Maintenance Payments Owed To			
Other Assets (Itemize)						
			TOTAL MONTHLY PAYMENTS		$140.00	
TOTAL ASSETS	A $26,199		NET WORTH (A minus B) $ 23,679		TOTAL LIABILITIES	B $2,520

SCHEDULE OF REAL ESTATE OWNED (If Additional Properties Owned Attach Separate Schedule)

Address of Property (Indicate S if Sold, PS if Pending Sale or R if Rental being held for income)		Type of Property	Present Market Value	Amount of Mortgages & Liens	Gross Rental Income	Mortgage Payments	Taxes, Ins. Maintenance and Misc.	Net Rental Income
			$	$	$	$	$	$
TOTALS →			$	$	$	$	$	$

LIST PREVIOUS CREDIT REFERENCES

	Creditor's Name and Address	Account Number	Purpose	Highest Balance	Date Paid
B	First Virginia Trust Company		Car Loan	$4,000	
B	First Virginia Trust Company – BAC	4335-150-033-798			

B–Borrower C–Co-Borrower

List any additional names under which credit has previously been received _____

AGREEMENT: The undersigned applies for the loan indicated in this application to be secured by a first mortgage or deed of trust on the property described herein, and represents that the property will not be used for any illegal or restricted purpose, and that all statements made in this application are true and are made for the purpose of obtaining the loan. Verification may be obtained from any source named in this application. The original or a copy of this application will be retained by the lender, even if the loan is not granted.
I/we fully understand that it is a federal crime punishable by fine or imprisonment, or both, to knowingly make any false statements concerning any of the above facts as applicable under the provisions of Title 18, United States Code, Section 1014.
CHECK ONE (if applicable) Yes ☐ No ☐ I/we hereby authorize loan approval details to be furnished to my/our real estate broker in order to facilitate processing of the transaction.

Victoria E. Fowler Date 6/3/77   Date _____
Borrower's Signature   Co-Borrower's Signature

VOLUNTARY INFORMATION FOR GOVERNMENT MONITORING PURPOSES

If this loan is for purchase or construction of a home, the following information is requested by the Federal Government to monitor this lender's compliance with Equal Credit Opportunity and Fair Housing Laws. The law provides that a lender may neither discriminate on the basis of this information nor on whether or not it is furnished. Furnishing this information is optional. If you do not wish to furnish the following information, please initial below.

BORROWER: I do not wish to furnish this information (initials) _____ CO-BORROWER: I do not wish to furnish this information (mitials) _____

	BORROWER		CO-BORROWER	
RACE/ NATIONAL ORIGIN	☒ American Indian, Alaskan Native ☐ Asian, Pacific Islander ☐ Black ☐ Hispanic ☒ White ☐ Other (specify)	SEX ☒ Female ☐ Male	☐ American Indian, Alaskan Native ☐ Asian, Pacific Islander ☐ Black ☐ Hispanic ☐ White ☐ Other (specify)	SEX ☐ Female ☐ Male

FOR LENDER'S USE ONLY

(FNMA REQUIREMENT ONLY) This application was taken by B. Martindil W (mail) 6/4/77 , a full time employee of
                                         Interviewer   Date
Perpetual Federal Savings, in a face to face interview with the prospective borrower.

					Given	Mailed	Initial
Appraised Value $ 38,600	Gross Mo. $ 1,600 P.I.T.I. $ 405 Debt $ 545			HUD Booklet	X		BM
Loan-to-Value Ratio 93 %	Income 25 % 34 %			Good Faith	X		BM

Loan Approved: $ 35,900 @ 9¼ % payable at $ _____ per month in 30 years plus taxes.   Settlement in Sept.

Subject to Sale @ $ 38,538 with $ equity cash. -- % Service Charge.

	Yes	No
Completion Inspection	X	
Release of Liens	X	
Private Mortgage Ins.	X	
Rescindable Transaction		X
Flood Insurance		X

Two
Executive Committee

FHLMC 65 Rev. 3/77   REVERSE   FNMA 1003 Rev. 3/77

Series KBI II

KETTLER BROTHERS, INC.   (Job No. 32348   )
BUILDERS — REALTORS
19110 MONTGOMERY VILLAGE AVENUE, GAITHERSBURG, MD. 20760 — TELEPHONE (301) 948-4000

This Agreement OF SALE entered into this 22nd   day of   May   , 19 77 , by and between Kettler Brothers, Inc , a Maryland corporation, hereinafter referred to as Seller, and

Victoria E. Fowler

hereinafter referred to as Purchaser.

Witnesseth

In consideration of a deposit in the sum of   One thousand five hundred and 00/100

(Cash)
($ 1,500.00   ) Dollars (Note for   7   days) paid by Purchaser to Seller, Seller agrees to sell and Purchaser agrees
(Check)

to buy:

Lot   #3   , Block   , Subdivision   Plat 277, Clubside, Montgomery Village

County,   Montgomery   , State   Maryland

Known as   #3 Ridgeline Drive   , with Seller's   Concord

Model, Front Style   L-11-B   dwelling completed thereon, for a price of   Thirty-seven

thousand eight hundred and 00/100

($ 37,800.00   ) Dollars, on the following terms and conditions:

1. Purchaser agrees to make payment as follows:
   a. A cash payment of   One thousand nine hundred and 00/100

   of which the above deposit shall be a part . . . .   ($ 1,900.00   )
   b. By proceeds of loan to be obtained by Purchaser in the amount of   Thirty-five thousand nine hundred and 00/100

   payable in monthly installments of approximately ($ 301.88   )
   representing principal and interest, with interest at 9¾ % or prevailing rate at
   time of settlement, secured by a first deed of trust on the premises . . . .   ($ 35,900.00   )
   c. The aforementioned loan is to be secured through
      Source provided by Seller
   d. By note payable to Seller in the amount of

   ($ N/A   )

   payable ($) monthly with balance due and payable five (5)
   years from date of same, with interest at   % secured by a deferred purchase
   money second deed of trust on the premises. Said note shall be due and payable
   in full in the event of sale, transfer or conveyance of property set forth above, at
   option of note holder.
   If Purchaser shall have been given notice of opportunity to rescind pursuant to
   the Federal Truth in Lending Laws and Regulations and shall not have elected to
   rescind within the time allowed, Purchaser shall, at or prior to settlement, so
   certify in writing
                        Total Purchase Price . . . . . .   ($ 37,800.00   )

   Purchaser agrees to cooperate in obtaining a firm commitment from the above named lending institution for a first deed
   of trust loan and shall, upon obtaining or accepting such commitment furnish Seller with satisfactory evidence thereof; if
   within thirty (30) days from the date hereof, Seller has not received satisfactory evidence of such commitment, Seller
   may, at its option at any time thereafter, return the deposit to Purchaser, whereupon this agreement shall be null and
   void. Trustees in all deeds of trust shall be named by the parties secured thereby.

2. Seller agrees to execute and deliver at settlement a special warranty deed conveying marketable title good of record. The
   property shall be conveyed subject to any covenants, conditions and restrictions of record and utility easements and rights
   of way now in existence or which may be hereafter required by the appropriate authorities in the interim period between
   the time of the date of execution of the within contract and the settlement thereunder, but free and clear of all liens and
   encumbrances except as otherwise provided herein. If there is a title defect which cannot be readily cured by legal action,
   the Seller shall return the deposit to Purchaser and this agreement shall become null and void. If legal action is necessary
   to perfect title, such action shall be taken promptly by and at the Seller's expense, whereupon the time specified herein for
   full settlement shall thereby be extended for the period necessary for such action. The Seller shall not be liable for any
   claim or damages by reason of any defect in title. Settlement shall be made at the office of the Attorney searching the title.
   Deposit with said Attorney of the deed of conveyance and such other papers as are required by the terms of this contract
   shall be deemed and construed as a good and sufficient tender of performance of the terms hereof

3. Seller assumes the risk of loss or damage to said property by fire or other casualty until the executed deed of conveyance
   is delivered at settlement.

4. Seller shall deliver possession of the premises to Purchaser at settlement. Taxes, water rent, insurance, interest on existing
   encumbrances, if any, annual Washington Suburban Sanitary Commission or other local or state government benefit
   charges, amortized water and sewer house connection fees and all other charges of assessments, if any, against the property
   shall be adjusted to the date of settlement and assumed thereafter by the Purchaser. Further, in the event subject property is heated by domestic fuel oil, Purchaser shall pay for any fuel located and stored thereon.

5. Examination of title, tax certificate, conveyancing, notary fees, transfer taxes, if any, state revenue stamps, survey if
   required, and all recording charges, including those for purchase money trust, if any, are to be at the cost of the Purchaser, who hereby authorizes the Seller to order the examination of title from
                        Betts, Clogg, and Murdock   ;

   provided however, that if upon examination, the title should be found defective and is not remedied as aforesaid, the
   Seller hereby agrees to pay the cost of the examination of the title.

{ THE PURCHASER HAS THE RIGHT TO SELECT THE TITLE INSURANCE COMPANY, SETTLEMENT, }
{ OR ESCROW COMPANY OR TITLE ATTORNEY }

KB 11 76

6. The Seller and Purchaser agree to make full settlement in accordance with subparagraphs a and b below or as soon thereafter as a report on the title can be secured if promptly ordered and subject to Seller's standard checkout (final inspection) of premises.

    a. Upon completion of the dwelling house, Seller shall give Purchaser 30 days written notice of the date of settlement and Purchaser agrees to make full settlement on such date.

    b. If the Purchaser shall fail to make full settlement in accordance with the terms hereof, the deposit herein provided for may be forfeited at the option of the Seller, in which event the Purchaser shall be relieved from further liability hereunder, or, without forfeiting the deposit, the Seller may avail itself of any legal or equitable rights or remedies which it may have under this contract.

7. The Purchaser has the option of cancelling this contract and receiving back his deposit in the event construction is not completed within 365 days from the date of acceptance hereof by the Seller, except where delay is caused by action required to perfect title in accordance with paragraph 2 hereof or except for delay occasioned by circumstances beyond the control of the Seller caused by one or more of the following: An Act of God, a national, state or local emergency, a strike, imposition of restrictions upon materials, failure of municipality or public utility company to provide necessary utilities, unusual soil conditions, or other valid cause which Seller could not foresee or anticipate, provided the same is beyond the control of the Seller to correct or remedy in the exercise of care and diligence. In the event there is a delay in the period of construction covered by the foregoing provision, settlement shall be extended for a reasonable period of time.

8. In the event government codes and regulations affecting this property are changed after the date of the contract that requires additional cost to the Seller, the Seller may, at its option, require Purchaser to pay for those costs. Upon such request, Purchaser shall, within 15 days after receipt of written notice, agree to pay such costs or may cancel their contract and the deposits will be returned whereby both parties will be relieved of all further obligations.

9. At the time of settlement, the Seller shall have substantially completed the dwelling house in accordance with its general construction standards for the community within which the subject dwelling is located. A copy of such general construction standards has been furnished Purchaser and such standards are hereby incorporated herein by reference. Provided, however, that any and all items listed on Seller's standard final inspection and check-out forms designated "Inside Check-out" and "Outside Check-out" shall be completed within a reasonable time by Seller after settlement.

10. At settlement, the Seller agrees to provide and the Purchaser agrees to accept a HOW Program Home Warranty Agreement respecting the dwelling house located on the subject property. A copy of said agreement has been furnished Purchaser and is incorporated herein by reference.

11. The Purchaser may, by selections from the Seller's *Standard Construction Options*, add to the basic plan for the model selected, provided however:

    a. That such selection must be made at *one time only* and must be agreed upon in writing on Seller's form; and

    b. That if the Seller's standard price for selections agreed upon increases the purchase price stated above, the deposit shall be increased by the amount required for such selection and paid in cash; and

    c. That it is understood that this provision does not permit the Purchaser to select any *standard construction* option if construction has proceeded beyond the stage where the option is available in the normal course of Seller's standard construction practices

Purchaser may make such *interior decorating* and *color selections* from Seller's standard selections as have not already been made, provided that such selections are completed and delivered to Seller in writing in time to be incorporated in Seller's production schedule and that any overages are paid in cash at the time the selections are made. Seller shall exercise reasonable care to see that all extra items are performed; however, Seller's responsibility for omission of any extra item shall be limited to the agreed price thereof, and any such omission shall not invalidate this agreement. Seller reserves the right to make such changes as become necessary in Seller's opinion by site or job conditions. Seller reserves the right to substitute materials or equipment of comparable quality, and to make necessary structural changes which are in accordance with the applicable building codes. All grading and landscaping, including the disposition of trees and control of waterflow shall be at the discretion of the Seller, and Seller assumes no responsibility for trees left on the premises, if any.

12. Purchaser hereby acknowledges receipt of a copy of the official subdivision plat of record containing the lot which is the subject of this agreement.

13. Purchaser has been furnished and has read copy of Declaration of Covenants, Conditions and Restrictions together with Supplementary Declaration of Covenants, Conditions and Restrictions applicable to the subdivision within which Purchaser's lot is located. Purchaser hereby accepts said documents and agrees to be bound by the provisions thereof.

    Purchase price includes a finished powder room. Purchaser agrees to pay first years mortgage insurance premium at settlement. Purchaser affirms that she is purchasing as her primary (principal) residence and will owner occupy the property.

14. Purchaser hereby acknowledges that Seller, prior to this sale, offered the opportunity to review the Master Plan for the area in which this property is located and the Purchaser has either viewed the same or has waived that privilege. Further, the Seller has disclosed to Purchaser the relative location of any airport or heliport, as defined in the County zoning ordinance, existing within a five mile radius of the property.

15. This agreement shall not be assigned without the express written consent of Seller being first had and obtained.

16. The terms of this agreement shall be binding upon the parties hereto, their heirs, executors, administrators, successors and permitted assigns. The provisions hereof shall survive execution and delivery of the deed aforesaid and shall not be merged therein. This is the entire and final agreement between the parties hereto and they shall not be bound by any terms, conditions, statements, warranties or representations, oral or written, not herein contained. This contract shall become final and binding when accepted in writing by an authorized official of Seller and deposited in the mail (ordinary, certified or registered) addressed to Purchaser.

By _____
                (Sales Representative)

5/22/77
_____
(Date)

_____
            (Purchaser)
Victoria E. Fowler

_____
(Date)

_____
(Purchaser)

KETTLER BROTHERS, INC.

_____
        Authorized Official of Seller

_____
(Date)

ARROWHEAD   5/76

K E T T L E R   B R O T H E R S ,   I N C.

PLAN COMPLETION CONFERENCE / FINAL ALTERNATE SELECTIONS

JOB # __32348__   LOT __#3__

HOUSE MODEL __Concord__   MODEL # __11 - B__

State of Completion at Time of this Conference __Under roof__

OPTIONS   KITCHEN APPLIANCES

K-100 G.E. Standard Package - Color __Harvest Wheat__

KITCHEN CABINETS

K-281 Kitchen Counter Tops __204-58   Butcher Block__

CERAMIC TILE

P-400 Ceramic Tile Bath #1   __Wall   103 Gold Fleck__

P-401 Ceramic Tile Bath #2   __Wall   103 Gold Fleck__

All bath floors shall receive resilient flooring (See color selection sheet)

ELECTRIC FIXTURES

E-290 Dining Room __Columbia Light Chandelier #3943__

E-291 Foyer _____ __Columbia Foyer Fixture #2401__

TOTAL OF ALTERNATE ITEMS	$ __738.00__
Original Contract Price	$ __37,800.00__
TOTAL Contract Price	$ __38,538.00__
Less: Original Deposit (With Contract) $ __1,500.00__	
Additional Deposit Herewith $ __738.00__	
TOTAL Deposits	$ __2,238.00__
Balance Due at Settlement	$ __36,300.00__

Please sign below, so that all purchase orders may be placed immediately

__5/22/77__   __5 22 7__
   (DATE)   (DATE)

__Victory E. Fowler__   KETTLER BROTHERS, INC.
(PURCHASER) Victoria E. Fowler   BY: _____

                                      Checked by: _____

_____
(PURCHASER)

PERPETUAL FEDERAL SAVINGS AND LOAN ASSOCIATION
11th and E Streets, Northwest
Washington, D. C. 20004

Real Estate Settlement Procedures Act
GOOD FAITH ESTIMATES OF CLOSING COSTS

Settlement Charges:
(The following headings correspond with those of the HUD Form-I, Settlement
Sheet, Section L which you will receive at settlement.)

801.	Loan Origination Fee _____ %	$ _____
803.	Appraisal Fee	75.00
804.	Credit Report	11.00
805.	Lender's Inspection Fee	
902.	Mortgage Insurance Premium for 12 Months	359.00
1101.	Settlement or Closing Fee	
1103.	Title Examination	
1104.	Title Insurance Binder	
1105.	Document Preparation	
1106.	Notary Fees	
1107.	Attorney's Fees 1101 - 1106	282.07
1109.	Title Insurance - Lender's Coverage	89.75
1201.	Recording Fees:	
	Deed $ 9.00 Mortgage $ 18.00	27.00
1202.	City/County Tax/Stamps	
	Deed $_____ Mortgage $_____	N/A
1203.	State Tax Stamps	
	Deed $ 169.56 Mortgage $_____	169.56
1204.	Transfer Taxes	
	County $ 385.38 State $ 192.69	578.07
1301.	Survey	60.00
1303.	Tax Service	2.00
	TOTAL Estimated Closing Costs	$ 1,653.45

NOTE: The above Good Faith Estimates of Closing Costs are made pursuant to
the requirements of the Real Estate Settlement Procedures Act (RESPA). These
figures are only estimates and the actual charges due at settlement may be
different. This form does not cover all items you will be required to pay in
cash at settlement, for example, deposits in escrow for real estate taxes and
insurance. You may wish to inquire as to the amounts of such other charges,
which you may be required to pay at settlement.

I/We hereby acknowledge receipt of the HUD Special Information Booklet and the
Good Faith Estimates of Closing Costs.

Victoria E. Fowler	6/10/77		
Victoria E. Fowler			
Name	Date	Name	Date

Application Number ___ 250357 ___

Property Address ___ #3 Ridgeline Drive ___

Gaithersburg, Maryland 20760

Federal National Mortgage Association

REQUEST FOR VERIFICATION OF EMPLOYMENT

FNMA

INSTRUCTIONS: LENDER- Complete items 1 thru 7. Have applicant complete item 8. Forward directly to employer named in item 1.

EMPLOYER-Please complete either Part II or Part III as applicable. Sign and return directly to lender named in item 2.

PART I - REQUEST

1. TO *(Name and address of employer)*	2. FROM *(Name and address of lender)*
C & P Telephone Company of Maryland 8858 Georgia Avenue Silver Spring, Maryland 20910	Perpetual Federal Savings & Loan 11th and E. Streets, N.W. Washington, D.C. 20004

3. SIGNATURE OF LENDER	4. TITLE	5. DATE	6. LENDER'S NUMBER *(optional)*
Donald D. Wigg	Loan Officer	6/77	

I have applied for a mortgage loan and stated that I am now or was formerly employed by you. My signature below authorizes verification of this information.

7. NAME AND ADDRESS OF APPLICANT *(Include employee or badge number)*	8. SIGNATURE OF APPLICANT
Victoria E. Fowler, 1804 Seminary Road, Maryland	*Victoria E. Fowler*

PART II - VERIFICATION OF PRESENT EMPLOYMENT

EMPLOYMENT DATA	PAY DATA		

9. APPLICANT'S DATE OF EMPLOYMENT	12A. CURRENT BASE PAY (Enter Amount and Check Period) ☒ ANNUAL ☐ HOURLY ☐ MONTHLY ☐ OTHER ☐ WEEKLY *(Specify)* $ 19,200	12C.FOR MILITARY PERSONNEL ONLY	
July, 1962		PAY GRADE	
10. PRESENT POSITION		TYPE	MONTHLY AMOUNT
Staff Associate	12B. EARNINGS	BASE PAY	$ 1,600.00

11. PROBABILITY OF CONTINUED EMPLOYMENT	TYPE	YEAR TO DATE	PAST YEAR	RATIONS	$
Definitely	BASE PAY	$	$	FLIGHT OR HAZARD	$
13. IF OVERTIME OR BONUS IS APPLICABLE, IS ITS CONTINUANCE LIKELY?	OVERTIME	$	$	CLOTHING	$
	COMMISSIONS	$	$	QUARTERS	$
OVERTIME ☐ YES ☐ NO				PRO PAY	$
BONUS ☒ YES ☐ NO	BONUS	$	$	OVER SEAS OR COMBAT	$

14. REMARKS *(if paid hourly, please indicate average hours worked each week during current and past year)*

Mrs. Fowler has been with the company for almost 15 years. She is a consciencious and highly regarded employee.

PART III - VERIFICATION OF PREVIOUS EMPLOYMENT

15. DATES OF EMPLOYMENT	16. SALARY/WAGE AT TERMINATION PER (Year) (Month)(Week)
	BASE _____ OVERTIME _____ COMMISSIONS _____ BONUS _____

17. REASON FOR LEAVING	18. POSITION HELD

The above information is provided in strict confidence in response to your request.

19. SIGNATURE OF EMPLOYER	20. TITLE	21. DATE
Jack Jones	Assistant Director of Personnel	6/8/77

The information on this form is Confidential. It is to be transmitted directly to the lender, without passing through the hands of the applicant or any other party.

PREVIOUS EDITIONS MAY BE USED UNTIL OCT. 1, 1977

FNMA Form 1005
July 77

Federal National Mortgage Association

REQUEST FOR VERIFICATION OF DEPOSIT

INSTRUCTIONS: LENDER - Complete Items 1 thru 8. Have applicant(s) complete Item 9. Forward directly to depository named in Item 1.
DEPOSITORY - Please complete Items 10 thru 15 and return DIRECTLY to lender named in Item 2.

PART I - REQUEST

1. TO (Name and address of depository)	2. FROM (Name and address of lender)
First Virginia Bank P.O. Box 123 Falls Church, Virginia 14690	Perpetual Federal Savings & Loan 1111 E. Street, N.W. Washington, D.C. 20004

3. SIGNATURE OF LENDER	4. TITLE	5. DATE	6. LENDER'S NUMBER (Optional)
William C. Mack	Loan Officer	6/8/77	250357

7. INFORMATION TO BE VERIFIED

TYPE OF ACCOUNT	ACCOUNT IN NAME OF	ACCOUNT NUMBER	BALANCE
Checking	Victoria E. Fowler	4-69-412-9	$ 700.00
Savings	Victoria E. Fowler	3-61-214-8	$2,700.00
Loan	Victoria E. Fowler	6-11-321-1	$2,520.00
			$

TO DEPOSITORY: *I have applied for a mortgage loan and stated in my financial statement that the balance on deposit with you is as shown above. You are authorized to verify this information and to supply the lender identified above with the information requested in Items 10 thru 12. Your response is solely a matter of courtesy for which no responsibility is attached to your institution or any of your officers.*

8. NAME AND ADDRESS OF APPLICANT(s)	9. SIGNATURE OF APPLICANT(s)
Victoria E. Fowler 1804 Seminary Road Falls Church, Virginia 22041	*Victoria E. Fowler*

TO BE COMPLETED BY DEPOSITORY

PART II - VERIFICATION OF DEPOSITORY

10. DEPOSIT ACCOUNTS OF APPLICANT(s)

TYPE OF ACCOUNT	ACCOUNT NUMBER	CURRENT BALANCE	AVERAGE BALANCE FOR PREVIOUS TWO MONTHS	DATE OPENED
Checking	4-69-412-9	$ 700.00	$ 700.00	6-1-75
Savings	3-61-214-8	$2,700.00	$2,700.00	6-1-75
Loan	6-11-321-1	$2,520.00	$2,520.00	1-1-76
		$	$	

11. LOANS OUTSTANDING TO APPLICANT(s)

LOAN NUMBER	DATE OF LOAN	ORIGINAL AMOUNT	CURRENT BALANCE	INSTALLMENTS (Monthly/Quarterly)		SECURED BY	NUMBER OF LATE PAYMENTS
6-11-321-1	1-1-76	$3,500.00	$2,520.00	$140	per month	Automobile	none
		$	$	$	per		
		$	$	$	per		

12. ADDITIONAL INFORMATION WHICH MAY BE OF ASSISTANCE IN DETERMINATION OF CREDIT WORTHINESS:
(Please include information on loans paid-in-full as in Item 11 above)

Subject to the requirements of the Fair Credit Reporting Act, the information provided in Items 10 thru 12 is furnished to you in strict confidence in response to your request. The accuracy of such information is not guaranteed.

13. SIGNATURE OF DEPOSITORY	14. TITLE	15. DATE
James N. Carbi, Jr.	Assistant Treasurer	6-12-77

This form is to be transmitted directly to the lender and is not to be transmitted through the applicant or any other party.

★ ★ ★ ★ THIS FORM MUST BE REPRODUCED BY LENDER ★ ★ ★ ★

FNMA Form 1006
Rev. Dec. 75

NAME AND ADDRESS OF BUREAU MAKING REPORT	REPORT TYPE

The Credit Bureau Inc.
Regional Center
P. O. Box 1617 Washington, D.C. 20013
1345 University Boulevard
Langley Park, Maryland 20783

REPORT TYPE:
☐ IN FILE ☐ SINGLE REF. ☐ TRADE
☐ EV&T ☒ FULL ☐ PREV. RES.

DATE RECEIVED	DATE MAILED	CBR REPORT
11/7/77.	11/10/77	

DATE TRADE CLEARED	DATE EMPL. VERIFIED	INCOME VERIFIED
11/77	11/77	YES NO X

CONFIDENTIAL crediscope® REPORT   FOR: 491FS84834

IN FILE SINCE:

☐ Member
Associated Credit Bureaus, Inc.

INQUIRED AS:
Perpetual Fed. Savings

4/19/73

REPORT ON (SURNAME): MR., MRS., MISS.	SOCIAL SECURITY NUMBER:	SPOUSE'S NAME:
Fowler Victoria E.	323-19-5644	

ADDRESS:	CITY:	STATE:	ZIP CODE	RESIDENCE SINCE:	SPOUSE'S SOC. SEC. NO.
1804 Seminary Rd.	Falls Church Va.		22041		

PRESENT EMPLOYER	POSITION HELD:	MONTHLY INC.	SINCE
C & P Telephone Company, Potomac Md.	Staff Assoc.	$ 1,600	7/2/60

DATE OF BIRTH	NUMBER OF DEPENDENTS			
10/10/44	1	☐ OWNS	☐ BUYING	☒ RENTS

FORMER ADDRESS:	CITY:	STATE:		FROM:	TO:
9621 Fillmore Ave.	Alexandria Va.			7/75	7/76

FORMER EMPLOYER	POSITION HELD:	MONTHLY INC.	FROM:	TO:
		$		

SPOUSE'S EMPLOYER	POSITION HELD:	MONTHLY INC.	FROM:	TO:
		$		

SPECIMEN
All entities fictitious

CREDIT HISTORY

★ Bus./ID Code	Rptd.	Opnd.	H/C	Trms.	Bal.	P/D	RT	30/60/90	MR	DLA/Account No.
491BB25185	1st Virginia Bank									
	07/77	09/75	5015	36$139	1950		I1	00 00 00		
	07/77	09/76	3497	36$97	00		I1	00 00 00	06/77	

BAC out of area trade.

I*4910N22006	Central Charge									
	06/77	08/75			00		R1	00 00 00		220547210
*491LZ29805	Hechinger									
	05/77		60		00		01	00 00 00		12312000
*491DC8200	Sears									
	04/77	09/74	93	10	00		R1	00 00 00	01	5450153491909
*491DC5479	Woodward & Lothrop									
	04/77	09/75	180		00		R1	00 00 00	09/75	21775621
U*906DC136	M Wards									
	12/76	12/76					R0	00 00 00		1Y206922117

This information is furnished in response to an inquiry for the purpose of evaluating credit risks. It has been obtained from sources deemed reliable, the accuracy of which this organization does not guarantee. The inquirer has agreed to indemnify the reporting bureau for any damage arising from misuse of this information, and this report is furnished in reliance upon that indemnity. It must be held in strict confidence, and must not be revealed to the subject reported on, except by reporting agency in accordance with the Fair Credit Reporting Act.

RESIDENTIAL APPRAISAL REPORT

File No.

Borrower/Client	Victoria E. Fowler
Property Address	3 Ridgeline Drive

Census Tract 7008.04 Map Reference 60-FU342

City Gaithersburg County Montgomery State Maryland Zip Code 20760

Legal Description Lot 3 Plat 277 Clubside, Montgomery Village

Sale Price $38,538.00 Date of Sale 5/22/77 Property Rights Appraised ☐ Fee ☐ Leasehold ☐ DeMinimis PUD(FNMA only ☐ Condo ☒ PUD)

Actual Real Estate Taxes $ _____ (yr) Loan charges to be paid by seller $ _____ Other sales concessions

Lender Perpetual Federal Savings & Loan Assoc Lender's Address 500 Eleventh St., Northwest, Washington, DC

Occupant N/A Appraiser Thos. J. Owen & Son, Inc. 20004

NEIGHBORHOOD

Location	☐ Urban	☒ Suburban	☐ Rural
Built Up	☐ Over 75%	☒ 25% to 75%	☐ Under 25%
Growth Rate ☐ Fully Dev.	☒ Rapid	☐ Steady	☐ Slow
Property Values	☒ Increasing	☐ Stable	☐ Declining
Demand/Supply	☐ Shortage	☒ In Balance	☐ Over Supply
Marketing Time	☐ Under 3 Mos.	☒ 4–6 Mos.	☐ Over 6 Mos.

Present Land Use 100% 1 Family ___ % 2–4 Family ___ % Apts. ___ % Condo ___ % Commercial

___ % Industrial ___ % Vacant ___ %

Change in Present Land Use ☒ Not Likely ☐ Likely (*) ☐ Taking Place (*)

(*) From _____ To _____

Predominant Occupancy ☒ Owner ☐ Tenant ___ % Vacant

Single Family Price Range $ 35,000 to $ 45,000 Predominant Value $ 40,000

Single Family Age New yrs to 2 yrs Predominant Age 1 yrs

	Good	Avg.	Fair	Poor
Employment Stability	☒	☐	☐	☐
Convenience to Employment	☒	☐	☐	☐
Convenience to Shopping	☒	☐	☐	☐
Convenience to Schools	☒	☐	☐	☐
Adequacy of Public Transportation	☒	☐	☐	☐
Recreational Facilities	☒	☐	☐	☐
Adequacy of Utilities	☐	☒	☐	☐
Property Compatibility	☒	☐	☐	☐
Protection from Detrimental Conditions	☒	☐	☐	☐
Police and Fire Protection	☒	☐	☐	☐
General Appearance of Properties	☒	☐	☐	☐
Appeal to Market	☒	☐	☐	☐

Note: FHLMC/FNMA do not consider the racial composition of the neighborhood to be a relevant factor and it must not be considered in the appraisal.

Comments (including those factors, favorable or unfavorable, affecting marketability) Subject neighborhood is a well planned community of modest priced townhouse dwelling units representing but one sector of the "Kettler Built" Montgomery Village project which offers homes ranging in price from the low $30,000.00 to over $100,000.00. Quarterly Home Owners Association fee of $54.00 provides for swimming pools, tennis courts, bike paths, tot lots, lake, and amphitheater.

SITE

Dimensions 22.00' x 42.00' x 42.00' x 22.00' = 924 Sq. Ft. or Acres ☒ Corner Lot

Zoning classification (Town Sector) Residential Present improvements ☒ do ☐ do not conform to zoning regulations

Highest and best use: ☒ Present use ☐ Other (specify) When Complete

	Public	Other (Describe)	OFF SITE IMPROVEMENTS	Topo	Average
Elec.	☒		Street Access: ☐ Public ☒ Private	Size	Average
Gas	☐		Surface Asphalt	Shape	Average
Water	☒		Maintenance: ☐ Public ☒ Private	View	Average
San.Sewer	☒		☒ Storm Sewer ☒ Curb/Gutter	Drainage	Average
		☒ Underground Elect. & Tel. ☒ Sidewalk ☒ Street Lights	Is the property located in a HUD Identified Special Flood Hazard Area? ☒ No ☐ Yes		

Comments (favorable or unfavorable including any apparent adverse easements, encroachments or other adverse conditions) Subject site is typical of the lots within Clubside, in that groups of lots are platted back to back without the benefit of a rear yard. The end unit location of subject site enhances its desirability.

IMPROVEMENTS

☐ Existing (approx. yr. blt.) 19 ___ No. Units 1 Type (det, duplex, semi/det, etc.) Design (rambler, split level, etc.) Ext 50% Walls 50%

☐ Proposed ☒ Under Construction No. Stories 2 End of Row Townhouse Brick/Frame

Roof Material Composition Gutters & Downspouts ☐ None Aluminum Window (Type): Wooden double hung Insulation ☐ None ☐ Floor

☐ Storm Sash ☒ Screens ☐ Combination ☒ Ceiling ☐ Roof ☒ Walls

Foundation Walls – 0 % Basement ☐ Floor Drain Finished Ceiling –

☐ Outside Entrance ☐ Sump Pump Finished Walls –

☐ Crawl Space ☐ Concrete Floor – % Finished Finished Floor –

☒ Slab on Grade Evidence of: ☐ Dampness ☐ Termites ☐ Settlement

Comments Improvements to be constructed in accordance with the plans and specifications for the "Concord" model style dwelling.

ROOM LIST

Room List	Foyer	Living	Dining	Kitchen	Den	Family Rm.	Rec. Rm.	Bedrooms	No. Baths	Laundry	Other
Basement											
1st Level	x	x	"L"	x					½	x	Utility
2nd Level								2	1		

Finished area above grade contains a total of 5 rooms 2 bedrooms 1½ baths.

Kitchen Equipment: ☒ Refrigerator ☒ Range/Oven ☒ Disposal ☒ Dishwasher ☒ Fan/Hood ☐ Compactor ☐ Washer ☐ Dryer ☐

HEAT: Type HeatPump Fuel Elec. Cond. Good AIR COND: ☒ Central ☐ Other ☒ Adequate ☐ Inadequate

INTERIOR FINISH & EQUIPMENT

Floors	☐ Hardwood ☒ Carpet Over SubFlr ☐	
Walls	☒ Drywall ☐ Plaster ☐	
Trim/Finish	☐ Good ☒ Average ☐ Fair ☐ Poor	
Bath Floor	☐ Ceramic ☒ Composition Tile	
Bath Wainscot	☐ Ceramic ☒ Drywall	
Special Features (including fireplaces): Smoke Detector	

PROPERTY RATING

	Good	Avg.	Fair	Poor
Quality of Construction (Materials & Finish)	☐	☒	☐	☐
Condition of Improvements	☒	☐	☐	☐
Rooms size and layout	☐	☒	☐	☐
Closets and Storage	☐	☒	☐	☐
Plumbing—adequacy and condition	☒	☐	☐	☐
Electrical—adequacy and condition	☒	☐	☐	☐
Kitchen Cabinets—adequacy and condition	☐	☒	☐	☐
Compatibility to Neighborhood	☒	☐	☐	☐
Overall Livability	☐	☒	☐	☐
Appeal and Marketability	☒	☐	☐	☐

ATTIC: ☒ Yes ☐ No ☐ Stairway ☐ Drop-stair ☒ Scuttle ☐ Floored

Finished (Describe Unfinished potential storage ☐ Heated

CAR STORAGE: ☐ Garage ☐ Built-in ☐ Attached ☐ Detached ☐ Car Port

No. Cars N/A ☐ Adequate ☐ Inadequate Condition

Effective Age New Yrs. Est. Remaining Economic Life 60 Yrs.

PORCHES, PATIOS, POOL, FENCES, etc. (describe) Wooden side yard privacy fencing.

COMMENTS (including functional or physical inadequacies, repairs needed, modernization, etc.) Subject improvements are typical of other improvements previously erected and under construction in the "Clubside" section of Montgomery Village offering an average degree of functional utility.

VALUATION SECTION

Purpose of Appraisal is to estimate Market Value as defined in Certification & Statement of Limiting Conditions (FHLMC Form 439/FNMA Form 1004B). If submitted for FNMA, the appraiser must attach (1) sketch or map showing location of subject, street names, distance from nearest intersection, and any detrimental conditions and (2) exterior building sketch of improvements showing dimensions.

COST APPROACH

Measurements		No. Stories		Sq. Ft.
19.50' x 25.08'	x	2	=	978.12
2.00' x 14.00'	x	2	=	56.00
1.33' x 5.33'	x	2	=	14.18
x	x		=	
x	x		=	
x	x		=	

Total Gross Living Area (List in Market Data Analysis below) 1048.30

Total on functional and economic obsolescence: No functional or economic obsolescence observed.

ESTIMATED REPRODUCTION COST – NEW – OF IMPROVEMENTS:

Dwelling 1048 Sq. Ft. @ $ 28.00	=	$29,344.00
— Sq. Ft. @ $ —	=	—
Extras Smoke Detector	=	50.00
Porches, Patios, etc. Privacy Fencing	=	400.00
Garage/Car Port N/A Sq. Ft. @ $ —	=	—
Site Improvements (driveway, landscaping, etc.)	=	1,500.00
Total Estimated Cost New	=	$31,294.00

	Physical	Functional	Economic	
Less Depreciation $ —	$ —	$ —	= $(—)

Depreciated value of improvements . . . . = $31,294.00
ESTIMATED LAND VALUE . . . . = $ 8,000.00
(If leasehold, show only leasehold value)

INDICATED VALUE BY COST APPROACH $39,294.00

MARKET DATA ANALYSIS

The undersigned has recited three recent sales of properties most similar and proximate to subject and has considered these in the market analysis. The description includes a dollar adjustment, reflecting market reaction to those items of significant variation between the subject and comparable properties. If a significant item in the comparable property is superior to, or more favorable than, the subject property, a minus (-) adjustment is made, thus reducing the indicated value of subject; if a significant item in the comparable is inferior to, or less favorable than, the subject property, a plus (+) adjustment is made, thus increasing the indicated value of the subject.

ITEM	Subject Property	COMPARABLE NO. 1	Adjustment	COMPARABLE NO. 2	Adjustment	COMPARABLE NO. 3	Adjustment
Address	3 Ridgeline Drive	Lot 6 Clubside Montgomery Village		Lot 15 Clubside Montgomery Village		Lot 21 Clubside Montgomery Village	
Proximity to Subj.		Same Section		Same Section		Same Section	
Sales Price	$38,538.00	$37,892		$37,800		$37,800	
Price/Living area	$36.77	$36.16		$36.07		$36.07	
Data Source	Contract/Appr.	Contract/Appraisal		Contract/Appraisal		Contract/Appraisal	
Date of Sale and Time Adjustment	5/77	5/77		3/77		5/77	
Location	Average	Average		Average		Average	
Site/View	Good/Average	Good/Average		Good/Average		Good/Average	
Design and Appeal	Average/Average	Average/Average		Average/Average		Average/Average	
Quality of Const.	Average	Average		Average		Average	
Age	New	New		New		New	
Condition	New	New		New		New	
Living Area Room Count and Total	Total 5 | B-rms 2 | Baths 1½	Total 5 | B-rms 2 | Baths 1½		Total 5 | B-rms 2 | Baths 1½		Total 5 | B-rms 2 | Baths 1½	
Gross Living Area	1048 Sq.Ft.	1048 Sq.Ft.		1048 Sq.Ft.		1048 Sq.Ft.	
Basement & Bsmt. Finished Rooms	N/A	N/A		N/A		N/A	
Functional Utility	Average	Average		Average		Average	
Air Conditioning	Central	Central		Central		Central	
Garage/Car Port	N/A	N/A		N/A		N/A	
Porches, Patio, Pools, etc.	Privacy Fence	Privacy Fence		Privacy Fence		Privacy Fence	
Other (e.g. fireplaces, kitchen equip., heating, remodeling)	Smoke Detector	Smoke Detector		Smoke Detector		Smoke Detector	
Sales or Financing Concessions	Conventional	Conventional		Conventional		Conventional	
Upgrade/Options	$738.00	$92.00	+ 646	N/A	+ 738	N/A	+ 738
Net Adj. (Total)		☒ Plus; ☐ Minus $ 646		☒ Plus; ☐ Minus $ 738		☒ Plus; ☐ Minus $ 738	
Indicated Value of Subject		$38,538		$ 38,538		$ 38,538	

Comments on Market Data: Considered excellent, reflecting recent sales involving the same model style unit. The only adjustments required were for alternate selections which were prepriced by the builder.

INDICATED VALUE BY MARKET DATA APPROACH . . . . $ 38,538

INDICATED VALUE BY INCOME APPROACH (If applicable) Economic Market Rent $ N/A /Mo. x Gross Rent Multiplier _____ = $ —

This appraisal is made ☐ "as is" ☐ subject to the repairs, alterations, or conditions listed below ☒ completion per plans and specifications.

Comments and Conditions of Appraisal: Subject to new house completion in accordance with the plans and specifications for the "Concord" model home and release of liens. *See title binder for conditions of home owners Association.

Final Reconciliation: The Market Data Approach has been given the most extensive consideration due to the excellence of recent reliable data. The Cost Approach has been utilized primarily as a reasonable check in the absence of comparable lot sales. The Income Approach is not considered applicable herein.

This appraisal is based upon the above requirements, the certification, contingent and limiting conditions, and Market Value definition that are stated in

☒ FHLMC Form 439 (Rev. 7/77)/FNMA Form 1004B filed with client _____ September 20, 19 65 ☐ attached.

If submitted for FNMA, the report has been prepared in compliance with FNMA form instructions.

I ESTIMATE THE MARKET VALUE, AS DEFINED, OF SUBJECT PROPERTY AS OF July 8, 19 77 to be $ 38,600.00

Appraiser(s) *Robert C. Kidwell*
Robert C. Kidwell

Review Appraiser (If applicable) _____
Thornton W. Owen, Jr. ☐ Did ☒ Did Not Physically Inspect Property

FHLMC Form 70 Rev. 7/77   REVERSE   FNMA Form 1004 Rev. 7/77

FRONT

STREET SCENE

MORTGAGOR: Victoria E. Fowler

ADDRESS: 3 Ridgeline Drive
            Gaithersburg, Maryland

MGIC

MORTGAGE GUARANTY INSURANCE CORPORATION
a subsidiary of MGIC Investment Corporation

Regional Office addresses on back of pad

Instant Mortgage Loan Insurance Application

SIMPLY COMPLETE THE FOLLOWING AND SELECT PREMIUM PLAN, THEN DATE AND SIGN

Perpetual Federal Savings and Loan Association   08-001-1-1030

LENDER NAME   MGIC LENDER NUMBER

1111 E Street, N.W., Washington, D.C.   20004

LENDER ADDRESS   STREET   CITY   STATE   ZIP

Victoria E. Fowler

BORROWER(S) NAME(S)

SELECT ANNUAL OR SINGLE PREMIUM PLAN, THEN ⊠ ONE BOX.

USE FOR STANDARD COVERAGE

MGIC COVERAGE	LOAN TO VALUE	ANNUAL PREMIUM PLAN		SINGLE PREMIUM PLANS				
				4 YRS.	5 YRS.	7 YRS.	10 YRS.	15 YRS.
25%	OVER 90-95%	1% 1st.yr. ¼% ann. ☒ 4	½% ea. 1st. 3yrs. ¼% ann. ☐ 8		1¾% ☐ B	2% ☐ 3	2½% ☐ 6	2¾% ☐ O
	OVER 80-90%	¾% first year ¼% annually ☐ 52		1¼% ☐ 59			2¼% ☐ 51	2½% ☐ 5L
20%	OVER 90-95%	¾% first year ¼% annually ☐ F		1½% ☐ G	1¾% ☐ H	2¼% ☐ J	2½% ☐ K
	OVER 80-90%	½% first year ¼% annually ☐ 2		1% ☐ 9			2% ☐ 1	2¼% ☐ L
	80% AND UNDER	¼% first year ¼% annually ☐ C		¾% ☐ M	1% ☐ N		1½% ☐ E
10%	80% AND UNDER	.15% first year .15% annually ☐ 6C		.6% ☐ 6M	.8% ☐ 6N	1% ☐ 6E

USE FOR FHLMC/FNMA/GNMA (COVERAGE TO 75%)

MGIC COVERAGE	LOAN TO VALUE	ANNUAL PREMIUM PLAN		SINGLE PREMIUM PLAN*	
22%	OVER 90-95%	.8% first year ¼% annually ☐ 44		2.4% ☐ 40	
17%	OVER 80-90%	.4% first year ¼% annually ☐ 32		2% ☐ 3L	

*Provides coverage until loan is amortized to 80% of original value not to exceed 15 years.

Check if requesting:
☒ FHLMC Underwriting Analysis
☐ Completion of FHLMC Form 13SF

CONSTANT RENEWAL PLAN ☒
(optional)

OTHER PREMIUM PLANS

Indicate Plan Code : _____

IMPORTANT! ATTACH COPIES OF THE DOCUMENTS LISTED BELOW

☒ COPY OF LENDER'S LOAN APPLICATION   ☒ COPY OF CURRENT APPRAISAL REPORT WITH PHOTO
☒ COPY OF CURRENT CREDIT REPORT   ☐ MORTGAGE PAYMENT RECORD (REFINANCE ONLY)
☒ VERIFICATION OF EMPLOYMENT   ☒ COPY OF SALES CONTRACT

COMPLETE THIS SECTION IF MISSING OR DIFFERENT FROM LOAN APPLICATION

AMOUNT OF LOAN   AMORTIZATION PERIOD   INTEREST RATE   MONTHLY PAYMENT (includes P & I, taxes, condo fee, insurance, MGIC)

$ YEARS   % $

TYPE OF PROPERTY (CHECK ONE)   WILL BORROWER OCCUPY PROPERTY?
☐ ONE FAMILY DETACHED   ☐ CONDOMINIUM   ☐ 2-4 FAMILY   ☒ YES   ☐ NO

FOR IMMEDIATE TELECOMMITMENT REPLY, PLEASE COMPLETE THE FOLLOWING:

AREA CODE/TELEPHONE NUMBER   202-638-7181   PERSON TO CONTACT   Judy Willis

7/15/77

DATE   BY LENDER'S AUTHORIZED REPRESENTATIVE

01-0114 (3/76) SE   SUBMIT WHITE AND YELLOW COPIES TO MGIC

The full service

Mortgage Guaranty Insurance Certificate

a combination Commitment Certificate

MGIC

Mortgage Guaranty Insurance Corporation

MGIC Plaza
Milwaukee, Wisconsin 53201

a subsidiary of
MGIC Investment Corporation

Mortgage Guaranty Insurance Corporation hereby agrees to insure the Lender against loss on the Mortgage loan described below, subject to the terms and conditions of the specified Master Policy, and the conditions noted below, if any. The Certificate of Insurance shall become effective on the mortgage consummation date.

Insured Lender's Name and Mailing Address

PERPETUAL FEDERAL SAVINGS & LOAN ASSN
500 11TH STREET NW
WASHINGTON   DC   20004

Master Policy Number	Commitment/ Certificate No.	Commitment Effective Date	Commitment Expiration Date	Amount of Coverage
08-001-1-1030	1,000000	7/20/77	7/20/78	TOP 25%

$ 35,900.00   amount of loan insured. Amortization period   30   years.

4	$ 359.00	1% OF LOAN AMOUNT FOR 1ST YEAR, WITH ANNUAL RENEWALS AT 1/4% OF PRINCIPAL BALANCE DUE AT BEGINNING OF EACH RENEWAL YEAR.

Borrower Name: FOWLER VICTORIA E
Property: #3 RIDGELINE DRIVE
                GAITHERSBURG   MD   20760

SP   38538
AV   38600

P & I	295.46	TRUTH		PREMIUM	BASIS-PTS	YRS	MON PREM
INITIAL		IN	10 YR	1,132.50	30	FIRST	7.43
PREMIUM	359.00	LENDING LIFE		2,213.02	39	LAST	.72

The Company has caused this Commitment/Certificate to be signed and sealed by its duly authorized officers in facsimile to become effective as its original seal and signatures and binding on the Company.

Mortgage Guaranty Insurance Corporation

Leon T. Kendall
President

John Lelonni
Secretary

CC416783

LENDER CERTIFICATION

The undersigned certifies that the above loan transaction has been consummated, the applicable premium has been paid, the buyer-seller affidavit (if applicable) and other documents necessary to satisfy the above conditions, if any, have been forwarded to the Company.

Mortgage Consummation Date (effective date of certificate)	Lender Loan No.	Remittance Amount	Authorized Signature of Lender	Date
9/9/77	6-203— 7981-5	$ 359.00	*Judy Wells*	9/12/77

01-0039A (9/76)

ORIGINAL CERTIFICATE — LENDER RETAIN

PERPETUAL FEDERAL SAVINGS AND LOAN ASSOCIATION
11th & E Streets, N. W.
WASHINGTON, D. C. 20004
Phone: 783-7700

Application No.   250357

Date: August 1, 1977

FIRST TRUST REAL ESTATE LOAN COMMITMENT

This Association has approved and hereby agrees to make a loan to the applicant named herein to be secured by a First Deed of Trust on the hereinafter described real estate on the following terms and conditions:

Name(s) of Borrower(s): __VICTORIA E. FOWLER__

Amount of Loan $ __35,900.00__   Term __30 YRS.__   Simple Interest Rate __9.250__ *

Sales Price $ __38,538.00__   Minimum Cash Payment $ __EQUITY CASH.__

Payable $ __302.83**__ monthly including principal and interest, plus one-twelfth of annual real estate taxes.
__IT IS UNDERSTOOD THAT THE APPLICANT IS TO OCCUPY THE PROPERTY__
__AS HIS PRINCIPAL RESIDENCE.__
__THIS LOAN IS TO BE PARTIALLY INSURED WITH PRIVATE MORTGAGE INSUR-__
__ANCE AND THE COMMITMENT IS SUBJECT TO THE APPROVAL OF THE PROPOSED__
__LOAN BY THE INSUROR.__
** __INCLUDES PRIVATE MORTGAGE INSURANCE PREMIUM EQUAL TO ONE-QUARTER__
__OF ONE PER CENT OF THE LOAN AMOUNT.__
__ALSO SUBJECT TO A COMPLETION INSPECTION AND FURNISHING A__
__SATISFACTORY RELEASE OF LIENS.__

PROPERTY OFFERED AS SECURITY: __LT 3, CLUBSIDE-MONT.VILL.,__

__3 RIDGELINE DRIVE, GAITHERSBURG, MD__

Charges to be collected at settlement and remitted to Perpetual Federal Savings and Loan Association:

Credit Report $ __11.00__ PREPAID   Appraisal Fee $ __75.00__ PREPAID
Private Mortgage   Service Charge $ __.00__
Insurance Premium $ __359.00__
In addition to the above charges, an escrow for real estate taxes must be paid at settlement.

GENERAL CONDITIONS

1. This loan is to be made in accordance with the laws of the jurisdiction where the property is located. The terms, agreements and covenants of the loan and the note and deed of trust evidencing the loan shall be governed by the laws of said jurisdiction. The note, deed of trust, legal description and all other documents required in connection with this loan shall be on the forms designated by this Association.
2. **Title Insurance**—Title work for this loan must be ordered by you or your agent. A satisfactory Mortgagee Title Insurance Policy will be required. The Mortgagee's Title Insurance Policy is for the protection of the mortgagee only and we suggest that you obtain information about an Owners Title Insurance Policy from your Title Company or Title Attorney.
3. **Survey**—A recent survey certified by a registered land surveyor showing all improvements, building restriction lines, joint driveways, easements and rights-of-way, if any, must be received and approved prior to our sending loan closing instructions.
4. **Insurance**—The property is to be insured at all times to the satisfaction of this Association with a Mortgagee Clause in favor of Perpetual Federal Savings and Loan Association. Please sign the enclosed insurance form and return with your acceptance of this commitment.
5. **Credit Reports**—A satisfactory credit report on the applicant shall be obtained by the Association at the cost of the applicant.
6. **Prepayment**—The borrower may prepay the loan in part or in full at any time with interest to the end of the month in which prepayment is made.
7. **Refinance**—If this loan commitment is for the purpose of refinancing any existing encumbrances, the outstanding balance of the existing encumbrance will be deducted from the proceeds of the new loan.
8. **Disclosure Statement.**—A Loan Disclosure Statement as required by Federal Law and Federal Reserve Regulation Z is enclosed. This statement must be signed and returned with your acceptance of this commitment.
* Please see item #4 of this statement of Annual Percentage Rates.
9. This Association shall be the sole judge of the satisfactory compliance with all the conditions of this commitment and the representations made on the loan application. We reserve the right to refuse consummation of this loan if in our opinion the conditions hereof have not been satisfactorily met, or if we find substantial differences from representations made on the application.
10. Written acceptance of this commitment must be made within 15 days from the date issued. Settlement must be made in the month of AUGUST, 1977 ; otherwise this commitment will become null and void.

PERPETUAL FEDERAL SAVINGS AND LOAN ASSOCIATION

By: *R. Lamond Jones*

This commitment is hereby accepted and receipt is acknowledged of a copy of this agreement on this the __3rd__ day of __August__, 19__, prior to the signing of the indebtedness contracted in connection with the above loan.

Victoria E. Fowler
VICTORIA E. FOWLER

PLEASE RETAIN ORIGINAL FOR YOUR RECORDS AND RETURN SIGNED YELLOW COPY

MD 2M 3/77

Conventional Loan For
Purchase of Principal
Residence
MD

PERPETUAL FEDERAL SAVINGS AND
LOAN ASSOCIATION
Washington, D. C.
DISCLOSURE STATEMENT OF LOAN

Borrower(s): **VICTORIA E. FOWLER**

Property: **3 RIDGELINE DRIVE, GAITHERSBURG, MD**

1. Principal and interest at the rate of **9.250** % is to be paid in **360** equal monthly installments of $ **302.83**** each. Interest from the date of settlement to the end of the month will be due on the first day of the month following settlement. In addition to the payment of principal and interest the borrower is required to pay one-twelfth of the annual real estate taxes monthly.

2. Principal Amount of this Mortgage Loan . . . . $ **35,900.00**
   Less: PREPAID FINANCE CHARGES

   ~~PRIVATE MORTGAGE INSURANCE PREMIUM~~ $ **359.00**
   _____ $ _____

   TOTAL PREPAID FINANCE CHARGES . . . . $ **359.00***
   AMOUNT FINANCED . . . . $ **35,541.00***

3. Charges Not Part of Finance Costs:

   Recording Cost:
   Deed $ **14.00**   City/Co. Transfer Tax $ **385.38**
   Deed of Trust $ **18.00**   State Transfer Tax $ **192.69**
   Recording Release   Documentary Tax Stamps $ **169.57**
    of Trust $ **16.00**   Other $ **.00**
   Taxes (balance of
        year) $ **.00***

   These charges do not include all settlement costs. A complete list of settlement charges can be obtained from the title company or title attorney who will settle this case.

   / *NOTE: Any figures in Section 2 & 3 above with asterisks are estimated /

4. Expressed as an ANNUAL PERCENTAGE RATE the FINANCE CHARGE is **9.50** %

5. The borrower will pay a late charge not to exceed three cents (3¢) for each dollar ($1.00) of the total monthly payment which is not paid within fifteen (15) days after due date thereof, to cover the extra expense involved in handling late payments.

6. Lender's security interest in this transaction is a Deed of Trust on property located at **3 RIDGELINE DRIVE, GAITHERSBURG, MD** .

7. Said Deed of Trust covers all property described therein with any after acquired property located thereon and any future advances the terms of which are described therein.

8. The borrower may prepay the loan in part or in full at anytime with interest to the end of the month in which prepayment is made.

9. The terms of this loan are subject to modification in the event of sale or conveyance of the property.

INSURANCE

Property Insurance required in connection with this loan may be obtained by the borrower through any company of his choice. The lender may refuse to accept the borrower's insurer for reasonable cause.

The minimum coverage required in connection with this transaction will be Fire and Extended Coverage in the amount of $ **35,900.00** . If the borrower desires this insurance to be obtained by Perpetual the cost will be $ **111.00** for the first **1** year(s) permium.

I hereby acknowledge receipt of the disclosure made above and affirm my acceptance of your offer of a loan dated **August 1, 1977** Application No. **250357** .

                                                    Victoria E. Fowler
                                        Borrower   **VICTORIA E. FOWLER**

8/3/77
Date   Borrower

**INCLUDES PRIVATE MORTGAGE INSURANCE PREMIUM

Loan Application Number 250357

MEMORANDUM & CERTIFICATE OF HAZARD INSURANCE
("CERTIFICATE")

This is to certify to Perpetual Federal Savings & Loan that there is in force

a Hazard Insurance Policy No. 18891564_____ of the ___Allstate_____

Insurance Company, with an inception date of ___9/9/77____ , in the amount of

$36,000.00_____ on the dwelling(s) located at (complete street address)

___#3 Ridgeline Drive, Gaithersburg, Maryland 20760_____

against the perils of at least fire and extended coverage for a term of ___1__ years

with an annual premium of $69.00_____ and with a mortgage clause in favor of

Perpetual Federal Savings & Loan Association.

> It is understood and agreed by the Agency designated
> and signed below that should the insurance protection
> specified above terminate for any reason, due notice
> will be given to Perpetual Federal Savings & Loan Association.

NAME INSURED Victoria E. Fowler_____

AGENCY___Allstate: Sears, Roebuck and Co. Building_____ DATE_8/31/77__

ADDRESS__7103 Democracy Blvd., - Bethesda, Maryland 20034 BY *(signature)*
                                                              (Agent's signature)

Executed copy should be returned at least three business days before settlement to:

> Mortgage Loan Department
> Perpetual Federal Savings & Loan Association
> 1111 "E" Street, N.W.
> Washington, DC   20004

PFID 1027

COMMONWEALTH LAND
TITLE INSURANCE COMPANY
(a stock company)   PHILADELPHIA, PENNSYLVANIA

COMMITMENT FOR TITLE INSURANCE

Commitment No.
801 – 365457

File No.___3062 MV_____

SCHEDULE A

1. Effective Date: **20th**   day of   **August, 1977**   , at   **4:30**   .M.

2. Policy or Policies to be issued: Amount

   (a)   ALTA Owner – 1970   ☐ Form B   ☐ Form A $ _____
          (Amended 10-17-70)
   Proposed Insured:

          Victoria E. Fowler

   (b) ☐   ALTA Loan Policy – 1970 (Amended 10-17-70) $35,900.00_____

Proposed Insured:

☒ Conv ☐ FHA ☐ VA

Perpetual Federal Savings and Loan Association

3. The estate or interest in the land described or referred to in the Commitment and covered herein is
and is at the effective date hereof vested in   Kettler Brothers, Inc. (a Maryland Corporation)

4. The land referred to in this Commitment is situated in the County of   Montgomery
   State of   Maryland   and described as follows:

Lot numbered 3, in the subdivision known as, "Plat 277, Lots 3 through 49,
Being a resubdivision of Lots 182 to 195, CLUBSIDE, Part of Section 2-A,
MONTGOMERY VILLAGE", as per Plat thereof duly recorded among the Land Records
of Montgomery County, Maryland in Plat Book 100 at Plat 11262.

Property Address: #3 Ridgeline Drive
                  Gaithersburg, Maryland 20760

SETTLEMENT DATE: September 9, 1977

Betts, Clogg & Murdock
PO Box 2186
Gaithersburg, Maryland 20760

Countersigned:
            James G. Hollis   Authorized Officer or Agent
American Land Title Association Commitment – 1966
Schedule A   Valid Only If Schedule B and Cover Are Attached
Form 1004-2 (6-77)
                ORIGINAL

Commitment No. '801-365257

File No.   3062 MV

Schedule B — Section 1

The following are the requirements to be complied with:

1. Instrument creating the estate or interest to be insured must be executed and filed for record, to-wit:

   a.   Proper deed vesting fee simple title to Victoria E. Fowler.

   b.   Deed of Trust from above named party securing Perpetual Federal Savings and
      Loan Association in the amount of $35,900.00.

2. Pay the full consideration to, or for the account of, the grantors or mortgagors.

3. Pay all taxes, charges, assessments, levied and assessed against subject premises, which are due and payable.

4. Satisfactory evidence should be had that improvements and/or repairs or alterations thereto are completed; that contractor, sub-contractors, labor and materialmen are all paid; and have released of record all liens or notice of intent to perfect a lien for labor or material.

5.   FREE & CLEAR

Schedule B — Section 2

Schedule B of the policy or policies to be issued will contain exceptions to the following matters unless the same are disposed of to the satisfaction of the Company:

1. Defects, liens, encumbrances, adverse claims or other matters, if any, created, first appearing in the public records or attaching subsequent to the effective date hereof but prior to the date the proposed Insured acquires for value of record the estate or interest or mortgage thereon covered by this Commitment.

CONTINUED

NOTE: AN OWNER'S POLICY ISSUED IN CONNECTION WITH THIS COMMITMENT WILL CONTAIN THE FOLLOW-
ING PRE-PRINTED EXCEPTIONS:
1. Rights or claims of parties other than Insured in actual possession of any or all of the property.
2. Unrecorded easements, discrepancies or conflicts in boundary lines, shortage in area and encroachments which an accurate
   and complete survey would disclose.
3. Unfiled mechanics' or materialmen's liens.

American Land Title Association Commitment 1966
Schedule B   **ORIGINAL**
Form 1004-7 (10-74)

Commitment No. 801-365257

File No. 3062 MV

Schedule B — Section 2

    Schedule B of the policy or policies to be issued will contain exceptions to the following matters unless the same are disposed of to the satisfaction of the Company:

1. Defects, liens, encumbrances, adverse claims or other matters, if any, created, first appearing in the public records or attaching subsequent to the effective date hereof but prior to the date the proposed Insured acquires for value of record the estate or interest or mortgage thereon covered by this Commitment.

2. Taxes subsequent to those for the levy ending June 30, 1977.

3. Washington Suburban Sanitary Commission taxes, charges and assessments subsequent to those for the calendar year ending December 31, 1976.

4. Minimum building restriction lines established by owner's dedication on the recorded plat.

5. Restrictive covenants as recorded in Liber 3592 at folio 299, and Liber 4903 at folio 338, Liber 4903 at folio 356 and Liber 4903 at folio 425.

6. Right of Way to Potomac Electric Power Company recorded in Liber 676 at folio 369.

7. Agreement to Washington Surburban Sanitary Commission recorded in Liber 4726 at folio 86.

8. Subject to a five (5) foot water easement as shown on said plat.

9. Party wall rights.

NOTE: Policy insures that the building restriction lines and restrictive covenants set forth herein have not been violated and a future violation thereof will not cause a forfeiture or reversion of title.

Plat 276, Plat Book 100 at Plat 11262

NOTE: AN OWNER'S POLICY ISSUED IN CONNECTION WITH THIS COMMITMENT WILL CONTAIN THE FOLLOW-
ING PRE-PRINTED EXCEPTIONS:
1. Rights or claims of parties other than Insured in actual possession of any or all of the property.
2. Unrecorded easements, discrepancies or conflicts in boundary lines, shortage in area and encroachments which an accurate
   and complete survey would disclose.
3. Unfiled mechanics' or materialmen's liens.

American Land Title Association Commitment 1966
Schedule B — Section 2
Form 1004-6 (9-75)   **ORIGINAL**

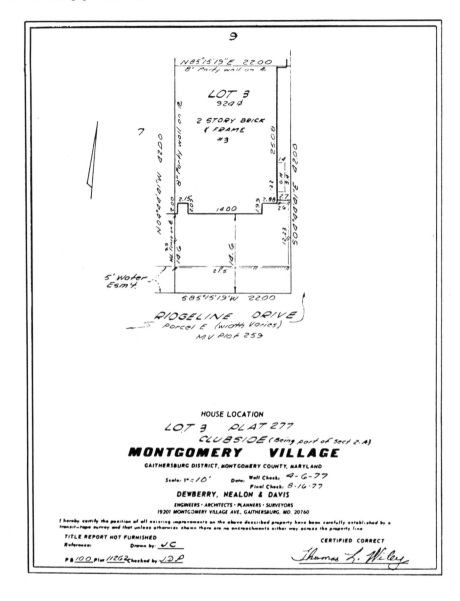

HOUSE LOCATION

LOT 3   PLAT 277

CLUBSIDE (Being part of Sect 2.A)

MONTGOMERY VILLAGE

GAITHERSBURG DISTRICT, MONTGOMERY COUNTY, MARYLAND

Scale: 1"=10'   Date: Wall Check: 4-6-77
Final Check: 8-16-77

DEWBERRY, NEALON & DAVIS

ENGINEERS · ARCHITECTS · PLANNERS · SURVEYORS
19201 MONTGOMERY VILLAGE AVE., GAITHERSBURG, MD. 20760

I hereby certify the position of all existing improvements on the above described property have been carefully established by a transit—tape survey and that unless otherwise shown there are no encroachments either way across the property line

TITLE REPORT NOT FURNISHED

Reference: Drawn by: JC

CERTIFIED CORRECT

PB 100 Plat 1126 Checked by: JDP

Thomas L. Wiley

HOME
OWNERS
WARRANTY
CORPORATION

National Housing Center
15th and M Streets, N.W. Washington, D.C. 20005

Single Family Home
Final Enrollment

ENROLLMENT NO.

(1) HOW COUNCIL OF __Suburban Maryland Home Builders Association__   LOCAL COUNCIL NO. | 2 | 1 | 7 | 8 |

(2) PARTICIPATING BUILDER (NAME) __Kettler Brothers, Incorporated__   BUILDERS REG. NO. | 1 | 3 | 3 | 7 | 2 |

(3) LEGAL DESCRIPTION OF HOME TO BE ENROLLED __#3 Ridgeline Drive__

__Gaithersburg__   __Maryland__   __Montgomery__
    City   State   County

(4) ESTIMATED START OF CONSTRUCTION   MONTH _____ YEAR _____

(5) IS THE HOME BEING ENROLLED UNDER THE GRANDFATHER OR GREAT GRANDFATHER CLAUSE? _____ YES   __X__ NO

(6) CHECK ONE   __X__ GOVERNMENT CODE AND INSPECTION SYSTEM IN THIS LOCATION APPROVED BY HOW   _____ IT IS NECESSARY FOR HOW TO PROVIDE THE CODE AND CONSTRUCTION INSPECTIONS

(7) ADMINISTRATIVE FEE DEPOSIT: **$30.00** + _____ = __$30.00__
    Administrative Fee Deposit   Inspection Fee (If Applicable)   Remit This Amount

(8) SIGNATURE, BUILDER REPRESENTATIVE _____   DATE _____

(9) SIGNATURE, LOCAL COUNCIL REPRESENTATIVE _____   DATE _____

If the answers to lines 10 through 21 inclusive are ALL identical to a previously enrolled unit, you may insert number of that unit and skip to line 22.
Lines 10-21 inclusive are identical to unit # _____.

(10) TYPE OF UNIT				(16) HEATING SYSTEM	FUEL	____ GAS	__X__ ELECTRICITY	Heat __X__ Pump
____ DETACHED	TWO FAMILY ____ SIDE BY SIDE	__X__ THREE OR MORE IN A ROW			TYPE	__X__ WARM AIR	____ BASEBOARD	____ OTHER
(11) TYPE OF STRUCTURE				(17) AIR CONDITIONING SYSTEM	TYPE	__X__ CENTRAL	WINDOW/THRU ____ THE WALL	____ NONE
____ ONE STORY	__X__ TWO STORY	____ SPLIT LEVEL	____ OTHER		FUEL	____ GAS	__X__ ELECTRICITY	____ OTHER
(12) LOT DATA	Sq. Ft. (Approximate) of Individual Lot	ESTIMATED MARKET VALUE		(18) HOME IS SERVED BY INDIVIDUAL SEPTIC SYSTEM			____ YES	____ NO
	__946 Square Feet__	$6,000.00						
(13) SIZE OF HOME	Sq. Ft. Finished Floor Area	No. Bedrooms	No. Bathrooms	(19) EXTERIOR WALLS		__X__ ½ masonry; ½ frame*		
	1058 Square feet	2	1½			SOLID MASONRY		____ FRAME
(14) CAR STORAGE				(20) IF FRAME, EXTERIOR WALL SURFACE IS	__X__ PLYWOOD/HARDBOARD PANELS			____ STUCCO
____ GARAGE	____ CARPORT	__X__ NONE			____ BOARD SIDING	____ MASONRY VENEER		____ OTHER
(15) IF GARAGE/CARPORT				(21) FOUNDA- TION	CONST	____ POURED CONCRETE	____ BLOCK	____ OTHER
____ ONE CAR	____ TWO OR MORE CARS				TYPE	____ FULL/PARTIAL BASEMENT	____ CRAWL SPACE	
						__X__ SLAB ON GRADE	____ STRUCTURAL SLAB	

(22) PURCHASERS NAME	LAST	FIRST	MIDDLE	SPOUSE, IF APPLICABLE	FIRST	MIDDLE
	Fowler	Victoria	E.			

(23) STREET ADDRESS OF HOME	NO.	STREET			
	#3	Ridgeline Drive,			
	CITY		STATE		ZIP CODE
	Gaithersburg,		Maryland		20760

(24) DATE OF BEGINNING OF INITIAL WARRANTY PERIOD. CHECK WHICHEVER OCCURRED FIRST AND SUPPLY DATE.		TITLE __X__ TRANSFER	FIRST _____ OCCUPANCY	DATE	MO. 9	DAY 9	YEAR 77

(25) PERMANENT MORTGAGE LENDER

NAME __Perpetual Federal Savings and Loan Assc__   STREET 11th and E. Streets, N.W.

CITY __Washington, D.C.__   STATE D.C.   ZIP CODE 20004

(26) CALCULATION OF BALANCE DUE

__.002__	X	__$37,800.00__	=	$75.60	− **$30**	=	**REMIT THIS AMOUNT** $45.60
ADMIN. FEE AND INS. PREM.		FINAL SALES PRICE			ADMIN. FEE DEPOSIT		BALANCE DUE HOW BY BUILDER (MINIMUM $20)

(27) THIS IS TO CERTIFY THAT THE HOME AT THE ABOVE LOCATION IS SUBSTANTIALLY COMPLETE AND READY FOR OCCUPANCY. THE WORK REMAINING TO BE DONE, IF ANY, IS OF A MINOR NATURE INVOLVING ONLY NORMAL "PUNCH LIST" ITEMS. ALL STRUCTURAL ELEMENTS ARE TOTALLY COMPLETED. THE ELECTRICAL, HEATING AND PLUMBING SYSTEMS (AND AIR CONDITIONING SYSTEM, IF ANY) ARE OPERATIONAL.

SIGNATURE, BUILDER REPRESENTATIVE _____   DATE __9/8/77__

LOCAL COUNCIL REPRESENTATIVE _____   DATE _____

Copyright, 1976
Home Owners Warranty Corporation
HOW 100B

NATIONAL COPY

MD
2/77

PERPETUAL FEDERAL SAVINGS AND
LOAN ASSOCIATION
Eleventh & E Streets, N.W.
Washington, D.C. 20004

LOAN CLOSING INSTRUCTIONS TO: SEPTEMBER 3   ,1977

BETTS, CLOGG AND MURDOCK   Title Co.   P.F.S.
                                  Case No. 3062 MV   Case No.250357

                                  Title Insurance from: COMMONWEALTH

This Association has approved a loan as follows to be secured by a first deed of trust.
Your office is to make the settlement and the proceeds of the loan will be disbursed to your
office for final closing.

Within 30 days after settlement this Association is to receive a Mortgagee Title
Insurance Policy from the company shown above which insures us that the deed of trust securing
the loan is a good first lien and that there are no exceptions other than those in the above
referenced title insurance binder as it may be amended in accordance with verbal or written
instructions from this Association.

Name of Borrower(s)____**VICTORIA F. FOWLER**_____

Mailing Address:_____

Security Property:____**3 RIDGELINE DRIVE**_____

Lot____**LT 3**_____ Block_____ Subdivision____**CLUBSIDE-MONT.VILL.**

                                                         Monthly Payment
Amount of Loan $__**35,900.00**___ Interest Rate__**9.250**__% Principal & Int.__**295.35**

Our commitment is subject to sale at $__**38,538.00**__ with $___**2,638.00**___ Cash Down.

INTEREST FROM DATE OF SETTLEMENT TO THE END OF SETTLEMENT MONTH WILL BE DUE AND PAYABLE ON
THE FIRST DAY OF THE FIRST MONTH AFTER SETTLEMENT. WE WILL BILL THE BORROWER FOR THIS AMOUNT.

THE FIRST MONTHLY PAYMENT OF PRINCIPAL, INTEREST AND TAXES WILL BE DUE ON THE FIRST DAY OF
THE SECOND MONTH AFTER SETTLEMENT AND FUTURE PAYMENTS WILL BE DUE ON THE FIRST DAY OF EACH
MONTH THEREAFTER. FINAL DUE DATE TO BE INCLUDED IN NOTE WILL BE COMPUTED AS FOLLOWS:
            YEARS FROM THE 1st DAY OF THE 1st MONTH FOLLOWING SETTLEMENT DATE.
                         COLLECT IN SETTLEMENT
_____ Insurance Premium for fire & extended coverage $ FURNISHED
          policy for $_____for _____years.
          (One-twelfth of the annual premium will be included
          in the monthly payment to cover renewals.)
   X   Approved "Certificate of Insurance" from borrower must be in our
          possession three (3) business days prior to settlement.
          Real Estate Tax Escrow for _____1____ Months $_____

          Credit Report $_____11.00 PREPAID
          APPRAISAL FEE   **75.00 PREPAID**
          PRIVATE MORTGAGE INSURANCE PREMIUM $ **359.00**
          /DO NOT CALL FOR OUR FUNDS UNTIL THE CASE IS READY FOR CLOSING/

ALL OF OUR CHARGES WILL BE DEDUCTED (EXCLUDING A PAY OFF OF OUR EXISTING LOAN, IF APPLICABLE,
ON A PURCHASE MONEY TRANSACTION) AND YOU WILL RECEIVE A NET CHECK

This loan must be settled in _____SEPTEMBER_____

If this is a REFINANCE TRANSACTION, you are to complete the following forms, obtain the
borrowers signature and furnish them copies per attached instructions.

     [ ]   Notice of Right to Rescind and Post Card

     [X]   Statement of Interest and Other Charges

We must be furnished the following items:

_____

_____

                    (SEE REVERSE SIDE FOR FURTHER INSTRUCTIONS)

ONE COPY OF THE NOTE AND DEED OF TRUST TO BE GIVEN BORROWER AT SETTLEMENT.

TRUSTEE ON THE DEED OF TRUST TO BE SUBURBAN TRUST COMPANY.

We must be furnished the following items:

1. One legible copy of the borrowers' and sellers' settlement statement which contains a statement signed by each of them that they have received a copy.

2. The settlement officer must acknowledge, on the settlement statement, receipt of the amount shown as balance due from the purchaser.

Other Requirements:

All taxes and special assessments due at the date of disbursement must be paid and an estimated tax amount is to be held by this office for any pending special assessment.

All U.S., State, County or D.C. tax liens filed against any one or all of the owners even though not a lien against the property, must be satisfied and released.

DISBURSEMENT PROCEDURE - PURCHASE MONEY TRUST
RECORDED IN MARYLAND

Settlement should not be scheduled until you have ascertained that all parties are known to be available for settlement.

When you are ready for settlement, including receipt of our written closing instructions, a phone call requesting our funds must be made to this office two business days before settlement.

The call should be made by one of your staff to one of the persons listed at the end of these instructions. Please be sure they have the case available to discuss it with our party. We will pull our case while your representative remains on the phone in order to determine if we are ready to disburse.

We will need to obtain from you at that time the annual real estate taxes in order that we can complete the monthly tax escrow. We will furnish you at that time the necessary information to complete the Maryland Statement of Interest and Other Charges which was enclosed with our instructions.

Our checks will be payable to the borrowers and the settlement firm or attorney and must be picked up on the day of settlement by the purchaser in person and brought to the settlement.

We will make our check available to the borrower to pick up at any one of our offices which they designate. You will be required to furnish this information at the time you call for the check.

SETTLEMENT MUST NOT BE HELD ON A PURCHASE MONEY TRANSACTION
UNLESS YOU HAVE OUR FUNDS AT SETTLEMENT.

Our funds will be disbursed with the stipulation that by the close of business of the second (2nd) day following settlement (exclusive of weekends and holidays) all executed loan settlement documents be in our hands; otherwise, our funds must be returned at that time.

If this Association holds the present trust on the property, your check for the pay-off must be in our hands within seven (7) days from the date of the settlement.

Requests for Disbursements:

Call 638-7181 Ask for any of the following:

Mrs. Ratterree   Mrs. Fink   Mrs. Kyle

BETTS, CLOGG & MURDOCK

ROCKVILLE AND GAITHERSBURG, MARYLAND

OWNER'S AFFIDAVIT

State of Maryland

County of Montgomery

Personally appeared before me, the undersigned Notary Public, **Philip J. Raymond,** **Asst. Vice President** of KETTLER BROTHERS, INC. who after being first duly sworn deposes and says that KETTLER BROTHERS, INC., is the owner of the premises situated in the County of Montgomery, State of Maryland, known as:

Lot 3   Clubside

3 Ridgeline Drive

Gaithersburg, Maryland

and that all improvements thereon have been satisfactorily completed;

That said improvements were made under its own supervision, no general contractor having been employed;

That all bills incurred in the construction of the improvements have been paid in full and that there are no mechanics' or materialmen's liens against said premises and no claims for labor, services, or materials furnished in connection with the construction or repair of the improvements upon said property which remain unpaid, except:

Further, that there are no chattel mortgages or conditional bills or sale affecting any fixtures or any mantels, awnings, door or window screens, or any plumbing, lighting, heating, cooking, refregerating or ventilating apparatus used in connection with the improvements upon said property:

That this afficavit is made for the purpose of inducing Betts, Clogg & Murdock to insure the title to said property without exception to claims of mechanics, materialmen, laborers and suppliers.

Philip J. Raymond, Asst. Vice President

Sworn to and subscribed before me this ___9___ day of ___September___, 19 77

NOTARY PUBLIC

Ruthe B. Emler

(N.P. Seal)   My commission expires: ___7/1/78___

Perpetual
Federal Savings

State Of Maryland Required Disclosure

Statement of Interest and Other Charges

Borrowers___Victoria E. Fowler_____

Property Address___#3 Ridgeline Drive, Gaithersburg, Maryland 20760_____

Total Principal Amount of Loan . . . . $ 35,900.00_____

Anticipated Total Amount of Interest to be collected
during term of loan provided the correct amount of all
monthly payments are made when due, all insurance
premiums are paid when due, all shortages in the tax
escrow account are immediately paid and that there is
full compliance with all of the terms, conditions and
provisions of the promissory note and deed of trust $ 70,626.15_____

Annual Effective Rate of Simple Interest . . . . . .   _____9.250_____ %

_____September 9_____ , 19 77__

The above statement was received by the undersigned prior to signing
the promissory note and deed of trust.

Victoria E. Fowle
Victoria E. Fowler
_____

Mortgage Loan Dept. — Eleventh and E Streets, Northwest ● Washington, D.C. 20004 ● Telephone (202) 638-7181

NOTE

US $ .35,900.00 . . . .   .Gaithersburg,. Maryland. . . . .
                                                      City   *State*

.September. 9th. . . . ., 19.77.

FOR VALUE RECEIVED, the undersigned ("Borrower") promise(s) to pay Perpetual Federal Savings and Loan Association, or order, the principal sum of. —
.THIRTY. FIVE. THOUSAND. NINE. HUNDRED. AND. NO/100. — Dollars, with interest on the unpaid principal balance from the date of this Note, until paid, at the rate of .9,250— — — — — — — —.
— percent per annum. Principal and interest shall be payable at the office of said Association in Washington, District of Columbia, or such other place as the Note holder may designate, in consecutive monthly installments of. .TWO. HUNDRED. NINETY. FIVE. AND. 35/100— —
— Dollars (US $. .295.35. . . . .), on the. . . . .
. . . .first. . . . .day of each month beginning. .November. 1. . . . ., 19.77. Such monthly installments shall continue until the entire indebtedness evidenced by this Note is fully paid, except that any remaining indebtedness, if not sooner paid, shall be due and payable on. . .October. 1,. 2007. . . . .

If any monthly installment under this Note is not paid when due and remains unpaid after a date specified by a notice to Borrower, the entire principal amount outstanding and accrued interest thereon shall at once become due and payable at the option of the Note holder. The date specified shall not be less than thirty days from the date such notice is mailed. The Note holder may exercise this option to accelerate during any default by Borrower regardless of any prior forbearance. If suit is brought to collect this Note, the Note holder shall be entitled to collect all reasonable costs and expenses of suit, including, but not limited to, reasonable attorney's fees.

Borrower shall pay to the Note holder a late charge of three (3) percent of any monthly installment not received by the Note holder within fifteen (15) days after the installment is due.

Borrower may prepay the principal amount outstanding in whole or in part. The Note holder may require that any partial prepayments (i) be made on the date monthly installments are due and (ii) be in the amount of that part of one or more monthly installments which would be applicable to principal. Any partial prepayment shall be applied against the principal amount outstanding and shall not postpone the due date of any subsequent monthly installments or change the amount of such installments, unless the Note holder shall otherwise agree. in writing.

Presentment, notice of dishonor, and protest are hereby waived by all makers, sureties, guarantors and endorsers hereof. This Note shall be the joint and several obligation of all makers, sureties, guarantors and endorsers, and shall be binding upon them and their successors and assigns.

Any notice to Borrower provided for in this Note shall be given by mailing such notice by certified mail addressed to Borrower at the Property Address stated below, or to such other address as Borrower may designate by notice to the Note holder. Any notice to the Note holder shall be given by mailing such notice by certified mail, return receipt requested, to the Note holder at the address stated in the first paragraph of this Note, or at such other address as may have been designated by notice to Borrower.

The indebtedness evidenced by this Note is secured by a Deed of Trust, dated. .September. 9,. 1977. . . . . . .
. . . ., and reference is made to the Deed of Trust for rights as to acceleration of the indebtedness evidenced by this Note.

                                          Victoria E. Fowler. . . . .(Seal)
                                          Victoria E. Fowler

. . . .#3. Ridgeline. Drive. . . . .(Seal)

. . . . .Gaithersburg,. Maryland. .20760. . .   : . . . .(Seal)
            Property Address   *(Execute Original Only)*

MARYLAND—1 to 4 Family—6/75—**FNMA/FHLMC UNIFORM INSTRUMENT**   3M 1/77

DEED OF TRUST

THIS DEED OF TRUST is made this............9th.............. day of .September........,
19.77., among the Grantor, .VICTORIA E. FOWLER...
.... (herein "Borrower"), ...
...SUBURBAN TRUST COMPANY................................ (herein "Trustee"), and the Beneficiary,
Perpetual Federal Savings and Loan Association, a corporation organized and existing under the laws of the United
States of America, whose address is 11th and E Streets, N.W., Washington, D.C. (herein "Lender").

BORROWER, in consideration of the indebtedness herein recited and the trust herein created, irrevocably grants
and conveys to Trustee, in trust, with power of sale, the following described property located in the County of
....Montgomery........................., State of Maryland:

Lot numbered 3 in the subdivision known as "Plat 27,,Lots 3   thru 49, Being a
resubdivision of Lots 182 at 195, CLUBSIDE, Part of Section 2-A, MONTGOMERY VILLAGE"
as per Plat thereof duly recorded among the Land Records of Montgomery County,
Maryland in Plat Book 100 at Plat 11262.

SEPT-13-77 PAID 9464 CLK.CT.M.C. -ACK   14.00

James G. Hollis

1977 SEP 13 PM 1:36
CLERK'S OFFICE
MONTG.CO.MD.

which has the address of.. #3 Ridgeline Drive, Gaithersburg, Maryland. .20760................,
............................(herein "Property Address");

TOGETHER with all the improvements now or hereafter erected on the property, and all easements, rights,
appurtenances, rents (subject however to the rights and authorities given herein to Lender to collect and apply such
rents), royalties, mineral, oil and gas rights and profits, water, water rights, and water stock, and all fixtures now or
hereafter attached to the property, all of which, including replacements and additions thereto, shall be deemed to be
and remain a part of the property covered by this Deed of Trust; and all of the foregoing, together with said property
(or the leasehold estate if this Deed of Trust is on a leasehold) are herein referred to as the "Property";

To SECURE to Lender (a) the repayment of the indebtedness evidenced by Borrower's note dated .September ..
9, 1977......(herein "Note"), in the principal sum of..THIRTY FIVE THOUSAND NINE HUNDRED AND ...
NO/100----------------------------.Dollars, with interest thereon, providing for monthly installments
of principal and interest, with the balance of the indebtedness, if not sooner paid, due and payable on............
October 1, 2007........................; the payment of all other sums, with interest thereon, advanced
in accordance herewith to protect the security of this Deed of Trust; and the performance of the covenants and
agreements of Borrower herein contained; and (b) the repayment of any future advances, with interest thereon, made
to Borrower by Lender pursuant to paragraph 21 hereof (herein "Future Advances").

Borrower covenants that Borrower is lawfully seised of the estate hereby conveyed and has the right to grant and
convey the Property, that the Property is unencumbered, and that Borrower will warrant and defend generally the
title to the Property against all claims and demands, subject to any declarations, easements or restrictions listed in a
schedule of exceptions to coverage in any title insurance policy insuring Lender's interest in the Property.

MARYLAND—1 to 4 Family—6/76—FNMA/FHLMC UNIFORM INSTRUMENT

1M 7/77

UNIFORM COVENANTS. Borrower and Lender covenant and agree as follows:

1. Payment of Principal and Interest. Borrower shall promptly pay when due the principal of and interest on the indebtedness evidenced by the Note, prepayment and late charges as provided in the Note, and the principal of and interest on any Future Advances secured by this Deed of Trust.

2. Funds for Taxes and Insurance. Subject to applicable law or to a written waiver by Lender, Borrower shall pay to Lender on the day monthly installments of principal and interest are payable under the Note, until the Note is paid in full, a sum (herein "Funds") equal to one-twelfth of the yearly taxes and assessments which may attain priority over this Deed of Trust, and ground rents on the Property, if any, plus one-twelfth of yearly premium installments for hazard insurance, plus one-twelfth of yearly premium installments for mortgage insurance, if any, all as reasonably estimated initially and from time to time by Lender on the basis of assessments and bills and reasonable estimates thereof.

The Funds shall be held in an institution the deposits or accounts of which are insured or guaranteed by a Federal or state agency (including Lender if Lender is such an institution). Lender shall apply the Funds to pay said taxes, assessments, insurance premiums and ground rents. Lender may not charge for so holding and applying the Funds, analyzing said account or verifying and compiling said assessments and bills, unless Lender pays Borrower interest on the Funds and applicable law permits Lender to make such a charge. Borrower and Lender may agree in writing at the time of execution of this Deed of Trust that interest on the Funds shall be paid to Borrower, and unless such agreement is made or applicable law requires such interest to be paid, Lender shall not be required to pay Borrower any interest or earnings on the Funds. Lender shall give to Borrower, without charge, an annual accounting of the Funds showing credits and debits to the Funds and the purpose for which each debit to the Funds was made. The Funds are pledged as additional security for the sums secured by this Deed of Trust.

If the amount of the Funds held by Lender, together with the future monthly installments of Funds payable prior to the due dates of taxes, assessments, insurance premiums and ground rents, shall exceed the amount required to pay said taxes, assessments, insurance premiums and ground rents as they fall due, such excess shall be, at Borrower's option, either promptly repaid to Borrower or credited to Borrower on monthly installments of Funds. If the amount of the Funds held by Lender shall not be sufficient to pay taxes, assessments, insurance premiums and ground rents as they fall due, Borrower shall pay to Lender any amount necessary to make up the deficiency within 30 days from the date notice is mailed by Lender to Borrower requesting payment thereof.

Upon payment in full of all sums secured by this Deed of Trust, Lender shall promptly refund to Borrower any Funds held by Lender. If under paragraph 18 hereof the Property is sold or the Property is otherwise acquired by Lender, Lender shall apply, no later than immediately prior to the sale of the Property or its acquisition by Lender, any Funds held by Lender at the time of application as a credit against the sums secured by this Deed of Trust.

3. Application of Payments. Unless applicable law provides otherwise, all payments received by Lender under the Note and paragraphs 1 and 2 hereof shall be applied by Lender first in payment of amounts payable to Lender by Borrower under paragraph 2 hereof, then to interest payable on the Note, then to the principal of the Note, and then to interest and principal on any Future Advances.

4. Charges; Liens. Borrower shall pay all taxes, assessments and other charges, fines and impositions attributable to the Property which may attain a priority over this Deed of Trust, and leasehold payments or ground rents, if any, in the manner provided under paragraph 2 hereof or, if not paid in such manner, by Borrower making payment, when due, directly to the payee thereof. Borrower shall promptly furnish to Lender all notices of amounts due under this paragraph, and in the event Borrower shall make payment directly, Borrower shall promptly furnish to Lender receipts evidencing such payments. Borrower shall promptly discharge any lien which has priority over this Deed of Trust; provided, that Borrower shall not be required to discharge any such lien so long as Borrower shall agree in writing to the payment of the obligation secured by such lien in a manner acceptable to Lender, or shall in good faith contest such lien by, or defend enforcement of such lien in, legal proceedings which operate to prevent the enforcement of the lien or forfeiture of the Property or any part thereof.

5. Hazard Insurance. Borrower shall keep the improvements now existing or hereafter erected on the Property insured against loss by fire, hazards included within the term "extended coverage", and such other hazards as Lender may require and in such amounts and for such periods as Lender may require; provided, that Lender shall not require that the amount of such coverage exceed that amount of coverage required to pay the sums secured by this Deed of Trust.

The insurance carrier providing the insurance shall be chosen by Borrower subject to approval by Lender; provided, that such approval shall not be unreasonably withheld. All premiums on insurance policies shall be paid in the manner provided under paragraph 2 hereof or, if not paid in such manner, by Borrower making payment, when due, directly to the insurance carrier.

All insurance policies and renewals thereof shall be in form acceptable to Lender and shall include a standard mortgage clause in favor of and in form acceptable to Lender. Lender shall have the right to hold the policies and renewals thereof, and Borrower shall promptly furnish to Lender all renewal notices and all receipts of paid premiums. In the event of loss, Borrower shall give prompt notice to the insurance carrier and Lender. Lender may make proof of loss if not made promptly by Borrower.

Unless Lender and Borrower otherwise agree in writing, insurance proceeds shall be applied to restoration or repair of the Property damaged, provided such restoration or repair is economically feasible and the security of this Deed of Trust is not thereby impaired. If such restoration or repair is not economically feasible or if the security of this Deed of Trust would be impaired, the insurance proceeds shall be applied to the sums secured by this Deed of Trust, with the excess, if any, paid to Borrower. If the Property is abandoned by Borrower, or if Borrower fails to respond to Lender within 30 days from the date notice is mailed by Lender to Borrower that the insurance carrier offers to settle a claim for insurance benefits, Lender is authorized to collect and apply the insurance proceeds at Lender's option either to restoration or repair of the Property or to the sums secured by this Deed of Trust.

Unless Lender and Borrower otherwise agree in writing, any such application of proceeds to principal shall not extend or postpone the due date of the monthly installments referred to in paragraphs 1 and 2 hereof or change the amount of such installments. If under paragraph 18 hereof the Property is acquired by Lender, all right, title and interest of Borrower in and to any insurance policies and in and to the proceeds thereof resulting from damage to the Property prior to the sale or acquisition shall pass to Lender to the extent of the sums secured by this Deed of Trust immediately prior to such sale or acquisition.

6. Preservation and Maintenance of Property; Leaseholds; Condominiums; Planned Unit Developments. Borrower shall keep the Property in good repair and shall not commit waste or permit impairment or deterioration of the Property and shall comply with the provisions of any lease if this Deed of Trust is on a leasehold. If this Deed of Trust is on a unit in a condominium or a planned unit development, Borrower shall perform all of Borrower's obligations under the declaration or covenants creating or governing the condominium or planned unit development, the by-laws and regulations of the condominium or planned unit development, and constituent documents. If a condominium or planned unit development rider is executed by Borrower and recorded together with this Deed of Trust, the covenants and agreements of such rider shall be incorporated into and shall amend and supplement the covenants and agreements of this Deed of Trust as if the rider were a part hereof.

7. Protection of Lender's Security. If Borrower fails to perform the covenants and agreements contained in this Deed of Trust, or if any action or proceeding is commenced which materially affects Lender's interest in the Property, including, but not limited to, eminent domain, insolvency, code enforcement, or arrangements or proceedings involving a bankrupt or decedent, then Lender at Lender's option, upon notice to Borrower, may make such appearances, disburse such sums and take such action as is necessary to protect Lender's interest, including, but not limited to, disbursement of reasonable attorney's fees and entry upon the Property to make repairs. If Lender required mortgage insurance as a condition of making the loan secured by this Deed of Trust, Borrower shall pay the premiums required to maintain such insurance in effect until such time as the requirement for such insurance terminates in accordance with Borrower's and Lender's written agreement or applicable law. Borrower shall pay the amount of all mortgage insurance premiums in the manner provided under paragraph 2 hereof.

Any amounts disbursed by Lender pursuant to this paragraph 7, with interest thereon, shall become additional indebtedness of Borrower secured by this Deed of Trust. Unless Borrower and Lender agree to other terms of payment, such amounts shall be payable upon notice from Lender to Borrower requesting payment thereof, and shall bear interest from the date of disbursement at the rate payable from time to time on outstanding principal under the Note unless payment of interest at such rate would be contrary to applicable law, in which event such amounts shall bear interest at the highest rate permissible under applicable law. Nothing contained in this paragraph 7 shall require Lender to incur any expense or take any action hereunder.

8. Inspection. Lender may make or cause to be made reasonable entries upon and inspections of the Property, provided that Lender shall give Borrower notice prior to any such inspection specifying reasonable cause therefor related to Lender's interest in the Property.

9. Condemnation. The proceeds of any award or claim for damages, direct or consequential, in connection with any condemnation or other taking of the Property, or part thereof, or for conveyance in lieu of condemnation, are hereby assigned and shall be paid to Lender.

In the event of a total taking of the Property, the proceeds shall be applied to the sums secured by this Deed of Trust, with the excess, if any, paid to Borrower. In the event of a partial taking of the Property, unless Borrower and Lender otherwise agree in writing, there shall be applied to the sums secured by this Deed of Trust such proportion of the proceeds as is equal to that proportion which the amount of the sums secured by this Deed of Trust immediately prior to the date of taking bears to the fair market value of the Property immediately prior to the date of taking, with the balance of the proceeds paid to Borrower.

If the Property is abandoned by Borrower, or if, after notice by Lender to Borrower that the condemnor offers to make an award or settle a claim for damages, Borrower fails to respond to Lender within 30 days after the date such notice is mailed, Lender is authorized to collect and apply the proceeds, at Lender's option, either to restoration or repair of the Property or to the sums secured by this Deed of Trust.

Unless Lender and Borrower otherwise agree in writing, any such application of proceeds to principal shall not extend or postpone the due date of the monthly installments referred to in paragraphs 1 and 2 hereof or change the amount of such installments.

10. Borrower Not Released. Extension of the time for payment or modification of amortization of the sums secured by this Deed of Trust granted by Lender to any successor in interest of Borrower shall not operate to release, in any manner, the liability of the original Borrower and Borrower's successors in interest. Lender shall not be required to commence proceedings against such successor or refuse to extend time for payment or otherwise modify amortization of the sums secured by this Deed of Trust by reason of any demand made by the original Borrower and Borrower's successors in interest.

11. Forbearance by Lender Not a Waiver. Any forbearance by Lender in exercising any right or remedy hereunder, or otherwise afforded by applicable law, shall not be a waiver of or preclude the exercise of any such right or remedy. The procurement of insurance or the payment of taxes or other liens or charges by Lender shall not be a waiver of Lender's right to accelerate the maturity of the indebtedness secured by this Deed of Trust.

12. Remedies Cumulative. All remedies provided in this Deed of Trust are distinct and cumulative to any other right or remedy under this Deed of Trust or afforded by law or equity, and may be exercised concurrently, independently or successively.

13. Successors and Assigns Bound; Joint and Several Liability; Captions. The covenants and agreements herein contained shall bind, and the rights hereunder shall inure to, the respective successors and assigns of Lender and Borrower, subject to the provisions of paragraph 17 hereof. All covenants and agreements of Borrower shall be joint and several. The captions and headings of the paragraphs of this Deed of Trust are for convenience only and are not to be used to interpret or define the provisions hereof.

14. Notice. Except for any notice required under applicable law to be given in another manner, (a) any notice to Borrower provided for in this Deed of Trust shall be given by mailing such notice by certified mail addressed to Borrower at the Property Address or at such other address as Borrower may designate by notice to Lender as provided herein, and (b) any notice to Lender shall be given by certified mail, return receipt requested, to Lender's address stated herein or to such other address as Lender may designate by notice to Borrower as provided herein. Any notice provided for in this Deed of Trust shall be deemed to have been given to Borrower or Lender when given in the manner designated herein.

15. Uniform Deed of Trust; Governing Law; Severability. This form of deed of trust combines uniform covenants for national use and non-uniform covenants with limited variations by jurisdiction to constitute a uniform security instrument covering real property. This Deed of Trust shall be governed by the law of the jurisdiction in which the Property is located. In the event that any provision or clause of this Deed of Trust or the Note conflicts with applicable law, such conflict shall not affect other provisions of this Deed of Trust or the Note which can be given effect without the conflicting provision, and to this end the provisions of the Deed of Trust and the Note are declared to be severable.

16. Borrower's Copy. Borrower shall be furnished a conformed copy of the Note and of this Deed of Trust at the time of execution or after recordation hereof.

17. Transfer of the Property; Assumption. If all or any part of the Property or an interest therein is sold or transferred by Borrower without Lender's prior written consent, excluding (a) the creation of a lien or encumbrance subordinate to this Deed of Trust, (b) the creation of a purchase money security interest for household appliances, (c) a transfer by devise, descent or by operation of law upon the death of a joint tenant or (d) the grant of any leasehold interest of three years or less not containing an option to purchase, Lender may, at Lender's option, declare all the sums secured by this Deed of Trust to be immediately due and payable. Lender shall have waived such option to accelerate if, prior to the sale or transfer, Lender and the person to whom the Property is to be sold or transferred reach agreement in writing that the credit of such person is satisfactory to Lender and that the interest payable on the sums secured by this Deed of Trust shall be at such rate as Lender shall request. If Lender has waived the option to accelerate provided in this paragraph 17, and if Borrower's successor in interest has executed a written assumption agreement accepted in writing by Lender, Lender shall release Borrower from all obligations under this Deed of Trust and the Note.

If Lender exercises such option to accelerate, Lender shall mail Borrower notice of acceleration in accordance with paragraph 14 hereof. Such notice shall provide a period of not less than 30 days from the date the notice is mailed within which Borrower may pay the sums declared due. If Borrower fails to pay such sums prior to the expiration of such period, Lender may, without further notice or demand on Borrower, invoke any remedies permitted by paragraph 18 hereof.

Non-Uniform Covenants. Borrower and Lender further covenant and agree as follows:

18. Acceleration; Remedies. Except as provided in paragraph 17 hereof, upon Borrower's breach of any covenant or agreement of Borrower in this Deed of Trust, including the covenants to pay when due any sums secured by this Deed of Trust, Lender prior to acceleration shall mail notice to Borrower as provided in paragraph 14 hereof specifying: (1) the breach; (2) the action required to cure such breach; (3) a date, not less than 30 days from the date the notice is mailed to Borrower, by which such breach must be cured; and (4) that failure to cure such breach on or before the date specified in the notice may result in acceleration of the sums secured by this Deed of Trust and sale of the Property. The notice shall further inform Borrower of the right to reinstate after acceleration and the right to assert in the foreclosure proceeding the non-existence of a default or any other defense of Borrower to acceleration and sale. If the breach is not cured on or before the date specified in the notice, Lender at Lender's option may declare all of the sums secured by this Deed of Trust to be immediately due and payable without further demand and may invoke the power of sale and any other remedies permitted by applicable law. Lender shall be entitled to collect all reasonable costs and expenses incurred in pursuing the remedies provided in this paragraph 18, including, but not limited to, reasonable attorney's fees.

If Lender invokes the power of sale, Lender shall mail or cause Trustee to mail written notice of sale to Borrower in the manner prescribed by applicable law. Trustee shall give notice of sale by public advertisement for the time and in the manner prescribed by applicable law. Trustee, without demand on Borrower, shall sell the Property at public auction to the highest bidder at the time and place and under the terms designated in the notice of sale in one or more parcels and in such order as Trustee may determine. Trustee may postpone sale of all or any parcel of the Property by public announcement at the time and place of any previously scheduled sale. Lender, or Lender's designee, may purchase the Property at any sale.

Trustee shall deliver to the purchaser Trustee's deed conveying the Property so sold without any covenant or warranty, expressed or implied. The recitals in the Trustee's deed shall be prima facie evidence of the truth of the statements made therein. Trustee shall apply the proceeds of the sale in the following order: (a) to all costs and expenses of the sale, including, but not limited to, Trustee's fees of . . . . . % of the gross sale price, reasonable attorney's fees and costs of title evidence; (b) to all sums secured by this Deed of Trust; and (c) the excess, if any, to the person or persons legally entitled thereto.

19. Borrower's Right to Reinstate. Notwithstanding Lender's acceleration of the sums secured by this Deed of Trust, Borrower shall have the right to have any proceedings begun by Lender to enforce this Deed of Trust discontinued at any time prior to the earlier to occur of (i) the fifth day before sale of the Property pursuant to the power of sale contained in this Deed of Trust or (ii) entry of a judgment enforcing this Deed of Trust if: (a) Borrower pays Lender all sums which would be then due under this Deed of Trust, the Note and notes securing Future Advances, if any, had no acceleration occurred; (b) Borrower cures all breaches of any other covenants or agreements of Borrower contained in this Deed of Trust; (c) Borrower pays all reasonable expenses incurred by Lender and Trustee in enforcing the covenants and agreements of Borrower contained in this Deed of Trust and in enforcing Lender's and Trustee's remedies as provided in paragraph 18 hereof, including, but not limited to, reasonable attorney's fees; and (d) Borrower takes such action as Lender may reasonably require to assure that the lien of this Deed of Trust, Lender's interest in the Property and Borrower's obligation to pay the sums secured by this Deed of Trust shall continue unimpaired. Upon such payment and cure by Borrower, this Deed of Trust and the obligations secured hereby shall remain in full force and effect as if no acceleration had occurred.

LIBER 5 0 1 3 FOLIO 8 0 1

20. Assignment of Rents; Appointment of Receiver. As additional security hereunder, Borrower hereby assigns to Lender the rents of the Property, provided that Borrower shall, prior to acceleration under paragraph 18 hereof or abandonment of the Property, have the right to collect and retain such rents as they become due and payable.

Upon acceleration under paragraph 18 hereof or abandonment of the Property, Lender shall be entitled to have a receiver appointed by a court to enter upon, take possession of and manage the Property and to collect the rents of the Property, including those past due. All rents collected by the receiver shall be applied first to payment of the costs of management of the Property and collection of rents, including, but not limited to, receiver's fees, premiums on receiver's bonds and reasonable attorney's fees, and then to the sums secured by this Deed of Trust. The receiver shall be liable to account only for those rents actually received.

21. Future Advances. Upon request of Borrower, Lender, at Lender's option prior to release of this Deed of Trust, may make Future Advances to Borrower. Such Future Advances, with interest thereon, shall be secured by this Deed of Trust when evidenced by promissory notes stating that said notes are secured hereby. At no time shall the principal amount of the indebtedness secured by this Deed of Trust, not including sums advanced in accordance herewith to protect the security of this Deed of Trust, exceed the original amount of the Note.

22. Release. Upon payment of all sums secured by this Deed of Trust, Lender or Trustee shall release this Deed of Trust without charge to Borrower. Borrower shall pay all costs of recordation, if any.

23. Substitute Trustee. Lender at Lender's option may from time to time remove Trustee and appoint a successor trustee to any Trustee appointed hereunder by an instrument recorded in the city or county in which this Deed of Trust is recorded. Without conveyance of the Property, the successor trustee shall succeed to all the title, power and duties conferred upon the Trustee herein and by applicable law.

The undersigned agree(s) that notwithstanding anything to the contrary previously stated in the foregoing Deed of Trust, the following additional covenants shall be in full force and effect:

ADDITIONAL COVENANTS. Borrower and lender further covenant and agree as follows:

24. The lender may, at its option, and as a condition of its consent to any transfer of title to the property. subject to this indebtedness, require a fee of not more than one (1) per cent of the unpaid balance of the loan.

25. Upon the full payment of the indebtedness hereby secured, the lender shall request the Trustee to release and reconvey the property described herein unto the borrower, or the party or parties then claiming under him, at his or their expense, including a trustees' fee of $10.00.

In the event that a 100% interest in this loan secured by this Deed of Trust is sold to the Federal Home Loan Mortgage Corporation, these ADDITIONAL COVENANTS, Numbers 24 and 25, shall become null and void; all other terms and covenants of the Deed of Trust remaining in full force and effect.

IN WITNESS WHEREOF, Borrower has executed this Deed of Trust.

Victoria E. Fowler .... (Seal)
Victoria E. Fowler   —Borrower

.... (Seal)
        —Borrower

STATE OF MARYLAND, . . MONTGOMERY . . . . County ss:

I Hereby Certify, That on this . . . . . 9th . . . . day of . September . . . . , 19 .77., before me, the subscriber, a Notary Public of the State of Maryland, in and for the . . . county aforesaid . . . . , personally appeared . . . . VICTORIA E. FOWLER . . . . , known to me or satisfactorily proven to be the person(s) whose name(s) . . . . . . is . . . . subscribed to the within instrument and acknowledge that . . he . . executed the same for the purposes therein contained.

As WITNESS: my hand and notarial seal.

My Commission expires:

July 1, 1978

James G. Hollis   Notary Public

STATE OF . . MARYLAND, MONTGOMERY . . , ... County ss:

I Hereby Certify, That on this . . . . . . 9th . . . . day of . September . . . . , 19 .77., before me, the subscriber, a Notary Public of the State of . Maryland . . . . and for the . county aforesaid . . . . , personally appeared . . DAVID E. BETTS, ... , the agent of the party secured by the foregoing Deed of Trust, and made oath in due form of law that the consideration recited in said Deed of Trust is true and bona fide as therein set forth and that the amount of the loan secured by the foregoing Deed of Trust was disbursed by the party or parties secured to the Borrower or to the person responsible for disbursement of funds in the closing transaction or their respective agent at a time no later than the execution and delivery by the Borrower of this Deed of Trust; and also made oath that he is the agent of the party or parties secured and is duly authorized to make this affidavit.

As WITNESS: my hand and notarial seal.

My Commission expires:

July 1, 1978

James G. Hollis   Notary Public

———————————————— (Space Below This Line Reserved For Lender and Recorder) ————————

NOTE:
AFTER RECORDING TRUST
PLEASE RETURN TO:
PERPETUAL FEDERAL S & L ASSN.
500 - 11th STREET, N.W.
WASHINGTON, D. C. 20004

HUD 1 (5-75) Page

CASE NO. 3062MV   DATE: September 9, 1977

Additional information and/or explanation of items reported on Pages 1 and 2:

Sec. _____ Line _____ _____

Sec. _____ Line _____ _____

Sec. _____ Line _____ _____

Sec. _____ Line _____ _____

Sec. _____ Line _____ _____

Sec. _____ Line _____ _____

Sec. _____ Line _____ _____

Sec. _____ Line _____ _____

Sec. _____ Line _____ _____

Sec. _____ Line _____ _____

Information relative to rents, taxes, assessments and principal and interest due on encumbrances must be furnished to us by others. Therefore, we cannot assume liability for the accuracy of information so acquired. Subject to timely receipt of funds and documents due from others, disbursements set forth in preceding pages will be made within ten days from date of settlement.

The firm of Betts, Clogg & Murdock is a binder and policy issuing agent of the title insurer, and as such, prepares and issues all documents relative to title insurance, including, but not limited to; Interim Title Insurance binders and endorsements, Mortgagee Title Insurance policies and endorsements, Owners Title Insurance policies and endorsements. For the performance of such services, the firm, pursuant to Public Law 93-533 Section 8 (C) (B), receives a fee equal to 60 % of the total established insurance premium, as approved by the Insurance Commissioner for the State of Maryland.

This Settlement Statement is approved and receipt of a copy thereof is hereby acknowledged.

KETTLER BROTHERS, INC.

_____   _____
Buyer-Borrower   Victoria E. Fowler   Seller

_____   _____
Buyer-Borrower   Seller

 3 Ridgeline Drive   _____
Address   Address

_____   _____
Phone   Phone

Certified to be a true and correct copy of original Settlement Statement consisting of 3 pages.

BETTS, CLOGG & MURDOCK

by: _____
James G. Hollis

THIS STATEMENT IS SUBJECT TO AUDIT

HUD-1 Rev. 5/76

Form Approved
OMB NO. 63-R-1501

A. U.S. DEPARTMENT OF HOUSING AND URBAN DEVELOPMENT	B. TYPE OF LOAN

BETTS, CLOGG & MURDOCK
19130 MONTGOMERY VILLAGE AVENUE
GAITHERSBURG, MARYLAND 20760
948-2776

SETTLEMENT STATEMENT

1. ☐ FHA 2. ☐ FmHA 3. ☐ CONV. UNINS.
4. ☐ VA 5. ☐ CONV. INS.

6. File Number: 3062MV   7. Loan Number:

8. Mortgage Insurance Case Number:

C. NOTE: *This form is furnished to give you a statement of actual settlement costs. Amounts paid to and by the settlement agent are shown. Items marked "(p.o.c.)" were paid outside the closing; they are shown here for informational purposes and are not included in the totals.*

D. NAME OF BORROWER:	E. NAME OF SELLER:	F. NAME OF LENDER:
Victoria E. Fowler	Kettler Brothers, Inc.	Perpetual Federal Savings and Loan Association

G. PROPERTY LOCATION:	H. SETTLEMENT AGENT:	I. SETTLEMENT DATE:
#3 Ridgeline Drive Gaithersburg, Maryland	Betts, Clogg & Murdock	September 9, 1977
	PLACE OF SETTLEMENT: 19130 Montgomery Village Ave. Gaithersburg, Maryland 20760	

J. SUMMARY OF BORROWER'S TRANSACTION			K. SUMMARY OF SELLER'S TRANSACTION		
100. GROSS AMOUNT DUE FROM BORROWER:			**400. GROSS AMOUNT DUE TO SELLER:**		
101. Contract sales price	37,800	00	401. Contract sales price	37,800	00
102. Personal property			402. Personal property		
103. Settlement charges to borrower *(line 1400)*	1,959	20	403. Survey	60	00
104. Alternate Selections	738	00	404. Alternate Selections	738	00
105.			405.		
Adjustments for items paid by seller in advance			*Adjustments for items paid by seller in advance*		
106. City/town taxes to			406. City/town taxes to		
107. County taxes 76.73 to 6/30/78	62	01	407. County taxes to		
108. Assessments to			408. Assessments to		
109. Front Foot Benefit 344.64 to 12/31	107	65	409. Front Foot Benefit to		
110. Transfer of Escrow Account			410. Transfer of Escrow Account		
111.			411.		
112.			412.		
120. GROSS AMOUNT DUE FROM BORROWER	40,666	86	**420. GROSS AMOUNT DUE TO SELLER**	38,598	00
200. AMOUNTS PAID BY OR IN BEHALF OF BORROWER:			**500. REDUCTIONS IN AMOUNT DUE TO SELLER:**		
201. Deposit or earnest money	2,238	00	501. Excess deposit *(see instructions)*		
202. Principal amount of new loan(s)	35,900	00	502. Settlement charges to seller *(line 1400)*		
203. Existing loan(s) taken subject to			503. Existing loan(s) taken subject to		
204.			504. Payoff of first mortgage loan		
205.			505. Payoff of second mortgage loan		
206.			506. Deposit held by seller	2,238	00
207.			507.		
208.			508.		
209.			509.		
Adjustments for items unpaid by seller			*Adjustments for items unpaid by seller*		
210. City/town taxes to			510. City/town taxes to		
211. County taxes to			511. County taxes 76.73 to 6/30/78	14	72
212. Assessments to			512. Assessments to		
213. Front Foot Benefit to			513. Front Foot Benefit 344.64 to 12/31	236	99
214.			514.		
215.			515.		
216.			516.		
217.			517.		
218.			518.		
219.			519.		
220. TOTAL PAID BY/FOR BORROWER	38,138	00	**520. TOTAL REDUCTION AMOUNT DUE SELLER**		
300. CASH AT SETTLEMENT FROM/TO BORROWER			**600. CASH AT SETTLEMENT TO/FROM SELLER**		
301. Gross amount due from borrower *(line 120)*	40,666	86	601. Gross amount due to seller *(line 420)*	38,598	00
302. Less amounts paid by/for borrower *(line 220)*	(38,138	00)	602. Less reductions in amount due seller *(line 520)*	(2,489	71)
303. CASH (☒ FROM) (☐ TO) BORROWER	2,528	86	**603. CASH (☒ TO) (☐ FROM) SELLER**	36,108	29

−2−

L. SETTLEMENT CHARGES		PAID FROM BORROWER'S FUNDS AT SETTLEMENT		PAID FROM SELLER'S FUNDS AT SETTLEMENT	
700. TOTAL SALES/BROKER'S COMMISSION based on price $ @ % =					
Division of Commission (line 700) as follows:					
701. $ to					
702. $ to					
703. Commission paid at Settlement					
704.					
800. ITEMS PAYABLE IN CONNECTION WITH LOAN					
801. Loan Origination Fee %					
802. Loan Discount %					
803. Appraisal Fee to Perpetual Federal POC		(75.00.00)			
804. Credit Report to POC		(11.00.00)			
805. Lender's Inspection Fee					
806. Mortgage Insurance Application Fee to					
807. Assumption Fee					
808.					
809.					
810.					
811.					
900. ITEMS REQUIRED BY LENDER TO BE PAID IN ADVANCE					
901. Interest from to @ $ /day					
902. Mortgage Insurance Premium for 12 months to MGIC		359	00		
903. Hazard Insurance Premium for years to					
904. years to					
905.					
1000. RESERVES DEPOSITED WITH LENDER					
1001. Hazard insurance months @ $ per month					
1002. Mortgage insurance months @ $ per month					
1003. City property taxes months @ $ per month					
1004. County property taxes 1 months @ $ 87.00 per month (estimated)		87	00		
1005. Annual assessments months @ $ per month					
1006. Est. ½ buy months @ $ per month		320	00		
1007. months @ $ per month					
1008. months @ $ per month					
1100. TITLE CHARGES					
1101. Settlement or closing fee to					
1102. Abstract or title search to					
1103. Title examination to					
1104. Title insurance binder to					
1105. Document preparation to					
1106. Notary fees to					
1107. Attorney's fees to Betts, Clogg & Murdock		274	00		
(includes above items numbers; 1101, 02, 03, 05 & 06 *)*					
1108. Title insurance to BCM & Commonwealth Land Title		95	00		
(includes above items numbers; 1104 *)*					
1109. Lender's coverage $ 95.00					
1110. Owner's coverage $ 50.80 ($145.80)					
1111. Tax Certificate to Montgomery County		2	00		
1112.					
1113.					
1200. GOVERNMENT RECORDING AND TRANSFER CHARGES					
1201. Recording fees: Deed $ 10.00 ; Mortgage $ 18.00 ; Releases $		28	00		
1202. City/county tax/stamps: Deed $; Mortgage $					
1203. State tax/stamps: Deed $ 167.20 ; Mortgage $		167	20		
1204. Transfer Taxes: County (1%) $378.00 State (1/2%) $189.00		567	00		
1205.					
1300. ADDITIONAL SETTLEMENT CHARGES					
1301. Survey to Seller		60	00		
1302. Pest inspection to					
1303. Escrow for payment of water bill					
1304.					
1305.					
1400. TOTAL SETTLEMENT CHARGES (enter on lines 103, Section J and 502, Section K)		1,959	20		

HUD-1 Rev. 5/76

TheMortgage Corporation
Federal Home Loan Mortgage Corporation

MORTGAGE SUBMISSION VOUCHER
CONVENTIONAL WHOLE LOAN & PARTICIPATION PROGRAMS
1—4 Family Home Mortgages

This form must be completed in detail (both light and shaded areas) before a loan can be properly processed by the FHLMC Regional Office.

▼ Tab Set	▼ Tab Set	▼ Tab Set
FHLMC Loan No.	Seller's Loan No. 6-412-5813-8	Purchase Contract Number

NOTE DATA (Copy from Note)

Date of Note (Use 6 digits Example: 05/21/76) Mo. Day Year (Use date of note or date of final disbursement whichever is later) 9 9 77	Original Loan Amount $ 35,900.00 .xx	Interest Rate 9.250 % (6-1/8 should be 6.125)
Monthly Installment—Principal & Interest only $295.35	First P&I Installment is due on Mo. Day Year 11/10/77 (use 6 digits Example: 01/28/76)	Original Note Term 360 months (Example: 30 year mortgage would be entered as 360)
☐ COMPLETE IF FLEXIBLE PYMT. LOAN $_____ Minimum Monthly Pymt ___ Months		

CREDIT DATA (Copy from Application)

Borrower (Last name, First, Middle Initial) Fowler, Victoria E.	Age 33	Years on this job 1	☐ self-employed	Number of Dependents other than Spouse 0 (If none, indicate by a zero)
Co-Borrower (Last name, First Middle Initial)	Age —	Years on this job —	☐ self-employed	

Purpose of Loan		Loan Type (Check if applicable)	
☒ Purchase for Owner Occupancy	☐ For Rental (Not Owner Occupied)	☐ Condominium Loan	
☐ Refinance (Owner Occupied)	☐ Borrower's Construction Loan (Owner Occ.)	☐ Leasehold Loan ☒ PUD Loan	

SOURCE OF GROSS MONTHLY INCOME (omit cents)	MONTHLY HOUSING EXPENSE (omit cents) Enter monthly costs even if not collected by Seller	DETAILS OF PURCHASE (Do not complete if a Refinance)
Borrower: Base Income $ 1,600 .xx	First Mortgage (P&I only) $ 295 .xx	Purchase Price (Do not include closing costs and prepaid escrow) $ 38,538 .xx
Co-Borrower: Base Income $ .xx	Secondary Financing (P&I only) $ .xx	Cash Down (Include amount of deposit) $ 2,638 .xx
All Other Income $ .xx	Hazard Insurance Premium $ 12 .xx	Trade, Lot or Other Equity $ .xx
TOTAL $1,600 .xx	Real Estate Taxes, Special Assessments and DeMinimis PUD Assessments $ 72 .xx	2nd Mortgage Amount $ .xx
	Mortgage Insurance Premium $ 7 .xx ☐ Total Premium Prepaid	Loan subsidy payment $ .xx ☐ HOAP or_____
TOTAL ALL OTHER OBLIGATIONS $ 140 .xx per month	Dues (Homeowners' Assoc. Charges) $ 18 .xx	☒ Must be completed if Condo or PUD (not DeMinimis)
Include alimony, child support and debts with more than 7 payments outstanding as of date of application. DO NOT include payments listed under Monthly Housing Expense	Ground Rent or Other (Specify) $ .xx	☐ Must be completed if Leasehold
	$ 404 .xx TOTAL	

Answer the following questions YES or NO. If "NO", the documentation submitted to FHLMC must contain a satisfactory explanation.

yes Has the source and amount of cash down payment as shown above been verified?

yes Has the borrower's and co-borrower's base income as shown above been verified?

yes Are ALL applicable obligations shown on Application and Credit Report included in "TOTAL ALL OTHER OBLIGATIONS" above?

yes Is the Application and Credit Report clear of the following: (a) Slow payment items?

(b) Pending or existing lawsuits or judgments? (c) History of bankruptcy?

yes Are the payments on this mortgage current (not more than 30 days past due) and, if applicable, have they been current for the past 12 months?

MORTGAGE INSURANCE (Complete if Applicable)

Mortgage Insurer (See Exhibit V Seller's Guide Conventional Mortgages for 2 digit Code Numbers) 07 Code Number	Mortgage Insurance Certificate No. (This Loan)

APPRAISAL DATA (Copy from Appraisal)

Property Address (Number and Street) 3 Ridgeline Drive	City Gaithersburg,	State MD. Zip / 20760
No. of Dwelling Units 1	Actual age of Dwelling 0 Years (If new enter 0)	Total No. of Rooms (Do not count baths)
Total No. of Bedrooms 2	Total No. of Baths 1½ (Show 1½ bath 15 Do not use decimal)	Total Finished Livable Area 1048 Sq. Ft.
Land Value $ 8,000 .xx	Total Appraised Value $ 38,600 .xx (Use the Appraiser's final market value estimate)	Name of Condominium, PUD or Subdivision

Answer the following questions YES or NO.

yes Is the NEIGHBORHOOD Section of the appraisal clear of factors adversely affecting marketability?

yes Is the SITE Section of the appraisal clear of adverse conditions?

yes Is the property located outside a HUD identified Flood Control Area?

yes Are the Sections of the appraisal relating to IMPROVEMENTS clear of functional or physical inadequacies?

If any answer is "NO," _____ (Name of Loan Officer), has reviewed the file and determined that the Appraisal Report clearly defines any significant detrimental conditions affecting long term marketability and stability and the loan amount and term reflect these conditions.

DOCUMENTATION

Items 1 through 5 must be included with each home mortgage submitted. Submit 6, 7, & 8 if required.

(1) Mortgage Note (Original if whole loan, copy if participation)

(2) Loan application (FHLMC Form 65)*

(3) Credit Report (Factual Data report if LTV exceeds 90% and in SMSA)* (Attach Verif. of Employment if Cr. Rpt. does not verify employment).

(4) Appraisal Report (Signed appropriate FHLMC Form) (Attach Form 442 if appraisal subject to completion)

(5) Photographs (Front and street elevation)

_____ (Initials) PREPARED THIS FORM AND IS RESPONSIBLE FOR ITS ACCURACY

(6) Profit and Loss Statement or latest Federal Tax Return (required if mortgagor is self-employed)*

LOANS OVER 1 YEAR OLD—ADDITIONAL REQUIREMENTS

(7) Payment record for past 12 months*

(8) Seller/Servicer 1—4 Family Property Inspection Report (FHLMC Form 452)

*(Present owner if loan has been assumed)

FHLMC 13SF 5-76

302

CASE STUDY: FEDERAL HOUSING ADMINISTRATION IN-SURED MORTGAGE LOAN

This residential mortgage loan is insured by FHA under Section 221(d)(2). Before FHA will insure any mortgage loan, it must approve both the borrower and the structure. This approval process begins with the *application for appraisal* which is submitted to FHA by the mortgage lender.

After the FHA receives an estimate of value, it issues a *conditional commitment* which contains requirements relative to the real estate that must be satisfied before insurance will be approved. The processing of the loan itself is basically the same as the previous two in that the borrower's credit, employment and financial liquidity must be verified. This information and all other pertinent facts are submitted to FHA for approval in a formal *application for mortgage insurance.*

The remainder of the closing process is much the same as previous cases. The mortgage note in this case is called a *mortgage bond.*

After closing, applicable documents are submitted to HUD, which issues a *mortgage insurance certificate.* This loan is to be sold and is warehoused for an interim period with a commercial bank. On the designated date, the mortgage, note and associated documents are shipped to the buyer and FHA is finally informed of the transaction.

The following documents are required for a mortgage loan insured by the Federal Housing Administration and warehoused by a commercial bank before being sold to a savings association:

1. Residential loan application-credit questionnaire

2. Qualifying worksheet

3. Purchase agreement

4. Good faith estimate of closing costs

5. Receipt of information booklet

6. Amendatory clause

7. Appraisal fee receipt

8. FHA Form 2800-1 Application for Appraisal

9. FHA Form 2800-2 Notice of Acceptance of Application

10. FHA Form 2800-5 Conditional Commitment

11. FHA Form 2800-6 Statement of Appraisal Value

12. Photographs

13. Request for verification of employment

14. Request for verification of deposit

15. Credit report

16. Down payment statement

17. FHA Form 2900-1 Application for Mortgage Insurance

18. FHA Form 2900-4 Firm Commitment

19. Loan commitment

20. Mortgagor's certification

21. Flood insurance affidavit

22. Mortgagor's affidavit of title and name

23. Title insurance policy (not included in this case)

24. Survey (not included in this case)

25. Truth in lending statement—Regulation "Z"

26. Termite warranty

27. Tax certification

28. Fire insurance certification

29. Settlement instructions

30. HUD-1 settlement statement

31. Mortgage bond (note)

32. Mortgage

33. HUD transmittal letter

34. Mortgage insurance certificate

35. Warehouse note

36. Warehouse receipt

37. Compliance warranty

38. Shipping instructions

39. Assignment of mortgage

40. HUD Form 92080, Mortgage Record Change

KENNEDY MORTGAGE CO.

518 MARKET STREET • CAMDEN, NEW JERSEY 08101

P.A. (215) 925-7225   N.J. (609) 365-6800

Applicant Interviewed by __Frank J. Simone__
(Kennedy Employee)

BROKER __Bon-Air__   CREDIT APPLICATION AS OF __5/11/78__

PROPERTY ADDRESS __51 Brunswick Lane   Willingboro, N.J.__   PURCHASE PRICE $ __25,000.00__

LOAN REQUESTED $ __24,650__   INTEREST RATE __8½&½__ % FOR __30__ YEARS

TYPE OF LOAN: F.H.A. ☒ __221d2__ VA. ☐ Conv. ☐   DO YOU INTEND TO: OCCUPY ☒ RENT ☐

MY NAME AS SIGNED ON THE AGREEMENT OF SALE IS: Soc. Sec. # __163-03-8503__

__John Smith__   AGE: __37__   MILITARY STATUS: _____

MY WIFE'S FULL NAME __Ella C. Smith__   AGE: __33__   Soc. Sec. # __163-43-3128__

OUR PRESENT ADDRESS IS __540 S. 4th St.   Camden, N.J.__   NUMBER OF YEARS: __5yrs.__
*IF LESS THAN TWO YRS GIVE PREV. ADDRESS

PHONE __541-0528__

AGES OF DEPENDENTS OTHER THAN WIFE __8, 4__   YEARS MARRIED __8__   EVER DIVORCED __NO__ Husband ☐ Wife ☐   BUSINESS PHONE _____

Employment

		Monthly Income
Husband's occupation __Truck Driver__	Husband's base pay	$ __476.67__
Employer's name and address __George Jacobs Clothing__	Other earnings (explain) __OT__	__143.00__
__305 Rt. 70 East__	Wife's base pay	__667.33__
__Cherry Hill, N.J.__ years employed __10mos__	Other earnings (explain)	
Wife's occupation __Nurses Aid__	Gross income, other Real Estate	
Employer's name and address __Cooper Hospital__	Other (explain)	
__6th & Stevens St.__		
__Camden, N.J.__ years employed __2½__		
IF HUSBAND'S EMPLOYMENT IS LESS THAN 2 YEARS COMPLETE THIS LINE		__1287.00__
Previous Occupation __Maintenance__ Yrs __5 yrs.__ Employer's Name and Address __Echelon Mall-Evesham Rd.-Voorhees Twsp__		

Previous Monthly Housing Expense

		Real Estate Owned
Mortgage payment or rent	$ __125.00__	NONE ☒
Fire Insurance		Address
Taxes, Special Assessments		Type of Mtge _____ Orig. Amt _____ Pres. Bal. _____
Maintenance		Lender and Address
Heat and Utilities	__40.00__	Is property to be Sold? _____ Leased? _____ Rented? _____
TOTAL $	__165.00__	Presently under A of S? _____ Sold on Assumption? _____
		Terms of lease or rental

Assets for Closing

		CREDITORS	Mo Pymt.	UnPd. Bal.	Acct. No.	Purpose
CK. Bank Accounts __Heritage Bank -Pennsauken, N.J.__	150.00	Sears	20	500.00		Household
SAV __Heritage Bank -Pennsauken, N.J.__	355.00	Singers	114	250.00		Household
Cash on Hand	500.00	1st Nat'l Bk	77.95	960.00		Auto
Marketable Securities	N/A					
Other (Savings Bonds, Pension Funds, Etc.)	N/A					
OTHER ASSETS (A) TOTAL $	1005.00	CREDIT REFERENCES: __Grants__				
Cash deposit on purchase	750.00					
Auto Year __73__ Make/Model __Buick__	3000.00					
Auto Year ___ Make/Model ___		LIFE INSURANCE				
Personal Property and Furniture	9000.00	Amt. $ _____ Cash Value $ _____ Annual Prem. $ _____				
Value of Real Estate						
(B) TOTAL $	12750.00	TOTAL $ _____ $ _____				

RACE or ETHNIC ORIGIN: (Check One)
White (Non-Minority) ☐   Spanish American ☐   Oriental ☐   Negro/Black ☒   American Indian ☐   Other Minority ☐

FHA Only:

1. HAVE YOU SOLD PROPERTY WITHIN THE LAST 24 MOS. WHICH HAD AN FHA MTGE.? __No__ IF YES, GIVE FHA CASE NO. _____ BUYER'S NAME _____ DID BUYER INTEND TO OCCUPY? _____
PROPERTY ADDRESS _____ ORIG. MTGE. AMT. $ _____ BAL. WHEN SOLD $ _____

2. HAVE YOU EVER BEEN OBLIGATED ON A HOME LOAN, OR HOME IMPROVEMENT LOAN WHICH RESULTED IN FORECLOSURE, DEED IN LIEU OF FORECLOSURE OR JUDGMENT? _____ IF YES, GIVE PROP. ADD. and LENDER

THIS IS NOT A LOAN COMMITMENT

THIS IS AN APPLICATION FORM AND IS NOT A COMMITMENT TO LEND MONEY. NO ORAL STATEMENT SHALL CONSTITUTE A LOAN COMMITMENT OF KENNEDY MORTGAGE CO. IF KENNEDY MORTGAGE CO. APPROVES YOUR APPLICATION, A SEPARATE, CLEARLY IDENTIFIED, WRITTEN LOAN COMMITMENT WILL BE TRANSMITTED TO YOU. NO OTHER WRITING SHALL CONSTITUTE A LOAN COMMITMENT OF KENNEDY MORTGAGE CO.

I hereby grant to Kennedy Mortgage Co., or its designee, the right to process the above mortgage loan and agree to pay, at settlement on the terms set forth above or such other terms as I may accept, a service charge of 1% of the mortgage amount.

This application (including NB63-1 RESPA) is made by the undersigned for the purpose of obtaining a mortgage loan and the statements and information herein are to the best of our knowledge and belief true, correct and complete. Kennedy Mortgage Co. is hereby authorized to verify the statements contained herein, by communicating with any of the persons or institutions named herein and to make any corrections required as a result of verified data received and to transfer the data as verified and corrected from this application form to the official FHA or VA application forms and submit them to me for my signature.

In compliance with the Fair Credit Reporting Act, this notice is to inform you that in connection with your application for a mortgage loan:
   (1) An investigative consumer report may be made as to your character, general reputation, personal characteristics and mode of living, and
   (2) Additional information as to the nature and scope of the report, if one is made, will be furnished to you, upon written request, within a reasonable time after you receive this notice.
Your acknowledgement of this statement gives Kennedy Mortgage Co. the authority to release credit information to the broker for the purpose of expediting the handling of your mortgage application.

__John Smith__   __Ella Smith__
Applicant   Wife of Applicant

KENNEDY MORTGAGE CO.

518 MARKET STREET • CAMDEN, NEW JERSEY 08101 • 609-365-6800 215-925-7225 215-925-7612

PRELIMINARY QUALIFYING WORKSHEET FHA/VA

S.P. $ 25,000.00

Mort. $ 24,650.00

Buyer John & Ella Smith

Property 51 Brunswick Lane

Willingboro, New Jersey

Monthly Gross Income	$ 1339.00		
Less Income Tax	$ 186.70		
Net Monthly Income		$ 1152.30	(A)
Principal & Interest	$ 189.56		
Real Estate Taxes	$ 85.00		
Hazard Insurance	$ 8.00		
MIP (If Applicable)	$ 10.23		
Maintenance (See chart below)	$ 24.00		
Utilities (See chart below)	$ 88.00		
Total Housing Expenses		$ 404.79	(B-1)
Plus: Other Recurring Charges (More than 12 months to pay)		$ 189.95	
Total Monthly Expenses		$ 594.74	(B-2)

FHA

Divide Net Monthly Income (A) into total housing expenses (B-1) and total monthly expenses (B-2) as follows:

$$\frac{B\text{-}1}{A} = \underline{\quad 35 \quad} \% \text{ (maximum)} \qquad \frac{B\text{-}2}{A} + \underline{\quad 51 \quad} \% \text{ (maximum)}$$
$$(35\%) \qquad\qquad\qquad\qquad\qquad\qquad\qquad (50\%)$$

VA

Subtract Total Monthly Expenses (B-2) from Net Monthly Income (A) to determine remaining income after all fixed expenses.

        (A)
     -(B-2)
     Remaining Income

Veteran qualifies if remaining income is more than:

Single Person	$350.00	Veteran, Spouse & 3 children	$530.00
Veteran & Spouse	$350.00	Veteran, Spouse & 4 children	$580.00
Veteran, Spouse & 1 child	$420.00	Veteran, Spouse & 5 children	$630.00
Veteran, Spouse & 2 children	$480.00	Veteran, Spouse & 6 children	$670.00
	(add $40.00 per each additional child)		

* Maintenance:
  Under 20 years - $4.00 per room
  Over 20 years - $5.00 per room
  Multi-Family (2-3-4) - Add 20% to Gross of above
  Hazard Ins: $3.25/$1,000 of mortgage amount

** Utilities & Service:
  All properties except electric heated $40.00
  Electric heated - $20.00
  Heat: Coal or gas - $8.00 per room;
         Electric $110.00 per mo. or flat-
         charge (Re: Budget Plans.)

NB# 36
3/77

Agreement for Sale 025D   Kennedy

This Agreement, MADE THIS ....10th....*day of*........May...........*19*..78

Between........ Eugene S. Thomas & Janet H., his wife   ....

....

of the First Part, hereinafter called the "Seller" and ....John Smith and................

...........Ella..C.,..his..wife..

of the Second Part, hereinafter called the "Buyer."

Witnesseth *That the Seller and Buyer respectively agree to sell and buy* **ALL** that certain premise known as 51 Brunswick Lane, lying and being at Willingboro, in the Township of Willingboro, County of Burlington, State of New Jersey, shown and designated as Lot 16, in Block 225, on Subdivision Map of Buckingham Park, Willingboro, Section 12, filed in the office of the County Clerk of Burlington County on March, 1958.

for the price of ....Twenty-five..Thousand------------------($25,000)...*Dollars.* *under the following conditions:*

1. *A payment of* ....Seven..Hundred..and..Fifty------------($750.00)...*Dollars* *made herewith and held in the escrow account of*   , *is to be applied on account of the purchase price, upon the compliance by the Buyer with this agreement.*

2. *Settlement is to take place at* ....Fellman..Realty................................

Pennypacker..Drive..&..Rt...130,..Willingboro,..N.J....................................

on or before the ..31st....*day of* ....August........, *19* 78, *at* 5:00.....*o'clock* .P..M., *which time is of the essence of this agreement, when the Seller shall deliver a special warranty deed for the said premises, and the balance of the purchase price is to be paid or secured as follows:*

This Agreement is contingent upon Buyer obtaining a commitment for an F.H.A. first mortgage upon the premises in the amount of $24,250. for a term of 30 years at an interest rate of 8½% or such rate of interest as is charged for F.H.A. mortgages at time of settlement. Seller will pay buyers closing costs, not exceeding $650.

Such part of purchase price, if any, unpaid at time of settlement, is to be delivered to..............

.....................................Any..reputable..title..company................................

to be disbursed after....said..title................................*Company has completed the necessary continuation search to cover the record date of said deed.*

3. *In the event of the Buyer not making settlement in accordance with the terms hereof the payment or payments made on account shall, at the Seller's option, be forfeited as liquidated damages for the failure of the Buyer to settle; or be applied on account of the purchase price.*

4. *The title to be delivered shall be a marketable title and insurable by a New Jersey title insurance company and shall be free and clear of all encumbrances, including municipal liens except as herein stated. The seller shall only pay for all municipal improvements which have been installed or are being installed at the time of final settlement. Seller warrants that he has made a full disclosure of his knowledge of all contemplated improvements affecting the subject premises. The title is to be subject to all existing restrictions of record, the seller, however, guarantees that there are no restrictions in any conveyance or plans of record affecting said premises which will prohibit the use and/or occupancy thereof as* ..a..single..family..residence................................*and the premises shall be conveyed in the same condition as the same now are, reasonable wear and tear excepted, and the seller warrants that the plumbing, heating, air conditioning and electrical systems and appliances included in this sale are to be in working order at the time of settlement and agrees to leave the premises in "broom clean" condition. Seller's warranty is valid through the day and hour of settlement but in no way obligates seller beyond completion of final settlement. Cost for inspection to determine the condition of the above mentioned systems shall be borne by the Buyer.*

5. *In the event that such title cannot be made by the Seller as above, and the Buyer is unwilling to accept such title as the Seller can make, then at Buyer's option, the above payment or payments shall be returned to the Buyer, together with the reasonable expenses of examining the title and making survey, or the Buyer may prosecute any legal or equitable action to which the Buyer may be entitled.*

6. *Actual possession is to be given to the Buyer on the day of settlement, except as herein stated* ....None... *If the Buyer accepts possession, with the Seller's consent, before the time of settlement, said possession shall be governed by a written lease to be executed between the parties hereto at time of execution of this agreement. Buyer shall have the right to inspect premises immediately prior to settlement.*

7. *Taxes, water and sewer charges, property rentals, escrow funds and other current charges including fuel oil if any, shall be adjusted as of date of settlement, unless possession be given prior thereto, in which case all such adjustments shall be made as of the date of delivery of possession.*

8. *The seller shall pay for the drawing of the deed and realty transfer fee, but all searches, title insurance, collateral bond, if any and other conveyancing expenses are to be borne by the Buyer.*

9. *It is understood and agreed that the Seller shall provide and pay for an inspection for wood damaging insects by a reputable exterminating firm. In the event of any termite or other wood damaging insect activity, Seller shall pay the cost of treatment to eliminate the condition and fully restore any structural damage.*

10. *Buyer hereby agrees to fully cooperate with the agent in making mortgage application to mortgage company within ten days of signing agreement of sale, and to provide any information or execute any necessary forms to accomplish the intent of effect of this agreement.*

11. *This Agreement constitutes the entire agreement between the parties and no verbal representation by the Broker or his representatives shall have any binding effect unless in writing.*

12. *The risk of loss or damage to said premises by fire or otherwise is on the Seller until title passes.*

13. *This agreement includes all fixtures, permanently attached to the building or buildings herein described and appurtenances also specifically includes the following items: existing storm sash, screens, storm doors, shades, rods and brackets used for drapes and curtains, existing shrubs, trees, and plantings.*

14. Seller warrants that the plumbing, heating, electrical systems and any mechanical appliances shall be in good working condition at the time of settlement, and the buyer has the option to reinspect these systems and appliances prior to that time. HOWEVER, failure to do so indicates acceptance "AS IS".

15. The risk of loss or damage to the property by fire or otherwise is the responsibility of the sellers until title passes.

16. The seller shall provide the buyer with a negative termite report or be responsible for the arrest of such activity, if prevailing.

17. Commission of 7% shall be divided as follows: 3½% to Fellman Realty, 3½% to Bon Air Realty. 7% commission shall be paid by the sellers.

The words "Seller" and "Buyer" in this agreement shall be construed to mean both the plural and singular number and to mean not only the party thereby designated, but also, his, her, or their respective heirs, executors or administrators; or in the event that either or both parties are corporations, its or their successors.

In Witness Whereof, *the parties hereto have hereunto set* our hands and seals
.. dated the day and year first above written.

SIGNED, SEALED AND DELIVERED
IN THE PRESENCE OF

Eugene S. Thomas   *Eugene S. Thomas* [L. S.]

Janet Thomas   *Janet Thomas* {L. S.]

John Smith   *John Smith* [L. S.]

Ella C. Smith   *Ella Smith* [L. S.]

THIS IS A LEGALLY BINDING CONTRACT. IF NOT UNDERSTOOD, SEEK COMPETENT ADVICE.

Agreement
for
Sale of Real Estate

AMENDMENT TO APPLICATION

Date___May 11, 1978___

NOTE: You may apply for the loan in your own name or you may wish your spouse (if any) to be a co-applicant. There is no requirement for your spouse (if any) to apply or otherwise become obligated to repay the debt except to the extent that your spouse's income and/or assets are necessary to qualify you for the loan. However, your spouse may be required to execute the security instrument (i.e., Mortgage or Deed of Trust.)

1. Title will be vested in what names?___John & Ella C. Smith___

2. How will title be held? (Tenancy)___Tenants in entirety___

3. Note will be signed by?___John & Ella C. Smith___

"GOOD FAITH ESTIMATES"

This list gives an estimate of most of the charges you will have to pay at the settlement of your loan. The figures shown, as estimates, are subject to change. The figures shown are computed based on sales price and proposed mortgage amount as stated on your loan application. The numbers listed on the left correspond with those on the HUD-1 Uniform Settlement Form you will be required to execute at settlement. For further information about these charges, consult your Special Information Booklet.

Estimated Settlement Charges

801	Loan Origination Fee	$ 242.50
805	Inspection Fee	20.00 (if any)
806	Mortgage Application Fee	65.00
901*	Interest	177.00
902	Mortgage Insurance Premium	N/A
1107	Attorney's Fees	N/A
1108	Title Insurance	270.00
1201	Recording Fees	25.00
1202	City/county tax/stamps	N/A
1203	State tax/stamps	N/A
1301	Survey	75.00

*This interest calculation represents the greatest amount of interest you could be required to pay at settlement. The actual amount will be determined by which day of the month your settlement is conducted. To determine the amount you will have to pay, multiply the number of days remaining in the month in which you settle times the daily interest charge for your loan.

"THIS FORM DOES NOT COVER ALL ITEMS YOU WILL BE REQUIRED TO PAY IN CASH AT SETTLEMENT, FOR EXAMPLE, DEPOSIT IN ESCROW FOR REAL ESTATE TAXES AND INSURANCE. YOU MAY WISH TO INQUIRE AS TO THE AMOUNTS OF SUCH OTHER ITEMS. YOU MAY BE REQUIRED TO PAY OTHER ADDITIONAL AMOUNTS AT SETTLEMENT."

In accordance with the Real Estate Settlement Procedure Act of 1974, I/we acknowledge receipt of the Settlement Costs Booklet. I/we also acknowledge receipt of the notice required by the Equal Credit Opportunity Act which is located on the inside back cover of the Settlement Cost Booklet. By signing this form, we acknowledge receipt this date of a duplicate copy of this form including the "Good Faith Estimates" of settlement costs, the Settlement Costs Booklet with the notice required by the Equal Credit Opportunity Act.

John Smith
Applicant

Ella Smith
Co-applicant

THIS MUST ·BE RETURNED TO KENNEDY MORTGAGE CO.

THIS IS NOT TO BE REMOVED FROM THE FILE

THIS IS NOT A LOAN COMMITMENT

RE: John & Ella Smith

K# 800,000

Address 51 Brunswick Lane

FHA/VA Commitment #

THIS IS AN APPLICATION FORM AND IS NOT A
COMMITMENT TO LEND MONEY. NO ORAL STATE-
MENT SHALL CONSTITUTE A LOAN COMMITMENT OF
KENNEDY MORTGAGE CO. IF KENNEDY MORTGAGE CO.
APPROVES YOUR APPLICATION, A SEPARATE, CLEARLY
IDENTIFIED, WRITTEN LOAN COMMITMENT WILL BE
TRANSMITTED TO YOU. NO OTHER WRITING SHALL
CONSTITUTE A LOAN COMMITMENT OF KENNEDY
MORTGAGE CO.

RECEIPT OF INFORMATION BOOKLET

I acknowledge that on 5/11/ , 1978, I received a copy of
the ·booklet entitled "Settlement Costs".

/s/ John Smith
(Purchaser)
/s/ Ella Smith
(Purchaser)

I have received the FHA Conditional Commitment or VA Certificate of
Reasonable Value showing the appraised value of the property.
I have received a copy of the brochure entitled "Watch Out for Lead
Paint Poisoning".

/s/ John Smith
(Purchaser)
/s/ Ella Smith
(Purchaser)

To Employer:

I have recently made application for a home mortgage loan to be
insured by the Federal Housing Administration. Please accept this
as your authorization to release to Kennedy Mortgage Co. all requested information relative to my employment.

/s/ John Smith
(Purchaser)
/s/ Ella Smith
(Purchaser)

To Purchaser:

Please sign one of above for each place of employment.

NB#150
Rev.7/75

KENNEDY MORTGAGE CO.

518 MARKET STREET . CAMDEN, NEW JERSEY 08101 . 609-365-6800 215-925-7225 215-925-7612

RE: 51 Brunswick Lane

Willingboro, NJ

"It is expressly agreed that, notwithstanding any other provisions of this contract, the purchaser shall not be obligated to complete the purchase of the property described herein or to incur any penalty by forfieture of earnest money deposits or otherwise unless the seller has delivered to the purchaser a written statement issued by the Federal Housing Commissioner setting forth the appraised value of the property for mortgage insurance purposes of not less than $25,000.00 which statement the seller hereby agrees to deliver to the purchaser promptly after such appraised value statement is made available to the seller."

"The purchaser shall, however, have the privilege and option of proceeding with the consummation of this contract without regard to the amount of the appraised valuation made by the Federal Housing Commissioner."

Janet H. Thomas   _Eugene S. Thomas_
                                  SELLER

John Smith
                                  BUYER

Elly Smith
                                  BUYER

John Ahern , KMCo.
                                  MORTGAGEE

The amount inserted in the above amendatory clause shall be an amount sufficient to support the mortgage requested. This amount must be inserted at the time this form is signed by the Seller and Buyers. If it is not, we shall have to return it for completion prior to submission to FHA.

NB#53
7/75

KENNEDY MORTGAGE CO.

11 ALLISON DRIVE • CHERRY HILL, NEW JERSEY 08003

N. J. 609-424-9300, 9312 • P. A. 215-925-2625, 7225

Camden, N. J., ...5/13........................19 78

K# 800,000................................

RECEIVED OF .... John and Ella Smith ....

....

............Sixty-Five and 00/100.................................. Dollars

Check ☒X$ ....65.00.................. Cash ☐ $ ....

To Cover the Following:
☒ FHA, VA, CONV Appraisal Fee
☒ Credit Report, Photos
☐ Extension, Conversion Fee
☐ FHA, VA Builder's Appraisal
☐

Property Address:

House No. ....51........... Lot ...Brunswick...... Block ....Lane......

City...Willingboro................................ State ...New Jersey......

Received by...
Cashier

Countersigned by ....Letty Alicea..............................
Representative

CA# 1

Receipt is not valid unless signed by both representative and cashier

Form Approved $\mathbf{14}\ L$
OMB No. 63-R1366

FHA MORTGAGEE NO. *(Please Verify)* 30257-8	U.S. DEPARTMENT OF HOUSING AND URBAN DEVELOPMENT FEDERAL HOUSING ADMINISTRATION	FHA CASE NO.	351-132092-221

MORTGAGEE'S APPLICATION FOR PROPERTY APPRAISAL AND COMMITMENT FOR MORTGAGE INSURANCE UNDER THE NATIONAL HOUSING ACT	PROPERTY ADDRESS 51 Brunswick Lane Willingboro, NJ

☐ SEC. 203(b) ☒ SEC. 221d2

MORTGAGEE Name and Address including ZIP Code *(Please Type)*
(Please locate address within corner marks)

⌐　　　　　　　　　　　　　　　　　　　　　¬

Kennedy Mortgage Company
11 Allison Drive
Cherry Hill, New Jersey

L　　　　　　　　　　　　　　　　　　　　　⌐

Telephone No. 424-9300

This form is a request for an appraisal and a commitment to insure a loan on an individual property.

We cannot process incomplete applications.
Rejecting them is costly.
Please help by giving us well prepared applications.
Keep all entries within alloted spaces.

EXISTING HOUSE ☒	Name of Occupant *(or person to call if unoccupied)* Contact Fellman Realty for access	Tel. No. 871-7970	Key Encl ☐ *(If unfurnished)*

Mon. & Yr. Completed 16 yrs☐ Never Occup. ☒ Vacant　　Occupied by ☐ Owner ☐ Tenant at $　Per Mo. ☒ Furn. ☐ Unfurn.

PROPOSED ☐ SUBSTAN. REHAB ☐ UNDER CONSTR ☐	Builder's Name & Address Including ZIP Code	Tel. No.	Model Identification

☐ Zins ☐ First Subm. 　Prob. Repeat Cases ☐ Yes ☐ No 　Prev. Proc. as FHA Case No.

Mineral Rights Reserved
☒ No ☐ Yes *(Explain)*

Utilities	Public	Comm	Individual
Water	☒	☐	☐
Gas	☒	☐	☐
Elect.	☒	☐	☐

☐ Underground Wiring

Sanitary	Sewer ☒	Sept. Tank ☐	Cess Pool ☐

Living Units

SPEC. ASSESS. Prepayable. $ _____ Non-Prepay. $ _____	LOT 65 x 100 ☐ Irr ☐ Acres _____ Sq. Ft
Int _____ % Ann. Pay. $ _____ Unpd. Bal. $ _____ Rem. Term _____ Yrs	GENERAL LOCATION:
ANN. R. EST. TAXES $ 910 　ANN. FIRE INS. $	SALE PRICE $ 25,000

EQUAL OPPORTUNITY IN HOUSING

Federal laws and regulations prohibit discrimination because of race, color, religion, sex, or national origin in the sale or rental of residential property. Numerous state statutes and local ordinances also prohibit such discrimination. In addition, section 805 of the Civil Rights Act of 1968 prohibits discriminatory practices in connection with the financing of housing.

If FHA finds there is noncompliance with any applicable antidiscrimination laws or regulations, it may discontinue FHA business with the violator.

LEGAL DESCRIPTION *(Attach one page if necessary)*

Owners: Eugene & Janet Thomas
　　　　140 E. Central St.
　　　　Moorestown, New Jersey ACQ. 1971
Broker: Bon-Air / Fellman

Please consider the following TITLE EXCEPTIONS in value:

SHOW BELOW: Shape, location, distance from nearest intersection and street names. Mark N at NORTH point

220'　☐　CENTRAL
14th　↓

N

Please consider the following
Equipment in value:

LEASEHOLD	Ground Rent *(Per Yr)* $	Lease is: ☐ 99 years	☐ Renewable	☐ FHA Approved	Expires

In submitting this application for a conditional commitment for mortgage insurance, it is agreed and understood by the parties involved in the transaction, that if, at the time of application for a Firm Commitment, the identity of the seller has changed, the application for a Firm Commitment will be rejected and the application for a Conditional Commitment will be reprocessed upon request by the mortgagee.

It is further agreed and understood that in submitting the request for a Firm Commitment for mortgage insurance, the seller, the purchaser and the broker involved in the transaction shall each certify that the terms of the contract for purchase are true to his best knowledge and belief, and that any other agreement entered into by any of these parties in connection with this transaction is attached to the sales agreement.

BUILDER/SELLER'S AGREEMENT: All Houses: The undersigned agrees to deliver to the purchaser FHA's statement of appraised value. Proposed Construction: The undersigned agrees, upon sale or conveyance of title within one year from date of initial occupancy, to deliver to the purchaser FHA Form 2544, warranting that the house is constructed in substantial conformity with the plans and specifications on which FHA based its value and to furnish FHA a conformed copy with the purchaser's receipt thereon that the original warranty was delivered to him. All Houses: In consideration of the issuance of the commitment requested by this application, I (we) hereby agree that any deposit or down payment made in connection with the purchase of the property described above, whether received by the undersigned or an agent of the undersigned, shall upon receipt be deposited in escrow or in trust or in a special account which is not subject to the claims of my creditors and where it will be maintained until it has been disbursed for the benefit of the purchaser or otherwise disposed of in accordance with the terms of the contract of sale.

Signature: ☒ Mortgagee ☐ Builder ☐ Seller ☐ Other 　*Letty Alicea* 　5/13　19 78

MORTGAGEE'S CERTIFICATE: The undersigned mortgagee certifies that to the best of its knowledge all statements made in this application and the supporting documents are true, correct and complete.

Signature/Title of Mortgagee Officer: *Letty Alicea* 　Loan Officer　5/13　19 78

WARNING: Section 1010 of Title 18, U.S.C. provides: "Whoever, for the purpose of . . . influencing such Administration . . . makes, passes, utters, or publishes any statement, knowing the same to be false . . . shall be fined not more than $5,000 or imprisoned not more than two years, or both."

FHA FORM NO. 2800-1 Rev. 7/76

MORTGAGEE - AFTER COMPLETING THE FORM DETACH THIS SHEET. SEND REST OF FORM TO FHA OFFICE

Form Approved
OMB No 63-R1 366

FHA MORTGAGEE NO.

30257-8

U.S. DEPARTMENT OF HOUSING AND URBAN DEVELOPMENT
FEDERAL HOUSING ADMINISTRATION

NOTICE OF ACCEPTANCE OF
MORTGAGEE'S APPLICATION FOR PROPERTY APPRAISAL
AND COMMITMENT FOR MORTGAGE INSURANCE UNDER
THE NATIONAL HOUSING ACT

☐ SEC. 203(b) ☒ SEC. 221d2

FHA CASE NO 351-132092-221

PROPERTY ADDRESS

51 Brunswick Lane
Willingboro, NJ

MORTGAGEE

Kennedy Mortgage Company
11 Allison Drive
Cherry Hill, New Jersey

YOUR APPLICATION HAS
BEEN ACCEPTED and assign-
ed the FHA Case Number shown
above. You will be billed, on a
monthly statement, the applicable fee which will be identified by the FHA Case Number.
Retain this notice to reconcile
future statements.

DATE STAMP

RETURN TO MORTGAGEE

FHA FORM NO 2800-2 Rev 7/76

Form Approved
OMB No 63-R1 366

FHA MORTGAGEE NO.	U.S. DEPARTMENT OF HOUSING AND URBAN DEVELOPMENT FEDERAL HOUSING ADMINISTRATION	FHA CASE NO.
30257-8		351-132092-221

CONDITIONAL COMMITMENT FOR MORTGAGE INSURANCE UNDER THE NATIONAL HOUSING ACT

☐ SEC 203(b) ☒ SEC. 221d2

PROPERTY ADDRESS

51 Brunswick Lane
Willingboro, NJ

MORTGAGEE

Kennedy Mortgage Company
11 Allison Drive
Cherry Hill, New Jersey

ESTIMATED VALUE OF PROPERTY.... $ *25,000*

COMMITTED FOR INSURANCE *D. W. Williams*

COMMITMENT

Issued	*5/25*	19 *78*
Expires	*11/25*	19 *78*

7 MONTHLY EXPENSE ESTIMATE

Fire Ins	$ *6.00*
Taxes	$ *75.00*
Condo Com Exp $	*—*
Maint & Repairs $	*20.00*
Heat & Utilities	$ *50.00*

ESTIMATED CLOSING COST $ *700*

COMMITMENT TERMS MAX MORT AMT $ *25,000* NO. MOS *360* MAX INTEREST *8¼* %

☒ EXISTING ☐ PROPOSED
(See Gen. Cond. 3)

Improved Living Area *1328* Sq Ft

INFORMATION

The estimates of fire insurance, taxes, maintenance/repairs, heat/utilities and closing costs are furnished for mortgagee's and mortgagor's information. They may be used to prepare FHA Form 2900, Application for Credit Approval, when a firm commitment is desired.

GENERAL COMMITMENT CONDITIONS

1. MAXIMUM MORTGAGE AMOUNT AND TERMS -
(a) **OCCUPANT MORTGAGORS:** the mortgage amount and term set forth in the heading are the maximum approved for this property assuming a satisfactory owner-occupant mortgagor. The maximum amount and term in the heading may be changed depending upon FHA's rating of the borrower, his income and credit.

(b) **NONOCCUPANT MORTGAGORS:** If the mortgagor does not occupy the house, the law limits the maximum mortgage amount to not exceed 85% of the maximum amount available to an eligible mortgagor who will occupy the house (85% of value if Sec. 203(I) or 221). In the case of nonoccupant mortgagors, the firm commitment when issued will reduce the mortgage amount and terms below that stated in the heading.

(c) **COMMITMENT CHANGES:** The Commissioner may, upon request of the approved mortgagee, change the mortgage amount and term set forth in the heading. If the application is accompanied by a VA CRV, changes will be made only if VA issues an amendment.

(d) **FLOOD INSURANCE COMMITMENT CONDITIONS:** This commitment is issued on the condition that if the property is located in a flood hazard area as identified on the latest FIA Flood Hazard

Boundary Map in effect for the community prior to the date of closing, the property will be covered by flood insurance in accordance with FHA Regulation 203.16a.

2. FIRM COMMITMENT: - A firm commitment to insure a loan will be issued upon receipt of an Application for Credit Approval. FHA Form 2900, executed by an approved mortgagee and a borrower satisfactory to the Commissioner.

3. COMMITMENT TERM: - This commitment shall expire **SIX MONTHS** from the issue date in the case of an EXISTING HOUSE or **ONE YEAR** from its date in the case of PROPOSED CONSTRUCTION. *(FHA classifies all cases as either "EXISTING" or "PROPOSED" for the purpose of determining when a commitment expires. Accordingly, a house, even though still under construction, may be classified as an existing house if it was not approved by FHA or VA prior to the beginning of construction.)*

4. CANCELLATION: - This commitment may be cancelled after 60 days from the date of issuance if construction has not started, unless the mortgagee has disbursed loan proceeds.

5. PROPERTY STANDARDS: - All commitment conditions, repairs, or alterations proposed in the application or on the drawings and specifications returned herewith, shall equal or exceed the FHA Minimum Property Standards.

SPECIFIC COMMITMENT CONDITIONS *(Applicable when checked)*

1. ☐ HEALTH AUTHORITY APPROVAL: - Execution of Form 2573 by the Health Authority indicating approval of the water supply and/or sewage disposal installation is required. (Approval by letter or Health Authority Form may be used.)

2. ☒ TERMITE CONTROL: - (a) EXISTING HOUSE - Furnish certificate from a recognized termite control operator that the house and other structures within the legal boundaries of the property shows no evidence of active termite infestation. (b) PROPOSED CONSTRUCTION - Furnish one copy of Termite Soil Treatment Guarantee FHA Form 2052.

3. ☐ PREFABRICATOR'S CERTIFICATE: - Provide Prefabrication Certificate required by related Engineering Bulletin.

4. ☐ CARPET UNDERFLOORING: - Notice of subflooring or finish flooring installed under carpet shall be posted at a conspicuous location within the dwelling.

5. ☐ SUBDIVISION REQUIREMENTS:-Comply with Requirements No. _____

from Report dated _____ for _____
_____ Subdivision.

6. ☐ BUILDER'S WARRANTY: - The builder shall execute FHA Form 2544. Builder's Warranty.

7. ☐ PROPERTY INSPECTIONS: - A notice of construction status shall be given by Form 2289X, letter or telephone at the time indicated below:
a. Proposed Construction Cases:
(1) ☐ Notification shall be given for all Proposed Construction Cases at least two work days before "beginning of construction" and as may be instructed below.
(2) ☐ When the building is enclosed, structural framing completely exposed and roughing-in of plumbing, heating and electrical work installed and visible.
(3) ☐ When construction completed and property ready for occupancy.
b. ☐ REPAIRS: Notify FHA upon completion of required repairs.
c. ☐ CERTIFICATE OF COMPLETION: A certificate stating that the mortgagee has examined the proposed or required repairs and that they have been satisfactorily completed will be accepted.

8. ☐ VA INSPECTIONS: - Furnish a copy of a clear VA final report.

9. ☐ ASSURANCE OF COMPLETION: - If the required repairs cannot be completed prior to submission of closing papers, a Form 2300 escrow in the amount of $ _____ (or such additional amount as the lender desires) may be established as the means to assure completion.

10. ☐ SELLER'S AGREEMENT AND ESCROW FOR EXISTING PROPERTIES FINANCED UNDER SECTION 235-Section 518.

This commitment is issued on the condition that if the mortgage is to be insured under Section 235, the seller will execute an agreement to reimburse HUD for expenses incurred in repairing structural or other defects with respect to the property being sold. The form of agreement shall be prescribed by the Secretary and a seller who is not the occupant of the property will deposit 5 percent of the sales price in escrow with the mortgage in accordance with the terms of the agreement.

11. SECTION 223
☐ This Commitment is issued under Section _____ Pursuant to Section 223e.

12. ☒ SECTION 221(d)(2)
The Maximum Insurable mortgage for a mortgagor other than a displaced family presenting a Certificate of Eligibility, FHA Form 3476, is $ *25,700*.

13. CODE ENFORCEMENT
☒ Submit a statement from Public Authority that the subject property meets Code Requirements. If the mortgage encumbering the property is to be insured under Section 221(d)(2) a code compliance inspection is required.

14. REQUIRED CERTIFICATIONS.
☐ ☐ Electrical ☐ Heating ☐ Roofing ☐ Plumbing

15. EXPIRATION DATE: - The Total Value stated above is based ☐ on Veterans Administration Certification of Reasonable Value, case number _____ , dated _____
Regardless of General Commitment Condition Number 3, above, this commitment expires on _____

16. ☐ See special conditions No. _____ below or on attached sheet.

FHA FORM NO. 2800 5 Rev 7/76

SEND TO MORTGAGEE AFTER AUTHORIZED AGENT SIGNS

Form Approved
OMB No 63-R1366

FHA MORTGAGEE NO. 30257-8	U.S. DEPARTMENT OF HOUSING AND URBAN DEVELOPMENT FEDERAL HOUSING ADMINISTRATION	FHA CASE NO. 351-132092-221

STATEMENT OF APPRAISED VALUE FOR A MORTGAGE TO BE INSURED UNDER THE NATIONAL HOUSING ACT

☐ SEC. 203(b) ☒ SEC. 221d2

PROPERTY ADDRESS

51 Brunswick Lane
Willingboro, NJ

MORTGAGEE

Kennedy Mortgage Company
11 Allison Drive
Cherry Hill, New Jersey

ESTIMATED VALUE OF PROPERTY .... $ 25,000

COMMITTED FOR INSURANCE

D. W. Williams

COMMITMENT:

Issued 5/25 1978
Expires 11/25 1978

Fire Ins	$ 6.00
Taxes	$ 75.00
Condo Com Exp	$ —
Maint & Repairs	$ 20.00
Heat & Utilities	$ 50.00

ESTIMATED CLOSING COST .... $ 200

DEFINITION OF VALUE

The Federal Housing Commissioner has valued the above identified property for mortgage insurance purposes in the amount equal to the sum of the estimated value of property plus the estimated closing cost.

FHA'S estimate of "Value" ("Replacement Cost" in Section 213 or 220) does not fix a sales price, except when the mortgage is to be insured under section 235(i); does not indicate FHA approval of a purchaser of the property; nor does it indicate the amount of an insured mortgage that would be approved.

"VALUE OF PROPERTY" IS FHA'S ESTIMATE OF THE VALUE OF THE PROPERTY.

"Closing Costs" is the FHA estimate of the cost of closing a mortgage loan on the property. These costs may be paid by either the buyer or the seller.

The maximum mortgage which FHA can insure is based on the sum of the value of the property plus the estimate of closing costs. Under those sections of the National Housing Act (such as 213 or 220) where the maximum mortgage amount must be based on estimated replacement cost, the "Value of Property shall be deemed to mean replacement cost for mortgage insurance purposes."

"Replacement Cost" is an estimate of the current cost to reproduce the property including land, labor, site survey and marketing expense but excluding payments for prepaid expenses such as taxes and insurance and closing costs.

If the contract price of the property is equal to or less than "Value of Property", and the buyer pays closing costs, a part of the closing costs can be included in the mortgage. IF THE CONTRACT PRICE OF THE PROPERTY IS MORE THAN "VALUE OF PROPERTY" AND THE BUYER PAYS THE CLOSING COSTS, THE BUYER IS PAYING MORE FOR THE PROPERTY THAN FHA'S ESTIMATE OF ITS VALUE.

The law requires that FHA mortgagors receive a statement of "appraised value" prior to the sale of the property. If the sales contract has been signed before the mortgagor receives such a statement, the contract must contain, or must be amended to include the following language:

"It is . . . agreed that, ... the purchaser shall not be obligated to complete the purchase . . . or to incur any penalty . . . unless the seller has delivered to the purchaser a written statement setting forth . . . the value of the property (excluding closing costs) not less than $ _____. The purchaser shall have the privilege . . . of preceding with . . . this contract without regard to the amount of the . . . valuation."

ADVICE TO HOME BUYERS

EXISTING PROPERTIES- WHERE THE APPLICATION INVOLVES AN EXISTING PROPERTY, FHA MAKES AN APPRAISAL ONLY TO DETERMINE THE PROPERTY'S VALUE. AN APPRAISAL DOES NOT IN ANY WAY WARRANT THE CONDITION OF THE PROPERTY. POTENTIAL BUYERS SHOULD EXAMINE THE PROPERTY CAREFULLY AND TAKE ALL NECESSARY PRECAUTIONS BEFORE SIGNING A PURCHASE CONTRACT. THE FHA DOES NOT HAVE AUTHORITY TO PROVIDE FINANCIAL ASSISTANCE IN CONNECTION WITH MAKING NEEDED REPAIRS.

ADVANCE PAYMENTS - Make extra payments when able. You pay less interest and have your home paid for sooner. Notify the lender in writing at least 30 days before the regular payment date on which you intend to make an advance payment.

DELINQUENT PAYMENTS - Monthly payments are due the first day of each month and should be made on or before that date. The lender may make a late charge up to 2 cents for each dollar of any payment more than 15 days late. If you fail for 30 days to make a payment, or to perform any other agreement in the mortgage, your lender may foreclose. You could lose your home, damage your credit, and prevent your obtaining further mortgage loans. If extraordinary circumstances prevent your making payments on time, see your lender at once. If you are temporarily unable to make your payments because of illness, loss of job, etc., your lender may be able to help you. Ask your lender to explain FHA's forbearance policy. **YOUR CREDIT IS AN IMPORTANT ASSET; DON'T LOSE IT THROUGH NEGLECT.**

MORTGAGE INSURANCE PREMIUM - The FHA charges a mortgage insurance premium-in the amount of ½ of 1% a year on the average outstanding principal obligation for the preceding 12 months without taking into account delinquent payments or prepayments. 1/12 of the mortgage insurance premium due each year is collected in the borrower's monthly mortgage payment to allow the lender to accumulate, one month prior to the premium due date, sufficient funds to pay the mortgage insurance premium.

TAXES, ASSESSMENTS, AND INSURANCE - Send your lender bills for taxes, special assessments, or fire insurance that come to you. The fire insurance the lender requires you to carry usually covers only the balance of the loan. Check this with your lender. You may wish to take out additional insurance so that if the house is damaged your loss will be covered as well as the lender's. If your home is damaged by fire, windstorm, or other cause, write your lender at once. Taxes for the coming year can't be known until the bills are received. If they exceed the amount accumulated from your payments, you will be asked to pay the difference. If they are less, the difference will be credited to your account. The same is true of fire insurance. Some States allow homestead or veteran's tax exemptions. Apply for any exemption to which you may be entitled. When it is approved, notify your lender.

CLOSING COSTS - In the heading is FHA's estimate of anticipated closing costs, such as fees for preparation of mortgage instruments, attorney's fees, title insurance, origination fees and documentary stamp taxes. The estimate does not include charges for such prepayable items as taxes, fire insurance.

NEW CONSTRUCTION - When FHA approves plans and specifications before construction, the builder is required to warrant that the house conforms to approved plans. This warranty is for 1 year following the date on which title is conveyed to the original buyer or the date on which the house was first occupied whichever occurs first. If during the warranty period you notice defects for which you believe the builder is responsible, ask him in writing to correct them. If he fails to do so, notify the HUD/FHA Field Office in writing. Mention the FHA case number shown above. If inspection shows the builder to be at fault, FHA will try to persuade him to make correction. If he does not, you may be able to obtain legal relief under the builder's warranty and where a structual defect is involved the FHA has authority to provide financial assistance in connection with making corrections. Most builders take pride in their work and will make justifiable corrections. They cannot be expected to correct damage caused by ordinary wear and tear or by poor maintenance. Keeping the house in good condition is the owner's responsibility.

IF YOU SELL - If you sell while the mortgage exists, the buyer may finance several ways. Understand how these arrangements may affect you. Consult your lender.
1. You may sell for all cash and pay off your mortgage. This ends your liability
2. The buyer can assume the mortgage and pay the difference between the unpaid balance and the selling price in cash. If the FHA and the lender are willing to accept the buyer as a mortgagor, you can be released from further liability. This requires the specific approval of the lender and the FHA.
3. The buyer can pay the difference in cash and purchase subject to the unpaid mortgage balance. FHA or lender approval is not necessary **BUT YOU REMAIN LIABLE FOR THE DEBT. IF THE BUYER DEFAULTS, IT COULD RESULT IN A DEFICIENCY JUDGMENT AND IMPAIR YOUR CREDIT STANDING.**

(METHODS 1 AND 2 ARE PREFERABLE TO METHOD NUMBER 3)

OPERATING EXPENSES - In the heading are FHA estimates of monthly costs of taxes, heat and utilities, fire insurance, maintenance and repairs. The estimated figures will probably have to be adjusted when you receive the actual bills. **BEAR IN MIND THAT IN MOST COMMUNITIES TAXES AND OTHER OPERATING COSTS ARE INCREASING.** The estimates should give some idea of what you can expect the costs to be at the beginning. In some areas FHA's estimate of taxes may also include charges such as sewer charges, garbage collection fee, water rates, etc.

☐ "THIS HOUSING WAS CONSTRUCTED BEFORE 1950. THERE IS A POSSIBILITY THAT IT MAY CONTAIN SOME LEAD PAINT THAT WAS IN USE BEFORE THAT TIME". THE LENDING INSTITUTION IS REQUIRED TO PROVIDE YOU WITH A COPY OF THE BROCHURE ENTITLED "WATCH OUT FOR LEAD PAINT POISONING".

AMOUNT TO BE BORROWED

When you borrow to buy a home, you pay interest and other charges which add to your cost. A larger down payment will result in a smaller mortgage. Borrow as little as you need and repay in the shortest time.

FHA FORM NO. 2800-6 Rev. 7/76

SEND TO MORTGAGEE FOR DELIVERY TO HOME BUYER

SUBJECT PROPERTY

STREET SCENE

05695   51 Brunswick

Previous Editions Obsolete

FHA FORM NO. 2004-G Rev. 5/75 VA FORM NO. 26-8497 Rev. 5/75	VETERANS ADMINISTRATION and U. S. DEPARTMENT OF HOUSING AND URBAN DEVELOPMENT FEDERAL HOUSING ADMINISTRATION	FORM APPROVED OMB NO. 63-R1288

REQUEST FOR VERIFICATION OF EMPLOYMENT

INSTRUCTIONS: Lender – Complete Items 1 through 6. Have applicant complete Items 7 and 8. Forward the completed form directly to the employer named in Item 1.
Employer – Complete Items 9A through 15 and return form directly to lender named in Item 2.

PART I   REQUEST

1. TO: (Name and Address of Employer):	2. FROM: (Name and Address of Lender):
George Jacobs Clothing 305 Rt. 70 East Cherry Hill, New Jersey	Kennedy Mortgage Co. 11 Allison Drive Cherry Hill, NJ 08003

3. Signature of Lender: Letty Alicea	4. Title of Lender: Processor	5. Date: 5/13/78	6. HUD-FHA or VA Number:

I certify that this verification has been sent directly to the employer and has not passed through the hands of the applicant or any other interested party.	I have applied for a mortgage loan and stated that I am employed by you. My signature below authorizes verification of this information.

7. Name and Address of Applicant:	8. Employee's Identification Number: 456-795
John Smith 540 S. 4th St. Camden, New Jersey	*John Smith* Signature of applicant

PART II   VERIFICATION

9 A. Is applicant now employed by you? ☒Yes ☐No	10A. Position or Job Title: Porter/Truck Driver	11. TO BE COMPLETED BY MILITARY PERSONNEL ONLY.
9B. Present Base Pay is $ 2.75 This amount is paid: ☐Annually ☒Hourly ☒Monthly ☐Other (Specify) ☐Weekly		Pay Grade:
	10B. Length of Applicant's employment: From 11/19/75	Base Pay $
		Rations $
9C. EARNINGS LAST 12 MONTHS Amount $ 3797.10	10C. Probability of continued employment: Permanent Position	Flight or Hazard $
Basic Earnings $		Clothing $
Normal Hours worked per Week: 40	10D. Date Applicant left:	
Overtime Earnings $ 4.12-1/2 ☒Regular 8 hrs. ☐Temporary	10E. Reason for leaving:	Quarters $
Other Income $		Pro-Pay $
☐Regular ☐Temporary		Overseas or Combat $

12. REMARKS:

13. Signature of Employer: *Tom Kelly*	14. Title of Employer: Bookkeeper	15. Date: 5/18/78

RETURN DIRECTLY TO LENDER

05695   51 Brunswick

FHA FORM NO. 2004-G Rev. 5/75 VA FORM NO. 26-8497 Rev. 5/75	VETERANS ADMINISTRATION and U. S. DEPARTMENT OF HOUSING AND URBAN DEVELOPMENT FEDERAL HOUSING ADMINISTRATION	FORM APPROVED OMB NO. 63-R1288

REQUEST FOR VERIFICATION OF EMPLOYMENT

INSTRUCTIONS: Lender – Complete Items 1 through 6. Have applicant complete Items 7 and 8. Forward the completed form directly to the employer named in Item 1.
Employer – Complete Items 9A through 15 and return form directly to lender named in Item 2.

PART I   REQUEST

1. TO: (Name and Address of Employer):	2. FROM: (Name and Address of Lender):
Echelon Mall Evesham Rd. Voorhees Twsp, N.J. ATT: Maintenance Personnel	Kennedy Mortgage Co. 11 Allison Drive Cherry Hill, NJ 08003

3. Signature of Lender: Letty Alicea	4. Title of Lender: Processor	5. Date: 5/13/78	6. HUD-FHA or VA Number:

I certify that this verification has been sent directly to the employer and has not passed through the hands of the applicant or any other interested party.

I have applied for a mortgage loan and stated that I am employed by you. My signature below authorizes verification of this information.

7. Name and Address of Applicant: John Smith 540 S. 4th St. Camden, New Jersey	8. Employee's Identification Number: *John Smith* Signature of applicant

PART II   VERIFICATION

9 A . Is applicant now employed by you? ☐Yes ☒No	10A. Position or Job Title: Maintenance	11. TO BE COMPLETED BY MILITARY PERSONNEL ONLY.
9B. Present Base Pay is $ _____ This amount is paid: ☐Annually ☐Hourly ☐Monthly ☐Other (Specify) ☐Weekly	10B. Length of Applicant's employment: 5 years	Pay Grade:

| 9B. Present Base Pay | 10B. Length | Base Pay $ |
| Rations $ |

9C. EARNINGS LAST 12 MONTHS	10C. Probability of continued employment:	
Amount $		Flight or Hazard $
Basic Earnings $		Clothing $
Normal Hours worked per Week:	10D. Date Applicant left: 11/16/75	
Overtime Earnings $ _____ ☐Regular ☐Temporary	10E. Reason for leaving: New job	Quarters $
Other Income $ _____ ☐Regular ☐Temporary		Pro-Pay $
		Overseas or Combat $

12. REMARKS:

13. Signature of Employer: *Edgar Brown*	14. Title of Employer: Bookkeeper	15. Date: 5/18/78

RETURN DIRECTLY TO LENDER

Previous Editions Obsolete

05695   51 Brunswick Lane

Previous Editions Obsolete

FHA FORM NO. 2004-G Rev. 5/75 VA FORM NO. 26-8497 Rev. 5/75	VETERANS ADMINISTRATION and U. S. DEPARTMENT OF HOUSING AND URBAN DEVELOPMENT FEDERAL HOUSING ADMINISTRATION	FORM APPROVED OMB NO. 63-R1288

REQUEST FOR VERIFICATION OF EMPLOYMENT

INSTRUCTIONS: Lender – Complete Items 1 through 6. Have applicant complete Items 7 and 8. Forward the completed form directly to the employer named in Item 1.
Employer – Complete Items 9A through 15 and return form directly to lender named in Item 2.

PART I   REQUEST

1. TO: (Name and Address of Employer): Cooper Hospital 6th & Cooper Sts. Camden, NJ ATT: Personnel	2. FROM: (Name and Address of Lender): Kennedy Mortgage Co. 11 Allison Drive Cherry Hill, NJ 08003

3. Signature of Lender: Letty Alicea	4. Title of Lender: Processor	5. Date: 5/13/78	6. HUD-FHA or VA Number:

I certify that this verification has been sent directly to the employer and has not passed through the hands of the applicant or any other interested party.	I have applied for a mortgage loan and stated that I am employed by you. My signature below authorizes verification of this information.

7. Name and Address of Applicant: Ella C. Smith 540 S. 4th St. Camden, NJ	8. Employee's Identification Number: 2020 Signature of applicant

PART II   VERIFICATION

9A. Is applicant now employed by you? ☒Yes ☐No	10A. Position or Job Title: Aide I Nursing	11. TO BE COMPLETED BY MILITARY PERSONNEL ONLY.	
9B. Present Base Pay is $ 3.85 This amount is paid: ☐Annually ☒Hourly ☐Monthly ☐Other (Specify) ☐Weekly		Pay Grade:	
	10B. Length of Applicant's employment: 4/8/74 to present	Base Pay	$
		Rations	$
9C. EARNINGS LAST 12 MONTHS ~~Year to date as of pay~~ Amount $ period 7/17 $4627.05	10C. Probability of continued employment: Permanent	Flight or Hazard	$
Basic Earnings $ N/A		Clothing	$
Normal Hours worked per Week: 40	10D. Date Applicant left:		
		Quarters	$
Overtime Earnings $ ☐Regular ☐Temporary N/A	10E. Reason for leaving:	Pro-Pay	$
Other Income $ ☐Regular ☐Temporary N/A		Overseas or Combat	$

12. REMARKS:

13. Signature of Employer: *Sally Brown*	14. Title of Employer: Personnel Manager	15. Date: 5/18/78

RETURN DIRECTLY TO LENDER

800,000   51 Brunswick La

FHA FORM NO. 2004-F (Rev. 12/75) VA FORM NO. 26-8497a (Rev.12/75)	VETERANS ADMINISTRATION AND U. S. DEPARTMENT OF HOUSING AND URBAN DEVELOPMENT FEDERAL HOUSING ADMINISTRATION	OMB NO. 63-R0266 Approval Expires 4/7C

REQUEST FOR VERIFICATION OF DEPOSIT

INSTRUCTIONS: *LENDER - Complete Items 1 through 7. Have applicant complete Items 8 and 9. Forward directly to bank or other depository named in Item 1.*
BANK or DEPOSITORY - Please complete Items 10 through 13. Return directly to Lender named in Item 2.

PART I - REQUEST

1. TO: (Name and Address of Bank or other Depository)	2. FROM: (Name and Address of Lender)
Heritage Bank Rt. 130 & Hylton Rd. Pennsauken, New Jersey	Kennedy Mortgage Company 11 Allison Drive Cherry Hill, New Jersey 08003

3. I certify that this verification has been sent directly to the bank or other depository and has not passed through the hands of the applicant or any other interested party. Signature of Lender: Letty Alicea	4. Title: Processor	5. Date: 5/13/78 6. FHA or VA Number:

7. STATEMENT OF APPLICANT:

7A. Name and Address of Applicant:	7B. TYPE OF ACCOUNT	BALANCE	ACCOUNT NUMBER
Ella C. Smith 540 S. 4th St. Camden, New Jersey	CHECKING	$ 150	500 847 9
	SAVINGS	$ 1,355	05010550 1
	CERTIFICATE OF DEPOSIT	$	

8. I have applied for a mortgage loan and stated that I maintain account(s) with the bank or other depository named in Item 1. My signature below authorizes that bank or other depository to furnish the lender named in Item 2 the information set forth in Part II. Your response is solely a matter of courtesy for which no responsibility is attached to your institution or any of your officers. *Ella Smith* Signature of Applicant	7C. TYPE OF LOAN	BALANCE	ACCOUNT NUMBER
	SECURED	$	
	UNSECURED	$	
	9. Date: 5/13/78		

PART II - VERIFICATION

10A. Does Applicant have any outstanding loans ? ☐ Yes ☒ No (If Yes, enter total in Item 10B.)	CURRENT STATUS OF ACCOUNTS			

10B. TYPE OF LOAN	MONTHLY PAYMENT	PRESENT BALANCE	11A. Is account less than two months old? (If Yes, give date account was opened in Item 12B)	CHECKING ☐ Yes ☒ No	SAVINGS ☐ Yes ☒ No	CERT. of DEPOSIT ☐ Yes ☐ No
SECURED	$	$	11B. Date the account was opened.			
UNSECURED	$	$	11C. Present Balance	$ 66.79	$ 1,346.89	$
10C. Payment Experience: ☒ Favorable			11D. Is account other than individual, e.g., Joint or Trust? (If Yes, explain in Remarks.)	☒ Yes ☐ No	☒ Yes ☐ No	☐ Yes ☐ No
☐ Unfavorable (If Unfavorable, explain in Remarks.)			11E. Is account satisfactory? ☐ Yes ☐ No			

12. REMARKS:

Balances as of 5/16/78

The above information is provided in response to your request.

13A. Signature of Official of Bank or other Depository: *Ben Savings*	13B. Title: Audit Division	13C. Date: 5/18/78

THIS INFORMATION IS FOR THE SOLE PURPOSE OF ASSISTING THE APPLICANT IN OBTAINING A MORTGAGE LOAN.
RETURN DIRECTLY TO LENDER

＊U.S. GOVERNMENT PRINTING OFFICE 1976 671 543 194♯

CREDIT BUREAU ASSOCIATES

817 CARPENTER STREET • CAMDEN, NEW JERSEY 08101

K# 800000

FHA STANDARD FACTUAL DATA REPORT

Date 5/16/78 mh ___ Social Security Number: 136 30 5830

FHA Case Number _____
☐ Acquired Property   ☐ Other than Acquired Property
EO Case Number _____
CPD Case Number _____
OI Case Number _____
ILS Case Number _____
PILB Case Number _____
HC Case Number _____
VA Loan Number _____
USDA-FHA Number _____

Name _____ Smith, John & Ella C.
Address _____ 540 So. 4th Street
Camden, N.J.   SINCE: 1972

Property Address
51 Brunswick Lane
Willingboro, N.J.

Credit Report Order Dated 5/13/78 ___ From:
☐ FHA or ☒ FHA Mortgagee:
☐ EO: ☐CPD: ☐OI:
☐ ILS: ☐ PILB; ☐HC,
☐ FHA Sales Broker: ☐ VA Sales Broker:
☐ VA: ☐VA Lender: ☐USDA-FHA

Credit Report Order Received by Contract Agency on _____ (date)

Credit Report Mailed on 5/18/78 ___ to: (date)
☐ FHA or ☐ FHA Mortgagee:
☐ EO: ☐ CPD: ☐ OI;
☐ ILS: ☐ PILB; ☐HC;
☐ VA; ☐VA Lender; ☐ USDA-FHA

(No reference shall be made in this report to race, creed, color, or national origin.)

1.A Do name & address Agree with Information Shown on Request For Report. If Not, Explain. **Yes**	B Subject Date of Birth 8/30/38-11/30/42

1.C Marital Status – No. of Dependents **Married   2 (8,4)**   1.D Length of Time Married **10/8/68**   1.E Did You Learn of any Separation or Divorce ☐Yes ☒No

2.A Name of Employer   **Verified**
George Jacobs, Clothing-305 Rt 70 E, Cherry Hill, N.J.
2.B Position Held – Length of Present Employment **Truck Driver   10/75**

Has His Employment Status Changed Within the Past Four Years?
Yes-Echelon Mall, Voorhees Twp., N.J. Verified
INCOME: **$143, wk, est.**

3.A If Wife is Employed, Give Name of Her Employer **Maint. 10/74 to 10/75**
Housewife
3.B Position Held – Length of Present Employment

Has Her Employment Status Changed Within the Past Four Years?
- - -
INCOME:

1. Amplify his business history. (This report shall contain information as to the subject's previous employment status, location and salary, if there has been a change in employment status within the past four years.)
2. The reporting bureau certifies that: (a) public records have been checked for judgments, foreclosures, garnishments, bankruptcies, chattels, liens, and other legal actions involving the subject with the results indicated below; or (b) equivalent information has been obtained through the use of a qualified public records reporting service with the results indicated below. (Give details.) (The records of real estate transfers which do not involve foreclosures may be excluded.) If no public records to report indicate NONE in this block. ☐
3. The reporting bureau certifies that the subject's credit record in the payment of bills and other obligations has been checked (a) ☒through the credit accounts extended by the designated credit grantors under the Classes and Trades identified in the contract for the community in which the subject resides with the results indicated below; or, (b) ☒through accumulated credit records of such credit grantors of the community in which the subject resides, with the results indicated below.

CREDIT HISTORY

TYPE OF BUSINESS	ORIGINAL ACCOUNT OPENED	DATE OF LAST TRANS. Mo. Yr.	HIGH CREDIT	BALANCE OWING	AMOUNT PAST DUE	PAYMENT TERMS	PAYING RECORD
Singer Co.		8/74	$600.	$240.		As agreed,	$14. mo.
GMAC		9/68	$3300.	0		Paid satis.	36 mos.
1st Nat'l S.J.		4/75	$2300.	$1200.		Delinq. 30 days, twice,	
				current since 12/75	30 @ 80.		
Sears		4/75	$400.	$350.		As agreed	
		9/70	$700.	$265.		As agreed.	$14. mo.

Subjects paying $125. month to Ed Ashley (unlisted number)

PUBLIC RECORDS: Judgment satisfied 6/11/73 no amt. to Edward Ashley, Jr.

PREPARED BY   NAME OF REPORTING BUREAU   CITY   STATE
Credit Bureau Associates, Camden, N.J.

REPORT FOR
C 31 Kennedy Mtg. Co.

TOTAL COST OF CREDIT REPORT

TUMBLE OVER.
WRITE FROM TOP DOWN.

The information in this report is provided under contract between the Department of Housing and Urban Development - Federal Housing Administration and Credit Bureau Associates. The information is not to be divulged to anyone other than the named Department of Housing and Urban Development organizational elements, Veterans Administration and USDA-Farmers Home Administration, except as required by Public Laws 91-508, 93-579, and 94-239 and the Contract.

Re: **Name** John & Ella Smith

Property 51 Brunswick Lane

Willingboro, N.J.

K# 800,000

The Federal Housing Administration requires that each applicant for a home loan submit evidence that money to be used for the down payment and settlement charges was derived from personal assets, and not borrowed in any way.

In order to comply with this regulation we request that you accurately complete the following statement with all pertinent information:

I hereby certify that the funds used for the deposit in the amount of $ 750.00 to purchase subject property, paid on 5/11/78 by cash/check drawn on Heritage Bank came from the following:

[X] $_____Savings Bank Account (Name of Bank) Cooper Hosp. Credit Union

[ ] $_____Cash on Hand Savings from earnings.

[ ] $_____Savings Bonds which were derived from earnings

[ ] $_____Proceeds from sale of present home

[ ] $_____Other -- Explain_____

In addition, I further certify that the balance of the funds due at settlement, approximately $ 300 will be obtained from:

[X] Savings in Bank Account (Name of Bank) Heritage Bank

[X] Cash-on-hand Savings from earnings

[ ] Savings Bonds that were derived from earnings

[ ] Net proceeds from sale of present home

[ ] Other -- Explain_____

We further state that none of the money used in this transaction is or will be borrowed.

We are aware of the following:

SECTION 1010 of TITLE 18, U.S.C., "Federal Housing Administration transaction," provides: "Whoever, for the purpose of influencing in any way the action of such Administration makes, passes, utters or publishes any statement, knowing the same to be false shall be fined not more than $5,000., or imprisoned not more than two years, or both."

This statement is true and correct to the best of my knowledge.

_____5/11/78_____   *John Smith*
        Date   Mortgagor

                              Ella Smith
                              Mortgagor

NB #68
7/75

Form Approved
OMB No 63—R1062

U. S. DEPARTMENT OF HOUSING AND URBAN DEVELOPMENT FEDERAL HOUSING ADMINISTRATION	2. FHA Case No. 351-132092

1. MORTGAGEE'S APPLICATION FOR MORTGAGOR APPROVAL AND COMMITMENT FOR MORTGAGE INSURANCE UNDER THE NATIONAL HOUSING ACT

☐ SEC. 203(b) ☒ SEC. 221
(NOTE: See reverse for Privacy Act Statement)

5. MORTGAGEE - Name, Address & Zip Code *(Please Type)*

Kennedy Mortgage Co.
11 Allison Drive
Cherry Hill, NJ   08003

(Please locate address within corner marks)

3. PROPERTY ADDRESS 51 Brunswick Lane Willingboro, NJ

4. MORTGAGORS:

Mtgor. John Smith   Sex M Age 37
Co-Mtgor. Ella C. Smith   Sex F Age 33
Address 540 S. 4th Street, Camden, NJ

Married yes Yrs. 8 No. of Dependents 2 Ages 8, 4

Co-Mortgagor(s)   Sex   Age(s)

(Check One)
☐ White *(Non-Minority)* ☐ American Indian ☐ Spanish American
☒ Negro/Black ☐ Oriental ☐ Other Minority

6. MORTGAGE APPLIED FOR →

Mortgage Amount	*Interest Rate	No. of Months	Monthly Payment Principal & Interest
$24,650	8-1/2%	360	$189.56

7. PURPOSE OF LOAN:

Finance Constr. ☐ on Own Land
Finance ☒ Purchase
Refinance ☐ Exist. Loan
☐ to Exist. Prop.
Finance Impr.
☐ Other

MORTGAGOR WILL BE: ☒ Occupant ☐ Landlord ☐ Builder ☐ Escrow Commit. Mortgagor

8. ASSETS

Cash accounts Heritage Bank	$1,346.89
Cash on Hand	400.00
Marketable securities	
Other (explain)	
OTHER ASSETS (A) TOTAL	$1,746.89
Cash deposit on purchase	750.00
Other (explain) '73 Buick	3,000.00
Furniture & Personal Prop.	9,000.00
(B) TOTAL	$14,496.89

9. LIABILITIES

	Monthly Payt.	Unpd. Bal.
Automobile	$	$
Debts, other Real Estate		
Life Insurance Loans		
Notes payable	80.00	1,200.00
Credit Union		
Retail accounts		
NAME Sears ACCOUNT NO.	14.00	265.00
Singer	14.00	240.00
Sears	20.00	350.00
If more space is needed, attach schedule. TOTAL	$128.00	$2,055.00

10. EMPLOYMENT

Mortgagor's occupation Porter
Employer's name & address George Jacobs Clothing
305 Rt. 70 East
Cherry Hill, NJ   years employed 11/75

Co-Mtgor. occupation Nursing Aide
Employer's name & address Cooper Hospital
6th & Cooper Sts.
Camden, NJ   years employed 4/74

11. MONTHLY INCOME

Mortgagor's base pay	$476.67
Other Earnings (explain) ot	143.00
Co-Mtgor. base pay	667.33
Other Earnings (explain)	
Gross Income, Real Estate	
Other (explain)	
TOTAL	$1,287.00

12. SETTLEMENT REQUIREMENTS

(a) Existing debt (Refinancing only)	$
(b) Sale price (Realty only)	25,000.00
(c) Repairs & Improvements Seller to pay	50.00
(d) Closing Costs Seller paying $650.00	
(e) TOTAL (a+b+c+d) Acquisition cost	25,050.00
(f) Mortgage amount	24,650.00
(g) Mortgagor's required investment(e—f)	400.00
(h) Prepayable expenses	350.00
(i) Non-realty & other items	
(j) TOTAL REQUIREMENTS (g+h+i)	750.00
(k) Amt.pd. ☒ cash ☐ Other (explain)	750.00
(l) Amt. to be pd ☒ cash ☐ Other (explain)	---
(m) Tot. assets available for closing (B)(A)	$513.68

13. FUTURE MONTHLY PAYMENTS

(a) Principal & Interest	$189.56
(b) FHA Mortgage Insurance Premium	10.06
(c) Ground rent (Leasehold only)	
(d) TOTAL DEBT SERVICE (a+b+c)	199.62
(e) Hazard Insurance	8.00
(f) Taxes, special assessments	78.00
(g) TOTAL MTG. PAYT. (d+e+f)	285.62
(h) Maintenance & Common Expense	17.00
(i) Heat & utilities	68.00
(j) TOTAL HSG. EXPENSE (g+h+i)	370.62
(k) Other recurring charges (explain)	202.00
(l) TOTAL FIXED PAYT. (j + k).	$572.62

14. PREVIOUS MONTHLY HOUSING EXPENSE

Mortgage payment or rent	$125.00
Hazard Insurance	
Taxes, special assessments	
Maintenance	40.00
Heat & Utilities	
Other (explain) TOTAL	$165.00

15. PREVIOUS MONTHLY FIXED CHARGES

Federal, State & Local income taxes	$146.30
Prem. for $ Life Insurance	
Social Security & Retirement Payments	74.00
Installment account payments	128.00
Operating Expenses, other Real Estate	
Other (explain)	
TOTAL $	348.30

16. Do you own other Real Estate ☐ Yes ☒ No Is it to be sold ☐ Yes ☐ No FHA mortgage ☐ Yes ☐ No Sales Price $ Orig-Mtg Amt $
Unpaid Bal. $ Address Lender

17. MORTGAGOR'S CERTIFICATE -- I ☒ have ☐ have not received a copy of the FHA Statement of Value (FHA Form 2800-6) or Veterans Administration Certificate of Reasonable Value (VA Form 26-1843) showing the estimated value of the property described in this application. Have you sold a property within the last year which had an FHA mortgage? ☐ Yes ☒ No. If "Yes" was the mortgage paid in full? ☐ Yes ☒ No. If "No" give FHA Case Number ____, buyer's name ____, property address ____, date of transfer ____. lender's name and address ____ original mortgage amount $____. unpaid balance when sold $____. Did buyer intend to occupy ? ☐ Yes ☒ No. Have you ever been obligated on a home loan, home improvement loan or a mobile home which resulted in foreclosure, transfer of title in lieu of foreclosure, or judgement? ☐ Yes ☒ No. If "Yes" attach statement giving full details including date, property address, name and address of lender, FHA or VA Case Number, if any, and reasons for the action. If dwelling is covered by this mortgage is to be rented, is it a part of, adjacent or contiguous to any project, subdivision, or group of rental properties involving eight or more dwelling units in which you have any financial interest? ☐ Yes ☐ No. If "Yes" give details. Do you own four or more dwelling units with mortgages insured under any title of the National Housing Act? ☐ Yes ☒ No. If "Yes" submit FHA Form 2561. The Mortgagor certifies that all information in this application is given for the purpose of obtaining a loan to be insured under the National Housing Act and is true and complete to the best of his knowledge and belief. Verification may be obtained from any source named herein. *NOTE: The interest rate shown in Item 6 is the FHA VA maximum rate in effect on the date of this commitment and may increase prior to closing unless buyer and lender agree otherwise.

Signature(s) ____ Date ____ 19__

18. MORTGAGEE'S CERTIFICATE -The mortgagee certifies that all information in this application is true and complete to the best of its knowledge and belief. Signature *Letty Alicia*   Loan Officer Date 5/25 19 78

WARNING: Section 1010 of Title 18, U. S. C., "Federal Housing Administration transactions," provides "Whoever, for the purpose of ... influencing in any way the action of such Administration ... makes, passes, utters, or publishes any statement, knowing the same to be false ... shall be fined not more than $5,000 or imprisoned not more than two years, or both".

FHA FORM NO 2900-1 Rev 2/76   FHA COPY — FILE IN CASE BINDER

Form Approved
OMB No. 63—R1062

U.S. DEPARTMENT OF HOUSING AND URBAN DEVELOPMENT FEDERAL HOUSING ADMINISTRATION	FHA Case No. 351-132092

FIRM COMMITMENT FOR
MORTGAGE INSURANCE UNDER THE NATIONAL HOUSING ACT

☐ SEC. 203(b)   [X] SEC. 221

PROPERTY ADDRESS	51 Brunswick Lane Willingboro, NJ

Mtgor.	John Smith	Sex M Age 37
Co-Mtgor.	Ella C. Smith	Sex F Age 33
Address	540 S. 4th Street, Camden, NJ	

Kennedy Mortgage Co.
11 Allison Drive
Cherry Hill, NJ   08003

Married yes Yrs. 8	No. of Dependents 2	Ages 8, 4
Co-Mortgagor(s)		Sex Age(s)

(Check One)
1 ☐ White *(Non-Minority)*   3 ☐ American Indian   5 ☐ Spanish American
2 [X] Negro/Black   4 ☐ Oriental   6 ☐ Other Minority

MORTGAGE APPLIED FOR →	Mortgage Amount $24,650	Interest Rate 8-1/2%	No. of Months 360	Monthly Payment Principal & Interest $189.56

[X] **ACCEPTED:** A note and mortgage described above or as modified below will be insured under the National Housing Act provided one of the mortgagors will be an owner-occupant and all conditions appearing in any outstanding commitment issued under the above case number and those set forth below are fulfilled.

☐ MODIFIED AND ACCEPTED AS FOLLOWS:	Mortgage Amount $	Interest Rate %	No. of months	Monthly Payment Principal & Interest $

ESTIMATE OF VALUE AND CLOSING COSTS

VALUE OF PROPERTY $25,000
Closing Costs .... $ 700
TOTAL *(For Mortgage Insurance Purposes)* ... $ 25,700

ADDITIONAL CONDITIONS

☐ 2544 - Builders warranty required.   ☐ Owner-occupancy NOT required. *(Delete (c) · Mortgagor's Certificate)*
(See Item(s) _____ on Addendum to Commitment)

Improved Floor Area 1328 Sq. Ft.

☐ The property is to be insured under Section 221 (d) (2); a code compliance inspection is required.

THIS COMMITMENT EXPIRES:

DATE OF THIS COMMITMENT

11/25, 1978
(Expiration Date)

D. W. Williams
(Authorized Agent for the Federal Housing Commissioner)

5/25, 1978
Newark
(Field Office)

INSTRUCTIONS TO MORTGAGEE: Forward to the insuring office: (1) this commitment signed by the mortgagee and mortgagor; (2) a copy of the note, bond or other credit instrument; (3) a copy of the mortgage or other security instrument; (4) a copy of the settlement statement, (Form HUD-1) signed by the mortgagee which itemizes all charges and fees collected by the mortgagee from the mortgagor and seller; and (5) FHA Mortgage Insurance Certificate completed with case number, Section of the National Housing Act, mortgage amount, property address, mortgagors' names and mortgagee's name and address.

MORTGAGOR'S CERTIFICATE - The undersigned certifies that:
(a) The mortgaged property, including removable equipment items shown on any outstanding commitment issued under the above case number and those set forth above, will be owned by me free and clear of all liens other than that of such mortgage.
(b) I will not have outstanding any other unpaid obligations contracted in connection with the mortgage transaction or the purchase of the said property except obligations which are secured by property or collateral owned by me independently of the said mortgaged property, or obligations approved by the Commissioner.
(c) One of the undersigned is the occupant of the subject property. (NOTE: Delete item (c) if owner occupancy not required by commitment).
(d) All charges and fees collected from me as shown in the settlement statement have been paid from my own funds, and no other charges have been or will be paid by me in respect to this transaction.
(e) Check Applicable Box:
☐ This was a refinancing transaction; sale of property was not involved.
☐ Purchase of the lot was a separate transaction; dwelling was built for occupancy by me.
☐ The FHA Statement of Appraised Value or VA Certificate of Reasonable Value was given to me prior to my signing the purchase contract for the property.
☐ The FHA Statement of Appraised Value or VA Certificate of Reasonable Value was not received by me prior to my signing the contract to purchase, but the contract to purchase contained the following language: "It is expressly agreed that, notwithstanding any other provisions of this contract, the purchaser shall not be obligated to complete the purchase of the property described herein or to incur any penalty by forfeiture of earnest money deposits or otherwise unless the seller has delivered to the purchaser a written statement issued by the Federal Housing Commissioner setting forth the appraised value of the property (excluding closing costs) of not less than $ _____ which statement the seller hereby agrees to deliver to the purchaser promptly after such appraised value statement is made available to the seller. The purchaser shall, however, have the privilege and option of proceeding with the consummation of the contract without regard to the amount of the appraised valuation made by the Federal Housing Commissioner."
(IF THE AMENDMENT PROCEDURE WAS NECESSARY, THE DOLLAR AMOUNT USED IN THE AMENDATORY CLAUSE IS INSERTED IN THE ABOVE BLANK.)
(f) Neither I, nor anyone authorized to act for me, will refuse to sell or rent, after the making of a bona fide offer, or refuse to negotiate for the sale or rental of, or otherwise make unavailable or deny the dwelling or property covered by this loan to any person because of race, color, religion, sex, marital status or national origin. I recognize that any restrictive covenant on this property relating to race, color, religion, sex, marital status or national origin is illegal and void and any such covenant is hereby specifically disclaimed. I understand that civil action for preventative relief may be brought by the Attorney General of the United States in any appropriate U.S. District Court against any person responsible for a violation of this certification. *NOTE: The interest rate shown is the FHA-VA maximum rate in effect on the date of this commitment and may increase prior to closing unless buyer and lender agree otherwise.

Signature: *John Smith   Ella Smith*   Date: 6/10 1978

MORTGAGEE'S CERTIFICATE - The undersigned certifies that to the best of its knowledge:

Date _____, 19 ___

(a) None of the statements made in its application for insurance nor in the Mortgagor's Certificate are untrue or incorrect.
(b) The conditions listed above or appearing in any outstanding commitment issued under the above case number have been fulfilled.
(c) Complete disbursement of the loan has been made to the Mortgagor, or to his creditors for his account and with his consent.
(d) The security instrument has been recorded and is a good and valid first lien on the property described.
(e) No charge has been made to or paid by the Mortgagor except as permitted under FHA Regulations.
(f) The copies of the credit and security instruments which are submitted herewith are true and exact copies as executed and filed for record.
(g) It has not paid any kickbacks, fees or consideration of any type, directly or indirectly, on or after May 1, 1972, to any party in connection with this transaction except as permitted under Section 203.7(a)(6) of the FHA Regulations and administrative instructions issued pursuant thereto.

Mortgagee *(Please use FHA imprint stamp, or other approved device.)*

NOTE: If commitment is executed by an agent in name of the mortgagee, the agent must enter the mortgagee's code number and type code number in blocks below.	
Code	Type

4
(Signature and title of officer)
H. Eugene Brown

FHA FORM NO. 2900-4 Rev 2/76   **MORTGAGEE - AFTER CLOSING, COMPLETE CERTIFICATES AND RETURN TO FHA. SEE INSTRUCTIONS ABOVE**

KENNEDY MORTGAGE CO.

11 ALLISON DRIVE • CHERRY HILL, NEW JERSEY 08003 • N. J. 609-424-8300, 9312 • P. A. 215-925-2626, 7225

Mr. & Mrs. John Smith
540 South 4th Street
Camden, NJ

Date: May 25, 1978

Borrower: John & Ella Smith

Property: 51 Brunswick Lane
           Willingboro, NJ

K#   800000

Dear Mr. & Mrs. Smith:
We are pleased to inform you that your application for a mortgage
loan on the captioned property has been approved by the Federal
Housing Administration/Veterans Administration in the

AMOUNT OF $24,650.00   **FOR A TERM OF** 30   **YEARS**

with monthly payments to principal and interest of $ 189.56
plus 1/12 of the annual cost of real estate taxes, hazard insurance premium and FHA mortgage insurance premium if applicable, as
evidenced by its commitment dated May 25,   19 78

This commitment is valid only if the following conditions are met:

1. All FHA/VA conditions and repairs must be completed prior to
    settlement. All Certifications, Guarantees and Inspection re-
    ports must be in this office and acceptable prior to sched-
    uling a date for settlement.
    The Maximum Insurable mortgage for a displaced family presenting a
    Certificate of Eligibility, FHA Form 3476, is $25,700.00. Submit a
    statement from Public Authority that the subject property meets Code
    Requirements. Electrical & roofing certifications required. See
    attached VC-3, VC-25, VC-39, & VC-44. Replace broken windows where **over

2. Compliance with all regulations governing FHA or VA mortgages
    at time of closing, as applicable. If a VA loan, the guarantee
    must be 60% of the loan or $17,500, whichever is less.

3. A discount or placement fee of 5% of the mortgage amount shall
    be paid by the seller of the property to us at time of settle-
    ment. This fee cannot be paid by the purchaser. Discount sub-
    ject to change without notice if not settled within commitment
    period.

4. A service charge of 1% of the mortgage amount shall be paid by
    the borrower at the time of settlement.

5. This loan shall bear the maximum interest rate and service
    charges allowable by FHA/VA at the time of settlement, but not
    less than 8½%. In the event an interest rate higher than the
    present rate is authorized by Federal Housing Administration/
    Veterans Administration and is in effect at the time this loan
    is ready for closing, it is agreed that it shall be closed at
    whatever the maximum interest rate is on that date.

6. Please forward two current Report of Title to this office AS
    SOON AS POSSIBLE in order that we may prepare the mortgage
    papers. Prior to arranging an hour for settlement, please con-
    tact this office for a mutually satisfactory time.

7. Two copies of a current final survey. (show: walks, driveways,
    easements, rights of ways, house type and location on lot, etc.)

8. Fire insurance policies must be written for a term of three
    years and include extended coverage. Homeowners policies or a
    continuous policy will be acceptable with a mortgagee clause to
    Kennedy Mortgage Co. and/or its assignee, 518 Market Street,
    Camden, New Jersey. NOTE: Fire insurance policies must be

NB#-26
7/75

K# 800-000
FHA# 351-132092-221

MORTGAGOR'S CERTIFICATION

This is to certify that prior to signing closing documents, we have:

1. Received a copy of the FHA commitment including a list of the required specific conditions.

2. Received a copy of mechanical and structural certifications called for in the commitment and purchase contract.

3. Received a copy of the inspections report from the local code enforcement officer.

We have examined these documents and have thoroughly inspected the property and are satisfied with the documents and repairs or condition of the property.

WE further certify that the settlement at closing of this mortgage loan was substantially as indicated on the application for a firm commitment; that there are no charges, credits, refunds or agreements that would affect the acquisition price or mortgage amount in this transaction.

Signed: _John Smith_   6/10/78
                MORTGAGOR   DATE

           Ella Smith   6/10/78
                CO-MORTGAGOR   DATE

Attested to: _Calvin D Miller_   6/10/78
                ATTORNEY/TITLE COMPANY   DATE

E H Brown   6/10/78
          AUTHORIZED MORTGAGEE   DATE

CL 793-A
2/76

Date: June 10, 1978

Re: K# 800-000

TO WHOM IT MAY CONCERN:

This is to certify that if flood insurance is required on my/our property, that KENNEDY MORTGAGE CO., and/or its Assignees, has my/our permission to obtain a flood insurance policy and make the necessary charges to me/us through my/our escrow account.

_____
John Smith

_____
Ella C. Smith

Sworn and subscribed:

Before me this _6_ :

Day of _June_   1978:

_____

CL# 102
9/75

K# 800-000

MORTGAGOR'S AFFIDAVIT OF TITLE AND NAME AFFIDAVIT

STATE OF NEW JERSEY   )
: SS.
COUNTY OF Burlington   )

    John Smith and Ella C. Smith, his wife
(hereinafter called Deponent)
of full age, being duly sworn according to law upon oath, depose(s) and say(s):

THAT DEPONENT is/are the grantee in a Deed dated the   10th   day of   June , 1978,
recorded or intended to be recorded in the   clerk   Office of   Burlington
County, covering premises commonly known as   51 Brunswick Lane
Township of Willingboro, NJ

THAT DEPONENT intends to occupy the premises in question.

THAT there do not appear of record, in any Court of the United States, or the State of New
Jersey, or any District thereof, or in the New Jersey Supreme Court, against Deponent, any
Judgments, Decrees, Recognizances, Bailbonds, Bonds of Sheriff, Bankruptcies or action tend-
ing to Bankruptcy, nor are there any suits or proceedings in equity which affect the title
or possession of the premises in question.

THERE are no Unemployment Compensation, New Jersey Alcoholic Beverage or Federal Social
Security taxes due and unpaid from Deponent.

DEPONENT is/are at least 21 years of age.

DEPONENT were married to each other at
on   , 19   , and have never been married to any other person now living.

LAST NAME of Deponent(s) is spelled   Smith   , and no other way.

DEPONENT(s) have/has not been known by any other name during the past twenty (20) years,
except that the maiden name of   Ella. C. Smith   **was**
          , and that   Ella C. Smith   and
    Ella Smith   is the same person, and that
        and   is the same person.

THE above statements and representations are made by deponent in order to induce KENNEDY
MORTGAGE CO. to grant the mortgage loan referred to herein and to induce the title
insurance company selected to insure the mortgage loan when made and to issue its title
insurance policy in favor of KENNEDY MORTGAGE CO., or its Assignee.

_____
John Smith

SWORN TO AND SUBSCRIBED
BEFORE ME THIS   10th
DAY OF   June , 19 78.

_____
Ella C. Smith

_____
Chas. Greene

CL#353
Rev. 7/75

REGULATION "Z" TRUTH IN LENDING STATEMENT

DATE OF MAILING: May 25, 1978   K# 800000

BORROWERS _____ John & Ella Smith

PROPERTY ADDRESS _____ 51 Brunswick Lane, Willingboro, NJ

MAILING ADDRESS _____ 540 South 4th Street, Camden, NJ

MORTGAGE AMOUNT: $ 24,250.00   INTEREST RATE: 8½ % TERM: 30   YEARS

The finance charge on this mortgage will begin to accrue on the date of closing.

The mortgage amount shall be repaid in 360 monthly installments of principal and finance charge exclusive of mortgage insurance premium of $ 186.48 each. "In addition, the monthly payments will include additional amounts for mortgage insurance premiums. These additional amounts will range from $ 10.06 in the first payment to $ .47 in the last mortgage payment that is due."

The first payment will become due on the 1ST day of the 2ND month following the day of closing.

THE TOTAL FINANCE CHARGE TO BE PAID BY YOU OVER THE LIFE OF THE LOAN IS AS FOLLOWS:
1. Total interest over the life of your loan. $ 42,882.80 e
2. Total F.H.A. Mortgage Insurance Premium over the life of your loan. $ 2,520.55 e
3. Total Private Mortgage Insurance Premium over the life of your loan. $ ---

                              TOTAL $ 45,403.35 e

The finance charge calculated in accordance with federal regulations and expressed as an ANNUAL PERCENTAGE RATE IS   9.75   %.

PREPAID FINANCE CHARGES AND REQUIRED DEPOSIT BALANCES

In addition to the amounts shown at the left you will pay certain other charges at settlement not considered finance charges. These charges include the following:

Service Charge	$ 242.50 e *	
Placement Fee paid by Seller 5	$ 1,212.50 e	
Adjusted Interest (Estimated)	$ 39.48 e *	Recording Fees-Deed $ 15.00 e *
Prepaid Mtge. Ins. Premium	$ 20.14 e *	Recording fees-Mortgage $ 15.00 e *
Amortization Schedule	$ 1.00 e *	*XXXXXXXXXXXX Survey $ 75.00 e *
One Year Private Mtge. Ins.	$ ---	* Title Insurance $ 239.87 e *
		Preparation of Documents $ 25.00 e *
TOTAL	$ 1,515.62 e *	Appraisal and Credit Report $ 70.00 e *
		Notary Fees $ 5.00 e *

AMOUNT FINANCED

                              TOTAL $ 444.87 e *

Amount of Loan $ 24,250.00
Less Prepaid Finance Charges & Required Deposit Balances $ 1,515.62 e

TOTAL AMOUNT FINANCED $ 22,734.38 e

LATE CHARGES - If any installment is more than 15 days late   4   % of that installment is payable by Borrower to Lender as a late charge.

PREPAYMENT PENALTY CLAUSE - You have the privilege to prepay the mortgage upon payment of the following amount:

(X) FHA-NONE   ( ) VA-NONE   ( ) Conventional - _____

INSURANCE - You must obtain fire and extended coverage on at least the original amount of the loan, with a loss payable clause to the lender. This insurance may be purchased from any insurance company subject to Lender's rejection for a reasonable cause.

SECURITY - Lender's security interest in this transaction is a first lien on the property specified above, more particularly described in the mortgage to be recorded in this transaction. The lien extends to all after-acquired property and secures future advances on the terms set forth in the mortgage.

APPLICATION SUBMITTED BY John & Ella Smith, 540 South 4th Street, Camden, NJ
                          (NAME)   (ADDRESS)

NB# 13 - 1/77 Signatures: *John Smith*
                          Ella Smith

877-8871

Centralized Exterminating Co
of Burlington County
39 BONNIE LANE
WILLINGBORO, N.J. 08046

𝔚arranty

𝔅e 𝔍t 𝔎nown 𝔗hat, on this _____9th_____ day of
__November__ 19 _76_____ Centralized Exterminating
Company made a careful visual inspection of all accessible*

areas of the property located at _51 Brunswick Lane,_

Willingboro, N.J., including sounding of accessible
structural members and there is no evidence of termite or
other wood destroying insect infestation,** and if such infestation previously existed, it has now been eliminated and any
visible damage due to such infestation that renders the wood
unserviceable has been corrected.

This certification shall be warranted for a period of one (1)
year. Any infestation during the warranty period shall be
eliminated by the certifying exterminator at no cost to the
purchaser.

All warranties contained in the foregoing report of a visual
inspection are concerned only with the presence or suspected
presence of live active termites or other wood destroying
insects.

* *Accessible — Clearly visible, open and unobstructed surfaces: areas
and surfaces behind or under covered ceilings, floors, crawlspaces,
furniture, and painted surfaces are considered not accessible.*

***Infestation means live or active evidence of termites or other wood
destroying insects.*

_____
Authorized Inspector

K#   800-000

NAME   John Smith, etux

T A X   C E R T I F I C A T I O N

To be FULLY COMPLETED and SIGNED by Closing Agent at Settlement.

Return Form with ALL Closing Documents to:

KENNEDY MORTGAGE CO.

PROPERTY:

Street   51 Brunswick Lane,

~~City~~ Township of Willingboro County   Burlington   State   New Jersey

Lot   16   Block   225   Section

Subdivision

Prior Record Owner   Eugene S. Neufeld, etux

TO THE CLOSING AGENT: If taxes are due, you are instructed to pay them from loan proceeds, and furnish this office with receipted bills.

I hereby certify that Real Estate Taxes for_____(Give year and if partial tax payment, indicate which portion--e.g. 1st half 19_: 2nd quarter 19___, etc.) have been/will be paid by_____ (Indicate Attorney, Title Company, Seller or Purchaser).

Check (X)   (Fill in Names below of S. D., City/Town, etc.)

TO: _____   School District_____

       _____   City/Town_____

        X   County *Burlington*_____

       _____   Special assessment or ground rent_____

_____ 3 Months tax escrow collected at Settlement to be deposited to the

Mortgagors escrow account in the amount of $ 229.77 . Next tax bill due

Sept. 30 197 8 .

_____   *Alven D Miller*
Date of Settlement   Signature of Closing Agent
  6/10/78

CL# 756
REV. 7/75

1103

INSURANCE CERTIFICATION

RE: K#800,000
SMITH, John
51 Brunswick Lane
Willingboro, New Jersey

The undersigned hereby certifies that it has in its possession, a fire insurance policy with extended coverage, now in force and written in accordance with your requirements as set forth in your Servicing Agreement, that the amount of coverage is sufficient to preclude any mortgagor from being a co-insurer of any part fo the risk but in no event less than the amount of the mortgage and that such insurance will be continuously maintained from this date forward.

The undersigned also certifies that this insurance is in the name of the record owner and contains (or we have ordered and will obtain) a non-contributory standard mortgagee clause in your favor covering all buildings on the premises.

KENNEDY MORTGAGE CO.

H. EUGENE BROWN
Vice President-Treasurer

IC# 26
8/77 Rev.

KENNEDY MORTGAGE CO.

818 MARKET STREET • CAMDEN, NEW JERSEY 08101 • 609-365-6800 215-925-7226 215-925-7612

K# 800-000
TITLE CO. Towne & Country Abst. Co.
TITLE CO. NO. TCA-NJ-106,853

INSTRUCTIONS FOR SETTLEMENT

Settlement Date 6/10/78   Mortgage Amount $ 24,650.00
TO: Towne & Country Abst. Co.   Mortgagors John Smith, etux
Address _____   Property Address 51 Brunswick Lane
                                        Township of Willingboro, NJ

KENNEDY MORTGAGE CO. hereby designates you as agent to act in its behalf in closing this
mortgage loan, in accordance with the specific instructions pertaining to this mortgage, and
as an approved attorney (or agent of the Title Insurance Company listed herein. You may
not make a charge for any service which you render in connection with the mortgage closing in
our behalf and must comply with the following instructions and those previously outlined in
our Mortgage Settlement Guide.

The enclosed Mortgage Proceeds check is a "NET CHECK". IT IS ENTRUSTED TO YOU SUBJECT TO
STRICT COMPLIANCE with ALL the following instructions and conditions and may not be used unless you comply with same. Discount charges due us from the Seller/s, as stated below, have
been deducted in advance:

                    Mortgage Amount $ 24,650.00
                    Less Discount (-) $ 1,232.50
                    Net Check Enclosed $ 23,417.50

This check may NOT be used unless you have the mortgagor's sign all copies of attached "NET
CHECK AUTHORIZATION" (CL#314), witness their signatures, and return one copy to us with the
settlement papers (give one copy to Mortgagor and retain one copy.)

1. PLEASE FORWARD all completed settlement papers to our Closing Administrator within 24
   hours after settlement in the enclosed return envelope. In the event of a delay in disbursement or in the return of our settlement papers extending beyond 24 hours, call our
   Closing Administrator at 609-365-6800(N.J.) or 215-WA-5-7225(Phila.)

2. PLEASE COLLECT AND FORWARD your check payable to KENNEDY MORTGAGE CO. for the following.
   Checks must be returned with the settlement papers. (We will not accept seller's or
   mortgagor's personal checks.)

   A. COLLECT FROM MORTGAGORS (ESCROWS)
      Two months Mortgage Insurance Premium.............................$ 10.24
      3 months Tax Escrows (per your comp.) ($ 76.59 per month).......$ 229.77
      _____ months School Tax (per your computation)....................$ —
      Two Months Fire Insurance (per your computation)..................$ 14.58
      Two Months Flood Insurance (when required-per your computation)....$ —
      Mortgage Interest Adjustment from_____to_____@_____%......$
   NOTE: Pay at settlement, all current taxes, municipal charges and added assessments
         through_____. If tax bill is not available, provide adequate escrows
         for payment
      Application/ Appraisal $_____
      Photos $_____
      Credit Report $_____
      Prepaid Mtge. Ins. Premium $_____
                                      $_____
                                      $_____
      Amortization Schedule $_____
      Inspection Fee $_____
      Buyers Fee $_____

   B. COLLECT FROM SELLERS (draw combined check for fees and a separate check for repair escrow)
      Termite Inspection Fee $_____
      Repair Inspection Fee $_____

DO NOT DISBURSE OUR MORTGAGE PROCEEDS CHECK UNTIL YOU HAVE RECEIVED AUTHORIZATION FROM THIS
OFFICE RE: THE FOLLOWING:

CL#100-1
7/75

HUD-1 Rev. 5/76   OMB NO. 63-R-1501

A.		B. TYPE OF LOAN
U. S. DEPARTMENT OF HOUSING AND URBAN DEVELOPMENT SETTLEMENT STATEMENT		1. ☒ FHA 2. ☐ FmHA 3. ☐ CONV. UNINS. 4. ☐ VA 5. ☐ CONV. INS. 6. File Number: 7. Loan Number: 8. Mortgage Insurance Case Number: 351-132092-221

C. NOTE: *This form is furnished to give you a statement of actual settlement costs. Amounts paid to and by the settlement agent are shown. Items marked "(p.o.c.)" were paid outside the closing; they are shown here for informational purposes and are not included in the totals.*

D. NAME OF BORROWER:	E. NAME OF SELLER:	F. NAME OF LENDER:
John Smith & Ella C., h/w	Eugene S. Thomas & Janet H., h/w	Kennedy Mortgage Co.

G. PROPERTY LOCATION:	H. SETTLEMENT AGENT:	I. SETTLEMENT DATE:
51 Brunswick Lane Willingboro, NJ Burlington County	PLACE OF SETTLEMENT: Fellman Realty Willingboro, NJ	6/10/78

J. SUMMARY OF BORROWER'S TRANSACTION		K. SUMMARY OF SELLER'S TRANSACTION	
100. GROSS AMOUNT DUE FROM BORROWER:		**400. GROSS AMOUNT DUE TO SELLER:**	
101. Contract sales price	25,000.00	401. Contract sales price	25,000.00
102. Personal property		402. Personal property	
103. Settlement charges to borrower (line 1400)	1,191.00	403.	
104.		404.	
105.		405.	
Adjustments for items paid by seller in advance		*Adjustments for items paid by seller in advance*	
106. City/town taxes 5/11 to 6/10	109.85	406. City/town taxes 5/11 to 6/10	109.85
107. County taxes to		407. County taxes to	
108. Assessments to		408. Assessments to	
109.		409.	
110.		410.	
111.		411.	
112.		412.	
120. **GROSS AMOUNT DUE FROM BORROWER**	26,300.85	420. **GROSS AMOUNT DUE TO SELLER**	25,109.85
200. AMOUNTS PAID BY OR IN BEHALF OF BORROWER:		**500. REDUCTIONS IN AMOUNT DUE TO SELLER:**	
201. Deposit or earnest money Fellman Re.	750.00	501. Excess deposit (see instructions)	
202. Principal amount of new loan(s) Kennedy M.	24,650.00	502. Settlement charges to seller (line 1400)	5,052.64
203. Existing loan(s) taken subject to		503. Existing loan(s) taken subject to	
204. Closing Costs	650.00	504. Payoff of first mortgage loan PSFS	9,961.33
205.		505. Payoff of second mortgage loan 1st Ntl Bk	4,836.25
206.		506. Closing Cost	650.00
207.		507.	
208.		508.	
209.		509.	
Adjustments for items unpaid by seller		*Adjustments for items unpaid by seller*	
210. City/town taxes to		510. City/town taxes to	
211. County taxes to		511. County taxes to	
212. Assessments to		512. Assessments to	
213. Water & Sewer	7.55	513. Water & Sewer	7.55
214.		514.	
215.		515.	
216.		516.	
217.		517.	
218.		518.	
219.		519.	
220. **TOTAL PAID BY/FOR BORROWER**	26,057.55	520. **TOTAL REDUCTION AMOUNT DUE SELLER**	20,507.77
300. CASH AT SETTLEMENT FROM/TO BORROWER		**600. CASH AT SETTLEMENT TO/FROM SELLER**	
301. Gross amount due from borrower (line 120)	26,300.85	601. Gross amount due to seller (line 420)	25,109.85
302. Less amounts paid by/for borrower (line 220)	(26,057.55)	602. Less reductions in amount due seller (line 520)	(20,507.77)
303. CASH (☒ FROM) (☐ TO) BORROWER	243.30	603. CASH (☐ TO) (☐ FROM) SELLER	4,602.08

L. SETTLEMENT CHARGES		PAID FROM BORROWER'S FUNDS AT SETTLEMENT	PAID FROM SELLER'S FUNDS AT SETTLEMENT
700. TOTAL SALES/BROKER'S COMMISSION based on price $ @ % =			
Division of Commission (line 700) as follows:			
701. $ 875.00 to Fellman Realty			
702. $ 875.00 to Bon-Air Agency			
703. Commission paid at Settlement			1,750.00
704.			
800. ITEMS PAYABLE IN CONNECTION WITH LOAN			
801. Loan Origination Fee 1 % Kennedy Mortgage		246.50	
802. Loan Discount 5 % Kennedy Mortgage			1,232.50
803. Appraisal Fee to			
804. Credit Report to			
805. Lender's Inspection Fee			
806. Mortgage Insurance Application Fee to			
807. Assumption Fee			
808. Amortization Schedule Kennedy Mortgage		2.00	
809.			
810.			
811.			
900. ITEMS REQUIRED BY LENDER TO BE PAID IN ADVANCE			
901. Interest from 5/11 to 6/10 @ $ /day		81.48	
902. Mortgage Insurance Premium for months to			
903. Hazard Insurance Premium for years to Warner Agency		87.44	
904. years to			
905.			
1000. RESERVES DEPOSITED WITH LENDER			
1001. Hazard insurance 2 months @ $ 7.29 per month		14.58	
1002. Mortgage insurance 2 months @ $ 10.24 per month		20.48	
1003. City property taxes 3 months @ $ 76.59 per month		299.77	
1004. County property taxes months @ $ per month			
1005. Annual assessments months @ $ per month			
1006. months @ $ per month			
1007. months @ $ per month			
1008. months @ $ per month			
1100. TITLE CHARGES			
1101. Settlement or closing fee to T & C Abstract			35.00
1102. Abstract or title search to T & C Search		25.00	
1103. Title examination to			
1104. Title insurance binder to			
1105. Document preparation to			
1106. Notary fees to			
1107. Attorney's fees to			
(includes above items numbers;)			
1108. Title insurance to T & C Abstract		258.75	
(includes above items numbers;)			
1109. Lender's coverage $			
1110. Owner's coverage $			
1111. Tax Assessment & Survey Ins.		30.00	
1112.			
1113.			
1200. GOVERNMENT RECORDING AND TRANSFER CHARGES			
1201. Recording fees: Deed $ 10.00 ; Mortgage $ 8.00 ; Releases $ Canc Mort		18.00	16.00
1202. City/county tax/stamps: Deed $ 87.50 ; Mortgage $			87.50
1203. State tax/stamps: Deed $; Mortgage $			
1204. Processing		12.00	
1205.			
1300. ADDITIONAL SETTLEMENT CHARGES Escrow			200.00
1301. Survey to James Jarvis		70.00	
1302. Pest inspection to Central Exterminating			215.25
1303. Inspection & Water Bill Fellman			77.75
1304. Spain Contractors			1,272.99
1305. Shell Escrow			165.75
1400. TOTAL SETTLEMENT CHARGES *(enter on lines 103, Section J and 502, Section K)*		1,191.00	5,052.64

1306.   Shell Escrow   95.00   HUD-1 Rev. 5/76

FHA FORM NO. 9151
Revised September 1970

K# 800-000

This form is used in connection with mortgages insured under the one- to four-family provisions of the National Housing Act.

NEW JERSEY MORTGAGE BOND

FHA CASE NO.

351-132092-221

KNOW ALL MEN BY THESE PRESENTS: That John Smith and Ella C. Smith, his wife
hereinafter called the obligor S , are held and
firmly bound unto KENNEDY MORTGAGE CO.
11 Allison Drive, Cherry Hill, NJ
a corporation organized and existing under the laws of the State of New Jersey
hereinafter called the obligee, in the penal sum of Forty Nine thousand Three hundred and
00/100------ Dollars ($ 49,300.00), to be paid to the said obligee, or to its certain attorney, successors, or assigns; for which payment well and truly to be made the obligor S do hereby
bind themselves, their heirs, executors, administrators, successors, and assigns, jointly and severally, firmly by these presents.

Sealed with their seal S and dated the 10th day of June , in the year One Thousand Nine Hundred and seventy eight

THE CONDITION OF THE ABOVE OBLIGATION IS SUCH, that if the above-bounden obligor S shall well and truly pay or cause to be paid to the obligee, or to its certain attorney, successors, or assigns, at its principal office in Camden, New Jersey , or such other place as the obligee or its certain attorney, successors, or assigns shall designate, in writing, the just and full sum of
Twenty four thousand six hundred fifty & 00/100 Dollars ($ 24,650.00),
with interest from date at the rate of eight and one half per centum (8½ %)
per annum on the unpaid balance until paid, said principal and interest to be paid in monthly installments of
One hundred eighty nine & 56/100---Dollars ($ 189.56), commencing on the
first day of August ,1978 , and on the first day of each month thereafter until the principal and interest are fully paid, except that the final payment of principal and interest, if not sooner paid, shall be due and payable on the first day of July ,2008 , privilege being reserved to pay this obligation in whole, or in an amount equal to one or more monthly payments on the principal that are next due, on the first day of any month prior to maturity; Provided, however, that written notice of an intention to exercise such privilege is given at least thirty (30) days prior to prepayment and provided further that in the event this debt is paid in full prior to maturity, and at that time it is insured under the provisions of the National Housing Act, all parties liable for the payment of same, whether principal, surety, guarantor, or endorser, agree to be jointly and severally bound to pay the holder of this bond an insurance premium charge of one per centum (1%) of the original principal amount hereof, except that in no event shall the adjusted premium exceed the aggregate amount of premium charges which would have been payable if the mortgage had continued to be insured until maturity; such payment to be applied by the holder hereof upon its obligation to the Secretary of Housing and Urban Development, on account of mortgage insurance; and shall make all other payments provided to be made by the mortgage of even date herewith, and shall in every other respect keep and perform all the covenants and agreements contained in this bond and the said mortgage without any fraud or other delay, then the above obligation to be void, otherwise to remain in full force and virtue.
In the event that any payment shall become overdue for a period in excess of fifteen (15) days, a "late charge" of two cents (2¢) for each dollar ($1) so overdue may be charged by the holder hereof, for the purpose of defraying the expense incident to handling the said delinquent payment.
In addition to the foregoing installments of principal and interest, the obligor S promise(s) to make monthly payments in the amounts, and to be applied in the manner, set forth in the mortgage securing this bond.
And it is expressly agreed that the obligor S herein, their heirs, executors, administrators, successors, and assigns, shall not make or claim any deduction from or credit on the interest herein, and in the mortgage securing this bond agreed to be paid, by reason or on account of or for any tax or taxes, assessed or to be assessed on the real estate described in said mortgage or any part thereof; and that should any default be made in the payment of any monthly installment on account of principal and interest, or any part thereof, or any of the other payments to be made by the obligor S under the provisions of the mortgage securing this bond on the day whereon the same is payable, as provided in this bond (it being agreed that a default in the payment of any installment under this bond shall exist only if not made good prior to the due date of the next such installment) or in said mortgage, or should any ground rent, tax or installment thereof, assessment, water rent, or other municipal or governmental rate, charge, imposition, or lien be hereafter imposed or acquired upon the premises described in said mortgage, the payment of which is not otherwise provided for therein, become due and payable and remain unpaid for the space of thirty (30) days, and from henceforth, that is to say, after the lapse or expiration of either of said periods, as the case may be, the above first-mentioned principal sum, or so much thereof as may at the time of such default remain unpaid, with all the arrearage of interest thereon, and all other payments provided in said mortgage securing this bond, to be made by the obligor S at the option of the said obligee, its successors and assigns, shall become and be due and payable immediately thereafter, although the period may not have then expired, anything herein contained to the contrary thereof in anywise notwithstanding, and the said obligee may at its option also pay any such premium of fire or other insurance, ground rent, tax or installment thereof, assessment, or water rent in arrears as aforesaid, and the amount so paid shall be added to and become part of the principal sum secured hereby and by said mortgage, and shall be payable on demand with interest at the above rate.
Signed, sealed, and delivered
in the presence of

H E Brown

J C Johnson

John Smith [L. S.]

Ella Smith [L. S.]
Ella C. Smith

[L. S.]

[L. S.]

GPO 899-394

K# 800-000

T/CO.# TCA-NJ-106,853

> This form is used in connection with mortgages insured under the one- to four-family provisions of the National Housing Act.

STATE OF NEW JERSEY
FHA FORM NO. 2151m
Revised June 1971

FHA# 351-132092-221

MORTGAGE

THIS INDENTURE, made the **10th** day of **June** in the year of our Lord One Thousand Nine Hundred and **seventy eight**

Between **John Smith and Ella C. Smith, his wife**
of the **Township** of **Willingboro** in the County of
Burlington and State of **New Jersey**
hereinafter with **their** heirs, executors, administrators, successors, and assigns called the Mortgagor, and

KENNEDY MORTGAGE CO.
11 Allison Drive, Cherry Hill, NJ

, a corporation organized and existing under the laws of **the State of New Jersey** , hereinafter with its successors and assigns called the Mortgagee,

WHEREAS, the said **Mortgagors are** justly indebted to the Mortgagee in the sum of **Twenty four thousand six hundred fifty and 00/100----------**Dollars ($ **24,650.00**) with interest thereon, as evidenced by a certain bond or obligation bearing even date with these presents, conditioned for the payment of the said sum to the Mortgagee, its certain attorney, successors or assigns, at its principal office in **Camden, New Jersey** , or at such other place as the Mortgagee may designate in writing, the said principal and interest to be payable in monthly installments of **One hundred eighty nine and 56/100------------------------**Dollars ($ **189.56**), commencing on the first day of **August** ,19 **78**, and on the first day of each month thereafter until the principal and interest are fully paid, except that the final payment of principal and interest, if not sooner paid, shall be due and payable on the first day of **July 2008**

NOW THIS INDENTURE WITNESSTH, that the Mortgagor, for better securing the payment of the said sum of money mentioned in the condition of the said bond or obligation, with interest thereon according to the true intent and meaning thereof, and also for and in consideration of the sum of One Dollar ($1) to **them** in hand paid by the Mortgagee, at or before the ensealing and delivery of these presents, the receipt whereof is hereby acknowledged, has granted, bargained, sold, aliened, released, conveyed and confirmed, and by these presents does grant, bargain, sell, alien, release, convey and confirm unto the said Mortgagee or to its certain attorney, successors or assigns, forever.

ALL th **at** tract or parcel of land, situate, lying and being in the **Township** of **Willingboro** in the County of **Burlington** in the State of New Jersey:

BEING more particularly described according to legal description attached hereto and made a part hereof.

THIS IS A PURCHASE MONEY MORTGAGE.

AND BEING the same land and premiese which Eugene S. Thomas and Janet H. Thomas, his wife by indenture dated the 10th day of June, 1978 and intended to be forthwith recorded, granted and conveyed unto the said John Smith and Ella C. Smith, his wife, in fee.

Together with the following removable items: range.

TOGETHER with all and singular the tenements, hereditaments and appurtenances thereunto belonging or in anywise appertaining, and the reversion or reversions, remainder and remainders, rents, issues and profits thereof, AND ALSO all the estate, right, title, interest property, possession, claim and demand whatsoever, as well in law as in equity, of the Mortgagor, of, in and to the same, and every part and parcel thereof, with the appurtenances, and also, all materials, equipment, furnishings or other property whatsoever installed or to be installed and used in and about the building or buildings now erected or hereafter to be erected upon the lands herein described which are necessary to the complete and comfortable use and occupancy or such building or buildings for the purposes for which they were or are to be erected, including in part all awnings, screens, shades, fixtures, and all heating, lighting, ventilating, refrigerating, incinerating and cooking equipment and appurtenances thereto (the Mortgagor hereby declaring that it is intended that the items herein enumerated shall be deemed to have been permanently installed as part of the realty); TO HAVE AND TO HOLD the above granted and described pre-

All of the covenants and conditions herein contained shall be for the benefit of, and bind the heirs, executors, administrators, successors and assigns of, the respective parties hereto. If more than one joins in the execution hereof as Mortgagor or any be of the feminine sex, the pronouns and relative words herein used shall be read as if written in plural or feminine, respectively.

IN WITNESS WHEREOF, the said Mortgagor S ha ve hereunto set   their   hand S   and seal S   , the day and year first above written.

Signed, sealed, and delivered in the presence of:

_____   *John Smith*   [L.S.]
                                         John Smith
_____   *Ella Smith*   [L.S.]
                                         Ella C. Smith
                                         _____   [L.S.]
                                         _____   [L.S.]

STATE OF NEW JERSEY }
                     } ss:
COUNTY OF Burlington }

BE IT REMEMBERED, That on this   10th   day of   June   , in the year One Thousand Nine Hundred and seventy eight   , before me the subscriber   a personally appeared   John Smith and Ella C. Smith, his wife   who I am satisfied   are   the Mortgagor S in the within Indenture named; and I having first made known to   them   the contents thereof,   they   acknowledged that   they   signed, sealed, and delivered the same as   their   voluntary act and deed for the uses and purposes therein expressed.

IN WITNESS WHEREOF, I have hereunto set my hand and official seal this   10th   day of   June   , 19 78

                                    Ed D Brown

Prepared By   Alvin D. Miller, Esq.   _____

Received for Record on the   11th   day of   June   , A.D. 19 78   at   3:10   o'clock P.M. and recorded in Book No. 1020   of Mortgages, at Page 37

                                    Sam Grey
                                    Recorder

THE MORTGAGOR CERTIFIES THAT A TRUE COPY OF THE MORTGAGE HAS BEEN RECEIVED

John Smith   *Ella Smith*
John Smith   Ella C. Smith

KENNEDY MORTGAGE CO.

818 MARKET STREET • CAMDEN, NEW JERSEY 08101 •

609-365-6800 215-925-7225 215-925-7612

HUD
519 Federal St.
Camden, NJ 08103

DATE ___June 10, 1978___

RE: K# ___800-000___

FHA# ___351-132092-221___

PROPERTY: ___51 Brunswick Lane___

___Township of Willingboro, NJ___

MORTGAGOR: ___John Smith, etux___

Gentlemen:

In connection with the captioned loan, we enclose the following closing papers for your review:

- (X) Copy of Mortgage
- (X) Copy of Bond
- (X) Settlement Sheet
- (X) Mortgage Insurance Certificate
- (X) FHA Firm Commitment
-     MC Conditions
- ( ) Proof of Previous Property Sold
- ( ) Minimum Net Proceeds of Previous Property
- ( ) Proof of Bills Paid (see set-up sheet)
- ( ) Prepayable amounting to $_____
- ( )
- ( )
- ( ) Housing Code
- ( ) Non-discrimination Certificate
-     Certifications of FHA Conditional Commitment
- ( ) Termite
- ( ) Roofing and Flashing
- ( ) Plumbing
- ( ) Heating
- ( ) Electrical (underwriters)
- ( ) Water
- ( )   ( ) Health Authority
-            ( ) Chemical/Bacterialogical
- ( ) Sewer
-            ( ) Health Authority
-            ( ) Contractor
- ( ) Water Proofing
- ( ) Builder's Warranty
- ( ) CL# 727, Buyer's Approval on Inspection (PA-FHA)
- ( ) Inspections: ( ) K ( ) FHA ( ) VA
- ( ) Escrow Agreements: ( ) Special ( ) FHA
- ( ) Letter of Assignment
- ( ) 2561 Form, Mortgagor's Contract with Respect to Hotel
-            and Transient Use of Property
- ( ) Special Conditions (DE FHA)
- ( ) Waiver ( ) Lot ( ) Easements ( ) Party Wall ( ) Side Wall
- ( ) Refund Letter
- ( )
- (X) Mtgrs. Cert.
- (X) CL# 793

Please endorse the attached Mortgage Insurance Certificate and return to the attention of H. E. Brown.

Very truly yours,

H. E. Brown

Kennedy Mortgage Co.

Enclosures
CL# 3A
3/77

| FHA CASE NO. | U.S. DEPARTMENT OF HOUSING AND URBAN DEVELOPMENT FEDERAL HOUSING ADMINISTRATION | FHA FORM NO. 9100-1 REV. 6/66 |

351-132092-221

Mortgage Insurance Certificate

Smith, John & Ella C., h/w
MORTGAGORS *(Last Name First)*

SECTION **221**   NATIONAL HOUSING ACT

51 Brunswick Lane
PROPERTY ADDRESS

MORTGAGE AMOUNT $ **24,650.00**

Willingboro Twp., NJ 08046
CITY, STATE & ZIP CODE

Kennedy Mortgage Co.
11 Allison Drive
Cherry Hill, NJ

This Certificate, when endorsed on the reverse hereof, is evidence of insurance of the mortgage loan described herein under the indicated Section of the National Housing Act (12 USC 1701 et seq.) and Regulations of the Federal Housing Commissioner (24 Code of Federal Regulations 200.1 et seq.).

MORTGAGEE'S NAME AND ADDRESS

Mortgage insurance certificate

HERITAGE BANK N.A.

TRUST RECEIPT

Date June 10, 1978

Re: Mortgage Co. No. K# 800-000

FHA or VA No. 351-132092-221

Property Address   51 Brunswick Lane, Willingboro, Twp.,NJ

Name   John Smith and Ella C. Smith, his wife

The undersigned (hereinafter called the 'Trustee') acknowledges receipt from the **HERITAGE BANK** N.A. (hereinafter called 'Bank') of the instruments and papers listed on the reverse side hereof, which instruments and papers are the property of the Bank, acquired in connection with the promissory notes likewise listed on the reverse side hereof. A security interest in said instruments and papers remains in, or will remain in, or has passed to, or will pass to the Bank.

In consideration of the delivery thereof the Trustee agrees to hold in trust for and subject to the security interest of the Bank as its property and to use said instruments and papers for the following purposes and for no other purpose: for the purpose of effecting delivery and sale of the loan evidenced by the instruments and papers to with no authority to make any other disposition thereof whatsoever either by way of conditional sale, pledge, mortgage, creation of another security interest, or otherwise. All of the said acts shall be for the account of, but without expense to, the Bank. The Trustee agrees that a copy of their delivery transmittal letter will be simultaneously mailed to the Bank within 7 days of the date hereof and further agrees that they will account to Bank by remitting the principal and interest due when payment is received from the purchaser in same form as received or by arranging with the purchaser to remit the total amount due directly to the Bank. The Trustee agrees that the right of the Bank to the proceeds of sale or other disposition shall not be deemed to be waived by any words or conduct of the Bank, or by any knowledge by the Bank of the existence of such proceeds.

The Trustee agrees upon demand to return said instruments and papers or their monetary equivalent to the Bank and further agrees that in no case will said instruments and papers be removed from the Bank's physical possession for a period in excess of a 21 day term.

The Trustee also agrees to keep said instruments and papers and the proceeds thereof separate and readily capable of identification as the property of the Bank, to make entries in its records showing that such instruments and papers and proceeds are held for the account of the Bank, and to permit the Bank to examine the instruments and papers and the records of the Trustee relating thereto at any time during usual business hours.

The Bank may at any time cancel this trust and take possession of said instruments and papers and any proceeds thereof, wherever and in whatever form they may be, and for such purpose the Bank or its representatives may, without legal process, enter any premises where such instruments and papers or proceeds are located. The Bank may require the Trustee to assemble the instruments and papers and make them available to the Bank at a place to be designated by it which is reasonably convenient to the Bank and the Trustee. Any notice of sale, disposition or other intended action by the Bank, sent to the Trustee at the address specified below or at such other address of the Trustee as may from time to time be shown on Bank's records, at least five days prior to such action, shall constitute reasonable notice to the Trustee. The expense of retaking, preparing for sale, selling and disposing of the instruments and papers shall include attorneys' fees and legal expenses incurred by the Bank, all of which the Trustee agrees to pay.

The Trustee also agrees to keep the instruments and papers fully insured at the expense of the Trustee against loss or damage by fire, theft, marine risks or otherwise, the insurance policies to be satisfactory to and payable to the Bank, and to be delivered promptly on demand, and the insurance money received for any loss shall be subject to the trust herein contained in the same manner as the instruments and papers themselves.

If this Agreement is signed by two or more parties, it shall be the joint and several obligation of such parties.

The rights of the Bank specified herein shall be in addition to, and not in limitation of the Bank's rights under the Uniform Commercial Code, as amended from time to time, or any other statute or rules by law conferring rights similar to those conferred by said Code; and under the promissory notes listed on the reverse side hereof.

KENNEDY MORTGAGE CO.

11 Allison Drive, Cherry Hill, NJ
Address

June 10, 1978
Date

7/74

Ann Little
ANN LITTLE   ASS't SECRETARY

By *H Eugene Brown*
H. EUGENE BROWN   Authorized Signature
VICE PRESIDENT TREASURER

HERITAGE BANK N.A.
Cherry Hill, New Jersey

TIME COLLATERAL NOTE

$ __23,417.00__   __June 10_____ , 19 __78__

__On demand_____ after date, the undersigned promise to pay to the order of **HERITAGE BANK** N.A. (herein called the "Bank") at its head office or any branch office the sum of __TWENTY THREE THOUSAND FOUR HUNDRED__ __SEVENTEEN AND 00/100---__ Dollars

($ __23,417.00_____), together with interest from the date hereof at the rate of _____ % per annum.

1. To secure the payment of the note and any other liabilities of the undersigned to the Bank, whether now existing or hereafter arising, the undersigned grant to the Bank a security interest in the following collateral:

   (a) __K# 800-000__

      __51 Brunswick Lane, Township of Willingboro, NJ__

      __John Smith and Ella C. Smith, his wife__

      together with proceeds and products thereof.

   (b) Any amounts which the Bank from time to time, may owe to any of them, including any balance or share of any deposit or other account. This right is in addition to the Bank's right of set-off

   (c) Any other property, tangible or intangible, owned by or which the undersigned have an interest which is or may hereafter be in the possession or control of the Bank.

2. If other liabilities of any of the undersigned to the Bank are in existence when this note is paid, then, notwithstanding the surrender of this note, the Bank may retain the collateral and have all rights and remedies available to it including those granted or referred to in this note.

3. The Bank may vote the collateral; collect all dividends thereon; take control of any proceeds; notify any person obligated on the collateral of the Bank's security interest therein and to make payments directly to the Bank; and transfer all or part of the collateral into the name of itself or its nominee.

4. If the Bank negotiates or transfers this note the Bank may deliver all or any part of the collateral to the transferee or holder who shall succeed to the rights of the Bank. Upon such negotiation or transfer the Bank shall be relieved and discharged from any liability or responsibility in connection with the transferred collateral but all rights of the Bank shall be preserved with respect to any collateral retained by it.

5. The Bank shall have no duty to collect or protect the collateral or any proceeds, to preserve rights of the undersigned against prior parties; to realize on the collateral in any particular manner or seek reimbursement from any particular source.

6. The Bank, at its election, may grant any extensions, postponement of time of payment, indulgence, or permit any substitutions exchange or release of collateral and may add to or release any parties primarily or secondarily liable.

7. The undersigned and all endorsers waive protest.

8. The undersigned assume full responsibility for taking any necessary steps to protect any of the collateral in the Bank's possession including without limitation, the exercise of any rights respecting the collateral. The Bank shall have exercised reasonable care in the preservation and protection of the collateral if it takes such action for that purpose as the undersigned shall request in writing but no omission to comply with any such request of itself shall be deemed failure to exercise reasonable care.

9. The Bank may

   (a) date this note as of the date of the making of the loan,

   (b) complete any blank spaces in the note according to the terms upon which the loan is granted and

   (c) cause the signature of one or more co-makers in addition to the original number to be added at any time or times without notice to the undersigned.

10. If this note is placed in the hands of an attorney for collection the undersigned shall pay an amount equal to 20% of the unpaid principal and interest as an attorney's fee, which amount the undersigned agree is reasonable.

11. If payment of this note is made by any co-maker or endorser the Bank is authorized, at its election, to surrender the collateral to the person making such payment.

12. The undersigned shall be in default hereunder and this note and any other obligations of the undersigned to the Bank, at the election of the Bank, shall become immediately due and payable at any time the Bank deems itself insecure and in all events upon occurrence of any of the following:

   (a) Failure to pay when due the principal of or interest on the note.

   (b) Change in the condition or affairs, financial or otherwise, of the undersigned or of any endorser, guarantor or surety for the liability of the undersigned to the Bank which in the opinion of the Bank impairs the Bank's security or increases its risk.

   (c) Death of any of the undersigned, termination of business of or commencement of any insolvency proceedings by or against any of the undersigned, or if any of them becomes insolvent.

   (c) If this note is secured by a security agreement then upon the occurrence of any event of default under the terms of the security agreement.

13. This note and the rights and remedies of the Bank with respect to all collateral in which the Bank has a security interest by this note or otherwise shall be governed by the law of New Jersey.

KENNEDY MORTGAGE CO.

   (Borrower's name)

By _____
  H. EUGENE BROWN
  VICE PRESIDENT-TREASURER

CO-MAKER _____

CO-MAKER _____
  ANN LITTLE
  ASS'T SECRETARY

24-71A 5/74

Haven Savings and Loan Association
621 Washington Street
Hoboken, New Jersey 07030

Gentlemen:

    In consideration of your purchase of FHA and VA mortgages
as set forth in your commitment of   May 27th, 1978   ,
we hereby warrant that in connection with any closing Federal Reserve
Regulation "Z", The Real Estate Settlement Procedures Act of 1974,
and the Equal Opportunity Act and Regulation "B" was complied with,
and that evidence of such compliance will be included in the documents
submitted.

    We further agree to indemnify you and save you harmless from
any liability imposed upon you in connection with any such loan assigned
to you, because of non-compliance with said regulation.

        KENNEDY MORTGAGE CO.

BY
        H. Eugene Brown

        Vice President and Treasurer

Notary

IC#25

Haven Savings and Loan Association
621 Washington Street
Hoboken, New Jersey 07030

KENNEDY MORTGAGE CO.
518 MARKET STREET · CAMDEN NEW JERSEY 08101

Re: K#800,000
Name: SMITH, John
Address: 51 Brunswick Lane
Willingboro, N.J.

Gentlemen:

We enclose the following documents as indicated for your review and purchase:

X Original Mortgage	X Borrower's Affidavit
___ Copy of Mortgage	X Statement of Settlement (HUD #1)
___ Original Modification Agreement	___ Ledger Card
___ Copy of Modification Agreement	X Amortization Schedule
X Original Bond/Note	X Survey
X Assignment of Mortgage to	___ Survey Affidavit
___ Investor-Copy (X)	___ Waiver
X Title Policy	X Certificate of Insurance
___ Title Policy Endorsement	___ Fire Insurance Policy
X Report of Title - Easement &	X Kennedy Corporate Resolution
___ Restrictions Attached	X Disclosure Statement
___ MGIC or Private Insurer Certificate	___ Escrow Agreement
X Copy of Insurance Transfer Form	___ Kennedy Inspection Report
___ Original Insurance Transfer has	X Termite Certification
___ been filed	X Flood XXXXXXXXX Certification
___ MGIC or Private Insurer Commitment Form	* To Follow
X MGIC/XGX Certificate	X Tax Certification
X Indemnification Letter	X Declaration No-Offset

1. Kindly examine the enclosures as soon as possible and wire transfer the amount due for the account of Kennedy Mortgage Co., together with a schedule and breakdown to: Heritage Bank, Route 70 Executive Campus, Cherry Hill, New Jersey 08034 Acct. #623-560-0

2. The bank will accept New York funds through:
It is important that your schedule identifies loans being paid. Please include interest adjusted to date the bank will receive funds and send a copy of the schedule and breakdown of payment to Kennedy Mortgage Co., Attention: Accounting Department.

3. Please direct all correspondence and inquiries concerning the acceptability of this loan delivery package to Kennedy Mortgage Co., 518 Market St., Camden, N.J. 08101, Attention: H. Eugene Brown, Vice President.

MORTGAGE STATEMENT

Breakdown of Monthly Payment:

Principal and Interest..........$ 189.56
MIP.............................$ 10.24
Hazard Insurance................$ 7.29
Taxes and Assessments...........$ 76.91

Total Present Monthly Payment....$ 284.00

Principal Balance After: 12/1/76
payment which has been received;
$ 24,650.00

Total Now Held in Escrow Account:
$ 264.83

KENNEDY MORTGAGE CO. hereby certifies to you that all monthly payments due on this loan from the Borrower have been paid to the above date and that the total escrow account funds shown above have been received and are being held by us in a special account.

DATE: July 11, 1978

By: *Kelly Thomas*
Loan Delivery Department

KNOW ALL MEN BY THESE PRESENTS that **KENNEDY MORTGAGE CO.,** a corporation organized and existing under the laws of the State of New Jersey, with its principal office in the City and County of Camden and State of New Jersey, for and in consideration of the sum of One Dollar, lawful money of the United States of America, and other good and valuable consideration, to it in hand paid by

Haven Savings and Loan Association

, a corporation organized and existing under the laws of New Jersey with its principal office in 621 Washington Street, Hoboken, New Jersey

, hereinafter referred to as ASSIGNEE, at or before the ensealing and delivery of these presents, the receipt whereof is hereby acknowledged, has granted, bargained, sold, assigned, transferred and set over, and by these presents does grant, bargain, sell, assign, transfer and set over unto the said ASSIGNEE and its successors and assigns, without recourse against it, the said Kennedy Mortgage Co., all that certain indenture of mortgage covering premises situate in the Township of Willingboro, County of Burlington, State of New Jersey

Being 51 Brunswick Lane

dated June 10 19 78 , and recorded in the office of the REGISTER OR CLERK of Burlington County in book 1218 of mortgages, at pages 1073 &c., made and executed by John Smith and Ella C. Smith, his wife

hereinafter referred to as MORTGAGOR, to said Kennedy Mortgage Co., in the principal sum of $ 24,650.00 , payable with interest on unpaid balances at the rate of 8½ % per annum, in monthly installments as therein noted, upon which there remains due an unpaid principal balance of $ 24,650.00

TOGETHER with the hereditaments and premises in and by said indenture of mortgage particularly described and granted, or mentioned and intended so to be, with the appurtenances, and the bond or obligation in said indenture of mortgage mentioned and thereby intended to be secured and all incidental or supplemental documents, or instruments, if any, secured or intended to be secured thereby, and all moneys due and to grow due thereon, and all its estate, right, title, interest, property, claim and demand in and to the same.

To have and to hold the same unto the said ASSIGNEE and its successors and assigns, to its and their proper use, benefit and behoof forever, subject, nevertheless, to the equity of redemption of said MORTGAGOR in said indenture of mortgage named, and the heirs, executors, administrators, successors and assigns of said MORTGAGOR therein.

And it, the said Kennedy Mortgage Co., does hereby covenant, promise and agree to and with the said ASSIGNEE that there is now due and owing upon the said bond and mortgage the sum of money hereinabove specified as the unpaid balance due thereon, with interest at the rate specified hereinabove on same from August 1 19 78

In WITNESS WHEREOF, the said Kennedy Mortgage Co., has caused its corporate seal to be hereto affixed and these presents to be duly executed by its proper officers this 18th day of July 19 78

KENNEDY MORTGAGE CO.

BY: J. J. Bernardo, Jr. Sr. Vice President

ATTEST: Marc S. Reed Assistant Secretary

KENNEDY MORTGAGE CO.
CORPORATE
SEAL
1975
NEW JERSEY

STATE OF NEW JERSEY } ss.

COUNTY OF CAMDEN }

BE IT REMEMBERED that on this 18th day of July , in the year of our Lord one thousand nine hundred and seventy- eight , before me, the subscriber, A Notary Public of New Jersey, personally appeared J.J. Bernardo, Jr. Sr. Vice President

of Kennedy Mortgage Co., who I am satisfied is the person who signed the within instrument and he acknowledged that he signed, sealed with the corporate seal and delivered the same as such officer aforesaid, and that the within instrument is the voluntary act and deed of such corporation, made by virtue of a Resolution of its Board of Directors.

(Notary Public of N.J. signature)

PREPARED BY: ALVIN D. MILLER, ESQ.
CL #277 - 12 72

NOTARY PUBLIC OF NEW JERSEY
My Commission Expires Jan. 15, 1978

K # 800-000
FHA/VA # 351-132092-221
TITLE CO. Towne & Country Abst. Co.
TITLE CO. # TCA-NJ 106,853

Assignment of Mortgage

KENNEDY MORTGAGE CO.

TO

Dated:

Premises: 51 Brunswick Lane
Township of Willingboro, NJ

Received in the .... *office*
of the County of ....
on the .... *day of* ....
A. D. 19   *, at* .... *o'clock*
in the ....*noon, and recorded*
in Book .... *of*
Assignment of Mortgages for said County on
pages ....

U. S. DEPARTMENT OF HOUSING AND URBAN DEVELOPMENT
OFFICE OF FINANCE AND ACCOUNTING

MORTGAGE RECORD CHANGE

HUD—92080
February 1974

(For Insured Loans Only – Not for Commitment Assignments)

TO: U.S. DEPARTMENT OF HOUSING AND URBAN DEVELOPMENT OFFICE OF FINANCE AND ACCOUNTING MORTGAGE INSURANCE ACCOUNTING ATTN: BILLING CONTROL BRANCH WASHINGTON, D.C. 20412	**1.** INDICATE TYPE OF ACTION **CHANGE OF HOLDING** **CHANGE OF MORTGAGOR** **MORTGAGEE OR SERVICER** *(Home Mortgages Only)* ☒ Sale of Mortgage ☐ Credit of new Mortgagor not Approved by HUD-FHA ☐ Change of Servicer ☐ Credit of new Mortgagor Approved by HUD-FHA Under 2210 Procedure.

(IMPORTANT: Please check all applicable blocks)

INSTRUCTIONS: Submit the original only to HUD within 30 days from the date of change for home or multifamily mortgage. **This notice will not be acknowledged.** The panels are to be completed as follows:
Sale of Mortgage: It is the buyer's responsibility to submit this form. Panels 1, 2, 3, 5, 6, 9, 11, and 13 should be completed by the seller. Panels 7, 8, 10, and 12 should be completed by the buyer. Completion of panels 9 and 10 constitutes official mortgagee signatures as well as notice to HUD that this insured loan has been sold in accordance with HUD regulations. Seller and buyer agree that the buyer hereby succeeds to all rights and assumes all obligations of the seller under the HUD contract of insurance. Upon HUD's receipt of this notice, the seller will be released from its obligations under the contract of insurance.
Change of Servicer: Panels 1, 2, 3, 5, 7, 8, 10, and 12 shall be completed.
Change of Mortgagor: Panels 1, 2, 3, 4, 5, 7, 8, 10, and 12 shall be completed. If a mortgagee marks the form indicating that a new home mortgage borrower has HUD-approved credit, HUD will accept this notice as mortgagee certification that all HUD requirements have been met. On all changes involving Section 222 cases, panel 13 shall be completed. On home mortgage assumptions by an eligible serviceman, attach the original executed DD Form 802, Certificate of Eligibility, plus all copies and check this block. ⟶ ☐

2. ORIGINAL AMOUNT OF MORTGAGE	**3.** FHA CASE OR PROJECT NO.	SECTION OF ACT CODE
▲ $ 24,650.00	▲ 351-132092	▲ 221

4. NAME OF NEW MORTGAGOR *(Change of Mortgagor only)*
▲

5.   *(Month)*   *(Year)*
MATURITY DATE ⟶ July 1, 2008

6. *(Complete this panel for Projects only)*

CONSTRUCTION IS: ☐ COMPLETED   ☐ UNCOMPLETED

7. DATE OF THIS NOTICE			**8.** DATE OF TRANSFER		
MO.	DAY	YEAR	MO.	DAY	YEAR
▲ 7	21	78	7	21	78

9. SELLING MORTGAGEE *(Code No., Name, Address & ZIP Code—Use Stamp or Other Approved Device)*

Kennedy Mortgage Co.
518 Market Street
Camden, NJ 08101
▲

10. HOLDING MORTGAGEE *(Code No., Name, Address & ZIP Code—Use Stamp or Other Approved Device)*

Haven Savings & Loan Assn.
621 Washington Street
Hoboken, NJ 07030
▲

11. NAME OF PRESENT MORTGAGOR *(Or Previous Mortgagor if Mortgagor Change)*

John Smith and Ella C., h/w

12. SERVICER TO WHICH FUTURE PREMIUM NOTICES SHOULD BE SENT *(Code No., Name, Address & ZIP Code—Use Stamp or Other Approved Device)*

Kennedy Mortgage Co.
518 Market Street
Camden, NJ 08101

13. PROPERTY ADDRESS

51 Brunswick Lane
Township of Willingboro, NJ

▲ *(Do not show Military Branch for Section 222 Cases)*

Chapter 14

Income-Property
Mortgage Loan
Case Study

The following income-property mortgage loan case is an actual submission from a mortgage lender to an institutional investor. Almost all names, facts and figures are noted as actually submitted. A few have been changed to protect the privacy of the parties, however.

As reproduced in this chapter, the case is complete enough for an investor to decide on the worthiness of this investment. Certain documents, such as plans and specifications, certain financial statements, survey and plot plan, which are typically included in a submission are deleted in this case because of the difficulty of condensing these documents to book size.

This case is not intended to be a representation of a complete income-property mortgage loan file. As reproduced, it does not contain, among other documents, the necessary commitment from the insurance company, the executed note and mortgage, or specific closing instructions. These documents are discussed elsewhere in this text and would be redundant in this chapter.

A SUBMISSION

FOR A

FIRST MORTGAGE LOAN

ON

FOREST CENTRAL ONE

A PROPOSED OFFICE BUILDING

TO BE LOCATED ON

NORTH CENTRAL EXPRESSWAY AT

BONNER STREET

IN

DALLAS, TEXAS

Presented to

ROBERT F. MACSWAIN

HARTFORD LIFE INSURANCE COMPANY

by

RICHARD E. C. MILLER, JR.

THE MORTGAGEBANQUE, INC.

6900 FANNIN STREET

SUITE 500

P. O. BOX 20074

HOUSTON, TEXAS 77025

THE MORTGAGEBANQUE, Inc.

May 11, 1977

Mr. Robert MacSwain
Assistant Secretary
Hartford Life Insurance Company
690 Asylum Avenue
Hartford, Connecticut 06115

                              Re: Forest Central One Office Building
                                    North Central Expressway at Bonner Street
                                    Dallas, Texas

Dear Bob:

Enclosed please find a first mortgage loan submission on the above-captioned
property which includes, the loan application, a narrative fair market value
appraisal and other supporting documentation. Plans and specifications are
being forwarded under separate cover.

Briefly summarizing this loan request:

Loan Amount:	$1,900,000
Rate:	9.50%
Servicing:	1/8 of 1%
Term:	30 years
Call Option:	in 15th loan year
Prepayment Privilege:	In full after seven (7) years with payment of 5% penalty declining 1% per year to a minimum of 1%.
Commitment Term:	Twelve (12) months.
Funding:	(See Loan Offering enclosed)
Standby Fee:	2% in form of Letter of Credit
Corporate Guaranty:	Southern Union Realty Company

Bob, we will be forwarding the 1976 year-end statement on Southern Union Gas
Company in a couple of days. The year-end on Southern Union Realty will be
completed next week. I think the 1976 Annual Report of the Southern Union Gas
Company will address those questions you raised concerning the future thrust of
the company, operation in a regulated environment, diversification, etc.

Also, though not noted in the enclosed material, it is contemplated that
leasing and management of the subject building will be handled by Coldwell-
Banker. I hope any pertinent questions you may have can be answered by
the enclosed materials; if however, you have additional questions, please
do not hesitate to call me. As I mentioned in our last phone conversation,
I spent the better part of a week in Dallas recently strictly for the purpose
of establishing the current status of the "Class A" suburban office market.
I came away most impressed. Without exception, everyone I consulted including
representatives of Coldwell Banker, Trammell Crow, The Vantage Companies, The
Swearingen Company, Baldwin-Harris, Ray Nasher Investments, etc. attested to
the strength of the market and the fact that the timing of this development

6900 Fannin St. Suite 500, P. O. Box 20074   Houston, Texas 77025 (713) 797-9899 couldn't be better. In summary, my findings were that current rental rates are $7.50 to $8.50 per square foot and operating expenses range from $2.65 to $2.95 per square foot. This particular loan was underwritten at $8.00 rents and $2.75 expenses. We are requesting rental achievement based on $7.86 (65½¢ P.S.F./mo.) rents; however, I would estimate that only the first few leases would be executed at this low of a rate.

Again, Bob, we are most appreciative of Hartford's consideration of this loan request and we hope that the proposal can be taken to committee at the earliest possible date. Thank you again.

Very truly yours,

Richard E. C. Miller, Jr.
Assistant Vice President

RECM:cjm

LOAN OFFERING

TERMS OF APPLICATION:

Applicant's Name:	Southern Union Realty Company
Applicant's Address:	First International Building Dallas, Texas
Project Name:	Forest Central One Office Building
Address of Security:	North Central Expressway at Bonner Street
Zoning:	I-1; use restricted to office building, motel/hotel, or restaurant development within Forest Central Park.
Loan Amount:	$1,900,000
Interest Rate:	9.50%
Term:	30 years
Payout:	30 years (call option in 15th year).
Refundable Standby-Fee:	2% of loan amount in form of negotiable irrevocable letter of credit.
Prepayment Privilege:	In full after 7 years upon payment of 5% prepayment penalty; penalty will decline 1% per year to a minimum of 1%.
Personal Guaranty:	None
Funding Date:	Second Quarter 1978
Leasing Requirement and Advance of Funds:	Lender will pay to Borrower $1,525,000 when the Building has been completed and the City of Dallas, or other appropriate governmental authority, has issued its Certificate of Occupancy. Monthly amortization payments to be made by Borrower on such amount shall be $12,823.03. In addition, within eighteen (18) months from the date of closing, Borrower, at its sole option, shall have a right to, and Lender shall make, the following increase to the Loan, subject to the following conditions:

352

Leasing Requirement and
Advance of Funds (Cont.):

(i) If 25,500 square feet of the Building has been rented under leases providing for at least $204,000 of aggregate annual rentals, then Borrower shall have a right to increase the Loan in the additional amount of $175,000; **or**

(ii) If 41,500 square feet of the Building has been rented under leases providing for at least $332,000 of aggregate annual rentals, then Borrower shall have the right to increase the loan in the additional amount of either $175,000 or $375,000.

It is understood and agreed that monthly amortization of payments to be made by the Borrower under the Loan or any increase thereof, shall be based on a term of thirty (30) years from the date of closing the original Loan of $1,525,000, and shall be based on a 10.10 annual loan constant, with any adjustment in principal payments calculated to be paid upon the end of such thirty-year term or the calling of the Loan as provided for herein.

LOAN STATISTICS:

Physical Data:

2.862 Acres of Land, or 124,669 Square Feet of Land.

69,166 Gross Square Feet of Building Area including Atrium.

56,630 Gross Square Feet of Building Area excluding Atrium.

51,075 Net Rentable Square Feet of Building Area.

207 On-site parking spaces

247: 1 Ratio

4.05 On-site parking spaces per 1,000 Net Rentable Square Feet

27.73% building coverage of site

3.60: 1.0 Ratio, Land Area to Building Area

Economics:

Stabilized Gross Annual Income (@ $8.00 rent)	408,600	($8.00/sf)
Vacancy and Rent Loss, Estimated as 5%	($ 20,430)	
Stabilized Effective Gross Annual Income:	$388,170	($7.60/sf)
Stabilized Ad Valorem Taxes	$ 38,300	($0.75/sf)
Fixed & Operating Expenses (36.2% of EGI)	$140,630	($2.75/sf)
Net Operating Income Before Depreciation	$247,540	($4.85/sf)

Appraisal:

Justified Capitalization Rate is 9.5%

Market Value is estimated to $2,600,000 which is 5.96 times estimated land value and 10.5 times estimated net operating income before depreciation, and equals $37.59 per gross square foot of building area.

353

Loan Ratios:

Loan is $1,900,000
Loan is 73% of estimated Market Value.
Loan is 4.36 times land value.
Loan is $27.47 per gross square foot of
  building area.
Loan equals 4.65 times Gross Annual Income.
Loan equals 4.89 times Stabilized Effective
  Gross Annual Income.
Loan equals 7.68 times Net Annual Income.

Default Point:

Annual Debt Service	$191,900
Fixed & Operating Expenses	$140,630
DEFAULT POINT	$332,530

Coverage:

Based on stabilized rentals, occupancy can
decline 18.62% to 81.38% ($6.51/s.f./yr.)
and still cover default point.

Estimated net operating income before depreciation can decline 27.09% to 72.91% and
still cover annual interest on the loan.

Stabilized Gross Annual Income equals 2.13
times debt service.

Stabilized Effective Gross Annual Income
equals 2.02 times debt service.

Estimated Net Operating Income Before Depreciation equals 1.29 times debt service.

Note:

Although the economic rent for the subject
property is $8.00 per square foot, the bor-
rower has requested that rental achievement
be based on $7.75 rents. It is my recommenda-
tion that rental achievement be based on $7.86
rents ($0.655/s.f./mo.). Underwriting this
loan based on a rental factor of $7.86/s.f.
results in the following:

Gross Annual Income		
51,075 s.f. @ $7.86/s.f.	$	401,449.50
5% Vacancy	($	20,072.50)
E.G.I.	$	381,377.00
Expenses	($	140,630.00)
Net Income	$	240,747.00
Cap @ 9.5%	Value =	$2,534,179.00
Loan Justified		$1,900,600.00
Debt Service Coverage		1.25

Loan Balances:

	Balance	P.S.F. Building (Gross s.f.)	P.S.F. Land
5th Year	$1,827,800	$26.43	$14.66
10th Year	$1,713,800	$24.77	$13.74
15th Year	$1,529,500	$22.11	$12.26
20th Year	$1,235,000	$17.85	$ 9.90
25th Year	$ 760,000	$10.98	$ 6.09

Summary and Recommended Action:

This is a first mortgage loan request on a
proposed two-story atrium office building
to be built on the southeast corner of the
North Central Expressway and Bonner Street
in north Dallas. The site is located in
Forest Central, a 27-acre master-planned

office park located at the southeastern
intersection of North Central Expressway
and Forest Lane. Forest Central, a joint
venture of Southern Union Realty Company and
Windward Corporation, will eventually contain
approximately 400,000 square feet of "Class A"
office space and will represent an investment
of approximately $25 Million. The subject
property will be the first building constructed
in the park. The building, of contemporary
design, will contain 51,075 square feet of
net rentable area and will have an adequate
number of on-site parking spaces at grade
level. The building will be extremely energy-
efficient owing primarily to the fact that the
developer is a wholly-owned subsidiary of a
major utility company. Both the architect,
Broadnax-Phenix, and the general contractor,
Pence Construction, are of the highest
integrity. It is therefore anticipated that
the completed project will possess quality
and workmanship second to none.

The developer of the property is Southern
Union Realty Company, a subsidiary of
Southern Union Gas Company. Southern Union
Realty has a current net worth of approximately
$4,000,000. Southern Union Gas has a net
worth in excess of $163 Million and earned
over $250 Million after tax last year.
While the note evidencing the debt on the
subject property will not have the guaranty
of Southern Union Gas Company due to legal
complications which would arise with the
State Utility Commission, it is evident that,
due to the corporate visibility and the
inherent community responsibility the parent
company has, it is extremely doubtful default
would ever be permitted on this loan.

In summary, this loan is recommended unequivo-
cably for the following principal reasons:

1. First and foremost, strength of the
   "Class A" office market in the subject
   neighborhood.

2. Superb location.

3. Excellent design.

4. Quality of Construction.

5. Capability of the developer.

6. Financial strength behind the developer.

7. Conservative nature of loan request.

It is therefore recommended that this loan
be approved as submitted.

Richard E. C. Miller, Jr.
Assistant Vice President

Borrower Southern Union Realty Company
Property Forest Central One Office Building

Legal 2.86 Acres out of the M. J. Sanchez Survey, A-1272 and also being a part of Block A/7319 Forest Central #2, an addition to the City of Dallas, Dallas County, Texas

LOAN REQUEST

Loan Amount	Term	Interest Rate	Debt Service
$ 1,900,000	30 Yrs. 0 Mos.	9.50 %	$ 191,900

Value or Purchase Price	Equity or Cash Payment	% Loan to Value	Default Point
$ 2,600,000	$ 700,000	73 %	$ 332,530

SECURITY

Year Built	Building Type	Construction
Proposed	Office Bldg.	Masonry/steel

Square Feet	Parking	Other Facilities
51,075 sf (NRA)	207 cars 247 s.f./ space	
Lot Size 124,669 s.f.		

ECONOMICS

GROSS ANNUAL INCOME	$ 408,600	100.0%
Taxes $ 38,300		
Ins. $ 2,500		
TOTAL FIXED & OPER. EXPENSES	-$ 140,630	34.4 %
P & I	-$ 191,900	46.9 %
VACANCY & PROFIT MARGIN	$ 76,070	18.7 %

THE MORTGAGEBANQUE, INC.

May 10, 1977

Mr. Robert MacSwain
Assistant Secretary
Hartford Life Insurance Company
690 Asylum Avenue
Hartford, Connecticut 06115

Re: Forest Central One Office Building
     North Central Expressway at Bonner
     Street
     Dallas, Texas

Dear Mr. MacSwain:

In connection with a request for a first mortgage loan on the above-captioned
property, you will find attached hereto my appraisal of the Market Value in
fee simple of the proposed two-story atrium office building known as Forest
Central One. The subject site contains 2.862 acres and is legally described
as:

> 124,669 square feet of land out of the M. J. Sanchez Survey, A-1272
> Dallas, Dallas County, Texas.

Market Value is defined as the highest price in terms of money a property will
bring if exposed on the open market allowing a reasonable period of time for
both buyer and seller to become fully informed as to all the uses to which the
property is adaptable and for which it is capable of being used, neither party
acting under duress.

I hand you herewith my report which describes my method of approach and contains
data gathered in my investigation.

I hereby certify that I have inspected the property and the plans and that all
the data gathered in my investigation is from sources believed to be reliable.

After a thorough analysis of all the data contained herein, it is my opinion, as
of the tenth of May, 1977, that the Market Value in fee simple of the subject property, subject to satisfactory completion of the building according to plans and
specifications, assuming good materials and workmanship, and properly leased
under competent management, is in the amount of:

TWO MILLION SIX HUNDRED THOUSAND DOLLARS

($2,600,000)

Respectfully submitted,

Richard E. C. Miller, Jr.
Richard E. C. Miller, Jr.
Assistant Vice President

6900 Fannin St. Suite 500, P.O. Box 20074   Houston, Texas 77025 (713) 797-9899

TABLE OF CONTENTS

SUBJECT PROPERTY

SUBJECT SITE

SUMMARY OF SALIENT FACTS

Building Type:	Office Building (Atrium-type)
Location:	S. E. Corner of North Central Expressway and Bonner Drive, Dallas, Texas
Land Area:	2.86 acres 124,669 square feet (±)
Building Area:	Gross Square Feet (including atrium): 69,166 s.f. Gross Square Feet (excluding atrium): 56,630 s.f. NRA: 51,075 s.f.
Building Efficiency:	91.69% (Excluding atrium)
Number of Stories:	Two
Number of Elevators:	One
Upper Floor NRA Per Elevator:	25,537.50 s.f.
Basement Area:	- 0 -
On-Site Parking Spaces:	207
Parking Spaces Per 1,000 S.F. NRA:	4.05
NRA/Space:	247
Building Coverage of Site:	27.73%

PHYSICAL VALUATION

Class "A" Office Building 56,630 s.f. @ $32.50/s.f.	$1,840,000
Parking Lot	75,000
Fees	118,000
Interest, Marketing, Leasing, Taxes, Insurance, Etc.	90,000
Total Less Land	$2,123,000
Land Value	436,000
Total Physical Valuation	$2,559,000

ECONOMIC VALUATION

			P.S.F.
Gross Annual Rental Income 51,075 s.f. @ $8.00 p.s.f.	$408,600		
Vacancy @ 5%	(20,430)		
Effective Gross Income		$388,170	
Expenses			
Taxes	$ 38,300		.75
Insurance	2,500		.05
Utilities	41,000		.80
Janitorial	18,000		.35
Other	40,830		.80
Total		$140,630	$2.75

Net Income Before Recapture $247,540

Justified Overall Capitalization Rate: 9.50%

Economic Valuation $247,540   = $2,605,604   Say, $2,600,000
                        .095

MARKET VALUATION

G.R.M. from Market = 6.5

    6.5 x $408,600   = $2,655,900   Say, $2,656,000

FINAL VALUE ESTIMATE

Physical Value Estimate $2,559,000

Economic Value Estimate $2,600,000

Market Value Estimate $2,656,000

Final Value Estimate $2,600,000

IDENTIFICATION OF THE PROPERTY

The subject property is a proposed two-story atrium office building containing
51,075 square feet of net rentable area to be located in the Forest Central
Office Park in North Dallas, Texas. The improvements will be located on a 2.86
acre tract out of the M. J. Sanchez Survey, A-1272, and being also a part of Block
A/7319, Forest Central #2, an addition to the City of Dallas, Dallas County, Texas.

The subject property fronts 330.83 feet in the east line of the North Central
Expressway right-of-way, 376.28 feet in the south line of Bonner, and approximately
320 feet in the west line of Forest Central Drive. A complete legal description
of the property is found in the Addenda to this report.

PURPOSE OF THE APPRAISAL

The purpose of the appraisal is to estimate the market value of the subject
property as of May 10, 1977, assuming satisfactory completion of the improvements.

DEFINITION OF MARKET VALUE

Market Value is defined as the highest price in terms of money a property

will bring if exposed on the open market allowing a reasonable period of time
for both buyer and seller to become fully informed as to all the uses to which
the property is adaptable and for which it is capable of being used, neither party
acting under duress.

PROPERTY RIGHTS APPRAISED

The property rights appraised are those of fee simple title to the subject
property.

STATEMENT OF OWNERSHIP

The subject property is appraised assuming ownership by Southern Union Realty
Company.

DATE OF THE APPRAISAL

The date on which the value estimate applies is May 10, 1977, assuming satisfactory completion of all improvements.

CITY DATA

The subject property is located in the City of Dallas, Texas. Dallas is a bustling
business capital. It is a diversified community whose prosperity depends upon a
broad root system rather than a few dominant economic interests. In the southern
half of the U. S. - east of Los Angeles - Dallas is first in wholesale sales, and
in size of banks and volume of banking business. It has more insurance company
home offices than any other city in the country. It is a major center for conventions,
trade shows and market shows; and it has greater hotel/motel facilities than any other
Southwestern city. At the Dallas Convention Center, Dallas has more meeting and
exhibit space under one roof than any city in the nation. Dallas is also a major
retail market, one of the key cities of the oil industry, and is one of America's
major transportation centers - air, rail, motor freight and inter-city bus lines.
Its comprehensive and modern merchandise marts (apparel, furniture, housewares,
giftware, etc.) are the buying centers for retail merchants in many states.

Dallas takes pride in its homes and home surroundings; its educational, cultural and spiritual resources; and its entertainment/recreational attractions.

Dallas population data (Bureau of Census, 1970 Final): City of Dallas, 844,401; County of Dallas, 1,327,321; and Dallas Standard Metropolitan Statistical Area, 1,555,950.

NEIGHBORHOOD DATA

The subject neighborhood is considered to be what is locally known as the North Central Corridor. This area extends along either side of the North Central Expressway, from Fitzhugh Avenue to the LBJ Freeway, I-635. The neighborhood is primarily commercial and is characterized by a preponderance of medium to high rise office buildings from two to twenty stories in height and a variety of retail establishments from the smaller strip centers to the 1.6 million square foot NorthPark Center. Buildings most comparable to the subject property, i.e., those containing "Class A" office space begin in the 6000 block of North Central Expressway and extend to the LBJ Freeway.

The following office buildings located in the subject neighborhood are considered to be generally comparable to the subject: the 6060 Building, 6060 North Central Expressway; Expressway Tower, 6116 North Central Expressway; University Tower, 6400 North Central Expressway; Energy Square, 4925 Greenville Avenue; Meadows Building, 5646 Milton; Campbell Center, 8350 North Central Expressway; Two North Park, 8950 North Central Expressway; Greenville Park Tower, Walnut Hill at Greenville Avenue; Meadow Park Central, 10300 Central Expressway; Meadow Park North, 10400 North Central Expressway; Royal Gardens, 10830 North Central Expressway; Royal Central Tower, 11300 North Central Expressway; North Haven Central, 11311 and 11333 North Central Expressway; and Keystone Park, 13777 North Central Expressway. All of these buildings are comparable to the subject in that they contain "Class A" space. The term "Class A" space denotes new, or effectively new offices of high quality finish in a building with excellent location and access to primary vehicular traffic arteries. It is assumed that "Class A" office buildings are professionally managed, have relatively large floor sizes, are architecturally functional and efficient, and have a generally high quality of tenancy.

Within the subject neighborhood is also found the most prestigious shopping center in the city. NorthPark Center contains over 1,600,000 square feet of gross leasable area. Within the shopping center are four major stores, Neiman Marcus, Lord & Taylor, J. C. Penny, and Titche's as well as over 135 shops in the air-conditioned mall. NorthPark is located on North Central Expressway at Northwest Highway, 2.5 miles south of the subject property.

Approximately two blocks east of the subject property is Park Central, a 300-acre business park developed by The Trammell Crow Company and the Equitable Life Assurance Society of the United States. Park Central consists of several medium to high-rise office buildings, a multi-story Marriott Inn, the Olla Podrina specialty shopping center, and Medical City Dallas which includes a 353 bed general hospital and professional building. The office buildings in Park Central consist of Park Central I, a six-story building containing 120,000 square feet which is in excess of 95% occupied, Park Central II, a nine-story, 135,000 square foot building which is effectively full; Park Central III, a 21-story, 500,000 square foot building occupied by the J. C. Penny Company; the J. C. Penny Center, a 250,000 square foot office building 100% occupied by J. C. Penny; and Park Central V a 210,000 square foot building which is 100% occupied, principally by Anderson-Clayton. Park Central will represent an investment well in excess of $1 Billion when completed.

SITE DATA

The site is graded flat and drainage appears to be good. The site is approximately 520 feet above mean sea level. A preliminary soil investigation was made by Soil Consultants, Inc. of Arlington, Texas. Subsoil to a depth of four feet is of tan and grey calcareous clay with limestone fragments. All utilities services including electric power, telephone, sanitary sewer, gas and water are available to the site. All streets on which the property fronts are paved concrete with concrete curbs and gutters. Access to the subject site is from the North Central Expressway service road via Bonner Street, a four-lane boulevard (80' R.O.W.) or from Forest Lane via Forest Central Drive, also a four-lane boulevard (74' R.O.W.). The site is accessible from the central business district in less than ten minutes driving time; the distance is approximately 8½ miles.

ZONING

The subject site is zoned I-1 by the City of Dallas, however, development is
further restricted by deed restrictions imposed by Forest Central, the office
park in which the subject site is located. Uses permitted in an I-1 district
include utility and service uses (sewer treatment plants require a Specific Use
Permit); institutional, educational and special uses (cemeteries, foster homes,
kindergartens, day camps, fraternity houses, dormitories, rehabilitation centers,
hospitals, and nursing homes require a Special Use Permit); food and beverage
service uses; office, professional and financial uses; retail sales uses (except
pawn shops and secondhand stores); recreational, social and entertainment uses;
transportation type uses (heliports require Special Use Permit); motor vehicle and
related uses (auto parts, outside display and auto auctions require Special Use
Permit), storage, processing and commercial uses; and industrial and manufacturing
uses except batching plants, animal slaughter houses, and building mover temporary
storage.

Perhaps more important than zoning, are the deed restrictions imposed by the
developer. The restrictions permit that the building sites shall solely be
used for office buildings, hotels, motels, and restaurants.

DESCRIPTION OF THE IMPROVEMENTS

The 2.862 acre subject tract will be improved with a two-story garden-type office
building with interior atrium. The gross building area, including atrium, is
69,166 square feet; not including the atrium, the gross building area is 56,630
square feet. The net rentable area of the building is 51,075 square feet. The
paved parking area will comprise 68,000 square feet and will provide parking for
207 standard size cars. The pertinent improvement data can be summarized in tabular
form as follows:

Architect:	Brodnax, Phenix, and Associates, A.I.A.
Gross Building Area (including Atrium):	69,166 square feet
Gross Building Area (excluding Atrium):	56,630 square feet
Net Rentable Area (BOMA):	51,075 square feet
Building Efficiency:	74%

Lot Coverage:	28%
Age:	Proposed construction
Foundation:	5" reinforced concrete
Exterior Walls:	Face brick, 1/4" bronze glass and insulated 1/4" bronze spandrel.
Window Type:	1/4" solar bronze plate glass (PPG)
Roof:	5" built up on insulated concrete fill on corrugated metal deck.
Interior Walls:	5/8" firecode gypsum board.
Ceilings:	5/8" x 2' x 4' suspended acoustical tile lay-in panels with exposed white enameled grid equal to Chicago Metallic Snap Grid System.
Heating and A/C:	Central, multi-zoned, electric.
Restrooms:	3 men, 3 women, per floor
Parking Lot:	Asphalt paved, 207 cars, spaces 9 feet wide.
Elevator:	2500 lb. capacity, 125 f.p.m.
Other:	Attractive landscaping

HIGHEST AND BEST USE

"Highest and best use" is often defined as "the most profitable legal use to which a property can be put, or that use which will yield the highest net return on the investment over a period of time." A study of the office market in the subject neighborhood reveals a strong demand for "Class A" office space. The rents obtainable in the marketplace, at present, can adequately cover all expenses of operation including debt service and provide investors a reasonable return on the equity dollars invested. In addition, current costs of construction, though high, enable structures to be built which can compete effectively in the marketplace given the current costs of financing.

The location of the proposed improvements, in a restricted office park, is excellent in that the site affords the amenities most "Class A" office tenants desire. Therefore, it is the opinion of the appraiser that the proposed use, that of a garden-type office building, is the highest, best, and most profitable use of the subject property.

COST APPROACH

In order to arrive at an estimate of value for the property by the cost approach,

the market value of the subject land is first determined through an analysis of
recent sales of vacant property in the neighborhood. The value of the land is
then added to the reproduction cost new of the improvements less any depreciation
to arrive at an estimate of the market value of the property. The following pages
contain data concerning the recent sales of vacant land with characteristics
comparable to the subject property.

COMPARABLE LAND SALES

Sale #1:
  Sec LBJ Freeway and North Central Expressway

  Seller: Harry O. Pulliam

  Buyer: E. Greg Liechty & Dyer Investment Corporation

  Legal Description: Part of Blocks 7621 and 7624

  Date of Sale: March 14, 1974 Recorded: 74058/585

  Size: 21,535 acres Zoning: "LC"

  Amount Paid: $3.50/square foot (terms with 19% down)

  Comments: Part of this tract is bisected by a DP & L
         easement, which restricts site utility.

Sale #2:
  SEC LBJ Freeway and Shroeder Road

  Seller: Ted A. Howard, Jr.

  Buyer: T. C. Strickland

  Legal Description: Part of Block 7623

  Date of Sale: March 23, 1971 Recorded: 71057/1751

  Size: 9.4186 acres Zoning: "LC" & "I-1"

  Amount Paid: $433,000, or $1.05/square foot

  Comments: This tract subsequently sold on March 27, 1972 to
         Shelly Baker as part of a package of several
         properties. Baker is asking $4.00/square foot
         and recently refused $2.00/square foot offer.

Sale #3:
  S/S LBJ Freeway, East of Shroeder Road

  Seller: Paulette P. Campbell

  Buyer: Gene McCutchin & Robert G. Vial

  Legal Description: Part of Abstract #1486 (Block 7623)

  Date of Sale: January 8, 1967 Recorded: 69007/1170

  Size: 5.2964 acres Zoning: "I-1"

  Amount Paid: $1.50/square foot

Comparable Land Sales (Cont.)

Sale #4:   NEC LBJ Freeway and Greenville Road

    Seller: Deal Development Company

    Buyer: Vantage Properties, Inc.

    Legal Description: Block 8416   Zoning: "PD-44" (Commercial)

    Date of Sale: December 11, 1973   Recorded: 73242/659

    Size: 21.167 acres (gross), 19.738 acres (net)

    Amount Paid: $1.55/square foot (net acreage basis)

Sale #5:   SEC North Central Expressway & Walnut Hill Lane

    Seller: F. E. Edmondson

    Buyer: Herman Evans, Tr. (Metro Dev. Co. & Annuity Board of
                                              Southern Baptist Conv.)

    Legal Description: Part of Blocks 5457 and 5459

    Date of Sale: April 8, 1975   Recorded: 75069/1001-11

    Size: 32.233 acres (gross area) Zoning: "R"
                             25.663 acres (net usable-estimated)

    Amount Paid: $1.75/square foot (gross area); $2.20/square foot
                                                      (net usable area - est.)

    Comments: Sale included part of "Glen Lakes Country Club"
                             and golf course. The lake covers an area of approx-
                             imately 6.57 acres. After deducting for this lake,
                             the net usable area of this tract is estimated to be
                             25.663 acres, which indicated the above adjusted price
                             of $2.20/square foot. The purchasers state they have
                             recently refused a $2.75/square foot offer and are
                             asking $3.50/square foot.

Sale #6:   E/S North Central Expressway, North & South of
                                       Walnut Hill Lane

    Seller: General Conf. Corp. - 7th Day Adventists

    Buyer: John W. Haney & Craig O. Cannon

    Legal Description: Part of Abstracts #177 & 996, and Block 5459

    Date of Sale: September 4, 1974   Recorded: 74173/1245

    Size: 25.886 acres   Zoning: "R" - "0-2" - "TH-3"

    Amount Paid: $4.12/square foot (Terms with 25% down, 5 yrs.
                                               I.0., plus balloon)

Sale #7:   W/S North Central Expressway, 340' South of
                                       Meadow Park Road

    Seller: General Conference Corp. - 7th Day Adventists

    Buyer: Barshop Motel Enterprises, Inc.

    Legal Description: Part of Tract 31, Block 7294

    Date of Sale: September 14, 1972 Recorded: 72187/0801

Size:	2.86 acres $\pm$ Zoning: "0-2" & Neigh. Svc.
Amount Paid:	$3.50/square foot
Comments:	A new "La Quinta Motor Inn" and restaurant has been completed on this land.

Sale #8:   NEC Central Expressway and Blair

Seller:	Orlena M. Nichols
Buyer:	A. Robert Beer, Tr.
Legal Description:	Lot 8, Block 1/7292, Dixon Subdivision
Date of Sale:	December, 1970 Recorded: 70249/1695
Size:	36,729 square feet
Amount Paid:	$156,000 ($110,830 vendors lien note), or $4.25/sf

Sale #9:   E/S North Central Expressway, 323' South of Meadow Road

Seller:	Howard Slywter
Buyer:	Peter W. Baldwin
Legal Description:	Part of Block 7292
Date of Sale:	October 3, 1973 Recorded: 73195/810
Size:	7.336 acres Zoning: "0-2"
Amount Paid:	$2.50/square foot
Comments:	This became additional land for the expansion of the "Meadow Park North" office development.

Sale #10:   NEC Central Expressway and Meadow Road

Seller:	Morris Shwiff, et al
Buyer:	Transland Investments
Legal Description:	Lot 3, Block 7291
Date of Sale:	December, 1970 Recorded: 70236/1527
Size:	1.41 acres (61,420 sf) Zoning: "0-2"
Amount Paid:	$240,000, or $3.90/square foot
Comments:	The price includes $20,000 in sitework and surface drainage required to utilize the land. Purchasers later developed the new "Meadow Park North" office building on this site.

Sale #11:   NWC Central Expressway and Meadow Road

Seller:	W. W. Caruth, Jr.
Buyer:	Cullum Development Co.
Legal Description:	Part of Block 7289
Date of Sale:	December 23, 1970 Recorded: 70247/2254
Size:	13.213 acres (575,560 sf) Zoning: "SC"

Amount Paid:	$1,726,674, or $3.00/square foot
Comments:	This site is now improved with a new shopping center "Meadow Central Mall." The corner was ground-leased to Shell Oil for a minimum $2,100/mo., indicating a value of approximately $14.00/square foot.

Sale #12:   W/S North Central Expressway between Meadow Road and Royal Lane

Seller:	W. W. Caruth, Jr., et al
Buyer:	George Yamini Co.
Legal Description:	Part of Abstract #177, Block 7291
Date of Sale:	December, 1972
Size:	88 acres $\pm$ Zoning: "MF-2" - "MF-3" - "0-2"
Amount Paid:	$2.00/square foot (gross) - 7 yr. option price on 5 parcels $1.45/square foot (discounted-adjusted)
Comments:	The buyer contracted for this large tract at the $2.00/sf option price covering five (5) different parcels of land over a 7-year period. Since the above date (12/72), the buyer has exercised the following two options:

Option #1:   April 23, 1973 - 12.32 acres - Site of 495-unit "Foxmoor" Apartments

Option #2:   April 19, 1974 - 13.14 acres - Site of 438-unit "Cobblestone" Apartments.

A discounted allowance for the terms and the carry costs involved in this option sale indicates an adjusted overall price of approximately $1.45/s.f.

Sale #13:   E/S Central Expressway, 200' South of Manderville

Seller:	Continental Telephone Service Corp.
Buyer:	Briarwood Development
Date of Sale:	October, 1970 Zoning: "I-1"
Size:	2.263 acres (98,576 sf) Recorded: 70207/781
Amount Paid:	$246,440, or $2.50/square foot
Comments:	This land was purchased by Sellers in May, 1967 for $1.75/square foot. Resale reflects an increase of 74¢/square foot over 3½ years, or approximately 12%/year.

Sale #14:   11300 North Central Expressway

Seller:	Peter P. Stewart
Buyer:	Mitchell Rasansky, et al
Legal Description:	Lot 1, Block 7290
Date of Sale:	May 28, 1971 Recorded: 71114/1544
Size:	2.523 acres Zoning: "I-1" & "FP" ("I-1")
Amount Paid:	$3.05/square foot

Comments:	The new "Royal Central Office Building" is now on this site. Purchasers were required to fill some of the back portion of the land that was designated flood plain.

Sale #15:   11400 Block of North Central Expressway

Seller:	Michael Spolane
Buyer:	Roberts Buick, Inc.
Legal Description:	Part of Block 7281
Date of Sale:	April 15, 1970 Recorded: 70106/170
Size:	1.30 acres (56,577 sf) Zoning: "I-1" & "FP" ("I-1")
Amount Paid:	$3.00/square foot (terms with 24% down)
Comments:	This tract was acquired to expand the purchaser's land area and operations.

Sale #16:   S/S Forest Lane, E. of (with frontage) North Central Expressway

Seller:	W. G. Cullum & Company, et al
Buyer:	Southern Realty Co. & Forest Central Joint Venture
Legal Description:	Part of Abstracts #177 and #1272
Date of Sale:	September 6, 1973 Recorded: 73175/2450
Size:	24.496 acres Zoning: "HC"
Amount Paid:	$1.30/square foot (Terms with 29% down)
Comments:	Buyer plans to develop and sell off commercial/ retail sites @ $3.50/sf to $5.00/sf (1-acre size).

Sale #17:   W/S North Central Expressway, 2,000' North of Forest Lane

Seller:	Lola Mae Stephenson
Buyer:	Dallas Power & Light Co.
Legal Description:	Part of Block 7750
Date of Sale:	September 25, 1974 Recorded: 74188/693
Size:	1.0 acre (43,550 sf) Zoning: "HC"
Amount Paid:	$174,200, or $4.00/square foot

Sale #18:   E/S Central Expressway, South of LBJ Freeway

Seller:	Henry Aaron Weinberger
Buyer:	Jerry E. Hayes
Legal Description:	Part of Block 7749
Size:	1.2 acres Recorded: 73055/2389
Amount Paid:	$100,000, or $1.92/square foot Zoning: "LC"
Comments:	Vacant land with about 10% - 15% in flood plain.

DATA SUMMARY

COMPARABLE LAND SALES

Sale No.	Date of Sale	Acreage	Price/S.F.	Indicated Value Per Sq. Ft. *
1	3/14/74	21.535	$3.50	$6.19
2	3/23/74	9.4186	1.05	1.23
3	1/8/69	5.2964	1.50	2.22
4	12/11/73	21.167	1.55	2.88
5	4/8/75	25.663	2.20	3.69
6	9/4/74	25.886	4.12	7.29
7	9/14/72	2.86	3.50	4.55
8	12/70	.84	4.25	6.03
9	10/3/73	7.336	2.50	3.10
10	12/70	1.41	3.90	5.53
11	12/23/70	13.213	3.00	5.31
12	12/72	88 ±	1.45	2.82
13	10/70	2.263	2.50	3.55
14	5/28/71	2.523	3.05	4.14
15	4/15/70	1.30	3.00	4.26
16	9/6/73	24.496	1.30	2.41
17	9/25/74	1.0	4.00	4.72
18	3/19/63	1.2	1.92	2.38

* Adjustments were made on the following basis:
   Time, Size, and Zoning

LAND VALUE ESTIMATE

An analysis was made of sales of properties with characteristics similar to the subject. A primary consideration of the appraiser was to choose only those properties which had frontage either on North Central Expressway north of Northwest Highway and south of LBJ Freeway, or on LBJ Freeway east of North Central Expressway and west of Abrams Road. Sales in this area were considered to be most comparable to the subject property.

The analysis revealed the following:

1. At least eighteen sales of vacant tracts have taken place in recent years.

2. The size of the tracts varied from 36,729 square feet to 88 $\pm$ acres.

3. All tracts had freeway frontage.

4. All had zoning which would permit office building construction (except Sale #5).

5. The sales prices ranged from $1.05 to $4.25 per square foot.

In order to arrive at a supportable opinion of value for the subject property several assumptions had to be made. First, it was assumed, and conversations with local brokers confirmed, that land values in the subject neighborhood have appreciated at a minimum rate of 6% per year. Second, it is assumed that for tracts in excess of 10 acres in size the per-unit value is reduced 25% as compared to a tract the size of the subject. And third, it is assumed that a tract larger than 20 acres will have a per-unit value 50% less than the subject. Therefore, after adjusting all sales for time and size (no adjustment was made for location since all tracts had freeway frontage and comparable access), a range of adjusted values was arrived at. These values ranged from $1.23 to $7.29 per square foot. The tracts most comparable to the subject were felt to be Sales #7 and #14. These tracts had unadjusted values of $3.50 and $3.05 per square foot respectively and adjusted values of $4.55 and $4.14 per square foot. After taking all factors into consideration, it is the opinion of the appraiser that the subject property has a fair market value, as of the date of this report, equal to $3.50 per square foot, or $436,341, rounded to:

FOUR HUNDRED THIRTY SIX THOUSAND DOLLARS

$436,000
(Land Only)

COST APPROACH

Class "A" Office Building 56,630 s.f. @ $32.50 p.s.f.	$1,840,000
Parking Lot 60,000 s.f. @ $1.25	75,000
Fees:	
Contractor	50,000
Architect/Engineering	25,000
Legal/Accounting	5,000
Permanent Financing	19,000
Construction Financing	19,000
Taxes/Insurance During Construction	15,000
Interest During Construction	75,000
Reproduction Cost New Less Depreciation	$2,123,000
Depreciation	- 0 -
Reproduction Cost New	$2,123,000
Land Value	436,000
Total	$2,559,000

Value Indicated by Cost Approach:

TWO MILLION FIVE HUNDRED FIFTY NINE THOUSAND DOLLARS

($2,559,000)

INCOME APPRAOCH

The first step in arriving at an estimate of value by the income approach is to form an opinion as to the economic rent for the subject property. Economic rent is defined as the amount of money a property should produce based on actual rentals being received from similar properties with like amenities in the same or similar location as of the effective date of the appraisal. An investigation was made of comparable properties in the subject neighborhood. The results of this investigation, found on the following pages, contain information concerning the rental rates quoted by competing buildings and the amount of space these projects currently have available.

RENTAL MARKET

The Dallas office building rental market can be broken down into eight identifiable sub-markets: the central business district, the North Central Expressway, North Dallas, L.B.J. Freeway, Oaklawn - Turtle Creek, Stemmons-Love Field, Oak Cliff, and East Dallas. The subject property is located in the North Central Expressway sub-market which extends generally from the central business district to the L.B.J. Freeway and slightly beyond. Presently there are approximately 2.5 million square feet of Class A office space in the North Central sector. It is conservatively estimated that 0.5 million square feet of new space can be absorbed in the North Central sub-market this year.

Currently, agents for office buildings comparable to the subject property are quoting rates in the range of $7.50 to $8.50 per square foot. Average occupancy for comparable properties is well in excess of 90%. A summary of a rental survey taken the week of May 1, 1977, is found on a following page.

RENT COMPARABLES

1

6060 Building
6060 North Central Expressway

Gross Building Area:	232,500 s.f.
Net Rentable Area:	205,000 s.f.
Current Leasing Status:	90%
Current Rental Rate:	$7.50 / s.f.

Comments: Completed in 1972; current occupancy reflects a recent loss of a 10,000 s.f. user which moved into the same building as its corporate parent; rents to go to $8.00 shortly.

2

Expressway Tower
6116 North Central Expressway

Gross Building Area:	219,000 s.f.
Net Rentable Area:	152,000 s.f.
Current Leasing Status:	98%
Current Rental Rate:	$8.00 / s.f.

Comments: Built in 1966; owned by Clint Murcheson, owner of Dallas Cowboys; building is virtually full despite a relatively unaggressive leasing program.

3

University Tower
6400 North Central Expressway

Gross Building Area:	121,750 s.f.
Net Rentable Area:	99,200 s.f.
Current Leasing Status:	80%
Current Rental Rate:	$7.00 / s.f.

Comments: This building is not actually comparable to the subject since the University
Tower would be classified as a "high B" rather
than a "Class A" building. This building,
though having a good location, has had a
history of poor management. It has recently
been sold and the new owners have dramatically
improved the situation. The current management feels confident that occupancy will be
up to 95% by August 1977. Rents will be increased to $7.50 shortly.

4

Meadows Building (foreground)
5646 Milton

Gross Building Area:	200,000 s.f.
Net Rentable Area:	175,000 s.f.
Current Leasing Status:	100%
Current Rental Rate:	$7.25 / s.f.

Comments: Completed in 1955; has a history
of excellent management; tenant turnover is
virtually nonexistent; leasing manager feels
he could get higher rents, but wants to maintain the highest tenant satisfaction.

5

One Energy Square (background)
4925 Greenville Avenue

Gross Building Area:	267,000 s.f.
Net Rentable Area:	235,000 s.f.
Current Leasing Status:	100%
Current Rental Rate:	$8.50 - $9.50,
	depending on suite finish

Comments: Completed in 1974; leased almost
exclusively to petroleum-related firms.
Another tower is contemplated.

6 & 7

Campbell Centre I and II
8350 North Central Expressway

Gross Building Area:	480,000 s.f. each
Net Rentable Area:	360,000 s.f. each
Current Leasing Status:	I: 98% II: 65% Preleased
Current Rental Rate:	I: $8.00 (average) II: $8.50 to $10.75 per s.f.

Comments: I: completed 1973, effectively full.
II: still under construction; first
tenants should take occupancy
in June.

8

Two North Park
8950 North Central Expressway

Net Rentable Area:	205,000 s.f. (both buildings)
Current Leasing Status:	100%
Current Rental Rate:	$8.00 / s.f.

Comments: Developed by Raymond Nasher; completed 1975; most comparable to subject property.

9

Meadow Park Central (foreground)

Net Rentable Area: 140,600 s.f.

Current Leasing Status: 100%

Current Rental Rate: $8.00 / s.f.
                        Going to $8.50, 8-1-77

<u>Comments</u>: Build in two phases; well received by
markets; excellent management (Baldwin-Harris).

10

Meadow Park North (background)

Net Rentable Area: 38,500 s.f.

Current Leasing Status: 100%

Current Rental Rate: Currently
                                  quoting $8.50

<u>Comments</u>: Built in 1972.

11

Royal Gardens
10830 North Central Expressway

Gross Building Area: 71,500 s.f.

Net Rentable Area: 63,000 s.f.

Current Leasing Status: 92%

Current Rental Rate: $7.25-$7.50

Comments: Completed in 1971; owned by Hinton
Mortgage.

12

Royal Central Tower
11300 North Central Expressway

Net Rentable Area: 62,000 s.f.

Current Leasing Status: 95%

Current Rental Rate: $7.75 / s.f.

Comments: Completed in 1972.

NORTH CENTRAL EXPRESSWAY

OFFICE RENTAL SUMMARY

No.	Building	Date Built	Stories	NRA Total	% Leased	Current Rate
1	6060 Building	1972	8	205,000	90%	$ 7.50
2	Expressway Tower	1966	15	152,000	98	8.00
3	University Tower *	1966	11	99,200	80	7.00
4	Energy Square	1974	14	235,000	100	8.50 - 9.50
5	Meadows Building	1954	10	175,000	100	7.25
6	Campbell Center I	1972	20	360,000	98	8.00
7	Campbell Center II	Unf.	20	360,000	65	9.00 - 10.75
8	Two North Park	1975	8	205,000	100	8.00
	Greenville Bank *	1976	10	115,000	80	8.00
9	Meadow Park Central	1970	5	140,600	100	8.00
10	Meadow Park North	1972	3	38,500	100	8.00
11	Royal Gardens	1971	4	63,000	92	7.25
12	Royal Central Tower	1972	6	62,000	95	7.25

* Not Comparable

ECONOMIC RENT AND GROSS INCOME ESTIMATE

To estimate the economic rent for the subject property, an analysis was made of all those properties in North Central Expressway from Mockingbird Lane to Forest Lane which appeal to the "Class A" office tenant. This study revealed that rents ranged from $7.25 to $10.75 per square foot. Those properties most comparable to the subject are currently experiencing rents in the $7.50 to $8.00 range. The Two North Park office park developed by Raymond Nasher, the developer of NorthPark Center, was felt to be most comparable to the subject property. Two North Park consists of two buildings comprising a total of 205,000 square feet. The buildings are located across North Central Expressway from NorthPark Center. The newer building of the two, an eight-story structure, was completed in 1975 and reached 98% occupancy in less than twelve months.

Due to the similarity of location, freeway access, and amenities offered to tenants, it is felt that the subject property should experience very similar rents to Two North Park. Therefore, it is the opinion of the appraiser that the economic rent for the subject property is $8.00 per square foot.

VACANCY LOSS FACTOR

Due to the multi-tenant nature of the subject property it is felt that a five percent vacancy factor would be appropriate. Even after the building reaches 100% occupancy, there will be leases expiring periodically and new tenants moving in. Since many leases do not commence until physical occupancy takes place and since it often takes two or more weeks to get suites ready for new occupancy, it is safe to assume that over the economic life of the property, an average vacancy of 5% will be experienced.

EXPENSES

In order to make an accurate estimation of the expenses of operation the subject property is likely to incur, the appraiser interviewed owners and managers of properties comparable to the subject. The results of these interviews are summarized in the following operational expense estimate.

TAXES

The subject property is located within the taxing jurisdictions of the State of Texas, the County of Dallas, the City of Dallas, and the Richardson Independent School District.

An analysis of comparable properties revealed that, on a per square foot basis, total real estate taxes ranged from a low of $0.58/s.f. on the INA Building at 1421 W. Mockingbird Lane to $0.86/s.f. on the Anderson-Clayton Building in Park Central. Additionally, it was noted that the 3530 Forest Lane Building, which shares many characteristics with the subject, pays a total of $50,029 in real estate taxes on a net rentable area of 71,000 square feet, or $0.71 per square foot. Therefore, it was felt that an estimate of $0.75 per square foot or $38,300 per year is reasonable and appropriate.

INSURANCE

Conversations with local agents and with building managers indicate that fire and extended coverage for a building with the design and structural characteristics similar to the subject property, would cost approximately $2,500 per year, or $0.0489 per square foot.

MANAGEMENT

Estimates from building management firms in the Dallas area indicate that the building could be managed efficiently and competently for a fee of $1,000 per month, or $12,000 per year. On per square foot basis, this equals $0.2349.

UTILITIES

Due to the fact that the subject building is being designed with energy considerations receiving a high priority, it is felt that total utility costs should equal approximately $41,000 per year, or slightly over 80¢ per square foot. An energy analysis by Pittsburg Plate and Glass engineers confirms this finding. It should be noted, however, that certain less energy-efficient buildings in this area are currently experiencing utility bills equivalent to $1.00 per square foot annually.

JANITORIAL SERVICE

The estimated cost of cleaning services including all janitorial supplies is $1,500 per month, or $18,000 per year. This equals $0.3524 per square foot.

GENERAL AND ADMINISTRATIVE

General and administrative expenses for twelve-month period are expected to be no more than $5,000 which equals $0.0978 per square foot.

REPAIRS, MAINTENANCE, AND SUPPLIES

The total annual expenditures for these items should equal approximately $13,300 per year, $0.2604 per square foot.

SECURITY

Security services for the building should cost approximately $700.00 per month. This equals $8400 per year, or $0.1644 per square foot.

ELEVATOR

A service contract for the elevator will cost approximately $52.50 per month. The annual charge equals $0.0123 per square foot.

TRASH REMOVAL

Trash removal services for the subject property will cost approximately $125 per month or $1,500 per year ($0.0294 per square foot).

TOTAL EXPENSES

The total annual operating expenses for the subject property are estimated to be $140,630. Expressed on a per unit basis the expenses equal $2.75 per square foot.

NET INCOME

It has previously been noted that the gross annual rental from the subject building is estimated to be $8.00 per square foot or $408,600. From this figure, it was felt that a vacancy factor of 5% should be deducted. An effective gross income of $388,170 is therefore realized. When total annual expenses of $140,630 are deducted from the effective gross income, a net income figure of $247,540 results.

CAPITALIZATION

As can be seen, capitalization rate of 9.50% was assumed. Capitalizing the net income of $247,540 at 9.50% results in a value estimate by the income approach of $2,605,604, rounded to

TWO MILLION SIX HUNDRED THOUSAND DOLLARS

($2,600,000)

PRO FORMA OPERATING STATEMENT

			P.S.F.
Gross Annual Rental Income 51,075 S.F. @ $8.00 psf	$408,600		
Vacancy	(20,430)		
Effective Gross Income		$388,170	
Expenses			
Taxes	$ 38,300		$0.7500
Insurance	2,500		0.0489
Management	12,000		0.2349
Utilities	41,000		0.8027
Janitorial	18,000		0.3524
General and Administrative	5,000		0.0978
Building Maintenance & Supplies	13,300		0.2604
Security	8,400		0.1644
Elevator	630		0.0123
Trash Removal	1,500		0.0294
		$140,630	$2.75
Net Income Before Recapture		$247,540	

MARKET DATA APPROACH

The third method by which the market value of the subject property is estimated

is through the market data approach. This approach to value involves the com-

parison of the sales prices of similar type projects on the basis of sales prices

paid per square foot, per unit, per room, etc. Additionally, a comparison can be

made of sales prices paid as a multiple of the gross income or the net income the

property was producing at the time of sale to arrive at a value estimation by the

market data approach. The following pages contain data concerning recent sales of

office buildings in the Dallas area.

IMPROVED PROPERTY SALES

1. Douglas Plaza Building - SEC Douglas Avenue and Luther Lane (Preston
    Center) Dallas, Texas

Date of Sale:	December 27, 1973	Recorded: 73252/131
Seller:	Douglas Plaza Corp.	
Buyer:	The Manufacturers Life Insurance Co. (Canada)	
Legal Desc.:	Tract 11, Block 5623	
Land Area:	47,040 S.F. (1.08 acres)	
Building:	8-story twin tower office building built 1965, and 2-story parking garage. Commercial/Medical office tenants with lobby retail space; gross building area = 104,099 S.F.; net leaseable area = 83,720 S.F.; parking garage (under lease) = 115,169 S.F.	

Sales Price:	$3,256,800
Mortgage Balance (orig. $1,950,000 @ 6 1/2%)	1,669,079
Equity Requirement	$1,587,721

	Actual	Pro-Forma
Gross Income:		
Tenant Income	$486,945	$ 523,000
Less: Vacancy	-0-	26,150
Effective Gross-Tenants	$486,945	$ 496,850
Parking Garage Lease	18,750	18,750
Concession Income	600	600
Total Effective Gross	$506,295	$ 516,200
Less: Operating Expenses	216,445	205,000
Net Income	$289,850	$ 311,200
Less: Debt Service	163,315	163,315
Cash Throw-off	$126,535	$ 147,885

Sale Price/SF Bldg. (Gross Area	$ 31.29	$ 31.29
Overall Capitalization Rate	8.90%	9.56%
Equity Dividend Rate	8.0%	9.31%
Gross Rent Multiplier	6.43 x	6.00 x

2. Locke Medical Building - NWC of Harry Hines and Record Crossing (6011 Harry Hines Blvd.) Dallas, Texas

Date of Sale: April 10, 1975   Recorded: 75072/1168
Seller: Adele N. Locke
Buyer: Phoenix Mutual Life Insurance Company
Legal Desc.: Part of Dallas City Block 6059
Land Area: 1.687 acres (73,486 S.F.)
Building: 9-story medical office building (built 1960) with commercial space on first floor; occupancy of 95%. Gross Area - 95,302 S.F.; Net Rentable Area - 69,343 S.F., for an efficiency of 72.8%. This building is located across the street from St. Paul's

Sales Price: (All cash) $2,600,000

Gross Income	$445,364
Vacancy & Expenses Allowance	199,100
Net Income	$246,264

Sales Price/SF (Gross Area)	$27.28/S.F.
Sales Price/SF (NRA)	$37.49/S.F.
Overall Capitalization Rate	9.47%
Equity Dividend Rate	9.47%
Gross Rent Multiplier	5.84 x

3. Hillcrest 635 - SEC LBJ Freeway & Hillcrest Rd. Dallas, Texas

Date of Sale: January 5, 1976   Recorded: 76000/1904
Seller: L and N Consultants
Buyer: Systech Properties, 1976
Legal Desc.: Part of Block A/7467
Land Area: 10.636 acres
Building Area: 2-story garden office complex (built 1972); Gross Area = 243,276 S.F.; NRA = 212,112 S.F., for an efficiency of 87.2%; overall occupancy at date of sale = 92%, with average rents of $6.33/S.F.

Sale Price

New Mortgage (10%, 30 years)	$5,800,000
Equity Required (Cash)	2,000,000
TOTAL	$7,800,000

Gross Income	$1,402,800
Vacancy Allowance	84,200
Effective Gross Income	$1,318,600
Expenses	517,000
Net Income	$ 801,600
Debt Service	611,088
Cash Flow	$ 190,512

Sale Price/S.F. (Gross Area)	$32.06/S.F.
Sale Price/S.F. (NRA)	$36.77/S.F.

Overall Capitalization Rate   10.28%

Equity Dividend Rate   9.53%

Gross Rent Multiplier   5.56 x

Note: This property is current under contract for sale at a reported price
       of $10,000,000 and is due to close shortly. While this sale cannot be
       confirmed as of the date of this appraisal, it indicates a G.R.M. of
       6.5 based on reported current average rents of $7.25/S.F.

4. Preston Forest Tower - 5925 Forest Lane, Dallas Texas

Date of Sale: May 25, 1973   Recorded: 73106/890
Seller: W. B. Rasansky, et al
Buyer: The Manufacturers Life Insurance Co.
Legal Desc.:   Part of Dallas City Block 6379
Land Area: 1.898 acres (82,688 S.F.)
Building: 5-story masonry building (built 1966). 40% of tenants are
                medical/professional; Gross Area - 55,000 S.F.; Net Rentable
                Area - 43,912 S.F., for an efficiency of 79.8%; major tenants
                include Meyers and Rosser Drugs and State Farm Insurance Agency;
                free parking for 150 spaces; average rental @ $6.46/S.F.

Sale Price (all cash) $1,675,890

Gross Income $283,540
Vacancy & Expenses   120,540
Net Income $163,000

Sales Price/S.F. (Gross Area) $30.47/S.F.
Sales Price/S.F. (NRA) $38.16/S.F.
Overall Capitalization Rate   9.73%
Equity Dividend Rate   9.73%
Gross Rent Multiplier   5.91 x

Note that a review of the aforediscussed sales reveals that the gross rent
multiplier is the best unit of comparison which is logical since buildings
such as these are sold on the basis of the income they can generate. Thus,
a summary of the sales is as follows:

Sale	Date of Sale	Gross Building Area	Gross Annual Income	Total Sales Price	GRM
1	12/73	104,099 S.F.	$ 523,000	$ 3,256,800	6
2	4/75	95,302	445,364	2,600,000	5.84
3	1/76	243,276	1,402,800	7,800,000	5.56
3-A	5/77	243,276	1,537,812(est.)	10,000,000	6.50
4	5/73	55,000	283,540	1,675,890	5.91

Note that the gross rent multipliers ranged from 5.56 to 6.50. Since Sale #3
is most comparable to the subject property, a gross rent multiplier of 6.50
would appear appropriate for the subject property. Applying a 6.50 multiplier

to the subject property's estimated gross annual income of $408,600 would indicate a value via the Market Data Approach of $2,656,900.

<u>TWO MILLION SIX HUNDRED FIFTY SIX THOUSAND DOLLARS</u>

($2,656,000)

CORRELATION AND FINAL ESTIMATE OF VALUE

The value estimates indicated by the three approaches to value are as follows:

Cost Approach	$2,559,000
Income Approach	$2,600,000
Market Data Approach	$2,656,000

The cost approach provides an excellent estimate of value if the building is new and the improvements reflect the highest and best use of the land. Both of the criteria are met with the subject property. The market data approach reflects the reaction of buyers and sellers in the marketplace. An analysis of recent sales, especially with respect to the relationship sales price bears to the gross income the property produces, provides a good indication of market value. Of the three approaches, the market data approach is the most subjective and therefore, the least reliable. The income approach usually provides the best indication of value for commercial properties. Purchasers are more concerned with the income the property will produce than its reproduction cost. In the present case, there is sufficient data to provide an excellent indication of value by the income approach. Additionally, the competitive position of this office building and its ability to provide an excellent return on invested capital were also given strong consideration. As a result, the income approach was felt to provide the best indication of fair market value. Therefore, after consideration of all the factors which influence value, I have estimated the market value of the subject property to be:

TWO MILLION SIX HUNDRED THOUSAND DOLLARS
($2,600,000)

The fair market value is allocated as follows:

Land	$ 436,000
Improvements	2,164,000
Total	$2,600,000

Richard E. C. Miller, Jr.
Richard E. C. Miller, Jr.

ASSUMPTIONS AND LIMITING CONDITIONS

This appraisal is subject to the following limiting conditions:

The legal description is assumed to be correct.

The appraiser assumed no responsibility for matters legal in character nor renders any opinion as to the title which is assumed to be good and marketable, and that it does not violate any applicable codes, ordinances, statutes, or other governmental regulations.

All existing liens and encumbrances have been disregarded and the property is appraised as though free and clear under responsible ownership and competent management.

The appraiser assumes there are no concealed or dubious conditions of the subsoil or the improvements which would have a tendency to render the property more or less valuable than similar properties.

I believe the information identified in this report as being furnished to me by others to be from reliable sources, however, no further responsibility is assumed for its accuracy.

The possession of this report, or a copy thereof, does not carry with it the right of publication or reproduction, nor may it be used for any purpose except substantiation of the value estimated in whole or in part, without the previous written consent of the appraiser and in any event, only with proper qualifications.

The valuations in the report apply only so far as the properties are improved to their highest and best use, and are not applicable under other patterns of use. All component parts of the property are valued only as a part of the whole property.

The sketch included in this report is only for the purpose of assisting the reader in visualizing the property and is not based on the survey.

I am not required to give testimony or attendance in court by reason of this appraisal with reference to the property in question, unless arrangements have been previously made therefor.

CERTIFICATE OF APPRAISAL

I hereby certify that I have no interest, present or contemplated,
in the property and that neither the employment to make the appraisal
nor the compensation is contingent on the value of the property. I
certify that I have personally inspected the property and that
according to my knowledge and belief, all statements and information
in this report are true and correct, subject to the underlying
assumptions and contingent conditions. Based upon the information
contained in this report and upon my general experience as an appraiser,
it is my opinion that the Market Value, as defined herein of the
subject property as of May 10, 1977, assuming satisfactory completion
of all improvements is:

TWO MILLION SIX HUNDRED THOUSAND DOLLARS

($2,600,000)

Richard E. C. Miller, Jr.

QUALIFICATIONS OF THE APPRAISER

Richard E. C. Miller, Jr.

I. Education

Bachelor of Arts degree (History major, Geology minor). Conferred by Louisiana State University, May, 1968

Master of Business Administration Degree (Finance concentration). Conferred by Louisiana State University, December, 1971

II. Additional Education

Real Estate Principles and Practices - Louisiana State University Spring, 1972

Real Estate Appraisal and Investment - Louisiana State University Spring, 1972

Course I, School of Mortgage Banking - Notre Dame University Spring, 1973

Course I-A, American Institute of Real Estate Appraisers - Villanova University, Summer, 1973

Case Study Seminar on Income Property Financing - Michigan State University, Fall, 1973

MBA Seminar on FNMA Condominium and Planned Unit Development Financing Houston, Texas, Summer, 1974

Course II, School of Mortgage Banking - University of Houston Spring, 1975

III. Current Status

Presently employed by The MortgageBanque, Inc. as Assistant Vice President Commercial Loans. Responsibilities include the origination of income property loans in the Houston metropolitan area and surrounding counties and the preparation of real estate appraisals of properties for both The MortgageBanque, Inc. and the mortgage loan investors The MortgageBanque, Inc. represents. Specific experience includes the appraisal of single-family and multi-family residential properties, including townhouses, in the area of income properties, the appraisal of office warehouses, single purpose industrial and commercial properties, office buildings, including medical professional buildings, shopping centers, retail facilities, and unimproved land.

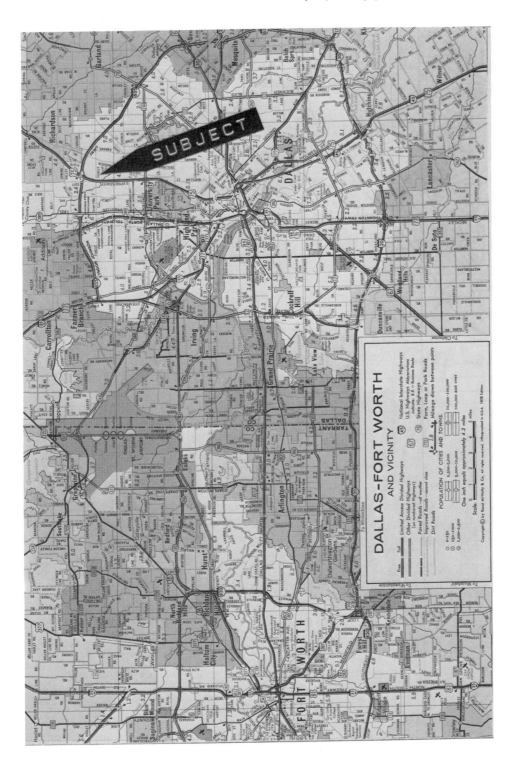

SUBJECT PROPERTY

Northwest Corner of Subject Tract
Bonner Street Entrance to Forest Central Tract
North Central Expressway Service to Road in Foreground

SUBJECT PROPERTY

Northeast Corner of Subject Site
Intersection at Bonner Street and Forest Central Avenue
North Central Expressway in Background

SUBJECT PROPERTY

North Central Expressway Frontage
Picture Taken from Shoulder of Expressway
Service Road in Foreground

SUBJECT PROPERTY

Looking East from
North Central Expressway Service Road

STREET SCENE

Bonner Street Looking West
Subject Property is to the Left

STREET SCENE

Forest Central Avenue Looking North
Subject Property is to the Left

NEIGHBORHOOD PROPERTY

Medical City Dallas
Subject Property is one block
east, one block south

NEIGHBORHOOD PROPERTY

Park Central V
Subject is four blocks south.

LEGAL DESCRIPTION

The subject property may be legally described as :

Being a tract of land situated in the M. J. Sanchez
Survey, Abstract No. 1272 and being also a part of
Block A/7319, Forest-Central #2, an addition to the
City of Dallas according to the revised plat thereof
filed Volume 76012, Page 0060, Deed Records, Dallas
County, Texas, and being more particularly described
as follows:

Beginning at a point in the east line of North Central
Expressway and the south line of Bonner Street
(80' R.O.W.), said point of intersection being also the
southwest Corner of Block A/7319.

THENCE N 89° 45' 35" E along the said south line of
Bonner Street, 376.28' to a point for corner in the west
line of Forest Central Drive (74' R.O.W.);

THENCE S 0° 14' 25" E along the said west line of Forest
Central Drive to a point for corner. Said point being
the beginning of a curve to the left, having a central
angle of 24° 59' 05" and a radius of 537.00';

THENCE in a southerly direction along said curve 234.17
feet to a point for corner at end of curve;

THENCE S 25° 13' 30" E along said west line of Forest Central
Drive 20.62 feet to a point for corner;

THENCE S 89° 45' 35" W 287.24 feet to a point for corner;

THENCE S 0° 14' 25" E 20.00 feet to a point for corner;

THENCE S 89° 45' 35" W 148.00 feet to a point for corner in
the aforementioned east line of North Central Expressway;

THENCE N 0° 14' 25" W along the said east line of North
Central Expressway 330.83 feet to the PLACE OF BEGINNING and
containing 2.862 acres of land, more or less.

Glossary of Real Estate and Mortgage Lending Terms

— A —

AAA tenant. A tenant with the highest credit rating.

Abandonment of property. A property status indicating the property has been abandoned, is not being maintained, and is not offered for sale or rent.

Abstract of title. A written history of the title transaction or condition bearing on the title to a designated real estate. An abstract of title covers the period from the original source of title to the present and summarizes all subsequent instruments of public record by setting forth their material parts.

Acceleration clause. A common provision of a mortgage, trust deed and note providing that the entire principal shall become immediately due and payable in the event of default.

Accrued interest. The interest earned for the period of time that has elapsed since interest was last paid.

Acknowledgment. A formal declaration, attached to or a part of an instrument, made before a duly authorized officer (usually a notary public) by the person who has executed the instrument, who declares the execution to be a free act and deed.

Acre. A measure of land, 43,560 square feet.

Action to quiet title. A court action to remove any interest or claim to the title to real property. To remove a cloud on the title.

Administrator. A person appointed by a probate court to administer the estate of a person who died intestate (without a will).

Ad valorem. "According to the value," used in connection with taxation.

Advance. In real estate, a partial disbursement of funds under a note. Most often used in connection with construction lending.

Advance commitment (conditional). A written promise to make an investment at some time in the future if specified conditions are met.

Adverse possession. The right by which someone occupying a piece of land might acquire title against the real owner, if the occupant's possession has been actual, continuous, hostile, visible, and distinct for a statutory period of time.

Affidavit. A sworn statement in writing before a proper official, usually a notary (see acknowledgement).

After-acquired property. Property acquired after the execution of a security agreement and which will serve as additional security for the underlying debt.

Agent. One who legally represents another, called a principal, from whom authority has been derived.

Agreement for sale. A written document in which the purchaser agrees to buy certain real estate (or personal property) and the seller agrees to sell under stated terms and conditions. Also called sales contract, binder, or earnest money contract.

Air rights. The ownership of the right to use, control or occupy the air space over designated real estate.

Alienation. To transfer real property from one person to another.

ALTA. American Land Title Association. A national association of title insurance companies, abstractors, and attorneys, specializing in real property law. The association speaks for the title insurance and abstracting industry and establishes standard procedures and title policy forms.

Amenity. An aspect of a property that enhances its value. Examples are off-street reserved parking within a condominium community, the nearness of good public transportation, tennis courts, or a swimming pool.

AMMINET. Automated Mortgage Market Information Network. A nationwide electronic quotation system designed for listing VA, FHA, conventional single-family and multifamily loans, and GNMA securities. The system can be expanded to include commercial property loans and mortgage participations. The network handles buy and sell offers that participating subscribers enter into the system through their own terminals. It is operated by a non-profit corporation the directors of which are selected from several national trade associations.

Amortization. Gradual debt reduction. Normally, the reduction is made according to a predetermined schedule of installment payments.

Amortization schedule. A table showing the amounts of principal and interest due at regular intervals and the unpaid balance of the loan after each payment is made.

Annual percentage rate (APR). A rate which represents the relationship of the total finance charge (interest, loan fees, points) to the amount of the loan.

Application. A form used to apply for a mortgage loan and to record pertinent information concerning a prospective mortgagor and the proposed security.

Appraisal. A report by a qualified person setting forth an opinion or estimate of value. Also, the process by which this estimate is obtained.

Appraised value. An opinion of value reached by an appraiser based upon knowledge, experience, and a study of pertinent data.

Appraiser. A person qualified by education, training, and experience to estimate the value of real and personal property.

Appreciation. An increase in value, the opposite of depreciation.

Appurtenance. Anything attached to the land and thus part of the property, such as a barn, garage, or an easement.

Assessed valuation. The value that a taxing authority places upon real or personal property for the purpose of taxation.

Assessment. The process of placing a value on property for the strict purpose of taxation. May also refer to a levy against property for a special purpose, such as a sewer assessment.

Assignee. The person to whom property or a right is assigned or transferred.

Assignment of mortgage. A document that evidences a transfer of ownership of a mortgage from one party to another.

Assignment of rents. An agreement between a property owner and mortgagee specifically fixing the rights and obligations of each regarding rent transferred to a mortgagee if a mortgagor defaults.

Assignor. A person who transfers or assigns a right or property.

Assumption. A written agreement by one party to pay an obligation originally incurred by another.

Assumption fee. The fee paid to a lender (usually by the purchaser of real property) resulting from the assumption of an existing mortgage.

Assumption of mortgage. Assumption by a purchaser of the primary liability for payment of an existing mortgage or deed of trust. The seller remains secondarily liable unless specifically released by the lender.

Attachment. A seizure of defendant's property by court order as security for any judgment plaintiff may recover in a legal action.

— B —

Balance sheet. A financial statement showing assets, liabilities and the net worth as of a specific date.

Balloon mortgage. A mortgage with periodic installments of principal and interest that do not fully amortize the loan. The balance of the mortgage is due in a lump sum at the end of the term.

Balloon payment. The unpaid principal amount of a mortgage or other long-term loan due at a certain date in the future. Usually the amount that must be paid in a lump sum at the end of the term.

Band of investment. A method of deriving capitalization rates by weighting the return on and of various interests in real estate.

Bankrupt. A person, firm or corporation, who, through a court proceeding, is relieved from the payment of all debts after the surrender of all assets to a court appointed trustee.

Base rent. The minimum fixed guaranteed rent in a commercial property lease.

Basis point. 1/100 of 1 percent. Used to describe the amount of change in yield in many debt instruments, including mortgages.

Basket provision. A provision contained in the regulatory acts governing the investments of insurance companies, savings and loan associations, and mutual savings banks. It allows for a certain small percentage of total assets to be placed in investments not otherwise permitted by the regulatory acts.

Beneficiary. The person designated to receive the income from a trust, estate or trust deed.

Bequeath. A transfer of personal property by will.

Bill of sale. A document in writing that transfers title to personal property.

Binder, insurance. A written evidence of temporary hazard or title coverage that only runs for a limited time and must be replaced by a permanent policy.

Blanket mortgage. A lien on more than one parcel or unit of land frequently incurred by subdividers or developers who have purchased a single tract of land for the purpose of dividing it into smaller parcels for sale or development.

Bona fide. In good faith, without fraud.

Borrower. One who receives funds with the expressed or implied intention of repaying the loan in full.

Breach. Violation of a legal obligation.

Break-even point. In residential or commercial property, the figure at which occupancy income is equal to all required expenses and debt service.

Broker. The person who, for a commission or a fee, brings parties together and assists in negotiating contracts between them.

Building code. Local regulations that control design, construction, and materials used in construction. Building codes are based on safety and health standards.

Bundle of rights. The rights or interests a person has in property. It is the exclusive right of an individual to own, possess, use, enjoy and dispose of real property.

Buy-sell agreement. An agreement entered into by an interim and a permanent lender for the sale and assignment of the mortgage to the permanent lender when a building has been completed. Often the mortgagor is a party to this agreement on the theory that the mortgagor should have a contractual right to insist that the permanent lender buy the mortgage.

– C –

Call provision. A clause in the mortgage or deed of trust giving the mortgagee or beneficiary the right to accelerate payment of the mortgage debt in full on a certain date or on the happening of specified conditions.

Capital. Money used to create income, either as investment in a business or income property. The money or property comprising the wealth owned or used by a person or business enterprise. The accumulated wealth of a person or business. The net worth of a business represented by the amount by which its assets exceed liabilities.

Capitalization. The process of converting into present value a series of anticipated future installments of net income by discounting them into a present worth using a specific desired rate of earnings.

Capitalization rate. The rate which is believed to represent the proper relationship between real property and the net income it produces.

Cash flow. The income from an investment after gross income is subtracted from all operating expenses, loan payments, and the allowance for the income tax attributed to the income.

Cash-on-cash return. The rate of return on an investment measured by the cash returned to the investor based on the investor's cash investment without regard to income tax savings or the use of borrowed funds.

Certificate of occupancy. Written authorization given by a local municipality that allows a newly completed, or substantially completed structure to be inhabited.

Certificate of reasonable value (CRV). A document issued by the VA establishing maximum value and loan amount for a VA guaranteed mortgage.

Certificate of title. A statement furnished by an abstract or title company or an attorney to a client stating that the title to real estate is legally vested in the present owner.

Chain of title. The history of all the documents transferring title to a parcel of real property, starting with the earliest existing document and ending with the most recent.

Chattel. Personal property.

Closing. The conclusion or consummation of a transaction. In real estate, closing includes the delivery of a deed, financial adjustments, the signing of notes, and the disbursement of funds necessary to the sale or loan transaction.

Closing costs. Expenses incidental to a sale of real estate, such as loan fees, title fees, appraisal fees, and others.

Closing statement. A financial disclosure accounting for all funds received and expected at the closing, including the escrow deposits for taxes, hazard insurance, and mortgage insurance for the escrow account.

Cloud on title. Any conditions revealed by a title search that adversely affect the title to real estate. Usually they cannot be removed except by a quit-claim deed, release, or court action.

CMB. Certified Mortgage Banker. A professional designation of the mortgage banking industry.

Coinsurance. A sharing of insurance risk between insurer and insured depending on the relation of the amount of the policy and a specified percentage of the actual value of the property insured at the time of loss.

Collateral. Any property pledged as security for a debt.

Collection. Procedure followed to bring the mortgage account current and to file the necessary notices to proceed with foreclosure when necessary.

Commercial loan. A mortgage loan on property that produces income.

Commercial paper. Short-term unsecured promissory notes of large firms sold to meet short-term capital needs.

Commission. An agent's fee for negotiating a real estate or loan transaction.

Commitment. An agreement, often in writing, between a lender and a borrower to loan money at a future date subject to compliance with stated conditions.

Commitment fee. Any fee paid by a borrower to a lender for the lender's promise to lend money at a specified date in the future. The lender may or may not expect to fund the commitment.

Community property. In some western and southwestern states,, a form of ownership under which property acquired during a marriage is presumed to be owned jointly unless acquired as separate property of either spouse.

Common law. An unwritten body of law based on general custom in England and used to an extent in the United States.

Comparables. An abbreviation for comparable properties used for comparative purposes in the appraisal process; facilities of reasonably the same size and location with similar amenities; properties which have been recently sold, which have characteristics similar to property under consideration, thereby indicating the approximate fair market value of the subject property.

Compensating balance. A demand deposit usually required by a commercial bank as a condition for extending a line of credit or a bank loan.

Compound interest. Interest paid on original principal and on the accrued and unpaid interest which has accumulated.

Condemnation. The court proceedings for taking private property under the right of eminent domain for public use with just compensation to the owner.

Condominium. A form of ownership of real property. The purchaser receives title to a particular unit and a proportionate interest in certain common areas. A condominium generally defines each unit as a separately-owned space to the interior surfaces of the perimeter walls, floor and ceilings.

Constant. The percentage of the original loan paid in equal annual payments that provide for interest and principal reduction over the life of the loan.

Construction contract. An agreement between a general contractor and an owner-developer stating the specific duties the general contractor will perform according to blueprints and specifications at a stipulated price and terms of payment.

Construction loan. A short-term, interim loan for financing the cost of construction. The lender makes payments to the builder at periodic intervals as the work progresses.

Construction loan agreement. A written agreement between a lender and a builder or borrower in which the specific terms and conditions of a construction loan, including the schedule of payments, are spelled out.

Construction loan draw. The partial disbursement of the construction loan, based on the schedule of payments in the loan agreement. Also called takedown.

Contract. An oral or written agreement to do or not to do a certain thing.

Conventional loan. A mortgage loan neither insured by FHA nor guaranteed by VA.

Cooperative. A form of multiple ownership of real estate in which a corporation or business trust entity holds title to a property and grants the occupancy rights to particular apartments or units to shareholders by means of proprietary leases or similar arrangements.

Corporation. An artificial person created by law with certain rights, privileges and duties of natural persons.

Correspondent. A mortgage banker who services mortgage loans as a representative or agent for the owner of the mortgage or investor. Also applies to the mortgage banker's role as originator of mortgage loans for an investor.

Cost approach. An appraisal technique used to establish value by estimating the cost to reproduce the improvement, allowing for depreciation, then adding in the fair market value of the land.

Coupon rate. The annual interest rate on a debt instrument. In mortgage lending, the term is used to describe the contract interest rate on the face of the note or bond.

Covenant. A legally enforceable promise or restriction in a mortgage. For example, the borrower may covenant to keep the property in good repair and adequately insured against fire and other casualties. The breach of a covenant in a mortgage usually creates a default as defined by the mortgage or deed of trust and can be the basis for foreclosure.

Credit deal. A mortgage made based primarily on the credit of a borrower or tenant with a net lease.

Credit report. A report to a prospective lender on the credit standing of a prospective borrower, or tenant used to help determine credit worthiness.

Curtesy. The common law interest a husband had in the real estate owned by the wife at the time of her death.

– **D** –

Debenture. An unsecured debt instrument backed only by the general credit standing and earning capacity of the issuer.

Debt coverage ratio. The ratio of effective annual net income to annual debt service.

Debt service. The periodic payment of principal and interest earned on mortgage loans.

Deed. A written legal document which purports to transfer ownership of land from one party to another.

Deed in lieu. A deed given by a mortgagor to a mortgagee to satisfy a debt and avoid foreclosure.

Deed of reconveyance. The transfer of legal title from the trustee to the trustor (the borrower) after the trust deed debt is paid in full.

Deed of trust. In some states it is the document used in place of a mortgage; a type of security instrument conveying title in trust to a third party covering a particular piece of property; used to secure the payment of a note; a conveyance of the title land to a trustee as collateral security for the payment of a debt with the condition that the trustee shall reconvey the title upon the payment of the debt, and with power of the trustee to sell the land and pay the debt in the event of a default on the part of the debtor.

Deed Restriction. A limitation placed in a deed limiting or restricting the use of real property.

Default. A breach or nonperformance of the terms of a note or the covenants of a mortgage or deed of trust.

Default point. See break-even point.

Defeasance clause. The clause in a mortgage that gives the mortgagor the right to redeem property upon the payment to the mortgagee of the obligation due.

Deficiency judgment. A court order to pay the balance owed on a loan if the proceeds from the sale of the security are insufficient to pay off the loan.

Delinquent. The status of a mortgage with a payment past due.

Delivery. The legal, final and absolute transfer of a deed from seller to buyer in such a manner that it cannot be recalled by the seller; a necessary requisite to the transfer of title; in mortgage banking, the physical delivery of loan documents to an investor or agent in conformance with the commitment.

Demand note. A note that is due whenever the holder demands payment.

Deposit. A sum of money given to bind a sale of real estate, or a sum of money given to assure payment or an advance of funds in the processing of a loan. Also known as earnest money.

Depreciation. A loss of value in real property brought about by age, physical deterioration or functional or economic obsolescence. Broadly, a loss in value from any cause. The opposite of appreciation.

Depreciation allowance. The accounting charge made to allow for the fact that the asset may become economically obsolete before its physical deterioration. The purpose is to write off the original cost by distributing it over the estimated useful life of the asset. It appears in both the profit and loss statement and the balance sheet.

Developer. A person or entity who prepares raw land for building sites, and sometimes builds on the sites.

Development loan. A loan made for the purpose of preparing raw land for the construction of buildings. Development may include grading and installation of utilities and roadways (see construction loan).

Disbursements. The payment of monies on a previously-agreed-to basis. Used to describe construction loan draws.

Discount. In loan originations, a discount refers to an amount withheld from loan proceeds by a lender. In secondary market sales, a discount is the amount by which the sale price of a note is less than its face value. In both instances, the purpose of a discount is to adjust the yield upward, either in lieu of interest or in addition to interest. The rate or amount of discount depends on money market conditions, the credit of the borrower, and the rate and terms of the note.

Discount point. See point.

Disintermediation. The flow of funds out of savings institutions into short-term investments in which interest rates are higher. This shift normally results in a net decrease in the amount of funds available for long-term real estate financing. Also the market condition that exists when this shift occurs.

Dower. The rights of a widow in the property of her husband at his death.

Due-on-sale clause. See alienation clause.

— E —

Earnest money. See deposit.

Easement. Right or interest in the land of another entitling the holder to a specific limited use, privilege, or benefit such as laying a sewer, putting up electric power lines, or crossing the property.

ECOA. Equal Credit Opportunity Act. ECOA is a federal law that requires lenders and other creditors to make credit equally available without discrimination based on race, color, religion, national origin, age, sex, marital status, or receipt of income from public assistance programs. Also known as Regulation "B".

Economic rent. The rent that a property would bring if offered in the open market at the fair rental value. Not necessarily the contract rent.

Economic value. The valuation of real property based on its earning capabilities.

Effective gross income (personal). Normal annual income including overtime that is regular or guaranteed. It may be from more than one source. Salary is generally the principal source, but other income may qualify if it is significant and stable.

Effective gross income (property). Stabilized income that a property is expected to generate after a vacancy allowance.

Effective rate. The actual rate of return to the investor. It may vary from the contract rate for a variety of reasons. Also called yield (see yield).

Eminent domain. The right of a government to take private property for public use upon payment of its fair value. It is the basis for condemnation proceedings (see condemnation).

Encroachment. An improvement that intrudes illegally upon another's property.

Encumbrance. Anything that affects or limits the fee simple title to property, such as mortgages, leases, easements, or restrictions.

Equity. In real estate, equity is the difference between fair market value and current indebtedness, usually referring to the owner's interest.

Equity of redemption. The common law right to redeem property during the foreclosure period. In some states the mortgagor has a statutory right to redeem property after a foreclosure sale.

Equity participation. Partial ownership of income property, given by the owner to the lender, as part of the consideration for making the loan.

Escalator clause. A clause providing for the upward or downward adjustment of rent payments to cover specified contingencies, such as the provision in a lease to provide for increases in property tax and operating expenses.

Escheat. The reversion of property to the state if the owner dies intestate and without heirs.

Escrow. A transaction in which a third party, acting as the agent for the buyer and the seller, carries out instructions of both and assumes the responsibilities of handling all the paperwork and disbursement of funds.

Escrow analysis. The periodic examination of escrow accounts to determine if current monthly deposits will provide sufficient funds to pay taxes, insurance and other bills when due.

Escrow payment. That portion of a mortgagor's monthly payments held by the lender to pay for taxes, hazard insurance, mortgage insurance, lease payments, and other items as they become due. Known as impounds or reserves in some states.

Estate. The ownership interest of an individual in real property. The sum total of all the real and personal property owned by an individual at time of death.

Estoppel letter. A statement that in itself prevents its issuer from later asserting different facts.

Eviction. The lawful expulsion of an occupant from real property.

Exclusive listing. A written contract giving a licensed real estate agent the exclusive right to sell a property for a specified time, but reserving the owner's right to sell the property alone without the payment of a commission.

Exclusive right to sell. The same as exclusive listing, but the owner agrees to pay a full commission to the broker even though the owner may sell the property.

Executor. A person named in a will to administer an estate. The court will appoint an administrator if no executor is named. Executrix is the feminine form.

— F —

Fair market value. The price at which property is transferred between a willing buyer and a willing seller, each of whom has a reasonable knowledge of all pertinent facts and neither of whom is under any compulsion to buy or sell.

Fannie Mae. See Federal National Mortgage Association.

Farmers Home Administration (FmHA). An agency within the Department of Agriculture which operates principally under the Consolidated Farm and Rural Development Act of 1921 and Title V of the Housing Act of 1949. This agency provides financing to farmers and other qualified borrowers who are unable to obtain loans elsewhere. Funds are borrowed from the U.S. Treasury.

Federal Home Loan Mortgage Corporation (FHLMC). A private corporation authorized by Congress to provide secondary mortgage market support for conventional mortgages. It also sells participation sale certificates secured by pools of conventional mortgage loans, their principal and interest guaranteed by the federal government through the FHLBB. Popularly known as Freddie Mac.

Federal Housing Administration (FHA). A division of HUD. Its main activity is the insuring of residential mortgage loans made by private lenders. It sets standards for construction and underwriting. FHA does not lend money, plan, or construct housing.

Federal National Mortgage Association (FNMA). A privately-owned corporation created by Congress to support the secondary mortgage market. It purchases and sells residential mortgages insured by FHA or guaranteed by VA, as well as conventional home mortgages. Popularly known as Fannie Mae.

Fee simple. The greatest possible interest a person can have in real estate.

Fiduciary. A person in a position of trust and confidence for another.

Financial intermediary. A financial institution which acts as a middleman between savers and borrowers by selling its own obligations or serving as a depository and, in turn, lending the accumulated funds to borrowers.

Financing package. The total of all financial interest in a project. It may include mortgages, partnerships, joint venture capital interests, stock ownership, or any financial arrangement used to carry a project to completion.

Financing statement. Under the Uniform Commercial Code, this is a prescribed form filed by a lender with the registrar of deeds, or secretary of state to perfect a security interest. It gives the name and address of the debtor and the secured party (lender), along with a description of the personal property securing the loan. It may show the amount of indebtedness.

Finder's fee. A fee or commission paid to a broker for obtaining a mortgage loan for a client or for referring a mortgage loan to a broker. It may also refer to a commission paid to a broker for locating a property.

Firm commitment. A lender's agreement to make a loan to a specific borrower on a specific property. An FHA or PMI agreement with a designated borrower to insure a loan on a specific property.

First mortgage. A real estate loan that creates a primary lien against real property.

Fixture. Personal property that becomes real property when attached in a permanent manner to real estate.

Floor loan. A portion or portions of a mortgage loan commitment that is less than the full amount of the commitment. It may be funded upon conditions less stringent than those required for funding the full amount. For example, the floor loan, equal to perhaps 80 percent of the full amount, may be funded upon completion of construction without occupancy requirements, but substantial occupancy of the building may be required for funding the full amount of the loan.

FNMA. See Federal National Mortgage Association.

Forbearance. The act of refraining from taking legal action despite the fact that a mortgage is in arrears. It is usually granted only when a mortgagor makes a satisfactory arrangement by which the arrears will be paid at a future date.

Foreclosure. An authorized procedure taken by a mortgagee or lender under the terms of a mortgage or deed of trust for the purpose of having the property applied to the payment of a defaulted debt.

Forward delivery. The delivery of mortgages or mortgage-backed securities to satisfy cash or future market transactions of an earlier date.

Front-end money. Funds required to start a development and generally advanced by the developer or equity owner as a capital contribution to the project.

Freehold estate. An estate in real estate that could last forever.

— G —

Gap financing. An interim loan given to finance the difference between the floor and the maximum permanent loan as committed (see floor loan).

Garnishment. A proceeding that applies specified monies, wages, or property to a debt or creditor by proper statutory process against a debtor.

Government National Mortgage Association (GNMA). On Sept. 1, 1968, Congress enacted legislation to partition FNMA into two continuing corporate entities within HUD. GNMA has assumed responsibility for the special assistance loan program and the management and liquidation function of the older FNMA. Also, GNMA administers the mortgage-backed securities program which channels new sources of funds into residential financing through the sale of privately-issued securities carrying a GNMA guaranty. Popularly known as Ginnie Mae.

GNMA futures market. A regulated central market in which standardized contracts for the future delivery of GNMA securities are traded.

GNMA mortgage-backed securities. Securities, guaranteed by GNMA, that are issued by mortgage bankers, commercial banks, savings and loan associations, savings banks and other institutions. The GNMA security holder is protected by the "full faith and credit of the U.S." GNMA securities are backed by FHA, VA or FmHA mortgages.

Grantee. The person to whom an interest in real property is conveyed.

Grantor. The person conveying an interest in real property.

Gross rent multiplier. A figure used to compare rental properties to determine value. It gives the relationship between the gross rental income and the sales price. Synonyms are gross multiplier, and gross income multiplier.

Ground rent. The earnings of improved property allocated to the ground itself after allowance is made for earnings of the improvement. Also, payment for the use of land in accordance with the terms of a ground lease.

Guaranteed loan. A loan guaranteed by VA, FmHA or any other interested party.

— H —

Hazard insurance. A contract whereby an insurer, for a premium, undertakes to compensate the insured for loss on a specific property due to certain hazards.

Hedging. In mortgage lending, the purchases or sale of mortgage futures contracts to offset cash market transactions to be made at a later date.

Highest and best use. The available present use or series of future uses that will produce the highest present property value and develop a site to its full economic potential.

Holdback. That portion of a loan commitment not funded until some additional requirement such as rental or completion is attained (See floor loan). In construction or interim lending it is a percentage of the contractor's draw held back to provide additional protection for the interim lender, often in an amount equal to the contractor's profit given over when the interim loan is closed.

Home Owners Loan Corporation (HOLC). An agency formed in 1933 to help stabilize the economy. The HOLC issued government guaranteed bonds to lenders for delinquent mortgages and then refinanced homeowner indebtedness.

Homeowners policy. A multiple peril policy commonly called "package policy". It is available to owners of private dwellings and covers the dwelling and contents in the case of fire or wind damage, theft, liability for property damage, and personal liability.

Homestead estate. In some states, the home and property occupied by an owner are protected by law up to a certain amount from attachment and sale for the claims of creditors.

HUD. The Department of Housing and Urban Development established by the Housing and Urban Development Act of 1965 to supersede the Housing and Home Finance Agency. It is responsible for the implementation and administration of government housing and urban development programs. The broad range of programs includes community planning and development, housing production and mortgage credit (FHA), equal opportunity in housing, research and technology.

Hypothecate. To give a thing as security without the necessity of giving up possession of it.

— I —

Impound. See escrow payment.

Income and expense statement. The actual or estimated schedule of income and expense items reflecting net gain or loss during a specified period.

Income approach to value. The appraisal technique used to estimate real property value by capitalizing net income (see capitalization).

Income property. Real estate developed or improved to produce income.

Industrial park. A controlled development designed for specific types of businesses. These developments provide required appurtenances including public utilities, streets, railroads sidings, auto parking, and water and sewage facilities.

Installment. The regular periodic payment that a borrower agrees to make to the mortgagee.

Institutional lender. A financial institution that invests in mortgages carried in its own portfolio. Mutual savings banks, life insurance companies, commercial banks, pension and trust funds, and savings and loan associations are examples.

Insurance. A contract for indemnification against loss.

Insured loan. A loan insured by FHA or a private mortgage insurance company.

Interest. Consideration in the form of money paid for the use of money, usually expressed as an annual percentage. Also, a right, share, or title in property.

Interim financing. Financing during the time from project commencement to closing of a permanent loan, usually in the form of a construction loan or development loan.

Intestate. To die leaving no valid will.

Investor. The holder of a mortgage or the permanent lender for whom a mortgage lender services the loan. Any person or institution investing in mortgages.

Involuntary lien. A lien imposed against property without consent of an owner. Examples include taxes, special assessments, federal income tax liens, mechanics liens, and materials liens.

– J –

Joint tenancy. An equal undivided ownership of property by two or more persons, whose survivors take the interest upon the death of any one of them.

Joint venture. An association between two or more parties to own or develop real estate. It may take a variety of legal forms including partnership, tenancy in common, or a corporation. It is formed for a specific purpose and duration.

Judgment. That which has been adjudicated, allowed, or decreed by a court.

Judgment lien. A lien upon the property of a debtor resulting from the decree of a court.

Judicial foreclosure. A type of foreclosure proceeding used in some states that is handled as a civil lawsuit and conducted entirely under auspices of a court.

Junior mortgage. A lien subsequent to the claims of the holder of a prior (senior) mortgage.

– K –

Kicker. A term describing any benefit to a lender above ordinary interest payments. It may be an equity in a property or a participation in the income stream.

– L –

Land contract. A contract ordinarily used in connection with the sale of property in cases where the seller does not wish to convey title until all or a certain part of the purchase price is paid by the buyer. The financing vehicle is often used when property is sold on a small downpayment.

Landlord. Owner or lessor of real property.

Late charge. An additional charge a borrower is required to pay as penalty for failure to pay a regular installment when due.

Lease. A written document containing the conditions under which the possession and use of real or personal property are given by the owner to another for a stated period and for a stated consideration.

Leaseback. See sale-leaseback.

Leasehold. An interest in real property held by virtue of a lease.

Leasehold mortgage. A loan to a lessee secured by a leasehold interest in a property.

Legal description. A property description recognized by law which is sufficient to locate and identify the property without oral testimony.

Legal lists. A term describing investments that life insurance companies, mutual savings banks, or other regulated investors may make under a state charter or court order.

Lessee (tenant). That person(s) holding rights of possession and use of property under terms of a lease.

Lessor (landlord). The one leasing property to a lessee.

Leverage. The use of borrowed money to increase the return on a cash investment. For leverage to be profitable, the rate of return on the investment must be higher than the cost of the money borrowed (interest plus amortization).

Lien. A legal hold or claim of one person on the property of another as security for a debt or charge. The right given by law to satisfy debt.

Limited partnership. A partnership that consists of one or more general partners who are fully liable and one or more limited partners are liable only for the amount of their investment.

Line of credit. An agreement by a commercial bank or other financial institution to extend credit up to a certain amount for a certain time to a specific borrower.

Lis pendens. A notice recorded in the official records of a county to indicate that there is a pending suit affecting the lands within that jurisdiction.

Loan. A sum of money loaned at interest to be repaid.

Loan submission. A package of pertinent papers and documents regarding specific property or properties. It is delivered to a prospective lender for review and consideration for the purpose of making a mortgage loan.

Loan-to-value ratio. The relationship between the amount of the mortgage loan and the appraised value of the security expressed as a percentage of the appraised value.

— M —

MAI (Member, Appraisal Institute). The highest professional designation awarded by the American Institute of Real Estate Appraisers.

Marketable title. A title that may not be completely clear but has only minor objections that a well-informed and prudent buyer of real estate would accept.

Market approach to value. In appraising, the market value estimate is predicated upon actual prices paid in market transactions. It is a process of correlation and analysis of similar recently sold properties. The reliability of this technique is dependent upon the degree of comparability of each property with the subject property, the time of sale, the verification of the sale dates, the absence of unusual conditions affecting the sale, and the terms of the sale.

Market rent. The price a tenant pays a landlord for the use and occupancy of real property based upon current prices for comparable property.

Market value. The highest price that a buyer, willing but not compelled to buy, would pay, and the lowest a seller, willing but not compelled to sell, would accept.

Maturity. The terminating or due date of a note, time, draft, acceptance, bill of exchange, or bond. The date a time instrument or indebtedness becomes due and payable.

Metes and bounds. A description in a deed of the land location in which the boundaries are defined by directions and distances.

Moratorium. A period during which a borrower is granted the right to delay fulfillment of an obligation.

Mortgage. A conveyance of an interest in real property given as security for the payment of a debt.

Mortgage-backed securities. Bond-type investment securities representing an undivided interest in a pool of mortgages or trust deeds. Income from the underlying mortgage is used to pay off the securities (see GNMA mortgage-backed securities).

Mortgage banker. A firm or individual active in the field of mortgage banking. Mortgage bankers, as local representatives of regional or national institutional lenders, act as correspondents between lenders and borrowers.

Mortgage banking. The packaging of mortgage loans secured by real property to be sold to a permanent investor with servicing retained for the life of the loan for a fee. The origination, sale, and servicing of mortgage loans by a firm or individual. The investor-correspondent system is the foundation of the mortgage banking industry.

Mortgage broker. A firm or individual bringing the borrower and lender together and receiving a commission. A mortgage broker does not retain servicing.

Mortgage company. A private corporation (sometimes called a mortgage banker) whose principal activity is the origination and servicing of mortgage loans which are sold to other financial institutions.

Mortgage discount. The difference between the principal amount of a mortgage and the amount for which it actually sells. Sometimes called points, loan brokerage fee, or new loan fee. The discount is computed on the amount of the loan, not the sales prices.

Mortgagee. A person or firm to whom property is conveyed as security for a loan made by such person or firm (a creditor).

Mortgagee in possession. A mortgagee who, by virtue of a default under the terms of a mortgage, has obtained possession but not ownership of the property.

Mortgage insurance. The function of mortgage insurance (whether government or private) is to insure a mortgage lender against loss caused by a mortgagor's default. This insurance may cover a percentage of or virtually all of the mortgage loan depending on the type of mortgage insurance.

Mortgage life insurance. A type of term life insurance often bought by mortgagors. The amount of coverage decreases as the mortgage balance declines. In the event that the borrower dies while the policy is in force, the debt is automatically satisfied by insurance proceeds.

Mortgage insurance premium (MIP). The consideration paid by a mortgagor for mortgage insurance either to FHA or a private mortgage insurance (PMI) company. On an FHA loan, the payment is one-half of one percent annually on the declining balance of the mortgage.

Mortgage note. A written promise to pay a sum of money at a stated interest rate during a specified term. It is secured by a mortgage.

Mortgage portfolio. The aggregate of mortgage loans held by an investor, or serviced by a mortgage lender.

Mortgagor. One who borrows money giving a mortgage or deed of trust on real property as security (a debtor).

Mutual mortgage insurance fund. One of four FHA insurance funds into which all mortgage insurance premiums and other specified revenue of the FHA are paid and from which losses are met.

Mutual savings bank. A state chartered financial institution, located primarily in the Northeast, that is a heavy purchaser of mortgage loans.

— N —

Negative cash flow. Cash expenditures of an income producing property in excess of the cash receipts.

Net income. The difference between effective gross income and the expenses including taxes and insurance. The term is qualified as net income before depreciation and debt service.

Net lease. A lease calling for the lessee to pay all fixed and variable expenses associated with the property. Also known as a pure net lease, as opposed to a gross lease. The terms net-net and net-net-net are ill-defined and should be avoided.

Net worth. The value of all assets, including cash, less total liabilities. It is often used as an underwriting guideline to indicate an individual's credit worthiness and financial strength.

Net yield. That part of gross yield that remains after the deductions of all costs, such as servicing, and any reserves for losses.

Nondisturbance agreement. An agreement that permits a tenant under a lease to remain in possession despite any foreclosure.

Notice of default. A notice recorded after the occurrence of a default under a deed of trust or mortgage or a notice required by an interested third party insuring or guaranteeing a loan (FHA, VA, or PMI).

Novation. The substitution of a new contract or obligation between the same or different parties. The substitution, by mutual agreement, of one debtor for another or one creditor for another whereby the existing debt is extinguished.

– O –

Obsolescence. The loss of value of a property occasioned by going out of style, by becoming less suitable for use, or by other economic influences.

Open-end mortgage. A mortgage with a provision that the outstanding loan amount may be increased upon mutual agreement of the lender and the borrower.

Option. A contract agreement granting a right to purchase, sell, or otherwise contract for the use of a property at a stated price during a stated period of time.

Origination fee. A fee or charge for the work involved in the evaluation, preparation, and submission of a proposed mortgage loan.

Originator. A person who solicits builders, brokers, and others to obtain applications for mortgage loans. Origination is the process by which the mortgage lender brings into being a mortgage secured by real property.

– P –

Package mortgage. A mortgage or deed of trust that includes items which are technically chattels, such as appliances, carpeting, and drapery.

Par. The principal amount of a mortgage with no premium or discount.

Participation loan. A mortgage made by one lender, known as the lead lender, in which one or more other lenders, known as participants, own a part interest, or a mortgage originated by two or more lenders.

Percentage lease. A lease in which a percentage of the tenant's gross business receipts constitutes the rent. Although a straight percentage lease is occasionally encountered, most percentage leases contain a provision for a minimum rent amount.

Personal property. Any property that is not real property.

PITI (principal, interest, taxes, and insurance). The principal and interest payment on most loans is fixed for the term of the loan; the tax and insurance portion may be adjusted to reflect changes in taxes or insurance costs.

Plans and specifications. Architectural and engineering drawings and specifications for construction of a building or project including a description of materials to be used and the manner in which they are to be applied.

Point. An amount equal to one percent of the principal amount of an investment or note. Loan discount points are a one-time charge assessed at closing by the lender to increase the yield on the mortgage loan to a competitive position with other types of investments.

Police power. That right by which the state or other governmental authority may take, condemn, destroy, impair the value of, limit the use of, or otherwise invade property rights. It must be affirmatively shown that the property was taken to protect the public health, public morals, public safety, or the general welfare.

Preclosing. A transaction preceding the formal closing, often used to distinguish between transactions affecting title to real property where there are events that appear to be the formal closing.

Premium. The amount, often stated as a percentage, paid in addition to the face value of a note or bond. Also, the charge for insurance coverage.

Prepayment fee. A consideration paid to the mortgagee for the prepayment privilege. Also known as prepayment penalty or reinvestment fee.

Prepayment privilege. The right given a borrower to pay all or part of a debt prior to its maturity. The mortgagee cannot be compelled to accept any payment other than those originally agreed to.

Principal. The amount of debt.

Principal balance. The outstanding balance of a mortgage, exclusive of interest and any other charges.

Priority. As applied to claims against property, priority is the status of being prior or having precedence over other claims. Priority is usually established by filing or recordation in point of time, but may be established by statute or agreement.

Private mortgage insurance (PMI). Insurance written by a private company protecting the mortgage lender against loss occasioned by a mortgage default.

Proforma statement. A financial or accounting statement projecting income and performance of real estate within a period of time (usually one year) based on estimates and assumption.

Purchase money mortgage. A mortgage given by the purchaser of real property to the seller as part of the consideration in the sales transaction.

− Q −

Quitclaim deed. A deed that transfers (with no warranty) only such interest, title or right a grantor may have at the time the conveyance is executed.

− R −

Real estate investment trust (REIT). A financial institution which can own and hold mortgages on real estate and pass earnings from these assets on free of tax to the corporation but taxable to shareholders.

Real estate owned (REO). A term frequently used by lending institutions as applied to ownership of real property acquired for investment or as a result of foreclosure.

Real property. Land and appurtenances, including anything of a permanent nature such as structures, trees, minerals, and the interest, benefits and inherent rights thereof.

Realtor. A real estate broker or an associate holding active membership in a local real estate board affiliated with the National Association of Realtors.

Recapture. An owner's recovery of money invested in real estate, usually referring to a depreciation allowance.

Recision. The cancellation or annulment of a transaction or contract by the operation of law or by mutual consent.

Reconveyance. The transfer of the title of land from one person to the immediate preceding owner. It is used when the performance of debt is satisfied under the terms of a deed of trust.

Recorder. The public official in a political subdivision who keeps records of transactions affecting real property in the area. Sometimes known as a registrar of deeds or county clerk.

Recording. The noting in the registrar's office of the details of a properly executed legal document, such as a deed, mortgage, a satisfaction of mortgage, or an extension of mortgage, thereby making it a part of the public record.

Redemption, right of. The right allowed by law in some states whereby a mortgagor may buy back property by paying the amount owed on a foreclosed mortgage, including interest and fees.

Refinancing. The repayment of a debt from the proceeds of a new loan using the same property as security.

Release of lien. An instrument discharging secured property from a lien.

Remainder. That part of an estate that remains after the termination of a prior estate.

Rent. Consideration paid for use or occupancy of property, buildings, or dwelling units.

Reproduction cost. The money required to reproduce a building under current market conditions less an allowance for depreciation.

RESPA. Real Estate Settlement Procedures Act.

Restrictive covenant. A clause in a deed limiting use of the property conveyed for a certain period of time.

Return on equity. The ratio of cash flow after debt service to the difference between the value of property and the total financing (see cash-on-cash return).

Reverse leverage. A situation that arises when financing is too costly. It results when total yield on cash investment is less than the financing constant on borrowed funds (see negative cash flow).

Reversion. A right to future possession retained by an owner at the time of a transfer of an owner's interest in real property.

Reversionary clause. A clause providing that any violations of restrictions will cause title to the property to revert to the party who imposed the restriction.

Right of survivorship. In joint tenancy, the right of survivors to acquire the interest of a deceased joint tenant.

Right-of-way. A privilege operating as an easement upon land, whereby a land owner, by grant or agreement, gives another the right to pass over land (see easement).

— S —

Sale-leaseback. A technique in which a seller deeds property to a buyer for a consideration and the buyer simultaneously leases the property back to the seller, usually on a long-term basis.

Sandwich lease. A lease in which the "sandwiched party" is a lessee, paying rent on a leasehold interest to one party, and also is a lessor, collecting rents from another party or parties.

Satisfaction of mortgage. The recordable instrument given by the lender to evidence payment in full of the mortgage debt. Sometimes known as a release deed.

Savings and loan association. A mutual or stock association chartered and regulated by either the federal government or a state. S&Ls accept time deposits and lend funds primarily on residential real estate.

Secondary financing. Financing real estate with a loan, or loans, subordinate to a first mortgage or first trust deed.

Secondary mortgage market. An unorganized market where existing mortgages are bought and sold. It contrasts with the primary mortgage market where mortgages are originated.

Secured party. The party holding a security interest or lien; may be referred to as the mortgagee, the conditional seller, or the pledgee.

Security. The collateral given, deposited, or pledged to secure the fulfillment of an obligation or the payment of a debt.

Security instrument. The mortgage or trust deed evidencing the pledge of real estate security as distinguished from the note or other credit instrument.

Security interest. According to the U.C.C., Uniform Commercial Code, security interest is a term designating the interest of the creditor in the property of the debtor in all types of credit transactions. It thus replaces such terms as chattel mortgage, pledge, trust receipt, chattel trust, equipment trust, conditional sale, and inventory lien (see financing statement).

Seller-servicer. FNMA term for an approved corporation that sells and services mortgages for FNMA.

Servicing. The duties of the mortgage lender as a loan correspondent as specified in the servicing agreement for which a fee is received. The collection for an investor of payments, interest, principal, and trust items such as hazard insurance and taxes, on a note by the borrower in accordance with the terms of the note. Servicing also consists of operational procedures covering accounting, bookkeeping, insurance, tax records, loan payment follow-up, delinquency loan follow-up, and loan analysis.

Soft costs. Architectural, engineering, and legal fees as distinguished from land and construction costs.

Special warranty deed. A deed containing a covenant whereby the grantor agrees to protect the grantee against any claims arising during the grantor's period of ownership.

Specific performance. A remedy in a court of equity compelling the defendant to carry out the terms of an agreement or contract.

SREA. The designation of an appraiser who is a member of the Society of Real Estate Appraisers. The designations are: senior residential appraiser (SRA), senior real property appraiser (SRPA), and senior real estate analyst (SREA).

Standby commitment. A commitment to purchase a loan or loans with specified terms, both parties understanding that delivery is not likely, unless circumstances warrant. The commitment is issued for a fee with willingness to fund in the event that a permanent loan is not obtained. Such commitments are typically used to enable the borrower to obtain construction financing at a lower cost on the assumption that permanent financing of the project will be available on more favorable terms when the improvements are completed and the project is generating income.

Standby fee. The fee charged by an investor for a standby commitment. The fee is earned upon issuance and acceptance of the commitment.

Statute of frauds. A state law requiring that certain contracts be in writing. In real estate, a contract for the sale of land must be in writing to be enforceable.

Statute of limitations. A law that limits the length of time in which a lawsuit must be commenced or the right to sue is lost. It varies from state to state.

Step-down-lease. A lease calling for one initial rent to be followed by a decrease in rent over stated periods.

Step-up-lease. A lease calling for one initial rent followed by an increase in rent over stated periods.

Subject to mortgage. When a purchaser buys subject to a mortgage but does not endorse the same or assume to pay mortgage, a purchaser cannot be held for any deficiency if the mortgage is foreclosed and the property sold for an amount not sufficient to cover the note (see assumption of mortgage).

Sublease. A lease executed by a lessee to a third person for a term no longer than the remaining portion of the original lease.

Subordinate. To make subject to, or junior to.

Subordination. The act of a party acknowledging, by written recorded instrument, that a debt due is inferior to the interest of another in the same property. Subordination may apply not only to mortgages, but to leases, real estate rights, and any other types of debt instruments.

Subrogation. The substitution of one person for another in reference to a debt, claim, or right.

– T –

Takeout commitment. A promise to make a loan at a future specified time. It is commonly used to designate a higher cost, shorter term, back-up commitment as a support for construction financing until a suitable permanent loan can be secured.

Tandem plan. A mortgage assistance program in which GNMA agrees to purchase qualified, below-market interest rate mortgages at prices favorable to sellers. The mortgages purchased by GNMA are accumulated and periodically sold at auction as either GNMA securities or whole mortgages. As the subsidy cost of the program, GNMA absorbs the difference between the price it paid for the loan and the market price paid by the investor. If the seller or assignee assumes GNMA's obligation to purchase, then GNMA will pay the seller a differential of the excess of the specified purchase price over a published interim selling price (ISP). The term is also used to describe any of the many forms of special assistance programs sponsored by GNMA to affect mortgage finance activity and costs.

Tax deed. A deed on property purchased at public sale for nonpayment of taxes.

Tax lien. A claim against property for the amount of its due and unpaid taxes.

Tenancy. A holding of real estate under any kind of right of title. Used alone, tenancy implies a holding under a lease.

Tenancy at will. A holding of real estate that can be terminated at the will of either the lessor or the lessee, usually with notice.

Tenance by entirety. The joint ownership of property by a husband and wife where both are viewed as one person under common law that provides for the right of survivorship.

Tenancy in common. In law, the type of tenancy or estate created when real or personal property is granted, devised or bequeathed to two or more persons, in the absence of expressed words creating a joint tenancy. There is no right of survivorship (see joint tenancy).

Tenant. One who is not the owner but occupies real property under consent of the owner and in subordination to the owner's title. The tenant is entitled to exclusive possession, use and enjoyment of the property, usually for a rent specified in the lease.

Term. The period of time between the commencement date and termination date of a note, mortgage, legal document, or other contract.

Testate. The estate or condition of leaving a will at death.

Title. The evidence of the right to or ownership in property. In the case of real estate, the documentary evidence of ownership is the title deed which specifies in whom the legal state is vested and the history of ownership and transfers. Title may be acquired through purchase, inheritance, devise, gift, or through foreclosure of a mortgage.

Title insurance policy. A contract by which the insurer, usually a title insurance company, agrees to pay the insured a specific amount for any loss caused by defects of title to real estate, wherein the insured has an interest as purchaser, mortgagee, or otherwise.

Triple A tenant. See AAA tenant.

Trust deed. The instrument given by a borrower (trustor) to a trustee vesting title to a property in the trustee as security for the borrower's fulfillment of an obligation (see deed of trust).

Trustee. A fiduciary who holds or controls property for the benefit of another.

— U —

Underwriting. The analysis and matching of risk to an appropriate rate and term.

Unencumbered property. A property the title to which is free and clear.

Uniform Commercial Code (UCC). A comprehensive law regulating commercial transactions. It has been adopted, with modification, by all states.

Usury. Charging more for the use of money than allowed by law.

— V —

Vacancy factor. A percentage rate expressing the loss from gross rental income due to vacancy and collection losses.

VA certificate of reasonable value. The VA issues a certificate of reasonable value at a specific figure, agreeing to guarantee a mortgage loan to an eligible qualified veteran buyer upon completion and sale of the house. The veteran must be aware of the VA's appraised value of the property.

Valuation. See appraisal.

Variable rate mortgage. A mortgage agreement that allows for adjustment of the interest rate in keeping with a fluctuating market and terms agreed upon in the note.

Vendee. The party to whom personal or real property is sold.

Veterans Administration (VA). The Servicemen's Readjustment Act of 1944 authorized this agency to administer a variety of benefit programs designed to facilitate the adjustment of returning veterans to civilian life. The VA home loan guaranty program is designed to encourage lenders to offer long-term, low down payment mortgages to eligible veterans by guaranteeing the lender against loss.

— W —

Warehousing. The borrowing of funds by a mortgage banker on a short-term basis at a commercial bank using permanent mortgage loans as collateral. This form of interim financing is used until the mortgages are sold to a permanent investor.

Warranty deed. A deed in which the grantor or seller warrants or guarantees that good title is being conveyed, as opposed to a quit-claim deed that contains no representation or warranty as to the quality of title being conveyed.

Waste. Damage to real estate by neglect or other cause.

Will. A written document providing for the distribution of property at death.

Wrap-around. A mortgage which secures a debt that includes the balance due on an existing senior mortgage and an additional amount advanced by the wrap-around mortgagee. The wrap-around mortgagee thereafter makes the amortizing payments on the senior mortgage. An example is when a land-owner has a mortgage securing a debt with an outstanding balance of $3,000,000. A lender now advances the same mortgagor another $1,500,000 and undertakes to make the remaining payments due on the $3,000,000 debt and takes a $4,500,000 wrap-around junior mortgage on the real estate to secure the total indebtedness.

— Y —

Yield. In real estate, the term refers to the effective annual amount of income which is being accrued on an investment. Expressed as a percentage of the price originally paid.

Yield to maturity. A percent returned each year to the lender on actual funds borrowed considering that the loan will be paid in full at the end of maturity.

— Z —

Zoning. The act of city or county authorities specifying the type of use to which property may be put in specific areas (see restriction).

Index